7

May 1–September 18, 1777

Paul H. Smith, Editor

Gerald W. Gawalt, Rosemary Fry Plakas, Eugene R. Sheridan
Assistant Editors

LIBRARY OF CONGRESS   WASHINGTON   1981

6/2394
5/0

This volume is printed on permanent/durable paper.

Library of Congress Cataloging in Publication Data (Revised)

Main entry under title:

Letters of delegates to Congress, 1774–1789.

Includes bibliographical references and indexes.

1. United States. Continental Congress—History—Sources—Collected works.   I.   Smith, Paul Hubert, 1931–
JK1033.L47   Z663.L35   973.3'12   76–2592
ISBN 0–8444–0177–3 (set)
ISBN 0–8444–0350–4 (v.7)

For sale by the Superintendent of Documents, U.S. Government Printing Office
Washington, D.C. 20402

Editorial Method and Apparatus

In its treatment of documents this edition of delegate letters strives to achieve a middle ground between facsimile reproduction and thorough modernization. The original spelling and grammar are allowed to stand except in cases where editorial changes or insertions are required to make the text intelligible. For example, when a badly misspelled word is misleading, the correct spelling is inserted in roman type in brackets after the word. Moreover, words omitted through oversight have been supplied at appropriate places in italic type in brackets. Obvious slips of the pen and inadvertent repetitions are usually silently corrected. Capitalization and punctuation have been standardized according to certain conventions. Each sentence begins with a capital letter, as do all proper and geographic names as well as days of the week and months of the year. Doubtful cases have been resolved in favor of modern usage; otherwise the usage of the original texts has been followed. Generally, abbreviations, contractions, and monetary signs are preserved as they appear in manuscript except when they are ambiguous or misleading. On the other hand, the thorn and the tilde are consistently expanded. "Ye" always appears as "The," for instance, and "recvd" as "received." Likewise, "pr." and "℘" are always expanded to "per," "pre," or "pro," as the case demands. Finally, superscript letters are always lowered to the line.

Gaps in the text are indicated by ellipses in brackets for missing words and by blank spaces in brackets for missing numbers. Conjectural readings are supplied in roman type in brackets, and editorial insertions in italic type in brackets. Material canceled in manuscript but restored to the printed text is included in italic type in angle brackets ("square parentheses"). Marginalia in letters are treated as postscripts, and postscripts which appear without explicit designation are supplied with a *P.S.* in brackets. Documents are arranged chronologically, with more than one document of the same date being arranged alphabetically according to writer. Documents dated only by the month or by the year are placed at the end of the respective month or year. Place-and-date lines always appear on the same line with the salutation regardless of their position in the manuscript.

A descriptive note at the foot of each entry provides abbreviations indicating the nature and location of the document when it was copied for this project, except for privately owned manuscripts whose ownership is fully explained. The descriptive note also contains information on

the document's authorship if explanation is necessary, and endorsements or addresses are quoted when they contain more than routine
information. Other editorial practices employed in this work are explained in the sections on editorial apparatus which follow.

TEXTUAL DEVICES

The following devices will be used in this work to clarify the text.

[. . .], [. . . .]	One or two words missing and not conjecturable.
[. . .]^1, [. . . .]^1	More than two words missing; subjoined footnote estimates amount of material missing.
[ ]	Number or part of a number missing or illegible.
[ ]^1	Blank space in manuscript; explanation in sub-joined footnote.
[roman]	Conjectural reading for missing or illegible matter; question mark inserted if reading is doubtful.
[*italic*]	Editorial insertion in the text.
⟨*italic*⟩	Matter crossed out in manuscript but restored.

DESCRIPTIVE SYMBOLS

The following symbols are used in this work to describe the kinds
of documents drawn upon. When more than one symbol is used in the
descriptive note, the first to appear is that from which the main text is
taken.

RC	recipient's copy
FC	file copy
LB	letterbook copy
MS	manuscript
Tr	transcript (used to designate not only contemporary and later handwritten copies of manuscripts, but also printed documents)

LOCATION SYMBOLS

The following symbols, denoting institutions holding the manuscripts
printed in the present volume, are taken from *Symbols of American
Libraries,* 11th ed. (Washington: Library of Congress, 1976).

CSmH	Henry E. Huntington Library, San Marino, Calif.
Ct	Connecticut State Library, Hartford
CtHi	Connecticut Historical Society, Hartford
CtNlHi	New London Historical Society, New London, Conn.

CtY	Yale University, New Haven, Conn.
DLC	Library of Congress
DNA	National Archives and Records Service
DNDAR	Daughters of the American Revolution, Washington, D.C.
ICHi	Chicago Historical Society
ICarbS	Southern Illinois University, Carbondale
InU	Indiana University, Bloomington
M–Ar	Massachusetts Archives, Boston
MB	Boston Public Library
MH–H	Harvard University, Houghton Library
MHi	Massachusetts Historical Society, Boston
MMhHi	Marblehead Historical Society, Marblehead, Mass.
MdAA	Maryland Hall of Records, Annapolis
MdAN	United States Naval Academy, Annapolis
MdBJ–G	John Work Garrett Library, Johns Hopkins University, Baltimore, Md.
MdFreHi	Historical Society of Frederick County, Frederick, Md.
MdHi	Maryland Historical Society, Baltimore
MeHi	Maine Historical Society, Portland
MiU–C	William L. Clements Library, University of Michigan, Ann Arbor
N	New York State Library, Albany
NHi	New-York Historical Society, New York
NN	New York Public Library
NNC	Columbia University, New York
NNPM	Pierpont Morgan Library, New York
Nc–Ar	North Carolina State Department of Archives and History, Raleigh
NcU	University of North Carolina, Chapel Hill
Nh–Ar	New Hampshire Division of Archives and Records Management, Concord
NhD	Dartmouth College, Hanover, N.H.
Nj	New Jersey State Library, Trenton
NjGbS	Glassboro State College, Glassboro, N.J.
NjMoHP	Morristown National Historical Park, Morristown, N.J.
NjP	Princeton University, Princeton, N.J.
NjR	Rutgers University, New Brunswick, N.J.
OClWHi	Western Reserve Historical Society, Cleveland, Ohio
PHC	Haverford College, Haverford, Pa.
PHarH	Pennsylvania Historical and Museum Commission, Harrisburg
PHi	Historical Society of Pennsylvania, Philadelphia
PPAmP	American Philosophical Society, Philadelphia

PPRF	Rosenbach Foundation, Philadelphia
PU	University of Pennsylvania, Philadelphia
R–Ar	Rhode Island State Archives, Providence
RHi	Rhode Island Historical Society, Providence
RNHi	Newport Historical Society, Newport, R.I.
RPJCB	John Carter Brown Library, Providence
ScHi	South Carolina Historical Society, Charleston
Vi	Virginia State Library, Richmond
ViHi	Virginia Historical Society, Richmond
ViU	University of Virginia, Charlottesville
ViW	College of William and Mary, Williamsburg, Va.

ABBREVIATIONS AND SHORT TITLES

Abbreviations and short titles frequently cited in the present volume are identified below.

Adams, *Diary* (Butterfield)
Adams, John. *Diary and Autobiography of John Adams*. Edited by Lyman H. Butterfield et al. 4 vols. Cambridge: Harvard University Press, Belknap Press, 1961.

Adams, *Family Correspondence* (Butterfield)
Butterfield, Lyman H., et al., eds. *Adams Family Correspondence*. Cambridge: Harvard University Press, Belknap Press, 1963–.

Am. Archives
Force, Peter, ed. *American Archives: Consisting of a Collection of Authentick Records, State Papers, Debates, and Letters and Other Notices of Publick Affairs*. 5th series, 3 vols. Washington: U.S. Government Printing Office, 1848-53.

Burnett, *Letters*
Burnett, Edmund C., ed. *Letters of Members of the Continental Congress*. 8 vols. Washington: Carnegie Institution of Washington, 1921-36.

DAB
Dictionary of American Biography. Edited by Allen Johnson and Dumas Malone.

DNB
Dictionary of National Biography. Edited by Sir Leslie Stephen and Sir Sidney Lee.

Evans, *Am. Bibliography*
Charles Evans. *American Bibliography*. 12 vols. Chicago: Privately printed, 1903-34.

Franklin, *Writings* (Smyth)
Franklin, Benjamin. *The Writings of Benjamin Franklin*. Edited by Albert Smyth. 10 vols. New York: Macmillan Co., 1905-7.

Jay, *Papers* (Morris)
 Jay, John. *John Jay, the Making of a Revolutionary: Unpublished Papers, 1745-1780*. Edited by Richard B. Morris et al. New York: Harper & Row, 1975.
JCC
 U.S. Continental Congress. *Journals of the Continental Congress, 1774-1789*. 34 vols. Edited by Worthington C. Ford et al. Washington: Library of Congress, 1904–37.
Jefferson, *Papers* (Boyd)
 Jefferson, Thomas. *The Papers of Thomas Jefferson*. Edited by Julian P. Boyd et al. Princeton: Princeton University Press, 1950–.
Journals of N.Y. Prov. Cong.
 New York. *Journals of the Provincial Congress, Provincial Convention, Committee of Safety and Council of Safety of the State of New York, 1775-1777*. 2 vols. Albany: T. Weed, 1842.
Lafayette, *Papers* (Idzerda)
 Idzerda, Stanley, et al., eds. *Lafayette in the Age of the American Revolution: Selected Letters and Papers, 1776-1790*. Ithaca: Cornell University Press, 1977–.
Lee, *Letters* (Ballagh)
 Lee, Richard Henry. *The Letters of Richard Henry Lee*. Edited by James C. Ballagh. 2 vols. New York: Macmillan Co., 1911-14.
Md. Archives
 Archives of Maryland. Edited by William H. Browne et al. Baltimore: Maryland Historical Society, 1883–.
Morgan, *Naval Documents*
 Morgan, William James, et al., eds. *Naval Documents of the American Revolution*. Washington: Department of the Navy, 1964–.
N.C. State Records
 North Carolina. *The State Records of North Carolina*. Edited by Walter Clark. Vols. 11-26. Winston and Goldsboro, N.C.: M.I. and J.C. Stewart et al., 1895-1914.
N.H. State Papers
 New Hampshire. *Provincial and State Papers*. 40 vols. Concord, 1867-1943.
NYHS Collections
 Collections of the New-York Historical Society.
Pa. Archives
 Pennsylvania Archives. 9 series, 119 vols. in 120. Philadelphia: J. Severns & Co., 1852-56; Harrisburg: State printer, 1874–1935.
Pa. Council Minutes
 Pennsylvania. *Minutes of the Supreme Executive Council of Pennsylvania, from its Organization to the Revolution*. 6 vols. [*Colonial*

Records of Pennsylvania, vols. 11-16] Harrisburg: Theo. Fenn & Co., 1852–53.

Paullin, *Marine Committee Letters*
Paullin, Charles O., ed. *Out-Letters of Continental Marine Committee and Board of Admiralty, 1776–1780.* 2 vols. New York: Printed for the Naval History Society by the De Vinne Press, 1914.

PCC
Papers of the Continental Congress. National Archives and Records Service. Washington, D.C.

PMHB
Pennsylvania Magazine of History and Biography.

Shipton, *Harvard Graduates*
Shipton, Clifford K. *Biographical Sketches of Those Who Attended Harvard College.* Sibley's Harvard Graduates. Boston: Massachusetts Historical Society, 1873–.

Sullivan, *Letters* (Hammond)
Sullivan, John. *Letters and Papers of Major-General John Sullivan.* Edited by Otis G. Hammond. 3 vols. Collections of the New Hampshire Historical Society, vols. 13–15. Concord: New Hampshire Historical Society, 1930–39.

Warren-Adams Letters
Warren-Adams Letters, Being Chiefly a Correspondence among John Adams, Samuel Adams and James Warren. 2 vols. Massachusetts Historical Society Collections, vols. 72–73. Boston: Massachusetts Historical Society, 1917–25.

Washington, *Writings* (Fitzpatrick)
Washington, George. *The Writings of George Washington.* Edited by John C. Fitzpatrick. 39 vols. Washington: U.S. Government Printing Office, 1931–44.

Wharton, *Diplomatic Correspondence*
Wharton, Francis, ed. *The Revolutionary Diplomatic Correspondence of the United States.* 6 vols. Washington: Government Printing Office, 1889.

Acknowledgments

To the Library of Congress, the Congress of the United States, and the Ford Foundation this edition owes its existence. It is fitting, therefore, that we take this opportunity to acknowledge the foresight of the Library's administration in planning a timely and comprehensive observance of the American Revolution Bicentennial, of the Congress in funding a Bicentennial Office in the Library, and of the Ford Foundation in making a generous grant in support of this project as a scholarly contribution to the celebration of the Bicentennial era. It is with the most profound gratitude that the editors acknowledge their appreciation to all those who bore responsibility for the decisions that made possible these contributions. Our appreciation is also extended to the innumerable persons who have contributed to enriching the holdings of the Library of Congress to make it the premier institution for conducting research on the American Revolution.

The photocopies of the more than twenty thousand documents that have been collected for this project have been assembled through the cooperation of several hundred institutions and private persons devoted to preserving the documentary record upon which the history and traditions of the American people rest, and it is to their work that a documentary publication of this nature should ultimately be dedicated. Unfortunately, the many individual contributors to this collecting effort cannot be adequately recognized, but for permission to print documents appearing in the present volume we are especially grateful to the following institutions: the American Philosophical Society, Boston Public Library, British Museum, John Carter Brown Library, Chicago Historical Society, William L. Clements Library, Columbia University, Connecticut Historical Society, Connecticut State Library, Dartmouth College, Daughters of the American Revolution, Historical Society of Frederick County, John Work Garrett Library, Glassboro State College, Harvard University, Haverford College, Henry E. Huntington Library, Indiana University, Maine Historical Society, Marblehead Historical Society, Maryland Hall of Records, Maryland Historical Society, Massachusetts Archives Division, Massachusetts Historical Society, Pierpont Morgan Library, Morristown National Historical Park, National Archives and Records Service, New Hampshire Division of Archives and Records Management, New Jersey State Library, New London County Historical Society, Newport Historical Society, New-York Historical Society, New York Public Library, New York State Library, North Carolina State

Department of Archives and History, University of North Carolina, Pennsylvania Historical and Museum Commission, Historical Society of Pennsylvania, University of Pennsylvania, Princeton University, Rhode Island Historical Society, Rhode Island State Archives, Rosenbach Foundation, Rutgers University, South Carolina Historical Society, United States Naval Academy, Virginia Historical Society, Virginia State Library, University of Virginia, Western Reserve Historical Society, College of William and Mary, and Yale University. And in addition we express our thanks and appreciation to the following persons: Mrs. Elsie O. Sang and Mr. Philip D. Sang and Capt. J. G. M. Stone.

This work has benefited not only from Edmund C. Burnett's pathfinding 8-volume edition of *Letters of Members of the Continental Congress* but also from the generous cooperation of the editors of several other documentary publications with a common focus on the revolutionary era. From them the Library has borrowed heavily and to them it owes a debt it can never adequately acknowledge. It is a pleasure to give special thanks to the editors of the papers of John Adams, Benjamin Franklin, Thomas Jefferson, Henry Laurens, James Madison, and George Washington. Finally, we owe thanks to the historians who have served on the Advisory Committee on the Library's American Revolution Bicentennial Program, and especially to Mr. Julian P. Boyd, Mr. Lyman H. Butterfield, and Mr. Merrill Jensen, who generously act as an advisory committee for the *Letters* project.

Paul H. Smith
American Revolution Bicentennial Office
Manuscript Division

Chronology of Congress

May 1   Considers possible hostilities against Portugal; appoints Arthur Lee commissioner to Spain.

May 3   Exonerates Gen. Philip Schuyler from charges of misusing public funds.

May 5   Debates Articles of Confederation.

May 7   Appoints Ralph Izard commissioner to Tuscany.

May 9   Appoints William Lee commissioner to Berlin and Vienna.

May 14   Debates reorganization of the quartermaster department.

May 20   Resolves to emit an additional $5 million.

May 22   Appoints Gen. Philip Schuyler to command of the northern department.

May 29   Considers draft address to the inhabitants of the United States.

June 3   Appoints committee to oversee the defense of Pennsylvania.

June 4   Empowers General Washington to offer rewards to encourage British desertions.

June 6   Directs Secret Committee and Marine Committee to make an accounting of their proceedings and expenditures.

June 10   Reorganizes the commissary department.

June 11   Receives committee report on "ways and means for defraying the expence of the current year."

June 14   Adopts the United States flag; disciplines Deputy Muster Master Gunning Bedford for issuing a challenge to delegate Jonathan Dickinson Sergeant for remarks made in Congress.

June 17   Memorializes Gen. David Wooster for bravery during the defense of Danbury, Conn.

June 18   Orders George Morgan to convene an Indian conference at Fort Pitt.

June 23   Resumes debate on Articles of Confederation; hears New York complaint against inhabitants of "the New Hampshire Grants."

June 30   Rebuffs movement to establish Vermont statehood.

July 1   Adopts instructions for commissioners to Vienna, Berlin, and Tuscany.

July 3   Adopts instructions for the commissioner to the United Provinces; dispatches troops to suppress Delaware and Maryland loyalists.

July 5   Creates Committee of Commerce to replace the Secret Committee.

July 7   Condemns Generals Greene, Knox, and Sullivan for an "attempt to influence" Congress.

July 11   Appoints committee to proceed to camp "to make a diligent enquiry into the state of the army."

July 14   Receives news of the retreat from Ticonderoga and Mount Independence.

July 16   Appoints committee to confer with the French officer du Coudray on his "agreement" with Commissioner Silas Deane.

July 23   Dismisses 12 naval officers to make an "example" of "combinations of officers to extort increase of pay and allowances."

July 25   Appoints committee to study the defense of the southern frontier; commends Colonels Barton and Meigs for "enterprize and valour" in capturing General Prescott and conducting an expedition on Long Island.

July 29   Orders an inquiry into the evacuation of Ticonderoga and Mount Independence.

July 31   Commissions the marquis de Lafayette a major general.

August 1 Begins inquiry into Commissioner Silas Deane's contracts with foreign officers.

August 4 Appoints Gen. Horatio Gates to replace Gen. Philip Schuyler as commander of the northern department.

August 5 Begins consideration of Committee to Camp report on the "state of the army."

August 7 Directs General Washington "to negotiate an exchange of prisoners with the enemy."

August 8 Records first roll call vote—on motion to promote Brig. Gen. Benedict Arnold.

August 11 Directs implementation of General Washington's proposals for defense of the Delaware.

August 15 Agrees to accept parole of prominent Pennsylvania dissidents seeking to avoid exile to Virginia.

August 20 Directs mustering of the Pennsylvania militia; dispatches New Jersey militia to New York to relieve troops for frontier defense.

August 21	Endorses General Washington's proposal to march his main army toward the Hudson River; receives news of American victory at Bennington, Vt.
August 22	Learns of British invasion of the Chesapeake; alerts Washington to the British threat to Philadelphia and issues call for the Pennsylvania, Delaware, Maryland, and Virginia militia.
August 26	Requests Pennsylvania and Delaware to apprehend and disarm the "notoriously disaffected" within their states.
August 28	Reverses decision to parole prominent Pennsylvania dissidents and orders their removal from the state.
September 1	Orders inquiry into the failure of Gen. John Sullivan's expedition against Staten Island.
September 4	Orders further call-up of Pennsylvania and New Jersey militia.
September 6	Directs clothier general to provide clothing bounties to troops.
September 8	Rebukes Silas Deane for exceeding his authority in negotiating agreements with foreign officers in France.
September 9	Orders General Washington to write Congress at least twice daily "advising the position and movements of the armies."
September 10	Adopts "ways and means" motion to pay interest accruing on loan office certificates in bills of exchange on the commissioners at Paris.
September 11	Learns of the American defeat at Brandywine Creek.
September 12	Directs Gen. Israel Putnam to reinforce Washington's army.
September 14	Orders General Sullivan's recall until the inquiry ordered into his conduct is completed; resolves to convene in Lancaster, Pa., if the evacuation of Philadelphia becomes necessary.
September 15	Orders investigation of a conspiracy rumored to be impending in Pennsylvania.
September 16	Grants General Washington broad powers to punish military officers and to impress supplies for the army; orders removal of supplies from Philadelphia.
September 18	Evacuates Philadelphia.

List of Delegates to Congress

This section lists both the dates on which delegates were elected to terms falling within the period covered by this volume and the inclusive dates of their attendance. The former are generally ascertainable from contemporary state records, but the latter are often elusive bits of information derived from the journals of Congress or extrapolated from references contained in the delegates' correspondence, and in such cases the "facts" are inevitably conjectural. It is not possible to determine interruptions in the attendance of many delegates, and no attempt has been made to record interruptions in service caused by illness or brief trips home, especially of delegates from New Jersey, Delaware, Maryland, and Pennsylvania living within easy access of Philadelphia. For occasional references to such periods of intermittent service as survive in the correspondence and notes of various delegates, see the index under individual delegates. Until fuller information is provided in a consolidated summary of delegate attendance in the final volume of this series, the reader is advised to consult Burnett, *Letters,* 2: xxxix-lxxiii, for additional information on conjectural dates of attendance. Brief biographical sketches of all the delegates are available in the *Biographical Directory of the American Congress, 1774–1971,* and fuller sketches of more than half of the delegates can be found in the *Dictionary of American Biography.*

CONNECTICUT

Eliphalet Dyer
    Elected: October 10, 1776
    Attended: June 25 to September 18, 1777
Samuel Huntington
    Elected: October 10, 1776
    Did not attend in 1777
Richard Law
    Elected: October 10, 1776
    Attended: June 25 to September 18, 1777
Roger Sherman
    Elected: October 10, 1776
    Attended: May 1 to July 2, 1777
William Williams
    Elected: October 10, 1776
    Attended: June 25 to September 18, 1777

Oliver Wolcott
  Elected: October 10, 1776
  Attended: May 1–2, 1777

DELAWARE

George Read
  Elected: November 8, 1776
  Attended: May 1–10?; September 9?–18, 1777
James Sykes
  Elected: February 22, 1777
  Did not attend May to September 1777
Nicholas Van Dyke
  Elected: February 22, 1777
  Attended: June 2 to August 15? 1777

GEORGIA

Nathan Brownson
  Elected: October 9, 1776; June 7, 1777
  Attended: May 1; August 23 to September 18, 1777
Button Gwinnett
  Elected: October 9, 1776
  Died May 19, 1777
Lyman Hall
  Elected: October 9, 1776; June 7, 1777
  Did not attend May to September 1777
John Houstoun
  Elected: October 9, 1776
  Did not attend in 1777
Edward Langworthy
  Elected: June 7, 1777
  Did not attend May to September 1777
George Walton
  Elected: October 9, 1776; June 7, 1777
  Attended: May 1 to September 18, 1777
Joseph Wood
  Elected June 7, 1777
  Did not attend May to September 1777

MARYLAND

Charles Carroll of Carrollton
  Elected: February 15, 1777
  Attended: May 5 to July 21? 1777
Samuel Chase
  Elected: February 15, 1777
  Attended: July 21 to September 18, 1777

William Paca
   Elected: February 15, 1777
   Attended: May 5? to June 28; August 13–22? 1777
Benjamin Rumsey
   Elected: February 15, 1777
   Attended: May 1–5, 1777
William Smith
   Elected: February 15, 1777
   Attended: May 1–5?; July 5?–September 18, 1777
Thomas Stone
   Elected: February 15, 1777
   Did not attend in 1777

MASSACHUSETTS

John Adams
   Elected: November 15, 1776
   Attended: May 1 to September 18, 1777
Samuel Adams
   Elected: November 15, 1776
   Attended: May 1 to September 18, 1777
Francis Dana
   Elected: November 15, 1776
   Did not attend May to September 1777
Elbridge Gerry
   Elected: November 15, 1776
   Attended: May 1 to September 18, 1777
John Hancock
   Elected: November 15, 1776
   Attended: May 1 to September 18, 1777
James Lovell
   Elected: November 15, 1776
   Attended: May 1 to September 18, 1777
Robert Treat Paine
   Elected: November 15, 1776
   Did not attend in 1777

NEW HAMPSHIRE

Josiah Bartlett
   Elected: December 24, 1776
   Did not attend in 1777
Nathaniel Folsom
   Elected: April 1, 1777
   Attended: July 21 to September 18, 1777

George Frost
  Elected: April 1, 1777
  Attended: May 16 to September 17, 1777
Matthew Thornton
  Elected: December 24, 1776
  Attended: May 1–2, 1777
William Whipple
  Elected: December 24, 1776
  Attended: May 1 to June 18, 1777

NEW JERSEY

Abraham Clark
  Elected: November 30, 1776
  Attended: May 29? to September 18? 1777
Jonathan Elmer
  Elected: November 30, 1776
  Attended: May 1 to September 18, 1777
Jonathan Dickinson Sergeant
  Elected: November 30, 1776
  Attended: May 1 to September 7, 1777
John Witherspoon
  Elected: November 30, 1776
  Attended: May 1 to September 13? 1777 (Probably returned briefly
  to Princeton twice during this period)

NEW YORK

George Clinton
  Elected: April 21, 1775
  Did not attend in 1777
James Duane
  Elected: April 21, 1775; May 13, 1777
  Attended: May 1 to September 18, 1777
William Duer
  Elected: March 29, 1777; May 13, 1777
  Attended: May 1 to September 18, 1777
William Floyd
  Elected: April 21, 1775
  Did not attend May to September 1777
John Jay
  Elected: April 21, 1775
  Did not attend in 1777
Francis Lewis
  Elected: April 21, 1775
  Attended: May 1–13, 1777 (Returned to Baltimore on Marine Com-
  mittee business for a part of this period)

Philip Livingston
  Elected: April 21, 1775; May 13, 1777
  Attended: May 1 to August 8? 1777
Robert R. Livingston
  Elected: April 21, 1775
  Did not attend in 1777
Gouverneur Morris
  Elected: May 13, 1777
  Did not attend in 1777
Lewis Morris
  Elected: April 21, 1775
  Did not attend May to September 1777
Philip Schuyler
  Elected: April 21, 1775; May 13, 1777
  Attended: May 1–26, 1777
Henry Wisner
  Elected: April 21, 1775
  Did not attend in 1777

NORTH CAROLINA

Thomas Burke
  Elected: December 20, 1776; May 4, 1777
  Attended: May 1 to September 18, 1777
Cornelius Harnett
  Elected: May 4, 1777
  Attended: July 22 to September 18, 1777
Joseph Hewes
  Elected: December 20, 1776
  Did not attend in 1777
William Hooper
  Elected: December 20, 1776
  Did not attend May to September 1777
John Penn
  Elected: May 4, 1777
  Attended: June 23 to September 18, 1777

PENNSYLVANIA

William Clingan
  Elected: September 14, 1777
  Did not attend September 1777
George Clymer
  Elected: February 22, 1777
  Attended: May 1–19; June 9 to September 9, 1777

Samuel Duffield
  Elected: September 14, 1777
  Did not attend Congress
Benjamin Franklin
  Elected: February 5, 1777
  Did not attend in 1777
Robert Morris
  Elected: February 5, 1777
  Attended: May 1 to September 18, 1777
Joseph Reed
  Elected: September 14, 1777
  Did not attend in 1777
Daniel Roberdeau
  Elected: February 5, 1777
  Attended: May 1–9; May 26? to September 18, 1777
Jonathan Bayard Smith
  Elected: February 5, 1777
  Attended: May 1 to August 22, 1777
James Wilson
  Elected: February 22, 1777
  Attended: May 1–29?; June 28 to September 13? 1777

RHODE ISLAND

William Ellery
  Elected: May 4, 1776; May 7, 1777
  Attended: May 1–4; May 31 to June 16? 1777
Stephen Hopkins
  Elected: May 3, 1776; May 7, 1777
  Did not attend in 1777
Henry Marchant
  Elected: May 7, 1777
  Attended: May 31 to September 18, 1777

SOUTH CAROLINA

Thomas Heyward
  Elected: January 10, 1777
  Attended: May 1 to September 18, 1777
Henry Laurens
  Elected: January 10, 1777
  Attended: July 22 to September 18, 1777
Arthur Middleton
  Elected: January 10, 1777
  Attended: May 1 to September 18, 1777

Charles Pinckney
    Elected: January 21, 1777
    Did not attend in 1777
Paul Trapier
    Elected: January 21, 1777
    Did not attend Congress

VIRGINIA

Benjamin Harrison
    Elected: October 10, 1776; May 22, 1777
    Attended: May 1–2?; May 30? to September 18, 1777
John Harvie
    Elected: May 22, 1777
    Did not attend May to September 1777
Thomas Jefferson
    Elected: June 20, 1776
    Did not attend in 1777
Joseph Jones
    Elected: May 22, 1777
    Attended: August 11 to September 18, 1777
Francis Lightfoot Lee
    Elected: June 20, 1776; May 22, 1777
    Attended: May 1 to September 18, 1777
Richard Henry Lee
    Elected: June 20, 1776; June 24, 1777
    Attended: May 1 to June 15; August 12 to September 18, 1777
George Mason
    Elected: May 22, 1777
    Did not attend Congress
Thomas Nelson
    Elected: June 20, 1776
    Probably did not attend May to September 1777 (obtained leave
    May 8)
Mann Page
    Elected: December 4, 1776
    Attended: May 1 to July ? 1777
George Wythe
    Elected: June 20, 1776
    Did not attend in 1777

Illustrations

View of Philadelphia   endpapers

"An East Prospect of the City of Philadelphia; taken by George Heap from the Jersey Shore, under the Direction of Nicholas Scull Surveyor General of the Province of Pennsylvania." This detail is from an engraving by Thomas Jefferys based on an etching of the city published in Thomas Jefferys, *A General Topography of North America and the West Indies. Being a Collection of All the Maps, Charts, Plans, and Particular Surveys, That Have Been Published of That Part of the World, Either in Europe or America* (London: R. Sayer, 1768).

Philip Schuyler   35

An aristocratic Albany, N.Y., landlord, Schuyler was one of the more controversial figures to mount the congressional stage during the Revolution. Named commander of the northern military department in June 1775, one of the three general officers Congress drew from its own ranks when creating the Continental Army, Schuyler soon demonstrated greater aptitude for supplying the army than for field command, in part because a major element of the northern army consisted of New Englanders, who took a dim view of his aristocratic pretensions. Although he skillfully organized the invasion of Canada led by Gen. Richard Montgomery in 1775, he did not escape censure for its failures, and the chronic problems that continued to plague the northern department throughout 1776 conspired to reduce still further his standing both in and out of Congress. New England delegates who longed to replace him with Horatio Gates listened sympathetically to rumors that he had mishandled public funds and even harbored secret sympathies for the British. Schuyler's own intemperate letters to Congress played into the hands of his opponents. By early 1777 it appeared that his congressional support had evaporated when he was admonished for criticizing Congress and Gates was granted an independent command in the northern department. But in April Schuyler thwarted his critics by resuming his seat in Congress, where he narrowly won vindication of his conduct and regained undisputed command over the northern department. His victory was only temporary, however, and scarcely three months after his departure from Philadelphia—where he had also served briefly as military commander of the city while in Congress—he was superseded by Gates for ineffectively opposing

Gen. John Burgoyne's advance into northern New York. He subsequently returned to Congress in 1779-80 and served conspicuously on the committee at headquarters seeking to restore morale to the army during the summer of 1780. After the war he served several terms as state senator and was twice elected to the United States Senate, from which he resigned in ill health in 1798, six years before his death in 1804.

Prints and Photographs Division, Library of Congress.

James Lovell's May 30, 1777, Letter to George Washington   157

A former Boston schoolmaster, Lovell became well known when he was imprisoned in 1775 on suspicion of spying in British-held Boston and was taken to Halifax. Upon his exchange he was elected to Congress in 1776 and served there almost without interruption from 1777 to 1782, establishing an unmatched record of continuous attendance at Congress. As one of the few delegates fluent in French he was named to the Committee for Foreign Affairs and chairman of the Committee on Foreign Applications. In the latter capacity he was often engaged in the thankless task of denying promises to foreign officers made by the American commissioners in France, who often seemed out of touch with congressional and military realities. During 1777 the stream of foreign volunteer officers reached flood stage, and Lovell and a congressional majority in frustration denounced several of the agreements approved by the commissioners and recalled Silas Deane, the chief offender, for exceeding his authority. A blunt and outspoken man, Lovell admitted to taunting his opponents in debate when he detected inconsistencies in their arguments. He became one of General Washington's harshest critics during the winter of 1777–78. He continued as a public officeholder after his retirement from Congress in 1782 and in the federal era was naval officer for Boston, from 1789 until his death in 1814.

Manuscript Division, Library of Congress.

Thomas Heyward, Jr.   210

Heyward, a South Carolina lawyer, was educated at the Middle Temple in London. He took an active role in the revolutionary movement as a member of the assembly, the council of safety, and the provincial congress in South Carolina before being elected a delegate to Congress in 1776. He represented his state in Congress from 1776 to 1778, during which time he became a signer of the Declaration of Independence and took part in the debates on the Articles of Confederation. Although he generally remained in the background and never won acclaim for great accomplishments, he served on several committees and much of the evidence on his congressional service survives in the form of the correspondence of the Committee for Foreign Affairs of which he was a member. Returning to South Carolina, he served as a captain of artillery in the state militia and was taken by the British in the capture of Charleston in 1780, remaining a prisoner for over a year. Reentering public life after his release, Heyward served South Carolina in both legislative and judicial capacities until he retired to private life in 1789. Because so little of his correspondence survives, a characteristic that he shares with many delegates from the southern colonies where climate and events have wreaked havoc on the historical record, Heyward's contributions in Congress are difficult to assess.

Engraving by J. B. Longacre from a miniature. In John Sanderson, *Biography of the Signers to the Declaration of Independence,* vol. 4 (Philadelphia: R. W. Pomeroy, 1823).

Henry Marchant 298

A Newport lawyer who had attended the College of Philadelphia and read law with the noted Massachusetts lawyer Edmund Trowbridge, Marchant was connected with one of Rhode Island's most prominent political families through his marriage to a daughter of Samuel Ward. The breadth of his intellectual and personal interests was attested to by his long friendship and correspondence with the well-known scholar-divine Ezra Stiles. Marchant entered Congress in 1777 imbued with a strong belief in the wisdom of the people, which was at times reflected in his stand on issues that came before Congress. Thus when he opposed Philip Schuyler because the New York general lacked popular support, the secretary of Congress noted in his record of the debates that Marchant "has a great Opinion of the Judgment of the people. It is generally pure, uncorrupt and well founded." He was indefatigable as a committeeman during his tenure in Congress (from 1777 to 1779), devoting his greatest energies to the demands of the Marine Committee and the Board of Treasury. Although reelected to Congress in 1783 and 1784, Marchant declined to attend and instead devoted himself to the Rhode Island General Assembly, where from 1784 to 1790 he distinguished himself as a defender of Rhode Island's commercial interests and an exponent of the federal constitution. After ratification of the new constitution, Marchant was appointed a United States district court judge in Rhode Island, an office he held until his death in 1796.

Etching by Max Rosenthal. Prints and Photographs Division, Library of Congress.

George Clymer 349

Clymer was a Philadelphia merchant who played an active role in

Pennsylvania politics during the decade of prerevolutionary ferment and was elected to the Pennsylvania Council of Safety in 1775. He served as one of two Continental treasurers in 1775-76 and was one of the men Pennsylvania elected to Congress in July 1776 to replace her four delegates who had opposed independence. He therefore became a signer of the Declaration of Independence, although he was not present to vote for its adoption. As a delegate he drew several special assignments that exploited his business acumen. He was named to make an inspection tour on the supply and condition of the northern army in October 1776, and he was a member of the executive committee that remained in Philadelphia when Congress fled to Baltimore during the winter of 1776-77. Subsequently he was engrossed in the business that came before the Board of Treasury and the Board of War, and in July 1777 he was named to the Committee to Camp to inquire into the state of the army and "the causes of the complaints in the commissary's department." After he withdrew from Congress he spent four months at Fort Pitt as a commissioner to report on conditions on the western frontiers, but he returned to Congress to serve two additional terms in 1780-82. He was a member of the federal convention in 1787 and was elected to the first federal Congress, but after serving briefly in two appointive capacities during Washington's administration he retired from public life in 1796 and devoted himself to private interests until his death in 1813.

Pennsylvania Historical and Museum Commission.

Charles Thomson's Notes of Debates, July 26, 1777   381

Students of the American Revolution often find Secretary Thomson's journals of Congress more tantalizing than satisfying. His principles for recording congressional proceedings have come down to us in the following statement, published in 1827, three years after his death. "With respect to the taking the Minutes: what congress adopted, I committed to writing; with what they rejected, I had nothing farther to do; and even this method led to some squabbles with the members, who were desirous of having their speeches and resolutions, however put to rest by the majority, still preserved upon the Minutes." That he nevertheless sometimes recorded the substance of debates in greater detail is apparent from his notes that survive for July 24, 25, 26, and 28, 1777. Two pages from those of July 26—sparked by a motion to appoint Horatio Gates to the command of the northern department in the place of Philip Schuyler—have been reproduced here to underscore the fragmentary nature of the official journals of Congress, which contain not a word on the subject recorded in the notes illustrated here.

Charles Thomson Papers, Manuscript Division, Library of Congress.

Bennington Broadside, August 18-22, 1777   531

This John Dunlap broadside announcing Gen. John Stark's recent victory at the battle of Bennington was a public reminder that Gen. John Burgoyne's invasion of New York had encountered serious difficulties. To boost American morale the committee of intelligence on September 2 transmitted a number of these broadsides to Washington to distribute among his men so "that the troops may be made acquainted with and emulate the conduct of their brave northern and eastern brethren." Although this publicity could have been interpreted as an implied rebuke to his generalship, Washington promptly distributed the broadsides among his troops and showed no signs of irritation with the committee. Congress found to its distress, however, that events in the northern department failed to improve the army's capabilities against General Howe's southern attack, as events at Brandywine Creek were to prove just over a week later.

Rare Book and Special Collections Division, Library of Congress.

William Howe   591

As commander in chief of the British army in North America from October 1775 to May 1778, General Howe was often at the center of American concerns, although during much of 1777 his activities were more puzzling than threatening. Despite General Washington's brilliant victories over Howe's forces at Trenton and Princeton during the winter of 1776–77, most observers feared that the Continental Army would be no match for Howe's regulars in 1777 and that he would soon recover the initiative and momentum that had been his the preceding campaign. Howe's dawdling during the early months of the new campaign baffled Washington and Congress. Howe seemed unable to focus his strategic plans, and not until the first of September when they learned he had disembarked an army at Head of Elk on Chesapeake Bay were the Americans able to prepare specific plans to oppose his march. His presence in Maryland dominated the delegates' correspondence during the following days, and although Philadelphia was presumed to be his objective there was little agreement on how to respond to his presence. His August 27 proclamation calling on Americans to seek pardon and subscribe an oath of allegiance underscored his dual purpose in America, for Howe was both military commander and peace commissioner empowered to negotiate with American leaders. The strength of the loyalists in the middle colonies and the chronic weakness of the Pennsylvania government fed apprehensions that Americans lacked the will to resist his invasion, and the military engagement between his regulars and Washington's army at Brandywine Creek on September 11 demonstrated their powerlessness to check the redcoats. On September 18 Congress simply abandoned the Pennsylvania capital and adjourned to Lancaster, leaving Howe to occupy Philadelphia unopposed on the 26th.

From *An Impartial History of the War in America* (London & Carlisle, 1780).

After a summer of uncertainty, Congress learned of Gen. William Howe's intentions when on August 22 word reached Philadelphia of the British invasion of the Chesapeake. Moving to impede the march of Howe's army north from Head of Elk, where it had been disembarked, Washington took up positions on Brandywine Creek early in September, but Howe's assault on General Sullivan's position above the main American army collapsed Washington's defenses. The day after receiving letters from Washington and his military secretary Col. Robert H. Harrison describing the defeat at Chadd's Ford, Congress ordered a broadside published to alert the public to the dangers that now faced them. The defeat left Philadelphia open to Howe's continued advance and within a week Congress evacuated the Pennsylvania capital for Lancaster.

Rare Book and Special Collections Division, Library of Congress.

The son of a Lebanon, Conn., Congregational pastor, Williams was educated for the ministry but turned from his father's path as a young man to become a merchant. He was an active opponent of British measures before the Revolution and held several local positions before he was elected to Congress in 1776. Although he did not reach Philadelphia until three weeks after the Declaration of Independence was adopted, he did take his seat in Congress in time to affix his signature to the engrossed document, the deed responsible for much of the attention since accorded him. He served on several committees charged with meeting the needs of the army and was appointed to the Board of War in October 1777. His congressional service is known largely through his correspondence with his brother-in-law Commissary Joseph Trumbull and his father-in-law, Gov. Jonathan Trumbull. Although that correspondence reveals him as one of the delegates most preoccupied with the "awful Frown of divine Providence," he repeatedly reaffirmed his faith that God would ultimately save the American cause. Returning to Connecticut in December 1777, Williams held a number of state and local offices, including a long tenure in the Windham probate and county courts.

Portrait by James J. Sawyer, 1873, after John Trumbull, Independence National Historical Park Collection.

LETTERS OF DELEGATES

7

May 1–September 18, 1777

TO CONGRESS

Jonathan Elmer to Elias Boudinot

Dear Sir   Philadelphia 1st May 1777

As General Washington has directed that the Bills of Exchange ordered by Congress to be purchased & sent to New York for the support of our suffering prisoners there should be transmitted to you for that purpose; I take the liberty of mentioning to you the name of my Brother-in-Law John Gibbon for whose Exchange you may probably remember I applied to his Excellency not long ago, but by reason of the particular obstacles relating to the general Cartel could not then obtain it.

Mr. Gibbon was taken prisoner in Character of a private Soldier belonging to a Company of Militia commanded by one Captn. Mashall of Col. Potter's Battalion from Cumberland County New Jersey on their retreat from Mount Holly the 24th of December last. He was in the sugar House in New York about 4 or 5 weeks ago. I mention these particulars that you may the more readily find where he now is, & as Mr. Richd. H. Lee informs me that the Committee (of which he is a member) have purchased a Bill of £600 which I expect will be immediately transmitted to you for the use of the prisoners, I must beg the favour of you not to fail letting him have a proportional share of that money.

I have several times endeavoured to transmit money to him, but know not whether ever he received it & from the best intilligence I can get he is in a suffering situation; If you should therefore in the course of your negociations, have it in your power by means of any of your friends residing in New York or otherwise to render him any service, by furnishing him with money, procuring his Exchange or enlargement upon Parole, or even mitigating the severity of his Imprisonment, I shall esteem it as a singular favour & will chearfully satisfy you for any expence or trouble you shall be at in doing it. Whenever you have an opportunity of hearing from him I should be glad of a line from you that I may acquaint his family of it.

I am (with my respects to Mrs. Boudinot), Your most obedient & very Hble servt.   Jonathn. Elmer

P.S. I am desired to mention to you one Joel Westcott first Lieut. in Capt. West's Company of Col Lambt. Cadwallader's Pennsylvania Battalion who was taken at Fort Washington, & informed his wife about 3 weeks ago that he was at Flat Bush on Long Island & in great want of necessaries.

3

RC (DLC). Addressed: "To Elias Boudinot Esquire near Baskenridge." Endorsed: "Recd. May 5 & Answd. same day."

James Lovell to Horatio Gates

Sir   May 1st 1777

You will see by the resolutions sent to you at this time that new Ideas are taking place here in regard to the western side of Tyconderoga.[1]

I apprehend you will be better informed than we are what expectations you can form with confidence about the number of eastern troops and the exact time when they will arrive to a certain necessary amount for your plans. An *absolute* order to relinquish the western Lines & fort was pushed for, but you find did not prevail. You certainly have not such a predilection for them as to run great risques of losing yr. Reputation in their defence with a few troops, if only a few can be had. Nor are you of such a disposition as to leave them without much consideration, if they appear to be highly essential to our defence, and you receive according to yr. wishes troops & military stores. If, after the liberty which is given to you, stores to a considerable amount and a number of men should be taken from you on the western side you will never hear the last of it. On this, I speak strongly, not fearing that I shall deter yr. Judgment & Spirit from deciding justly according to circumstances on the spot of deliberation.

But, another matter besides the foregoing will be upon yr. mind, on which you will expect to hear from me by this bearer.

The affairs to the northeast are in a critical situation for the state of N. York in particular. Disaffection, as you see, is greatly prevalent; and those who profess well to our cause judge & say that there is but one single man who can keep their subjects united against the common enemy; and that *he*[2] stands on our books as commandr. in chief in the middle, or, as it is sometimes called, the northern departmt; that his presence is absolutely necessary in his home quarters for their immediate succour & service as well as that of the united states necessarily connected; that if he returns, he is a Genl. without an army or a Military Chest; And, "why is he thus disgraced"?

It is said that it is nonsense to give you the command of the northern army at Tyconderoga and confine you to that fort and mount Independence where you cannot have an extensive idea of the defence of the frontier of the eastern states, but only of one spot where the enemy are not obliged to confine their operations, and, as it were knock their heads against a single Rock. And if you are not so confined you intirely destroy the idea of their Chief to whom they profess devotion unbounded. How this matter will be untangled I can not now exactly determine, but I suspect not intirely agreable to yr. *sentiments*. I wish to have these explicitly & minutely by the first opportunity after the receipt of this. I wish some course coud be taken which would suit you both. It is plain that all the northern army can not be intended for the single Garison of Ty. Who then has the distribution of the Numbers? This must depend upon one opinion or their can be no decision in the defence of the northern frontiers. It is an unhappy circumstance that such is the altercation at the opening of this campaign so early by the foreign enemies of these states.

In every condition I wish you health, prosperity and honor, being sincerely Yr. friend & humb Servt.   J. Lovell

RC (NHi).
   1 See John Hancock to Horatio Gates, April 29, 1777.
   2 Philip Schuyler, who was at this time attending Congress as a delegate from New York. For further information on the reinstatement of General Schuyler to the northern command, see Philip Schuyler's Memorial to Congress, May 6; and Lovell to Gates, May 22, 1777.

Marine Committee to Aquilla Johns

Sir   May 1. 1777
A Resolution of Congress this day passed has suspended the Command of Captain James Nicholson in the Continental service for a limitted time, and we think it necessary to inform you thereof, requiring you to act in all things necessary on board of the Virginia Frigate during this suspension.[1]

You are to discharge immediately on receipt hereof all such Men as have not received the Continental bounty and suscribed the Articles, you are to preserve strict discipline on board the ship and keep all the people belonging to her not included in the above discription constantly on board, employing them in such services as may be necessary for preparing her for Sea and in all matters that Occur we expect you to perform the duty of an Active Attentive Officer, vested with a temporary command until further orders from this Board.

We are sir, Your Friends & Servants

LB (DNA: PCC Miscellaneous Papers, Marine Committee Letter Book). Addressed: "Lieut. Aquilla Johns, commanding officer of the Frigate Virginia."
   1 See following entry.

Marine Committee to Thomas Johnson

Sir,   In Marine Committee. May 1. 1777

The President will inclose you certain resolves of Congress relative to the contempt offered by Captain James Nicholson against the Executive power of the State of Maryland.[1]

The Marine Committee have directed Wm Lux Esqr. the Marine Agent at Baltimore to serve the Said Nicholson with a Copy of them,[2] and to inform your Excellency of the time of Such service. The Committee have also ordered the Commanding Officer on board the Frigate Virginia to set at Liberty all persons who have not Signed the Marine Articles and received the Continental bounty.[3] We request your Excellency to give the President of Congress the most early notice whether or not Capt Nicholson makes such concessions to the Executive power of the state as they shall require within the limited time. We have the honor to be, yr. Excellencys Most obedt. Servts,

John Hancock	Wm. Whipple
Phil. Livingston	Oliver Wolcott
Tho Burke	Richard Henry Lee
	William Ellery

RC (MdAA). In a clerical hand and signed by Burke, Ellery, Hancock Lee, Livingston, Whipple, and Wolcott.

[1] See *JCC,* 7:318–19. For a discussion of Maryland's controversy with Captain Nicholson, see Marine Committee to James Nicholson, April 29, 1777, note.

[2] On this day the Marine Committee also wrote this brief note to William Lux, the Continental prize agent in Maryland: "You'll please to Serve Captain James Nicholson with the inclosed Copies of Resolves of Congress in presence of Some one or more Credible persons and inform Governor Johnston and this Committee of the time of such Service." PCC, item 70, 1:207.

[3] See preceding entry.

Maryland Delegates to Thomas Johnson

Sir   Philadelphia May 1st. 1777

We embrace this oppertunity by Your returnd express, to acknowledge receipt of your favor of the 26th Ult.[1] The multiplicity of business before congress, made it impossible to dispatch the express sooner than has been done.

We have the honour to inclose your Excy. coppy of the Resolutions of Congress, respecting Capt Nicholsons very indecent & Imprudent behavior, to your self & Council as well as his infringmt. on the liberties of the people. We have the pleasure to assure yr. Excellency that Congress were Unanimous in expressing their warmest disapprobation of Capt. Nicholsons Conduct, & that he had not the least incouragement to proceed in this business in the manner he has done, & we are of oppinion he would have been dismissd the service immediatly, but many Gentlemen thought him a good officer & were willing to believe your Excelly & Councill would Accept of Such Submissions & Acknowledgments as he ought immediatly to make.

By letters yesterday from Genl. Washington we were informd that the enemy had landed 1500 or 2000 men on the Sound near Fairfield, Conecticut, & had marchd to Danbury abt. 25 Miles into the country where we had a large Magazine, that they had destroyed abt. 5000 bbls of Pork, & 3000 Barrells of Flour, Burnt the greatest part of The Town.[2] We had not above 50 regular troops at this post. The Militia, however, collected next morning Under Generals Arnold & Worster (& a few regulars) in the whole About 600, & harassd them on their retreat. We killed 12 of the Enemy, took 13 Prisoners, the Number of Wounded not Known, our loss very trifling. Genl. Worster Mortaly Wounded & one or two other officers. They retreated on board their Ships, more like a flight than a retreat. From every accot. recd. if we had had nearly an equal number of Troops these robers would have been taken proper care of. We have the Honour to be yr. Excellencys, Most Obt. hble Serts,   W. Smith   B. Rumsey

P.S. The Enemy have burnt in this excursion the Towns of Danbury & Ridgfield. The Frigates at this place have Impressd Some Seamen, but we have not learnd that any complaints have been made on that head, therefore this State have winkd at this measure & incouraged it from the pressing necessity. Congress, nor even the Marine Committee have ever given any incouragement to this practice, nor we hope will congress ever give any incouragement to their officers to Interfere with the Internal police of any State.

RC (MdAA). Written by Smith and signed by Smith and Rumsey.

[1] The Maryland Council's April 26 letter to the Maryland delegates is in *Md. Archives,* 16:230.

[2] See John Adams to Abigail Adams, April 30, 1777, note.

Robert Morris to Thomas Johnson

Dear Sir   Philada. May 1st. 1777

I have seen with a good deal of Concern what appears to me an unfortunate dispute between your Excellency and Capt Nicholson in Consequence of his having followed the example of his Brother officers who have for sometime been Impressing men into the Naval Service of the Continent in this Port.

The practice of Impressing Seamen cannot be supported on any other

principle than Necessity and I am confident it is as pernicious to the
Commercial Interests of a Country as destructive of the Civil Liberty
of those Individuals who become its Victims. Under these opinions you
will readily see I cannot advocate the measure. Nothing but the prospect
of great Public advantages to result from a well manned navy would
have induced me to be silent whilst these things were doing here, but it
was properly the business of the Executive power of the State to notice
& stop the practice. They have not interfered & that probably because
they saw & Considered the force of *Necessity*. Perhaps no great disadvantages might have resulted to the State of Maryld had you only
checked this business so far as it had come before you by Complaints
from Individuals whose particular situations or Circumstances might
have called for exemption & protection. Remember I don't offer these
as fixed Sentiments or as proper considerations in a settled peaceable
Government, because I know they are inconsistant with it but in times
of Invasion & War, especially such a War as ours, it seems to me that
forcing out Militia against their will which I believe to have been much
practiced is an equal infringement of Liberty with the Impressing of
Men for a limited time for the Naval service & it is to be observed that
it has hitherto been the practice at the end of every Cruize or Voyage
made by our Continental Ships the men have had their liberty again.
In the British Navy they are generally impressed for Life. Thus much
in Paliation only. With respect to Capt Nicholson he certainly deserves
severe reprehension, the terms of his letter are quite unwarrantable &
not a single member of Congress offered to support him. You will see
that the Resolves of Congress place him in your power so far as he
values his Commission[1] & at present he is at the head of the American
Navy but I think the dispute unfortunate because I have been taught
to believe him an excellent & Capable officer, the loss of such a one will
be a real misfortune to the Continent & yet I think he ought to be
dismissed unless by satisfactory submission he attones for the offensive
Stile of his letter which I suppose to have been written in warmth inflamed by the Violence of that Species of Whiggism that savours more
of passion than true Patriotism, I am told he is of a high Spirit and
that it is doubtful if he will make the Concessions he ought. I wish not
to be guilty of an improper interferance & shall only repeat that if he was
dismiss'd the service it will be a heavy loss, especially as the next in
Command (Capt Manly) is vastly his inferiour in abilities, & knowing
as I do how much your Excellency wishes to promote the Service of
America, I coud not refrain from mentioning my notions on this Subject.
There is also another matter that gives me concern & that is the detention of Continental Troops on the Eastern Shoar to keep Tories in order
at a time when Genl Washington cou'd strike a Capital stroke was he
reinforced by those & others that ought to join him. I wish you wou'd

think of this & order them to march on, other means may be found to keep the Tories in order there, you will merit & require the thanks of the continent if you think proper to improve this hint, the resolve of Congress for detaining them was obtained in consequence of your letter to me on that Subject.[2] The arms that came on the Ship blown up at our Capes I am told were pretty generally damaged in the explosion,[3] the Continent had 2500 on board & for your State 500, but the Packages are all blown to pieces and the Muskets mixed, therefore of what is saved we must receive in proportion & I am now sending for the whole to this City to have them put in order & divided, that done I will inform your Excellency or the Council of Safety & deliver what I receive as my proportion to their order.

The Continent also recd when at Balto 52 bbls of the Powder I imported for your State, supposing it theirs, I will get an order for it & send the same down, for I think that Powder is still at Baltimore. I am very respectfully, Your Excellys most Obedient & very hble Servant,

Robt Morris

RC (MdAA).
    [1] See *JCC*, 7:318–19.
    [2] See John Hancock to Thomas Johnson and John McKinly, April 20, 1777, note.
    [3] See the Secret Committee's letters to Caesar Rodney of April 15, 25, and May 2, 1777.

Daniel Roberdeau to Benjamin Franklin

Dear Sir,   Philada. May 1st. 1777

Being one of the committee for Foreign applications I had it in my power to pay the more immediate attention to your recommendation of le Chevalier de Mauduit du Plessis and through Favor of Congress immediately procured him a Commission for Capt. of Artillery[1] and he was with out delay in two or three days after his arrival here forwarded to General Washington. I have met with irreparable Loss of my dr. Mrs. Roberdeau[2] which is such a source of Affliction that I shall not attempt the unnecessary work of informing you of the State of things here, knowing you will have intelligence from better hands by this Conveyance. I beg the favr. of a safe conveyance of the enclosed Letters. May God succeed your faithful Endeavours for our America. I am, Dr. Sir, Yr. most obt & very huml Sert,

Daniel Roberdeau

RC (PPAmP).
    [1] See *JCC*, 7:269, 272.
    [2] See Roberdeau to Elisha Hinman, April 7, 1777, note.

Benjamin Rumsey to Thomas Johnson

Sir   1777 May 1. Philada.

I promised the Officers of our State passing thro' this Town to write to you on a Subject that gives them much Concern. They have no Commissions and they say Government engaged to send them to this Place and if they are taken without they will be treated as private Soldiers. I could wish they might be satisfied.[1]

Congress being informed to Day by Genl. Schuyler that 100 Men of Colo. Richardsons Men were now in this City have ordered them up to Camp and given You a Power to detain 100 or as many out of any other Men of any of the weaker Battallions in Maryland as are here of that Battalion.[2]

An Act of Parliament has to Day been received making it Felony for our Men to fight on the Ocean agt the King of Britain. I have not seen or heard it. Mr. Smith has but does not remember it well enough to give a particular Acct.

The Enemy are landing their Cannon &c on Staten Island supposed to be for an Attack on this Town. This Dr. Witherspoon hath this Day received Advice off.

I am afraid the 2000 Arms will not be granted.[3] By a Letter from A. Lee of the 20th Feby from Bordeaux in his Way to Paris Burgoine with 10,000 Germans & 3000 British Troops are to attack Boston, How Philadelphia, Carlton the back Settlements &c. Yet we will take every favourable Opportunity We can to procure them. This will be from Carlisle I imagine.

I need not apologise for the Delay of the Express. My Colleague and myself have done all We could to send him off sooner but the House have been 3 Days squabling abt. what might have been done in three Minutes. I am Sir, your Excellency's most humble Servant,

                                                    Benjamin Rumsey

RC (MdAA).
[1] Although the correspondence on this subject apparently does not survive, Governor Johnson had responded to this plea for Maryland officers' commissions by May 13 when Rumsey's fellow delegate William Paca acknowledged receipt of the commissions requested. See William Paca to Thomas Johnson, May 13, 1777.
[2] See *JCC,* 7:284–86, 319.
[3] See Maryland Delegates to Thomas Johnson, April 28, 1777, note 2.

Secret Committee Minutes of Proceedings

                                                    May 1st. 1777.

Issued two drafts on the Contl. Treasurer, Michl. Hillegas Esqr.

at Baltimore, for 37,500 dlls. in favor of Mr. J. Steinmetzs, he having pd that sum here to Mr. Morris to be applied to public use.[1]

MS (MH–H).
[1] The following note in the copyist's hand appears at the foot of the page and is keyed at this point: "This was a mode of preventg. R. Morris from being chargd on the public books of the treasury, tho he pocketed the public Money. A Lee. All the paymts made when seperate from the Come. were transacted by the Marine Committee." For similar footnoted comments pertaining to Robert Morris found in this copy of the committee's "journal," see Secret Committee Minutes of Proceedings, April 24, 1777, note.

George Walton to Lachlan McIntosh

Philadelphia 1st May 1777
... "The preceeding subject having necessarily drawn me into the mention of this man [B. Gwinett][1] I cannot readily dismiss him; not from any partiality to his virtues, but from an abhorrence of his vices.[2] Mark him at the first moment of his arrival in that Country & trace him (if it be possible to follow him thro the great variety of his shiftings & turnings) down to the present crisis; and you will find no criterion by which you might fix any character. A mere Proteus in principle, he makes virtue subservient to his vices; to cover the multitude of the latter he affects to be possessed of the former. With the loudest clamorings for Liberty he would ruin the Country whose cause he pretends to advocate; and with the warmest declaration of Friendship he would stab the most virtuous of Characters. Counteract one machination and he will have recourse to another. Disgrace him for discovered crimes, he will seek a palliation and founds a reestablishment in the delusions of Patriotism. Has he not deserted all parties with which he was ever known to be engaged? Has he ever professed a friendship (save one perhaps [Lyman Hall]) but to betray?[3] Did he not consent to put you at the head of a Regiment when he could not keep it himself with a premeditated intention to ruin you? Did he not betray the trust of his Country when he was here [Philadelphia] respecting arms and ammunition for the second & third Battalions of Georgia Troops & Denying me the necessary support in getting them sent from hence or procuring an order on our Agent in Martinique to send a Vessel to Georgia with them, either of which could have been obtained. He without my knowledge applies to the secret committee; and assuring them with his accustomed confidence that he could mighty easily get them at the Mole, Hispaniola & I don't know how many places they readily furnished him with 20,000 dollars for the purpose of supplying these Battalions with Arms &c and they were to be ready long before the troops were raised.[4] Whether he has performed this

contract with the United States let Colonels Elbert & Screven declare. Thinking the continent, the State & myself ill used in this business I mentioned the matter with all the attendant circumstances in a public letter [5] to my late worthy friend Mr President Bulloch who I am informed sent the letter to the convention. The secretary delivered it to the Speaker (Mr Gw——tt) and he suppressed it. The iniquity of the proceeding speaks so loudly that it calls for vengeance &c &c. This self elected Demaacque [Demagogue] is dispised more or less every where. His election by his own vote is detested beyond measure. If he has not fascinated the senses of the whole people and has not the power of preserving the infatuation, he must, sooner or later atone for these things," &c &c.

Tr (DLC). Headed: "Extracts from another Letter of George Walton to General McIntosh dated Philadelphia 1st May 1777."

[1] Names in brackets, here and below, appear at the foot of the Tr, keyed with asterisks.

[2] For Walton's earlier criticism of Georgia President Button Gwinnett, see Walton to McIntosh, April 18, 1777.

[3] For Gwinnett's special friendship with Hall, see Charles F. Jenkins, *Button Gwinnett: Signer of the Declaration of Independence* (New York: Doubleday, Page & Co., 1926), p. 62.

[4] For more details about Gwinnett's contract, see Secret Committee Minutes of Proceedings, July 12, 1776.

[5] Not found.

John Adams to Abigail Adams

May 2. 1777 [1]

We have promoted Arnold, one Step this day, for his Vigilance, Activity, and Bravery, in the late Affair at Connecticutt. We shall make Huntingdon a Brigadier, I hope.[2]

We shall sleep in a whole Skin for some Time I think in Philadelphia, at least untill a strong Reinforcement arrives.

I want to learn, where Sir William Erskine with his Two Thousand Men, went after his Exploit at Danbury. Perhaps to Newport.

RC (MHi). Adams, *Family Correspondence* (Butterfield), 2:230.

[1] For a brief letter to Abigail and their children which Adams wrote the preceding day about Tammany, a seventeenth-century chief of the Delawares whose local popularity was turned to political ends in 1773 when Philadelphia radicals founded the Sons of Saint Tammany, see ibid., pp. 229–30.

[2] Benedict Arnold was promoted to major general on this date; Jedediah Huntington was promoted to brigadier general on May 12. *JCC*, 7:323, 347.

John Adams to James Warren

Dear Sir   May 2 1777

Dr Brownson, a Delegate from Georgia, in Congress, and a worthy, Spirited, sensible Man, a Native of Connecticutt will deliver you this.[1] He will be able to tell you much News, because he intends a circuitous Journey by Albany, and the New Hampshire Grants, who have lately made themselves a state, to Boston.

The British Demons have recd a little Chastisement in Connecticutt.

J. Adams

RC (MHi).

[1] Nathan Brownson had received leave of absence from Congress on May 1. *JCC*, 7:321.

Thomas Burke to Richard Caswell

Sir   Philadelphia May 2d 1777

I wrote you the day before yesterday by an Express going to Charlestown, and after I had sealed up the letter, some intelligence was opened in Congress, which I wrote on a slip of paper and put into the cover. I doubt not you will receive it.[1]

Mr Cochran of Cross Creek going home to day gives me an opportunity of giving you all the intelligence relative to that affair, which has been a little mischievous, and threatens consequences much more considerable than have happened. The inclosed paper contains the whole, as it was laid before Congress; except a few expressions of General Arnold, complaining of the behaviour of the Connecticut Militia, and of the supineness of the country which suffered such an insult without resistance or proper revenge. You will easily perceive that publishing such things would have no good effect.[2]

As Mr Cochran sets off at three to-day, and I shall be all the intermediate time engaged in Congress, I shall not have time to write by him to any friend who may be in the Assembly. I must therefore entreat you to give the members of Assembly this intelligence in the most public manner you can.

An insulting letter written by the Captain[3] of one of the Continental Frigates to the Governor of Maryland has excited great indignation in Congress. The Officer is suspended, and ordered in five days to make such satisfaction as the Governor and Council shall accept, or, failing, to be dismissed the service. Every Gentleman (a few only excepted) seemed to feel his own State injured in this insult, and they were determined that nothing less should do, than what would satisfy Maryland, and convince Officers that they were very far inferior to the

Magistrates of States, and must treat them with the most profound respect. I never had more hopes of Congress than I have now. All seem sensible that the honour and dignity of the Magistrates of the States ought to be preserved sacred and inviolable; whether for applying the force of the States, or restraining abuses, and suppressing ambition.

Your Excellency knows enough of my political creed to believe that this disposition is exceedingly pleasing to me. I have not time to add more, but that I have the honor to be, Your &c,

Thos Burke

Tr (Nc–Ar).

[1] This "intelligence" concerned the recent British raid on Danbury, Conn. See Burke to Caswell, April 30, 1777.

[2] On May 1 Congress read an April 30 letter from Washington to President Hancock containing numerous enclosures describing the Danbury raid and directed the committee of intelligence "to publish such extracts from them as they judge proper." Later, however, Congress rescinded this order and erased it from the journals. See *JCC,* 7:319; PCC, item 152, 4:121–45; and Washington, *Writings* (Fitzpatrick), 7:493–94.

[3] James Nicholson.

Committee for Foreign Affairs to the
Commissioners at Paris

Gentlemen   No. 1   In Committee for Foreign Affairs

The former of those Letters will serve to shew that at the Time of writing them we had nothing material to inform you of, and are now sent rather for your Amusement than instruction.

Philadelphia May 2d. 1777

Your dispatches dated Paris Feby 6th & 8th were safely recd about the middle of April.[1] We observe your Remarks on the Timerousness of the French Merchants respecting the forming Trading Companies which you say is occasioned by the change and fluctuation of News. That the Spirit for trade will always be governed by the rise or fall of Military strength is a maxim always to be admitted in the first attempts to establish a Commerce between any two Nations, because success in War is supposed to give Security or Protection to it; But this timidity ceases naturally as soon as a trade is opened for losing or gaining after *that* equally produces a Spirit of adventuring farther; Therefore, we wish to enter into a Commerce with them as soon as possible because as nothing can abridge or prevent their Profits but the Enemy making Prizes of their Vessels, the consequence will be, that they will either be encouraged by the gain, or aggravated by the loss to come to a Serious understanding with the Court of Britain. We advise you to be constantly holding up the great advantages which the Crown and Commerce of France would receive by possessing themselves of the West Indies, and We Trust to your Wisdom in making all the use possible of the English Newspapers as a channel thro' which to counteract the Tide of folly and falsehood of which you complain and rest assured that every Material Circumstance either for or against will be dispatched to you with the utmost expedition.

By Information from N York it appears that the more discerning part of the English Generals begin to give up the thought of Conquest, and of Consequence the fear of totally losing the trade of America must accompany the despair of Arms, therefore we conceive that the English Papers are calculated to deter the French merchants from beginning to taste the sweets of our Trade. Their falsehoods rightly understood are the Barometers of their fears, & in Proportion as the Political Atmosphere presses downward the spirit of Fiction is obliged to rise. We wish it to be understood that we pay too much respect to the Wisdom of the French Cabinet to suppose they can be influenced by such efforts of Visible despair, and that We have too much reverence for the Honor of the American Congress to prostitute its authority by filling our own Newspapers with the same kind of invented Tales which characterise the London Gazette.

We observe that General Howe in his Letter to administration printed in London Gazette of Decr. 30th apologizes for not having written to them since his taking possession of New York (nearly three months). Here is the proper field to speculate on Silence, because his business is conquest, ours, defence and repulse, and because likewise he has the sea more open to him than we have, had he any thing to send that would please; therefore silence on his part is always to be understood as a species of good news on ours.

The Congress highly approves your dividing yourselves to foreign Courts, and have sent Commissions for that Purpose and likewise Commissions for fitting out Privateers in France.[2] The Mercury from Nantz is safely arrived at Hampsh., the Amphitrite and Seine we are yet in hopes of.[3] We shall Notice the Conduct of Nicholas Davis. We have presented Marshal Maillebois Sentiments on the Mode of War to Congress who are greatly pleased therewith and entertain a high respect for the Author.[4]

Our last Accounts gave you the State of News down to March since which nothing material has happened. The Enemy wearied and disappointed in their Winters Campaign still continue in a State of dormancy at N York and Brunswick. The Congress is Returned to Philadelphia, Genl Washington remains at Morris Town and occupies the same Posts as when the last dispatches were sent you. The Principal object now is the Recruiting Service which has been greatly promoted by some late Resolves of Congress. Our Troops have been under inoculation for the Small Pox with good Success which Purgation we hope will be a means of preserving them from fevers in the Summer, however it will frustrate one cannibal Scheme of our Enemies who have constantly fought us with that disease by introducing it among our Troops.

When we look back to the beginning of last December and see our Army reduced to between two and three thousand men occasioned by the Expiration of the Time for which they were engaged, we feel ourselves exceedingly happy in Contemplating the agreeable Condition and prospect our affairs are now in, we have since that Period reduced the Enemy more than our whole Army at that time consisted of, and scarce a day passes in which they do not suffer either by Skirmishes or desertions.

The Congress have it in Contemplation to remove the Garrison from the present fort in the district of Ticonderoga to fort Independance in the same district which they judge will command that pass with greater advantage and is a much healthier Situation. We mention this as the Enemy will probably give an Air of Triumph to the evacuation should it be done. The distance between the two is about a quarter of a Mile.[5]

As Genl Howe is preparing a Bridge of Boats we think it possible that he might by a sudden and forced march, reach this City, but we are clearly of opinion that he would be ruined by the Event, and tho' we are not under much apprehension of such a movement yet we think it proper to give you the Case with our opinion thereon.

We are Gentlemen, your Obt. Hble Srvts,

Benja Harrison   Thos. Heyward Junr.

Robt Morris   James Lovell[6]

RC (PPAmP). In a clerical hand and signed by Harrison, Heyward, Lovell, and Morris. A duplicate, with the additional signature of John Witherspoon, is also in the Franklin Papers, PPAmP.

[1] The commissioners' February 6 letter is in Wharton, *Diplomatic Correspondence*, 2:261–65. Their letter of February 8 has not been found.

[2] See Richard Henry Lee to Arthur Lee, April 20, 1777; and *JCC*, 7:317–18.

[3] For further information on the arrival of the *Amphritrite* at Portsmouth, N.H., see *JCC*, 7:335; and *Warren-Adams Letters*, 1:318–19.

[4] See Richard Henry Lee to George Washington, April 16, 1777, note 2.

[5] Congress made its approval of this move contingent on General Gates' judgment that "the great point of preventing the enemy penetrating the country may be better obtained by applying his whole force to the strengthening and securing Fort Independence and the water defence of Lake George." *JCC*, 7:307.

[6] Although Lovell and Heyward were not officially elected to the Committee for Foreign Affairs until May 26, 1777, a deleted entry indicating their addition to the committee appears in the journals under the date April 17—the day the Committee of Secret Correspondence was transformed into the Committee for Foreign Affairs. *JCC*, 7:276, 8:385.

James Duane to Certain Members of the
New York Convention

Dear Gent.   Philad. 2d May 1777

The principal design of this is to recommend to your Attention Col. Thornton who will pass thro' Kingston in his way from Congress to New Hampshire of which State he is a Delegate.[1] You will find him to be very chearful and agreeable and you can collect from him every thing worthy of your attention which has passed here. I therefore need not enlarge.

Since our Arrival Four thousand Continental Troops have passed this Town or are now here on their way from the Southward to join General Washington. Many more are daily expected and particularly 3000 from North Carolina. They all undergo Innoculation which is a great, tho' necessary Impediment to the Assembling the Army. Congress's Ideas of being able to recruite more than 100 Battalions were too enlargd. However by all Accounts there are few or none of the Southern regiments which have less than 300 Privates. And if the Eastern States are not more deficient there will still be a formadable army; especially as some Battalions are much more compleat.

We shall write to Congress soon & shall then endeavour to be more particular with respect to the Levies and foreign Intelligence.

In the mean time permit me to assure you that, I am with the utmost Regard, Dear Gent, Your affect & most obedient Servant,

                                                           Jas Duane

RC (NNC). Addressed: "Honl Rob R. Livingston, John Jay Esqs, Gouverneur Morris, & Robert Yates Esqs."

[1] Matthew Thornton had received leave from Congress on May 1 to return home. *JCC*, 7:321.

John Hancock to Thomas Johnson

Sir,   Philada. May 2d. 1777

I had the Honour of receiving your Favour of the 26th Ulto and communicated the same to Congress; in Consequence whereof they passed the inclosed Resolves, a Copy of which as far as they respect Captain Nicholson, I have forwarded to him by this Express.[1]

Two Companies of Colo. Richardson's Battalion (which you had ordered to remain in Maryland in Pursuance of a Resolve of Congress) being at present in this City on their Way to Genl. Washington, the Congress have thought proper to detain them here, & have empowered you to replace them by detaining any two Companies of the weakest

Battalion now remaining in your State.[2] I have the Honour to be with great Respect, Sir, your most obed. & very hble Sert.

J.H. Presid.

LB (DNA: PCC, item 12A).
[1] See Marine Committee to James Nicholson, April 29, 1777, note.
[2] See *JCC,* 7: 284–86, 319.

Marine Committee to Benjamin Dunn

[May 2, 1777]

We are now at the second of May and as you have been detained here so long for want of Men it may probably be too late to take in Stores at the Mole and return to the Continent, therefore you may deliver the flour to Mr. Dupuy and immediately proceed on a Cruize which you may continue to the 10th day of July and then open the sealed Instructions given you herewith [1] by which you are to be governed after that time and if during your Cruize you fall in with the Randolph, Captain Biddle, or Andrew Doria, Captain Robinson, you must receive orders from them to Cruize in Concert. You have Signals enclosed to know them by and, We are, sir, Your hble servants.

LB (DNA: PCC Miscellaneous Papers, Marine Committee Letter Book). A continuation of Marine Committee to Benjamin Dunn, April 19, 1777.
[1] See Marine Committee Instructions, April 29, 1777.

Marine Committee to Isaiah Robinson

[May 2, 1777]

We are now at the second of May and as you have been detained so long for want of Men and may probably be some time longer before you get out to Sea we now direct that you embrace the first opportunity to push out and proceed for Cape François delivering the Letters given you herewith to Mr. Ceronio, also the Cargo, after which you need not take in any Stores nor attempt coming back to this Coast, but proceed from the Cape soon as possible on a Cruize which you may continue until the 10th day of July and then open the sealed Instructions [1] which are to govern you from that time. Should you fall in with the Randolph, Captain Biddle, you must receive Orders from him and Cruize in Concert.

We are sir, Your obed servants

P.S. We expect Captain Biddle to proceed to the Cape and he is directed to Convoy from thence the Brig Anne, Capt. Garrigues, and the Sloop Phoebe, Captain Gilbert. Should the Randolph not arrive you must convoy those two Vessels off the Coast of Hispaniola as they will take in the Stores intended for you.

LB (DNA: PCC Miscellaneous Papers, Marine Committee Letter Book). A continuation of Marine Committee to Isaiah Robinson, April 19, 1777.

[1] See Marine Committee Instructions, April 29, 1777.

Secret Committee Minutes of Proceedings

May 2d. 1777.

Come. met. Present Morris, Whipple, Lee. The Come. have agreed to allow S & J Penrose, Owners of the Ship Sally 70/ sterlg. per diem demurrage for the time sd. ship was detain in France, agreable to an Acct. they have deliverd in, & to pay them in bills of exchange for that & balance of trade due them for sd. vessel. Mr. B. Gibbes laid before the Come. an Estimate of what he supposes will be the amount of the sales of the Brige. Ann's cargo, lately purchasd of him by the Come.[1] Suppose 300 Casks Rice at 5 1/2 C.Wt. each is 1750 lb at 25 livs. &

Casks is 44950 livres—[2]	£2107.12
deduct for charges &c	207.12
	£1900.
Advance 100 per Ct. per Agreement	1900.
	3800
vessels value he payg. all Charges till Cargo delivered.	1800
	5600

Agreed that £5000 be advancd in part paymt. of the above Estimate, And an order was drawn on Mr. Morris in favor of sd. Gibbes for that Sum. Order on J. Gibson Esqr. favor Saml. Penrose & Co. for 4500 dlls being the price of the Sloop Phoebe purchased from them, & part paymt. for their bill on Stepn Ceronio for ballance of proceeds of sd. vessel's cargo in his hands.

MS (MH–H).

[1] See Secret Committee Minutes of Proceedings, April 24, 1777.

[2] The figures in the MS appear clearly as printed, but it seems probable that the copyist made one or more errors in transcription. For example, 300 casks of rice at 5 1/2 cwt. would weigh 1650 cwt., which at 25 livres per cwt. would cost 41,250 livres.

Secret Committee to Caesar Rodney

Sir   Philada. May 2d. 1777
   Not meeting with an opportunity to send down the annexd letter
soon as intended We have now employed Capt John Hun to go down
& get the Goods shipped up.[1] He will deliver you this letter & you'l
please to direct that all the Goods be committed to his management
and give him such advice or assistance as may be found necessary.
   On behalf of the Committee I am sir, Your obedt hble servt.
                                                    Robt Morris

RC (PHi). Written and signed by Morris.
   [1] Morris wrote this letter on the verso of the committee's April 25 letter to
Rodney. For a list of the cargo salvaged from the *Success,* see Rodney, *Letters*
(Ryden), p. 186.

Secret Committee to George Washington

Sir   In Secret Committee Philada. May 2d. 1777
   We are obliged to trouble your Excellency with the enclosed letter
for Mr Boudinot[1] containing a remittance of Six hundred pounds
Sterlg for the use of the Continental Prisoners in New York as we
do not know Mr Boudinots address & we have left the letter unsealed
for your perusal. We preferred Mr Franks's bills as they are drawn
on the Contractors in England, & may probably be the more readily
negotiated in New York. With the greatest respect & esteem, We are
Your Excellencys Obt hble servts,

         Robt Morris   Wm. Whipple

         Richard Henry Lee   Phil. Livingston

RC (DLC). Written by Morris and signed by Morris, Lee, Livingston, and
Whipple.
   [1] The committee's May 2 letter to Commissary of Prisoners Elias Boudinot,
which also was written by Morris and signed by Morris, Lee, Livingston, and
Whipple, states in part: "By order of Congress in consequence of a recommendation from His Excy. Genl. Washington we enclose herein to your care
a sett of Exchange . . . on Arnold Nesbitt, Adam Drummond and Moses Franks
Esqr. London, No. 12, at 30 days sight for Six Hundred pounds sterling . . . This
remittance is for the use of Continental Prisoners in New York . . . we refer you
to such instructions as His Excellency Genl. Washington has given or may give
you." *Parke-Bernet Galleries Catalog,* no. 2569 (May 16, 1967), item 38, p. 34.
For Washington's recommendations and response, see his April 26 and 28
letters to President Hancock and his May 5 letter to the Secret Committee in
Washington, *Writings* (Fitzpatrick), 7:476, 491; 8:18.

John Adams to James Warren

My dear Sir   Philadelphia April [i.e. May] 3. 1777

Yours of April 3d I recd.[1] I must confess that I am at a Loss to determine whether it is good Policy in Us to wish for a War between France and Britain, unless We could be sure that no other Powers would engage in it. But if France engaged, Spain will and then all Europe will arrange themselves on one side and the other, and what Consequences to Us might be involved in it, I dont know. If We could have a free Trade with Europe, I should rather run the Risque of fighting it out with George and his present Allies, provided he should get no other. I dont love to be intangled in the Quarrells of Europe, I dont wish to be under Obligations to any of them, and I am very unwilling they should rob Us of the Glory of vindicating our own Liberties.

It is a Cowardly Spirit in our Countrymen, which makes them pant with so much longing Expectation, after a French War. I have very often been ashamed to hear so many Whiggs groaning and Sighing with Despondency, and whining out their Fears that We must be Subdued unless France should step in. Are We to be beholden to France for our Liberties?

France has done so much already, that the Honour and Dignity and Reputation of Great Britain is concerned to resent it, and if she does not, France will trifle with her forever hereafter. She has recd our Ambassadors, protected our Merchant Men, Privateers, Men of War and Prizes—admitted Us freely to trade—lent Us Money and Supplied Us with Arms, Ammunition, and Warlike stores of every Kind. This is notorious all over Europe. And she will do more, presently, if our dastardly Despondency in the midst of the finest Prospects imaginable does not discourage her. The surest and the only way to secure her Arms in this Cause is for Us to exert our own. For Gods Sake then dont fail of a single Man of your Quota. Get them at any Rate, and by any Means, rather than not have them.

I am more concerned about our Revenue than the Aid of France. Pray let the Loan officers do their Part, that We may not be compelled to make Paper Money, as plenty and of course as cheap as Oak Leaves. There is so much Injustice in carrying on a war with a depreciating Currency that We can hardly pray with Confidence for success.

The Confederation has been delayed because the states were not fully represented. Congress is now full—and We are in the midst of it. It will soon be passed.

God prosper your new Constitution. But I am afraid you will meet the Disapprobation of your Constituents. It is a Pity you should be obliged to lay it before them. It will divide and distract them.

However their Will be done. If they suit themselves they will please me, your Friend

RC (MHi). In Adams' hand, though not signed.

[1] This letter to John Adams is in the *Warren-Adams Letters,* 1:309–10.

John Hancock to George Washington

Sir,   Philada. May 3d. 1777.

The enclosed Resolves, relative to a Variety of Subjects, are all that I have in Charge from Congress to forward at this Time.[1]

The additional Resolves respecting the Muster Masters were highly requisite to compleat that Department, and will, I trust, be punctually carried into Execution.[2]

You will perceive that Mr. Ludwick is appointed to superintend the Baking Business in the Army, which I make no Doubt he will do to the entire Satisfaction of the Troops, and in such a Manner as to save considerable Sums to the Public.[3]

The Conduct of Genl. Arnold on the late Expedition of the Enemy against the Town of Danbury being highly approved of by Congress, they have promoted him to the Rank of Major General.[4]

Your Favour of the 30th ulto. was duely received.[5] I have the Honour to be, with the greatest Respect & Esteem, Sir, your most obed. & very hble Servt.   John Hancock Presidt

RC (DLC). In the hand of Jacob Rush and signed by Hancock.

[1] In addition to those specifically mentioned in the text, Hancock also sent Washington May 1 and 3 resolves on reinforcements from Maryland, John Belton's "improved" musket, and miscellaneous appointments. *JCC,* 7:319, 324.

[2] Hancock sent Washington a John Dunlap broadside containing May 2 resolves for the prevention of fraudulent muster rolls. *JCC,* 7:322; and Washington Papers, DLC.

[3] See *JCC,* 7:323.

[4] Ibid.

[5] See Thomas Burke to Richard Caswell, May 2, 1777, note 2.

Francis Lightfoot Lee to Adam Stephen

Dear Sir,   Philadelphia May 3. 1777

An hundred times have I been going to write to you, & as often been interrupted. I hope you will not punish me too severely, by ceasing to let me know, now & then, what you are doing. We hear there are some appearances of the Enemy quitting the Jerseys, will you let them get off unhurt? Considerable reinforcements are coming forward, near 2000 are now marching from hence.

Great exertions will be made against us this campaign, our exertions must be proportioned; but I am sure it will not avail us much to have numbers in the feild, if they are not under proper discipline, of which I almost despair, so very shamefull has been the conduct of our Officers for some months past. Unless the Generals take extraordinary pains & examine minutely into every particular relative to the troops, disease & despondency will make them an easy prey to the Enemy. Cleanliness in lodging & diet, just payments, and martial exercises will make them invincible. Tis true your troops are at present raw; but you may remember that Epaminondas soon bro't his disheartend Countrymen to beat the best troops, then in the world; by his excellent discipline, & frequent judicious skirmishes. I know I incur the ridicule of the Orator who discoursed of war before Hanibal but I cant help it, the subject lies too heavy upon my mind. The stake we play for is not a common one.

Tis a pity so many of our stores were laid up in that nest of Tories at Danbury & its environs; the loss will not easily be repaired, & the disgrace is injurious. These things hurt us exceedingly with our own people, & have a bad influence abroad. God send you may soon give us something to put on the other side of the Account.

The Lottery managers informed me, they had sent Tickets to camp, so that I suppose you are supplied. May the genius of Liberty attend your steps & render you victorious over all its Enemies.

Farewell,   Francis Lightfoot Lee

RC (PPRF).

Benjamin Rumsey to Thomas Johnson

Sir   Philada. May 3d. 1777

I take the Liberty to inclose to your Excellency a Letter written by Major Forrest to Col. Ramsey on the Subject of the Officers Commissions.[1]

Many of them have passed thro' this Town in their Way to Camp and are exceedingly uneasy at not having them, they continually wait on the Delegates agreeable to the Expectations hinted at in the inclosed Letter and are greatly disappointed and much dejected at marching up without Commissions as they say they will be used but as common Men without them if they have the Misfortune to be taken by the Enemy.

Another Source of Discontent arises from the giving those Commissions Dated the 9th of April last to whom Commissions were before

given by the Commissioners on the 10th Decr. 1776. They say they
have been in the publick Service from that Time and it is hard they
should lose both their Rank and Pay.

A like Complaint is made by such as were appointed by the Commissioners. They think their Rank and Pay ought to be from the 10th
Decr. 1776 as the Want of Commissions was the only Reason they
were not made out for them.

At their pressing Entreaty I have a second Time wrote to your
Excellency and if the Matter appears to You of the same Importance
as to them beg You will send up the whole Arrangement to the Delegates and the Sentiments of our State relative to it. I have promised
them that if agreeable to You they should be sent to Camp.

I only wait for the Arrival of Mr. Paca to decamp, he is not yet
arrived or your Excellency might not possibly be troubled on the
Subject at all by, Your Excellency's Most humble Servant,

                                            Benjamin Rumsey

RC (MdAA).
[1] See Rumsey to Johnson, May 1, 1777, note 1.

William Whipple to John Langdon

My Dear Sir,   Philadelphia 3d May 1777

Your favor of the 12th ulto came to hand yesterday. I have not yet
heard of the arrival of the schooner (you mention) at Baltimore. However orders are given to dispatch her as soon as she arrives. I most
heartily lament with you the situation of our paper currency and am
sometimes almost ready to think with you that "all nature will not
support it." However another project is now on the tapis and if
that should fail, after a thorough trial we must endeavor to support the
war without for the war must be supported at all events till an honorable peace can be obtained.[1] In this I know you will agree with me
fully. But why do you suffer so much impudence from the Tories?
Is it possible that those pests to society should govern the town meetings
in the Metropolis of New Hampshire? I have much more to say to you
on this subject, but time not permitting must bid you Adieu.

                                            Wm Whipple

Tr (DLC).
[1] Whipple may have been referring to plans for obtaining foreign loans.
Congress had already authorized the commissioners at Paris to borrow £2
million sterling, and the possibility of other loans was under consideration. These
plans were central to the proposals presented to Congress on June 11 by the
committee appointed on May 15 "to devise ways and means for defraying the
expences of the present year." See JCC, 7:362, 8:453–57; Committee of Secret

Correspondence to the Commissioners at Paris, December 21, 1776, note 4;
and John Adams to Joseph Palmer, May 6, 1777.

John Adams to Abigail Adams

May 4. 1777

Inclosed with this you have an Evening Post,[1] containing some of
the tender Mercies of the Barbarians to their Prisoners.

If there is a Man, Woman or Child in America, who can read these
Depositions, without Resentment, and Horror, that Person has no soul
or a very wicked one.

Their Treatment of Prisoners, last Year added to an Act of Parliament, which they have made to enable them to send Prisoners to England, to be there murthered, with still more relentless Cruelty, in
Prisons, will bring our Officers and Soldiers to the universal Resolution
to *conquer* or *die*.

This Maxim, *conquer or die,* never failed to raise a People who
adopted it, to the Head of Man kind.

An Express from Portsmouth last night brought Us News of the
Arrival of Arms and ordnance enough to enable Us to take Vengeance
of these Foes of Human Nature.[2]

RC (MHi). Adams, *Family Correspondence* (Butterfield), 2:231.

[1] Probably a copy of the *Pennsylvania Evening Post*, May 3, 1777, which contained the last installment of the congressional report on British and German
barbarity in New Jersey during the preceding campaign. See Adams to Abigail
Adams, April 27, 1777; and *JCC*, 7:276–79.

[2] See Committee for Foreign Affairs to the Commissioners at Paris, May 2,
1777, note 3.

Charles Carroll of Carrollton to Charles Carroll, Sr.

Dr. Papa,   Pha. 4th May 1777

I got here yesterday by the half hour after two. Before this reaches
you will probably have heared of the expedition of the enemy into
Connecticut. They have destroyed, it is said, between 4 & 5 thousand
barrels of beef & pork & 25 hundred barrels of flour & some tents.
The exact amount of the damage done is not yet known.

An advanced party of Carleton's army by the last accounts from
Tionderoga was within 45 miles of that place. I am afraid Carleton
will be at Tionderoga before we can collect a force sufficient to
defend those lines. In that case Gen. Gates will probably evacuate
them & retire to fort independence on the eastern side of lake Champlain, & remove, if he has time, his canon & stores from the lines into

that fort. Congress have given discretionary orders to G. Gates to this
effect. Yesterday evening we received the following agreeable intelligence from Boston which you may certainly rely on, as Mr. Morris has
got the invoice of the goods. The ship Amphitrite is arrived at Portsmouth from France after a very long passage; she sailed from Havre
some time in Novr. Among a variety of other articles she has brought
the following: 53 brass field pieces (4 pounders) with all their necessary apparatus, a large assort. of ball, musket balls, primeers & intrenching tools, 6 thousand odd hundred muskets, a very great quantity
of gun powder, & &c. Mr. John Adams informed me that several
engineers & artillery men are come in the above vessel & that a
Colonel Conway in the Irish brigade is also come in to offer his services
to the united States.

Congress does not know the amount of G. Washington's army, and
I believe the general himself does not know it. What Howe will do is
uncertain—it is my opinion he will go up North River & try to join
Carleton. A letter from Docr. Arthur Lee dated on his way to
Madrid (the Date I can not learn) mentions that he had recd. a letter
from a correspondent in England informing him that Gen. Burgoyne
with ten thousand Germans & 3000 English was to attack Boston
early this Spring, that the transports had already sailed to take the
Germans on board. I believe it will be late in the year before this
reinforcement arrives.

Mr. Sam. Hanson will deliver you this letter. I think you will admire
his lady; she is not only beautiful, but appears to be of a sweet &
amiable temper. Molly & Mrs. Darnall & you will do all in yr. power
to make her stay at Douhoragen agreeable. How many commissioned
& noncommisioned officers do you imagine are in the pay of the
united States? Not less than 10,000. It is said 18 hundred are in this
city. Gen. Schuyler issued orders for them to attend him some day last
week at the State house, 200 only complyed with the order. Perhaps
the number of officers may be exaggerated, but it is agreed on all hands
that there [are] many more than 200. What do you think I pay a week
for my horse's food & stabling? Not less than £5.5.0 & £4 a week
for mine & my servant's board. If the Congress sits after two o'clock
I must dine at the Tavern; when it rises before 2 o'clock I shall dine at
my lodgings. There is another ship arrived at Portsmouth with the
above mentioned vessel & has brought 36 bales of cloth, 6 bales of
blanketts & furniture for light horse. A vessel which sailed from Nantes
with military stores is arrived at Martinico. The French in Martinico
have applied to Congress for commissions to cruize agt. the English
trade. Several commissions have been granted already. I think these
steps must inevitably draw on a war between France & England. The
Congress have not recd. any late advices from Docr. Franklin or
Dean. Docr. Lee is gone to Madrid. If we can stand this campaign I

think our independance will be secured. Carleton will, I am sure possess himself of our lines at Tionderoga, if he makes haste, & unless we can speedily collect an army at fort Independance on the east side of Lake Champlain opposite to Tionderoga, the Garrison of that fort consisting of 3000 under Gen. Wayne will I am afraid, fall into Carleton's hands, unless they retreat before he can invest them. I did intend to send this letter by Mr. Hanson, who will leave this city tomorrow to return home (he will take Douhoragen in his way) but as he will travel much slower than the post, and as I am desirous of your receiving the intelligence contained in this letter as early as possible I shall send it by Tuesday's post. I have seen several of our light horse. They really cut a good figure, & have a martial appearance, their horses (those I have seen) appear to be very good & are showy. If there should be any news of consequence before the post goes off, I will write again. My love to Molly & Mrs. Darnall. I am, yr. affectionate Son,

Ch. Carroll of Carrollton

RC (MdHi).

John Hancock to the States

Gentlemen,   (Circular) Philada. May 5th. 1777.

I have it in Charge from Congress to transmit the enclosed Resolves relative to sundry important Subjects and to urge your Compliance therewith.

The *Mode* therein recommended in order that Congress may be informed what Sums of Money have been advanced by the respective States for recruiting their Continental Battalions, and of the Expenditure of the same by the Officers, as it is the only effectual one that can be pursued, and the *Measure* is of the utmost Consequence to the United States, I make no Doubt you will immediately adopt *both*.[1] I beg Leave to refer your Attention to the Resolves, and have the Honour to be, Gentlemen, your most obed. & very hble Sert.[2]   J.H. Presid.

LB (DNA: PCC, item 12A).

[1] For these resolves of April 29, see *JCC,* 7:309–12.

[2] Hancock added this postscript to the letter he sent to the Connecticut Assembly: "Your favor by Mr Brown was duly received, & is now under the Consideration of the Board of War." Jonathan Trumbull Letterbooks, Ct. The letter referred to has not been identified.

John Adams to Abigail Adams

May 6. 1777

We have no News here but what comes from you—except that all is well and quiet at Ticonderoga, that We have four Thousand Troops there, and that they were not afraid of Carlton.

The Connecticutt People have given Sir Wm. Erskine a Concord and Lexington Drubbing. But I am very angry at our People for making a Magazine, so near the Water and among such a Gang of high Church Tories. The Loss however, will not be much felt, as We have many Magazines and a plentifull Supply.

Send our Men along and We shall drubb them yet effectually. Ample Vengeance will be yet taken, of these Disturbers of human Nature. ...[1] There is a chosen Curse, red with uncommon Wrath, yet reserved in the stores of Heaven for these, most mean and most wicked of Men.[2]

RC (MHi). Adams, *Family Correspondence* (Butterfield), 2:233-34.

[1] Suspension points in MS.

[2] Adams also wrote a brief letter to his four-year-old son, Thomas Boylston, on this day. Ibid., p. 234.

John Adams to Samuel Freeman

Sir   Philadelphia May 6. 1777

I had the Favour of your Letter of 23d Ult. by this days Post.[1]

As to the Petitions you mention, the Congress have made good no *Losses* to any Soldiers—nor any Accounts for Sickness, more than Pay, Rations, and Mileage.

I am much obliged to you for your Account of the several Acts passed by the assembly. It is very necessary that We should know here, the Proceedings of our Assembly. We often suffer much Anxiety, and indeed the public Cause often suffers from our Ignorance.

I am rejoiced above all Things that you have detached 2000 Men to Rhòde Island. It is the opprobrium of New England, that so small a Nest of Vermin has been so long unmolested at Newport.

We have no News here, but what you have had before. I hope you will hear of something done before long.

We have been insulted long enough. We have borne ever to[o] long Suffering. If something is not done soon I shall think Americans have very small souls.

I hope you will not fail a single Man of your Quota. Dont harbour the Thought of falling short. Send the Men along, for Gods Sake send them along, that We may suffer no more Surprises, and Disgraces, for Want of Men.

The Muster Master in this City, has mustered two hundred Men a day for Ten days Past. We shall have an Army, if the Lassitude of the Massachusetts dont discourage it. I am, with much Respect Sir, your servant,   John Adams

RC (MeHi).

[1] Freeman's April 23 letter to Adams is in the Adams Papers, MHi.

John Adams to Joseph Palmer

Dear Sir   Philadelphia May 6. 1777

I had a few days ago the Pleasure of receiving your Favour of the 16 ult.[1]

The Subject of Finances is the most important of any that can come under our Consideration. If We can Support these We can carry on the War with Vigour and probably with Success. But if We go on as We have We must suffer extream Distress. The Science of a Financier is to be learned only from Books or from Travels. I have Scarce a Moment to look into a Book and I never travelled. Some of our Bostonian Genius's who understand the Nature of Commerce and of Money must turn their Thoughts to those Subjects.

I think with you that We ought to negotiate with some foreign Power Loans of Cash; But this is attended with great Difficulty. We might possibly borrow, but there is a vast Risque in transporting the Money across the Sea.[2]

I know not what to say of the Lottery you say is in Contemplation. I dread the Effects of the Gambling Spirit that is abroad. Salt, Lead, Sulphur, Allum and Copperas are Articles of great Importance, but whether you cannot import them cheaper than you can make them (under all the Risques) I know not.

I wish you had informed me, how many Men of our Quota are raised and how many marched. We are suffering much for Want of Men. The surprises at Bound Brook, Peeks Kill and Danbury were all owing to this Cause. I hope and pray that our State will not fall a Man short of its Quota and that every Man will be sent to Ti and Morristown.

I Sincerely condole with you under Mrs Palmers Indisposition. Be pleased to make my Compliments to her and all the Family. I hope she will recover beyond your apprehensions.

I am &c,   John Adams

RC (PHC).

[1] Palmer's April 16 letter to Adams is in the Adams Papers, MHi.

[2] A committee appointed on May 15 to devise means to meet expenses proposed to avoid this danger by writing bills of exchange on the commissioners at Paris who would redeem them with funds raised through foreign loans and the sale of American supplies. Adams was one of a minority on September 10, 1777, voting against paying interest on loan office certificates in bills of exchange drawn on the commissioners at Paris. *JCC*, 7:362, 8:453–57, and 725. See also William Duer to Robert R. Livingston, May 28, 1777, note 3.

John Adams to James Warren

Dear Sir   Philadelphia May 6. 1777
About Ten Days ago, I had the Boldness to make a Motion that a Navy Board Should be established at Boston—certain Gentlemen looked Struck and Surprised—however it passed. I have moved, I believe fifteen Times, that a Nomination should take Place. Certain Gentlemen looked cold.

Two or three Days ago, the Nomination came on. Langdon, Vernon, Deshon, Dalton, Orne, Henley, Smith, Cushing, and Warren were nominated. This Day the Choice came on. At last Vernon, Warren and Deshon were chosen. The Board are to appoint their own Clerk who is to have 500 Dollars a year.[1]

I hope you will engage in this Business and conduct it with Spirit. You cannot be Speaker, and do this Duty too, I believe.[2]

I think the Town of Boston, will be offended. But I could not help it. This you will not mention. The salary for the Commissioners is 1500 Dollars a year. You will have the Building and fitting of all ships the appointment of officers, the Establishment of Arsenals and Magazines &c, which will take up your whole Time. But it will be honourable to be so capitally concerned in laying a Foundation of a great Navy. The Profit to you will be nothing. But the Honour and the Virtue, the greater.

I almost envy you this Employment. I am weary of my own, and almost with my Life. But I ought not to be weary in endeavouring to do well.

RC (MHi). In Adams' hand, though not signed.
    [1] On the creation of the Eastern Navy Board, see Adams to Warren, April 6, 1777.
    [2] Warren later told Adams that he was pressured into continuing as speaker of the Massachusetts House of Representatives: "When I came to Town it was with a full determination not to act as Speaker; but I was forced to accept for a few days." Warren to Adams, June 5, 1777, *Warren-Adams Letters,* 1:326. Warren remained speaker until May 27, 1778, when he was not reelected to the house of representatives and John Pickering succeeded him as speaker. Shipton, *Harvard Graduates,* 11:596; and Massachusetts House Journal, May 27, 1778, DLC(ESR).

James Duane to the New York Convention

Honourable Gentlemen,   Philad. 6th May, 1777.

Nothing of sufficient moment has happen'd since our last Letter to deserve your Attention. The Troops from the Southward are filing down towards General Washington, tho' not in such Numbers as cou'd be wished. He will however be soon at the Head of a respectable Force able to meet General Howe if he does not receive a very considerable Accession from Europe or from the disaffected among ourselves. Much as it might gratify you, there is not a sufficient Certainty to justify a Conjecture of the General's present Strength. When it can be done you shall be advised.

The Accounts from our Commissioners (or if you please Ambassadors) in France, Justify an Expectation that as well that Court as Spain will support the Americans in everything (at least) on this side of a Declaration of War. The Commissioners have procur'd very great Credit And for such Sums as leave it unquestionable that the Court of Versailles is at the Bottom their real Friend and privately supports their Applications. You may rely upon it that vast quantities of Artillery, Arms, Ammunition and Cloathing have been purchased on Credit for our use; no inconsiderable part of which is actually arrived. At the same time the French will in my Opinion be cautious of entering into an actual War till they find some decisive Advantage. When that approaches all Reserve will be laid aside. Great Brittain is at present in such humiliating Circumstances that she will bear every Insult rather than provoke a declaration of War. It was too great a condescention to hear the just Complaints of injur'd Americans! It was Treason against their Dignity to examine into their own Abuse of Power, to rectify their own Errors! What is the Conduct of this haughty nation at this Period of her disgrace? From her natural and inveterate Enemy she must bear every thing inflicted upon her, and dares hardly to complain.

Mr. Livingston and Mr Duer Join me in our most respectful Compliments to the Members of your honourable House.

I remain with the utmost Regard, Honl Gent., your most Obedient, humble Servant,   Jas Duane

RC (NjMoHP). *Journals of N.Y. Prov. Cong.*, 1:943. Salutation, place, and dateline supplied from Tr.

William Duer to the New York Convention

Sir,   Philadelphia, May 6th, 1777.

I have received your two favours of the 23d and 25th April,[1] the first relative to the accounts of teamsters, &c. in Westchester county, and the other in answer to mine of the [17] April.

I should have immediately sent off all the accounts in my possession by an express, but as Genl. Schuyler then thought of returning in two or three days, with the advice of my colleagues, I thought best to defer it, it being judged a much safer opportunity. Several letters have of late been opened on the road, and persons seized by the disaffected; should these accounts have met with such a fate, the public must have suffered extremely. I am extremely sorry that the unavoidable delay of Genl. Schuyler has occasioned the detention of these papers, but should he not be able to leave this place in three days from this time, which he now expects, I shall convey them in the safest manner possible.

The present opportunity not being considered by Mr. Duane and Mr. Livingston, as altogether safe, I think it is not advisable to write on any matters of importance.

I shall content myself with observing that we have surveyed our ground, and that we have no doubt but we shall make a successful attack on the points recommended to us.[2] The papers which I enclose you, will give you an insight into the news stirring here. The accounts of the arrival of the ship loaded with 52 field pieces and other ordnance, &c. may be depended upon. Her name is the Amphitrite, a 20 gun ship, chartered in France by Mr. Silas Deane. Mr. Livingston and Mr. Duane, both of whom are now busily engaged, desire me to present their respects to the Honourable Convention.

I am, sir, with great respect, Your obedt. hble. servt.

Wm. Duer.

Reprinted from *Journals of N.Y. Prov. Cong.*, 1:936. Addressed: "To the Honble. Pierre Van Cortlandt, Esqr."

[1] These letters are not in *Journals of N.Y. Prov. Cong.*

[2] "The points recommended," which were instructions adopted by the New York Convention on April 7, required the New York delegates to oppose the admission to Congress of any representatives from Vermont, to protest against Congress' appointment of Seth Warner—a Vermont leader—as commander of a regiment in New York, to send the convention all congressional resolutions that "may impliedly or expressly infringe the rights or jurisdiction of this state," and to withhold their consent from any plan of confederation until it had first been examined and approved by "this Convention or the future Legislature of this State." Ibid., 1:868–69.

Richard Henry Lee to Patrick Henry

Dear Sir,   Philadelphia May 6. 1777

Having written to you so lately by Express this chiefly serves to convey my wishes that another Delegate might be hastened here, for the reasons you will see in the inclosed note,[1] this moment put into my hands. By a late letter from France, we understand that our enemies have given up their plan of attacking Virginia for the present, in order to gratify their stronger resentment against New England. However, I greatly question their being able to do much against either, as a French & Spanish war seems inevitable. A curious Act of Parliament has passed to make our opposition on the land high Treason, and on the Sea Piracy—And directing a place of imprisonment in England until it is *convenient* to try the Offenders.[2] It is an acrimonious and foolish display of Tyranny. I am, with great respect, dear Sir, your most obedient and very humble servant,   Richard Henry Lee

RC (PU).
[1] Not found, but it probably concerned Thomas Nelson's inability to continue serving as a delegate. See Mann Page to John Page, this date, note 1.
[2] In the April 28 issue of the *New-York Gazette* a news item datelined London, February 8, reported that the House of Commons had approved Lord North's January 28 request "that leave be given to bring in a bill, to enable his Majesty to apprehend and secure all persons guilty of, or suspected to be guilty of high treason, in America, or of the crime of piracy on the high seas," which in essence meant suspension of the Habeas Corpus Act. For additional responses to this intelligence, see William Ellery to Nicholas Cooke, May 8; and Richard Henry Lee to Patrick Henry, May 13, 1777.

Mann Page to John Page

Dear Brother   Phila. May 6th 1777
I am much obliged to you for your Congratulations upon my Wife's Recovery. She is now restored to perfect Health. I wish our Friend Colo. Nelson was in a better Way than he is, for I really fear he will never again be able to attend to Business, the smallest Application affects his head. It will be Charity in the Assembly to send a Delegate immediately to relieve him. Rest from Business may be of Service to him, whereas if he stays he must inevitably die.[1] We have no News from the Jersies. The Enemy lately made an Excursion into Conecticut & destroyed a considerable Magazine at Danbury; of which & the arrival of the Amphitrite, General Washington has given our Governour as particular an Account as any I can furnish. Send us Men, & all will go well. Colo. Nelson, who knows more of the making the Seal, than any other of the Delegates, promises to enquire about it. As soon as it can be finished it shall be sent.[2] I am so much hurried with Business, & fatigued with writing a Number of other Letters that I must desire you to give my Love to my Sister, & conclude. I am, dear Sir, Your affectionate Brother,   Mann Page Junr.

RC (NjMoHP).

[1] Thomas Nelson's attendance in Congress in late April and early May 1777 cannot be ascertained precisely. Burnett credits him with attendance from April 30 to May 8, while a biographer recently suggested that Nelson arrived in Philadelphia around April 25 and eight days later suffered the stroke that hastened his return to Virginia. Burnett, *Letters*, 2:lxxii; and Emory G. Evans, *Thomas Nelson of Yorktown* (Williamsburg: Colonial Williamsburg Foundation, 1975), p. 64. Although Congress did not grant Nelson leave "for the recovery of his health" until May 8, it seems unlikely that he attended after his stroke, which probably had occurred before Page wrote this letter. *JCC*, 7:335. Furthermore, Nelson's entry under April 1777 in his account with Virginia included charges "to travelling to and from Phila" and "to attendance 8 days in Congress," suggesting that his services had been rendered primarily in April. Emmet Collection, NN.

At any rate Nelson was at his home in Hanover County, Va., on May 16 when he wrote to Speaker George Wythe requesting to be replaced in Congress. "A total inability to at[tend to business] having oblig'd me to quit the Congress, I beg leave, thro' you, to acquaint the Assembly with it, that they may appoint another Delegate; and I will take the liberty to advise, that this be immediately done, because Congress are now engag'd in forming the Confederation, in which Virginia is deeply interested.

"Nothing but necessity could have induced me to leave Congress at this critical time, & I hope I shall stand excus'd." Executive Communications, Vi. On May 22 George Mason was selected to relieve Nelson, and when Mason declined to serve, Richard Henry Lee was elected on June 24 to fill the vacancy.

[2] For details about making a seal for Virginia, see Thomas Jefferson to John Page, July 30, 1776.

Philip Schuyler's Memorial to Congress

To the honorable the Continental Congress

The Memorial of Major General Schuyler

Humbly sheweth   Phila. May 6th. 1777 [1]

That sundry Resolutions passed in your honorable House on the 15th Ultimo [i.e. March], conveying a severe Censure on your Memorialist for a supposed Contempt of the House deeply affect his Feelings both as an officer and a Citizen.

Your Memorialist with great Submission begs Leave to observe that these Resolutions appear to him to have been founded on a Misapprehension of his Letter to Congress of the 4th February,[2] and this he hopes to evince to the Satisfaction of the House.

He trusts that a Candor, rendered necessary on the principle of Self Justification will not give offence, so long as he confines himself within the Bounds of that Decency and Respect which are due to the grand Council of the united States.

For the Sake of perspicuity he begs Leave to recite the passages of his Letter on which the Resolutions of Congress were founded.

Philip Schuyler

"As Dr. Stringer had my Recommendation to the office he has sustained, *perhaps* it was a Compliment due to me, that I should have been advised of the Reasons for his Dismission."

These Expressions gave Rise to the following Resolutions.

"In Congress March 15th.

"Resolved that as Congress proceeded to the Dismission of Dr Stringer upon Reasons satisfactory to themselves, General Schuyler ought to have known it to be his Duty to have acquiesced therein.

"Resolved, that the Suggestion in General Schuyler's Letter to Congress, that it was a Compliment due to him to have been advised of the Reasons of Dr. Stringer's Dismission is highly derogatory to the Honor of Congress, and that the president be desired to acquaint General Schuyler that it is expected his Letters for the Future be written in a Stile more suitable to the Dignity of the Representative Body of these free and independent States, and to his own Character as their officer."

The other passage of your Memorialist's Letter which has given offence is in these words: "I percieve by some of the Resolutions that my Letter of the 30th December continued to the first of January [3] was received by Congress. I was in Hopes some Notice would have been taken of the odious Suspicion contained in Mr. Commissary Trumbull's intercepted Letter to the honorable W. Williams Esqr. I really feel myself chagrined on the Occasion. I am incapable of the Meaness he suspects me of, and I confidently expected Congress would have done me that Justice which it was in their power to give, and which I humbly conceive they ought to have done." [4]

Upon which Congress was pleased to resolve "That it is altogether improper and inconsistent with the Dignity of this Congress to interfere in Disputes subsisting among the officers of the army, which ought to be settled, unless they can be otherwise accommodated in a Court Martial agreeably to the Rules of the army, and that the Expressions in General Schuyler's Letter of the 4th of February, that he confidently expected Congress would have done him that Justice which it was in their power to give and which he humbly concieves they ought to have done, were, to say the least ill advised and highly indecent."

With Respect to the first Resolution your Memorialist begs Leave to observe, that the word acquiesce admits of a very extensive Construction and may either mean that your Memorialist ought to have obeyed your orders; that he ought to have been convinced of their Justice & propriety or that he was obliged to suppress his Sentiments concerning them.

If an obedience to your order was meant, your Memorialist assures this House that he caused the Letter from General Washington, covering the Dismission of Dr Stringer,[5] to be delivered to that Gentleman within half an Hour after its Receipt and that he prevailed on Dr

Stringer to continue in the Care of the Sick, and of the Hospital Stores, till the Arrival of Dr. Potts, by whom he was superceded. If this latter part of your Memorialist's Conduct which was dictated by common Humanity and a Regard to public Œconomy be deemed a Disobedience, he must plead guilty.

If by the word acquiesce a Belief of the Justice and propriety of the Measure was meant, your Memorialist begs Leave to observe, that Congress having made Rules for the Government of the army and its Followers and appointed a Mode of Trial, a general opinion has prevailed therein that all persons who enter the Military Service have a Right to be tried by these Rules, and if guilty to be punished.

The following Resolution of Congress of the 29th November ordering an Enquiry to be made into the Conduct of persons in the Medical Department, and which your Memorialist begs Leave to quote seems to justify this opinion, "That the General or commanding officer in each of the Armies cause strict Enquiry to be made into the Conduct of the Directors of the Hospitals and their Surgeons, Officers & Servants, and of the Regimental Surgeons, that if there had been any just Ground of Complaint in those Departments the offenders may be punished."

Your Memorialist begs Leave to observe, that tho' this Resolution did not come to his Hands till the 12th January when he was on public Business at Fish Kill, the Dismission of Dr Stringer took place on the 9th of that Month, a Circumstance which superceded the Enquiry which your Memorialist was on the point of instituting.[6]

The power of Congress to dismiss their Servants, without a formal Enquiry, your Memorialist, for his own part, never questioned; but its policy as a general Rule he humbly begs leave to observe, may be subject at least to one strong objection, it may tend to prevent Men of worth and abilities from affording to the public that assistance which they are capable of giving, from the apprehension that the Suggestions & Clamors too often arising from a Jealousy of Office might expose them to the Disgrace & Injury of a Dismission, without being heard in their own Defence.

If an Idea was intended to be conveyed by the Word *acquiesced,* that your Memorialist ought to have suppressed his Sentiments concerning the Resolutions of Congress, he is apprehensive that a principle would be held up of so broad a nature, as might sometimes be injurious to the public Interest. Should the great confidential Servants of Congress be precluded from the Indulgence of expressing their opinions or Sentiments on such of the Resolutions of your House as appear to them to affect the public Interest or to wound their own Feelings, Congress would certainly be deprived of many useful Suggestions, and one important Channel of Information, frequently arising from actual Experience be entirely cut off.

This Privilege your Memorialist from a Sense of Duty has exercised on several Occasions, in which Congress has not only acquiesced, but sometimes expressly approved of his Sentiments even when they did not coincide with their own Resolutions.

Among several Instances your Memorialist begs Leave to remind Congress of the Resolution of the 1st of July 1775 ordering him not to remove any of the Troops under his Command from New York.

That of the 8th January 1776 directing Shipwrights to be sent from New York and Philadelphia to build Batteaus at Fort George.

That of the 14th October last, withdrawing the Allowance of one and one third Dollar, as a Compensation to recruiting officers for inlisting Soldiers.

That for ordering Batteaumen to be raised in New York and several more, which your Memorialist humbly conceives were repealed or altered in Consequence of the Information he gave, and the Execution of others not insisted on, when your Memorialist pointed out the Objections to which they were liable.

It is true that when the Servants of the public give their Opinion of the Measures of Congress, Decency as well as Candor should be observed, and your Memorialist flatters himself that when his Motives for using the Expressions which have incurred Displeasure are duly compared and weighed, it will appear that he has not deviated from that Line. This, at least, he can conscientiously affirm that he hath in no Instance done it intentionally, Nothing having been more distant from his Thoughts, however they may be expressed, than to offend, or reflect upon, Congress.

Your Memorialist took it for granted that Congress was acquainted, that he had in a Manner forced Dr Stringer into the Service, that in August 1775 when Sickness was spreading through the Army under his Command at Tyonderoga with great Rapidity and they were not only destitute of competent medical assistance, but even of Medicine, the repeated Solicitations of your Memorialist, supported by the promisses of the late Mr. Lynch a Member of your honorable House (who was then at Albany) prevailed on Dr. Stringer to exchange an extensive and established practice for your Service, and to appropriate a large Stock of his own Medicines to the public use.

Your Memorialist begs Leave to observe that Dr Stringer, since his Dismission, without an Enquiry into his Conduct, imputes the Loss of a profitable Business, as well as that of his Medicines which cannot now be replaced, to your Memorialist, who, for that Reason, could not but be anxious to have it in his power to assign the Motives of Congress for taking that Measure.

When these Circumstances are attended to, and when it is considered that your Memorialist expressed his Wish of being informed of the Reasons for dismissing Dr Stringer, not as a Right, but merely as a

Matter of Compliment, and not from Impatience or Curiosity, but
with a View to obviate that Gentleman's Complaints, he flatters himself that the Expressions on which the first and second Resolutions
were founded will not appear in that unfavorable point of Light, in
which they have hitherto been considered. Conscious he is (and he
must again repeat) that he did not mean to wound the Dignity of
Congress, or to dispute their authority.

Your Memorialist begs Leave to tresspass on the patience of the
House, whilst he proceeds to the third Resolution which is founded,
as he hopes to evince, on Missapprehension.[7]

The Commissary General in a Letter to a Member of Congress, which
was accidentally made public, had accused your Memorialist with
detaining the Commission of Deputy Adjutant General of the Northern
Department which had been directed to be made out for Colo. John
Trumbull, the Commissary's Brother. An Imputation so injurious to the
Honor of your Memorialist could not be passed over in Silence: to
vindicate himself became a Duty, and the only Means by which it
could be effected were in the power of Congress because their honorable president must have known, and from his Candor & Regard for
Justice, been ready to declare, that the Commission had not at the
Time of writing that Letter been transmitted.

Your Memorialist entertained not the most distant Wish that Congress should interfere in the Dispute between him and Commissary
Trumbull, though the third Resolution is founded on such a Supposition. He applied only for their Testimony of the Fact, whether the
Commission had been transmitted to him or not: and very far was he
from apprehending that this could have given Offence or Displeasure,
even now he cannot but flatter himself, that upon a Revision it will not
appear to have been a presumptuous or unreasonable Request.

Without this Evidence how would it have been possible to convince
the World that the Suspicion was ill founded, or to have brought
Colonel Trumbull to a Court Martial for slandering his superior
Officer? Had this Mode been deemed by your Memorialist consistent
with the public Good.

Candor however obliges your Memorialist to confess, that, ignorant as
he was of the Sense of Congress in this point, he should not have
thought it a Transgression of the Bounds of his Duty, if he had directly
applied to them as a mediating power. May he be permitted to refer
it to their Consideration whether the Exclusion of an appeal to Congress
in Disputes between the great officers of the army, might not, in many
Instances, be attended with unhappy Effects?

What, he begs Leave to ask, must have been the Consequence, had
your Memorialist immediately arrested Major General Gates when,
on the Retreat of the Army from Canada, he disputed his Command?

Might it not have been greatly detrimental to the Service, especially as your Memorialist was under the Necessity at that Time to quit the army and to attend an Indian Treaty at the German Flatts? Would that Harmony have subsisted which was so necessary to the Good of the Service, which your honorable House so warmly recommended: and which your Memorialist trusts he can convince the whole World he has strenuously labored to cultivate?

In That Dispute, from a pure Zeal to the public Cause, your Memorialist waved the Rights of a superior Officer and appealed to Congress. They thought proper to take the Matter into Consideration, and passed the following Resolution.

"In Congress July 8th. 1776.

"Resolved, that General Gates be informed that it was the Intention of Congress to give him the Command of the Troops whilst in Canada: but had no Design to vest him with a superior Command to General Schuyler whilst the Troops should be on this Side Canada and that the president write to General Schuyler and General Gates stating this Matter and recommending to them to carry on the Military operations with Harmony & in such a Manner as shall best promote the public Service." They further directed their president to express their approbation of the Measures your Memorialist had taken on this Occasion.[8]

In the Case of Colonel Trumbull, if it be considered, that he was then Commissary General of all our Forces, that he accompanied the main Body of the Army under his Excellency General Washington, and that your Memorialist commanded in the Northern Department, might not great prejudices have accrued to the public Service if your Memorialist, as he had a Right to do, had arrested the Commissary General? Either the one or the other must at a very critical period have left his Station to attend the Enquiry and your Memorialist fears that if any Misfortune had followed such a Step, though he might have stood justified in the opinion of Congress, the world would have laid all the Blame upon him and he should have been censured for precipitation, Intemperance & Disregard to the public Good.

Your Memorialist, with Gratitude, begs Leave to remind Congress, that he has on many Occasions received their Thanks for the Zeal and unremitted Attention which he has shewn in the Service of his Country. He hopes he has studied to deserve them. His Feelings are deeply wounded whenever he reflects that on the Same Journals he is recorded as an intemperate person, who acted in Contempt of that Body whose Dignity he has endeavored to maintain with his Life and Fortune; he therefore hopes that the Honorable Congress will reconsider the Resolutions of the 15th of March and that they will adopt such Measures in Consequence as to their Justice and Wisdom shall appear meet and expedient,[9] and Your Memorialist Shall Ever Pray &c.[10]   Ph. Schuyler

MS (DNA: PCC, item 41). In the hand of John Lansing, Jr., and signed by Schuyler. Lansing was Schuyler's military secretary.

[1] General Schuyler prepared this memorial as part of his campaign to vindicate himself against what he regarded as unjust treatment by Congress. On March 15 Congress had reprimanded him for a sharply critical letter he had written to President Hancock on February 4, and on March 25 it had made Horatio Gates commander of the army at Ticonderoga, thereby removing the largest military force in the northern department from Schuyler's control. Yet these actions were also the result of long-standing dissatisfaction with Schuyler among several delegates—particularly the New Englanders—who were discontented with his military leadership and inability to get along with New England troops, resented the hectoring tone of some of his letters to Congress, and believed rumors that he corruptly mishandled public funds. Thus several factors had conspired to lower Schuyler's prestige and lead many delegates to want General Gates appointed commander of the northern department.

In order to answer his critics and regain control over the northern department, Schuyler, who was technically still a New York delegate, returned to Congress early in April, resolved either to win vindication or resign from the army. The immediate result of this move was a striking series of short-term successes for the much harried general. Ably supported by his fellow New York delegates, Schuyler secured the appointment on April 18 of a committee to examine his "conduct ... since he has held a command in the army of the United States." Next, he submitted his accounts to the Board of Treasury, which on May 3 cleared him of the charge of financial irregularities. And after he presented the memorial printed here, Congress expressed satisfaction with his explanation of his offending letter to President Hancock. Finally, on May 22 Congress granted Schuyler' main wish by confirming his command over the northern department, stipulating that it included "Albany, Ticonderoga, Fort Stanwix and their dependencies," thus making Gates his subordinate. Yet these resolves did not signify that Schuyler had won Congress' unreserved confidence. Those of the 22d passed by only a narrow margin—six states to three, with two divided and two absent, according to William Duer; five states to four, with two divided, according to James Lovell. It was not surprising, therefore, that after the fall of Ticonderoga in July, Schuyler's congressional support evaporated and Gates was made commander of the northern department on August 4, 1777.

For information on congressional dissatisfaction with Schuyler before April 1777, see Edward Rutledge to Robert R. Livingston, September 23, 1776; John Hancock to Schuyler, March 18, and to Gates, March 25, 1777; Benson J. Lossing, *The Life and Times of Philip Schuyler,* 2 vols. (1873; reprint ed., New York: Da Capo Press, 1973), 2:153–82; and Jonathan G. Rossie, *The Politics of Command in the American Revolution* (Syracuse: Syracuse University Press, 1975), pp. 107–53. Schuyler's mission to Philadelphia may be followed in *JCC,* 7:279, 326–27, 333–34, 336, 364, 371, 8:375; Schuyler to Richard Varick, April 16, 26, and to George Washington, May 18; James Lovell to Horatio Gates, May 1, 22, and to Oliver Wolcott, June 7; New York Delegates to the New York Convention, May 9; and William Duer to Robert R. Livingston, May 28, 1777. John Lansing, Jr., to Richard Varick, April 26, 1777, NNPM, indicates that Schuyler composed his memorial with the help of James Duane, William Duer, Philip Livingston, and Lansing himself. That Schuyler began work on this document in April is also indicated by the reference in the very first paragraph to a March 15 resolve as one of the "15th Ultimo."

For General Gates' dramatic reaction to Congress' May 22 resolves on the northern department, see Horatio Gates' Notes for a Speech in Congress, June 18, 1777.

Schuyler actually presented this memorial to Congress under cover of the following brief May 7 letter to President Hancock:

"I have done Myself the Honor to address the Honorable Continental Congress in a Memorial on the Subject Matter of their Resolutions of the 15th March last, & have taken the Liberty to inclose it.

"Permit me to intreat you to lay It before the House." Schuyler Papers, NN.

2 This letter is in PCC, item 153, 3:9–14.

3 For this letter, see ibid., 2:513–19.

4 Commissary General Joseph Trumbull's intercepted letter to Connecticut delegate William Williams of November 18, 1776, is in *Am. Archives,* 5th ser. 3:1497–98.

5 See Washington, *Writings* (Fitzpatrick), 7:28.

6 Shortly before meeting with the New York Convention at Fishkill, Schuyler had a highly revealing conversation with New York loyalist William Smith, which the latter recorded in his diary:

"General Schuyler . . . declares agt. the Disunion of the Empire, and speaks in Despair of the Abilities of the Colonies and with Disgust at the Conduct of their Leaders. . . .

"Unless Clothing & Covering can be found soon the Indian Interest will be lost. He has Nothing to give them—they are strongly solicited by the British Generals—Mr. Howe got two Men to them thro' Jersey to Susquehanna very lately—The Oneydas he says are as yet staunch. Mr. Howe desires them to take up the Hatchet.

"He has no Opinion of the New England People. He can get no Cannon from thence to supply the Loss of the Naval Victory & the Flight from Canada. He thinks the Miseries of the Country convert the Multitude daily, and he wishes Negotiations were opened for Peace.

"I informed him of all that passed with Ld. Drummond of which he had heard Nothing and seemed to be greatly surprised & declared that he would promote at Fishkill some Application in the Continental Congress for a Treaty of Reconciliation." William Smith, *Historical Memoirs from 12 July 1776 to 25 July 1778 of William Smith* . . . , ed. William H.W. Sabine, (New York: Colburn & Tegg, 1958), pp. 62–63. There is no evidence that Schuyler subsequently urged the New York Convention to support reconciliation with Great Britain, and it is only fair to point out that after his vindication by Congress his martial spirit rose, for on June 3 he met again with Smith, who regretfully confided to his diary that now the general "Talks with great Confidence in the Success of the American Opposition." Ibid., p. 150. Nevertheless, the pessimistic views that Schuyler expressed to Smith in January 1777 help to indicate why so many delegates were dissatisfied with his performance in the northern department. For an explanation of Smith's reference to "Ld. Drummond," see Lord Drumond's Notes, January 3–9, 1776.

7 That is, Congress' March 15 resolution against interfering in disputes between military officers.

8 See also John Hancock to Gates and to Schuyler, July 8, 1776.

9 Remainder of MS written by Schuyler.

10 On May 6 Schuyler, commander of Continental troops at Philadelphia, also wrote a letter to the Board of War in which he recommended that the Philadelphia "City Guards" continue to be "employed in Continental Duty, such as guarding ships, Batteaus, Hospitals, Goals, artillery &c," and accordingly that they be permitted to continue "to draw Provisions as usual." Schuyler Papers, NN.

Secret Committee Minutes of Proceedings

May 6th. 1777

Come. met. Present, Morris, Lee, Whipple, Livingston. Issued the folg. drafts on the Auditor general in favor Arch. Mercer & Philip Moore for 5333 24/90 dlls, being the valuation of their ship Polly charterd & insurd by the Come., said ship being carried in by the Seamen to Hallifax, as appears by the Captns protest, taken before G. Nutting, Notary public, on the 25th Feby. last. Do. in favor of Blair McCleneghan for 13,333 1/3 dlls being the valuatn. of his ship Adventure taken in this bay & destroyd by the Enemy,[1] as appears by the Capts. protest, sd. ship being charterd & insurd by the Come.

MS (MH–H).
[1] The *Adventure,* William Jones, master, returning from Hispaniola with salt, was burned by H.M.S. *Phoenix* on January 27, 1777. Morgan, *Naval Documents,* 7:1047.

John Adams to Abigail Adams

Philadelphia May 7. 1777

We have no News here, except what We get from your Country. The Privateers act with great Spirit, and are blessed with remarkable Success. Some Merchant ships are arrived this Week from Maryland. They were first chased by Men of War, in attempting to get into Cheasapeak Bay—they run from them and attempted Delaware Bay—there they were chased again. Whereupon they again shifted their Course for Cheasapeak and got in safe in spight of all the Men of War could do.

Thus you see We can and will have Trade, in spight of them....[1] And this Trade will probably increase fast. It requires Time for The Stream of Commerce to alter its Channell. Time is necessary, for our Merchants and foreign Merchants to think, plan, and correspond with each other. Time is also necessary for our Masters of Vessells and Mariners to become familiar with the Coasts, Ports and Harbours of foreign Countries—and a longer Time still is needfull for French, Spanish, and Dutch Masters and Mariners to learn our Coasts, and Harbours.

Yours, ever, ever yours.

RC (MHi). Adams, *Family Correspondence* (Butterfield), 2:234–35.
[1] Suspension points in MS.

Board of War to George Washington

Sir   War Office May 7th. 1777

I do myself the Honour of transmitting you the enclosed Papers by Order of the Board by whom I am directed to inform you that all the Military Stores, Arms &c in Possession of the Continental Agents at Boston, Portsmouth, & Providence are ordered to Springfield in Connecticut [*Massachusetts*] as a Place of greater Security where they are to be subject to your Excellency's Directions. The Agents are ordered to transmitt proper returns of what they send to Springfield which when received shall be sent to you.[1]

A Major Etherington who ranks as a Lieut Colonel gave his Parole as a Prisoner of War to the late Committee of Safety of this State & was permitted to go either to the West Indies or to England he to be forthcoming when called for by the States. I mention him at this Time as his Name was omitted in the List of Prisoners sent to your Excellency.[2]

I have the Honour to be, with great Respect, your very obedt Servt,
                                                         Richard Peters Secy

RC (DLC). Endorsed: "From Richd. Peters Esqr. with Genl. Gates's letter upon the necessity for defending the Highlands." On May 6 Congress had ordered that a copy of Horatio Gates' April 29 letter to President Hancock be sent to Washington. *JCC,* 7:329–30; and PCC, item 154, 1:173–80.

[1] Washington had recommended the removal of these stores to Springfield in a May 3 letter to President Hancock, which Congress read on the 5th and referred to the Board of War. As there is no mention of the order for removal in the journals, the board probably issued it on its own authority with Congress' consent. *JCC,* 7:330; PCC, item 152, 4:147–51; and Washington, *Writings* (Fitzpatrick), 8:7–8.

[2] Washington's May 10 reply to this letter is in Washington, *Writings* (Fitzpatrick), 8:36.

Philip Schuyler to George Washington

Dear Sir   Philadelphia May 7. 1777.

I am honored with Your Excellencys favor of the 3d.[1] It gives me Great pleasure that You approve of the Measure alluded to in my last but one.

Inclose You such a Return as I have been able to procure. Major Livingston is gone to Bristol & will send Your Excellency a Return of what Troops may be there.

Be pleased to order the inclosed to be forwarded by the first Conveyance to Kingston.

I am Dear Sir with every friendly wish & respectful Sentiment, Your Excys Most Obed. Hble servt.   Ph. Sch.

LB (NN).
[1] See Washington, *Writings* (Fitzpatrick), 8:11–12.

William Whipple to Josiah Bartlett

My Dear Sir,   Philadelphia 7th May 1777

Your favor of the 21st Ulto was handed me by Mr. Campney who was sent Express by G.W. Langdon with the dispatches that came in the Amphitrite.[1] This ship has been so long from France that she can bring nothing new. Another ship with a Similar cargo is arriv'd at Martineco after making several unsuccessful attempts to get into some of our ports. Some others are still expected, I wish they may not fall into the Enemies hands. It gives me Pleasure that a discovery is made of the Vilaneous money making scheme, for Heavens sake dont let the Villains escape the halter.[2] Sure I am they richly deserve it. Lenity to them will cost the lives of Thousands. It therefore is an indispensable duty to the Public to make examples of them. I beg leave to suggest whether it wod not be prudent to call in the money that is counterfited immediately. In Expectation that this plan will be adopted, I will endeavor to obtain an order on the loan office, to enable you to execute it. I have desir'd the Treasury to forward Proof sheets of every Emission which they promise me shall be done. Large quantities of Conterfit money has been sent out from N. York but I have not heard that any body has yet been deceiv'd by it. I am told its badly done.

Genl. Lee did not mention any perticular business. The copy of his letter which I sent you conveys every thing that I know respecting that matter.[3] The latest advices from France confirm me in the impropriety of his request, as the conference last summer was improv'd greatly to our disadvantage, that was a considerable means of preventing our having the stores last faul, that are now coming.

Colo. Thornton set out the 3d inst.[4] I endeavor'd to perswade him to tarry 'till Mr. Frost arriv'd, but without success. I hope I shall be excus'd if I leave this very soon after Mr. Frost arrives, for I assure you I am almost wore out. It has not been in my Power to mount my horse since I arriv'd from Baltimore, nor not more then twice while there. Without relaxation, & exercise, my constitution ('tho a very good one) will not stand this climate. I think it absolutely necessary that the state shod be as fully represented as possible, therefore hope a second Person will soon be sent after Mr Frost.

I agree with you, that we have many Difficulties to Encounter but doubt not we shall be able to surmount them all. Our internal & Secret Enemies embarrass us much more then is in the Power of all the force that can be rais'd by Great Britain, & nothing but the most vigorous exertions of civil authority can free us from those difficulties. The Laws shod be severe & executed with Rigour. This measure properly persued will surely have a very salutary Effect. The whip, Pilory, & Gibet shod be exercis'd freely, & those that the Laws will not hang should be immediately Banish'd & their Estates Confiscated, for keeping them among us will still subject us to the inconveniences arrising from their wicked Machinations. It is no time now to trifle. We must know who is for & who is against us & seperate the goats from the sheep. I inclose you a paper that has the test establish'd by S. Carolina. I think it a good one & wish, that, or something like it was adopted by our state. The Southern States are all acting vigourously, even Maryland, are takeing very decisive measures to rid themselves of their internal Enemies. And for the Honor & safety of New Hampshire I hope She will persue such measures as will frustrate the evil designs of the Enemies of America. Hoping soon to rejoice with you on the Successes of our arms, & a fair Prospect of establishing Happiness on the most permanant Basis Concludes me Your very affectionate Friend & Most Huml Sert.   Wm. Whipple

RC (NNPM).

[1] Josiah Bartlett's April 21 letter to Whipple is in the Josiah Bartlett Papers, NhHi, microfilm.

[2] The New Hampshire Assembly passed a law on June 25, 1777, that forfeited the property of fugitive counterfeiters to the state and prevented its transfer to other persons. *N.H. State Papers,* 8:603, 613.

[3] For further information on Gen. Charles Lee's proposal for a conference with members of Congress to discuss British reconciliation overtures, see Thomas Burke's Notes of Debate, February 21, 1777.

[4] Matthew Thornton had received permission from Congress to return home on May 1. *JCC,* 7:321.

William Ellery to Nicholas Cooke

Sir,   Philadelphia May 8th 1777

Inclosed is an Extract from a Letter written to the Committee of Correspondence by Arthur Lee Esqr. One of the Commissioners employed by the Congress at the Courts of France & Spain.[1] By this Extract the Necessity of destroying the British &c Forces on Rhode-Island before they may be reinforced fully and strongly appears. Boston it seems is to be attacked. Which Way it is to be attacked, if attacked, is unknown. The Distance from Providence to Boston is about forty six Miles—Two Days March only. It hath been and still is my Opinion that, if the Enemy intend to penetrate into New England, One of their Routes will be from the Head of our Bay or near it. If the Assembly should agree with Me in this Sentiment, no Arguments will be wanting to them, to comply with the Recommendation of Congress.[2] But should this not be the Case most certainly every possible Advantage ought to be taken of the divided State of the British Army to crush and destroy it.

In a late N. York Paper was published an Act of Parliament lately passed for apprehending, and imprisoning within the Realm of Britain, until January 1778, all Pirates & Traitors.[3] If I should be able to procure the Paper or a Copy of the Act before I close my Letter I will transcribe & transmit it to you. We must retaliate, and confine all the Prisoners We take. I fancy before the Campaign is out We shall be able to ballance Accounts with the Enemy. Recruits have come forward from the Southward very cleverly of late. I hope recruiting goes on in the Eastern States brisker than it did. The Quota of our State must not be deficient. The common Cause and our Reputation depend upon our Activity. The Enemy have used and are still using every Artifice they can, to increase Toryism, promote Desertions, and depretiate continental Dollars. Persons are employed in every State to propagate the first, Twenty four Dollars is offered for every Soldier that will desert and carry with him his Arms, a Less Sum for a Deserter without his Arms, to promote the Second; and to depretiate our Money it seems they have counterfeited large Sums and [dispersed] their Emissaries to spread their counterfeit Dollars [through] the States. I have seen a thirty Dollar counterfeit Bill. It was badly executed. We ought to be, methinks, as industrious to defeat as they are to contrive. It is high Time to treat Tories with proper uniform Severity, & to watch Strangers and perhaps One another with a jealous Eye. The Enemies of our own House, are more dangerous than external Foes. But it is my Business to inform not to direct.

I hope the Genl. Assembly will attend, if they should not have already done it, to the Letter which I wrote them desiring the earliest Information after the Appointment of Delegates. Our State is not represented in Congress now, and will not be until I shall have received authentick Advice of my being chosen, or another Delegate shall have arrived. Therefore let me intreat that it may be done, that the new Delegates may come forward immediately. The Circumstances of my Family require that I shall return as soon as possible to make some suitable Provisions for it, and my long constant attention in Congress demands Relaxation.[4]

Our Loss at Danbury turns out to be less than we imagined, and We have killed more of the Enemy; but We have not certain account of either. Every Thing in the Jersey statu quo. I congratulate your Honour on the Arrival of the Field-Peices. We shall take the Field under greater Advantages this than the last Campaign. Heartily wishing that the Success of it may be at least proportioned to our superior Advantages, that we may give our Enemies such convincing Proof of their Folly, Injustice and Cruelty as may induce them to drop the Contest, and thus this be our last Campaign, I am with great Respect, Yr Honor's most Obedt. hble Servt.   William Ellery

RC (RHi).

[1] Lee's letter to the Committee of Secret Correspondence is dated February 18 in Wharton, *Diplomatic Correspondence,* 2:272-73, but the extract enclosed in Ellery's letter is dated February 20. See William R. Staples, ed., *Rhode Island in the Continental Congress, 1765–1790* (Providence: Providence Press Co., 1870), pp. 139–40.

[2] See John Hancock to Certain States, April 16, 1777.

[3] See Richard Henry Lee to Patrick Henry, May 6, 1777, note 2.

[4] Not until May 31 was Ellery able to present to Congress the credentials certifying his recent reelection to a one year term as a Rhode Island delegate. See *JCC*, 8:408–9; and Ellery to Cooke, March 30, 1777, note 4. Ellery's previous term had expired on May 4.

John Adams to Nathanael Greene

Dear Sir   Philadelphia May 9. 1777

Yours of the 2d Instant came duely to hand.[1] The Indifference of the People about recruiting the Army, is a Circumstance which ought to make Us consider what are the Causes of it. It is not merely the Melancholly arising from the unfortunate Event of the last Campaign, but the Small Pox, and above all the unhappy State of our Finances, which occasion this Evil. There are other Circumstances which are little attended to which contribute much more than is imagined to this unfavourable Temper in the People. The Prevalance of Dissipation, Debauchery, Gaming, Prophaneness and Blasphemy terrifies the best People upon the Continent, from trusting their Sons and other Relations among so many dangerous snares and temptations. Multitudes of People, who would with chearfull Resignation Submit their Families to the Dangers of the sword, shudder at the Thought of exposing them to what appears to them the more destructive Effects of Vice and Impiety. These Ideas would be received by many with scorn. But there is not the less Solidity in them for that. It is Discipline alone that can Stem the Torrent. Chaplains are of great use, I believe, and I wish Mr Leonard might be in the Army, upon such Terms as would be agreeable to him, for there is no Man of whom I have a better opinion. But there is so much difficulty in accomplishing any Thing of the Kind, that I wish G. Washington would either appoint him, or recommend him to Congress.

The Utility of Medals has ever been impressed Strongly upon my Mind. Pride, Ambition and indeed what a Philosopher would call Vanity, is the Strongest Passion in human Nature, and next to Religion, the most operative Motive to great Actions. Religion, or if the fine Gentlemen please, Superstition and Enthusiasm, is the greatest Incentive and wherever it has prevailed, has never failed to produce Heroism. If our N. Englandmen were alone, and could have their own way, a great deal of this would appear, But in their present Situation, I fear We have little to expect from this Principle, more than the Performance of the People in the Camp. We ought to avail our selves then of even the Vanity of Men. For my own Part I wish We would make a Beginning, by Striking a Medal, with a Platone firing at General Arnold, on Horseback, His Horse falling dead under him, and He deliberately disentangling his feet from the Stirrups and taking his Pistolls out of his Holsters, before his Retreat. On the Reverse, He should be mounted on a Fresh Horse, receiving another Discharge of Musquetry, with a Wound in the Neck of his Horse. This Picture alone, which as I am informed is true History, if Arnold did not unfortunately belong to Connecticutt, would be sufficient to make his Fortune for Life. I believe there have been few such Scenes in the world.

We have not Artists at present for such works, and many other Difficulties would attend an Attempt to introduce Medals.

Taxation is begun in N.E. The Mass. raises 100,000 this year. The Regulation of Prices and the Embargo are Measures of which I could never see the Justice or Policy.

The Intimation in your Letter that the Enemy lost in killed, wounded and Prisoners 600 Men, surprizes me much; because it exceeds by at least two Thirds the largest account that has come from any other authority. I wish our N. England Men would practice a little honest Policy for their own Interest and Honour, by transmitting to Congress and publishing in the Newspapers, true states of the Actions in which they are concerned. The Truth alone would be sufficient for them, and surely they may be allowed to avail themselves of this shield of defence, when so many Arts of dishonest Policy are practiced against them.

Congress were too anxious for Ti. I wish our Army was encamped upon some Hill twenty Miles from the Waters of the Lake, or at least Ten.

We are alarmed here with frequent accounts of numerous Desertions from our Army. Is there no Remedy for this Evil. Howe is trying his Hand at Bribery. He is sending his Emmissaries all about, and scattering ministerial gold. They despair of the Effects of Force, and are now attempting Bribery and Insinuation which are more provoking than all their Cruelties. What Effect would these have in N. England?

Stracky the Secretary,[2] is an old Partisan at Electioneering, long hackneyd in the ways of Corruption, long a ministerial agent, in that dirty Work and the greatest Master of it, in the Nation, selected for that very Purpose to be sent here. Pray dont you Generals sometimes practice Methods of holding up such Characters among your Enemies, to the Contempt and Hatred of the Soldiery?

I find I have written a long Story. Excuse me, and believe me to be, with great Truth and Regard, your most obedient Servant.

FC (MHi).

[1] General Greene's May 2 letter to Adams is in the Adams Papers, MHi.

[2] See Henry Strachey's Notes on Lord Howe's Meeting with a Committee of Congress, September 11, 1776.

William Ellery to William Vernon

Dear Sir,   Phila May 9th 1777

Inclosed are Two Resolves of Congress by which you will see that a Navy-Board is established in Massachusetts Bay and that you are appointed One of the Commissioners.[1] You will please to let me know as soon as possible whether you accept the Appointment or not. If you should decline the Office you will write to the President & inform him of it. It is expected that you do no other Business while you are a Commissioner. I suppose you are in no great if any Business at present, and I presume the Duties of your Office will take up your whole Attention.

Billy[2] is at Princetown and well. The Armies in the Jersey Statu quo. The main Army fills up fast. The News of Carletons being on the Lake and advancing towards Tionderoga premature. We have a considerable Body of Troops there in good health and high Spirits. Forward the Expedition agst Rhode Island with all your might. I am in haste, Yrs   W Ellery

P.S. I sealed this before I recd. the Copy of the Resolutions & therefore was obliged to break the Seal, and have the Resolve cover the Letter instead of the Letter covering the Resolve.

RC (RHi).

[1] See JCC, 7:281, 331.

[2] Vernon's son William.

New York Delegates to the New York Convention

Gentlemen,   Philada. May 9th, 1777.

When we arrived here, it plainly appeared that great pains had been taken to injure the character of Major-General Schuyler.

No direct charge had been urged against him: a series of sly insinuations—that he was making an enormous fortune at the expense of the public; that he had converted the specie provided by Congress for the Canada service, to his own private purposes, and when he showed his feelings of some unworthy treatment, severe rebukes and animadversions on his expressions and his supposed want of respect to his superiors. Those were weapons, employed so successfully, as in the end produced some resolutions of Congress, paring away his authority to nothing. It took us some time to become acquainted with the new members, and to undeceive those who wished for conviction. We had in the mean time got a committee appointed to inquire into the General's conduct at large. That business went on heavily, and seemed to promise no conclusion; we, therefore, were under the necessity to take a more direct course. The General's account of the specie was, at his request, reëxamined; and after it had been passed by the commissioners at the treasury board, who made a full report in his favour, which was received by Congress and ordered to be published. This report, a printed copy of which is herewith transmitted, had a powerful effect on many of the members, who heard it with the utmost pleasure and frankly acknowledged that they had been deceived.[1]

The way being thus prepared, the General presented a memorial to Congress, stating such of their resolutions as conveyed censure upon him, justifying himself in every particular. This, after some debate, produced a unanimous resolution of Congress, that the memorial was satisfactory, and that the Congress entertained the same favourable opinion of the General as they entertained before the passing those resolutions.[2]

A complete and honourable vindication of the General's character and conduct being implied in that resolution, and the infamous charge of embezzling the specie effectually done away by the report from the treasury, we shall give ourselves no trouble about the proposed inquiry, especially as Congress came into the appointment of the committee with the utmost reluctance, almost every member declaring that there was no accuser or charge against the General, and that the inquiry was therefore unnecessary. All impediments being now removed, we shall proceed to take the most speedy measures for reinstating the General in his command.

In the critical situation of our affairs, his services are loudly called for. We, therefore, conceived that this business ought first to be despatched. It unavoidably occasioned some delay in the other matters committed to our charge, but you may be assured that they shall be attended to with all the zeal and diligence of which we are capable.

In the mean time we remain, with the utmost regard, honourable gentlemen, Your most obedt. humble servants,   Phil. Livingston,

Jas. Duane.

Reprinted from *Journals of N.Y. Prov. Cong.*, 1:941.

[1] See *JCC*, 7:326–27.

[2] See *JCC*, 7:336; and Philip Schuyler's Memorial to Congress, May 6, 1777.

Secret Committee to the Commissioners at Paris

Honorable Gentlemen,   Philadelphia 9th May 1777

This letter is intended to be delivered you by John Paul Jones Esquire an active and brave Commander in our Navy, who has already performed Signal Services in Vessels of little force and in reward for his Zeal, we have directed him to go on board the Amphitrite a French Ship of 20 Guns that brought in a valuable Cargo of Stores from Monsr. Hortalez & Co and with her repair to France. He takes with him his Commission, some Officers and Men, so that we hope he will under that Sanction make Some good Prizes with the Amphitrite, but our design in Sending him is (with the approbation of Congress) that you may purchase One of those fine Frigates that Mr Deane writes us you can get, and invest him with the Command thereof soon as possible. We hope you may not delay this business one Moment, but purchase in Such port or place in Europe as it can be done with most convenience & dispatch a fine fast sailing Frigate or larger Ship. Direct Captain Jones where he must repair to, and he will take with him his Officers and men towards manning her. You will assign him Some good House or Agent to supply him with every thing necessary to get the Ship speedily and well equipped and Manned, Somebody that will bestir themselves vigourously in the business and never quit until it is Accomplished.

If you have any plan or Service to be performed in Europe by Such a Ship that you think will be more for the Interest or honor of these States than Sending her out directly, Captain Jones is instructed to Obey your Order, and to Save repetition let him lay before you the instructions we have given him and furnish you with a Copy thereof. You can then judge what will be necessary for you to direct him in; and whatever you do will be approved as it will undoubtedly tend to promote the publick Service of this Country.

You See by this Step how much dependance Congress place in your advices and you must make it a point not to disapoint Capt Jones's wishes and our expectations on this Occasion.

We are Honorable Gentlemen, Your obedt hble Servants,

Robt Morris   Wm. Whipple

Richard Henry Lee   Phil. Livingston

RC (MdBJ–G). In a clerical hand and signed by Lee, Livingston, Morris, and Whipple.

Secret Committee to John Paul Jones

Sir,   Philadelphia May 9. 1777

On receipt of this letter you are to proceed to Portsmouth in New Hampshire where you will find the Amphitrite a French Ship of 20 Guns commanded by Monsr. N. Fautrel a Gentleman that has acquitted himself honorably of the charge he undertook, and we doubt not he will continue the Same good conduct for the remainder of the Voyage.

This Ship is to proceed from Portsmouth to Charles Town, South Carolina, to load with Rice &c, from thence She goes to France, and we have proposed that you Should go in her this Voyage taking your Commission and Appearing or Acting on Suitable Occasions as the Commander. We know not the number of men on board this Ship, but if Captain Fautrel accepts our propositions, you will examine the Ships force, both as to Guns and men and if the latter are insufficient you may recruit as many more to go with you as Shall be deemed Sufficient to enable you to take and man Such Prizes as may come in your way.[1] In this respect you will consult Mr Langdon to whom we Send Some Warrants to be filled up if you want Petty Officers. We think the Number of men Should be Sufficient to defend the Ship against any armed Merchantmen at the Same time it must be remembered that she is to carry a Cargo from Carolina, therefore too much room must not be taken up with Water Provisions &c. Mr Langdon is directed to put on board sufficient for you and your people, Capt Fautrel will do the same for his. This to prevent hesitation on that Subject and we desire you will give all the aid & assistance in your power to get this Ship away as expeditiously as possible. We have told Monsr. Fautrel that one Third of all Prizes taken by his Ship under Authority of your Commission Shall be appropriated to the use of his owners, himself, Officers and men, the other two Thirds to be divided between the United States, you and your Men agreeable to the Resolves of Congress, and this engagement must be strickly complied with, therefore if you Send any Prizes into any Ports of this Continent, Monsr. Fautrel and you must write the Agent to reserve One third for his use and to follow his orders respecting it. If you carry or Send prizes into France he will receive A Third, you and your people a third, and the other third you must Order to be remitted to the Honorable Benjamin Franklin & other American Commissioners at the Court of Versailles, Paris for the use of the United States. You will readily see the propriety and Necessity of preserving a Strict harmony and friendship with Monsr. Fautrel, this we recommend you to do at all events, give him every advice and Assistance in your power, and particularly endeavour to procure him good dispatch from Portsmouth & Charles Town. The Continental Agents Livinus Clarkson & John Dorsius will load the

Ship at the latter place, they will also render you any Service you may Stand in need of.

You will naturally suppose we do not remove you from the Ship you were so lately appointed to for the Sole purpose of making this voyage in the Amphitrite, we have other veiws and is only adopted as part of our plan which we expect will afford you an Opportunity of doing some Mischief to our Enemies and some good for yourself and the Country you have engaged to serve. We hope you may make many Prizes and thereby lodge Funds in Europe that will assist in executing the other part of our veiws. We are advised by our Commissioners at the Court of France that they can procure us some fine Frigates and as we have a desire to gratify you with the command of a fine Ship in firm dependance that you will make good use of her to serve and promote the Interest of America, we send you to France in the Amphitrite for these two purposes, first, to avail of her Guns & men to make a Cruizing voyage to France, and then to Obtain One of the Frigates mentioned. When Amphitrite arrives in France you will dispose of your Officers & Men so that they may remain in Safety at the Port whilst you proceed for Paris with the enclosed letter which you must deliver yourself. The Commissioners will procure you A fine Ship and the Officers and Men you take with you will assist towards manning her. The Commissioners will inform you what Port to repair to for this Ship, and whom you are to apply to for Supplies of every kind. We expect you will exert yourself to the Utmost to get the Ship they may appoint for you equipped, manned and fit for Service with the utmost expedition. We desire the Commissioners if they have any particular service for you to perform in Europe to give you the needful instructions, and if any Such you receive it is your business to execute their orders to the best of your power. Such Services as they may point out being performed, or if they order none, you will then enquire of them and of our Commercial Agents Wm Lee & Thomas Morris Esqrs. at Nantes or Bourdeaux if it be Necessary for you to receive on board any Stores or supplies for this Continent, and take in Such as may be ready. We hope you may obtain a fine Ship well equipped in every particular and that you'll be able to get her Officered & Manned. These things done you will steer for America making it your constant Study to take or destroy as many of the enemies Ships as possible during the Voyage. If you receive any dispatches from the Commissioners at Paris or the Commercial Agents for this or any Committee of Congress you must be very carefull of them and always have them ready to be Sunk if too heavy A Ship should attack you.

You will get into the first safe Port in these States that you can, with the dispatches if any you have. All prizes are to be addressed and give us notice immediately of your Arrival and Send an officer to the Continental Agents here, and to such persons in Europe as the

Commissioners or Commercial Agents may recommend for that purpose.

You remember that we ardently wish to have Strict discipline with good usage maintained in our Navy, that Prisoners are to be treated with humanity, that dilligence in making dispatch both in Port and at Sea, frugality in Expences and care of the Ship, her Stores & materials are absolutely necessary and if duely practiced cannot fail to recommend you to our Friendship and favour.

We are, Sir, Your hble Servants,

Robt Morris	Wm. Whipple
Richard Henry Lee	Phil. Livingston

RC (DNA: PCC, item 168). In a clerical hand and signed by Lee, Livingston, Morris, and Whipple.

[1] Jones' new commission was sent this day by the Marine Committee, accompanied by the following note: "The Congress have thought proper to authorize the Secret Committee to employ you [on] a voyage in the Amphitrite from Portsmouth to Carolina and France where it is expected you will be provided with a fine frigate and as your present Commission is for the Command of a particular Ship we now Send you a new one whereby you are appointed a Captain in our Navy and of course may command any Ship in the service. You are to obey the orders of the Secret Committee." PCC Miscellaneous Papers, Marine Committee Letter Book, fol. 90; and Paullin, *Marine Committee Letters*, 1:133. Because the French captain did not accept the conditions of Congress' proposal, these orders were never carried out. See Secret Committee Minutes of Proceedings, June 13, 1777; and Samuel E. Morison, *John Paul Jones, a Sailor's Biography* (Boston: Little, Brown and Company, 1959), pp. 99–100.

Secret Committee to John Langdon

Sir,   Philadelphia May 9 1777

We had the pleasure to receive your favour of the 22d April some days Since but could not reply sooner as it took some time to have the several French letters and papers rendered into English that they might be laid before Congress to obtain their orders for the disposition of the several articles that compose the Amphitrites Cargo, and We are now authorized to direct that you comply with such orders as the Board of War may think proper to give respecting the Military Stores, intrenching Tools &c, and with the Orders of the Cloathier General respecting the Article of Cloathing &c appertaining to that department.[1] Thus the entire Cargo will be disposed off between those two Branches. It only remains that we direct what is to be done with the Ship. We observe by your letter of the 21 Ultimo that you had determined to load the Ship Mercury with Masts, Spars &c which is well, as we had not at that time Sufficient documents to know what was best to be done with her. Whatever Cargo you Send by that Ship address the Same to Messrs. Rodrique Hortalez & Co by Bill of loading and

Invoice, freight as Per Contract, inclose the Invoice and bill of Loading in A letter directed to that house, and Send duplicates thereof inclosed to the Honorable Commissioners at the Court of France. Other Copies you will send to us. The letters for Monsr Hortalez & Co must be indorsed to be delivered to the following houses at which ever of the Ports the Ship happens first to arrive.

Messrs. Eyries & Le Coureur Merchts, at	Havre de Grace
Le Pellettier & Du Doyer	Nantes
David Gradis & Son	Bourdeaux
Heber de St Clement	Rochford
Le Conte Ancient Councellor to the Sovereign Council of Lisle de France	Rochelle
Le Baron	Brest
Dujat Ancient Secry of the Marine	L'Orient
Casinove	Bayonne

The more valuable you make the Cargo with Suitable articles the more agreeable to us and the more acceptable will it be on the other side.

With respect to the Amphitrite we want a More valuable remittance to be made by her, and therefore have wrote Captain Fautrell, that he must proceed from Portsmouth to Charles Town in South Carolina to load with Rice and Indico and we request your Assistance to procure him dispatch from Portsmouth. For this purpose youl please to advance him such money and procure him such Stores, provisions and necessarys, as he may need to get the Ship away, you will take his receipts for the amount of all you Supply him with expressing it to be for the Ships use. Let him Sign Several Copies and it may not be amiss to mention therein the Sterling amount at the Current Rate of Exchange to prevent disputes hereafter. One of these Receipts you will transmit to Messrs. Hortalez & Co by the Ship, and another by the Mercury if she remains after the Amphitrite, and the rest to us. We have formed a plan for making this Ships Guns of Some Service to us by opposing them to our enemies, for this purpose John Paul Jones Esqr a Captain in our Navy is directed to proceed to Portsmouth where he will call on you. We have proposed to Monsr. Fautrel that Captain Jones shall embarque with him on board the Amphitrite taking his Commission in order that the ship may thereby be Authorized to make prizes of British Ships during the remainder of her Voyage. We have proposed this to Mr. Fautrel and expect he will gladly embrace the offer. His number of men we do not know, but suppose they will not be sufficient, therefore we have wrote Captain Jones to examine the ship, her Guns &c and inlist on ship as many Petty Officers & men as he may think necessary to compleat this Ship for defence or to enable her to take any British Armed Trader.

In this business we beg you will assist all in your power. Herein you have twelve Blank Warrants for Petty Officers and you may fill them up with the names of Such Suitable persons as agree to go with Jones in the Several Stations wanted taking care that none but Suitable Men are engaged. Any Blanks that remain transmit them to the Honorable Benjamin Franklin, Silas Deane & Arthur Lee Esqrs American Commissioners at the Court of Versailles, committing the Packet to Captain Jones Care, with A Charge to Sink it if accident renders that precaution necessary.

It is possible Mr Fautrel may object to this Plan, for we dont See by the Agrement that he is bound to comply with it, and in that case you'l Send us back the Warrants and tell Captain Jones he must return to the command of the Ship he left, but this we don't expect will happen. On the Contrary we think Monsr. Fautrel will gladly fall in with our views & that Jones will go the Voyage. In this case you will supply him with Provisions for himself and Officers and Men during the Voyage, advance what money may be needful agreeable to resolves of Congress and transmit Accounts thereof to the Marine Committee with Captain Jones Receipts. You must charge that Committee with the advances made Captain Jones and his men on this Occassion. The advances made Monsr. Fautrel and the Captain of the Mercury must be Charged to the Secret Committee.

We doubt not your exertions to concur with our views and if any dificulties arise to remove them, and remain, Sir, Your Obedt Servants,

Robt Morris	Wm. Whipple
Richard Henry Lee	Phil. Livingston

P.S. Shou'd Capt Fautrell think the third of Prizes which we have offered him too small a share for the use of his Ship, You may agree to allow him half & let him & Capt Jones Sign in Writing to fix the bargain, but if he will accept a third you'l say nothing of the half.[2]

RC (Capt. J. G. M. Stone, Annapolis, Md., 1973). In a clerical hand and signed by Lee, Livingston, Morris, and Whipple.

[1] See *JCC*, 7:335–36.

[2] See *JCC*, 7:346–47.

John Adams to Abigail Adams

Philadelphia May 10. 1777

The Day before Yesterday, I took a Walk, with my Friend Whipple to Mrs. Wells's, the Sister of the famous Mrs. Wright, to see her Wax-work.[1] She has two Chambers filled with it. In one, the Parable of the Prodigal Son is represented. The Prodigal is prostrate on his Knees, before his Father, whose Joy, and Grief, and Compassion all appear in his Eyes and Face, struggling with each other. A servant Maid, at the Fathers command, is pulling down from a Closet Shelf, the choicest Robes, to cloath the Prodigal, who is all in Rags. At an outward Door, in a Corner of the Room stands the elder Brother, chagrined at this Festivity, a Servant coaxing him to come in. A large Number of Guests are placed round the Room. In another Chamber, are the Figures of Chatham, Franklin, Sawbridge, Mrs. Maccaulay, and several others. At a Corner is a Miser, sitting at his Table, weighing his Gold, his Bag upon one Side of the Table, and a Thief behind him, endeavouring to pilfer the Bag.

There is Genius, as well as Taste and Art, discovered in this Exhibition: But I must confess, the whole Scæne was disagreable to me. The Imitation of Life was too faint, and I seemed to be walking among a Group of Corps's, standing, sitting, and walking, laughing, singing, crying, and weeping. This Art I think will make but little Progress in the World.

Another Historical Piece I forgot, which is Elisha, restoring to Life the Shunamite's Son. The Joy of the Mother, upon Discerning the first Symptoms of Life in the Child, is pretty strongly expressed.

Dr. Chevots Waxwork, in which all the various Parts of the human Body are represented, for the Benefit of young Students in Anatomy and of which I gave you a particular Description, a Year or two ago, were much more pleasing to me. Wax is much fitter to represent dead Bodies, than living ones.[2]

Upon a Hint, from one of our Commissioners abroad, We are looking about for American Curiosities, to send across the Atlantic as presents to the Ladies.[3] Mr. Rittenhouse's Planetarium, Mr. Arnolds Collection of Rareties in the Virtuoso Way, which I once saw at Norwalk in Connecticutt, Narragansett Pacing Mares, Mooses, Wood ducks, Flying Squirrels, Redwinged Black birds, Cramberries, and Rattlesnakes have all been thought of.

Is not this a pretty Employment for great Statesmen, as We think ourselves to be? Frivolous as it seems, it may be of some Consequence. Little Attentions have great Influence. I think, however, We ought to consult the Ladies upon this Point. Pray what is your Opinion?[4]

RC (MHi). Adams, *Family Correspondence* (Butterfield), 2:235–36.

[1] For further information on Rachel Lovell Wells and her sister Patience Lovell Wright, see Charles C. Sellers, *Patience Wright, American Artist and Spy in George III's London* (Middletown, Conn.: Wesleyan University Press, 1976).

[2] For Adams' earlier description of the anatomical waxworks of Abraham Chovet, see Adams' Diary, October 14, 1774.

[3] Silas Deane suggested several possible "curiosities" in his November 28 letter to the Committee of Secret Correspondence and his December 3, 1776, letter to John Jay. Wharton, *Diplomatic Correspondence*, 2:200, 214.

⁴ Adams' letterbook contains a fragment of a letter dated May 10 that he may have intended to add to this letter to Abigail.

"We have at last accomplished a troublesome Piece of Business. We have chosen a Number of additional Ambassadors. Mr. Ralph Izzard of S. Carolina, a Gentleman of large Fortune, for the Court of the Grand Duke of Tuscany, and Mr. William Lee, formerly Alderman of London, for the Courts of Vienna and Berlin." See Adams, *Family Correspondence* (Butterfield), 2:237.

John Adams to Nathanael Greene

Philadelphia May 10. 1777

Yours of the 7th was brought me this Morning.[1] My Meaning was that if the Conduct of our Army had depended on me, I should have taken more Pains to have obtained exact Information of the Enemies Numbers, and our own, and should have considered every Inclination of the Enemies Intentions of coming to Philadelphia more particularly. Altho there is no doubt that Congress have authority to direct the military operations, yet I think they would be unwise to attempt it. This must be left to the General officers.

We have not the Information that you have respecting our own Force. There is not a Man in Congress who knows what Force you now have in N. Jersey. We have had no Returns a long time and the opinions of Gentn who come from Camp are very various. My Constituents have a Right to expect that I give my Council whenever it may be usefull; and my Constituents shall not be disappointed. If you knew how many dozens of my opinions are rejected where one is adopted, you would not think they had much Weight. But enough of this.

My opinion last Summer was very consistent I believe, with that in my last Letter. A Man may be humble before the Enemy, and proud before a Friend. Some who think too little of their Powers and Forces against the Enemy, think too highly of their own Importance, among their Friends, and treat the latter with less Delicacy than they would the former. For my own Part I care not how haughty Men are, to the Enemies of their Country, provided they have Regard to Truth & Justice, nor how humble they are among its Friends.

If by the finer Feelings of the Gentlemen of the Army, are meant their Moral Feelings, no Man detests more than myself, the Idea of hurting them. But if Vanity, and Pleasure is meant, I think, no Harm would be done by mortifying it. I am much mistaken and much misinformed, if the nice Feelings, the Pride, the Vanity, the Foppery, the Knavery and Gambling among too many of the officers, do not end in direct Endeavours to set up a Tyrant sooner or later, unless early Endeavours are used to controul them. I dont mean by this, any General Reflections upon the officers, most of whom I believe to be good Citizens at present, but by the Representations We hear there are so many of an opposite Character, that there is danger that the Contagion will Spread.

The Necessity of establishing an Army, Superiour to all our Enemies, is obvious, and, for my own Part, I dont See any Thing in the Power of Congress to do, to accomplish this great Purpose, but what has been done. If you think of any Thing more that is proper to be done, I should thank you for the Hint. I have Reason to believe upon very good Authority, that foreign Troops might be hired, both Germans, Swiss and French. What think you of the Policy of hiring them? The Waste of the Natives of the Country, in the Army, is a melancholly, and an alarming Consideration. We want People, for Agriculture, Manufactures, Commerce and war, both by Sea and Land.

FC (MHi).

[1] General Greene's May 7 letter to Adams is in the Adams Papers, MHi.

Charles Carroll of Carrollton to Charles Carroll, Sr.

Dr. Papa,   Saturday 10th May 1777.

The 2 inclosed Evening posts of the 6th & 8th instant with Bradfords last Wednesday's paper, which I suppose was forwarded as usual per post, will inform you pretty nearly of all the news. Our loss at Danbury was considerable. By G. Washington's letter to Congress we have lossed 1700 barrels of Pork, 50 of beef, 1000 tents and several other articles of less value as rum, rice, wheat, oats, flour &c the particulars of which I dont remember. The enemy make our loss much more considerable, but I believe they have exaggerated it a good deal. If we can get money, and support the credit of what is now in circulation, I am in hopes the enemy will not be able to make any considerable progress this campaign unless their reinforcements from Europe should be as great as they give out, and unless they arrive sooner than they arrived last year.

There remain great abuses in every department to be corrected: committees are nominated to inspect the Commissaries depart., measures are taken to prevent the shameful practices of officers defrauding their soldiers of their pay, thereby occasioning their desertion to the enemy & great discontents at camp.

The enemy by the latest advices from Camp remain quiet. Carleton is not yet come to Ticonderoga, nor have we any intelligence of his being on the way. G. Schuyler recd. yesterday letters from fort Stanwix informing him that the 6 nations & their allies would observe a perfect neutrality—this is a great point gained.

From all the information I can gather, and I have the opportunity of getting the best, the French nation is much disposed in our favor, so is the court, but prudential & cautious maxims of policy will prevent for some time, I think, their openly engaging in the war. We have already received very essential services from that People. Were our people more united & more spirited we should soon put an end to the war.

G. Schuyler has got the model of the flaxmill made for me; but it is at Saratoga, & God knows when & how I shall get it from thence.

I was yesterday reappointed one of the board of war, and consequently shall have my hands full.[1]

Do let me know whether the grapes & fruit have been much damaged by the frost.

A resolve has passed giving the enemy's vessels & cargoes to the crews who shall bring them into our ports. We perceive the enemy by a similar practice encourage our sailors to be guilty of highest perfidy & breach of trust, we must counteract them with their own arts. Several of our vessels from the perfidiousness of the crews, consisting chiefly of English sailors, have been carried into the enemys ports. The Aurora a valuable Tobacco ship, was by this means carried into Liverpool.

I hope your intended jaunt will be agreeable, but I would not have you set out unless the weather becomes more settled. My love to Molly & Mrs. Darnall. I am, yr. most affectionate Son,

Ch. Carroll of Carrollton

RC (MdHi).
[1] According to the journals, Carroll was added to the Board of War on May 8. *JCC,* 7:337.

John Hancock to Thomas Johnson

Sir, Philada. May 10th. 1777

I do myself the Honour of transmitting the enclosed Resolves in Obedience to the Commands of Congress. You will perceive it is their Desire, that in Conjunction with your Council, you should appoint Superintendants of the public Press at Baltimore as often as there may be Occasion by any of them declining to act, or otherwise neglecting the Office.[1] I beg Leave to refer your Attention to the Resolves as the Line of Conduct, and am, with great Respect, Sir, Your most obed. & very hble Servt. John Hancock, Presidt.

RC (MdAA).
[1] See *JCC,* 7:332. On May 28 the Maryland Council of Safety appointed William Aisquith, Zachariah Mackubbin, Jr., and Philip Rogers as "Superintendants of the Press, or Presses in Baltimore Town employed in printing the

Continental Bills of Credit, in the Room of those, who were appointed by Congress, and have discontinued in that Office." *Md. Archives,* 16:261.

John Hancock to George Washington

Sir,   Philada. May 10th. 1777.

I have Nothing further in Charge from Congress at this Time, except the enclosed Resolve, founded upon Complaints which, if not immediately enquired into and redressed, must be productive of the most fatal Consequences to the Army.

Nothing can so effectually lay the Foundation of Discontent, and of Course encourage a Spirit of Mutiny and Desertion among the Soldiers, as withholding their Pay from them; and to this Cause, there is too much Reason to apprehend, we must attribute the many Instances of Desertion of which we have daily Accounts.

The Congress therefore have taken the Matter into Consideration; and with a View of doing Justice to the injured Soldier, and exposing the Officer who neglects or designedly withholds his Pay, and to prevent the evil Effects of such Conduct on the public Cause, have recommended it to you to institute a Court of Enquiry to examine into the Behaviour of the Officers in this particular, and to see that their Men are regularly and honestly paid.[1] I beg Leave to refer your Attention to the Resolve,[2] and am, with Sentiments of the greatest Esteem, Sir, your most obed. & very hble Servt.

John Hancock, Presid

P.S. I am directed by Congress to request you will furnish them, by the Return of this Express, with an Account of the Number of the Troops you have at present. It is not expected in the Situation of the Army, without an Adjutant General, that you will be able to do it with any great Degree of Precision. What they desire is, that you will give them the best Information in your Power as to your Numbers and Strength.[3]

The Congress having recommended it to the States of Delaware & Pennsylvania to call out a Body of their Militia amounting in the whole to four Thousand five Hundred, and Preparations being made for their going into Camp, would wish to know, whether in your opinion, it is necessary to compleat this Business. They would by no Means interfere with any Plan you may have formed; and therefore leave it entirely to you to determine on the Expediency of the Measure, being desirous of co-operating with you in any Schemes you may have projected against the Enemy.[4]

I am, Sir, with the greatest Respect, your most obed Sert.

John Hancock Presidt

RC (DLC). In the hand of Jacob Rush and signed by Hancock.

[1] See *JCC,* 7:342–43. Washington explained the impracticability of complying with this resolve in a May 12 letter to Hancock. Washington, *Writings* (Fitzpatrick), 8:45–46. For the genesis of the resolve, see ibid., pp. 8–9.

[2] At this point in the MS Rush first wrote and then deleted the phrase "as the Line of your Conduct." The same phrase is also deleted in the LB of this letter. PCC, item 12A, fol. 202.

[3] Washington enclosed "a General Return of the Forces in Jersey" in his May 21 letter to Hancock. Washington, *Writings* (Fitzpatrick), 8:99.

[4] Congress had resolved on April 24 and 25 to request these reinforcements, and on May 12 Washington reluctantly admitted his need for them. Ibid., pp. 46–47; and *JCC,* 7:296, 299.

Richard Henry Lee to Thomas and Ludwell Lee

Philadelphia May 10th 1777

I heared with great pleasure that my dear children were safely arrived in France.[1] Before this intelligence reached me I had suffered much from apprehensions both for them and their worthy Uncles, in a Country (England) where every consideration of *virtue* and justice, is sacrificed to wicked resentment and views of Tyranny. The risk and danger of correspondence to Great Britain prevented me from writing to you whilst you remained in that Country, and not a want of affection, for whilst you continue to behave as well as you have done, my tenderest affection shall always be placed on you. The views I formerly entertained for my eldest Son must now be changed, with the great alterations that have taken place in the System of North America. Instead of the Church I would now have him as knowing as possible in Commerce, as well the Theory as the Practical part. For this purpose, if his good Uncle William should reside in France, my Son will be employed by him as Clerk or Agent in some capacity, by which a temporary support may be gained, and a lasting knowledge of business at the same time. But, whether he is under the immediate care of his Uncle, or any other Gentleman in France, I hope and insist that he pay the closest attention to business, and the greatest respect and obedience to him under whose care and patronage he lives. Every present and future good consequence will flow from such a conduct, and every evil from the contrary. Let my dear Son therefore, grave upon his mind, and faithfully practice this advice of his affectionate father. It will be of great importance to learn well the French language, and be able to speak, read, and write it with correctness and fluency. Our future commerce with France will be so extensive as to render this indispensible, and I desire it may not be neglected. If Gentlemen in France observe your attention to business and capacity for the discharge of it, there is no doubt but on your return to your own Country, you will be so trusted to conduct the business of foreign Merchants, as to be very useful to them, and profitable to yourself. Your[2]

FC (ViU). In Lee's hand and endorsed: "Copy of a letter to my Sons."

[1] Arthur Lee's March 19, 1777, letter, in which he informed his brother that Thomas was with John Schweighauser, a Nantes merchant, and that Ludwell was studying engineering at a military academy in Paris, is in the Lee Family Papers, MH–H.

[2] The letter ends abruptly here at midpage.

Robert Morris to George Washington

Dear Sir   Philada. May 10th. 1777

I have not taken the liberty of giving You any trouble for someti ne past and indeed I never do it but with great reluctance because I know how much your attention & time must be engaged in the most important pursuits.

The bearer of this the Marquis Armand de la Rouerie is entitled to my Warmest recommendations because he brought from his own Country letters to me that I am obliged to attend to & put great faith in as they come from persons Worthy of the utmost Credit. One of them is from Mr Deane who not only mentions him as a Gentn of Rank, good Family & Fortune but also as a Man of great Merit desiring my particular attention to him & that I shou'd supply him with Money which will be repaid in France by a Gentn to whom America is under the most important obligations. You will therefore excuse & oblige me at the same time by your favourable attention to Monsr. Armand for he chooses to pass by that Name & shoud he want money I will pay his drafts for what he Stands in need of. I find he is a little disgusted at an appointment made for him by Congress this day and I believe it was through the inattention of a Committee which I shall get set right again in a Short time.[1] I am Dr sir with the greatest esteem & affection, Your obedt hble sert.   Robt Morris

RC (DLC).

[1] The basis for Armand's disgust appears to have been that initially he was commissioned a major, although Morris immediately succeeded in having his rank changed to that of colonel. In any event, the May 10 journal entry pertaining to the commission of Charles Armand-Tuffin, chevalier de la Roüerie, indicates that Secretary Thomson originally wrote "major," which he subsequently deleted and replaced with the word "colonel." See PCC, item 1, 6:113; and *JCC,* 7:346. As James Lovell, chairman of the committee on foreign applications, later explained to Washington, "The promotion of Monsr. Armand by Congress to the rank of Colonel was a surprize to the Committee who had considered his pretensions, and rashly enough in all conscience had proposed a majority for him." Lovell to Washington, May 26, 1777. Armand's letter to Morris of April 16, 1777, is in the Robert Morris Papers, DLC. For the marquis' career in America,

see Townsend Ward, "Charles Armand Tuffin, Marquis de la Rouerie," *PMHB,* 2 (1878): 1–34.

Philip Schuyler to Israel Putnam

Dear General,   Philadelphia May 10. 1777.
Information having been given that Dr. Stapleton who attends Capt McPherson, by some Means or other informs himself of the Numbers of which Every Detachment of our Troops going to the Army is composed, It is doubtless with a View to inform General Howe thereof. It is therefore tho't best that he should be immediately removed to this Place, And if Capt. McPherson is not in a Condition to come with him that some skillful Surgeon of ours should attend that Gentleman. You will please to give the Necessary Orders.[1] Nothing new here.

I am Dear General, with real Esteem, Your Most Obed. Humble Servt.   Ph. Schuyler

LB (NN).
[1] See *JCC,* 7:344–45.

Secret Committee to John Langdon

Sir   In Secret Committee Philadelphia May 10 1777
We have your favours of the 17th and 21st instt. That of the 22d we acknowledge receipt of yesterday. With the first of these came Account of the outfitt of the Ship Mifflin and your Account Current, these Shall be examined in course and if any remarks are necessary thereon you Shall have them soon after. As to the Ballance we Shall make you a Remittance of More than the Amount by this conveyance.

We observe your having delivered that part of the Arms and Cloathing from the Cargo of the Mercury before any orders appeared from the Committees of Congress for that purpose, on which we Shall not Animadvert having happily got eased of that part of our troublesome business, by the Board of War being directed to take charge of the Military Stores & the Cloathier General of all cloathing and Materials suitable for it.[1] Consequently you will Account to them for your conduct in disposing of these things previous to the Receipt of their Orders.

We Remit you herein a draft of John Steinmetz & Wm Bell on Mr. Andrew Black of Boston for Seventeen Thousand five hundred dollars, which you'l please to receive and bring the same to our Credit. We will make you a further remittance soon as we know it to be necessary & are, Sir, Your Obedt hble serts,

                 Robt Morris   Wm. Whipple

                 Richard Henry Lee   Phil. Livingston

RC (Capt. J. G. M. Stone, Annapolis, Md., 1973). In a clerical hand and signed by Lee, Livingston, Morris, and Whipple.

[1] See the resolves of March 31, *JCC,* 7:211–12; and Secret Committee to Langdon, April 2, 1777.

Secret Committee to Jeremiah Powell

Sir,   In Secret Committee. Philadelphia May 10. 1777

. Your favour of the 21st Ultimo came duely with the pleasing Account of your having received from Mr Bingham a parcell of Muskets part of the Ship Seins Cargo landed in Martinico. The Continent are now happily pretty well provided for the Campaign and Men Seems the only thing wanting, a circumstance never expected at the commencement of the present War. The Board of war will give the Necessary Orders respecting these Arms, and thanking you for your attention to the publick Interest, We remain Sir, Your Obedt hble servants,

Robt Morris, Chair Man of the Secret Commee.

RC (M–Ar). In a clerical hand and signed by Morris. Addressed: "The Honorable Jer. Powell Esq President Massachusets Bay."

William Whipple to John Langdon

My Dear Sir,   Philadelphia 10th May 1777.

Your two favors of 21st and 22d were handed me the 3d inst by Mr. Champney. The arrival of the Amphitrite gives me double pleasure as she has been long expected and I had in my own mind given her over for lost. This ship has been so long from France that no intelligence can be expected from her. A packet is daily expected with dispatches from that country. A ship with a similar cargo to the Amphitrite is arrived at Martinico after unsuccessfully attempting to get into some of our ports. However we are now well furnished with materials to carry on the war, men only are wanting to use those materials. It grieves me that New Hampshire's quota should be so backward, though perhaps not more so than some other states, but it would be my pride to hear that her sons were first in the field. I think you did right in delivering arms and clothing to the troops. The clothing General tells me he has given orders for clothing all the troops. When I urged your sending your accounts quarterly I did not mean the accounts of those ships that were building; that I know is impossible. What I had in view was the prizes and those ships fitted out by order of the Secret Committee. I have applied to the Clerks of the Committees for accounts of the money sent you which I shall forward so soon as obtained.

I have urged the appointment of the officers for Roche's Ship and was in hopes of having it done so as to send the Commissions by this conveyance, but now despair of getting it done so soon. Roche's character is to be inquired into. I was not here when the orders were given for building that vessel but am told the orders were to rig her a brig and that she was to mount no more than 18 guns, but have lately been informed she is built for a ship and pierced for 20 Guns. I do not imagine that rigging her a ship will be very exceptionable but mounting 20 guns on her certainly will—as that alters her rate.[1]

A Navy Board is to be established at Boston.[2] The gentlemen who compose it are elected. You were in nomination, but as I thought you had rather continue in the business you are than to remove to Boston for a salary of 1500 dollars I did not urge your appointment. The gentlemen are Mr. Warren of Massachusetts, Mr. Varnum of Rhode Island and Mr. Deshon of Connecticut—to them I expect the case of Capt Roche will be referred.

Col Thornton set out the 3d inst. I enclose you his receipt for 65 dollars and told him his draft was refused payment which he promises to have settled without giving you any trouble in the matter.

I am now a single representative of the State of New Hampshire and an arduous task I have of it by advice from Col Bartlett. I suppose Mr Frost is on his way here. I heartily wish he was arrived, and hope some other gentleman will soon be dispatched after him. I shall set out soon after Mr Frost's arrival. I find my health absolutely requires exercise and relaxation. I have not had time to mount my horse since I arrived here from Baltimore nor more than twice while there. Such a life may suit some constitutions but will soon ruin mine.

Enclosed you have an order on the Loan Office for 40,000 dollars for account of Marine Committee. You will also receive from the Secret Committee an order on a gentleman at Boston for 17500, these sums I hope will serve you for the present.

You will receive directions from the Committee respecting the Amphitrite. She is to go to South Carolina. *Inter nos* I have not a very high opinion of the plan of sending Capt Jones in her, however if it succeeds I shall be very agreeably disappointed.[3] You no doubt will do your endeavour to assist in procuring men &c.

Our army is daily increasing and I hope will soon be in a condition to attack the enemy and either destroy or drive them from their posts. Their Ships are still very troublesome on this coast, though some vessels do escape them. I hope the Dove and Friend's adventure will be of the fortunate number, I have not yet heard of the sailing of the Morris, Gunnison from Virginia, but think she must be gone before this. I hope to send you the commissions in a few days—in the interim am sincerely yours,   Wm Whipple

Tr (DLC).

[1] For further information on the *Ranger,* see Whipple to Langdon, May 21, 1777.

[2] On the appointment of the Eastern Navy Board, see John Adams to James Warren, May 6, 1777.

[3] See the Secret Committee's letters to John Paul Jones and to John Langdon of May 9, 1777.

Board of War to George Washington

Sir   War Office May 11th. 1777

By Order of the Board I have the Honour of enclosing the Resolution of Congress herewith sent.[1] I have written to Governor Livingstone & General Putnam & as soon as their Answers are received they will be communicated to your Excellency.

Congress are desirous to be informed what Number of Men are now under your Excellency's Command in New Jersey as nearly as Certainty can be arrived at in the present Situation of the Army, in Order that a Judgment may be formed of the Propriety of hastning on a disbanding the Pennsilvania & Delaware Militia now embodying agreeable to the Request of Congress who would be glad of your Excellency's Opinion on the Subject & that you would inform them whether the disbanding the Militia would be safe & proper or would in anywise interfere with any Plan your Excellency has formed. From the distracted State of Pennsilvania there is no certain Prospect of their Quota speedily taking the Field & no Accounts have been received of those of the Delaware State being ready. Steps however are persuing in both States to comply with the Recommendation of Congress & Part of the Men are assembled.[2]

The Secretary of Congress mistook the State wherein Springfield is situate, it being in the Massachusetts & not the Connecticut State. I copied the Error in my Letter to your Excellency of the 7th inst informing you of the military Stores being ordered thither from Portsmouth, Boston & Providence.

I have the Honour to be, Your very obed & most hble Servt,

Richard Peters Secy

RC (DLC).

[1] See the May 10 resolve on certain prisoners at Princeton in *JCC,* 7:344–45, as well as Washington, *Writings* (Fitzpatrick), 8:48–49.

[2] See John Hancock to Washington, May 10, 1777, note 4.

Thomas Burke to Richard Caswell

Sir   Philadelphia May 11th 1777

A few days ago I received a letter from General Nash, announcing the death of General Moore; at the same time I received some letters recommending Col. Clark for promotion in his room. But altho. I have a very high opinion of Col. Clark as an active, vigilant, and gallant Officer, I can not be satisfied that it is right for me to make a nomination so far out of the usual line, unless I have first your Excellency's assurance that it will be satisfactory to my country. Therefore I have resolved to consult you thereupon, and suspend all proceedings relative thereto, until I shall be favored with your answer. I will beg leave also to suggest to you, that nothing but the command of my country shall make me nominate any man whose merit as a soldier is even suspected, altho he should stand first in order; and I believe our State is too jealous of her honor, and too zealous in the common cause, to give me any such command. Truly, Sir, our affairs have suffered very much through the insufficiency of our Officers, and I am one, among many in Congress, who are determined, so long as I have the honor of a seat, to keep a very strict watch over them. It shall not be my fault, if worthless drones consume the public treasure. It is but justice to say that we have some excellent officers, and our Commander in Chief is very justly admired by all the world.[1]

Nothing interesting has happened since my last, except the arrival of a French ship with military stores, which are exceedingly seasonable and important. In short we now only want men; and one vigorous campaign would give our affairs a very flourishing aspect. Our liberty would be established beyond all danger.

We have had no debates of any consequence in Congress except on the Confederation; all those I shall transmit you at once. It goes on very slowly, and I fear, the difficulty of preserving the independence of the States, and at the same time giving to each its proper weight in the public councils, will frustrate a Confederation altogether.[2]

I have had so short a notice of this opportunity that I can not be full on this subject: but as I give the most diligent attention to it, nothing material will escape me, and you shall be fully informed.

I have the honor to be &c Your Excellency's ob't serv't,

Thos Burke

Tr (Nc–Ar).

[1] Governor Caswell wrote to Burke on June 11 and stated that although he personally approved of Col. Thomas Clark's promotion, he could not guarantee the state's approval of it until he consulted with the North Carolina Assembly in November 1777. In any case Clark remained colonel of the First North Carolina Regiment for the rest of the war. *N.C. State Records,* 11:494; and F. B.

Heitman, *Historical Register of Officers of the Continental Army ...* (Washington [Baltimore]: Press of Nichols, Killam & Maffitt, 1893), pp. 41, 126.

[2] Burke attempted to solve this problem by moving that the Articles of Confederation be amended to make Congress a bicameral legislature consisting of a "General House" made up of delegates chosen proportionally by the states and a "Council of State" composed of one delegate from each state. This proposal, which foreshadowed the national legislature created by the Federal Constitution in 1787, was rejected by Congress because of the belief that it would entail "Delays in Execution," make Congress an "Executive Body resembling King &c.," permit "No Combination Except one or the other," and introduce "Ideas of Distinctions resembling British Constitution." Worthington C. Ford printed the text of Burke's undated plan as part of the entry in the journals for May 5, 1777, but although the journals reveal that Congress then considered the Articles of Confederation, the actual day Burke offered his plan or Congress rejected it can only be conjectured. See *JCC, 7*:328–29.

For a perceptive discussion of Burke's views on state sovereignty and contributions to congressional debates on the Articles of Confederation, see Jack N. Rakove, *The Beginnings of National Politics: An Interpretive History of the Continental Congress* (New York: Alfred A. Knopf, 1979), pp. 164–82.

Samuel Adams to Nathanael Greene

My dear Sir   Philad May 12 1777

Amidst your Hurry of Business and my own, I cannot help withdrawing myself for a Moment to throw on paper a single Sentiment for your Consideration. Europe and America seem to be applauding our Imitation of the Fabian Method of carrying on this War without considering as I conceive the widely different Circumstances of the Carthaginian & the British Generals. It will recur to your Memory that the Faction of Hanno in Carthage prevented Hannibals receiving the Supplys from them which he had a Right to expect and his Necessities requird. This left him to the Resources of his own Mind, and obligd him to depend upon such Supplys as he could procure from the Italians. Under such a Circumstance, it was the Wisdom of Fabius to put himself in the State of Defence but by no means of Inactivity—by keeping a watchful Eye upon Hannibal and cutting of his forraging & other Parties by frequent Skirmishes he had the strongest Reason to promise himself the Ruin of his Army without any Necessity of risqueing his own by a general Engagement. But General Howe (whom by the way I am not about to compare to Hannibal as a Soldier) has at all times the best Assurances of Supplies from Britain. There is no Faction there to disappoint him and the British Navy is powerful enough to protect Transports & provision Vessels coming to him. Hannibal despaird of Reinforcements from Carthage, but Howe has the fullest Assurances of early reinforcements from Britain & cannot fail of receiving them, unless a general War has taken place which I think is at least problematical. They are expected every Day. Would Fabius, if he were his

Enemy, pursue the Method he took with the Carthaginian General? Would he not rather attend to the present Circumstances, and by destroying the Army in Brunswick prevent as much as possible the Enemy increasing in Strength even if reinforcements should arrive or puting a total End to the Campaign if they should not. I am sensible our own Circumstances have been such, thro' the Winter past, as to make it impracticable to attempt any thing, but I hope we are or shall be very soon in a Condition to take a decisive part, and I do not entertain any Doubt but we shall see such an enterprizing Spirit as will confound our Enemies and give Assurances to the Friends of Liberty & Mankind that we still retain a just Sense of our own Dignity and the Dignity of our Cause and are resolvd by Gods Assistance to support it at all Hazzards. I am &c

FC (NN).

Charles Carroll of Carrollton to Charles Carroll, Sr.

Dr. Papa,   P.M. 12th May 1777.

The ship Seine which arrived at Martinico with military Stores for the united States in sailing from Martinico for Boston was taken by a English frigate the morning after she left Martinico: A considerable part of her cargo was landed, at Martinico, part of which is just arrived in a sloop which has got in to Sinapuxent inlet—consists principally of muskets.

The Govr. of Martinico Count D'Argou in concert with the continental agent at that place had concerted a wise scheme to prevent the Seine's falling into the enemy's hands. He wrote a letter to the Govr. of Miquelon artfully calculated to conceal the real destination of the vessel pretending she was destined to the Isle of Miquelon with military stores. The Capt. thro' his letters overboard, but the Pilot kept some papers which discovered the real voyage vizt. to Boston. However Count D'Argou has sent a spirited memorial to the Governor of Dominica demanding the restitution of the vessel as the French King's property. This matter may possibly afford a pretence to the French of declaring war agt. [Englan]d, if they should be thus inclined, tho' I think it there interest and ours too to remain quiet some time longer: they can, & have afforded us material assistance, and I have no doubt of the intention of that court to give us still further assistance.

We have no news from Camp: we had letters from Gen. Washington dated the 10th Morris;[1] and encampt. is marked out, it is said, at Bound Brook for ten thousand men. So we conjecture G. Washington intends moving to that place, which is but 5 miles distant from Brunswick. Col. Conway (mentioned in my letter to Molly)[2] informs me the

French have 60 ships of the line (mostly 74) ready for sea: he says
the ships are all new, or mostly new, & that a great reform has taken
place in the French service. I think we have a valuable acquisition in
Col. Conway. He speaks English well. I am, yr. affectionate Son,

Ch. Carroll of Carrollton

RC (MdHi).
[1] Washington's May 10 letter to Congress from Morristown is in PCC, item
152, 4:171–73, and Washington, *Writings* (Fitzpatrick), 8:34–36.
[2] Carroll's letter to his wife has not been found.

James Lovell to George Washington

Honored dear Sir   Philada. May 12th. 1777
    By the singular manner in which General Lee gives out his charac-
terizing opinions Monsr. Malmedy was exalted to a colonial rank in
Rhode Island which will be a source of pain to him contrary to the
intention of his mentioned zealous friend. Congress has aimed by passing over one continental gradation, from Major to Colonel, to lessen
that pain to this Gentleman, who is high in his professions of ambition
to give signal testimony, in the field, of his attachment to our cause. I
wish every one under your Excellency's command would fullfil all their
professions made at entrance into commission, that, so, one considerable portion of anxiety might be deducted from that load which falls
upon you in your virtuous superintendance of our armies.[1]
    The Bearer appears to me to be sensible & spirited. But, it was not
to pass compliments upon him that I now write, tho at his request. It
was rather that I might not appear backward to any call which affords
me opportunity of professing myself, Your Excellency's Obliged devoted Friend & Humble Servant,   James Lovell

RC (DLC).
[1] On May 11 Congress had resolved that "Monsieur Malmedy be promoted to
the rank, and the pay, of a colonel in the service of these United States," despite
the fact that Rhode Island had already granted him the rank of brigadier general. *JCC*, 7:288, 346. On Washington's inability to satisfy François, marquis de
Malmedy, see his May 16 letters to Malmedy and to President Hancock, Washington, *Writings* (Fitzpatrick), 8:68–72. On Malmedy's relations with Gen.
Charles Lee, see *NYHS Collections* 5 (1872): 322, 338, 342–43, 350–55.

Elbridge Gerry to Thomas Gerry

Dear Brother   Philadelphia May 13. 1777
    I am favoured with yours of April the 28th with the Inclosures; the
17 Bales contain as follows

No 1 to 5	171 pounds Twine	42 pieces fine Duck
6		10 pieces higher price
7 & 8		22 pieces second sort
9 & 10		18 pieces fine Holland Ditto
11 to 13		27 pieces fine Russia
		119 pieces

			Vars
14 to 16	83 do	Twine, 400 sail Needles	22 pieces Ticklenburg
			contg 1542
17		20 pieces do	1359
	254	42	2901

besides which Messrs Gardoquis mention 6 Bales

Contents		Vars
No 1	12 pieces Tent Cloth	573 3/5
2	10 pieces	632 4/5
3	12 do	730
4	12 do	763
5	10 ⎱	675 1/2
6	1 ⎰	3374 9/10
	10 do Contents not mentioned	
164 Yds Wrapper	67 pieces	

These I would have delivered to Capt Curtis or some other principal Sailmaker, & his receipt taken for the number of Yards which each peice contains together with the Weidth (& also for the Twine) to be made into Tents agreable to inclosed Directions without Delay. I shall take it as a Favour if You will employ some faithful person to deliver & measure it, as by the Cost, some peices contain more than others, where the *Vars* are not mentioned, & I am also unacquainted with *this* measure.[1] You will please to pay the person measuring the Cloth, & contract with the Sailmaker on the best Terms not allowing more than the Quarter Master General does here One Do per Tent per the inclosed Memo. The Tops are to be made of the best Duck, & the Sides of the other, the Wrapping may do for some of the Bottoms. These will be ordered to Tyonderoga as soon as made, & therefore no Time should be lost.

The Salt I have agreed to deliver in North Carolina for the Use of the Continent, & shall load the Vessel that Takes it with naval Stores or other produce for Bilbao. If You incline to engage I will freight your Vessel from Marblehead to Edenton in North Carolina, from thence to Bilbao & back to Marblehead, & will leave with our Friend Colo Orne what the Freight shall be. If not, pray engage or Freight a Vessel of 120 Tons, & insure on the Salt & premium for my Account from Marblehead to Edenton 6000 Dollars, agreeing with

the Owner on the best Terms You can, to take a Load of naval or
other Stores from thence to Bilbao, & procuring a Certificate that the
same is to be invested in military Stores, from the Board of War of
the State, if the same is necessary to clear the Stores at Carolina. The
Vessel is to be sent to Messrs. Hughes & Smith of Edenton aforesd. &
the Salt is to be delivered to the order of William Aylet Esqr. of
Virginia, Deputy Commissary General. Inclosed is the Commissary
General's Certificate for this purpose, which will excuse any Vessel
from the Embargo.

I shall write to the Gentleman at Carolina[2] & desire that on the
arrival of the vessel the Cargo may be ready.

The Arms belong to the State & are to be delivered to the Board
of war.

With respect to the Cannon, I shall probably want them for the
Vessel at Newburyport in which I shall be concerned one eighth.

The Fish being bad as Messr. Gardoquis inform me, came to a
miserable Market, but I must make the best of it.

My Regards to Mrs Gerry's & all Friends being yours, sincerely,

E Gerry

P.S. Pray let the Tents be finished in a fortnight or three Weeks after
the Cloth is delivered & inform me as soon as may be of the Number
that will be made by the Duck, And the Contract with the Tradesman.
This Expence must be paid by you in my behalf; & I think the prices
of making if there is any difference should be less with you than in
this place. The Needles & Twine not wanted may be sold to the sailmaker & deducted from his Account. With respect to Messr. Gardoquis
Letter I think it best not to forward them.

RC (MMhHi).
  [1] The vara, the Spanish yard, was a linear measure used in Spain, Portugal,
and Spanish America, varying according to locality but usually measuring about
33 inches. *OED*.
  [2] Not found.

John Hancock to the Massachusetts Council

Gentlemen,   Philada. May 13th. 1777.

I have the Honour of transmitting the enclosed Resolves, and forwarding at the same Time an Order on the Loan Office in Favour of
the President of the Council of your State, to be paid by him to Mr.
Allen the Agent for Indian Affairs in the Eastern Department, who is
to employ it in the Service of that Department.[1]

The Inhabitants of Nova Scotia in the Counties of Cumberland &
Sunbury, having adhered to the Cause of America and suffered for

their Attachment to it, the Congress have requested you will consider their Case, and adopt and carry into Execution, at the Expence of the United States, such Measures for their Relief, as you may think prudent & practicable.[2] I beg Leave to refer your Attention to the Resolve, and have the Honour to be, with great Respect, Gentlemen, your most obed Servt.   John Hancock Presidt

RC (M–Ar). In the hand of Jacob Rush and signed by Hancock.
  [1] See *JCC,* 7:313, 330–31.
  [2] See *JCC,* 7:313, 348–49.

Richard Henry Lee to Patrick Henry

Dear Sir,   Philadelphia 13th May 1777
    The inclosed infamous Act of Parliament is taken from the New York Gazette and its authenticity therefore not to be doubted.[1] The question upon this is, whether every State will not pass acts appointing places of security where the prisoners they take may be safely kept as pledges for the good usage of our people, or as objects of punishment in the way of retaliation? In proportion as our enemies loose the hopes of subduing us by open force, they endeavor more strenuously to sap us by corrupt influence and by the wicked machinations of their Tory friends. To put an effectual stop to the proceedings of the latter, will it not be necessary so to provide by law, as that every Tory may be precisely in the same situation if we succeed in this war, that we undoubtedly shall be if the enemy prevail. And what this latter will be, the inclosed Act of Parliament very plainly declares. The point is, how to distinguish previously the Whigs from the Tories. I believe, by a strict Test, and by appointing a General and a County board of Commissioners, with small but compitent funds to carry on quick correspondence with each other, and to search into the conduct of suspicious Residents, and of all unknown Passengers or Travellers. As you may rely upon it, that Tory machinations are now more wicked than ever, and their correspondence with each other, and their injurious communications not to be doubted. I wish some of the most sensible Whigs in our Assembly would take under consideration what I have here suggested the propriety of. The necessity of completing our Batallions is so obvious, that I suppose the Assembly will adopt the plan of drafting recommended by Congress,[2] and if they do, will it not be highly proper to have discreet recruiting Officers at every place where the Militia is assembled for the draft, who by clearly pointing out to the young Men the advantages of bounty, annual clothes, and land for those that voluntarily engage, may procure a sufficiency on the willing plan. Nor is it a bad argument with them to shew how safely and

easily they are carried thro the Small pox at the public expence, by the present plan of inoculation. Above all things my dear Sir, let us secure the credit of our money by a vigorous Taxation. Maryland has done so, and so have the Eastern States, and all must do it to procure public confidence in our funds and the stability of our currency.

Our Army is approaching the enemies lines and promises soon to be active. We have no late intelligence from France, tho we have reason every day to expect it. Capt Weks in the Continental Ship Reprisal of 16 guns & 100 & odd men has taken & sent into Port L'Orient a Lisbon packet of equal force to himself, with three Ships that were under her Convoy, and the provisions we have taken at Sea, more than compensate for the Danbury loss, since the latter was only 1700 barrels of Meat with some flour & grain, and we have brought in 5000 barrels of Meat bound to N. York.

Colo. Nelson is gone home ill, so that we three are here fixed to hard service. We deserve compassion and relief. I have no objection to a service however irksome, if it is so contrived that a reasonable relief may now and then be interposed, so as to ease the Individual, without injury to the public.

We learn lately, that the account of General Carletons approach to Ticonderoga was premature, and in the mean time a considerable reenforcement has arrived from the Eastward, so that we are no longer in pain for that Post.

I am, with much esteem, dear Sir, Yours sincerely,

Richard Henry Lee

RC (ViHi).
[1] See Lee to Henry, May 6, 1777, note 2.
[2] For the April 14 resolves on recruiting, see *JCC*, 7:261–63.

Richard Henry Lee to Samuel Purviance, Jr.

Dear Sir,   Philadelphia 13th May 1777

It gives me great pleasure to hear of Capt. Nicholsons reconciliation with the Government, altho it is not yet announced to us in form.[1]

The Tories I hope will not long have occasion to rejoice. They must either change their conduct, or abide the consequences shortly. I have not yet received the letter containing my brothers observations on Tobacco. I remember generally that observing on the different Tobaccos that suited different Markets he said that what grew on both sides of Potomac was the kind most used in France, and he thought it would not be prudent to send the finer kinds of Tobo. to France, but immediately to the markets that consumed it. As Holland, the Baltic &c.

Be so kind as inform your brother Robert that I took the liberty to request Mr. Blair McClanahin of this City would direct to his care in Baltimore for me a Cask of Spirit from Wilmington, and I beg the favor of him to have it well taken care of and sent to Potomac for me by the first safe conveyance. I would prefer its going by a Mr. Crump to any other, but by no means let it be sent by a John Bayne who sometimes comes to Baltimore from Potomac, as I have no opinion of that Man. Mr. Crump comes often from Potomac to Baltimore and is a good Man. If it goes by Crump, he knows where to land it, if by any other, desire it may be landed at Pecatone, the house of George Turberville esqr. on South Potomac river side, a little above the mouth of Yeocomico, and not far above Sandy Point.

I am Sir your most obedient servant,   Richard Henry Lee

[*P.S.*] Capt. Weeks has taken & sent into Port L'Orient a Lisbon Packet of 16 guns & 105 men with three Ships that she had under Convoy. The Packet was of equal force with Capt. Weeks & fought 2 hours. Our Army is approaching the enemies lines, and we may soon expect important intelligence.

RC (NjGbS).
   [1] For the details of Nicholson's conflict with Maryland authorities, see Marine Committee to James Nicholson, April 29, 1777, note.

Marine Committee to John Young

Sir   May 13th. 1777.
   You are to return to Senepuxent and after sending up the Stores you brought thither in the Independence, you are immediately to proceed out to Sea on a Cruize off the Capes of Delaware, keeping out side of the British men of war and so distant from them as may be necessary for your own security. You are to Cruize in such places as may be most likely for you to meet or fall in with American Ships or Vessels bound into this Port, taking care when you chase any such as you take for Americans to shew them Continental Colours, & when you speak them inform them of the British Cruizers in the Mouth of Delaware and Chesapeake Bay, advising them to get into the Inlets or if large ships to seek safety either in the Eastern or Southern States, you are to continue this Cruize for about three weeks some times to the Northward and some times to the Southward of Cape Henlopen and render every assistance and service in your power to such American Vessels as you fall in with during that time. We hope also that you may shew some good Prizes the way into some of the Inlets along the Coast. When this Cruize is finished you may put into any one of the

Said Inlets where you can with most convenience heave down the
Sloop and send an Officer or an Express to inform us where you are,
when you can be ready to Sail again, and what Stores and Provisions
you will want for a three months Cruize when we shall send fresh
orders and take measures for your being supplied.
    We are sir, Your hble servants

LB (DNA: PCC Miscellaneous Papers, Marine Committee Letter Book).

Medical Committee to Thomas Johnson

Sir   13th May 1777
    The Director General of the Continental Hospitals is much in want
of Spanish Flies and Suggests that the State over which you preside
has a considerable Quantity of them in Store. He has requested the
Medical Committee to apply for Such part as the State may Spare and
Accordingly we take the Freedom to request your Excellency to give
the Necessary orders for furnishing him with so much of that Medicine
as the particular Demand of your own Medical Departments will
admit. Whatever Quantity shall be delivered to the Director General
or his Order shall be replaced from the Continental Stores as soon as
possible, meantime it will be proper to charge it to the United States.
We doubt not that Your Excellency will Comply with this request if
not prevented by some very particular Circumstances, and we have
the Honor to be, Your Excellency's very Obedt Servts. Signed by Order
of the Medical Committee,   Jonathn. Elmer

RC (MdAA).

William Paca to Thomas Johnson

Dr Sir   13 May 1777.
    We recd. yours by the post & shall fill up the Commissions as you
request.[1] There is Nothing new since my last. A heavy firing was heard
yesterday near Bonam Town. There is no Doubt but a smart Skirmish
has been had with the Enemy. By General Washingtons Return last
Evening which I saw at the Presidents he had 6891 Men Eight hundred
of them sick but general Mifflin says the most of them with the small
Pox and so far recovered that about 500 of them would be able to turn
out & fight on an Emergency. Over & above these on their way from
Bristol we have above twelve hundred more. The above are regular

forces—the militia detachments in the Jerseys not included. The 6891 are privates enclusive of officers commisd. & non commissd. officers.

Pray has Capt. Nicholson made a satisfactory Submission?

My Complts to your Council. Yrs. affly.,   Wm Paca

[*P.S.*] You'll see in the papers an account of Capt. Wicke's Success. We have no certainty however of it.

RC (MeHi).
¹ Not found, but see Benjamin Rumsey to Thomas Johnson, May 1, 1777, note 1.

Secret Committee to Nicholas and John Brown

Gentlemen, In Secret Committee, Philadelphia April [*i.e.* May] 13. 1777¹

We received your favour of the 28th April advising the Safe arrival of 19 bales Blankets at Bedford from Nantes in France and inclosing Sundry Accounts, which shall be examined shortly when we will write to you and make a Remittance.

You will please to deliver those 19 bales Containing 980 Blankets to James Mease Esquire Cloathier General or to his order, and to no other order whatsoever, as the Resolves of Congress are expressly against their being put into any other hands & transmit us his or his Agents Receipt for the Same. We are Gentlemen, Your hble Servants,

> Robt Morris
>
> Richard Henry Lee
>
> Wm. Whipple

RC (RPJCB). In a clerical hand and signed by Lee, Morris, and Whipple.
¹ The minutes of the Secret Committee indicate that this letter was written following the reading of the Browns' April 28 letter at the committee's May 13 meeting. Journal of the Secret Committee, fol. 134, MH–H.

Secret Committee to Caesar Rodney

Sir   In Secret Committee. Philada. May 13th 1777

We are obliged to trouble you again to provide for us some Waggons to go down with Capt John Young of the Sloop Independance to Senepuxen to bring up from thence a quantity of Arms, Tents & Stores for the use of the Continent.¹ Capt Young will deliver this & inform you how many Waggons may be necessary for this Service. The Goods must be halled to Duck Creek & sent up from thence by Water in the same manner as those lately come up from Cape Henlopen² & we will engage the Shallop to come again. Cap Young will be supplied with Money to pay the expences but if it falls short we will pay any ballances that may remain to your or his order & we must also request you will send a suitable Guard with the Waggons, that every thing may come up in Safety. We are Sir, Your obedt hble servts,

Robt Morris

Richard Henry Lee

Wm Whipple

P.S. We have concluded to send down Mr Robt Purdy on this business. We request therefore that you will give him your assistance in doing the business as above.[3]

RC (PHi). Written by Morris and signed by Morris, Lee, and Whipple.

[1] For a list of the arms brought from Sinepuxent, Md., and delivered to Commissary Benjamin Flower, see Secret Committee Minutes of Proceedings, May 31, 1777.

[2] For the Secret Committee's earlier requests for Rodney's assistance, see their letters to him of April 15, 25, and May 2, 1777.

[3] On May 31 Morris wrote the following brief note to Rodney, apparently in response to letters Rodney had written on May 29 as an outgrowth of this request for assistance in hiring wagons. "I received both your letters of the 29th Inst. at the same time, one Contradicting the news contained in the other. I have paid these expresses & in future if you have occasion to send others be pleased to agree for the Sum they are to receive & mention it in your letters. The Congress pay 30/ per day for Waggons & have plenty of them at that rate." Universiteitsbibliotheek van Amsterdam.

Roger Sherman to Oliver Wolcott

Sir,   Philadelphia May 13th. 1777

I received the Enclosed letters by the Post this day. I now forward them to you by Jesse Brown. Nothing very material has been done in Congress Since You left it.[1] The Quarter Master Generals department has been regulated and Col. Jedediah Huntington & Col. Joseph Read were yesterday promoted to the Rank of Brigadiers. The Confederation has been twice entered upon, but not much progress made in it. The Commissary General is here, he has displaced his Deputy Wharton. Regulations are prepared to put that department on a good footing but not passed Congress. I hope you will Soon return with Some other of the Delegates; I want very much to return home. I am not very well—cannot endure So close attention to Business as is necessary when but one Delegate from the State is attending. Mr Ellery's time expired last week & he has no account of being reappointed.[2] Neither that State nor Delaware are now represented.

Mr. Duncan is about to dismiss his boarders. Colo. Whipple comes to Mrs Cheesman's to Morrow.

I am with due regards, your humble Servant,

Roger Sherman

RC (CtY).

[1] Congress had granted Wolcott leave of absence on May 2. *JCC,* 7:321.

[2] On the appointment of Rhode Island delegates, see William Ellery to Nicholas Cooke, March 30, note 2, and May 8, 1777, note 3.

John Adams to Abigail Adams

May 14. 77

Prices with you are much more moderate than here. Yesterday I was obliged to give Forty shillings Pen. Cur., Thirty Two L.M.[1] for one Gallon of Rum.

In my station here, I have Business with many Gentlemen who have occasion to visit me, and I am reduced to the Necessity of treating them with plain Toddy and Rum and Water—a Glass of Wine, once in a while to a great stranger, of uncommon Consideration.

The Prices of Beef, Pork, Veal, Mutton, Poultry, Butter, Cheese, Milk is Three Times higher, here than with you.

I live like a Miser, and an Hermit, to save Charges, yet my Constituents will think my Expences beyond all Bounds. My Love to Dr. Tufts. I have received two agreable Letters from him, which I will answer as soon as I can.[2]

RC (MHi). Adams, *Family Correspondence* (Butterfield), 2:238.

[1] That is, "lawful money."

[2] Cotton Tufts' April 14 and 24 letters to Adams are in Adams, *Family Correspondence* (Butterfield), 2:210–11, and 220–22.

Roger Sherman to Jonathan Trumbull, Sr.

Honored Sir   Philadelphia May 14th. 1777

Your letter to Congress was received and read, and then committed to the Board of War.[1] I am Sorry to hear that the Militia are no better Armed in this time of danger. I believe there are no Continental Arms to Spare at present, more are daily expected. If any are due to the State of Connecticut, it would be best to Send a particular account of the Number and request Congress that they be replaced as Soon as any Shall arrive. Congress has lately been employed in regulating the Several departments of the Army that the business may be properly conducted and frauds and abuse prevented. The Articles of Confederation have Several times come Under consideration but not much progress made therein. Rhode Island is not represented. Mr Ellery's time expired last week & he has no information of being reappointed. Letters as late as the 15th of April received from our Agent in Martineco Inform that our Trade receives all the protection that could be desired from the Govt of the French Islands, but no certain accounts whether a war will Soon take place between France & Britain.

Your Honr has probably Seen the late Act of Parliament for Sending the Americans to England & detaining them in prison without Bail or mainprize till the first of Jany. 1778. The best way to relieve our people who may fall into their hands, is by a vigorous exertion to get as many of theirs as possible into our custody, as nothing but the fear of retaliation will induce them to regard the laws of humanity.

The Gentleman who gave information of Governor Franklin's misbehaviour and the inattention of our Government to prevent it seemed displeased that any part of the information was contradicted by your Honrs letter.[2] I have no doubt but his information was good as to Govr Franklin's Misconduct. As to our Government being informed of it he says that he told Genll Parsons of it and Mr Burr of Fairfield was also informed of it. Mr Duer is Zealously engaged to Suppress Tories.[3]

The Congress promoted Colonels Huntington and Read to the rank of Brigadiers General on the 12th instant, the first on General Washington's request.[4] I wish for leave to return home for a Short time at least, but it wont do to leave the State of Connecticut unrepresented. I hope other Delegates will Soon arrive.

I am with great Esteem [and] regard Your Honrs. Obedient humble Servant,   Roger Sherman

RC (Ct).

[1] Trumbull's May 5 letter to Hancock, which was read in Congress on May 12, is in PCC, item 66, 1:333–36.

[2] On April 22 Congress had requested Governor Trumbull to place former New Jersey governor William Franklin in close confinement for violating his parole by distributing pardons offered by the Howe brothers. In his May 5 letter Trumbull had reported that he had complied with this request, but he denied that "any in Power" had had any knowledge of Franklin's activities and insisted that Franklin had operated "in covert of secrecy." According to accounts circulating in Connecticut, William Duer, who had informed Congress about Franklin, also had alleged that several members of the Connecticut General Assembly were among the recipients of these pardons. During its May session the assembly requested Trumbull to ask the Connecticut delegates to obtain evidence from Duer "respecting any secret plots and conspiracies" that involved receiving protection from the Howes. And in June, councillor Titus Hosmer asked William Williams to query Duer about the involvement of assembly members. But with the exception of Sherman's brief May 26 reply to Trumbull, no response on this point from Duer or any of the Connecticut delegates has been found. See *JCC,* 7:291; *A Historical Collection, from Official Records, Files, &c., of the Part*

Sustained by Connecticut, during the War of the Revolution, comp. Royal R. Hinman (Hartford: E. Gleason, 1842), p. 274; Burnett, *Letters,* 2:362n.4; John Hancock to Jonathan Trumbull, Sr., April 23, note 1; and Sherman to Jonathan Trumbull, Sr., May 26, 1777.
   [3] In apparent recognition of his zeal, Duer had been added to the "committee for suppressing toryism" on April 22. *JCC,* 7:291.
   [4] See *JCC,* 7:347.

John Adams to Abigail Adams

May 15. 1777

Gen. Warren writes me, that my Farm never looked better, than when he last saw it, and that Mrs. —— was like to outshine all the Farmers.[1] I wish I could see it. But I can make Allowances. He knows the Weakness of his Friends Heart and that nothing flatters it more than praises bestowed upon a certain Lady.

I am suffering every day for Want of my farm to ramble in. I have been now for near Ten Weeks in a drooping disagreable Way, loaded constantly with a Cold. In the Midst of infinite Noise, Hurry, and Bustle, I lead a lonely melancholly Life, mourning the Loss of all the Charms of Life, which are my family, and all the Amusement that I ever had in Life which is my farm.

If the warm Weather, which is now coming on, should not cure my Cold, and make me better I must come home. If it should and I should get tolerably comfortable, I shall stay, and reconcile my self to the Misery I here suffer as well as I can.

I expect, that I shall be chained to this Oar, untill my Constitution both of Mind and Body are totally destroyed, and rendered wholly useless to my self, and Family for the Remainder of my Days.

However, now We have got over the dreary, dismall, torpid Winter, when We had no Army, not even Three Thousand Men to protect Us against all our Enemies foreign and domestic; and now We have got together a pretty respectable Army, which renders Us tolerably secure against both, I doubt not, We shall be able to perswade some Gentleman or other, in the Massachusetts, to vouch safe, to undertake the dangerous Office of Delegate to Congress.

However, I will neither whine, nor croak. The Moment our Affairs are in a prosperous Way and a little more out of Doubt—that Moment I become a private Gentleman, the respectfull Husband of the amiable Mrs. A. of B. and the affectionate Father of her Children, two Characters, which I have scarcely supported for these three Years past, having done the Duties of neither.

RC (MHi). Adams, *Family Correspondence* (Butterfield), 2:238–39.
   [1] For James Warren's April 27 letter to Adams, in which he reported that "I

don't know but Mrs. Adams Native Genius will Excel us all in Husbandry," see
Warren-Adams Letters, 1:320.

John Hancock to George Washington

Sir,   Philada. May 15. 1777.
I do myself the Honour to enclose you sundry Resolves of Congress,[1]
accompanied with a Commission for Monsr. Armand, which I am to
request you will order to be delivered to him, as he is now at Head
Quarters.[2]
Ever since the Appointment of Brigadiers I have been waiting to be
informed of the Dates of their respective Commissions in Order to
settle their Rank in making out new ones. But as there is no Probability of my receiving this Information, & the Gentlemen themselves
will be at Head Quarters, I must request you will give Commissions to
them and ascertain their Rank by the Dates of their original Commissions. I have the Honour to be, with the utmost Esteem & Respect,
Sir, your most obedt. & very hble Servt.
                                                         John Hancock Presidt

RC (DLC). In the hand of Jacob Rush and signed by Hancock.
[1] These were resolves of May 10 and 12–14 on certain French officers, the
appointment of brigadier generals, postal service, Nova Scotia, Maj. Richard
Campbell, and the quartermaster's department. *JCC,* 7:346–49, 351–52, 355–59.
[2] In regard to Armand, see Robert Morris to Washington, May 10, 1777.

Philip Schuyler to William Livingston

Dear Sir   Philadelphia 15th May 1777.
Last Evening I was honored with Your Excellency's Favor of the
13th instant.
The Papers which it inclosed evince Lee to be a dangerous Character
and as he was taken near the Enemies Lines and as he has been, as
Mrs. Thompson declares, with them, he will fall within the Cognizance
of the Military.
Your Excellency & the Council of Safety will therefore please to
send him to this Town, his Confession to Major Tayler makes it necessary that the Major should attend with him, together with Thompson
& his Wife. And you will please to order such Other persons to Attend
as may be necessary.[1]
I am Dr. Sir, with Every Friendly Wish, Your Excellency's most
Obedt. Humble Servt.   Ph. Schuyler

LB (NN).
[1] Governor Livingston's May 13 letter to Schuyler discussed the case of a

certain John Lee, alias Brown, who had been caught near the British lines in New Jersey with a petition to General Howe. Lee claimed that he was apprehended as he was returning to the American lines to report what he had learned about the British forces, but Livingston scoffed at this story and asserted that Lee "is undoubtedly one of Hows Recruiters." Schuyler Papers, NN. Livingston's May 15 reply to this letter from Schuyler is in the same collection.

Charles Carroll of Carrollton to Charles Carroll, Sr.

Dr. Papa,   Phila. 14th [i.e. 16th] May 1777[1]

Inclosed you have the Pena. evening posts of Tuesday & Thursday. We this day received intelligence of a vessel arrived at Egg harbour with Cloths & between 3 & 4 thousand stand of arms from France. This vessel has brought English prints as late as the latter end of February & letters from our Commissioners in France dated sometime in March & one from Docr. Lee dated 23d March from Burgos in Spain.[2] The news brought by these dispatches are favourable. The King of Portugal is dead, & troops were filing off from the frontiers of Spain towards Portugal. Capt Weeks had brought into Port l'Orient 5 prises, among which was the Falmouth packet bound from that port to Lisbon. These vessels Weeks disposed of tho' not without difficulty at Port l'Orient. From the affected orders given him to depart, & the excuses made by him for delaying his departure at and last admitted with great seeming reluctance, it is plain, the French court wants to temporise & to gain time. The vessel which carried the dispatches from Congress to France of our Successes in the Jersies was just arrived at Nantes: no doubt the good news would encourage the French court to continue their assistance. To judge from Dor. Lee's letter Spain also is well inclined. By a letter from London of the 14th March to that gentleman the Ministry have altered their intended plan of operations. Owing to the difficulty of raising foreign mercenaries, they have determined to order the greatest part of their forces to fall down the St. Laurence & join Howe. If so, no attack will be made on Tionderoga this year. This piece of news corresponds with intelligence lately brought by some Indians from Canada, of which I advised you in my last. G. Arnold is in town. He says two officers who have lately come out of N. York & were well acquainted with some English officers were informed by them that their loss in their expedition to Danbury amounted in killed, wounded & prisoners & missing to 500, if so they have paid dear for the destruction of our magazine at that place.

All is yet quiet in the Jersies. I believe the enemy will attempt nothing of importance till they receive reinforcements. Gen. Washington disapproves of the inlisting servants & convicts in his letter of the 13 instant.[3]

Tell Molly they ask for making shoes 45/pair, tea £45.15. per pound. I can not give such prices, and I am sure she will commend me for it.

An English newspaper of some day in March (I forget the date) mentions the enemy's losses in the Jersies. The ministry allow our Generals outgeneraled theirs. However they stile it only a military check. My love to Molly & Mrs. Darnall. I am, yr. affectionate Son,

Ch. Carroll of Carrollton

RC (MdHi).

[1] From the contents of this letter it seems clear that Carroll actually wrote it on the 16th. The Thursday *Pennsylvania Evening Post* he enclosed was issued May 15, and the George Washington letter he discussed was read in Congress on May 16. Compare also Roger Sherman's May 16 letter to Jonathan Trumbull for references to letters from France and London which Sherman states "were this Day received."

[2] Apparently Arthur Lee's letter to the Committee of Secret Correspondence of March 8, 1777. See Wharton, *Diplomatic Correspondence,* 2:280, 292. For Silas Deane's and Benjamin Franklin's March 4 letter to the committee, see ibid., pp. 277–78.

[3] For Washington's May 13 letter to President Hancock, which according to the journals was read in Congress on May 16, see Washington, *Writings* (Fitzpatrick), 8:56–57; and *JCC,* 7:365.

Marine Committee to Hoysted Hacker

Sir: In Marine Committee, Philadelphia, May 16, 1777.

As we have now appointed you Commander of the Ship Columbus, you are to repair without delay to Providence, Rhode Island, and there put on board said Vessel, Provisions, etc. for a Four Months Cruize, using every endeavor to get fitted and manned with despatch.

When ready for the Sea, you are to proceed out against the Enemies' Transport Ships, coming to reinforce or supply their army at New York, and take, burn, sink or destroy as many of their vessels of every kind as you possibly can.[1]

You will employ your vessel in this manner until the 10th day of July next, when you are to break open the Sealed Instructions[2] enclosed herein and follow the orders there laid down for you.[3]

These instructions will direct your attention to an object of great importance, the execution whereof we have much at heart and on your part we expect that every thing in your power will be done to accomplish it. Should any misfortune happen to you be sure to destroy those instructions, and for that purpose keep them constantly slung with a weight to sink them, should there be occasion so to do.

We wish to see strict discipline supported in our Navy and the Seamen well treated, great care to be taken of the Ships, their materials and stores, and prisoners are to be treated with humanity, therefore recommend you will attend carefully to these points, as well as to keep us constantly advised of your proceedings.[4]

Wishing you health & Success we remain Sir, Your Friends & Servants.   John Hancock   Thos. Burke

　　　　　　　　　　Robt. Morris   Nathan Brownson

　　　　　　　　　　Richard Henry Lee   Phil. Livingston

　　　　　　　　　　　　　　　　　　　　　Wm. Whipple

Reprinted from *The Collector* 25 (March 1915): 53. LB (DNA: PCC Miscellaneous Papers, Marine Committee Letter Book).

[1] Captain Hacker was unable to carry out this mission because the British fleet kept him and his ship bottled up in Narragansett Bay throughout 1777. William J. Morgan, *Captains to the Northward: The New England Captains in the Continental Navy* (Barre, Mass: Barre Publishing Co., 1959), p. 78.

[2] Although these have not been found, they were probably the instructions proposing an attack on Britain's Jamaica fleet, for which see Marine Committee Resolutions, April 29, 1777.

[3] On this day the Marine Committee also wrote this letter to Daniel Tillinghast, the Continental prize agent in Rhode Island:

"Enclosed herein we send forward to you some blank warrants which are to be filled up with the names of suitable men for Petty officers on board the Ship Columbus, therefore we request that you will join with Captain Hacker to have good men appointed and transmit us a list of their names.

"We have ordered the Columbus out on a Cruize and request you will lend Captain Hacker every assistance in your power to get her to sea as soon as possible." PCC Miscellaneous Papers, Marine Committee Letter Book, fol. 112; and Paullin, *Marine Committee Letters,* 1:136.

[4] At this point the following paragraph appears in the LB: "Your exertions for the Public benefit will always command our esteem and freindship and we doubt not you will be dilligent in the service of your Country."

Roger Sherman to Jonathan Trumbull, Sr.

Sir,   Philadelphia May 16th. 1777

The President detained the express 'till to day waiting for the board of War to report on your Honrs letter. The Board took it into consideration this morning, but did not think it necessary to make any report to Congress on the contents as the resolution of Congress passed last December authorizing Your Honr to retain two Regiments for the defence of the State until further order has not been superceded.[1] Capt John Langdon has Informed the board of war that he had Sent about 3000 Arms to Connecticut to furnish the continental raised in that State. All the residue of the arms that were in the hands of the Agents in the Eastern States are ordered to be Sent to Springfield where a Laboratory is ordered to be erected, and the Board have agreed upon Sending an order to the Store keeper there to furnish as many more as are necessary for equipping the Troops in Connecticut upon proper muster rolls being produced to him. Letters were this Day received from France as late as the 25th of March but no material news, they related chiefly to commerce. London papers were received mentioning the Battles of Trenton and Princetown last winter, which were humiliating to the Ministry. They applaud the Conduct of our Generals. An extract of a letter from London mentions that the Enemies forces are to be removed from Canada to Joyn General Howe's Army, but we ought not to give so much Credit to it as to alter our plans for defence in the Northern department.

I am Sir with great regards, Your Honrs. Obedient humble Servant,
Roger Sherman

P.S. I Should think it advisable to represent to General Washington the necessity of having the Battalions Stationed in Connecticut. When the board of War had the matter under consideration the resolution of Congress was not before them, but they Supposed it was at General Washingtons option to call for the Troops when he might think proper.[2]
R.S.

RC (Ct).
[1] In the aftermath of the British raid on Danbury, Governor Trumbull had outlined the weak defense posture of his state in his May 5 letter to Congress, wherein he stressed the necessity of the return to Connecticut of two Continental regiments previously placed under his temporary direction by a December 10, 1776, congressional resolve and requested a share of recently imported arms. PCC, item 66, 1:333–36.
[2] Trumbull had already written to the general concerning this matter and in his May 11 reply Washington had explained why it would be impossible for him to comply with Trumbull's request for two regiments to guard the Connecticut coast. Washington, *Writings* (Fitzpatrick), 8:42–44.

John Adams to Abigail Adams

Philadelphia May 17. 1777

I never fail to inclose to you the News papers, which contain the most of the Intelligence that comes to my Knowledge.

I am obliged to slacken my Attention to Business a little, and ride and walk for the Sake of my Health, which is but infirm. Oh that I could wander, upon Penns Hill, and in the Meadows and Mountains in its Neighbourhood free from Care! But this is a Felicity too great for me.

Mr. Gorham and Mr. Russell are here with a Petition from Charlstown. It grieves me that they are to return without success. I feel, most exquisitely, for the unhappy People of that Town. Their Agents have done every Thing in their Power, or in the Power of Men to do, and the Mass. Delegates have seconded their Efforts to the Utmost of their Power, but all in vain.[1]

The Distress of the States, arising from the Quantity of Money abroad, and the monstrous Demands that would be made from Virginia, N. Jersy, N. York and elsewhere, if a Precedent should be once set, has determined the Congress, almost with Tears in their Eyes, to withstand this Application at present.

Every Man expressed the Utmost Tenderness and Humanity, upon the Occasion: But at the same Time every Man except the Mass. Delegates expressed his full Conviction of the ill Policy of granting any Thing at present.

RC (MHi). Adams, *Family Correspondence* (Butterfield), 2:239–40.

[1] The Charlestown, Mass., petition, asking for £163,405.3.8 lawful money, was read in Congress on May 14 and rejected two days later. Congress resolved that "Though the estimation of the damages sustained may be very moderate, and the great and early sufferings of the inhabitants of Charlestown entitle them to particular attention, yet the committee apprehend, that if Congress were to pay that valuation, claims, much more extensive, and of a similar nature, will be made by other sufferers, and subject the United States to the payment of sums of money, which, in the present exigency of their affairs, cannot be spared from the support of the present just and necessary war." Congress also rejected the committee's recommendation to urge state legislatures to relieve war victims. *JCC,* 7:354, 365–66; PCC, item 42, 2:23. See also Massachusetts Delegates to the Massachusetts Assembly, May 21, 1777.

A similar petition from the inhabitants of Falmouth, Cumberland Co., Mass., was read in Congress on March 1, 1776, but apparently no action was taken. *JCC,* 4:179.

Philip Schuyler to John Pemberton

Friend Pemberton,[1]   Philadelphia May 17. 1777.

Altho the Profession of Arms is contrary to the religious Tenets of Friends, Yet as that Society has on many Occasions exercised their Benevolence to Soldiers by making Contributions of Clothing & provision to them & by affording them medical Relief when in Sickness, I cannot entertain a Doubt but that the same humane Principle continues to influence their Conduct.

In this Confidence, I rely on their Aid in procuring me an immediate Supply of one thousand Blankets to be collected from Friends in this City for the purpose of covering Soldiers, who are braving the Rigours of a Campaign & hazarding their Lives, that Your Society in Common with all other Classes of Men may enjoy those Civil & religious Rights which have been transmitted them by their Ancestors.[2] You will therefore please to lay my Requisition before a Meeting of the Friends in this City assuring them, that reasonable Compensation will be made for the Blankets furnished.

I should hope for the Exertion of your Influence on an Occasion so important to the public Weal, If I did not entertain the fullest Confidence that a Request so reasonable in Its Nature and affording to the Friends an Oppertunity of evincing their Humanity and Patriotism would meet with a cheerful Compliance.

From a Total Want of personal Acquaintance with any of the Friends, I am induced to look up to You as a public Character, having seen Your name submitted to a Testimony of Friends at a Meeting of Suffertorys held in this City on the 20th of November last.

Please to Favor me with an Answer as soon as possible. I am &c. &c.

Ph. Schuyler

LB (NN).

[1] John Pemberton (1727–95) was a Quaker preacher in Philadelphia whose opposition to the war with Great Britain led in September 1777 to his arrest and imprisonment in Virginia. *DAB*. Schuyler enclosed this letter in a brief one of the same date to John's older brother Israel, one of Pennsylvania's most prominent Quaker merchants and philanthropists. "Inclose You a Letter," wrote the general to Israel, "which by its Direction You will see designed for Mr. John Pemberton. But being informed that he is out of Town & not likely to return soon, I beg You will read It, and communicate Its Contents to the Society of Friends in this City, of which I am advised You are a Member. You will please to signify to me Whether I may expect an Answer or not." Schuyler Papers, NN. For the refusal of the Quakers to comply with Schuyler's requests, see Schuyler to Israel Pemberton, May 22, 1777. For additional information on the plight of the Pembertons and Pennsylvania Quakers as they became engulfed in the revolution, see also Theodore Thayer, *Israel Pemberton, King of the Quakers* (Philadelphia: Historical Society of Pennsylvania, 1943), pp. 210-32.

[2] Schuyler also wrote a brief letter on this day to Quartermaster General Thomas Mifflin asking him to send 1,000 tents to the army in the northern department. Schuyler Papers, NN.

Philip Schuyler to George Washington

Dear Sir   Philadelphia 18th May 1777

I do myself the Honor to inclose your Excellency a Return of the Troops in the Town. We have not a Blanket to cover them with. The Quakers refused to furnish any to the Committee appointed to collect from the Inhabitants. I have written to John Pemberton on the Subject and am determined if they do not voluntarily afford us a thousand, to make Use of coercive Measures. This Jesuitical Set do us much Injury. The Board of War have reported to Congress that I ought again to be invested with the Command in the Northern Department, and that General Gates should continue to serve under me, or join your Excellency. This occasioned a warm Debate which will be renewed to Morrow.[1] I am Dr Sir, with the greatest Respect and Esteem, Your Excellency's most obedient hble Servant,   Ph. Schuyler

RC (DLC). In the hand of John Lansing, Jr., and signed by Schuyler.
[1] See *JCC*, 7:366, 371, 8:375; and Schuyler's Memorial to Congress, May 6, 1777, note.

Secret Committee Minutes of Proceedings

May 19th. 1777.

Committee met. Present—Morris, Lee, Whipple. Order on the Auditor genl. in favor of Ja. Wallace, for 3200 dlls being the value of his Brige. Polly, Capt. Lacy, taken by the Enemy's frigate Orpheus, on the 4th July last, as appears by the Capt's protest, sd. Brige. being charterd & insurd by the Come.[1]

MS (MH–H).
[1] For information relating to the chartering of the *Polly*, see Secret Committee Minutes of Proceedings, March 27, 1776, and June 4, 1777; and Secret Committee to Philip Lacey, May 14, 1776, note.

William Whipple to Josiah Bartlett

My Dear Sir   Piladelphia 19 May 1777

My last was by Mr. Champney since which I have not had the Pleasure of any of Yours. Mr. Frost arriv'd the 15th inst, by his Credentials I find I am superceeded, he tells me that was not the intention of the Court.[1] I also find by Your letters that it was there wish that I might tarry some time after Mr. Frosts arrival which I shall do, if I can with propriety, tho I wish to be on my way home before the weather is uncomfortably warm. A ship arriv'd a few days ago from Nants. She brings letters of the 20th March but no dispatches of very great importance, those are expected by a Packet which was to sail in two or three days. Perhaps she is already arriv'd, at some distant port. This ship is landing her Cargo at Cinnapucksen, several of the Enemies ships being still, in Delaware Bay; her cargo consists of Arms & Cloathing. The Reprisal has carried in to France five Prizes since the two she took on her passage from hence one of them a Packet from Falmouth for Lisbon. Capt Weeks writes he is cleaning his ship at 'Orant & has wrote to the Commissioners for leave to come home so he may be soon expected.

By a letter from Dr. Lee dated at Burgos in Spain (he being on his way to Madrid) large Quantities of Cloathing are prepareing in that Kingdom for this Country.[2] Some are already sent to the Havanna. This is done without application, he also says the King of Portugal is dead & that a large body of Spanish Troops are marching to the

Frontiers of Portugal. I shall set out in about a fortnight. Perhaps I may write you once more before I leave this, if anything happens worth communicating I certainly shall. In the mean time I am very sincerely Yours,   Wm. Whipple

[P.S.] Mr. Frost desires his Compliments.

RC (N).
¹ On April 1 the New Hampshire Assembly had "resolved, that Major-General Nathaniel Folsom, and the Honorable George Frost, Esq. be, and hereby are, chosen and appointed Delegates to represent this State in the Continental Congress." The absence of Whipple's name led him to believe that he had been superseded, although he had been elected to a one-year term commencing January 23, 1777. See *JCC,* 7:71, 365.
² See Arthur Lee to the Committee of Secret Correspondence, March 8, 1777, in Wharton, *Diplomatic Correspondence,* 2:280.

Board of War to George Washington

Sir   War Office May 20th. 1777
I do myself the Honour of enclosing all the Resolves of Congress I know of relative to the recruiting Allowance.¹ Much Complaint has been made as to its Sufficiency for the Support of both Officers & Soldiers. It was at the Time the Resolves were passed perhaps equal to the Expence incurred by recruiting Officers. At these times when all the Necessaries of Life are so enormously advanced the Allowance it is imagined is below the Mark. Some Officers however have learned the Art of supplying the Deficiency, while others more attentive to their Reputations than their Interest are Losers by the Service.
I have the Honour to be with the greatest Respect, your very obed. Servt,   Richard Peters Secy

RC (DLC).
¹ For these resolves, which were passed by Congress on November 7, 1776, and January 22, 1777, see *JCC,* 6:932, 7:55. Washington had requested copies of them in his May 10 letter to President Hancock. Washington, *Writings* (Fitzpatrick), 8:35–36.

William Duer to the New York Convention

Sir,   Philadelphia, May 20th, 1777.
I send by Mr. Carter an account of cash received and disbursed by the committee of Convention whilst in Westchester county; likewise a book in which is entered an account of the different brigades of teams employed for the purpose of removing families and forage.¹

Unless great care is taken in settling accounts with the teamsters, the public will be much imposed on; and this care can only be taken by persons who were acquainted with the transaction of business in the county of Westchester. Mr. Tomkins, one of the Representatives of the county of Westchester, is in my opinion the person best calculated to settle these accounts in such a manner as to do justice both to the individuals and to the public, as he is perfectly acquainted with the merits and services of the different claimants.

Genl. Schuyler expecting to leave this place from day to day for these twelve days, has induced me to defer sending you these papers; but as I think it is very uncertain whether he will leave this town in five or six days, I have thought it advisable to send them by Mr. Carter, by whom I flatter myself they will arrive safe.

I should not have carried these papers with me, but as I had not time to arrange my affairs after my return from Westchester to Esopus, I found it necessary to take them with me, and intended to have sent them properly stated by my clerk, whom I ordered to follow me to Philadelphia: this he neglected, so that I am obliged now to send them in a crude state; but Mr. Tompkins will be able to settle them in a proper manner.

I am, sir, with the greatest respect, Your obedt. hble. servt,

Wm. Duer.

Reprinted from *Journals of N.Y. Prov. Cong.*, 1:954. Addressed: "To the President of the Convention, or Council of Safety of the State of New-York."

[1] For the enclosed account, see ibid., pp. 954–55.

John Hancock to Jonathan Hudson

Sir,   Philada. May 20th. 1777

Your Letter of the 17th Inst. I duely recd. and laid before Congress, in Consequence of which they ordered you a farther Sum of twenty Thousand Dollars, and for which you will find enclosed a Warrant on Mr. Hillegas the Treasurer. I also enclose you a Resolution of Congress passed at the same Time respecting your future Advances to the Troops, to which I request your Attention, & is to be the Rule of your Conduct.[1]

I am Sir, with Respect, your very hbl Set.   JH Presid.

LB (DNA: PCC, item 12A).

[1] Jonathan Hudson was Continental paymaster in Baltimore. His May 17 letter to Hancock is in PCC, item 78, 11:161–62. In addition to approving Hudson's request for $20,000, Congress also informed him "that the arrearages due to the troops on their march from the southward, will be discharged at Philadelphia or Bristol; and that it is not the intention of Congress that he should advance larger

sums than are necessary to forward their march to head-quarters." *JCC*, 7:368. It should also be noted that in his letter Hudson acknowledged the receipt of Hancock's "favour of the 7th Inst per Post ... Covering a Warrant of Congress for Twenty Thousand Dollars." This "favour" has not been found, but see also *JCC*, 7:328; and Hudson to Hancock, May 1, 1777, in PCC, item 78, 11:149. For further information on Hudson, particularly concerning his private versus public transactions, see Robert Morris to Jonathan Hudson, this date.

John Hancock to George Washington

Sir,   Philada. May 20th. 1777.
   This will be delivered to you by Mrs. Graydon of this City, a very worthy Lady, whose Anxiety to see her Son Captain Graydon, now a Prisoner with the Enemy, is so great, that Congress have been induced to consent to her having an Interview with him. I am therefore to request your Attention to the enclosed Resolve on the Subject, and that you will give Directions for having it carried into Execution in such Manner as you may think will be most proper.[1] I have the Honour to be, with the greatest Esteem & Respect, Sir, your most obed. hble Servt.   John Hancock Presidt

RC (DLC). In the hand of Jacob Rush and signed by Hancock.
  [1] See *JCC*, 7:367. Alexander Graydon, a captain in the Third Pennsylvania Battalion, was captured by the British at Fort Washington in November 1776, paroled in July 1777, and exchanged in April 1778. In his memoirs he vividly describes his mother's trip to New York to intercede personally with General Howe to obtain his parole and President Hancock's chagrin at her success because of his fear that it might cast a favorable light on the British. Alexander Graydon, *Memoirs of a Life, Chiefly Passed in Pennsylvania within the Last Sixty Years* (Harrisburg: John Wyeth, 1811), pp. 241–63.

Richard Henry Lee to Thomas Jefferson

Dear Sir   Phila. May 20. 1777
   We are this moment informed here, that some evil disposed people (no doubt hired for the purpose) have industriously propagated among the N. Carolina Troops, and among the recruits of Virginia in the upper parts, *that the plague rages in our Army.* In consequence of which, it is said, the recruiting business stops, and desertions are frequent.[1] There never was a more infamous and groundless falsehood. The Army is extremely healthy, and the wise[st] methods are pursued to keep them so. I mention this dear Sir, that some adequate plan may be adopted to stop the progress of such wicked lies as are now, with industry circulated thro the Country. Force having failed our enemies,

fraud is substituted, and corruption is swiftly and silently pushed thro every quarter.

One plan, now in frequent use, is, to assassinate the Characters of the friends of America in every place, and by every means.

At this moment, they are now reading in Congress, an audacious attempt of this kind against the brave General Arnold.[2] Farewell dear Sir, I wish you happy,   Richard Henry Lee

[*P.S.*] Nothing new in Jersey.

RC (DLC). Jefferson, *Papers* (Boyd), 2:20.

[1] This "plague" rumor was not mentioned as a source of recruiting problems in the report of Col. Alexander Martin of the Second North Carolina Battalion that was read in Congress this day. Martin's May 10 letter from Fredericksburg, Va., which is in PCC, item 78, 15:189, explained that recruiting was slow because of sickness, death, discharges, and desertions and that North Carolina troops, after being delayed by their march to and from South Carolina, were marching northward with expedition.

[2] Benedict Arnold's May 20 letter requesting Congress to inquire into his conduct and that of his accuser, Lt. Col. John Brown, is in PCC, item 162, fol. 86. It was referred to the Board of War, whose members on May 23 reported their "entire satisfaction" with Arnold's "character and conduct, so cruelly and groundlessly aspersed" by Brown's handbill, printed in Pittsfield, Mass., on April 12. See *JCC,* 7:371, 373, 8:382; and Carl Van Doren, *Secret History of the American Revolution* (New York: Viking Press, 1941), pp. 154–60.

Robert Morris to Thomas Bromfield

Sir   Philada. May 20th. 1777

Your favr. of the 8th Inst. did not reach my Hands untill last Night & I embrace the first Opportunity to reply thereto but find myself good deal at a loss for want of those Letters you tell me Captn. Roche is possessed of as I am an entire Stranger to the Nature & intent of your Voy[age] except the particulars you have been pleased to inform me of.[1] I hope however that the Ship may have got Safe into Carolina where the Cargo will find ready Sale but not on such advantageous terms as in Virga. or here. The Approach to these Coasts however is infinitely more dangerous at this Time as the Ennemies Ships are numerous & vigilant in their endeavours to destroy our Trade. We must therefore agree Carolina was the best Destination the Ship could have had at this period & I hope a good Voyage will result to all parties concerned. I take the Liberty to inclose a few Lines to Mr. John Dorsius[2] who transacts the Business of my House in Chas. Town. In him you will find an honest Worthy Man well versed in Business ready to give you his advice or assistance if wanted. I find many Persons are going from these States towards Carolina to purchase Goods on Speculation so that you will not want customers for your

Cargo but it might probably be no bad part of your plan to sell in Carolina sufficient to load the Ship Union in Carolina with Rice & after dispatching her therewith & another Vessell if you chuse it for if your Cargo is of the Value I am informed it is you will have Funds Sufficient to Ship many Cargoes of produce. You might then travell towards Virga. with the remainder of the Cargo. It will sell well there & the Investment may then be made in Tobo. You can readily get information in Carolina of the best Way of removing your Goods to Virginia. This plan I only mention as it may probably promote the Interest of this Concern but Captn. Roche & you must finally determine for altho it is probable that I am interested Yet I know not to what extent on what terms nor am vested with any authority to advise or direct what should be done. I observe in your Instructions you are to attempt a division of the risque by exchanging Risques with other Merchts. but this you must confine to Carolina where you are because People this way can not know the Circumstances of your Expeditions in time to make such Agreements. However there is an Insurance Office in Carolina & perhaps it may be more eligible to make Insurance on part of the Cargoes sent from thence to France. I would order this to be done on a certain proportion of my Concern if I knew what it is. I advise you by all means to expedite the Union & send her away soon as you can because it is probable the British Cruizers may draw that way before long & watch that Port as closely as they have done others. I think you had best Ship Rice, Tobacco, Skins & Furrs if reasonable but no Indigo for that article is too dear & must continue so whilst it is necessary to Ship it in Small Vessells for the Sake of making remittances be the cost what it may. If you come towards Virginia I can & will be usefull to your operations in that country but in Carolina you are too distant for that Speedy Communication that coud make me usefull. I beg my Compts to Captn. Roche. Shall be expecting my Letters by him & on receipt of them shall write or do what may appear incumbent in consequence of them. I am, Sir, Your obedt. hble Sert.

Tr (CtHi).

[1] For additional information on the activities of Bromfield, see Robert Morris to Silas Deane, June 29, 1777.

[2] Not found.

Robert Morris to Jonathan Hudson

Sir[1]   Philada. May 20th. 1777

I have your letters of the 13th & 16th Inst. and from their Contents I am to suppose you have set out on your journey, however I direct this

to you at Baltimore & if you are gone I depend that those who Act
for you will send it after you to the care of Benjn. Harrison Junr
Esqr. I sent your letters to General Washington & the pay Master
General the day after they came to my hands. I am satisfyed with
your Shipping the flour on our joint Account & will receive the Net
proceeds of what you have ordered to be sold to be applyed in payment of such bills as you may draw on me for your own Account to
the extent of One Thousand pounds. I shall honor your drafts on me
to the Extent of Two thousand five hundred pounds on any Account,
however I now mean to alter these arrangements provided what I
shall now propose be agreed to by Carter Braxton Esqr. in Virginia.
It seems he has also determined on sending to Carolina to purchase
Goods and invites me to be Concerned. I will therefore send this letter
enclosed to him and propose that he shou'd join us & let this Speculation be in thirds. If he agrees to this you may extend the purchase
to Twelve or fifteen thousand Pounds this Cury provided the Goods
can be obtained on reasonable terms, and you must hurry them back
soon as possible for I believe so many People will go on this plan as
to raise prices in Carolina & fall them on their return this way. If
this is agreed to Mr Braxton must supply you with some money to
carry with you. I think five thousand pounds which I believe he can
readily do & the letters herewith will enable you to procure the
Remainder for drafts on me or on him but unless you can buy the
Goods cheap & bring them safe I think you had best not go so deep.
I shall desire Mr Braxton to meet you at Williamsburg & for that
purpose I alter my first design & enclose this letter open to him
instead of sending it to Baltimore. Draw your bills at as long sight as
you can & advise me regularly of your proceedings. I am, Sir, Your
hble servant,   Robt Morris

RC (PHarH).
    [1] Jonathan Hudson (d. 1786), who had been appointed by Congress on
January 18, 1777, deputy paymaster at Baltimore, was a merchant frequently
associated in commercial transactions with the firm Willing, Morris & Co. See
JCC, 7:48; and Robert Morris, *The Papers of Robert Morris, 1781–1784*, ed.
E. James Ferguson, et al., (Pittsburgh: University of Pittsburgh Press, 1973–),
1:414.

Virginia Delegates to George Wythe

Sir,   Philadelphia May 20th 1777
    We are favored with yours covering a resolve of Assembly to which
we shall pay due attention. The first Volume of the last edition of
the Journal of Congress, is now published, and shall be forwarded to
Williamsburg by the first opportunity.[1] This Volume reaches no

further than the 30th of December 1775. As our duty directs, so our inclinations lead to an immediate compliance with the desires of the House of Delegates, but we apprehend insurmountable difficulty in getting the manuscript journal, because the many secret articles cannot be exposed to a Copier, and neither the Secretary or ourselves have time to do it. The Printer has hitherto been delayed for want of paper, but now that is obtained, we shall urge the publication of the remaining Journal, and send it to you Sir, with all the dispatch in our power.

We have the honor to be with esteem and respect, Sir, your most obedient servants,   Richard Henry Lee

Francis Lightfoot Lee

Mann Page Jr

P.S. We shall endeavor to prevail with the Post Rider to take the Vol of Journal with him this Trip.

RC (Vi). Written by Richard Henry Lee. The original signatures have been clipped but were transcribed in the margin of the document.

[1] Copies of this volume of the journals were distributed among the delegates on June 2. See *JCC*, 8:412; and Evans, *Am. Bibilography*, no. 15683. For insight into the attitudes underlying the Virginia assembly's request for a manuscript copy of the journals, see Thomas Jefferson's May 16 letter to John Adams, where he explained that "in our assembly even the best affected think it an indignity to freemen to be voted away life and fortune in the dark." Jefferson, *Papers* (Boyd), 2:18–19.

John Adams to Abigail Adams

May 21. 1777

Dont be two much alarmed at the Report of an Attack of Boston. The British Court are pursuing a system which in the End I think they will find impolitick. They are alarming the Fears of the People, every where. Wentworths Letter was contrived to terrify Portsmouth.[1] Other Threats are given out against Boston. Others against the Eastern shore of Virginia and Maryland. Now Philadelphia is to be invaded—then Albany. Sometimes New London, at others N. Haven.

After all they will make but a poor Figure this Summer. There is some Reason to think, they have sent to Canada, for the Troops there by Water. Their Reinforcement from Europe, I think will not be great. Our Army is grown pretty strong. Pray let my dear Countrymen turn out, and not let a Man be wanting of their Quota.

The Enemy will find it impollitick to awaken the Apprehensions of so many People. Because when the Peoples Fears subside which most of them will, they will be succeeded by Contempt.

My Eyes are weak again, and I am in bad Health but I keep about. I ride every fair Morning and walk every pleasant Evening, so that I cannot write so often as I wish. Have received no Letter from you by the two last Posts.

The Country here looks most deliciously and the Singing Birds of which Species there is here a great Variety are inspired. The Spring is backward but promised great Fertility, Plenty and Abundance.

I wish I could see your Garden and little Farm.

RC (MHi). Adams, *Family Correspondence* (Butterfield), 2:243–44.

[1] This is apparently a reference to the captured February 3, 1777, letter of former New Hampshire Governor John Wentworth that Governor Jonathan Trumbull sent to Congress in March. Neither the extracts of the letter enclosed by Trumbull nor the letter itself, which Trumbull sent to the New Hampshire Assembly, has been located. *JCC,* 7:187; and PCC, item 66, 1:297. Wentworth's January 17, 1777, letter to his sister, Ann Fisher, was captured and widely publicized but it did not mention a direct threat to Portsmouth. In that letter he reported that "an army of 20,000 Russians and 12,000 Wirtenbergers &c. are engag'd and will be in N. England by June next, unless prevented by Peace." *N.H. Provincial Papers,* 7:394–95; and Shipton, *Harvard Graduates,* 13:670–71.

Massachusetts Delegates to the Massachusetts Assembly

Sir   Philadelphia May 21st. 1777

Mr. Gorham and Mr. Russel, Agents of the Town of Charlestown, have presented to Congress a Petition from the unfortunate Inhabitants of that Place, praying for a Compensation for their Losses.[1] The Petition was drawn in very decent & handsome Terms, containing a lively Description of the Distresses to which the unhappy Petitioners are reduced from a State of Ease & Affluence; and the Gentlemen who presented the Petition have urged every Motive which could either show the Justice & Policy of granting the Request, or which could move the Humanity & Charity of those who heard it.

These Endeavors of theirs have been seconded by your Delegates in Congress, but to no other Effect than to obtain a Committee to consider the Petition; whose Report, altho' it expresses much Sympathy with that virtuous People in Affliction, contains a Denial of their Request, on Account of the present Condition of the Finances of the United States: As the granting of Compensation, even in Part, at this Time, would set a Precedent for so many & so great Demands of a similar Nature that the public Treasury would not be able to spare so much from the necessary Calls of the War.

There was a great Deal of Delicacy shown thro the whole Debate upon this Subject. Every one wished it was in the Power of Congress to grant the desired Relief; most acknowledged the Justice of the Demand; but all agreed that, at present, it would be impolitic to grant it, except the Delegates from the Massachusetts Bay.

Upon a Motion that a small Part of the Losses should be made up, such was the Reluctance to giving a Negative that the previous Question was moved & put; so that a present Determination might not prejudice the Petitioners in any future Application.

It may be doubtfull whether such Petitions to Congress from particular Corporations, or Individuals in any State, are proper. Perhaps it would be better that each State shd. ascertain the Amount of its own Losses, in this Kind, and represent it to Congress; that so, in the End, some Adjustment may be made, between the several States.

That such an Adjustment will, sooner or later, be made is not doubted by Us, because, neither Equity nor sound Policy will admit that different States, contending in the same common Cause, having in View the same common Benefit, should be unequally loaded with Expence, or suffer disproportionate Losses. But as it is impossible to foresee what Course the War will take, or what State will be the greatest Sufferer, it is probable this Question will be postponed untill the End of the War.

In the mean Time, our Brethren and Neighbours, virtuously struggling together with us for every Thing that is valuable, and reduced from Prosperity to Adversity by the casual Stroke of War, must not be left to suffer unnoticed. This would be plainly repugnant to the Dictates of Humanity, to the Precepts of Christian Charity, to the Rules of common Justice and the soundest Policy;[2] a Chain of Motives which doubtless produced the Grants already made by the General Assembly of our State, for the immediate Subsistence of these Sufferers. But, as the unfortunate Petitioners were deprived of their necessary Tools & Materials for Business, it was remarked, by Gentlemen who pleaded for them in Congress, that an Advance sufficient to replace those Things would be a most essential Relief, and by far the most economical in the end. And it was suggested that such Estates of disaffected Persons as may be sequestered or confiscated, throughout the Limits of our Union, might be a Fund, to insure the Loan of Monies, for compensating patriotic Sufferers. This, however was not formally recommended. Each State is competent to the Business, if judged proper.

Having represented this affair as it has been conducted in Congress, we wish it to be communicated by you to the Honorable House, for any Improvement which their Wisdom may direct.

We have the Honor to be with much Respect, Sir, your most humble Servants,   John Hancock   John Adams
                                 Samuel Adams   Elbridge Gerry
                                                      James Lovell

RC (M–Ar). Written by Lovell and signed by Lovell, John Adams, Samuel Adams, Gerry, and Hancock. Addressed: "To the Speaker of the Honble. House of Representatives of Massachusetts Bay."

¹ For further information on Congress' rejection of the November 28, 1776, Charlestown petition, see John Adams to Abigail Adams, May 17, note.

² A variant copy of this letter, also in Lovell's hand but signed only by John Adams, Samuel Adams, and Hancock, completes this paragraph as follows:

"And, though we have had the pleasure of hearing the Delegates from the other States express an honorable full Confidence, built upon the Character of the Massachusetts, that the Petitioners would not be unaided in their Calamity by their own State; yet, we think it not improper for us to make a formal Sollicitation, thro your Honor, to the Court, in Behalf of the worthy, the distressed Inhabitants of Charlestown and all others in similar Circumstances within its Jurisdiction, and to request that their Case may be taken into Consideration, and some Assistance and Relief granted. There is scarcely another Instance of a Desolation so compleat as that which these Petitioners have suffered, their Implements & Accommodations for Business as well as their Habitations, Furniture & other Property being destroyed. Such Assistance therefore as would enable them to provide necessary Tools & Materials for Business would render them again useful Members of Society: and Sums for this Purpose might be more profitably employed for the Commonwealth than if they were in the public Treasury, or more unequally diffused among the People of the State." Edes Collection, MHi.

Roger Sherman to Oliver Wolcott

Sir   Philadelphia May 21, 1777

The enclosed Letters came to hand yesterday by the Post. I was in doubt Whether it was best to Send them back, or keep them till you return here. I hope it will not be long before a Delegation arives, that I may have leave of absence. I understand that an Inhabitant of Connecticut has been lately executed by a Sentence of a General Court Martial.¹ I think it dangerous to admit Citizens not connected with the army to be tried by a Court Martial. The resolution of Congress concerning Spies does not warrant it—that respects only Such as are not Subjects of any of the States. It is easy to accuse any person with being a Spy & to put his life into the power of a Court Martial. I have no doubt but that the person executed was an attrocious offender & deserved Death but if he was an Inhabitant of the State he ought to have been tryed before the Supr. Court. We have nothing new here since my last. General Arnold is here. Congress has ordered the Quarter Master General to procure and present to him a Horse properly caparisoned for his Bravery in attacking the enemy who m[arched] to Danbury, in which action he had one horse killed under him and another wounded.² A Committee is appointed to consider what Honors are due to the Memory of Genll. Wooster.³ There are different accounts of the day of his death. Some say Thursday, others

Friday and others Saturday. I wish that could be ascertained, & that I could be informed of his age. I have had an account of the Election in the Hartford paper. A few lines from you with Some account of the proceedings of the Assembly, will oblige your humble Servant

RC (CtHi). In Sherman's hand; signature has been clipped.
[1] According to the May 7 issue of the *Connecticut Journal* Daniel Griswold had been executed in New Haven on May 5.
[2] See *JCC,* 7:372–73.
[3] See *JCC,* 7:368–69.

William Whipple to John Langdon

My Dear Sir,   Philadelphia 21st May 1777
    Your favor of the 4th inst (No 6) came to hand this day. I had anticipated your desire in part having sent by Mr Campney some requisites which I hope are near at hand by this time. Mr. Frost arrived the 15th inst. By his credentials I find I am superseded, but as he tells me it was not the intention of the Assembly and is very desirous of my tarrying some time I shall not set out in less than two or three weeks when I think I shall bid farewell to Philadelphia and hope for the pleasure of taking you by the hand about the middle of June.
    I rejoice at the arrival of Miller and hope Smith will be as fortunate though I confess my hopes have but little foundation as the enemy's ships are very thick off the Capes of Virginia and Delaware and I understand many are now cruizing on your coast which doubles the risk.
    A ship arrived a few days ago at Cinapucksen from Nantz with 3 or 4000 arms and a large quantity of clothing. She brings no news that are at this time very interesting. All the public dispatches were to come in a packet that was to sail in a few days; perhaps she is already arrived at some distant port. Some other packets may also be expected soon. I expect to bring with me the Commissions for the new ship which is called the Ranger. I am inclined to think Capt Roche will not have the command of her; I do not interest myself either for or against him, but hope if he is removed a good man will have her.[1]
    I am with much esteem and respect, Your friend and humble Servt.
                                                          Wm Whipple

Tr (DLC).
[1] On June 14 Congress, at the urging of the Massachusetts Council, "suspended" Capt. John Roche and appointed John Paul Jones to the command of the *Ranger. JCC,* 8:464–65. See also Executive Committee to John Hancock, January 25, 1777, note.

John Adams to Abigail Adams

May 22 [*1777*]. 4 O Clock in the Morning

After a Series of the souerest, and harshest Weather that ever I felt in this Climate, We are at last blessed with a bright Sun and a soft Air. The Weather here has been like our old Easterly Winds to me, and southerly Winds to you.

The Charms of the Morning at this Hour, are irresistable. The Streakes of Glory dawning in the East: the freshness and Purity in the Air, the bright blue of the sky, the sweet Warblings of a great Variety of Birds intermingling with the martial Clarions of an hundred Cocks now within my Hearing, all conspire to chear the Spirits.

This kind of puerile Description is a very pretty Employment for an old Fellow whose Brow is furrowed with the Cares of Politicks and War.

I shall be on Horseback in a few Minutes, and then I shall enjoy the Morning, in more Perfection.

I spent last Evening at the War-Office, with General Arnold. . . .[1] He has been basely slandered and libelled.[2] The Regulars say, "he fought like Julius Cæsar."

I am wearied to Death with the Wrangles between military officers, high and low. They Quarrell like Cats and Dogs. They worry one another like Mastiffs. Scrambling for Rank and Pay like Apes for Nutts.

I believe there is no one Principle, which predominates in human Nature so much in every stage of Life, from the Cradle to the Grave, in Males and females, old and young, black and white, rich and poor, high and low, as this Passion for Superiority. . . . Every human Being compares itself in its own Imagination, with every other round about it, and will find some Superiority over every other real or imaginary, or it will die of Grief and Vexation. I have seen it among Boys and Girls at school, among Lads at Colledge, among Practicers at the Bar, among the Clergy in their Associations, among Clubbs of Friends, among the People in Town Meetings, among the Members of an House of Representatives, among the Grave Councillors, on the more solemn Bench of Justice, and in that awfully August Body the Congress, and on many of its Committees—and among Ladies every Where—But I never saw it operate with such Keenness, Ferocity and Fury, as among military Officers. They will go terrible Lengths, in their Emulations, their Envy and Revenge, in Consequence of it.

So much for Philosophy. I hope my five or six Babes are all well. My Duty to my Mother and your Father and Love to sisters and Brothers, Aunts and Uncles.

Pray how does your Asparagus perform? &c.

I would give Three Guineas for a Barrell of your Cyder—not one drop is to be had here for Gold. And wine is not to be had under Six or Eight Dollars a Gallon and that very bad. I would give a Guinea for a Barrell of your Beer. The small beer here is wretchedly bad. In short I can get nothing that I can drink, and I believe I shall be sick from this Cause alone. Rum at forty shillings a Gallon and bad Water, will never do, in this hot Climate in summer where Acid Liquors are necessary against Putrefaction.

RC (MHi). Adams, *Family Correspondence* (Butterfield), 2:245–46.
   [1] Suspension points in MS here and below.
   [2] The Board of War subsequently cleared General Arnold of "imputations upon his character, contained in an hand bill, dated Pittsfield, April 12, 1777, and subscribed John Brown." See *JCC*, 7:373, 8:382; and Richard Henry Lee to Thomas Jefferson, May 20, 1777, note 2.

Richard Henry Lee to George Washington

Dear General   Philadelphia 22d May 1777
   The subject of your letter of the 17th is a very important one, and whilst it deserves the greatest attention, is certainly involved in great difficulty.[1] Of one truth however, I beg you Sir to be convinced. That no desire *to get rid of importunity* has occasioned these appointments, but motives military and political meerly. These Adventurers may be divided into three Classes, some who came early and without any recommendation but apparent zeal, with Commissions shewing that they had been in service—Others that brought with them recommendations from our good friend the Count D'Argout General of Martinique, and from Mr Bingham the Continental Agent in that Island—A third Class includes those who come from France, generally under agreement with our Commissioners, or one of them at least. The strongest obligations rest upon us (tho' the inconvenience is great) to make good engagements with the latter, and if the second had been disregarded we might have offended a good & powerful Friend in Martinique who has done many good offices there, or have brought our Agent into disrepute. Among the first Class, I realy believe there are many worthless Men, and I Heartily wish we were rid of them. All this is true, and yet I feel the great force of your reasoning, and the many difficulties in the way of providing for them properly and that may be tolerably agreeable to them. It is of some consequence that we all, [in] our several departments, endeavor to smooth this rugged business as much as possible. When Gen. Conway was appointed, I did hope that as he knew most of them, and spoke both French & English well, that he might relieve you from the greater part of this difficulty, for realy, the discontented importunity of the greater part of these Gentlen is too much [to] be borne under our various & important attentions. I will prevail with the Committee for foreign applications to furnish you

with the most explicit views of Congress in every appointment, as well
as with the recommendations under which each appointment was and
is made. We have written both to France & to Martinique to stop the
further flow of these Gentlemen here, and after the letters arrive I
suppose we shall have no more. Many of the last Comers are, I believe,
Men of real merit, and if they will learn to express themselves tolerably in English, may be of service to the Army. The desire to obtain
Engineers and Artillerists was the principal cause of our being so over-
burthened. The first that came had sagacity enough quickly to discern
our wants, and professing competency in these branches They were
too quickly believed. And when our Commissioners abroad (in consequence of directions for this purpose) enquired for those Artists, Military Speculation was immediately up, and recommendations were
obtained from persons of so much consideration in France, that the
success of our applications then made it quite necessary not to neglect
them. And at this moment I am apprehensive that the discontent of
many may injure our cause abroad where we would wish it to stand
well. As you express it Sir, this affair requires great delicacy in its
management, as well in the account of our own Officers as on that of
these Foreigners.[2]

FC (PPAmP).
[1] For Washington's May 17 letter to Lee, in which he questioned the propriety of Congress' appointing numerous foreigners to military positions of high
rank, as well as his June 1 reply to this letter, see Washington, *Writings* (Fitzpatrick), 8:74–76, 159–61.
[2] Washington was the most likely recipient of a brief note Lee wrote on May
26 introducing a Mr. Demmere of Georgia, "who comes to the Army with a
strong desire of becoming a part of it." Fogg Collection, MeHi; and Lee, *Letters*
(Ballagh), 1:303.

James Lovell to Horatio Gates

Dear sir   Philada. May 22d. 1777
The Strange delays of Mr. Yancey here,[1] greatly mortifying to him,
have drawn me on day by day from an earlier acknowledgment of
your favor of Apr. 29th.
Indeed, I could not have related to you, before this time, any interesting decisions concerning such matters as have been moved in Congress connected with Tyconderoga.
Misconstructions of past resolves, and consequent jealousies, have
produced a definition of the *northern* department; and General Schyler
is ordered to take the command of it. The resolve also which was
thought to fix Head Quarters at Albany is repealed.[2]
It was said you *now* look upon yourself in the same command which

he *had* held. This was universally denied to be the *Intention* of sending
you to Tyconderoga to take command of the army *there*. The Debate
in March was about the Adjutancy *or* Tyconderoga; and it was decided
for the latter. In the present Debate I acknowledged it was my *hope* &
wish, at the time you went, and still continue to be, that the officer
who is at so very important a post shd. not be under the absolute orders
of another at 100 miles distance, in treaty with Indians or busied in the
duties of a Providore. This Idea was supported by several; and it is, of
itself, an irrefragible argument of the impropriety of distributing America
into departments. A commander-in-chief & Commanders of the seperate
armies is the only distinction which should be known. However, that
was contrary to our Journals. Besides, the army at Ty. and the force
at Stanwix &c. &c. at a distance were looked upon as different subjects; tho it appears you have other ideas than those had who directed
your destination. No single debate has been more tedious with us;—
having lasted whole days & being finally settled 5 to 4 & 2 divided.[3]

Your dating from Albany is counted by some irreconcileable with
the order to repair to Ty. I am sorry your letter to the President and
that to myself did not arrive 1 hour earlier, or, had not arrived at all.[4]

I will write to you by the first opportunity after this, if I do not
write again by Mr. Yancey.

Our Trouble has sprung from the difference between living in Albany
Providore to ones own army 100 miles off, and living there Providore
to another at the same distance, and that other not cordially liked.
Where is *soldier like* feeling in the first case? Dr Sir, Yr humb. Servt.

James Lovell

RC (NHi).

[1] Deputy commissary general James Yancey.

[2] Congress adopted this "definition" of the northern department this day, but
their action failed to halt the ongoing feud between Generals Gates and Schuyler.
When Gates received word of Congress' decision he immediately came to Philadelphia to protest the erosion of his authority entailed by this resolve. See *JCC,*
7:364, 8:375; New York Delegates to the New York Council of Safety, May 23
and June 19; and James Duane to Philip Schuyler, June 19, 1777.

[3] For further information on the vote in Congress, see William Duer to Robert
Livingston, May 28; Lovell to Oliver Wolcott, June 7; and Samuel Adams to
James Warren, July 31, 1777.

[4] General Gates' May 2, 11, and 14 letters to President Hancock were written
from Albany and read in Congress on May 10 and 22. *JCC,* 7:344, 8:375.
Lovell was almost certainly referring to Gates' May 11 letter containing a
resignation threat: "By the direction of Your Excellency's last Letter, I am led
to conceive, that some change is likely to take place in the Command of the
Northern Army; I cannot however prevail on myself to think that Congress has
any Fix'd design to Alter their former Resolution upon that head, but should
that unhappily be the Case, & I am to be Degraded; I beg Sir you will request
the Congress to give me an Honorable Dismission from their Service." PCC,
item 154, 1:189–92.

Philip Schuyler to Israel Pemberton

Respected Friend,   Philadelphia May 22d. 1777.[1]

Your Letter of Yesterday's Date advising me that mine of the 17th inst. had been laid before a Meeting of Friends convened for the Purpose of deliberating on Its Contents, I have taken into the most serious Consideration. The Sentiments conveyed in the first Paragraph are such as ought to influence every Member of Society of whatever religious Persuasion he may be, but more especially Christian, And altho' I differ with You on the Subject Matter of the next, I shall never the less not cease to respect & hold sacred the Rights of Conscience. From this Motive I shall no longer insist on a Contribution of Friends, for what they deem to be preparations for War: But as the first Principle of Human Nature is Self preservation; as we are engaged in a Conflict the Event of which must Either be a perfect Establishment of our Civil & Religious Priviledges or a Total Deprivation of both, It is a Duty incumbent on Us, in Order to avert the Latter, to embrace all Means made Lawful from the most evident Necessity, And altho' Friends cannot conscientiously give, Yet such is their Benevolence & Charity that I am sure rather than see Men suffer, they will acquiesce if We take at a just Valuation, a small Portion of What they can share. Directions must be given for that purpose & shall be conducted with all prudence & Tenderness for Civil Liberty, of which such an urgent & uncommon Case is capable.

On the other part of your Letter, I shall in General observe, that it is out of my sphere to enter into any political Disquisitions; that I am a Friend to All Mankind; that I wish to see Universal Happiness prevail & Every Member of every Society in the full Enjoyment of all their Rights; That my Application to the Friends for Blankets was forwarded on Information & Belief that they had not contributed on the Application of a Committee appointed by the Board of War; That I did not mean by the Discrimination to convey one disadvantageous Idea entertained of the Society of Friends; But meerly that they might be put on a Footing with the Other Members of the Community who as I was informed had Liberally contributed; That I shall waive animadverting on what was done by "some Rich Men & others in their private Stations";[2] And that I thank You for the present of the Book You have been so kind as to send me and that altho' my Time is much engrossed, I shall read It with great Attention, convinced from its Character, that my Heart will be mended thereby, altho' I should not fully subscribe to every Part of the Doctrine it contains.

I thank You for your Fervent Wish for my Real Peace & Happiness and with equal Good Will toward You, I remain with Respect, Your Friend & Very Humble servant.   P. Schuyler

LB (NN).
    [1] On this day Schuyler also wrote letters to Generals Washington and Israel
Putnam, asking them to detain James Fisher of Philadelphia, "a Notorious Tory
& one capable of giving Much Information to the Enemy," who was accompany-
ing Mrs. Alexander Graydon on her journey to New York to seek the release of
her son, a prisoner of war held by the British. Schuyler Papers, NN. See also
JCC, 7:367; and John Hancock to Washington, May 20, 1777.
    [2] Quotation closed editorially.

George Walton to Philip Schuyler

Dr Sir,   22d May [1777].
    I am plagued to death with the Indians.[1] Congress is so much en-
gaged about other important concerns, that it cannot attend to theirs.
I submit it to you therefore, whether it would not be best to furnish
them with some wampum & money, and send them away, with assurances of their business being attended to soon?
    Dr Sir, Yours sincerely,   Geo Walton

RC (PHi).
    [1] Although Walton was not added to the Committee on Indian Affairs until
June 30, he had been involved in efforts to pacify the Indians since January
1777 when he was appointed to deliver presents to the Indians assembling for the
treaty at Easton, Pa. See *JCC*, 7:62, 166; 8:508.

Thomas Burke to Richard Caswell

Sir   Philadelphia May 23d 1777
    Since my last nothing has occurred worth your attention except the
arrival of several supply ships, by which we have received many very
important articles for facilitating the ensuing campaign. Our army is
daily gaining strength, and I hope will before long be in a condition to
face the enemy to some advantage. The enemy are unaccountably inactive, and cautious to the last degree. It is supposed they expect reinforcements, but we have accounts from Europe which indicate that
they will in a great measure be disappointed. I have heard from our
troops who are now under inoculation at Alexandria in Virginia, and
two hundred who have had the small pox are on their march under
Cols Summer and Lytle. I was informed they were much in want of
shoes by reason of some disappointment in your Quartermaster's department. I applied to the Clothier General for a supply for them, and
General Schuyler immediately sent them under the care of an officer
to meet them at Baltimore.
    We are alarmed with a report brought hither by a Mr Tenant from

the Southward, that some persons in North Carolina have maliciously propagated a report that a very fatal infectious disease prevails in our army, and that the general belief thereof very much retards and injures the recruiting service. I am happy in having it in my power to declare that such report is entirely groundless and that our army is in very high health and spirits. The Congress have instituted a liberal medical arrangement, and put it under the immediate inspection of a Committee, of which I am a member. By this arrangement no diseased patients are suffered to remain in camp, not even any wounded patients who are incapable of duty: all such are immediately removed to hospitals remote from the quarters of the healthy troops, and, there, are carefully attended and supplied. Proper officers are appointed to superintend and direct every thing necessary for the sick and wounded, and to make regular returns to the medical Committee.[1] By the last return very few appeared sick, in proportion to the numbers in service; and by every account from officers daily in this City from camp we learn that the army is very healthy. This information will enable your Excellency to refute the falsehood, and take off the evil impressions it may have made, and I am satisfied your endeavours for so good a purpose will not be wanting.

Since my last we have made no progress in the business of Confederation. A difficulty occurs, which, I fear, will be insuperable: that is how to secure to each State its separate independence, and give each its proper weight in the public Councils. So unequal as the States are, it will be nearly impossible to effect this: and after all it is far from improbable that the only Conferation will be a defensive alliance.

Nothing of importance has been determined in Congress, except what is merely executory.

I must beg leave again to complain of my receiving no information from my constituents. You will excuse my uneasiness upon this account when you reflect, that I am charged with a very important trust, to which I feel myself very unequal, and in which I am most anxiously desirous of rendering every possible service to my country: that I have been without a Colleague ever since my arrival, and in great measure uninformed in what had been previously done. To be under such circumstances, and also uninformed of any contingencies which may make any alteration in the system of my country, you will readily admit is sufficient to make me uneasy. I shall however Sir, give unremitting attention to every matter which shall come before the Great Council of which I am a member, and decide on fixed principles and clear conviction as far as my understanding is competent. I doubt not my Country will believe my intentions to be what they wish, and my endeavours shall be the best my abilities will admit. I need not repeat my wish that greater services might be rendered by some abler hand.

I also beg leave to request your Excellency to inform me whether I am at liberty to return home during any time in this summer.[2]

Some ships are in the river, and the Marine of this State are ordered down. Some of us are resolved to go down, and observe at least the conflict, if any there may be. I am called away and therefore must conclude. Having the honor to be Your Excellency's most Obedient hum. Sert.   Thos Burke

P.S. In one of my letters I believe I mentioned that Georgia was of no use in Congress but to vote with Connecticut. This was owing I believe to this circumstance, only one Delegate was then present, who is by birth a Connecticut man.[3] Since then a Mr Walton has given his attendance, which was before interrupted by illness; and I perceive Georgia is now frequently divided when any question relates to Colonial politics, so that these two Delegates are of different principles, or different judgments.

Tr (Nc–Ar).

   [1] See *JCC,* 7:87, 231–37, 244–46.

   [2] Governor Caswell informed Burke on June 17 that he could return to North Carolina as soon as his colleagues Cornelius Harnett and John Penn arrived in Congress, but despite the fact that these two reached Philadelphia in July, Burke did not set out for home until the middle of October 1777. See *N.C. State Records,* 12:500–501; and Burke to Caswell, November 4, 1777.

   [3] Lyman Hall was the aspersed Georgia delegate. See Burke's Notes of Debates, February 24, 1777, note 9.

John Hancock to the Maryland and Pennsylvania Assemblies

Gentlemen,   Philada. May 23d. 1777.

The Necessity of having proper Laws to compel the Militia of your State to march for the Common Defense when called upon by the Exigency of our Affairs, has induced the Congress to pass the enclosed Resolve.[1]

It is also highly requisite, that the executive Power be authorized to limit not only the Time of their Service when called out, but likewise the Distance they may be ordered to march. I beg Leave to refer your Attention to the Resolve, and your Compliance therewith, & have the Honour to be, Gentlemen, your most obed & very hble Sev.

                                                      J.H. Presid.

LB (DNA: PCC, item 12A).

   [1] Congress was apparently prompted to pass this resolve in response to one of Washington's May 12 letters to Hancock, although in stating his concern the

general had referred expressly to the militia of Delaware and Pennsylvania. See *JCC*, 7:348, 369–70; and Washington, *Writings* (Fitzpatrick), 8:46–47.

Richard Henry Lee's Notes on Commissary Regulations

[May 23–June 10? 1777][1]

Great Expence to procure the Commissioners or they must be all appointed [here]. The evils of appointing [all?] here. How long will it be 'ere the appointments are made known [to] the persons met here and they agree on their Agents &c.[2]

Department expencive. Great abuses have happened but the present plan of Regulation calculated to prevent One Gentleman has purchased extensively why then appoint more. Speculatists have appeared as contending Bidders. Fault in [owing?] Commission. Members of [Congress?] inform of the price of Commodities.

MS (ViU). Written by Lee in pencil on the cover of a May 18 letter from Edmund Pendleton, Caroline County, Va.

[1] Lee probably wrote these cryptic notes between May 23 and June 10 in connection with his work on a committee charged with drafting new regulations for the commissary's department. The committee's initial report, which had been read and tabled on May 14, was debated in Congress and recommitted on May 23. Thus the 23d seems the earliest time that Lee could have addressed himself to this subject after he had received the May 18 Pendleton letter on which he penciled these notes. During the following two and a half weeks, the report on commissary regulations was debated in Congress on eight occasions and recommitted three times before a revised report, which divided the work of the department among nine salaried officials and their assistants, was approved on June 10. See *JCC*, 7:266–67, 280–81, 292, 354; 8:384, 386, 394, 405, 406, 409, 410, 414–15, 427, 433–48.

[2] In the margin next to this paragraph Lee wrote: "Board may do many good things why not a single person."

New York Delegates to the New York Council of Safety

Honble Gentlemen   Philadelphia May 23d. 1777

Since our arrival here we have not been honored, but with one public Letter, which we ascribe to the Multiplicity of Business in which our Convention has been involved. It was by accident that we procured a Copy of the ordinance for establishing a temporary Government in our State, which has enabled us to address ourselves to your honorable Body.

The new Delegation transmitted by the Secretary has reached us. Rest assured that our most zealous Efforts shall be strenuously exerted to promote the general Good and Happiness of the united States, as well as the Honor, Interest and Security of our more immediate Constituents.

General Schuyler is fully reinstated in his Command, every point being adjusted entirely to his and our Satisfaction. This Business with which more than the *Reputation* of our State was so closely connected required Address and great attention for Reasons which the General, who delivers this, can explain.

We shall now have Leisure to turn our Thoughts to the Subjects of our Instructions,[1] which we shall diligently pursue and flatter ourselves with the wished for Success. The Revolt in our State cannot but be considered as a dangerous and alarming Example. Every Country is plagued with profligate and ambitious Men who in Times like the present may find it their Interest, or be led by their Passions to bring on Revolutions. Good Policy must therefore dictate to all the Necessity of discouraging this factious and turbulent Spirit, and of securing to every State its proper Rights and Jurisdiction, as well against internal as foreign Enemies.

We fear the Consideration of the Boundaries of New York has, thro' the Multiplicity of Business, been deferred. If so, we submit to your honorable Body, whether it ought not now to be dispatched, especially as the Convention, by one of their Letters,[2] stood pledged, to give Congress full Information on that Subject, and we can assure you it is expected.

General Schuyler, one of our Brethren, will take an oppertunity of conferring with your Honorable Body, on some other points which materially concern our State; the Discussion of them here must be therefore unnecessary. Permit us only most earnestly to press you to pursue the plan of manufacturing salt in the Interior parts of our State, with unremitting Vigor. As long as the war continues we must, from the exposed Situation of our Sea ports, be distressed for this necessary article of Life, if we trust to a foreign Supply. A temporary Relief we shall endeavor to procure, tho' it must be at a most enormous Expence. We are confident that Congress will chearfully interpose every good office to assist us.

We are with the utmost Regard, Honorable Gentlemen, Your most obedient, humble Servants,   Phil. Livingston

                                                                    Jas. Duane

P.S. Mr Duer is Stept out & the General mounting which prevents his Signing this Letter.

RC (NHi). Written by William Duer and signed by Duane and Livingston, with a postscript by Duane.

[1] See William Duer to the New York Council of Safety, May 6, 1777, note 2.
[2] For the letter in question, which was written to President Hancock on March 1, see PCC, item 67, 2:25–26; and *Journals of N.Y. Prov. Cong.,* 1:777–79.

John Adams to Abigail Adams

Philadelphia May 24. 1777

We have an Army in the Jersies, so respectable that We seem to be under no Apprehensions at present, of an Invasion of Philadelphia—at least untill a powerfull Reinforcement shall arrive from Europe. When that will be and how powerfull, it is impossible to say: But I think, it will not be very soon, nor very strong.

Perhaps, the Troops from Canada may come round by Water. If they do, the whole Force they can make, with all the Reinforcements from Europe will do no great Things this Year. I think, our Cause will never again be in so low a state as it was last December—then was the Crisis.

There are four Men of War and four Tenders in Delaware Bay. The Roebuck, and a Fifty Gun ship, and two other Frigates, are the Men of War. They come up the River a little Way to get Water some times with Fear and Trembling, and dare not come up far enough to get fresh Water, but content themselves with brackish Water.

They go on shore sometimes to steal some lean Cattle, if any happen to wander into lonely Places, where they dare venture.

My Love to all.

RC (MHi). Adams, *Family Correspondence* (Butterfield), 2:246–47.

John Adams to Nathanael Greene

Philadelphia May 24. 1777

During the civil Wars in Rome, in the Time of Sylla,[1] and young Marius, after the death of the Elder Marius, Sylla commanded one Army against Mithridates King of Pontus, and Fimbria another. Both were in Arms against the Same foreign Enemy: but Sylla and Fimbria were equally Enemies to each other, commanding different Armies in the service of different Parties at Rome, which were disputing which had the legal Authority. Sylla patched up a Peace with Mithridates and marched against Fimbria. The two Generals fortified their Camps. The Soldiers of both Armies, of the Same Nation, the Same City, the Same Language, Religion, Manners, Tastes and Habits instead of Skirmishing with each other, when they met upon Parties for Forage, Saluted one another, with great Cordiality. Some from Fimbria's Camp, came Secretly into that of Sylla, to see their Friends. In these clandestine Visits, Syllas soldiers, instructed by their General, and furnished with Money, won over those of Fimbria by Secret Bribes. These returning, corrupted others: many came off in the Night. The desertion became General. Shame and Punishment lost their Influence, and at last whole Companies carried off their Colours to Sylla.

Fimbria finding himself betrayed, solicited an Interview with Sylla but being denied it, returned to Pergamus, entered the Temple of Esculapius, and ran himself through with his sword.[2]

After this Sylla began his March from Asia towards Italy. The two Consulls, Cinna and Carbo, hearing of his design ordered young Marius and other Leaders of their Party to raise Forces, and commit the Legions, required the assistance of the Samnites and formed different Armies to oppose him. At the next Election Scipio and Norbanus were chosen Consulls in the Room of Cinna & Carbo. Sylla landed at Brundusium and began his March, and was joined by Metellus Pius, a Proconsul, as Sylla was, and by Pompey. Sylla, who had brought back with him from Asia not more than Thirty Thousand Men, was much pleased with these Allies; because his Enemies had 450 Ensigns of Foot, in several Bodies, besides their Cavalry, the whole commanded by 15 General officers, at the Head of whom were Scipio and Norbanus, who as Consulls had the chief Command.

Sylla, as great a Master of Intrigue as of the military Art, surrounded by so many different Enemies, joined Craft to his Valour. Scipio was encamped near him. To him, Sylla sends deputies to make overtures, who artfully represented that he was grieved at the Calamities to which the Commonwealth must be exposed, by a civil War, whoever should prevail, and that he only desired to lay down his Arms with Honor. Scipio, Sincerely desiring Peace, and misled by such plausible Proposals, desired Time to communicate them to Norbanus, and agreed to a Truce between the two Camps in the mean Time. Syllas Soldiers, by favour of this Truce insinuated themselves into Scipios Camp, under Pretense of visiting their Friends, and having before in Fimbrias Affair learned the Artifice, brought over many to their Party with Bribes. Carbo said upon this, that in Sylla he had to encounter both a Fox and a Lion; but that the Lion gave him much less Trouble than the Fox.

Sylla, sure of a great Number of Scipios Soldiers, presented himself before his Camp. The soldiers upon Guard, instead of charging him, saluted him as their general, and let him into their Camp. He made himself master of the whole so suddenly, that Scipio knew nothing of it, untill he and his son were arrested in his own Tent.

The next year Carbo, and young Marius, 26 years old, were chosen Consulls. The Armies took the Field, as early as the Season would permit, in the Spring. Marius at the Head of 85 Cohorts, offered Battle to Sylla, who having a secret Intelligence in his Enemys Camp, accepted the Challenge. Both Armies fought with great Bravery, the soldiers of each Side resolving to vanquish or to die. Fortune had not yet declared for either, when some Squadrons of Marius's Army, and five cohorts of his left Wing that had been bribed with Silla's Money, caused a Confusion by their unseasonable Flight, as they had agreed with Sylla to do. Their Example drew many others after them: a general Terror Struck the rest of the Army, and it was at last more a Rout than a Battle.

Howe is no Sylla, but he is manifestly aping two of Syllas Tricks, holding out Proposals of Terms and bribing soldiers to desert but you see, he is endeavouring to make a Fimbria of somebody. Many of the Troops from Pensilvania, Maryland and Virginia, are Natives of England, Scotland and Ireland, who have adventured over here and been sold for their Passages, or transported as Convicts and have lived and served here as Coachmen, Hostlers, and other servants.

They have no Tie to this Country. They have no Principles. They love Howe as well as Washington, and his Army better than ours. These Things give Howe great opportunities to corrupt and Seduce them.

LB (MHi).

[1] Lucius Cornelius Sulla established himself as dictator of the Roman Empire in a two-year campaign, 83–82 B.C., following the Social War. George P. Baker, *Sulla the Fortunate: The Great Dictator* (London: John Murray, 1927), pp. 207–53.

[2] When Adams sent this letter to Greene, he apparently omitted the lengthy passage that continues from this point to the second to last paragraph, which was marked in the LB for insertion here. "The Revolutionary Correspondence of Nathanael Greene and John Adams," *Rhode Island History* 1 (July 1942): 73–74, prints the letter Greene apparently received, which was then in private hands.

Samuel Adams to Horatio Gates

My dear Sir   Philada. May 24 1777

I embrace this Moment of Leisure to let you know that, as I ought not, I have not forgot you. I well remember the last Words you said to me; but we were obligd to yeild to Numbers at a time when unluckily some were absent who would have turnd the Scale if they had been with us. The Bearer is able to let you into my whole Meaning. It is no great Cause of Boasting to say that five out of Eleven were in favor of any Measure—but so it was. I hope you will determine as I think you have ever done for the *publick Good*.[1] Had I time I would write you more fully. I will not be wanting hereafter. Assure yourself that I am very affectionately, Yours,   Saml Adams

RC (MH–H).
¹ For further information on the command in the northern department, see James Lovell to Horatio Gates, May 22, 1777.

Charles Carroll of Carrollton to Charles Carroll, Sr.

Dr Papa,   24th May 1777

There are ten ships in the Bay coming up towards Newcastle: 1 fifty gun ship, 1 forty four, 2 frigates, a Brig & 4 Tenders & a pilot boat, no transports. We imagine these ships are come up to water & get live stock.

The enemy are yet quiet: I suppose they will not attempt any thing of consequence till they receive reinforcements from Europe. By the time those reinforcements arrive, I hope G. Washington's army will be respectable. We have made no progress in the Confederacy, things of more immediate necessity have taken up our time. We are endeavouring to reform the Commissary's Department. The Quarter Master General's is put on a better footing. Pray have any considerable payts. been made to you since I left home? Has the Vineyard suffered? Last Sunday I rode to see the Vineyard 5 miles off from this city. It is in bad order. The vines are chiefly the murnier Burgundy, he has one sort (the names of which he knew not) of which I have bespoke cuttings. G. Cadwallader has promised to procure for me some rooted plants of Jones Vines. You remember they are mentioned in the Pena. Philosophical publication. I hear our assembly is to be called the 2d of next month. I shall not attend it, being determined to make a long session in Congress, and then enjoy a little quiet at Home. I assure you I am sick of public business, nothing but a strong Sense of duty, and the great importance of the cause we are engaged in could keep me here. G. Shuyler will Set off in a day or two to take the command in the northern Depart. This measure will greatly displease Gates, & perhaps occasion his resignation, but justice is due to Shuyler. Gates probably will go & command at Boston. His depart. is not yet fixed. I wish he would act as adjutant General, in which office I think he would be able to render the most essential services, but this I fear we shall not prevail on him to accept.

I hope you have had a pleasant jaunt and that it has agreed with you. If Mr. & Mrs. Ridout should be with you, please to present my complts to them and to all enquiring friends. My love to Molly & her Mama & little ones. I have sent my horses home, and by so doing accomodated Col. Jenifer. I directed Mr. Skerret to send my horses to Elkridge; they cost me £5.5.0. We are going a party of us down the river to see the fight, if there should be one. I am your affectionate Son,

                                                    Ch. Carroll of Carrollton

RC (MdHi).

William Paca to the Maryland Council

Gent.   Philad. Saturday, 12 oClock, 24 May 1777[1]

Enclosed you have the account of the printers of the Continental Money that will ascertain the Terms on which the money was printed.[2] I have examined the Barracks, they are all of a Size above & below each room 16 ft Square and about 9 ft in Height.

We have no Intelligence from the Camp except that the Enemy are fortifying the Town of Brunswick and have launched into water the Boats that were hoisted into Waggons to pass as it was conjectured the Delaware.

They play the very Devil with the Tories in Connecticut & New York. In a late Hunt for them several were apprehended with Commissions from Howe. They were immediately hung up & executed. Among them were two, one with a Captains the other with a Lieutenants Commission. These poor Dogs had no notion to the last Hour that they would be hanged, they thought and treated it as merely in Terrorem when they came to the Place of Execution. Why damn it says the Lieutenant the Rebels surely w'ont have the Impudence to hang us. By G—d says the Capt. it looks as if they would and I dare say they would if they dared. They had no Time for further Conversation.

Yesterday the Alarm Gun was fired and to Day an Express informs us of ten Sail coming up the River: a fifty Gun Ship—the Roebuck of forty four Guns—a Frigate—four Tenders—a Brig and two Pilot Boats. The Gondolas are gone down. The Congress has adjourned to go down in Barges to see the Sport.

Congress took up Capt Nicholsons Affair and were unanimously of opinion he had not made the Satisfaction he ought to have made and on Examination of the order from the Marine Committee with Respect to the impress'd men they found that Committee had acted very unwarrantably in explaining the Resolve of Congress on that Subject in such a narrow limited Sence.[3] Congress meant every man to be discharged without any discrimination of such as subscribed the Articles and took the Bounty and the Resolve was full & explicit to that Purpose. The Marine Committee were severely handled for presuming to explain at all the Resolve but the more reprehensible for giving a Sence to it which might have defeated the whole Design of it. Mr. Carroll & I were directed to prepare a fresh set of Resolutions. We did so one of which declared Capt. Nicholson dismiss'd from the Command of the Virginia frigate for not making that full satisfaction to the Governor & Council of Mary[lan]d which by a former Resolve of Congress he was ordered to do. A second resolve restored him to his Command on his explicit Disapprobation of his Letter & a third Resolve ordered the commanding officer of the Frigate to deliver up every impress'd man who should be considered such by any Persons the Governor & Council should send on Board for the Purpose of making the Enquiry. These Resolutions would have passed unanimously but Mr. Lewis coming up and assuring us of his having Conversations with our Council who declared they would be satisfied with the Concessions which were contained in Nicholsons first Letter and which were satisfactory to the Governor and Mr Lewis further assuring us that Capt. Nicholson had wrote a second Letter in Consequence thereof and discharged every man who did not chuse to remain, we have been induced from these assurances to postpone doing any thing in the matter till we hear further from you on the Subject. Mr. Lewis further says that Capt. Nicholson is about joining the Virginia arm'd Vessels with an Intent to attack the Man of War in the Bay. I can with pleasure inform you the Congress shewed a determined Spirit to give full Satisfaction on both points and I am confident they would have dismiss'd Capt. Nicholson without Hesitation if we had not proposed to restore him on his explicit disapprobation of his Letter which was the Satisfaction you in your's to him demanded: you may be further assured Capt. Nicholson had not even an Intimation from Congress or Committees to impress. I am surprised that Mr. Rumsey who was on the Marine Committee approved of the Explanation they gave the Resolve to discharge the impress'd men. Mr. Middleton who was also a member of that Committee told Congress he opposed it in the Marine Committee as an illegal assumption of Power. As the Question was agitated there how could our friend Rumsey suffer such a thing to be done? You'll be pleased to let us have a Line from you as soon as possible.

Generals Schuyler, Arnold & Miflin are in Town and propose to accompany us down to the expected Engagement.

Our Army begins to make a very formidable Figure. They were well [. . .] and handsomely uniformed in their D[. . . .] They are dress'd Soldier like from [. . .] to Shoe.

I am Gent, Yr. most obed hb. st.,   Wm. Paca

[*P.S.*] A fellow in this State was detected in inlisting men for the Enemy. He had actually carried five to Brunswick. He has been tried by a Court Martial and condemn'd to die. I am confident there are such villains in every State. We must next assembly make some Laws on this Subject.

RC (MdAA).
   [1] For two other letters Paca dated May 24 but undoubtedly wrote at later times, see Paca's letters to the Maryland governor and council printed below under the dates May 27 and May 29, 1777.
   [2] For the council's May 12 letter to the Maryland delegates inquring about the allowances made to printers of Continental money to which Paca is responding, see *Md. Archives*, 16:248.
   [3] For the Nicholson affair, see Marine Committee to James Nicholson, April 29, note, and the Marine Committee, Maryland Delegates, and Robert Morris letters to Thomas Johnson, May 1, 1777.

John Adams to Abigail Adams

May 25. 1777

At half past four this Morning, I mounted my Horse, and took a ride, in a Road that was new to me. I went to Kensington, and then to Point No Point, by Land, the Place where I went, once before, with a large Company in the Rowe Gallies, by Water. That Frolic was almost two Years ago. I gave you a Relation of it, in the Time, I suppose. The Road to Point No Point lies along the River Delaware, in fair Sight of it, and its opposite shore. For near four Miles the Road is as strait as the Streets of Philadelphia. On each Side, are beautifull Rowes of Trees, Buttonwoods, Oaks, Walnutts, Cherries and Willows, especially down towards the Banks of the River. The Meadows, Pastures, and Grass Plotts, are as Green as Leeks. There are many Fruit Trees and fine orchards, set with the nicest Regularity. But the Fields of Grain, the Rye, and Wheat, exceed all Description. These Fields are all sown in Ridges; and the Furrough between each Couple of Ridges, is as plainly to be seen, as if a swarth had been mown along. Yet it is no wider than a Plough share, and it is as strait as an Arrow. It looks as if the Sower had gone along the Furrough with his Spectacles to pick up every grain that should accidentally fall into it.

The Corn is just coming out of the Ground. The Furroughs struck out for the Hills to be planted in, are each Way, as straight as mathematical right Lines; and the Squares between every four Hills, as exact as they could be done by Plumb and Line, or Scale and Compass.

I am ashamed of our Farmers. They are a lazy, ignorant sett, in Husbandry, I mean—For they know infinitely more of every Thing else, than these. But after all the Native Face of our Country, diversified as it is, with Hill and Dale, Sea and Land, is to me more agreable than this enchanting artificial scæne.

May 27.

The Post brought me yours of May 6th and 9th.

You express Apprehensions that We may be driven from this City. We have No such Apprehensions here. Howe is unable to do any Thing but by Stealth. Washington is strong enough to keep Howe, where he is.

How could it happen that you should have £5 of counterfeit New Hampshire Money? Cant you recollect who you had it of? Let me intreat you not to take a shilling of any but continental Money, or Massachusetts—and be very carefull of that. There is a Counterfeit Continental Bill abroad sent out of New York but it will deceive none but Fools, for it is Copper Plate—easily detected, miserably done.

RC (MHi). Adams, *Family Correspondence* (Butterfield), 2:247–48.

John Adams to Thomas Jefferson

My dear Sir   Philadelphia May 26. 1777
I had this Morning, the Pleasure of your Favour of the Sixteenth
inst, by the Post; and rejoice to learn that your Battallions, were so
far fill'd, as to render a Draught from the Militia, unnecessary. It is
a dangerous Measure, and only to be adopted in great extremities,
even by popular Governments. Perhaps, in Such Governments Draughts
will never be made, but in Cases, when the People themselves see the
Necessity of them. Such Draughts are widely different from those made
by Monarchs, to carry on Wars, in which the People can see no Interest of their own nor any other object in View, than the Gratification
of the Avarice, Ambition, Caprice, Envy, Revenge, or Vanity of a
Single Tyrant. Draughts in the Massachusetts, as they have been there
managed, have not been very unpopular, for the Persons draughted are
commonly the wealthiest, who become obliged to give large Premiums,
to their poorer Neighbours, to take their Places.

The great Work of Confederation, draggs heavily on, but I dont
despair of it. The great and Small States must be brought as near
together as possible: and I am not without Hopes, that this may be
done, to the tolerable Satisfaction of both. Your Suggestion, Sir, that
any Proposition may be negatived, by the Representatives of a Majority
of the People, or of a Majority of States, shall be attended to, and I
will endeavour to get it introduced, if We cannot Succeed in our
Wishes for a Representation and a Rule of voting, perfectly equitable,
which has no equal, in my Mind.[1]

Nothing gives me, more constant Anxiety, than the Delays, in publishing the Journals.[2] Yet I hope, Gentlemen will have a little Patience
with Us. We have had a Committee constantly attending to this very
Thing, for a long Time. But we have too many Irons in the Fire, you
know for Twenty Hands, which is nearly the whole Number We have
had upon an Average Since, last fall. The Committee are now busy,
every day in correcting Proof Sheets, So that I hope We Shall Soon do
better.

A Committee on the Post office, too, have found, a thousand difficulties. The Post is now very regular, from the North and South,
altho it comes but once a Week. It is not easy to get faithfull Riders,
to go oftener. The Expence is very high, and the Profits, (so dear is
every Thing, and so little Correspondence is carried on, except in
franked Letters), will not Support the office. Mr. Hazard is now gone
Southward, in the Character of Surveyor of the Post office, and I hope
will have as good Success, as he lately had eastward, where he has put
the office into good order.

We have no News from Camp, but that the General and Army are
in good Spirits, and begin to feel themselves powerfull. We are

anxiously waiting for News from abroad, and for my own Part I am apprehensive of some insidious Maneuvre from Great Britain, to deceive Us into Disunion and then to destroy.

We want your Industry and Abilities here extreamly. Financiers, we want more than Soldiers. The worst Enemy, we have now is Poverty, real Poverty in the Shape of exuberant Wealth. Pray come and help Us, to raise the Value of our Money, and lower the Prices of Things. Without this, We cannot carry on the War. With it, we can make it a Diversion.

No poor Mortals were ever more perplexed than we have been, with three Misfortunes at once, any one of which would have been, alone, sufficient to have distressed Us. A Redundancy of the Medium of Exchange. A Diminution of the Quantity, at Markett of the Luxuries, the Conveniences and even the Necessaries of Life, and an Increase of the Demand for all these, occasioned by two large Armies in the Country.

I shall, ever esteam it a Happiness to hear of your Welfare, my dear Sir, and a much greater Still to see you, once more in Congress. Your Country is not yet, quite Secure enough, to excuse your Retreat to the Delights of domestic Life. Yet, for the soul of me, when I attend to my own Feelings, I cannot blame you. I am, Sir your Friend and most obedient Servant,   John Adams

RC (DLC). Jefferson, *Papers* (Boyd), 2:20–22.

[1] Jefferson had raised this issue as well as the following questions concerning the journals of Congress and the post office in his May 16 letter to Adams. Ibid., pp. 18–19.

[2] Congress voted on June 2 to distribute 20 copies of the journals to the delegates of each state. *JCC,* 8:412.

Richard Henry Lee to Patrick Henry

My dear Sir,   Philadelphia May 26. 1777

If I have contributed in any degree to your satisfaction or enabled you to combat false news intended to injure the cause of America, I am happy. I love the cause, and I have faithfully exerted myself to serve it well. Provided America be free and happy, I am not solicitous about the Agents that accomplish it. For this reason Sir, I look with indifference on the malice of my enemies, trusting that the wisdom of my Country will employ in its great concerns, such men only, as are of known uniform attachment to the cause of America, and who possess wisdom, integrity, and industry. But it has ever been my wish to deserve the esteem of virtuous men, and to stand well in their opinion. Upon this principle I hope for your pardon when I trouble you with a detail of the lease business.[1] From motives of private ease and as I thought of public good, if the same plan were generally adopted in Vir-

ginia, I determined some years ago to break up my quarters, and rent
out all my lands to a number of industrious men, who might benefit
themselves, and ease me of trouble at the same time. As the support of
a numerous family depended entirely upon those rents, I was brought to
the alarming situation of seeing that family infinitely distressed when
the Association took place, by the Tenants not paying me, assigning for
reason that they could not sell their produce. The present evil was then
great and pressing, and well knowing the determination of Great
Britain to push her ruinous system, which wd of course drive America
into a long and expensive war, that could only be supported by immense emissions of paper money, which falling in value with its excessive quantity would render my small income (but barely sufficient
with the greatest economy to maintain my family in the best times)
totally insufficient, I did propose to Colo Marshal (who was one of my
Tenants & a Collector for me in Fauquier) so early as August 1775 to
offer, by himself and Mr. Blackwell, to my Tenants, such a change of
rent as might enable them to pay, prevent my total ruin, and at the
same time be not injurious to them; since the plenty of money here
after which might lessen its value, would certainly raise the price of all
their produce. This proposition you will observe Sir, was made in
August 1775, at a time when emissions of money for this war were
scarcely begun, and when of course, the malignant insinuation of my
enemies could not have existed with me, that of depreciating a currency not yet in being. And it is worthy of remark, that in Augt. 1776,
the Tenants of Loudon County did themselves petition the Convention (if I forget not) to have their money rents changed to produce.
Colo. Marshall very much approved the reasonableness of my proposal,
and promised to offer the matter to the consideration of the Tenants.
I returned here to Congress, and Colo. Marshall soon after went into
the military line, so that nothing, that I know of, was done in this
business until March 1776 when yet very little money had been issued,
and when of course this alteration could not possibly have had the
least effect upon the credit of the paper money. At that time, for reasons already mentioned, I had for more than a year received little or
no support from my estate to the great injury of my family; and being
obliged to return here, I engaged Mr Parker of Westmoreland to go
up to Fauquier and propose to the Tenants to alter the rents to Tobacco at a price mutually to be agreed on. This he did, and returned
to me the alterations agreed on by all the Tenants near Fauquier Court
House, except two or three.[2] It was then upon two principles that this
change took place, first to put it in the power of the Tenant to pay me
what was then and might become due, and secondly to prevent thereafter the excessive and partial injury that might be derived to me from
emissions of paper money not then in existence. Would any but bad
Men, hardly pressed for argument against an innocent Character, have

misrepresented, and miscalled this absolutely faultless and justifiable conduct, a *design* to injure the public by depreciating the currency? But the truth is Sir, that certain evil disposed Men hate me partly for the same reason that I am devoted to destruction in the Enemies Camp, because I have served my Country with unremitting zeal and industry, and in concert with other generous friends to human liberty and the rights of America, have gone far towards defeating our enemies, and raising America triumphant over its cruel, vindictive, and determined foes. But it seems there are two other charges equally futile and false; the one, that I have favored New England to the injury of Virginia. The other, that as a Member of the Secret Committee I objected to their proceedings being laid before Congress, meaning to insinuate that I wished to conceal embezlement of the public money! The Wretch who carried, or sent this last account to Virginia, knows perfectly well that my total abstraction from every Commercial concern renders it impossible that I can propose any kind of good to myself from trading business of any sort. But I have a strong belief that a change is wished in order to remove obstruction feared from me, and to prepare the way for the execution of private plans in which the public will not be gainers. The affair alluded to is, I suppose, a very inconsiderate motion made at Baltimore for the Secret Committee to lay all its proceedings before Congress. I observed that so extensive a motion defeated the very end for which such a Committee was appointed, and might expose to danger valuable Cargoes that should be coming in, or that might be going out, particularly the former. The motion was narrowed, and even so it was agreed to. Mr. Morris the Chairman of the Committee who was here at the time, did by Letter so convince the Congress of the impropriety of the order even as it passed, that nothing more was said about it.[3] We did indeed expect at that very time the arrival of the valuable Stores that have since come in. The charge of favoring New England is so contemptibly wicked that I can scarcely bring myself to the trouble of refuting it, or to trespass on your time to read my observations on it. Our enemies and our friends too, know that America can only be conquered by disunion. The former, by unremitting art had endeavored to incite jealousy and discord between the Southern and Eastern Colonies, and in truth Sir they had so far prevailed that it required constant attention, and a firmness not to be shaken, to prevent the malicous art of our enemies from succeeding. I am persuaded as I am of my existence, that had it not been for Virginia and Jersey, with Georgia sometimes, that our Union would eer now have been by this means broken like a Potters vessel dashed against a rock and I heartily wish that this greatest of all political evils may not yet take place before a safe and honorable peace is established. I am sure it will not be the fault of many men that I know if this worst does not happen. I defy the poisonous tongue of slander to produce a single instance in which I have preferred the interest of New England to that of Virginia. Indeed I am at a Loss to know wherein their interests clash. The guilt of New England is that of a fixed determination against British Tyranny, & such I believe is the crime of Virginia in the eye of their common enemies. Most of the rest have entitled themselves to some hopes of pardon from the Tyrant, by weak, dividing, irresolute and pernicious conduct. One thing is certain, that among the Middle and Southern states Virginia had many enemies, arising from jealousy and envy of her wisdom, vigor, and extent of Territory. But I have ever discovered, upon every question, respect and love for Virginia among the Eastern Delegates. Folly and ingratitude would have marked the Representatives of Virginia had they shown disesteem for the latter, and attachment to the former. I have served my Country, Sir, to the best of my knowledge, and with fidelity and industry, to the injury of my health, fortune, and a sequestration from domestic happiness. I shall rejoice to find that others are employed, who will do the business better than I have done. It will always make me happy to reflect, that those Malignants who would represent me as an enemy to my Country, cannot make me so.

I am ready to give my enemies credit for more address than I thought they possessed—I mean the use they make of a good principle under cover of which to wound me. For this purpose the Delegates time of service is to be so limited as to reward a three years painful employ by dismission. The plan is precisely fitted for my ease, and thus the most malicious, groundless, and infamous slander is likely to succeed against an absent Man, who has labored to deserve a better fate. You will make what use you please of this letter. The business of war remains as when I wrote you last, except that the American Army is daily increasing, whilst that of the enemy is only added to by a few Tories as yet, tho they will I expect in a month or so be reinforced with 8 or 10,000 men from Europe, which will not make them so strong as when they began the Campaign last year, whilst our Army will be far more formidable. Gen. Washington has now about 10,000 regular Troops with him, and his numbers daily increasing. As far as we are able to learn the enemy have not now in Jersey so many as 5000. By accounts just from New York we hear of the death of Governor Tryon of the wounds he received in the expedition to Danbury, and also of the death of Colo. Woolcot from the same cause.[4] This was the Colonel that made such indecent observations of Gen. Washington's proposal in exchange of prisoners. Tis said that the Officers in N. York look very grave and say all hope of conquest over America is now gone, unless they can succeed in dividing us. The inclosed resolve of Congress is intended to prevent injury to the recruiting business and other public service in the absence of a General Officer from Virginia.[5]

I beg your pardon Sir for the trouble I have given you, and wish to be considered affectionately yours,   Richard Henry Lee

RC (NjR: Elsie O. and Philip D. Sang deposit).

[1] Lee had been left out of the delegation appointed by the Virginia Assembly on May 22, allegedly because of accusations that he was contributing to the depreciation of paper currency by requiring his tenants to pay their rents in produce or specie. When he took his seat in the Virginia house on June 20, Lee demanded an investigation of these charges and subsequently received the thanks of both houses for his services as a delegate and on June 24 was appointed to replace George Mason, who had declined to serve as a delegate. Lee reported the outcome in his June 25 letter to Landon Carter. "It was impossible for me to avoid feeling the unmerited illtreatment that I had received, but I have now the pleasure to inform you that the two houses have removed all bad impressions by their favorable approbation of my conduct; and they have directed me to return to Congress as one of their Delegates. This latter is a most oppressive business, and therefore unsought by me, but having put my hand to the plough I am bound to go through." Lee-Ludwell Papers, ViHi; and Lee, *Letters* (Ballagh), 1:303–4. For further discussion of this episode in relation to the passage of a Virginia act for regulating the appointment of delegates, see Oliver Perry Chitwood, *Richard Henry Lee, Statesman of the Revolution* (Morgantown: West Virginia University Library, 1967), pp. 136–42; and Jefferson, *Papers* (Boyd), 2:15–18.

[2] At this point Lee's draft varies considerably from the RC. Cf. Lee, *Letters* (Ballagh) 1:299–300.

[3] Although Robert Morris' letter on this subject has not been found it probably had been written in reaction to the Secret Committee's January 18 letter requesting his assistance in complying with the congressional order to the Secret Commitee to supply "a list of the articles which they have ordered in consequence of the directions of Congress, distinguishing how much is arrived and what is expected." See *JCC,* 7:45; and Secret Committee to Robert Morris, January 18, 1777.

[4] Reports that William Tryon, royal governor of New York and commander of the British expeditionary force, and Lt. Col. William Walcott had been killed at Danbury were unfounded.

[5] For this resolve of May 22, see *JCC,* 8:377.

Richard Henry Lee to John Page

My dear Sir,   Philadelphia 26 May 1777

Finding by your letter of this post to your brother that you suppose I have been negligent in my correspondence with you, my chief purpose here is to remove that charge. I do not remember which of us is debtor on the letter score, but as far as I do recollect I think I was the writer, not the Receiver of the last letter. However this may be, it appeared the less necessary for me to write, as I knew Mr. Page furnished you with regular intelligence of what passed in the war department, besides which, I had nothing worth troubling you with, or calling my attention from the busy scene around me.

I observe in the Gazette, your call upon our Countrymen to apply some of their attention to the business of philosophy.[1] Your reasoning is just, and I hope will have its due weight. I am sure that some among us have abundant necessity both for the study and the practise of the Moral part of that noble science. If this had been better learned, such an industrious attempt to injure my reputation in the opinion of my Countrymen would not have taken place. It has been a wicked industry, the most false, and the most malicious that the deceitful heart of man ever produced. I am not on my own account affected with this malice of my enemies, because I have long panted for retirement from the most distressing pressure of business that I ever had conception of. But my principal concern arises from the dreadful example my case presents, to cool the arder of patriotism, and prevent the sacrifice of private ease to public service. I ought at least to have been heared in my defence. But Sir I will not trouble you with my feelings.

The enemies expected reenforcements from Europe have not yet arrived, in consequence of which, our army in Jersey outnumbers theirs considerably, but since they do expect 8 or 10,000 men from beyond the Atlantic, and may bring the greatest part of their force round from Canada in order to make one last dying effort, it behooves us to be prepared to meet the desperate designs of desperate men. If no disappointment takes place, when their whole force is collected, I do not think they will be so strong as when the field was taken last year, and the American Army promises to be much more formidable. Skirmishing still continues, and still we keep the superiority, insomuch that by the late maneuvres of the enemy, it seems not improbable that they intend to quit Jersey soon. They paid severely for their provision destroying excursion to Danbury, where besides their disgraceful flight, they did not loose less than 450 or 500 men killed & wounded. Governor Tryon, late a Major General, and Colo. Wolcot, are both dead of the wounds they received in that chace. The last accounts from York tell us, that the British Officers look grave, and say, all hope of conquering America but by disuniting it is now lost. Great efforts will be made this year for that purpose, and no act or expence omitted to obtain by fraud what force has failed to procure, the Court favorite "Subduction of America."

We hear that in the West Indies French Privateers abound under Continental Commissions, which I think cannot fail to procure war if Great Britain is not dead to every feeling except resentment for the Virtue of their once affectionate brethren and fellow subjects. The inclosed pamphlet is well written, and will I hope amuse you. Be pleased to give my brother Thom the reading of it when you have finished it.

Adieu my dear Sir, I am your affectionate Kinsman,

Richard Henry Lee

[P.S.] I hope to see you e'er long in Williamsburg.[2]

RC (NN).

[1] In the *Virginia Gazette* (Purdie), May 16, 1777, Page, as president of the Virginia Society for Promoting Useful Knowledge, had presented arguments for continuing this scientific group during the war years and called for papers to be submitted for a volume of transactions.

[2] Lee was granted a leave of absence on June 5 and left Philadelphia on the 15th. See *JCC*, 8:420; and Lee, *Letters* (Ballagh), 1:305.

James Lovell to George Washington

Sir   Philada. May 26th. 1777

This will be delivered to you by a German officer who expresses much inclination to enter into the army under your command.[1]

The trouble which your Excellency receives from Foreigners commissioned by Congress has made the Committee, appointed to examine their pretensions, averse to offering any resolutions for places above the rank of subalterns.

The Bearer speaks English very well, and has an honorable character in a letter from Doctor Franklin, with 4 commissions proving his regular service.

I have told him that, notwithstanding these advantages, he cannot expect any place till you have pointed out a situation wherein he may subserve the interest of these United States.

The resolute importunity of some strangers of less desert has, I fear, gained the post which would be better filled by this modest veteran.

The promotion of Monsr. Armand by Congress to the rank of Colonel was a surprize to the Committee who had considered his pretensions, and rashly enough in all conscience had proposed a majority for him.[2]

With affectionate Respect, I am, Your Excellency's Most obedient Friend,   James Lovell

RC (DLC).

[1] In a June 4 reply, General Washington informed Lovell that he had recommended Maj. Henry Emmanuel Lutterloh to Gen. Thomas Mifflin for a position in the quartermaster general's department. Washington, *Writings* (Fitzpatrick), 8:178. See also Washington to Thomas Mifflin, May 31, 1777, ibid., p. 145n.31.

[2] See Robert Morris to George Washington, May 10, 1777, note.

Marine Committee to the Rhode Island Frigate Committee

Gentlemen   May 26th 1777

Your Letter of the 17th Feby lies before us requesting a Remittance

of Seven thousand Dollars, or an order on the Loan office of your State
for that sum. As you have in the latter part of your Letter given us
reason to hope that you would shortly forward to us compleat Accounts of the two frigates built under your Inspection, accompanied
with proper vouchers we think it will be more regular to wait the arrival of these Accounts before we advance any further sums. We assure you that when the said Accounts have passed this board the balance shall be punctually and speedily remitted to you.

We are Gentlemen, Your very hble servts

LB (DNA: PCC Miscellaneous Papers, Marine Committee Letter Book).

Mann Page to John Page

Dear Brother   Philadelphia, May 26th 1777.
In your Letter to me you refered me to Colo. Nelson for News, he
has left us for some time,[1] and as I was anxious to hear particularly
from Virginia, I took the Liberty of opening your Letter to him, which
I now enclose, that you may know its' fate. We have no News here,
except a Report which is well founded, that Genl. Tryon and Lieutt.
Colo. Wallcot are both dead of the Wounds which they recd. in their
expedition against Danbury. I shall be much obliged to you to send me
weekly the Journals of our Assembly, tho' I do not expect to stay long
to read them; for I understand there is to be an entire change in the
Delegation from Virga. I wrote you my sentiments upon that Head by
the last Post.[2] One thing I would wish you to urge to your friends in the
Assembly, which is that every person who is appointed a Delegate to
Congress should decline all foreign Commerce in which he may be
then engaged, & be bound during the time of his Delegation not to
enter into any foreign commercial Business, either directly on his own
Acct., or indirectly by joining in Partnership with any person whatever. The necessity we are under of making Returns in our Produce to
Europe for the Supplies which we have imported from thence for the
Use of our Army renders this Caution proper. This is generally pur-
chased· by Agents who are usually nominated by the Delegates of the
respective States. If the merchant Delegate should want a little honesty,
& should have Interest to get one of his Partners, who may be as little
scrupleous as himself, appointed an Agent, they may apply the Money
advanced for the public Service to their own Uses, & the Agent by
purchasing certain Commodities which his Partner the Delegate may
inform him will shortly be wanted by the Public, & afterwards by selling to the public at an advanced Price, they may replace the Money
which ought to have been laid out for the public, & by that means
make great Profit to themselves upon the ruin of the Continent. Again,

if the Person who exports the produce to foreign Ports or the Delegate should be concerned in Trade, they may manage their Affairs so that every Cargo which is taken by the Enemy will belong to the public, & everyone which arrives safe will be private Property. Neither is it possible to detect the Villainy, for the confidence placed in the Delegate, & the Opinion entertained of the Agent who has the Recommendation & Support of the Delegate will prevent all Suspicions; but if they should arise, & an Enquiry into the Matter be insisted on, they may by many artful ways evade a Settlement 'til they hear the Fate of the Cargoes which they have shiped. I do not know whether any thing of the Sort has happened, but it is best to guard against the worst.

As to the Seal I fear it cannot be made here; the Man who was employed about it is in Prison for [Tompson?]; Colo. Nelson promised to carry the Print to Virga which was left in the Care of Mr. Purviance at Baltimore when we came from thence. Please to give my Love to my Sister. I am dear Brother, Your's affectionately,

Mann Page Junr.

RC (ViW).

¹ See Mann Page to John Page, May 6, 1777, note 1.

² Page's letter to his brother on this subject has not been found, but he had not been included in the Virginia delegation appointed by the assembly on May 22 and announced in Purdie's *Virginia Gazette* on May 23, 1777.

Daniel Roberdeau to George Washington

My dear General   Philada May 26th. 1777¹

I have known nothing but Affliction ever since I had the honor of seeing you last and was a Subject of your great humanity and politeness, for which you have my most sincere thanks, when I was reduced to the lowest Ebb of Life in New Jersey, but the affliction I suffered in my own person and all the Sorrows of my whole life accumulated, are not to be compared with that awful stroke of Providence which deprived me of my Dr. Mrs. Roberdeau. I know your generous Breast feels for my distress with which I do not intend to take up more of your precious time than to offer it as an apology that I have not presented my acknowledgement sooner.

Congress has this day made a new arrangement of the Chaplains department by reducing that part of the Staff to one for each Brigade to be recommended by the Brigadier and appointed by Congress, with the pay, rations and Forrage allowed to Colonels.²

This new and honorable Establishment is designed to suppress the horrid Sins of Cursing, swearing and other Vices with which I am sorry to say our Army Vies with the most abandoned of the English Troops; to strengthen the Officers hands by publick and private exorta-

tions to obedience of General and Regimental Order; to discourage
Disertions by recommending the Service, to encourage Enlistments; to
recommend cleanlyness as a virtue conducive to health, and to repre-
hend the neglect of it. These and other valuable Ends with the
Countinance and concurrence of General Officers by the blessing of
heaven I doubt not may be answered by a careful choice and recommendation of pious Clergymen zealously attached to our glorious
Cause who will not begrudge the exertion of every nerve of the Service
but if Drones induced by the loaves and Fishes should creep into the
Army, the designs of Congress will be entirely defeated, to prevent
which I frankly confess has induced me to step out of my line on this
Occasion, and I beg you will not look upon it as an impudent intrusion
on you, when I assure you the honor of God, my Countries welfare,
your Comfort and that of every sober Officer and man in the Army
are my only motives. With submission I think an early recommendation
to Congress will be best in every view, particularly to prevent the application of such as would mar instead of promoting the Service, and as
I know you may have what influence you please with the Genl. Officers
in this measure, for these Reasons permit me to mention at the foot of
this some Gentlemen who would be of great Service in our Army, as
probably you are not as well acquainted with that order of Gentlemen,
zealously attached to our Cause, as I am. The Names that have occurred to me are chiefly of the Church I belong to, but believe me no
partiallity has influenced to this but my greater knowledge of such is
the occasion. The four last mentioned Gentlemen I am not personally
acquainted with but all the others I speak of from my own knowledge
as persons well qualified to serve the valuable purposes already mentioned. I plead no right to this freedom much less Do I presume on my
publick Character but solely from the motives I have professed above
and free from every solicitation.

Congress has this day refered to you the nomination of any of the
General Officers already appointed to the command of the horse. I
fear your censure of my freedom but relying on your candour I remain with unfeigned regard and profound Respect, Dear General, Yr.
much obliged & obt, huml Servt.   Daniel Roberdeau

Dr. John Livingston of the Dutch reformed Church of New York
Dr. John Rodgers Presbyterian of N.Y.
Mr. Elihu Spencer do. of Delaware
Mr. Alexr. McWhorter do. of New Jersey
Mr. James Caldwell do. do.
Mr. Geo. Duffield do. of Philada.
Mr.   Stillman Baptist of Boston
Mr. Wm. Gordon Presbyterian Jama. Plains
Mr.   McRoberts political character unknown, but popular of
    Virginia

Dr. Abiel Leonard of New England
Dr. Ladley of the Dutch reformed Church at New York
Mr.   Mason of New York

Whatever Clergymen Congress may appoint their present Connection I believe will be no hinderance.

RC (DLC).
    [1] Roberdeau probably misdated this letter, since it was motivated by a resolution of Congress that is recorded in the journals under the date May 27.
    [2] See *JCC,* 8:390–91.

Philip Schuyler to the Board of Treasury

Gentlemen,   Philadelphia May 26th. 1777
    Your Letter of the 4th of April[1] I received on the 9th. The Reasons which have induced so long a Silence on my Part are too Obvious to need Explanations.
    I am extremely sorry that You should have so widely misapplied a Paragraph in my Letter of the 14th of February to the Hono. Cont. Congress, as to suppose that I mean to designate the Treasury Board, "as Persons lending willing Ears to improbable Tales." I know not a Gentleman that held a Seat at that Board. I did not know who It was composed of, I was never advised that any of Its Members had entertained one Injurious Suspicion of me, and when I wrote that part of my Letter on which yours is founded, I had not the most distant Thought of the Treasury Board. I meant to allude to Committees who had taken the Liberty to try me for ruining our Affairs in Canada by withholding the Specie, which was sent for the Use of the Army in that Quarter.[2]
    These being the Facts, I trust that a Regard to Candor & Justice will induce Your Honorable Board to make such an Explanation of the severe Expressions contained in your Letter as are due to an injured Gentleman.[3] I am Gentlemen Your Most Obedt. Hble. servt.
                                                                P. Schuyler

LB (NN).
    [1] Not found.
    [2] See Schuyler to the Board of Treasury, April 27, 1777.
    [3] The Board's response to this letter is not known.

Philip Schuyler to John Hancock

Sir   Philadelphia May 26 1777.
    I do myself the Honor to return sincere thanks to Congress for the attention and Justice I have experienced, from that respectable Body,

since my arrival in this City. I entreat you Sir, to assure them that I entertain the most grateful Feilings on the Occasion, and that I shall by a steady and zealous perseverance in the Line of my Duty strive to merit a Continuance of their Confidence; that I shall most assiduously labour to introduce Discipline, Harmony and Œconomy, into that part of the Army committed to my immediate Care; that as I am the Officer of the united States, I shall make no Colonial Discriminations and deprecate every Measure that has the least Tendency to disunite or create Jealousies amongst us.

Permit me to suggest that I think one or two Troops of Horse may be speedily levied and accoutered in the Vicinity of Albany, and I believe much cheaper than in this part of the Country, that they would be very useful, and that if Congress should see Cause to order it to be done I could wish for their Direction in the Arrangement. Messrs. Winslow and Pierce the Deputy paymasters general in the Northern Department have made a written application to me requesting me to represent to Congress that their pay is small, and intreating an augmentation of it. Capt. Stevens also of the artillery has intreated me to advise Congress, that he last Year held the Rank of Major, but that on the new Arrangement he stands as a Captain only. He is a worthy officer and I believe would promote the Service if he was honored with a Brevet giving him the Rank of Major.

None of the officers of Colonel Livingston's Regiment, except Captain Hughes, have as yet received their Commissions. I wish to know if it is the pleasure of Congress that I should fill up the Commissions agreeable to the List I had the Honor to transmit to Congress.

Permit me, with all due Deference to the better Judgment of Congress, to suggest that the Mode of paying the army by abstract may be attended with some abuses, and that I should be extremely happy if I might be permitted to direct the pay-Masters in the Northern Department to conduct themselves in the Line pointed out by the orders of the 8h of February last, Copy whereof I had the Honor to enclose, which, with some small amendments, I should hope would effectually remedy the Evils, so much and so fully complained of.

If General Gates should not have appointed a Deputy Adjutant General and Deputy Judge advocate I should wish to be empowered to make temporary appointments until the pleasure of Congres was known.

As the Indians frequently inform me of certain Matters, said by them to be done or promised by the Commissioners of the middle Department, which Causes some Embarrassment in giving answers to them, I therefore wish that the Committee of Indian affairs may be directed from Time to Time to furnish the Commissioners with Copies of such Intelligence as may be received by Congress.[1]

I propose leaving this to Morrow, if agreeable to Congress, and beg their Commands. I am Sir, with every Sentiment of Respect & Esteem, Your most obedient and most humble Servant,   Ph. Schuyler

RC (DNA: PCC, item 153). In the hand of John Lansing, Jr., and signed by Schuyler.

[1] Congress took action on most of the requests in the foregoing five paragraphs on May 27. *JCC*, 8:391–92.

Roger Sherman to Jonathan Trumbull, Sr.

Honored Sir   Philadelphia May 26th 1777

I was honored with your favour of the 18th Instant which I received on the 24th after Congress adjourned. I have not Seen Mr. Duer Since, but I never heard from him or any other person any Such imputation on any member of Assembly as your Honr. mentions. I Shall enquire into the matter.[1]

I transmitted Your Honr a copy of the resolution of Congress concerning the two Battalions to be Stationed in Connecticut in my last.[2]

The Board of War has Sent orders to the Commissary of Military Stores at Springfield to Supply the Connecticut Troops with Arms and Accoutrements upon Authentic Muster rolls being produced to him. As to the Field pieces and other Stores for the use of the State General Washington is best able to determine whether they can be Spared. By the best accounts from New York the Enemy paid pretty dear for their excursion to Danbury, tis reported here that Governor Tryon is dead of his wounds. I imagine they wont be fond of making another incursion into Connecticut unless they could have Some greater object in view than any that I know of, however it is best to be prepared for them.

Tis most likely they will pursue the plan of joyning their two armies by the way of Hudson's River if they have a Sufficient force. At present our Army in New Jersy is Superior to theirs. Some capital Stroke may be Struck there Soon. We have no great expectation of their coming to this City.

General Schuyler is here. Congress has ordered him to the Northern department. The Eastern States were of opinion that it would best promote the Service, for him to have been with the Commander in Chief, & that would probably have been carried if Rhode Island had been represented. Some are apprehensive that his taking Command in the Northern department may interfere with General Gates's plans and be prejudicial to the Service at a time when the Campaign is expected to be opened.

The Commissary General is here. Congress is about to make Some new regulations in that department.[3]

A Committee is appointed to consider what Honors are due to the memory of General Wooster. Major General Arnold is here. Congress has ordered an elegant horse properly caparisoned to be presented to him.

I am with great Esteem & Regard, Your Honrs. Obedient humble Servant,   Roger Sherman

P.S. I Saw an account in the New Haven paper that one Griswold was executed as a traitor and Spy by the Sentence of a Court Martial.[4] If he was an Inhabitant of the State & not of the Army, I think he ought to have been tryed before the Superior Court. The resolution of Congress for the punishment of Spies respects only persons who are not inhabitants of any of the United States, or under the protection of their laws. We cant be too careful of Military incroachments. It is easy to accuse any person with being a Spy & So put his Life in the power of a Court Martial if that is allowed. The Case of Molesworth who was tryed and executed in this City was approved by Congress, but it was from necessity, because there was no Civil Courts established in this State.[5]   R.S.

RC (Ct).
    [1] See Sherman to Trumbull, May 14, 1777, note 2.
    [2] See Sherman to Trumbull, May 16, 1777.
    [3] Joseph Trumbull had been in Philadelphia since April 22 conferring with a congressional committee on the reorganization of the commissary department. For a discussion of developments leading to the adoption of new commissary regulations, see Elbridge Gerry to Joseph Trumbull, April 19, 1777, note 1.
    [4] See Sherman to Oliver Wolcott, May 21, 1777, note 1.
    [5] See John Hancock to Horatio Gates, March 31, 1777.

Charles Carroll of Carrollton to Charles Carroll, Sr.

Dr. Papa   27th May 1777. Pha.

There is nothing new Since my last. I have yours of the 20th instant from Annapolis. Altho' the law making the currencies a legal tender is certainly unjust, yet when the debtors tender no more than the interest, I would not write to them about the injustice of tendering the interest money at par. When they tender more than the interest, it would be proper to expostulate with them on the injustice of the proferred payt. You say Lewellen's Son did not tender the money. I wish you may not bring yourself into trouble about that law, altho it is unjust, it hath passed, & we must submit to it, or take the consequences of a refusal. The Congress is under a necessity of emitting 5 million more of Dollars. We are in hopes we shall not be obliged to put this whole Sum in circulation, as the Loan offices & lottery will supply us with nearly money sufficient to answer the remaining expences of this campaign.

I am in hopes we shall be able to negotiate a loan in Europe among those nations which are diposed to favour our cause. If this could be done to any considerable extent, it would supersede the necessity of any farther emissions; and if the several States would tax highly, those taxes together with the monies that might be borrowed on interest, would probably nearly answer the expences of next campaign, which I think will not be so expensive as the present, as our army & its different departments will be put on a more economical footing.

This State is in a very languid condition. The Govt. is feeble beyond conception, & yet a better, I fear, will not soon be established; nothing but an actual invasion can make Pena. exert itself with becoming vigour. It has great resources, but in the present State of things they lie dormant; a collection of blankets is now making from the Quakers. They refused to give voluntarily even on payt. so that a *Seeming* force has become necessary to procure that much wanted supply. I shall write again by next Saturday's post, if there should be anything worth writing. All is quiet in the Jersies. Wishing you a long continuance of your health I remain, yr. affectionate Son,

C. Carroll of Carrollton

RC (MdHi).

Elbridge Gerry to Unknown

My dear sir   Philadelphia 27th May 1777

Being now in Congress I am unable to reply to your last Favours, & have only Time to inclose You a Warrant on the Loan office for the Money due to You in Consequence of an Error attending the last Adjustt. of your Account. I suffer much from Want of Exercise & Relaxation, shall however not leave Congress while I am able to attend the Business, as I wish much to see several Matters compleated, particularly the Confederation, before my Return.

I am much in Haste sir your assured Friend & huml. sert.

E Gerry

RC (MB).

John Hancock to George Washington

Sir,   Philada. May 27th. 1777.

I have the Honour of transmitting at this Time sundry Resolves, to which I beg Leave to refer your Attention.[1]

From them you will learn, that Congress have ascertained the Limits of the Northern Department, and that they have ordered Genl. Schuyler to take the Command therein.[2]

The Regulations respecting Chaplains in the Army are highly necessary. By increasing their Pay, and enlarging the Bounds of their Duty, the Congress are in Hopes of engaging Gentlemen of superior Learning & Virtue to fill those Stations.[3]

Your several Favours to the 24th Inst. have been duely received and laid before Congress. I have the Honour to be, with perfect Esteem & Respect, Sir, your most obed. & very hble Servt.

John Hancock Presidt

RC (DLC). In the hand of Jacob Rush and signed by Hancock.

[1] In addition to those specifically mentioned in the text, Hancock also enclosed resolves of May 14–15, 22, and 26–27 on Virginia troops, Gen. Philip Schuyler, James Norris, Louis Fleury, certain French officers, light horse, pardons, and Capt. Ebenezer Stevens. *JCC*, 7:353, 362, 364, 8:380, 385–86, 390–91.

[2] See *JCC*, 8:375.

[3] See *JCC*, 8:390–91.

William Paca to the Maryland Governor and Council

Gent.   Five O Clock. 24 [27?] May 1777.[1]

By a Letter from Genl. Washington we are inform'd that seventeen Sail of Transports have arrived at New York and more are coming up in Sight. He also says by Accounts Tryon & Wolcot are dead of their Wounds.[2]

There are great Errors in the Names of the officers of the roster you sent up. Many of the officers also were not in our Service.

V. hb. St.   W Paca

[*P.S.*] I am informed by Col. Gunby that there is not one commissioned officer with Capt. Deams Company. The Capt. has resigned, two of the officers are Prisoners and the other no one can tell what is become of him. The Privates are all to eight or ten deserted. Not a field officer is at Camp of Col. William's Regiment. Our Troops and State are in Contempt.

RC (MdAA).

[1] Although Paca clearly dated this letter "24 May 1777," the letter General Washington wrote from Morristown on May 24 containing the intelligence Paca recounts here was not read in Congress until May 27. See *JCC*, 8:386. For another letter Paca misdated May 24, see his letter to the Maryland governor and council printed under the date May 29 below.

[2] Washington's May 24 letter to Congress is in PCC, item 152, 4:191–94, and Washington, *Writings* (Fitzpatrick), 8:114–17.

George Walton to George Washington

Dear Sir,   Philadelphia, 27 May, 1777.
Well aware of the many great objects which necessarily & constantly occupy your mind, I would not trouble you upon the present occasion, were I not pressed to it by the bearer. He is appointed to the command of the fourth Georgia Battalion, which is yet in great part to be raised, and that too in other states. I have suggested to him the several difficulties; I have told him, that, as Congress have required of the states certain quotas of troops, they would not, by any recommendation, embarrass them until those quotas were completed. Colonel White still urges that Georgia, oppressed by Savages on one side, & Floridians on the other, ought to be supported; and thinks he can, by a true representation, convince your Excellency that there is a necessity for more strength. If he should succeed in this, it is probable that you will recommend it to the southern states to suffer him to recruit a few companies.[1] I beg leave to suggest one thing; if the enemy's army should be directed this way in any part of the campaign, these companies, under a good Officer, would be at your Excellency's beck.
I am, with the greatest esteem & regard, Your Excellency's most obt. Sevt.   Geo Walton.

RC (DLC).
[1] Washington's reply of June 2, in which he pointed out that only Congress had the right to grant permission for recruiting in other states, is in Washington, *Writings* (Fitzpatrick), 8:169.

John Adams to Abigail Adams

Philadelphia May 28. 1777
An horrid cold Day for Election—warm work however, in the Afternoon, I suppose.[1]
You will see by the inclosed Papers, among the Advertisements, how the Spirit of Manufacturing grows. There never was a Time when there was such full Employment, for every Man, Woman and Child, in this City. Spinning, Knitting, Weaving, every Tradesman is as full as possible. Wool and Flax in great Demand.
Industry will supply our Necessities, if it is not cramped by injudicious Law—such as Regulations of Prices &c., Embargoes &c. These discourage Industry and turn that Ingenuity which ought to be employed for the general Good, into Knavery.

RC (MHi). Adams, *Family Correspondence* (Butterfield), 2:250.
[1] A reference to the election of councillors in the Massachusetts General Court, which took place on May 28–29, 1777. Massachusetts House Journals, DLC(ESR).

William Duer to John Jay

My dear Sir,   May 28th 1777

You have been undoubtedly surpris'd at my long Silence, but when I inform you what is Fact, that my principal Reasons for not writing have been want of Time, and of Satisfactory Matter, I flatter myself I shall Stand acquitted (if not with honor) at least as a Wilful Offender against the Laws of Friendship.

As General Schuyler expects to deliver this Letter in Person I shall refer you to him for the particular Manavres respecting his own affairs, and for the political Complexion of Affairs in Congress. From a very low Ebb at which our Affairs were when we arrived here we have recovered surprisingly and I may venture to say that the Eyes of all those who are not willfully blind are open, and that we may expect Justice to take Place with respect to our State.

I congratulate you on the Completion of the Task of forming and Organizing our New Government.[1] I think it upon the maturest Reflection the best System which has as yet been adopted, and possibly as good as the Temper of the Times would admit of. If it is well administerd, and some wise and Vigorous Laws pass'd at the Opening of the Session for watching, and defeating the Machinations of the Enemy & their Abettors, and for Supporting by Taxes, and other Means the Credit of the Circulating Money—it will be a formidable Engine of Opposition to the Designs of our Tyrannical Enemies—but I assure you I am not without my Fears concerning the Choice which will be made of those who are to set the Machine in Motion.

Our All Depends on it. It is very observable that in almost every other State where Government has been formd, and established either from the Contention of Parties, or from a Want of proper Power being vested in the Executive Branches—Disaffection has encreased prodigiously, and an unhappy langour has prevaild in the whole Political System. I sincerely wish that this may not be the Case with us, but that the new Government may continue to act with that Spirit, Integrity, and Wisdom which animated the Councils of the Old!

In this State Toryism (or rather Treason) stalks triumphant, the Credit of our Money is sapp'd by the Arts and Avarice of the Malignants and Monopolisers, and such is the desperate Situation of affairs, that nothing but desperate Remedies can restore these people to Reason and Virtue.

The Assembly is now convend, but I am afraid will not dare to lay a Tax to call in part of the large Sums of Money circulating in this State, or to pass vigorous Laws to crush the disaffected. All my hope is that the Spirit of Whiggism will at length break forth in some of the Populace, which (if well directed) may effect by Quackery a

Course which the regular State Physicians are either not adequate to, or unwilling to attempt.

A Spirit of this kind under the Name of *Joyce Junr.* has made his Appearance in Boston.[2] I should not be surpris'd if he was to travel Westward. It would be attended with these good Effects: it would either supply the Want of Vigor in the present Government or it would induce those whose duty it is to act with Spirit and Vigor. What think you of an Episcopalian Clergyman in this City praying last Sunday for the Lords Spiritual and Temporal—or rather what think you of the Congregation which heard him with Patience?

If in the midst of your Political Business you can now and then drop me a Line I will esteem it as a favor, and (if not regularly) I will by Starts when there is any thing worth communicating write to you.

A Word in the Ear of a Friend. When I was sent here I had some Idea that I was entering into The Temple of Public Virtue. I am disappointed and Chagrined. Genl. Schuyler will communicate my Sentiments and his own at large.

The *Chaste* Colo. Lee will I am credibly informed be left out of the new Delegation for Virginia which is now in Agitation. The mere Contemplation of this Event gives me Pleasure. My mind is full, and I wish to unburthen it; but Prudence forbids me.[3]

I condole with you on the Loss of your Aged Mother or rather should I not congratulate you that she is arrived in a secure and pleasant Haven from a Storm, which she was little calculated to bear? This Reflection I beleive has alleviated your Distress. May we be as Virtuous as your Parents should we live to be as old! From the rapid Increase of Villainy both Moral and Political, it is to be feard that we shall not increase in Virtue, as we may in Years. Remember me to all my Freinds, particularly to my Fellow-Labourors in the Council of *Conspiracy*.[4] Adieu, and beleive me Yours with much Esteem and Affection.   W Duer

[*P.S.*] I have deliverd Genl. Schuyler a Letter from your Friend Mr Dean in France.[5] I have had it some Time by me, but waited a safe Mode of Conveyance.

RC (NNC). Addressed: "To The Honble. John Jay Esqr, Chief Justice of the State of New York."

[1] The New York Convention had adopted a state constitution on April 20.

[2] Joyce, Jr., was the pseudonym used by a Boston mob leader whose real identity has never been established. Taking his name from an English officer who had arrested Charles I in 1647 and allegedly taken part in his execution two years later, Joyce, Jr., first appeared in Boston in 1774 as chairman of a committee of tarring and feathering. After disappearing during the British occupation of Boston, he returned to public view in April 1777 as the leader of a mob which drove five loyalists out of Boston and threatened to kill them if they set foot in the city again. R. S. Longley, "Mob Activities in Revolutionary Massachusetts," *New England Quarterly* 6 (March 1933): 126–28.

[3] Richard Henry Lee had opposed General Schuyler's reinstatement as com-

mander of the northern department. Contrary to Duer's expectation he was reelected as a Virginia delegate in June after he had been omitted from the slate of delegates elected in May. See Richard Henry Lee to Patrick Henry, May 26, note 1; and Duer to Robert R. Livingston, July 9, 1777.

[4] The New York Committee for Detecting Conspiracies, whose proceedings are available in *NYHS Collections,* vols. 57–58 (1924–25).

[5] Possibly Silas Deane's letter to Jay of December 3, 1776. Jay, *Papers* (Morris), 1:325–29.

William Duer to Robert R. Livingston

My dear Friend,   28 May 1777

Like an old Sinner who has deferr'd Repentance, I should almost be afraid to write to you after so long a Silence, if I did not trust that your Lenity would be a powerful Advocate in my favor, more particularly when I can with Truth assure you that my attention has been so engross'd in defeating the Designs of a Mischevious Combination, and in cultivating the Friendship of the Members from the Southern States that I have had little or no Time to write to you as fully as I have wishd.

I have now the Pleasure to inform you that in Spite of all the Arts and Influence made use of by the Eastern Delegates in conjunction with the Members from New Jersey—we have got Genl. Schuyler's Conduct fully justified, and himself reinstated in his Command in the Northern Department in as extensive a Manner as before. There was never I believe a more Difficult Card to play. Genl. Gates had the Address whilst at this Place to insinuate himself into the good Graces of even the honest Part of the House, and the wickedness to poison the Minds of most with Prejudices against Genl. Schuyler, which operated so strongly that nothing but Time and great Temper and address could have dispelled the Mist of Error which had clouded the Eyes even of those who were Friends to the great Cause, and to the State of New York.

His own merit however which they have had an opportunity of seeing, and the all powerful Influence of Truth assisted with Management at length effected all our wishes and we carried the Question upon his being reinstated in his Command in the Northern Department in the following manner.

Affirmative	Negative	
New York	New Hampshire	Delaware
Pensilvania	Massachusetts	Rhode Island
Maryland	Connecticut.	not represented.
Virginia		
North Carolina	Jersey; and	
South Carolina	Georgia divided.	

Dissentient from Virginia *Richard Henry Lee.*[1]

This Division will give you a pretty good general Idea of the political Complexion of the different States. But I must inform you that the Vote of Virginia is rather a Phenomenon, and that the Division of Jersey was owing to the Absence of Mr. Clark, and Mr. Sarjent whose political Line of Conduct lies to the Eastward of Biram's River.[2] Genl. Schuyler will inform you more fully on this Subject.

We shall now have Leisure to pay our Attention to the Matters recommended to us by the Convention, and (to make use of Lord Botetourt's Expression) I augur well of the Event of our Exertions. This you may be assurd of that we have recover'd a full Weight in the Scale of Politicks in this Place.

You will be as sorry to hear, as I am to inform you that a langour of the most alarming Nature prevails in this City and State—principally (from what I can judge) to be imputed to the Dispute about their Government, which rages with more Violence than ever. This City is a Vortex which sucks in the Disaffected, and monopolisers of all the Different States, by whose Acts and Traffic the Continental Money is depocketed far beyond what can possibly be imputed to the Quantity emitted. Unless some Wise and Vigorous Measures are speedily adopted for checking this Evil, I tremble for the Consequences. I entertain no doubt from a Variety of Circumstances but that the Main Plot of the Enemy is to war against the Credit of our Money.

At present unhappily for us they have too fair a Prospect of succeeding. You would be astonished, my dear Freind, at the Lukewarmness shewn by them both in and out of Congress who denominate themselves Whigs on this Subject—for my own Part I feel an Anxiety on the Occasion, which I have never experienced at any Period of this Contest, and so far as the Influence or Attention of an Individual can avail I am determin to exert myself in this important Matter. You will do essential Service to the public, and oblige a Friend in communicating your Ideas on the Means of recovering the Credit of our Money, and establishing Funds for the future Operations of the war. The sooner I can be furnished with your Thoughts the better as I [am] on a Committee for the last mentioned Purpose.[3]

My long Absence from my Private Affairs has thrown them into such Confusion that I cannot without almost ruining myself irreparably be absent from home much longer. I apply by this Opportunity to the Council of Safety for permission to be absent about a Month or 6 weeks, and that Mr. Morris may be orderd to attend.[4] I am very happy that he is returnd; he will do honor and essential Service to the State.

If I obtain Leave of absence, in which I sollicit your Influence, I shall do myself the Pleasure of spending some Days at Claremont. I entreat you to remember me in the most affectionate Manner to all under your Roof, and to beleive me, very Sincerely, Yours,

W Duer

[*P.S.*] As I write in hurry, you must excuse my Incorrectness, and the Heiroglyphics I make use of. I send you several News Papers.

RC (NHi). Addressed: "To The Honble. R. R. Livingston Junr. Esqr. at Kingston."

¹ For a full discussion of Schuyler's case, see Philip Schuyler's Memorial to Congress, May 6, 1777.

² Duer was disparaging Jonathan Dickinson Sergeant's support of New England's interests in Congress—Byram River is near the New York-Connecticut boundary.

³ On May 15 Congress ordered the Board of Treasury to prepare "an estimate of the public expences for the present year" and appointed a committee consisting of Duer, Robert Morris, and John Witherspoon "to devise ways and means for defraying the expences of the present year." The board and the committee submitted a joint report to Congress on June 11, suggesting that Congress meet its financial obligations by drawing bills of exchange on the American commissioners in Paris. Congress intermittently considered this report in the committee of the whole in June, August, and September, and despite the claims of some delegates that this would make America unduly beholden to France and fail to halt the depreciation of Continental currency, it brushed aside these objections and approved the use of this expedient on September 10, 1777. See *JCC*, 7:362, 8:453–57, 480, 648, 652–53, 689, 696–98, 702–3, 706–7, 709, 724–26, 730–31, 743; James Lovell to William Whipple, August 18, and to Oliver Wolcott, August 21; John Adams to James Warren, August 18; and Henry Laurens to John Gervais, September 5, 8, 9, and to John Rutledge, September 10, 1777.

⁴ Duer asked General Schuyler to relay his request for leave of absence to the council of safety, and when no reply from the council was forthcoming he wrote to it directly on June 19. In response the council decided on July 3 to request Duer to delay his return to New York until "the sense of Congress respecting our revolted subjects" in Vermont could be ascertained. Gouverneur Morris, who had been elected a delegate on May 13, did not attend Congress in 1777. See *Journals of N.Y. Prov. Cong.*, 1:981, 985; and Duer to the New York Council of Safety, June 19, 1777.

Secret Committee Minutes of Proceedings

May 28th. 1777

Come. met. Present Morris, Lee, Whipple, Lewis, Levingston. Rt. Bridges, Elias Boys, & Fergus McIlvaine owners of the ship Liberty, produced their Acct. for hire & valuation of sd. ship (She being taken by the enemy as appears by protest)—ballance due them per sd. Acct. £7003.10.0. The Come. on considerg the same agreed to pay 12000 dlls. in part, until they can be furnished with particular Accts. of the Monies advanced by their Agents, to the Capn. abroad. Accordingy.

an order was drawn for that sum, on the Auditr. genl. in favr. sd.
Owners. In consequence of a letter from Messrs. Hewes & Smith of
Edinton, datd. 20th March last to Robt. Morris Esqr. The Come. have
agreed to ensure the value of the Brige. Patty wch. they mention in
sd. letter to have purchased & loaded on public Acct. for Nantes, at
the Sum She cost, viz: 8,500 dlls for the voyage & to take sd vessel at
the above sum & allow a Comn. for purchasg. & pay any charges that
may have accrued. Bill of Exchange drawn by Messrs. Clarkson &
Dorsius of Charles-town, S. Carolina dated 29th March last favr Jas.
Nelson or order on Mr. Morris as Chairman of this Come. for
£5712.12.0 Peny. Curry was presented & an order drawn by the
Presidt. of Congress on the L. Officer of this State in favor of Jabez
Perkins for 15,233 54/90 dlls to be pd. in Certificates being amt. of
sd. Bill.

MS (MH–H).

William Whipple to Josiah Bartlett

Dear Sir,   Philadelphia 28th May 1777
    Your favor of the 9th inst came to hand Yesterday.[1] I am extreamly
sorry you shod be under the necessaty of filling up the Regiments with
eight & twelve months men as it appears to me there will always be a
difficulty in replacing them. I can conceive of no reason for an abatement in the spirits of the People unless it is that those miscreants who
are aiming at the distruction of their Country, are not treated with that
just severity which their Crimes deserve. What purpose will it answer
to fill the Goals? These Villains have all friend, & while they remain
with you 'tho they are in Goal they will be raising their parties, whereas
if they are under Ground or out of the Country they will soon be forgot. The necessaty of the Case will surely justify the most severe &
decisive measures, I am always for persueing lenitive measures, when
such will answer the purpose, but experience has tought us others must
be adopted.
    I am fully sensible of the necessaty you are under of a supply of
Military stores & shall do everything in My power to obtain them.
    I wish to know what Concurrent circumstances leed you to appre-
hend a speedy attackt. The Enemy certainly have no troops to spare
from N. York; nor can they have a considerable reinforcement from
Europe very soon, however there is no doubt its best to be prepared at
all points for which purpose the most Vigorous exertions shod be use'd.
It will by no means do to dispond because a few scatering Clouds pass
between us & the sun, proper Exertion will soon dispel them. We shod
never suffer Gloomy reflections to incomber the path, but look forward

to the Glorious prize, with a determination to obtain it, and all those difficulties that a Gloomy mind wod deem insupportable will be meer mushroons. As we get over difficulties no doubt new one will start up, but Pacience, & Vigorous persevereince will surmount them all. I wish I had some good news to send you to Chear you up, however I hope to bring you some shortly as I shall leave this so soon as I can get some necessary matters settled in Naval department, which (to my Grief) is not on so respectable a footing as I coud wish.

Our army is daily increasing. There is a report that a Lieut Col Walcot was kill'd on the retreat of the Enemy from Denbury, & that Govr, alias Major Genl. *Tryon* who commanded that notable Expedition, is dead of the wounds he receiv'd there.

I shod send you some new papers but have none by me & as the post hour is arriv'd have not time to send for any, must therefore bid you Adieu after assuring you that I am Sincerely Your Friend &c

                                                            Wm. Whipple

RC (NhD).
[1] Bartlett's May 9 letter to Whipple is in the Josiah Bartlett Papers, microfilm, NhHi.

Thomas Burke's Draft Address to the Inhabitants of the United States

Friends and fellow Citizens   [ante May 29, 1777][1]
We your Delegates in Congress address you at this Period in order to give you a Just Notion of your affairs and of the Exertions Necessary for compleating your Freedom and Happiness.

Our Enemy are unwearied in their Endeavours to seduce you from that honest and virtuous firmness wherewith you have united against their Usurpations. They pretend that your resistance do's not arise from a Sense of Violence done to your Rights, but from a Delusion into which you have been lead by Some designing men whose purpose is only to set up an Independant Dominion that they themselves may enjoy the supreme Power.

These Suggestions your own Experience can best refute, to you it is best known that they are false and Groundless, and every honest unprejudiced man will be convinced of it from a short View of the progress of the Contest.

The British Parliament expressly declared that they had and of Right ought to have Power to bind the Inhabitants of America in all Cases whatsoever. They proceeded to the Exercise of such Power by laying Taxes to be paid in America, and they Instituted arbitrary Courts supported by Military Force to Compel Obedience. This Tax, confessedly, was not laid for the Value of the revenue, but to form a precedent for exercising the Power when and to what Extent they pleased.

The Representatives of the People in their general Assemblies Complained of those Doings as violating the Rights of their Constituents. They knew it was their distinguished Privilege to give and grant their own Money, and to Consent to all Laws which they were bound to obey.

Soon as the Governors perceived the Assemblies were in Deliberation on this Subject they dissolved them. Other Representatives were chozen and those Extravagant Usurpations Still presented themselves as the greatest Grievance. When they entered on the Consideration of them they were again dissolved. This mode was pursued until the People every where became Sensible that no Opportunity would be given them ever to Complain. Necessity pointed out to them that they must have recourse to other Methods of representing their wrongs and requiring redress. Nature pointed out to them the mode they Adopted, and they were so reluctant to do any thing which might even appear a Deviation from Established Form, that they long forbore assembling in Towns and Counties and did not at length yield to the Necessity until they found every hope of redress any other way was lost.

When obliged to take this first Step the People proceeded with the utmost Caution. No tumult or disorder appeared, every man was impressed with an awful Sense of the Necessity he was under of Exercising that Right which Nature gave to every Man, and which the British Constitution expressly Assented, that of Consulting and resolving Concerning his Safety and Happiness, and each was determined to Exercise it no farther than the Necessity pressingly required.

In the most humble manner they declared their attachment to the Established Government, and even affection to the person of the Prince, they Complained of Wrongs which they modestly supposed to have arisen from no ill Intention or design in the Prince or Parliament, and they determined to Communicate their Sentiments to their Neighbors in Conventions of representatives Chosen and Instructed for this purpose. The same Necessity pressing at the Same time in every Colony, the same Sense of Wrong being every where felt, and Simple Nature every where Suggesting the same Expedient the meetings were every where held nearly at the same time, and they produced Conventions nearly at the Same time in every one of the present United States. Instructions from the People were nearly the Same in every Town and County, and they all Breathed ⟨nearly⟩ the same Spirit of humility, Moderation and Loyalty. All pointed out the Propriety of a Common Communication between the Different Colonies, and of Joint Supplications to the Throne for redress of Wrongs and Protection from Usurpations.

This produced the first Congress, and that Congress Confined itself entirely to Stating the Grievances of the People of America, Peti-[ti]oning the King for a redress of them, professing the most Loyal humility and recommending Frugality and A Suspension of Commerce, unless within a Certain time the Wrongs should be redressed.

It is fresh in every Ones Memory that their Petition was treated with the most Insulting Contempt. That another Congress Still fondly holding by the Hope that Britain would forego her unjust Claims and Harmony be Restored, most humbly entreated the King to point out Some Method by which the Complaints of America might find their way to him without offending him, but to this Petition, the lowest Condescention to which a free People ever Stooped, was refused even an Answer. This humiliating Measure which Nothing but the Extream reluctance of the People of America to seperate from Britain can Account for or Justify was as fruitless as every other, and Acts of Parliament were made to subject the persons and Properties of Americans every where to Military plunder and Execution. Regular Bands of Soldiers were marched into the Country under their officers to deal Hostile Murders and Ravages around them. A formidable Naval Force was employed to hinder the Commerce of populous Cities and thereby to reduce the poor Inhabitants to Wretchedness, and even to prevent their availing themselves of the Food which the Sea Washing their own Coasts afforded to their Industry—and it was expressly declared that no Mitigation of those violences could be obtained but by Submitting without Condition to the absolute Will of the Parliament of Great Britain, a Body composed of men unknown to and unchozen by the Inhabitants of America, and who showed but too little regard to the Rights of their own Constituents, and of human Nature.

The Conduct of the British Court towards the Americans in the repeated dissolutions of their Assemblies whenever they attempted to Complain, in disregarding their Complaints when offered in the most humble and supplicating Manner by their Representatives in Congress, in refusing even to point out a Mode whereby they might find an Inoffensive passage to the Royal Ear, in disregarding all Rules of Justice and humanity by Subjecting their persons and Properties to Military Violence and Endeavouring even to Starve them, and by denying any Mitigation of those Enormities, Unless absolute Submission Should be made, this Conduct of the B[ritish] C[ourt] left no room to doubt that they considered the Americans as objects merely of Dominion not of Government, of Plunder not of Protection, of Military Tyranny not of Legal administration of Justice. No choice was left but to Oppose Arms to Arms, or submit to the absolute dominion of Men whose pride and Cruelty is incurrable, and whose rapacity is without Bounds. No alternative was left to the Citizen but to rouse into a Soldier or Sink into a Slave and entail Servitude Irrevocably on his posterity.

Yet even after this altho the People of America Could not Hesitate to take Arms, they kept in view their much loved Constitutional Connection with Britain, and altho they knew that when Protection was denied them, and they were driven to arms for their Safety, all relation between them and the Crown of Britain was dissolved, yet they chose to overlook this, and so long as any Hope remained of obtaining it on Just and reasonable Grounds to leave every possible Avenue open to reconciliation, nor did they forego this pleasing tho Imaginary prospect until they found that Britain was arming Slaves, Savages, and foreign Mercenaries against them and that she was totally regardless of their sufferings and Intent only on Subduing them to absolute Slavery. It now became Folly to indulge any Hope of Reconciliation. The Americans were universally Sensible that in all her progress Britain was determined to Establish over them an unlimitted Tyranny, that nothing less would Satisfy her ambition, and to Effect this She would Not Scruple to Expose them to the Undistinguishing Plunder and Massacres of Slaves, Indians, and more unfeeling Mercenary Soldiers. All Connection with Britain became impossible Except as Slaves without Right or property, but what must be held at the Precarious Will and pleasure of her Ministers.[2] Reconciliation became the same thing as Slavery, Independence the same thing as Freedom. Independance was not the voluntary choice of America but the Alternative which she prefered to Servitude, for no other Choice but one of them was left.

Every Man in America knows that during the whole Progress until the Declaration of Independance Britain might have disarmed America and made her perfectly Happy by recalling her Fleets and armies, renouncing her claims to absolute Dominion and declaring she would be Satisfied with regulating Commerce. That the Declaration of Independance was adopted at length as a Measure of Necessity to which Britain herself had driven America, and every Man of Common Sense and Honesty must be convinced it is Necessary to maintain it. Because to give it up would be to Sink into the most abject Slavery to a People who have given the most convincing Proofs that they regard us only as objects of their rapine; whose Policy it must be to keep us always poor, dejected and oppressed in order to Subdue our Spirit of Resistance to their Tyranny and to blot out even the Memory of that Liberty which Animates us at present to defend our Rights under so many disadvantages. Even to suspend it would deprive us of the Confidence of Foreign Powers, and Consequently of their Friendship and assistance. Thus Britain could she prevail in this would deprive us of every prospect of Support and might pursue her purpose of enslaving us without danger of any Effectual resistance, and we should be deprived of every resource which enables us to make a stand for our Liberties.

In short it is manifest that from the Begining Britain has pursued a purpose of making the People of America Submit to her absolute

Dominion, and regardless of Right, Justice and humanity, has employed means the most destructive and Calamitous.

On the other Hand America has Supplicated with the most humble Voice and manner of Complaint, have prayed with most Submissive humility for Peace, Liberty and Safety, but in vain, and at length when forced to take Arms for self-preservation She raised them with reluctance against Britain even in Defence of her own Bosom, and at length unwillingly seperated altho she plainly saw that any further Connection must involve her in Circumstances worse than utter Perdition.

To maintain this Seperation is to maintain the Religion, Liberty and Property of ourselves and our Posterity, to renounce it is to Sink into the lowest meanness and Slavery.

May God remove every such thought from every American Breast! Welcome first the Life of the most uncivilized Savages! Welcome Death itself and everlasting Oblivion to our race!

Your own Experience, Fellow Citizens, will best bear Testimony to the Truth of the Facts here set forth. Your own Experience can best prove the Falshood of the Suggestion that you are deluded by Individuals who aim at Nothing but Power. You know how little Influence Individuals have over you. You know that every Man trusted or Employed by you is a creature of your free Choice, and by every choice you make and every act you do you manifest that you feel you are Sovereign and supreme, and Influenced by Nothing but a Conviction that you ought to be free, a Determined Resolution to remain so and to transmit freedom unimpaired to your Children. You well know that you Command Your Servants to Execute Certain Duties which tho arduous and dangerous they think they ought not to refuse because every Citizen is devoted to his Country, and ought Serve on such Duty as his Country shall think proper to require.

It is not Strange that our Enemies should have fallen at first into this Error, accustomed to a Country where only the Shadow of Liberty remains to the People, where Multitudes know no more of freedom than the Liberty of following their choice of *leaders,* where the most groce [gross] and wicked artifices are every day practiced in order to acquire Power and trust to Individuals who afterwards abuse them, to the purposes of avarice and Luxury, where the People in short are Considered as fit for Nothing but to toil that men of high birth and Fortune may ⟨riot on what⟩ live in Ease and Splender.. Accustomed to this it is not surprising they should expect to find the Same in America. They know not the Plenty which the fruitful Soil of America yields to the Hand which gives it Cultivation, that penury and oppressive Landlords are here equally unknown, that Americans undebauched by Luxury have few wants and these few are always supply'd by a chearful and Laborious Industry, that wanting nothing they have nothing to

Hope from Individuals, and no Individuals having Power or Inclination to hurt they have nothing from Individuals to fear. That each man has Leisure to Search out and understand what are his rights and that none Can Comprehend any reason why they should be given up to the absolute will of another. In Such a state as this no One is in a Situation to delude or be deluded, and the People of America well know that it is their State, altho of such the present race of Men in Britain have no Experience. But it is not to be believed that they Still Continue in this Error. They have Seen the People change their Servants frequently since they were compelled to take arms for their Defence, and yet the resistance has rather increased upon every change. They have seen the People in every State Erect Governments by their Sovereign authority, and in these Governments take special care that no Individuals should ever acquire any Influence over them. They have met with one Common Spirit of resistance every where in America, and that Spirit actuated the People without Distinction. This must undoubtedly have Convinced them long before this that the Americans are all apprehensive of Danger from the same Object and are Influenced by nothing but that Common Apprehension, and a firm resolution to meet it with Effectual Opposition.

But altho they cannot believe it they make use of it as an Engine wherewith to deceive the timorous and unwary amongst us. They put it as an argument into the mouths of their Emissaries, and Such Inhabitants of America, as are insensible of the Blessings of Freedom, Such as are unfeeling and mean spirited enough to prefer their present ease and oppulence to the Happiness of Milions now living and of Myriads yet unborn, Such as have wickedly determined for the Hopes of private advantages to assist in enslaving the Country which gave them birth, or Support, or altered them by the pleasing prospect of Liberty and plenty, Such endeavour to avail themselves of it, to excuse their Indolence, their selfishness or their Criminal Endeavours.[3] We flatter ourselves their are few of our fellow Citizens who answer this description, but we are sorry to find there are Some, and we warn you against all who use these arguments to you. Every Man who uses them is himself convinced of their falshood, and every Man to whom they are used need but apply one moment to his own Experience to refute them. We advise you therefore to Consider all such as men who wish you to Submit to the absolute Will of a People whose rapine as appears by their Treatment of Ireland and the East Indies can never be Satisfied, as long as the most Cruel Violence can Extort any thing from you.[4]

The War in which we are engaged for the defence of the Liberty Religion, and property of ourselves and our Posterity was begun under every disadvantage which a brave and virtuous People could struggle with. A powerfull and warlike oppressor whose Numbers of Inhabitants and boundless Commerce render her resources infinite and inexhaustable, with armies disciplined and officers Experienced, with a Fleet in every respect the Dread and Envy of the World—on our part Inexperience, ⟨want of Numbers,⟩ want of Commerce, of warlike stores and even of ⟨arms⟩, and of every resource but an Inextinguishable Love of Liberty and a Confidence in the Justice of Divine Providence. In this Situation were we opposed to that Power which a few years ago Shook the most formidable Monarchies in Europe and carried Terror all over the World, ⟨and who ungenerously as well as unjustly relying on her Superior Force insisted on binding us in all Cases whatever without our Consent, and on binding us to an absolute Submission to the Will and pleasure of her Corrupt and venal Ministers⟩. Not detered by such Disadvantages, nor despairing of Divine aid and Protection the Virtuous Inhabitants of America determined ⟨without Hesitation⟩ to resist all attempts to enforce such unjust and extravagant Claims, and to maintain that Freedom which Heaven had originally bestowed on Mankind, and which their Ancestors had wrested from the Hands of usurping Tyrants, and rendering it more valuable by their Blood shed in its defence transmitted Improved to their Posterity, chusing rather to trust to the Issue of any War however callamitous, than to the boundless and Insatiable rapine of Ministers who had a whole People once great and Free to corrupt, and Consequently Innumerable Minions to employ, whose avarice or Luxury must be Satiated with the plunder extorted from the Industrious Poor in America. The Events of the War hitherto have justified our Trust in Divine Providence, and prove to us that an all wise and beneficent God will never forsake men who have virtue enough to Struggle for those Blessings which he has bestowed upon them, and who will rely on his Protection against all superiority of worldly Power, for, our unfeeling Enemy, tho possessed of the advantages of superior Force, Discipline and Experience, and employing every Engine of Fraud and violence in a three years War have acquired only one City and a small Teritory round it which by reason of their superiority in shipping could not be defended and they have been baffled in every ⟨Considerable Enterprize⟩ attempt to Penetrate into the Country whether from Canada or the Sea. They have been forced to fly from Boston, and have been repelled and defeated with disgrace at Charlestown, and their Efforts against Virginia, North and South Carolina, either by Invasion from the Sea, by Inroads which they procured the Savage Indians to make on Western Frontiers or the Insurrections Excited by them among the Slaves, the Ignorant Highlanders, and disaffected Tories have been all repelled and suppressed, with little Damage to us; but with Irreparable Ruin to their Instruments. Their attempts against Pennsylvania were rendered abortive, their Troops defeated, and Captivated, and their Generals forced to retreat in order to save the remains of their army from utter destruction, altho this Enterprize was undertaken under the Conduct of their most experienced officers, with a numerous, well disciplined and well appointed army at a time when we had but few Troops, and these Few under every disadvantage. This Happy event was produced by the Superior Skill and Sagacity of our Commander in Chief, by the Indefatigable perseverance and Intrepidity of our fellow Citizens who composed the army under his Command great part of which consisted of the Militia of Philadelphia, and other parts of Pennsylvania, Jersey and Maryland, and above all by the peculiar Interposition of Divine Providence. Ever Since they have been confined to Straight Quarter and never attempted to pass without them but they are repulsed defeated or taken Prisoners.

The Campaign is now nearly ready to open. We have large Supplies of Arms and Military Stores, we have large Magazines of Provisions, and our Country abounds in plenty, for among other marks of Divine favor Heaven has blessed us with Extraordinary fruitfulness. Your Delegates in Congress have provided a liberal, and they Hope useful Establishment for the assistance and care of all who during the Course of the War may be afflicted with Wounds or diseases and are taking every precaution to preserve the Health of their fellow Citizens who must form the armies. Nothing is now wanting but the Zealous Exertions of our brave fellow Citizens to Compleat our armies, and to man our Navy, and to watch, detect, and suppress the Tories amongst us with Spirit and Vigilence.

For these purpose[s] we Exhort you every where to use every Effort for recruiting the Battalions from our brave and Magnanimous Youth, to whom must be due the Glory of Freeing their Country from Oppression, and bestowing Liberty and Happiness on their Families to be transmitted to future ages in a bright and improving Succession, to Apprehend all Deserters who not only disgrace themselves by quitting so Noble a Conflict, but Rob you of the Monies which have been advanced to them, to Seize and bring to legal punishment all who Endeavour to deceive any men into a Belief that they ought to Submit to the absolute Dominion of Britain or to renounce that Independance which alone can Secure us from it, in a Word to Employ the most vigorous and Zealous Vigilence in Executing the Laws Enacted by every State upon Offenders against the public cause. We have the Strongest Confidence that the men You entrust with the Power of making Laws will provide such as will be Competent to every desirable purpose, and we assure you that we shall not remit the greatest care, attention and Vigor in discharging the Duties you have Enjoyned us to perform.[5]

May the all bountiful, Merciful, and Gracious God enable us to Conclude the War in a short time, and with as little Misery to Mankind as possible, and so may he prosper our Endeavours as he knows our Intentions are void of ambition, and of every Motive but that of

Securing those Blessings which we derive from him as the Great and bountiful Father of Mankind. We hope Fellow Citizens that your Virtue and Piety will always merit his Divine Protection, and we humbly beseech him to make you the Care of his All righteous Providence.

MS (Nc–Ar). In the hand of Thomas Burke and endorsed by him: "Rough [*draft*] of an address to the People drawn when member of Congress in 1777."

¹ In order to mobilize popular support for the forthcoming campaign, Congress appointed Burke, William Duer, and James Wilson on April 30 "to prepare an address to the inhabitants of the thirteen United States, on the present situation of public affairs." On May 29 the committee submitted a draft address to Congress, written by Wilson and containing marginal comments by Burke, which reviewed the controversy between America and Great Britain and exhorted the American people to defend their rights vigorously against British tyranny. Congress read the address but took no further action on it. There is no explanation in the journals or in the delegates' surviving correspondence of Congress' failure to approve the address, but Wilson's bombastic style and occasional lack of clarity may have convinced many delegates that his work was unsuited for a popular audience. This conclusion is suggested by a marginal comment Burke made about Wilson's justification of the adoption of the Declaration of Independence: "This does not enter my Mind with sufficient force, clearness and Simplicity, neither the reasoning or motive is full, satisfactory or conclusive." PCC, item 24, fols. 233–39; and *JCC*, 7:314, 8:397–404. Burke's remark is reminiscent of Congress' reaction to one of Wilson's earlier literary efforts, for in February 1776 it had rejected his proposed address to the colonies on the grounds that it was "very long, badly written & full against Independence." See Richard Smith's Diary, February 13, 1776.

Burke doubtless drafted the address printed here sometime between his appointment to the committee on April 30 and the submission of Wilson's address to Congress on May 29. Burke's address differs greatly in content and style from Wilson's and a careful comparison of the two fails to reveal any influence by Burke on Wilson's work. As there is no known testimony of the three committee members about their work, it is impossible to determine why they preferred Wilson's draft to Burke's, which is in many respects a more vigorous statement.

² On a detached sheet Burke wrote what might be a variant draft of the preceding sentence: "By this the Political union between you and Great Britain was dissolved, and because you would not be slaves you were not suffered to be subjects."

³ After this sentence in the MS Burke first wrote and then deleted: "of all such we warn you to beware."

⁴ At this point Burke apparently decided to discontinue the present draft and start afresh. On the next MS page he first drew up an outline for a new draft—"1. General Situation of affairs. 2. Suggestions of the Enemy's Arts. 3. Cautions and Incentives—[traitors?], Deserters. Trace the Steps leading to Indepen[den]ce and Shew the Necessity of Defending that in order to prevent the claims of our Enemies"—and then wrote a salutation and paragraph identical to the opening of the present address. After this, however, he deleted both the outline and opening paragraph and resumed writing his original draft.

⁵ On a detached sheet Burke wrote a sentence that might have been intended for insertion near the end of this paragraph: "We advise you to be dilligent in bringing all such men to the Chastisement provided by Law for their Offenses, and Suppress and disappoint their Endeavours as you would prevent your Enemy from gaining an advantage over you."

Committee of Congress to Joseph Trumbull

29th May 1777

In Consequence of the preceding Resolution we request the favor of you to furnish us with the Papers therein mentiond.[1]

We are Sir, with due Respect, Your Obedt. Hble. Servt.

Wm. Duer

A. Middleton

RC (Ct.) Written by Duer and signed by Duer and Middleton.

[1] This note was written at the foot of a page below a resolution of this date appointing Duer, Middleton, and Thomas Burke as a committee to estimate the number of teams needed to carry supplies to Washington's army and calling upon Commissary Trumbull to provide them with "a particular state of all the magazines of provisions already laid up." *JCC,* 8:395.

William Paca to the Maryland Governor
and Council

Gentn.   Philad. 24.[29?] May 1777[1]

We were much disappointed in our Excursion on Saturday last. The Enemy would not come up, they lie still low down the river.

We have no Intelligence from Camp other than that Genl. Washington has moved to Boundbrooke and there encamped. There was a firing heard yesterday Morning, we suppose a Skirmish at the outposts.

I shall write you by every Post for I take it for granted you are anxious to be informed of every Event. Tryon it is said and the Impertinent Lieut. Col. Walcot are both dead of the wounds they got in the Danbury Affair.

I am Gent., yr. most obd. hble Set.   W Paca

RC (MdAA).

[1] Although Paca clearly dated this letter "24 May 1777," it was obviously written at a later time. The reference to "our Excursion on Saturday last" is to an event that occurred on the 24th; and General Washington's move to Boundbrook, mentioned in Paca's second paragraph, was explained in Washington's letters of May 28 to President Hancock and to Robert Morris, the first of which was read in Congress on the 29th. See William Paca to the Maryland Governor and Council, May 24, 1777; Washington, *Writings* (Fitzpatrick), 8:131–34, 134n.16; and *JCC,* 8:395. For another letter Paca misdated May 24, see his letter to the Maryland governor and council printed under the date May 27.

Board of War to George Washington

Sir   War Office May 30th. 1777

By Order of the Board I do myself the Honour of troubling your Excellency for Information on the Subject of our Prisoners who are with the Enemy. I am directed to enquire whether a Commissary has been sent in to supply them or in what Situation that Business now is & what Steps have been taken which have fallen within your Observation for the Relief of their Wants. The Board are desirous of collecting every necessary Information that they may be enabled to form a proper Judgment of that Part of General Howe's Letter which as they apprehend groundlessly throws upon Congress an Imputation of Neglect of proper Attention to their Officers & Soldiers in Captivity.[1]

The enclosed Letter from Genl Forman I am directed to transmitt to your Excellency as the best Judge of the Expediency of the Measure therein recommended.[2] Should you approve of it the Board will endeavour to comply with the Request.

The Board have been frequently applied to by Complainants against a certain Captain John Doyle of an independent Company raised in this State who is indebted but every where for almost all the Necessaries with which his Company were supplied. Enclosed is a Letter from a Gentleman to whom he owes a large Sum to pay which he has received Money from the Treasury. If this be not an Object unworthy of your Attention amidst your present more important Concerns it would be well to weed out of the Army a Person who has conducted himself so unbecoming the Character of a Gentleman & a Soldier. I have the Honour to be with the greatest Respect, Your very obedt & most humble Servt,   Richard Peters Secy

RC (DLC).

[1] Apparently Peters is referring to Gen. William Howe's May 22 letter to Washington in which he complained about the mistreatment Col. Archibald Campbell was suffering during his imprisonment in Massachusetts. Although Congress had more than two months before ordered better treatment for Campbell, who was being held as a hostage to guarantee good British treatment of Gen. Charles Lee, Howe was still dissatisfied with the conduct of the Massachusetts authorities. In response, Congress ordered Washington on June 10 to inform Howe that it "most sincerely laments the necessity to which they are driven by the cruel policy of their enemies, of entering into any resolutions which have any appearance of severity towards those prisoners of war who have fallen or may fall into our hands; but, there are not other means in our power of inducing our enemies to respect the rights of humanity." See JCC, 8:449–50; Washington, Writings (Fitzpatrick), 8:131–33; Howe to Washington, May 22, Washington Papers, DLC; and John Hancock to the Massachusetts Council, March 26, 1777.

[2] Brig. Gen. David Forman's May 27 letter to the Board of War, a copy of which is in Washington Papers, DLC, asked for some artillery pieces so that he could prevent British incursions into Sandy Hook. Washington declared in a

June 6 reply to the board that the artillery Forman requested would not "be of the least Service in his Situation." Washington, *Writings* (Fitzpatrick), 8:191.

Charles Carroll of Carrollton to Charles Carroll, Sr.

Dr. Papa,   Pha. 30th May 1777

We have a report that G. Mathews of the Guards was killed by the canonading last Monday. You will see some mention of this affair in the inclosed newspaper. Last night G. Arnold received a letter from G. Sullivan giving an account that two of the enemy's vessels, which have been cut down & turned into floating batteries had sailed from N. York & steared to the southward, from which circumstances I apprehend the enemy meditate an attack on this city. Tho I am persuaded they will not attempt it till they receive reinforcements from Europe. Part of their forces from Rhode Island have sailed to join G. Howe, who seems to be collecting his army together. The vessels above mentioned mount each 32 guns 24 & 18 pounders. Let me know all the occurrences in Maryd. We have no news of a late date from Tionderoga. G. Schuyler went off yesterday to take the command of the army in the northern department. My love to Molly, Mrs. Darnall & the little ones. God grant you health & a long enjoyment of it. I am, Yr. affectionate Son,

Ch. Carroll of Carrollton

RC (MdHi).

Committee for Foreign Affairs to the Commissioners at Paris

Philadelphia May 30th. 1777

We have delayed sending this Packet from a daily expectation of hearing from you, as some letters from France make mention of a quick sailing Vessel by [*which*] we were to receive despatches. Tho' it must be agreeable to you to hear frequently from us, yet as our letters by being taken might be of worse Consequence than being delayed, We are desirous of waiting for the safest opportunity, and when you hear not so often as you wish; remember, our Silence means our Safety. Acquainted as we are with the Situation and Condition of the Enemy, we well know, that the pompous Paragraphs in the London papers, are not the News which the Ministry *hear from* their Army but the News they *make for* them.

The Amphitrite is safely arrived at Portsmouth N. Hampshire. The Seine at Martinique, but is made a Prize of on her Passage from thence. We request you to expedite the Loan of Two Millions (which we have already sent you a commission for and now send you a duplicate of the same) for tho' we conceive the Credit of America to be as well founded at least as any in the world, having neither Debt nor Taxes on her Back when she began the War, yet she represents a Man who with a Vast Capital all in Property is unable to make new Purchases till he can either convert some of it into Specie, or borrow from hand to mouth in the mean Time. Britain is now fighting us, and the Greatest part of Europe negatively, by endeavouring to stop that Trade from us, to France, Spain &c which She has most effectually lost to herself, & we wish those Courts saw their Interest in the same Clear point of View, which it appears to us. We have little or no doubt of being able to reduce the Enemy by Land and we likewise believe that the united Powers of France, Spain and America would be able totally to expel the British fleet from the western Seas, by which the Communication for Trade would be openned, the Number of Interests reduced which have hitherto distracted the West Indies, and Consequently the Peace of all this Side the Globe put on a better foundation than it has yet ever been a Mutual Advantage as we Conceive to France, Spain and these States.

That Britain was formidable in the West Indies last War is true, but when it is Considered that her power there arose from her Possessions here or that she was formidable chiefly thro' us it is impossible to suppose that she can again arrive to the same pitch. Here she was assisted by Numberless Privateers—Here she supplied and partly manned her Navy, recruited and almost raised her Army for that service, in short, America last War represented Britain removed to this side the Atlantic. The scene is changed, and America now, is that to France and Spain, in point of Advantage, which she last War was to Britain. Therefore putting the Convenience which we might receive out of the Question, by their making an Attack on the West Indies, We are somewhat surprised that such Political Courts as France and Spain should Hesitate on a Measure so alluring and Practicable. We do not mention these Remarks because we suppose they do not occur to you, but to let you know *our* thoughts on the matter, and to give you every advantage by conveying our minds to you as well as our Instructions or Informations.

This Packet brings you compleat Setts of the Philadelphia News Papers filed in order for 17 Weeks, to which we refer you for account of little skirmishes &c.

We are Gentlemen, yr Obt. Hble Servts,

Benja Harrison	Jno Witherspoon
Robt Morris	Thos. Heyward Junr.
	James Lovell

RC (PPAmP). In the hand of Witherspoon and signed by Witherspoon, Harrison, Heyward, Lovell, and Morris. The FC in PCC, item 79, 1:61–64, is signed by Richard Henry Lee, Harrison, Heyward, and Lovell, but not by Morris or Witherspoon.

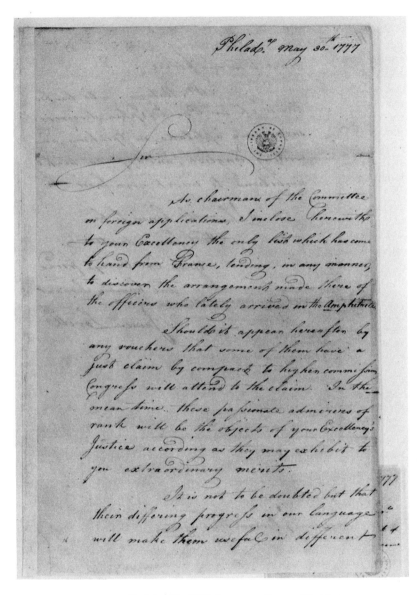

Philad.ª May 30. 1777

Sir

As chairman of the Committee on foreign applications, I inclose herewith to your Excellency the only list which has come to hand from France, tending, in any manner, to discover the arrangements made there of the officers who lately arrived in the Amphitrite.

Should it appear hereafter by any vouchers that some of them have a just claim by compact to higher commissions Congress will attend to the claim. In the mean time these passionate admirers of rank will be the objects of your Excellency's Justice according as they may exhibit to you extraordinary merits.

It is not to be doubted but that their differing progress in our language will make them useful in different

James Lovell's May 30, 1777, Letter to George Washington

James Lovell to George Washington

Sir   Philada. May 30th. 1777

As Chairman of the Committee on foreign applications, I inclose herewith to your Excellency the only list which has come to hand from France, tending, in any manner, to discover the arrangement made there of the officers who lately arrived in the Amphitrite.[1]

Should it appear hereafter by any vouchers that some of them have a just claim by compact to higher commissions Congress will attend to the claim. In the mean time these passionate admirers of rank will be the objects of your Excellency's Justice according as they may exhibit to you extraordinary merits.

It is not to be doubted but that their differing progress in our language will make them useful in different degrees in our service.

Mr. Maligny who has been this week in Philadelphia discovers a surprising aptitude in speaking and writing English, and appears highly ambitous to merit your favor.

I have the honor to be, With sincere devotion, Your Excellency's friend and humble Servant,   James Lovell

RC (DLC).
[1] This list of French officers, headed by Thomas Conway, is in the Washington Papers, DLC. Reports of the Committee on Foreign Applications dealing with several of the men on the list, including Conway and Louis, marquis de Fleury, are in PCC, item 25, fols. 10–17. Washington's June 6 response to Lovell is in Washington, *Writings* (Fitzpatrick), 8:193–94.

Richard Henry Lee to Arthur Lee

May 31st. [1777]

Since the above, the events of war have not been considerable. The Enemy, with about 2000 Men from N. York pushed up the Sound by water, and made a forced March thro a small part of Connecticut to surprise & destroy a Magazine of provisions laid up there for our Army. They succeeded in destroying about 1700 barrels of Salted Meat & some grain, with about 1000 barrels of flour. However, the Militia assembled quickly as possible under command of Generals Wooster & Arnold to the number of about 1500 and attacked the enemy as they were retreating to their Ships where with great difficulty, and much loss, they at length arrived. We learn that this trip has lessened their numbers at least 500. Among the wounded and since dead we are told they count Majr. General Govern. Tryon and a Colonel Wolcot. The loss of provisions has been amply made up to us by the Privateers who have taken 5000 barrels of Salted provisions coming to N. York from

Europe. In a variety of skirmishes lately we have beaten them, and in some of these, their best Troops have been foiled. By this opportunity Congress sends you a particular Commission as their Representative at the Court of Spain.[1] In my judgement, and it is an opinion founded on the most accurate information, the Independence, and security of N. America, cannot be said to be certain until an Alliance with Spain & France is procured, and in consequence, the British Arms, and Arts not solely employed for our ruin. You may be assured that this is of infinite consequence to your Country and therefore you will conduct yourself accordingly. And for the assistance of our finance, an extensive loan is indispensable. If any untoward accident should have befallen our brother the alderman, in which case I have desired my letters to him to be sent you for your perusal, the management of my boys must rest entirely with you and in that case, at all events, you will see the necessity of sending them both immediately to me.

Farewell my dear Brother.   Richard Henry Lee

P.S. It will be of great consequence that I hear from you frequently & fully. If your letters come anywhere to the Northward of Virginia, or if they go by the West Indies, let them be directed to the care of our brother Doctor Shippen in Philadelphia.   R.H.L.

I believe Tryon is not dead and we have not heard more of Colo Wolcot.

1. Letr to Committee March 8th
2. March 16th
3. March 29th
4. April 8
5. April 19

RC (ViU). A continuation of Richard Henry Lee to Arthur Lee, April 20, 1777.
[1] Although a draft of Arthur Lee's commission was read in Congress this day, it was not approved until June 5. *JCC,* 8:409, 420.

New York Delegates to the New York Council of Safety

Sir,   Philada. 31st May, 1777.

We transmit you the resolution of Congress, of 23rd May, 1777, relative to the manning and fitting out two galleys for the defence of the North river.[1] We wish that Mr. Morris who was desired by Convention to write on this subject, had transmitted his letter to the board of war through us, as we then should have been able (in all probability) to have obtained a resolution for fitting those gallies at the Continental expense.[2] For want of previous information, the resolution enclosed was passed without that attention which might otherwise have been paid to it.

We by no means are of opinion that there is any similarity betwixt the State of New-York and other States who have fitted out vessels of this nature.

The use of these vessels in Hudson's river is chiefly to protect the chain near the forts in the Highlands, and by that means keep up the communication betwixt the southern and eastern States. In other States they have been built for the purpose of protecting their own harbours and towns. The purpose, therefore, for which the vessels on Hudson's river are intended, being Continental, the expense ought, in our opinion, to be the same.

If the Council of Safety should be of the same opinion with us, and write to Congress on this subject, we shall procure a reconsideration of this resolution, and exert ourselves to make the fitting and manning these vessels a Continental charge. In the mean time, we think it will be for the interest and safety of the State to exert themselves in equipping and manning these vessels with the utmost despatch.[3]

We are directed by Mr. Lewis to inform you that the accounts of the sloop Montgomery will be forwarded in two or three days, together with the share of prize money due to the captors.[4]

We are, sir, with great respect, Your obedt. hble. servts.

Phil Livingston,

Wm. Duer.

P.S. Capt. Cook having no money to carry him out of town, we have furnished him with a loan of seventy dollars, for which we enclose you his receipt.

Reprinted from *Journals of N.Y. Prov. Cong.*, 1:958. Addressed: "To the Honble. Pierre Van Cortlandt, President of the Council of Safety of the State of New-York."

[1] See *JCC,* 8:383.

[2] Gouverneur Morris' May 13 letter to the Board of War requesting "your Assistance in procuring Men for two Gallies in Hudson's River" is in PCC, item 78, 15:197.

[3] In accordance with this advice, the council of safety wrote letters on June 17 to President Hancock and to the New York delegates, protesting Congress' failure to assume the cost of manning and outfitting the two galleys. However, the delegates decided to withhold these letters from Congress and not raise the issue of Continental financing because of their belief that Congress felt it had recently devoted too much of its time to New York affairs. See *Journals of N.Y. Prov. Cong.*, 1:966; and New York Delegates to the New York Council of Safety, July 8, 1777.

[4] See Francis Lewis to the New York Convention, January 16, 31, and March 12, 1777.

Secret Committee Minutes of Proceedings

[ca. May 31, 1777][1]

Come. met. Present Morris, Livingston, Whipple. Issued the followg. Drafts on the Treasurer at Balte. in favor of Mr. Stephen Steward for 37,333 1/3 dlls to pay for produce he is now purchasg. on public Acct. Do. on the Audr. genl. for 2666 2/3 favor Willm Gerrard, Beeker & Co. being part paymt. of the demands of the Owners of the Ship Mary, Capt. Tho. Kennedy, Charterd by the Come.[2] The followg. Stores part of the Sloop Independance Cargo from Martinico were brought up in wagons from Sinipuxent & deliverd to Benjn. Flower Comy. genl. of Mily Stores as per Rect. dated 31st. May. 272 Muskts. without Bayonets marked E.D.T., 401 Muskets with Bayonets—E.V. 2 Boxes Gunlocks, supposd 500—A.C.C.

MS (MH–H).
[1] This date has been assigned because of the reference in the entry to a receipt dated May 31.
[2] For information related to the aborted voyage of the *Mary,* see Morgan, *Naval Documents,* 7 : 155, 169, 220–21, 251–52, 385, 402, 1103.

John Adams to Abigail Adams

Monday, June 2. 1777[1]

Artillery Election! I wish I was at it, or near it.

Yours of the 18th reached me this Morning. The Cause that Letters are so long in travelling, is that there is but one Post in a Week who goes from hence to Peeks Kill, altho there are two that go from thence to Boston.

Riding every day, has made me better than I was, altho I am not yet quite well. I am determined to continue this Practice, which is very necessary for me.

I rejoice to find, that the Town have had the Wisdom to send but one Rep[resentative]. The House last Year was too numerous and unwieldy. The Expence was too great. I suppose you will have a Constitution formed this Year. Who will be the Moses, the Lycurgus, the Solon? Or have you a score or two of such? Whoever they may be and whatever Form may be adopted, I am perswaded there is among the Mass of our People a Fund of Wisdom, Integrity and Humanity, which will preserve their Happiness, in a tolerable Measure.

If the Enemy come to Boston again, fly with your little ones all of them to Philadelphia. But they will scarcely get to Boston, this Campaign.

I admire your Sentiments concerning Revenge.

Revenge, in ancient Days, you will see it through the whole Roman History, was esteemed a generous, and an heroic Passion. Nothing was too good for a Friend or too bad for an Enemy. Hatred and Malice, without Limits, against an Enemy, was indulged, was justified, and no Cruelty was thought unwarrantable.

Our Saviour taught the Immorality of Revenge, and the moral Duty of forgiving Injuries, and even the Duty of loving Enemies. Nothing can shew the amiable, the moral, and divine Excellency of these Christian Doctrines in a stronger Point of Light, than the Characters and Conduct of Marius and Sylla, Cæsar, Pompey, Anthony and Augustus, among innumerable others.

Retaliation, we must practice, in some Instances, in order to make our barbarous Foes respect in some degree the Rights of Humanity. But this will never be done without the most palpable Necessity.

The Apprehension of Retaliation alone, will restrain them from Cruelties which would disgrace Savages.

To omit it then would be cruelty to ourselves, our Officers and Men.

We are amused here with Reports of Troops removing from R. Island, N. York, Staten Island &c.—Waggons, Boats, Bridges &c. prepared—two old Indiamen cutt down into floating Batteries mounting 32 Guns sent round into Delaware R &c. &c. But I heed it no more, than the whistling of the Zephyrs. In short I had rather they should come to Philadelphia than not. It would purify this City of its Dross. Either the Furnace of Affliction would refine it of its Impurities, or it would be purged yet so as by fire.

This Town has been a dead Weight, upon Us—it would be a dead Weight also upon the Enemy. The Mules here would plague them more than all their Money.

RC (MHi). Adams, *Family Correspondence* (Butterfield), 2:253–54.

[1] Adams wrote a second letter this day to Abigail describing his June 1 visit to Rush Hill, home of Benjamin Rush's mother. Ibid., p. 252.

John Adams to Nathanael Greene

Dear Sir.   Phyladelphia June 2d. 1777

Yours of the 28 Ult. is before me.[1] It is certain that Religion and Morality have no less obligations upon Armies, than upon Cities and contribute no less to the Happiness of Soldiers than of Citizens. There is one Principle of Religion which has contributed vastly to the Excellence of Armies, who had very little else of Religion or Morality, the Principle I mean is the Sacred obligation of oaths, which among both Romans and Britans, who seem to have placed the whole of Religion and Morality in the punctual observance of them, have done Wonders.

It is this alone which prevents Desertions from your Enemies. I think our Chaplains ought to make the Solemn Nature and the Sacred obligation of oaths the favourite Subject of their Sermons to the Soldiery. Odd as it may seem I cannot help considering a serious sense of the Solemnity of an oath as the corner Stone of Discipline, and that it might be made to contribute more, to the order of the Army, than any or all of the Instruments of Punishment.

The Information you recd, that General Schuyler was about to be created President, and to hold his Command in the Army, was a Mistake. No Gentleman would have been willing for that, as I know. I am pretty sure at least that a vast Majority would have detested the Thought. G. Schuyler is reserved for another Fate. What that will be Time must discover.

It is, in my humble opinion, utterly improper that this Gentn. should hold a seat in Congress, and a Command in the Army, and I took the first opportunity to express my opinion of the Inconsistency and Danger of it. I think his Constituents much to blame for the late Choice of him. I shall think him much to blame if he does not immediately resign his seat. If he does not, I hope some Gentleman bring in a Motion, to destroy the Precedent, by obliging him to quit his seat or his Command. What the success of such a Motion will be, I know not, but I *(will certainly discharge my Duty to myself and my Constituents and Posterity)* believe such a Motion will be made.

I agree entirely in your sentiments concerning the Danger of entrusting so many important Commands to foreigners. Mr Deane I fear has exceeded his Powers. Mr Du Coudray shall never have my Consent to be at the Head of the Artillery.[2] And I believe he will have few advocates for placing him there. I hope none.

Pray what is your opinion of General Conway. He acquired a good Reputation here.

It gives me great Joy, Sir, to find by your Letter, that you begin to feel your Army to be respectable. We are anxious to hear from Peeks Kill what Numbers are collected there.

LB (MHi).

[1] General Greene's May 28 letter to Adams is in the Adams Papers, MHi.

[2] Despite Adams' apparent dismissal of Philippe Charles du Coudray's claims to be chief of artillery and engineers, he later wrote to James Warren that "Coudray has cost us dear, his Terms are very high, but he has done us such essential service in France, and his Interest is so great and so near the Throne, that it would be impolitick, not to avail ourselves of him." John Adams to James Warren, June 19, 1777.

Du Coudray's September 11, 1776, contract with Silas Deane promising to make him commander of the American artillery and engineers symbolized the problem of the applications of foreign officers. After a summer of turmoil over the issue during which Generals Greene, Knox, and Sullivan threatened to resign if Du Coudray's contract was honored, Congress sidestepped the confrontation by accepting Du Coudray's offer to serve as a volunteer. Although the decision is not noted in the journals, Adams recorded in his diary that Du Coudray had been named inspector general of ordance and military manufactures with the rank of major general. Further difficulty was avoided only because Du Coudray drowned in the Schuylkill River on September 15, 1777. See *Am. Archives,* 5th ser. 2:283; John Adams' Diary, September 18, 1777; and Edmund C. Burnett, *The Continental Congress* (New York: Macmillan Co., 1941), pp. 243–44. See also John Adams to Nathanael Greene, July 7, 1777.

Charles Carroll of Carrollton to Charles Carroll, Sr.

Dr. Papa,   2d June 1777. Pha.

I have your letter of the 28th ultimo. It is really vexatious that our hopes of making wine should be so often blasted by the unseasonable Springs, and the opportunities of making the experiment thus taken away. I shall not forget your Memorandum about the bass matting & ples. I much question whether any of the former is to be had here. In a former letter I answerd yr. quere about the vines cultivated in the Vineyard near this city. I think you did well to send Ashton back with his money: the transaction was with Mr. Lewis, and I think Mr. Lewis will have more honesty than to offer it in payment.

However if pay[men]ts are insisted on, we must receive them or loose our debts, we can only expostulate with our debtors on the injustice of their conduct, authorised it is true by an unjust law, but not by principles of honor or equity. Considerable Sums have been lent to the Continent, and I hear are daily lending, but yet our expenditures exceed our incomes. You say you will not lend the Continent? Can you lend to private persons? Can you invest your money in any thing valuable without a prodigious loss? For instance can you buy lands, negroes, or any thing useful without paying 5 nay 20 times their value? It appears to me we cannot dispose of our money on better terms than to the Continent. If we succeed, as I hope we shall, agt. G B, the money will be redeemed in time, & funded in the mean while. This currency is too generally dispersed, & the effects of a bankruptcy will be too fatal to our Independency, & livelihood of millions to suffer it to take place. I am in hopes, nay I have very little doubt, but we shall be able to obtain loans in Europe, which will enable us to call in a great deal of this paper, prevent the necessity of further emissions, & of course raise the credit of what will remain in circulation. High taxes & the punctual payt. of interest on the sums borrowed will also greatly contribute thereto, but more than all this, a Successful campaign, & union of all parties: the latter will surely be the consequence of the former. The Tories who have fled to the enemy are treated with contempt, & find themselves in a very uneasy situation. This I advance on pretty good authority, such as induces me to believe the intelligence to be true, and you know I am not apt to credit every tale. I ask what will you do with your paper money, if you keep it by you, & the enemy should get the better? In that case I presume you will lose the whole. Considering therefore how deeply we are interested in the final success of our arms, and that we can not do better for ourselves or our country than by lending to the Continent, I advise & desire you to lend. I am sure matters must be brought to a Crisis this Campaign, we shall either conquer, submit unconditionally, or a compromise will take place. Of these 3 events the former is the most probable (at least I think so) the last (a compromise) the most improbable. Again therefore I advise you to lend. Altho' an unjust law has been passed by the legislature of Maryd., it behoves us to be just to our country & help it all we can.

By letters this day recd. from G. Washington dated 31 ultimo,[1] we learn that the enemy have reinforced their army at Brunswick with two brigades from N. York. Part of these brigades consist of the troops lately brought from Rhode Island. It is said some troops have lately arrived from England or Canada, they have brought to Brunswick 200 wagons from N. York & Long Island. G. Washington thinks they intend an attack on this city, but the enemy give out they intend attacking his army; & I am of this opinion, for till they can defeat & disperse his army, the taking of Pha. will not bring them a whit nearer their journey's end. The Tories in N. York are in great consternation preparing to follow the enemy & leave that city. I hope many of them will take the advantage of the Amnesty published by the N. York Convention. Jersey is preparing a similar one, which I expect will be followed by good consequences, for the Tories as I said before, begin to be sick of their company & repent their conduct. I think you treated Lotbiniere as he deserved; I would not choose to be troubled with any more domestic chaplains. I did not receive by this post any letter from Molly. My love to her & her Mama. God grant you health & long continuance of it. I am, yr. affectionate Son,   C.C. of Carrollton

P.S. Mr. Curle at the boling green 14 miles from Port Royal on Rapahanock makes ash corks at 1/2 dollar the gross. If you find a safe opportunity do send me £100 in continental money, I shall want that sum to clear me of this city if I stay here to the beginning of next month. Perhaps my stay will be longer. It depends on our circumstances & the temperature of the weather.

RC (MdHi).
[1] For Washington's two letters of May 31 to President Hancock, see Washington, *Writings* (Fitzpatrick), 8:148–51; and *JCC,* 8:409.

William Whipple to John Langdon

My Dear Sir,   Philadelphia 2d June 1777
    Your favor of the 12th May came to hand the 27th of the same

month. I shall do all in my power to procure a supply of arms &c, but dare not be very sanguine in my hopes of success, as there is not a sufficient quantity arrived to furnish the army proposed to be raised. I am in hopes of leaving this in about a week as I am now waiting only to get some matters done in the Marine Department, which I wish to have done before my departure.

There is not the least probability of your obtaining liberty to appoint a Deputy, if you should have an opportunity and be disposed to go in the army, as no man will be allowed to hold a place in a civil department and a commission in the military at the same time. I have at last paid Messrs Wharton 585 dollars which they suppose to be about the balance of your account but they would not make a final settlement as their books were out of town and the mahogany you shipped them still unsold. I have their receipt for the sum paid them which I shall take with me; there now remain in my hands $960 which I hope to have the pleasure of delivering you in person.

I had wrote thus far when your's of the 16th ulto was handed me. I thank you for your good opinion of me and must defer saying any thing more on the subject of your letter till I have the pleasure of taking you by the hand which will be about the last of this month; in the mean time be assured I am with all due respect, Your friend and humble sevt,   Wm Whipple

Tr (DLC).

John Adams to John Sullivan

Dear Sir   Philadelphia June 3. 1777
I regret with you the Loss of Coll Stark, of whose Experience and Bravery, I have often heard the best accounts.[1] I knew not the Man but some Gentlemen represented him as unequal in Abilities to the high Command of a General officer.

I am extremely sorry to learn that you have been so great a Sufferer in the Loss of your Baggage &c upon several occasions. But in answer to your first Question I can only say, that Congress have hitherto refused to grant any Compensation to Sufferers of any Kind. Falmouth and Charlestown have both petitioned and been civilly refused.[2] Several officers Widows, in deplorable Circumstances, have petitioned and been refused. Several other officers have applied and been refused particularly Lord Sterling. So that I can give you, but cold comfort, respecting your Losses. As to your Second Question, I can give no possitive Answer, how Congress consider your Post. The Resolve of Congress in Words extends only to a Major General commanding in a Seperate Department.[3] But I believe General Gates was allowed for his Table under it, and I see no Reason why you should not.

What shall I say, about raising the Pay of General officers! Our Revenue! sir, our Revenue! What will become of it, and of us! With the Greatest objects in View that any Society ever beheld, the greatest evil to be avoided, and the greatest good to be obtained: with the fairest Prospects of Success that a fond, Sanguine Imagination could wish, We are in the utmost danger of Ruin, by a Failure in our Finances.[4]

RC (DLC).

[1] John Stark, colonel of the First New Hampshire Regiment, had resigned on March 22, 1777. *N.H. State Papers,* 8:518-19.

[2] See John Adams to Abigail Adams, May 17, 1777, note 1.

[3] On June 16, 1775, Congress had resolved that when any major general should "act in a separate department, he be allowed, for his pay and expence, three hundred and thirty-two dollars per month" beyond his regular pay of $166 per month. *JCC,* 2:93.

[4] For the continuation of this letter, see Adams to Sullivan, June 8, 1777.

John Adams to Abigail Adams

June 4. 1777

I wish I could know, whether your season is cold or warm, wet or dry, fruitfull or barren. Whether you had late Frosts. Whether those Frosts have hurt the Fruit, the Flax, the Corn or Vines, &c. We have a fine season here and a bright Prospect of Abundance.

You will see by the inclosed Papers, in a Letter from my Friend Parsons, a very handsome Narration of one of the prettiest Exploits of this War—a fine Retaliation for the Danbury Mischief. Meigs who was before esteemed a good Officer has acquired by this Expedition a splendid Reputation.[1]

You will see by the same Papers too, that the Writers here in Opposition to the Constitution of Pensilvania, are making a factious Use of my Name and Lucubrations. Much against my Will, I assure you, for altho I am no Admirer of the Form of this Government, yet I think it is agreable to the Body of the People, and if they please themselves they will please me. And I would not choose to be impressed into the service of one Party, or the other—and I am determined I will not inlist.[2]

Besides it is not very genteel in these Writers, to put my Name to a Letter, from which I cautiously withheld it myself.

However, let them take their own Way. I shant trouble myself about it.

I am growing better, by Exercise and Air.

I must write a Letter, in Behalf of Mr. Thaxter, to the Bar and Bench in Boston, in order to get him sworn, at July Court.[3]

Will my Brother, when the Time comes, officiate for his Brother at a Christening?

If it is a young Gentleman call him William after your Father—if a young Lady, call her Elizabeth after your Mother, and sister.

RC (MHi). Adams, *Family Correspondence* (Butterfield), 2:255–56.

[1] Gen. Samuel H. Parsons' May 25, 1777, letter to General Washington describing the destruction of a British foraging party at Sag Harbor, Long Island, was published in the *Pennsylvania Journal,* June 4, 1777.

[2] Benjamin Rush, using the pseudonym Ludlow, had cited John Adams' *Thoughts on Government* in a newspaper article criticizing the new Pennsylvania constitution's unicameral legislature. *Pennsylvania Journal,* May 28, 1777. Supporters of the constitution then counter-attacked Adams' pamphlet, spurring a reprint of it in the *Pennsylvania Gazette,* June 11, 1777. Rush's was apparently the first public revelation of Adams' authorship. See John Adams to John Penn, [March 19–27?, 1776], note 2; and Adams, *Family Correspondence* (Butterfield), 2:256n.2.

[3] Adams' letters to the Suffolk County Bar Association and the Suffolk County Court of Common Pleas have not been found, but see Abigail Adams to John Adams, August 27, 1777, ibid., p. 331.

Board of War to Horatio Gates

Dear General   War Office June 4th. 1777

Congress have received your Letters of the 29th April, May 2d & 24th. The several Matters have been attended to & what was thought immediately necessary was done.[1] The Paragraph relating to Light Horse mentioned in yours of the 29th April & your Reasons enclosed for your Opinion that the Enemy's Plan will be to go up the North River & endeavour to effect the old Scheme of a Junction with Carlton, were sent to General Washington for his Consideration & Directions were given that he should send the Horse if he could spare them.

Enclosed you have Copies of the Regulations as to Chaplains & a Resolve respecting the Appointment of an Ajutant General for the Northern Army.[2]

General Mifflin has forwarded one thousand Tents which it is hoped have before this reached you.

The Part of your Letter relative to Money is referred to the Treasury Board who will no Doubt report a Supply.[3]

Your Request as to Capt. Whitcombe's Corps being indulged with a Bounty equal to that given by the Eastern States cannot be complied with on Account of the *Precedent.*[4]

I have the Honour to be, with the greatest Regard, your very obedt Servt,   Richard Peters, Secy

RC (NHi).

[1] Gates' letters are in PCC, item 154, 1:173–85, 208–11. For Congress' response to them, see *JCC*, 7:330, 344, 8:390–91, 417–18.

[2] See *JCC*, 8:390–91.

[3] Burnett thought that Secretary Peters was referring here to a May 30 Gates letter, but in fact the reference is to the general's May 24 letter to President Hancock. Gates wrote his May 30 letter to Washington (who forwarded it to Congress) and did not even mention the financial needs of the northern army in it, but he did deal with this issue in his May 24 letter to Hancock, which Congress referred to the Board of Treasury on June 5. See *JCC*, 8:417–18; PCC, item 154, 1:208–11, 228; and Burnett, *Letters*, 2:378n.3.

[4] Gates discussed the case of Capt. Benjamin Whitcomb and his ranger corps in his May 24 letter to Hancock. Although Congress balked at Gates' request to increase the enlistment bounty paid to Whitcomb and his men, on July 17 it approved Gen. Philip Schuyler's payment to them of "3,066 2/3d dollars . . . over the usual bounty allowed by Congress" but directed that this sum "be charged to the State of Massachusetts bay; and that the corps be considered as part of their quota of continental troops." *JCC*, 8:561.

John Hancock to George Washington

Sir,   Philada. June 5th. 1777.

The enclosed Resolves are all I have in Charge from Congress to forward at this Time.[1]

General Mifflin having applied to Congress in Consequence of your Letter to him, he has their Permission to repair immediately to Head Quarters agreeably to his own Desire. I have made him acquainted with this Determination of Congress.[2]

In Order that you may be enabled to meet Genl. Howe upon his own Ground who has long since offered Rewards to induce the Soldiers of the American Army to desert, the Congress have authorized you to fix on such Rewards or Sum of Money as you may judge proper to encourage Deserters from the Enemy, both Horse and Foot. You will therefore be pleased to carry this Resolve into Execution in such Way as you may think most expedient, and best suited to answer the End.[3] I have the Honour to be, with the utmost Esteem and Respect, Sir, your most obed. & very hble Servt.   John Hancock Presidt

RC (DLC). In the hand of Jacob Rush and signed by Hancock.

[1] In addition to those mentioned in the body of the letter, Hancock also sent Washington resolves of May 29 and 30 and June 2 on the impressment of supply teams, artillery reinforcements, French officers, and Gen. Charles Lee. *JCC*, 8:396, 406, 411–12.

[2] See *JCC*, 8:416; PCC, item 161, fol. 12; and Washington, *Writings* (Fitzpatrick), 8:134–35.

[3] See *JCC*, 8:417. Washington had urged the need for such a policy in letters to Hancock of May 2 and June 3 as well as in one to Richard Henry Lee of June 1. Washington, *Writings* (Fitzpatrick), 8:8–9, 160–61, 172–75.

Secret Committee Minutes of Proceedings

June 5. 1777

Come met. Present Morris, Whipple, Livingston. Order on the Audr. Genl. in favr. Josha. Wallace, for 1162 2/3 dlls being for freight due on his Brigane. Polly, Capt. Lacey, from 15 March 1776 to 4th July followg. when sd. Brige. was taken by the Enemy, is 3 m[onth]s, 19 d[a]ys at £120 per is £436.0.0.[1] Charter party was signd by the Come. for the Brige. Betsey, Jn. Young Owner.

MS (MH–H).

[1] For other payments made to Wallace, see Secret Committee Minutes of Proceedings, May 19, 1777.

John Hancock to George Washington

Sir,   Philada. June 6th. 1777.

I do myself the Honour to transmit sundry Resolves, wherein you will perceive the Congress have expressed the most entire Satisfaction of your Conduct relative to the Cartel for the Exchange of Prisoners, and their Approbation of your Principles and Reasoning on that Occasion; insomuch that it is their Desire you will steadily adhere to them for the future.[1]

You will please to order a List of all the regimental Chaplains to be made out, and transmit it to Congress as soon as possible.[2]

Your Favours of the 1st, 3d, and 5th Inst. were duely received & immediately laid before Congress.[3] I have the Honour to be, with the most perfect Esteem and Respect, Sir, your most obed. & very hble Servt.   John Hancock Presidt

RC (DLC). In the hand of Jacob Rush and signed by Hancock.

[1] See *JCC*, 8:421; and Washington, *Writings* (Fitzpatrick), 8:131–34.

[2] See *JCC*, 8:421; and Washington, *Writings* (Fitzpatrick), 8:202–4.

[3] These letters are in PCC, item 152, 4:221–27, and Washington, *Writings* (Fitzpatrick), 8:168, 172–75, 182–83. The first letter mentioned by Hancock was apparently that of June 2 because there is no June 1 letter from Washington to Hancock in PCC or the Fitzpatrick edition of the general's writings.

James Lovell to Joseph Trumbull

Dear Sir   6th A.M. [June, 1777.]

I will not allow the Express by which I received your last to return without a Line, tho I can add nothing since I wrote to you last Evening by Genl. Mifflin.[1]

I wish, if you are not hurried out of your senses, that you would endeavour to convey to me some hint whereby an Accommodation should take place as to Mons Du Coudray and Genl. Knox.

The Officers of our Army must have a hard struggle in reconciling themselves to that monarchical devotion which is necessary in the adoption of Du Coudray's Command, as it appears to have been regulated in Mr Deane's Compact. I have but a poor Idea of that Gentleman's ability to guard against French finess and flattery. I believe the Arrival of Doctr. Franklin will be an Advantage to Mr. D. Yr Frd and Servt,

J L

Reprinted from Burnett, *Letters,* 2:379.
¹ Not found.

Charles Carroll of Carrollton to Charles Carroll, Sr.

Dear Papa,   Pha. 7th June 1777.

By a letter from General Poor, who commands at Tionderoga, dated the 27th past we are informed that the vanguard of the enemy's army was then within 50 miles of his garrison, which was weak & not well supplied with provisions. If the enemy push on with alacrity Poor must evacuate the lines at Tionderoga & retreat into mount Independance, where he may possibly hold out till our an army can be collected & march to his relief. Perhaps it will be impossible for him to save his military stores, cannon &c which are in the lines. However I have some faint hopes the enemy will proceed with their usual caution & delay. I wish our stores & troops at Tionderoga & mount Independance (opposite to Tionderoga) were removed to Fort Nicholson, called Chessire's in my journal.

It is the common opinion, and of General Washington also, that the enemy will soon march to this city thro' the Jersies. Some of their preparations indicate such an attack, but I can not help thinking they will only make a feint of marching this way to draw G. Washington from his strong camp at middle Brook, & then endeavour to force him to a battle before he regains his present advantageous post. If they fail in this scheme, Howe will probably turn his arms agt. the Province of N.Y. & in conjunction with Carleton endeavour to subdue it. The Enemy it is said have received about 1900 new recruits from Europe. Much depends on this campaign. I wish Gen. Washington's army was stronger & better provided than it is. Most, if not all the States, are very deficient in their quotas. I think the People grow tired of the war.

I wish you would look over the list of bonds, & get such renewed as are very near expiring. I wrote to you in my last for a supply of cash. I fancy there are frequent opportunities from Baltimore Town, I mean such as you might trust to. Simpson has sent me a pair of shoes for Molly. I shall get those for which she sent up the silk made immediately for 30/ a pair. Simpson asks 45/ & no dependance on him. Every thing is most exorbitantly dear in this city, in short the continental currency seems daily to depreciate. However I hope we shall surmount this the greatest, & all our other difficulties. What cannot wisdom, perseverance, & virtue affect? Yet we abound not in either. I have more confidence of success, from the blunders of our enemy than our own good conduct. My love to Molly & Mrs. Darnall. I wish you health & a long continuance of it. I am, yr affec Son,   Ch. Carroll of Carrollton

RC (MdHi).
   [1] For a copy of Gen. Enoch Poor's May 27 letter to Horatio Gates, which Gates had enclosed in a letter to Washington of May 30 and Washington had forwarded in a June 2 letter to President Hancock, see PCC, item 154, 1:228–30. See also Washington, *Writings* (Fitzpatrick), 8:168, and *JCC*, 8:417.
   [2] A reference to the journal he kept while on his mission as a commissioner to Canada in 1776, for which see Richard Smith's Diary, February 14, 1776, note.

Francis Lewis to the New York Council of Safety

Gentlm   Phila. 7th June 1777
   I have at length obtained a decree from the Commissrs. of Appeals relative to the Brign Minerva & Cargo, who have confirmed the sentance of the Admiralty Court at Baltimore, by which the Vessell & Cargo is restored to the Claimants. I shall set out for Baltimore on Monday next, collect the Registers Bill of cost &c there, when shall furnish you with all the accounts relative to the Montgomery's prizes.[1] Should you think my attendance necessary at Kingston or elsewhere, please to advise me.
   The Cross cut Saws & Cinnamon are here, I shall leave them under the direction of Mr. P Livingston, who advises me to dispose of the Cordage at Baltimore where it still remains, rather than send it to you as the transportation is at present hazardous.
   The 500 bushells of salt lately arived here, has been refused your Delegates by the Committee of Congress,[2] it being much wanted here, and at Ten dollars per bushell, your Delegates purpose to move the Congress for an applycation to the state of Virginia for what salt they can spare you, which, if can be obtained, may be forwarded by water (except twelve miles of land carriage) to Trentown if no interuption from the enemy, in the mean time it shall be my endeavor to procure salt, wherever it can be purchased untill I receive your orders to the contrary.[3] I have the honor to be, Gentlm, Your Obedt Huml Servt,
                                                        Fra Lewis

P.S. From the inclosed Account Currant you may nearly form a judgement of what the Captors moiety of prize money will be, provided you should be under the necessity of making a distribution before I can furnish you with all the accounts, which shall be compleated soon after my arrival at Baltimore.

RC (N).

¹ For some account of the disposition of the *Minerva,* a brigantine captured by the *Montgomery,* a New York privateer commanded by Capt. William Rogers, see Morgan, *Naval Documents,* 7:987, 1191–92: Lewis to the New York Convention, January 16 and 31 and March 12; and Lewis to William Allison and Robert R. Livingston, April 16, 1777. There are also legal records pertaining to this case in Records of the Supreme Court of the United States, Record Group 267, Case no. 15, DNA.

² The committee appointed on June 3 "to devise ways and means of supplying the United States with salt." *JCC,* 8:413.

³ Lewis had described his own efforts to obtain badly needed salt supplies for New York in a May 31 letter to the council of safety:

"Pursuant to the Resolves of the Honble Convention, dated the 1st April, directing me to invest a moiety of the nett proceeds in Salt, the which as it was not to be purchased in this state, I proceeded to Baltimore, in order to effect it there, and sent my son also to Virginia where I have been informed, is a considerable quantity, but not suffered to be taken out of the state without any applycation to the Governor from Congress.

"Within these few days arrived at Patuxent a Brign with 500 Bus[hels] of Salt for account of Congress, to whom Your Delegates are applying for the State of New York; If obtained shall forward it to Esopus in the most expeditious manner.

A partial transcript of this letter, described as "Copied from the manuscript then in the possession of Mr. Stan V. Henkels of Philadelphia," is in the Edmund C. Burnett Papers, DLC. Lewis' reference to "a moiety" is explained in Lewis to the New York Convention, March 12, 1777, note 4. On June 14 Congress did urge all the states to provide New York with salt. *JCC,* 8:465–66.

James Lovell to Oliver Wolcott

Sir   Saty. June 7th. '77

Your favor of May 24th should not have been this long unacknowledged but for a disagreable alteration at the post office. Letters being delivered in Congress after our assembling on Mondays cannot be answered by 2 oClock P.M. of the *same* day, when the rider again leaves the city. I may say at least that this is an *uncomplaisant* order of somebody or other.

By the vein of humour in which you wrote, I have concluded that you found your dear domestic connexions in a more favorable state of health than your fears boded, when I had last the pleasure of your company; and, under the impression of my Conclusions, I rejoyce with you.

I very much suspect a roguish transition of your ideas from one species of noble animals to another, when you say that *in Boston* the Hero of animadversions will be not only among friends, but such friends as "will not fail to conceal all the imperfections of their own party." Upon this suspicion, I might be disposed, as is usual in such cases, to wink att the truth of the ideas out of sight, and then altercate upon the remainder, to show my learning. But, having been an ear witness to *such like* proceeding, too, too often, since you left us, my stomach is not set for it at this present hour.

By 5 to 4 & 2 divided, the *northern* department has been lined out, and Genl. Schyler sent to take the command.[1] By a repeal of an old resolve, he will not appear to be *obliged* to make his Head Quarters at Albany, 100 miles from the army; nor is he *obliged* to go from that city except by *true military feelings*. Can you readily determine in your own mind where he will reside, from the data now before you? Genl. Gates will most assuredly not take the post of hazard both to his life & reputation to be under the absolute direction of a man 35 leagues off, in treaties with Indians or acting as a Providor to his army at the same distance. I daily expect to hear of Confusion from that Department.

The Compliments which you desired me to present were gratefully received by Mr. & Mrs. Duncan, at whose house, however, I do not lodge. He thought it not for his interest to entertain us more than a Week after you went away; and therefore desired us to accommodate ourselves elsewhere. I lodge at Mrs. Cheeseman's with Collo. Whipple, Judge Frost from N Hampshire and the Gentlemen who, you know, lodged there at yr. departure.

We have nothing foreign of any import, unless you will call news from the Mississipi foreign.[2] The Governour of New Orleans will accept a salute from a British Sloop of War which is watching our trade in that district. He has also ordered Spanish papers to be put on board our vessels at a certain Look-out before they can fall in with the Sloop of war, and the English papers to be conveyed to him by Land with several other friendly arrangements. You may recollect that Blankets &cc were to be lodged at New Orleans by the Spanish Ambassador to be *lent* to us. This I think is by no means for a News paper tho' I could not avoid giving you the agreable hint of it.

Should you be at Hartford when you receive this please to present my Complimts. to Capt. Ledlie & Family. I will endeavour to gain intelligence from his daughter, if the bearer of Mr. Morris's letter, from which I learnt the news on the other side, should be able to give me any. Mr. Morris not being in town at present I know not what course to pursue; but I will not neglect to write *if* I succeed.

I am, Sir, Your Friend & very humble Servant,   James Lovell

RC (CtHi).

[1] For further information on the question of command in the northern department, see Philip Schuyler's Memorial to Congress, May 6; and Lovell to Horatio Gates, May 22, 1777.

[2] Lovell is apparently referring to the receipt of Oliver Pollock's letters of May 4 and 5 to Robert Morris and Andrew Allen. See Secret Committee to Oliver Pollock, June 12, 1777.

John Adams to Abigail Adams

June 8. 1777

Upon an Invitation from the Board of War of Pensilvania, a Committee was appointed a few days ago to go down Delaware River and take a View of the Works there, erected with a View to prevent the Enemy from coming up to Philadelphia by Water. Mr. Duer, your humble servant and Mr. Middleton made the Committee.[1]

Yesterday we went, in three Boats, with Eight Oars each. Mr. Rittenhouse, Coll. Bull and Coll. Deane, went from the Pensilvania Board of War. General Arnold, General De Coudrai, an experienced French officer of Artillery, Monsr. Le Brune, an Engineer, and Mr. Rogers an Aid de Camp of Gen. De Coudray were in Company.

We had a Band of Musick in Company which is very agreable upon the Water.

We went first to Billingsport, about 10 Miles down the River on the Jersey side, where the River is obstructed with Vesseaux de Frizes, and where a large Fort is laid out with a great deal of Work done upon it.

We then came back to Fort Island, or Province Island, where the River is obstructed again, and the only Passage for shipps is commanded by a Fort of 18. 18. Pounders. Here lay the Fire ships, Fire Rafts, floating Batteries, Gallies and the Andrew Doria, and the fine new Frigate Delaware.

We then crossed the River and went to Red Point on the Jersey side, where Coll. Bull has thrown up the strongest Works that I have ever seen. Here We dined, and after Dinner Coll. Bull ordered out his Regiment upon the Parade, where they went through their Exercises and Maneuvres, very well.

We had a long Passage home and made it 9 o Clock before We reached the Wharf. We suffered much with the Heat, yet upon the whole it was an agreable day.

Upon our Return to Town We expected to hear some News but not a Word had been received. All is quiet still. How long will this Calm continue?

I begin to suspect We shall have an unactive Campaign—that How will shut himself up, in some impregnable Post, and lie still. We shall see, however, and I think We shall trouble him whether he moves or lies still.

RC (MHi). Adams, *Family Correspondence* (Butterfield), 2:259–60.
[1] The report of this committee, which had been appointed on June 3, advo-

cated strengthening the Delaware River defenses at Billingsport. *JCC,* 8:414,
451–52.

John Adams to John Sullivan

June 8. [1777]

This Moment I had yours of this days date put into my Hand.[1] I
am ashamed that I had not answered your other Letter before: But
my Apology for it, is ill Health, which has obliged me to devote my
Mornings and Evenings to Exercise and Relaxation.

The Information you give me, that Desertions from the Enemy are
plentifull, gives me Pleasure, but the Resolution of the Militia to turn
out and assist you, gives me much more. Nothing however contributes
so much to my Happiness, as the accounts I hear, that Discipline, order,
subordination, Cleanliness, Health and Spirits are so rapidly increasing
in our Army. All depends upon this. This will surely conduct us to
Honour, Glory, and Tryumph: as the Reverse would certainly end in
our Disgrace and Ruin.

There are two other Things upon which our Prosperity depends. The
one is the Reputation of our Loan offices, and the other is the Resolution of the Assemblies to proceed to tax the People as deep as they
can bare. If Men who have Money can be persuaded to lend it to the
Public: and if the assemblies can be convinced of the Necessity of proceeding to tax their Constituents: and if the People can be convinced
of this Sacred Truth, that it is their Interest to pay high Taxes, We
shall be able to avoid emitting more Money, and to sustain the Credit
of that already out. But, if not, our Money will be a Bubble and we
shall be in order in terrible Distress. We shall not lose the Cause, for
We will carry on the War by Barter: We will call in all the Plate: We
will march out all at once, and crush the Snakes in their Nests: We will
do any thing, rather than fail: But we shall be put to a great deal of
confusion and Perplexity. We have no News. Shall always be happy to
learn News from you, especially if it be good.

I am your Friend & most obedient servant,   John Adams

RC (DLC). A continuation of Adams to Sullivan, June 3, 1777.

[1] Sullivan's June 8 letter, chiding Adams for not responding to his May 15
letter and remarking on the high rate of British desertions, is in the Adams
Papers, MHi.

Francis Lightfoot Lee to Landon Carter

My dear Col.   Philadelphia June 8th. 1777

I have lately received several of your favors, for which I feel myself
much obliged, & should sooner have acknowleged it but that I waited

to have the pleasure of sending you a treatise on sugar making but as Doctor Bond has repeatedly disappointed me, I can no longer defer paying my respects to you. Mr. Fauntleroy shall have your letter, I can hardly think he will let his house be made use of when it is so disagreeable to his neighbours. It is certainly too much surrounded by Slaves, & the season very improper for if the infection shou'd by accident spread, the crops must inevitably be lost. The campaign is not yet opened, Genl. Howe is collecting his forces, but whether he means to act offensively, before he is reinforced, is uncertain. Some think he will be satisfied to keep himself secure. I think it is reduced to a certainty that G.B. cannot conquer America with her own forces or what she can procure in Europe. We have pretty good intelligence that our Enemies are satisfied of this, & are therefore determined to try this full force of corruption. We know they have many emissaries at work, & I fear the scheme has extended further than we are aware of. Mr. Towne coud not publish your peice, he said it was too long for the plan of his paper.[1]

I have received the number of your Tickets & shall inform you immediately of their fate, when the Lottery is drawn (which I hope will be soon) if I am here, but I hope soon of being with you, as I am very desirous of returning to my friends if without reputation, at least without disgrace.[2] My best respects to Sabine Hall. Your friend wishes you health & happiness.   Francis Lightfoot Lee

RC (ViHi).
[1] See Francis Lightfoot Lee to Landon Carter, April 15, 1777.
[2] See Virginia Delegates to George Wythe, June 10, 1777.

James Lovell to Horatio Gates

Dear sir   Philada. June 8th. [1777][1]

If yours of the 25th Ultimo is really a fourth, one has been intercepted; for I have recd. only those which I have before acknowledged of the 19th of Apr. & the 11th of May. I have but little expectation that this will come fairly to your hand; therefore I here insert a curse for the dirty scoundrel who shall be guilty of opening it.[2]

I am sorry I did not press you in my last to keep yourself easy till you could be called away from the northward with honour upon some occasion which must soon offer. I wish Boston was at present such a post of honor as to merit your acceptance. But without some more certain danger, and a number of troops of some figure, I cannot think it worthy of you. As danger is talked of in your quarter I doubt not your presence there will be most agreable to the Commander of the Department.[3] It is understood here that you have no objection to his residing with the army where you are; but you do not like to be controuled by a senior at a distance from the field of danger. I can only say at large I hope the army at Ty will not be ruined by any misunderstandings of its Leaders.

I am writing to you before the post arrives; I expect much fret when he delivers what is now on the road from you.

I have lost more flesh by the devilish arrangement than I shall recover again this season. I do not however wish *myself* under Ground nor *you*.

If you should receive this anywhere on the other side of the Jersies, I beg you would speedily give me one line in return.

The Governour of New Orleans is ready to do us every kind service. He will not allow harbour to British vessels, but gives Spanish papers to all the colony traders bound up the Mississipi, to secure them from a Sloop of War cruising in his neighbourhood. And he offers aid even to Cash if we make any Expedition that way.[4]

I am, Dear Sir, Your Friend & Servt.   James Lovell

RC (NHi).

[1] Although cataloged as a 1778 letter to William Alexander and located in the William Alexander Papers, this letter was clearly written in 1777 to Horatio Gates. Its contents indicate that it was written while Gates was commanding the American army at Fort Ticonderoga, shortly after Congress had reinstated Gen. Philip Schuyler as commander of the Northern Army and before Gates' dramatic June 18, 1777, appearance in Congress.

[2] There is more than a little irony in this sentence, since the letter's location in the Alexander Papers suggests that it may indeed have not "come fairly to your hand." Lovell's lament invites speculation that Alexander may have been "the dirty scoundrel" cursed here. Alexander's long-standing friendship with Philip Schuyler—Gates' bitter rival for the northern command—may have predisposed him to take advantage of opportunities to embarrass Gates and therefore to inspect Gates' correspondence as it passed through his headquarters near Morristown, N.J. In any event, it was Alexander who later brought the "Conway Cabal" against General Washington into the open in November 1777 by apprising Washington of a letter from Gen. Thomas Conway to Gates that disparaged the commander in chief. See Alan C. Valentine, *Lord Stirling* (New York: Oxford University Press, 1960), pp. 11, 13, 51–55, 95; and Freeman, *Washington,* 4:550.

[3] That is, Philip Schuyler.

[4] See Secret Committee to Oliver Pollock, June 12, 1777.

Charles Carroll of Carrollton to Charles Carroll, Sr.

Dr Papa,   10th June 1777. Ph[iladelphi]a.

The inclosed Pen[nsylvani]a packet will give you almost all the intelligence stirring here. The letter, of which an extract is published under the Ph[iladelphi]a head from a gentleman of eminence & character in the West Indies comes from Mr. Bingham the continental Agent at Martinico,[1] and therefore altho' the name of Charles Thompson is not signed, you may look upon the intelligence as authentick. There is a possibility that the answer of their High mightinesses may not be strictly true, and therefore it was thought prudent not to publish the intelligence as coming from Congress; but we believe the answer to be genuine, as it comes from our Agent, who writes that he thinks a war between England & France inevitable, as the subjects of each State begin to be exasperated agt. each other & to make reprisals. Gen. Washington writes of the 5th instant that by late intelligence recd. from G. Poor, the enemy, who had come up to Split Rock, & of which I advised you in my last, had fallen down the lake & returned, it was supposed to St. Johns. If the conjecture of G. Washington's informant from N. York be true that the late reinforcements (about 2000) arrived at that city came from Canada, it is most probable the enemy will not attack Tionderoga this year, but content themselves with the command of Lake Champlain, by which they will effectually prevent our invading Canada. The Enemy are certainly meditating an expedition by water, agt what place is uncertain, but the General & most others think agt. this City.

Colo. Sim this moment delivered me £100 from you with a letter from Molly of the 1st instant inclosing £40 of Miss Carroll's money. I will answer Molly's letter by the next post, she shall have her shoes by Col. Sim & some other things. I shall deliver Miss Lucy Leonard the memorandum for Miss Carroll. I beg you will act cautiously with respect to the continental money; remember the opposition of one man cannot counteract a law & you will only make yourself enemies. Upon my word, I would not generally incur the odium of a whole People for a million a year. Give my love to Molly & to little Poll. I am glad to hear by Col. Sim that her cold is going off. My love to Mrs. Darnall. I am, yr. affectionate Son,   C. Carroll of Carrollton

RC (MdHi).

[1] This brief extract of Bingham's letter, which appears in the June 10 issue of John Dunlap's *Pennsylvania Packet, or the General Advertiser,* reads simply: "I have herewith the honor to enclose you a copy of a Memorial presented by Sir Joseph York, the English Ambassador at the Hague, to their High Mightinesses the States General—and their answer thereto." For a discussion of Yorke's memorial protesting Dutch failure to halt illicit American trade at St. Eustatius and the unneutral act of returning the salute of an American ship, and the States General's refusal to comply with Britain's demands, see Daniel A. Miller, *Sir Joseph Yorke and Anglo-Dutch Relations, 1774-1780* (The Hague and Paris: Mouton & Co., 1970), pp. 51–59.

Secret Committee Minutes of Proceedings

June 10th. 1777

Come. met. Present, Morris, Whipple, Livingston. Agreable to verbal Instructns. recd from Congress the 9th inst. Resolvd. that this Come.

will import from N. Orleans on the Missisippi to the value of 40 or 50,000 dlls in Blankets, Strouds, & other Articles suitable for public use, That proper lists of sd. goods be sent forward to Mr. Oliver Pollock Mercht. there with orders that he purchase or charter three or four small suitable vessels & ship on each to the value of 10, or 12000 dlls of sd. goods & dispatch them for the first safe ports in these States. Also that he be authorizd, shoud he charter the vessels to have them justly valued & insure the valuation agst. any capture by the Enemy. Agreed with Robt. Morris Esqr. for his Drafts on Olivr. Pollock Esqr. for thirty thousd. dlls to be pd. at N. Orleans for wch Mr. Morris is to be paid in Dollars.[1]

MS (MH–H).
[1] See Secret Committee to Oliver Pollock, June 12, 1777.

Secret Committee to Robert Purviance and Samuel Purviance, Jr.

Gentn.   Philada. June 10th. 1777
The Secret Committee are now preparing their Accounts & papers in order to report the State of them & their proceedings to Congress[1] & for this purpose they must call on every body with whom they have transacted business to render in their Accounts speedily as possible. You will therefore be pleased to send us Acct Sales of the Goods put into your hands, Acct of the purchases you made by order of this Committee & Account Current the sooner the better. I am Sirs, Your Obedt hble servt. By order of the Commtee.   Robt Morris Chair Man

RC (MdHi). Written and signed by Robert Morris. Addressed: "To Messrs. Saml. & Robt. Purviance, Merchts., Baltimore."
[1] See JCC, 8:423–24.

Virginia Delegates to George Wythe

Sir   Philadelphia June 10th 1777
We shall be much obliged to you to inform the House of our earnest desire to have leave to return home immediately, & that other Gentlemen may be sent to fill our Places. What passed in the House previous to the last Election of Delegates is well known.[1] We do not presume to judge of the proceedings of the House farther than as they affect ourselves; in which case we hope to be excused if we are determined by our own feelings. From what then passed & our long and intimate ac-

quaintance with Colo. Lee, we are sorry to be obliged to think that however upright our Conduct may be, we may while absent, engaged in a very painfull Service, in an instant be deprived of what we esteem most valuable, our Reputation. It is impossible we can do our duty as we could wish, while our Minds labour under such melancholy impressions.

We love our Country, & will chearfully share it's Fate, whatever may be the Issue of the present Contest; but must be content to serve it in a more humble Station, less exposed to Envy Hatred & Malice.

We are, Sir, with great Esteem, Your obdt. hble. Servants,

Francis Lightfoot Lee

Mann Page Junr.

RC (ViU). Written by Page and signed by Page and Lee.

[1] For the assembly's displacement of Richard Henry Lee, see Richard Henry Lee to Patrick Henry, May 26, 1777, note 1. This protest resignation was apparently ignored in Virginia. Francis Lightfoot Lee continued to serve in Congress during the ensuing term—along with his brother Richard Henry, who was subsequently returned to Congress—but Page had also been dropped from the new delegation elected on May 22. This is the last known surviving letter written by Page as a delegate to Congress. His presence in Philadelphia after this date is not well documented, but he subsequently attested an account of Francis Lightfoot Lee "with the Commonwealth of Virginia" dated "Philadelphia July 3d. 1777." Signers of the Articles of Confederation, NNPM. Page had left Congress some time before July 21 when James Lovell mentioned his absence in a letter to William Whipple.

John Adams to James Warren

My dear Sir   Philadelphia June 11. 1777

The honourable Samuel Hewes[1] Esqr a Delegate in Congress from North Carolina from 1774 to 1777, being bound on a Journey to Boston for the Recovery of his Health, I do myself the Honour to introduce him to you.

He has a large share in the Conduct of our naval and commercial affairs, having been a member of the naval and marine Committees, and of the Secret Committee from the first.

I wish you would be kind enough to introduce him to some of our best Company, and give him a line to Dr Winthrop, that he may have an opportunity of seeing the Curiosities of Harvard Colledge. I have not Time to write the Dr.

What Mr Howes present Plan is, no Conjurer can discover. He is moving and maneuvring with his Fleet and Army, as if he had some Design, or other, but what it may be no Astrologer can divine.

It is disputed among the Writers, upon military Science, whether a Faculty of penetrating the Intentions of an Enemy or that of acquiring the Love of his soldiers is the first Quality of a General—but whether this Penetration holds the first or second Place, it cannot discover Designs that are not, and schemes that were never laid. Howes Behaviour Strongly indicates a Want of system.

Some conjecture he is bound to the West Indies, others to Europe, one Party to Hallifax, another to Rhode Island. This set sends him up the North River, that down the East River and the other up the Delaware. I am weary of Conjectures—Time will solve them.

One Thing is certain, that in the Jersies his whole Army was Seized with Terror and Amazement. The Jersy Militia have done themselves the highest Honour, by turning out in such great Numbers, and with such Determined Resolution. This was altogether unexpected to the British and Hessian Gentry. They were persuaded that the People would be on their Side, or at least unactive but when they found Hundreds who had taken their Protections and their oaths of allegiance, in Arms against them, and with terrible Imprecations, vowing Vengeance, their Hearts sunck within them and they sneaked away in a Panic. The Militia was dismissed too soon, and they took advantage of it, to come out again with their whole Army upon a predatory Expedition, but soon returned, and evacuated New Jersy altogether.

I am most apprehensive they will go to Rhode Island. If not, I think, unless they have prepared Reinforcements with such secrecy that no Intimations of them have reached Us, they will give Us but a languishing and inactive Campaign.

I hope you proceed in the Formation of a Constitution without any hurtfull Divisions, or Altercations. Whatever the Majority determine, I hope the minority will cheerfully concur in. The fatal Experience of Pensilvania has made me dread nothing so much as Disunion, upon this Point. God grant you may lay the Foundations of a great, wise, free and honourable People.

RC (MHi). In Adams' hand, though not signed.

¹ That is, Joseph Hewes. Adams may have been thinking momentarily of Boston merchant Samuel Hewes, a correspondent of Samuel Adams. See Samuel Adams to Samuel Hewes, July 7, 1777.

John Hancock to Benedict Arnold

Sir,   Philada. June 11th. 1777.

The Congress judges it highly necessary in the present Situation of our Affairs that an Officer of Experience and Reputation should be stationed at Trenton, and have therefore directed you to repair thither as soon as possible.¹

On your Arrival there you are to conduct yourself agreeable to the

Orders you may receive from the Commander in Chief. I am with great Respect, Sir, your most obed. & very hble Servt.

J.H. Presid.

LB (DNA: PCC, item 12A).
[1] See *JCC*, 8:432.

Jonathan Dickinson Sergeant to Gunning Bedford

Sir   Wednesday Evg. [June 11, 1777]
I do not recollect mentioning your Character or Name on any Occasion unless in Congress in the Course of Business. For my Conduct there, I conceive I am answerable only to that Body & to my Constituents.[1]

I flatter myself however that no *illiberal* Expressions have escaped me there respecting either You or any other subject.

I am, Yr. hble Servt.   Jona D Sergeant

FC (DNA: PCC, item 78).
[1] Sergeant was writing in response to an angry letter from Muster Master General Gunning Bedford, written at 8:30 in the evening on Wednesday June 11, stating that:

"You having reflected very illiberally on my character, & refusing to give me that satisfaction, which a gentleman is intitled to; without further ceremony I beg you will meet me at 6 oclock on Friday morning at the Center-House, armed with a Pair of Pistols.

"I wait impatiently your answer, & expect it immediately." PCC, item 78, 2:199.

It is not known when Sergeant delivered the remarks that offended Bedford or what was said that he found so objectionable. Bedford was so dissatisfied by Sergeant's reply, however, that he wrote to him in even stronger terms on the 12th:

"The reputation of a gentleman is not to be trifled with; you have attempted to injure mine, for which I expect the satisfaction of a man of honor.

"Your evasion is mean & pittiful; & so far from being an extenuation of the insult, the place where the aspertion was made rather heightens it. I have been much abused & illtreated by the arbitrary & ungenerous conduct of that house & have long wished to lay my hands on some one particular member, whome I could prove had traduced my character; I am at length so happy as to have fixed on one; & could only wish he was an object more worthy of resentment.

"I am by no means satisfied, Sir, with your answer. I am determined & fixed as to my conduct, & must insist on it, that you will either make me ample acknowledgements for what you have said, or meet me according to my appointment. I will accept of no excuse whatever, & shall expect no further trouble in the matter. If you refuse to make me the satisfaction I ask, or to meet me at the place appointed, remember I shall treat you as a scoundrel wherever I meet you, & publish you to the world as a person destitute of every spark of honor, a poltroon & a coward." Ibid., fols. 193–94.

When Sergeant submitted Bedford's letters to Congress on the 12th, the delegates were thrown into an uproar. Several, alarmed by the threat Bedford posed to freedom of debate, offered resolutions calling for his imprisonment and dismissal from office, but North Carolina delegate Thomas Burke persuaded Congress not to put any of these resolves to a vote, and at length on June 14 Congress contented itself with exacting an apology from the muster master general for committing "a high breach of the privileges of this house, in sending a challenge to one of the members of this house, for words spoken by him in this house, in the course of debate." *JCC,* 8:458–61, 466–67.

John Witherspoon to David Witherspoon

Dear David,   Philadelphia, June 11, 1777.

Having met with an accidental opportunity, though the time is very short, I have written a line or two to Mr. Smith,[1] and refer you to him for news. It gave us much pleasure to see you here lately, but much greater to understand from every quarter, that you behaved in such a manner in Virginia as was quite agreeable to all. I hope, my dear boy, if you continue to keep the path which I have chalked out to you, you will be useful, happy, and successful in life. Give great application to your studies, but above all be attentive to your moral conduct. It is my earnest desire that you should, as soon as possible, renew your baptismal engagements, agreeably to the conversation I had with you here. Remember, my beloved child, that those who have been trained up in the fear of God, cannot sin at so cheap a rate as others, and that the great advantages which you have had, and do still enjoy, must be accounted for.

I wish your accomplishment in every respect, and therefore bear with me while I put you in mind to prevent at any rate a habit of holding down your head, or keeping it on one side, or any other ungraceful habit. Let there be decency in your outward carriage, reserve and modesty in your conversation, and humility in your heart. . . .[2] I am, dear David, Your affectionate father,   Jno. Witherspoon.

P.S. If the enemy leave New Jersey, as there is some prospect at present, you shall have notice immediately. . . .

MS not found; reprinted from *Christian Advocate* 2 (October, 1824): 445.
    [1] No letters from Witherspoon to Samuel Stanhope Smith have been found.
    [2] Ellipses in Tr here and below.

John Hancock to William Livingston

Sir,   Philadelphia, June 12th, 1777.

You are hereby requested to order out forthwith five hundred of the militia of the state of New Jersey, to assist in completing the works now erecting at Billingsport for the defence of the river Delaware, it being of the utmost consequence that the fortifications at that place should be completed without delay.[1] By order of Congress,

John Hancock, Prest.

Reprinted from *Selections from the Correspondence of the Executive of New Jersey, from 1776 to 1786* (Newark, N.J.: Published by order of the legislature, 1848), p. 63.

[1] See *JCC*, 8:451–52. Hancock's letter to Governor Livingston is taken almost verbatim from this June 11 resolve.

Secret Committee to Oliver Pollock

Sir,   June 12th 1777

Your Letters of 4th & 5th May addressed to Andrew Allen & Robert Morris Esquires were laid before the Congress by the latter whereby we are informed that your new Governor Don Bernard de Galvez is much disposed to favour the Commercial Interest of the United States of America, and as we are appointed by the Honorable Congress to superintend the Management of such Trade as is necessary to be carried on for public Account we do ourselves the Honor of addressing a Letter to his Excellency on this Subject, it is here inclosed and you will please to deliver and if needful translate the same for him.[1]

The good Disposition you discover to our Cause and the Character you bear has determined us to employ you as our commercial Agent in New Orleans[2] in full Confidence that your Conduct in our Affairs will be such as will intitle you to our Approbation and future Favours, and should it at any Time be your Misfortune to fall into the hands of our Enemies as you have suggested, you have Liberty to claim the Protection of the United States of America as their commercial Agent resident at New Orleans and may depend that Congress will redeem you by Exchange or retaliate any Injuries or Indignities that may be offered you, and they have always a sufficiency of Prisoners in their Power to do this with Effect if our Enemies dare to treat ill those Persons that are entitled to our Protection.

Thus much we have said that you may produce if ever it becomes necessary, and now for Business of another kind. We learn from Capt Le Mere and his Passenger that there is Plenty of Blankets, Strouds and other dry Goods in New Orleans suitable for the Use of our Army. The Difficulties we meet in our attempts to import a sufficiency of those Things induces us to look for them in every Quarter and we have engaged Capt Le Mere to return directly back to New Orleans with this Letter and to return from thence for this Coast with a Cargo of such Goods as you may ship by him for our Account. You will find herein inclosed a List of the kinds of Goods that will best suit us and we hereby authorize you to purchase and ship the Value of forty or fifty thousand Dollars in those Articles but we would have these Goods come by three or four different Conveyances each Cargo of the Value of ten or twelve thousand Dollars. We depend on you to purchase these Goods on the best Terms you can obtain them and we authorize you to charter or buy three or four fast sailing suitable Vessels to bring the Goods to a safe Port on this Coast, observing however that we prefer chartering to buying, and would rather have them brought in French or Spanish Bottoms than any other, particularly we wish to have Capt Le Mere employed in this Business because he knows the Coast, and is acquainted with a proper Inlet where the Cargo may be safely landed. In order that you may be able to procure suitable Vessels on the best Terms on charter We agree that you may have each Vessel you charter valued by honest impartial Men judges of such things and you may on behalf of the United States of America insure on each Vessel the Sum she is valued at against all Risques of Seizure or Capture by the British &c. You will agree the Freight on the most moderate Terms you can either by the Month or by the Voyage, securing us Liberty to load the Vessels back to you loaden with Flour if it can conveniently be done and we hereby agree to pay the Freights you agree for and the Losses (if any) that may arise on the Insurances you agree to make for Account of the Owners of said Vessels, but if after all these Powers you should find it still out of your Power to charter suitable Vessels you may in that Case purchase on the best Terms in your power, one, two, three, or four small fast sailing Vessels suitable to bring the Goods observing that if you cannot get the Goods or cannot get Masters & Men to navigate the Vessels, in either of these Cases none must be bought, but we can hardly suppose such Impediments to arise, therefore if you do purchase, let the Vessels be well fitted & sound, get good Masters & dispatch them soon as you can enclosing by each Invoice & Bill Lading of the Goods shipped in each Vessel, and duplicates thereof by other good Conveyances. You will take Care to have the goods properly imbaled or packed in Bales, Casks &c so as to secure them as much as possible from Damage and proper Precautions must be taken to prevent any Danger of Seizure by British armed Vessels in the River Mississippi. We doubt not but your Governor & Officers in New Orleans will concur in doing what may be necessary for this purpose and we judge it might be best that the Goods should be shipped on board of Spanish Bottoms and cleared out as bound for the Havanna or Teneriffe, and if shipped on French Bottoms that they should be cleared out for Martinico or St Pierres & Miquilon altho the latter plan is become much suspected, and therefore most dangerous to be used. The Governor & Officers we suppose will readily grant the necessary Certificates & Passports and you will consult with them & seek their Concurrence in all that may be needful. We think also that you should make it a point not to let it be known that you have any orders to buy Goods on our Account. Capt LeMere will deliver all the Letters he carries to you and you need not give them out till your Business is done. When the Vessels are chartered or bought it should be kept perfectly secret if possible where they are bound, these precautions being necessary to prevent the Enemy getting Intelligence of what you are doing. In short, you must buy the Goods we want, cheap as possible, ship them to us soon and on as good Terms as you can, and avoid all in your Power letting it be known what you are about. Mr Morris has shewn us the Accounts you have rendered to Willing, Morris & Co. down to 15th Nov. 1776 when the Balance in their favour amot. to about 40 thousand, say 42,000 Dollars, and he has Reason to think this Balance has rather increased than decreased since that time, and as he is willing to accommodate us with these Funds for the purpose of making the Purchases, we now inclose you said Willing, Morris & Cos. draught of this Date at thirty Days Sight for fifteen thousand Dollars and one other their Draught at Sixty Days Sight for fifteen thousand Dollars indorsed payable to yourself, both which Sums you will place to our credit. Mr Morris also agrees that you may apply the remainder of his Houses Money in your Hands to our use to execute the Orders given you for Amount whereof your Draughts on us in their favour shall be punctually paid, or if it so happens that you have remitted any part of their Effects, so as to lessen the Balance due them, you may draw on us in favour of whom you please with equal Assurance that your Draughts will be paid and besides this we shall ship you Cargoes of Flour back in the Vessels and make you other Remittances to provide for future Purchases, because if we find you execute the present Order to Satisfaction we shall lay our Account in getting from you hereafter very considerable Supplies of useful & necessary Goods, and probably we may find it convenient to lodge Flour at the Cape to be sent you from thence in French Bottoms, respecting which be pleased to give us your Opinion and tell us also on what terms you can sell Bills on France or Spain, if we should authorize you at any time to draw on Madrid or Paris for Sums that may be necessary to execute our Orders. When you dispatch the Vessels with the Goods we have ordered, you will direct the Captains to avoid all Vessels at Sea and if examined by the British Ships of War on their voyages they should have a feasible Story to tell them to which the Log Book & Journals should be suited, and ultimately they are to push into any Port or Inlet on this Coast where they can get in most safely. The small Inlets between Cape Henlopen & Cape Charles of which there are several are most safe, there are also good Inlets between New York & Cape May and many in North Carolina. Wherever they arrive let them send an Express to

us with their Letters and an Account of their Arrival advising the Place
and such other Circumstances as they may think necessary and we shall
immediately return the needfull Instructions. You will instruct the
Masters of the Vessels to keep all the Letters & English Papers constantly slung with a Weight ready for sinking so that they may throw
them overboard rather than let them fall into the Enemies Hands. We
observe you mention to have paid Monies for the good of the Cause
of which you have kept no Account, but that you propose charging
such in future. You'll please to be cautious in such transactions, as any
Monies you may disburse for the Service of the United States which
they in Justice ought to pay, they will pay, but should you or any of
their Agents judge improperly and pay away Money under a Notion
of serving the States which they in Justice are not liable, it may be
difficult for you in such Cases to obtain Reimbursement all which we
mention for your Government.

It is not unlikely but at some future Day an Expedition may become
necessary in your Neighbourhood, and when that is the Case Congress
will no doubt avail themselves of the Governor's favourable Disposition
and of your Services so that you have every inducement to recommend
yourself to their Friendship by your good Management of our present
orders & not doubting but that will be the case We remain &c

Tr (DNA: PCC, item 50). Enclosed with Robert Morris' October 11, 1782,
report to a congressional committee regarding Pollock's services and settlement
of his accounts.

¹ Although Pollock apparently addressed these letters to "The Honble Andrew
Allen and Robert Morris, Committee of Congress," as he had an October 10,
1776, letter concerning a cargo that was subsequently received by the Secret
Committee, there is nothing in the journals of Congress to indicate that Allen
and Morris ever served together on a congressional committee that corresponded
with Pollock, and although both Morris and Allen were members of the Pennsylvania Committee of Safety in 1776 only Morris was a member of its sub-
committee for importing powder and arms. An Irish-born trader and planter,
Pollock (1737–1823) had spent a brief period during the late 1760s in Philadelphia cultivating mercantile connections before establishing himself in Havana
and finally settling in New Orleans. In 1776 he was serving as commercial and
real estate agent for the firm of Willing, Morris & Co. and actively supporting
American commercial interests in New Orleans. For copies of Pollock's October
10, 1776, letter, and several letters written in the spring of 1777, including the
May 5 letter mentioned here (in which he offers his commercial services and
reports Governor Galvez' interest in supporting an American expedition to
Pensacola), see PCC, item 50, 1:53–57. See also Morgan, *Naval Documents*,
3:1336–37; and Secret Committee Minutes of Proceedings, November 16, 1776.
Neither Pollock's May 4 letter nor the committee's letter to Galvez has been
found.

² According to Pollock's March 6, 1778, letter to the Committee of Commerce,
a copy of which is in PCC, item 50, 1:57–59, he did not learn of his appointment
as agent until March 4, when he received a November 21, 1777, letter of the
Committee of Commerce enclosing a duplicate of this Secret Committee letter,
but he had already been performing many of the tasks expected of such an

agent. For further details on Pollock's activities in behalf of the United States, see James A. James, *Oliver Pollock, the Life and Times of an Unknown Patriot* (New York: D. Appleton-Century Co., 1937).

Charles Carroll of Carrollton to Charles Carroll, Sr.

Dr Papa,   Pha. Friday P.M. 9 o'clock 13th June 1777.

Monsieur de Coudray an officer of ability and experience in the artillery and adjutant General in the Artillery of France is now attending on Congress waiting the ratification of the agreement made with him by Mr Deane in Paris. I much question whether Congress will confirm all the parts of the agreement, their Agent not being authorised to grant such conditions; but tho' they are very advantageous to Mr. de Coudray, and some of them of an important nature, yet I think they ought to be complied with, if the compliance will not create too much dissatisfaction in our army. Mr. de Coudray is certainly well connected in France, has had the confidence of 3 successive ministers of the war department, & has been very serviceable & instrumental in procuring for us 200 pieces of brass ordinance. He is moreover a man of letters, and certainly of distinguished merit in his profession, as he was appointed by the Ministry to superintend, under the Director General of Artillery, the casting of the new cannon in France, for it seems that court has been casting over a great quantity of its old ordinance on a new & improved model.

All accts from the army confirm the approaching movement of the enemy, & all agree that they are coming here, tho' their destination is not certainly known. The Secretary to our board returned yesterday from Camp; he says the men are healthy & in spirits and he thinks the army, tho' much smaller than what Gen. Washington commanded last Summer & fall, much more formidable. It is said Putnam has under him at Peaks Kills 5000. The articles of intelligence in Town's paper of the 12th instant, are said to be well grounded. Dessertion certainly prevails in the enemy's army. Within these 10 days, above 20 deserters have passed thro' this city; several of them I have seen, some I have spoken to, and they all agree that they have received no pay since their arrival at N. York. They say the British forces are in good health, but the Hessians sickly. The deserters I saw were fine, hearty fellows, and most of them tradesmen, they are gone into the country to work at their different trades. I shall not close this letter tonight. The attack with which this city is threatened has been productive of most salutary consequences. It has occasioned a coalition of parties: a Convention is to be called at a seasonable juncture for altering the Governt. if agreeable to the sense of a majority of the People, & Committees are appointed to collect that Sense, that is, whether they choose to have the Governt. altered or not. Col. Sam Meridith has reassumed his command in the militia; Cadwallader is sent for, & will no doubt follow Meredith's example; in five days, General Mifflin this day to be one, there would be 5 thousand militia collected at or near this city. 1100 met on the Common this day. Gen. Mifflin made them a spirited harangue, which was received with great applause. No Forces will be suffered to act as a neutral part, all must bear arms except Quakers, Monr. de Coudray, who was present at the review this day, spoke to me in high strains of compliment about the militia; he says they are the best Militia he ever saw. He is not a man of compliments, tho' polite, and therefore I lay the greater stress on his praises, as I believe them justly due. He farther remarked that Mifflin's harangue, great part of which he understood, called to his mind the times of Ancient Greece & Rome. I really am pleased with this gentleman, his address, tho' a Frenchman, is not elegant & easy, yet you may plainly see he has frequented & even been intimate with the Polite & Great. He seems to have studied more the arts & sciences than the Graces; yet his plain & unaffected manner, his good sense, & sweetness of temper gains upon us daily.

Saturday morning o'clock 14th June

About 1 o'clock last night I was awakened by an express to General Arnold, who lodges in this house. The express came from Bristol, & brings an account that the alarm guns from Rocky Hill & Princetown to Trenton were fired about 10 o'clock last night, a signal of the approach & movement of the enemy, and to alarm the militia of the Jersies, who have agreed to turn out & harass the enemy on their march. I can not help thinking it a false alarm, for I cannot persuade myself the enemy will hazard a march thro' the Jersies & an attack on this city, till they receive reinforcements either from Canada or Europe, and not above 1500 have yet arrived, and they are said to be sickly.

Monday's post will bring us interesting intelligence, which you may depend on being communicated to you by the post which will set off from this city next Tuesday. Please to present my complts to the Messrs. Howards & Capt. Ireland. I am, yr. most affectionate Son,

Ch Carroll of Carrollton

P.S. Do not forget to go over the list of bonds & examine which are near expiring.

RC (MdHi).

Committee for Foreign Affairs to the
Commissioners at Paris

Gentlemen   Philadelphia June 13th. 1777

Though the Dispatches prepared some Time since are not gone,[1] we think it best to write you again and give you an exact Account of the Situation of our Army & military Affairs to this Time. You were formerly made acquainted that immediately after our important Victory at Princeton on the 3d of January, General Washington took Post at Morris-Town, which appears to have been a well chosen Situation. From thence sending out Detachments of his Army, he speedily drove the Enemy from Hackensac, Chatham, Springfield, Westfield & Elizabeth Town; all which Places we have possessed ever since that Time, as well as Millstone and Princeton on the West, and Cranbury to the South, the Enemy having been confined to a narrow Communication upon Rariton River from Brunswick to Amboy 12 Miles. About ten Days ago, General Washington moved his Headquarters towards the Enemy, to a Place called Middle Brook about 8 Miles from Brunswick. He has now called in most of his outposts; and the Enemy have done the same, being chiefly collected about Brunswick, and just upon the Eve of some Movement, which is generally supposed to be intended against this City. We are taking every Measure to disappoint them, and have good Hopes, in Dependance upon divine Providence, as our Army has been augmenting daily for three Months past. It is given out that the Enemy intend to come up Delaware Bay with their Ships as well as by Land through New Jersey. It is probable that before the Vessel sails we shall have something to add upon this Subject.

In the northern Department Things are yet intirely quiet. We have a pretty strong Body at Tyconderoga. Some small Parties of the Enemy were up the Lake lately a considerable Way but are gone again & there is no Appearance of any important Motion soon. Whether this is owing to their not being ready, or to a Change in their Plan & the Army in Canada being ordered round to reinforce Genl. Howe, as some late Reports would make us believe, it is impossible to say with Certainty.

A third Body of our Troops is at PeeksKill upon Hudsons River, to defend the Passes towards Albany, and be ready to fall down upon New York, in case the greatest part of the Enemy's Army should be drawn from that Place. The Convention of that State has issued an Act of Indemnity, to encourage those who had been seduced to join the Enemy to return, which has had a very happy Effect.

Upon the whole, our Affairs wear as favorable an Aspect as at any Time since the Beginning of the War. And the Unanimity of all Ranks in the different States in Support of our Independence is greater than at any preceeding Period. The arbitrary Conduct, the Cruelty & Barbarity of the Enemy for the 26 Days in which they possessed some considerable part of New Jersey has been of Service to our Cause. See upon this Subject the Report of a Committee of Congress with the Proofs in the News Papers; which you may safely assure every Person

is a just & true but very small Sample of their Proceedings. We are
your most obedient, humble Servants,

Benja Harrison   Jno Witherspoon

Robt Morris   Ths. Heyward Junr

James Lovell

RC (PPAmP). Written by Lovell and signed by Lovell, Harrison, Heyward,
Morris, and Witherspoon.
¹ The last letter of the Committee for Foreign Affairs to the Commissioners at
Paris was that of May 30, 1777.

John Hancock to George Washington

Sir,   Philada. June 13th. 1777.
You will perceive from the enclosed Resolves, the fixed Determina-
tion of Congress to retaliate (as nearly as lies in their Power) on our
Enemies, should they think proper to send any of their Prisoners to
Great Britain, or to any other Part of the British King's Dominions
beyond Sea. This Resolution you will please to convey to Genl. Howe
as soon as possible, as it is of the utmost Importance.¹
If the sixteen additional Battalions are not all provided with Commanding Officers, the Congress, in Consequence of a Letter from Govr.
Caswell (an Extract of which I enclose you) have recommended
Colonel Abraham Shephard to the Command of one of the said Battalions, and doubt not you will honor him with the Appointment.² I
beg Leave to refer your Attention to the whole of the Resolves herewith transmitted.
Enclosed you have the Observations of Monsr. De Coudray on
Billingsport and the other Fortifications in this River, which I forward
for your Perusal.³ Every possible Measure is taking to render the Fortifications compleat.⁴
I have the Honour to be, with the utmost Esteem & Respect, Sir,
your most obed. & very hble Servt.   John Hancock Presidt

RC (DLC). In the hand of Jacob Rush and signed by Hancock. LB (DNA:
PCC, item 12A).
¹ See JCC, 8:449–50; and Washington, Writings (Fitzpatrick), 8:131–34,
182–83.
² See JCC, 8:450. The extract from North Carolina governor Richard Caswell's April 20 letter to Thomas Burke is in Washington Papers, DLC, and the
full text is in N.C. State Records, 11:456–57. Washington agreed to give
Colonel Sheppard command of a battalion to be raised in North Carolina, but
Sheppard failed to raise it in the alloted time and thus did not receive the
appointment. See JCC, 8:475; and Washington, Writings (Fitzpatrick), 8:475.
³ Hancock also enclosed resolves of June 7 through 11 on regimental pay-

masters, Apollos Morris, Benedict Arnold, the commissariat, ranking of officers, and the defense of the Delaware. *JCC,* 8:426–28, 432–48, 450–52.

⁴ After this sentence in the LB Hancock's secretary Jacob Rush first wrote and then deleted: "Your sevl. Favours to the   inst have been duely recd. and immediately laid before Congress."

Secret Committee Minutes of Proceedings

June 13, 1777

Come. met. Present Morris, Livingston, Whipple. Letters were received from Messrs. Fautreuil Commander of the French ship Amphitrite at Portsmouth, from J. Langdon Esqr. Contl. Agt. & from Capt. Jn. Paul Jones. Monsr. Fautreul hath declind the proposition made to him by the Come. of taking Capt. Jones on board his ship as Commander but is willing to proceed to Charles town on certain assurances be given him as per his sd. letter. Resolved That the sd. Letters be laid before Congress & that it is the opinion of this Come. that Capt. Fautrel shoud have the assurances given wch. he requires & be orderd round to Chs. town for a loading of Rice.¹ On considerg. the terms of agreemt. made with the Owners of the ship Mary & Elizabeth lying in the Inlet of Sinepuxent, the Come. finds that by Charter party, She is to be deliverd at this port, & is at the public risque until that time, & as it is now impracticable so to do (the enemys ships being so numerous in this bay) think best to charter her for a new voyage & have agreed with the Owners as follows. Sd. Ship is to be ballasted by the Owners & proceed when the Come. may direct to Virga. where She is to take on board 200 hhds of tobo. on public Acct. for any port in France, where She is to deliver the same, & bring back from thence any goods, wares & Merchandize, Arms & Ammunition that may be shippd on board by the Agents of the Come. to any safe port in these States when the voyage shall expire. The Come. are to insure that vessel, for sd. voyage, at £2700 Curry. & to allow 4 g[uinea]s per hhd. freight for tobo. & 2/6 sterlg. per foot, for the goods &c brought back.²

An order was drawn on Mr. Morris in favor of Ann Stewart wife of Jas. Stewart for £25 as a reward for his havg. taken up an Anchor & Cable belongg. to the ship Olive branch in this bay on the 7th Augt. last, wch. She was obligd to leave on the approach of the Enemy's ships of war, sd. ship being then charterd & insurd by the Committee.³

MS (MH–H).

¹ There is no mention of this matter in the journals, but for details on the committee's proposal, see Secret Committee to John Paul Jones, May 9, 1777.

² On September 3, 1777, committee members Robert Morris and Richard Henry Lee agreed to grant Capt. Peter Young of the *Mary & Elizabeth* a reward for having "faithfully & successfully performed a voyage to France & back

to this Continent with sd. ship on public Accts." Journal of the Secret Committee, fol. 141, Lee Papers, MH–H.

³ With the departure of William Whipple on June 18, the Secret Committee dwindled to two members (Robert Morris and Philip Livingston). Accordingly, on July 5, 1777, Congress created a new Committee of Commerce and vested it with all the powers that had been granted the Secret Committee. Although the remaining Secret Committee members were directed to close their accounts and transfer balances to the new committee, some accounts remained unsettled more than a year later when Congress, on September 4, 1778, authorized the remaining Secret Committee members to "employ proper persons for adjusting and closing the accounts of the Secret Committee." See *JCC,* 8:533–34; 12:878–79. The last entry in the journal, which the copyist indicated was in the hand of Robert Morris, was dated October 5, 1778, and reported that Morris and Francis Lewis met and agreed to hire a clerk. Journal of the Secret Committee, fol. 142, Lee Papers, MH–H.

John Adams to Abigail Adams

Phyladelphia June 14. 1777

This Week has produced an happy Reconciliation between the two Parties in this City and Commonwealth, the Friends of the new Constitution and those who wish for Amendments in it. . . .¹ Mifflin invited the People to assemble in the State House Yard, at the Desire of General Washington, who sent them an Account that the Motions of the Enemy indicated an intention to begin an Expedition, and that every Appearance intimated this City to be their Object.²

Mifflin made an Harrangue, in which he applauded the Exertions of the Citizens last December, ascribed the successes of Trenton and Princeton to their Behaviour and exhorted them to the same Spirit, Unanimity and Firmness, upon this occasion. Advised them to choose their Officers, under the new Militia Law and meet him in the common on Fryday.

The Citizens by loud shouts and Huzzas, promised him to turn out, and accordingly, they met him in great Numbers Yesterday.

Mean Time, Generals Armstrong, Mifflin and Reed, waited on the Assembly, to interceed with them, to gratify those who wished Amendments in the Constitution with an Appeal to the People.

The Pensilvania Board of War too, applied, for the same Purpose as you will see by one of the inclosed Papers.

The House agreed to it. Thus the Dispute is in a Way to be determined, and a Coalition formed.

June 15

Yesterday We had an Alarm, and News that the Enemy were on their March, towards Philadelphia in two Divisions—one at Shanks Mills 8 miles from Brunswick, the other at Ten Mile Run, about Ten

Miles from Brunswick on another Road, a Road that goes to Corells Ferry.

We feel pretty bold, here. If they get Philadelphia, they will hang a Mill stone about their Necks. They must evacuate N. Jersey. The Jersey Militia have turned out, with great Spirit. Magistrates and Subjects, Clergy and Laity, have all marched, like so many Yankees.

If How should get over the Delaware River, and We should not have an Army to stop him, Congress I suppose will remove, fifty or sixty Miles into the Country. But they will not move hastily.

Riding and walking, have given me tolerable Health, and I must confess my Spirits, notwithstanding the Difficulties We have to encounter, are very good.[3]

RC (MHi). Adams, *Family Correspondence* (Butterfield), 2:261–62.

[1] Suspension points in MS.

[2] An account of this public meeting appeared in the *Pennsylvania Gazette*, June 18, 1777.

[3] On June 16 Adams wrote Abigail a brief note complimenting her on the management of their finances and speculating on his next opportunity to return home. "I know not what would become of me, and mine," he stated, "if I had not such a friend to take Care of my Interests in my Absence.

"You will have Patience with me this Time, I hope, for this Time will be the last.

"I shall stay out this Year, if I can preserve my Health, and then come home, and bid farewell to great Affairs. I have a Right to spend the Remainder of my days in small ones." Adams, *Family Correspondence* (Butterfield), 2:267.

Board of War to the States

Sir,   War Office June 16. 1777.

By Order of the Board of War, I have the Honour of enclosing you two Resolves of Congress,[1] to the latter whereof, I wou'd particularly request yr. immediate Attention, as great Inconveniencies daily arise from the Lists of the Army not being completely returned.

You will be pleased also to render an Account to the Board of all Monies expended on Account of Prisoners of War & Sums paid to them. You will be pleased to be very exact in the Account, and see that no Charges are omitted as the Enemy are rigidly accurate in their Charges against the States on account of Prisoners. All Sums omitted will be lost by the State wherein the Charge was neglected to be made.

I have the honor to be, Your very obt. Servant.

Richard Peters Secy

RC (M–Ar). Addressed: "Honble President of the Council of the State of Massachusetts Bay." Slightly variant texts of this letter are in *N.H. State Records,* 8:587; *Journals of N.Y. Prov. Cong.,* 1:983; and *N.C. State Records,* 11:497.

These texts, considered in conjunction with the nature of the resolves enclosed, suggest that this letter was a circular letter sent to all the states.

[1] These were April 1 resolves stating that no Continental officer "shall take rank by virtue of a commission antedated, but rank shall be determined by the time of appointment, unless otherwise directed by a special resolution of Congress," and asking all the states to "forthwith transmit to the Board of War, exact lists of all officers appointed by them in the continental army, with the dates of their commissions and times of appointment." *JCC,* 7:217.

Board of War to George Washington

Sir   War Office June 16th. 1777

Immediately on my Arrival I attended to the several Things mentioned by your Excellency.[1] Two hundred Spears are sent me by General Mifflin.[2] I have ordered three hundred more to be made but the Workmen are going out with the Militia & complain of the Want of seasoned Stuff for the Shafts. They will I hope however be shortly completed. Should you choose any Alteration from those sent the Commissary Genl. of M. Stores will attend to the having it done. Would it not be better to have Slings to the Spears that they may be slung at the Men's Backs when they are using their rifles? Or are they to be used as Rests to keep the Rifle steady? There are one thousand Tin Cartridge Boxes already made in this City, Five hundred are sent on to your Excellency & the remainder waits your Orders. The five hundred Arms are also sent, altho' they can be but illy spared as our Stock here runs very low.

I received from Mr Tilghman & laid before the Board the Establishment of the Pay of the Light Dragoons. In the Troops passing thro' & raised in this City I have observed that they have Quarter Masters in every Troop who are Persons thinking themselves entitled to a superior Rank in the Army to that of a Serjeant. Is it your Excellency's Opinion that these Gentlemen should be left out of the Establishment or is there to be a Quarter Master & Qr. Mr. Serjeant to each Troop? If so no Pay is established for the Qr Mr of a Troop who perhaps in your Excellency's Opinion is an unnecessary Officer.[3]

I have the Honour to be with great Respect, your very obedt humble Servt,   Richard Peters Secy

RC (DLC).

[1] Secretary Peters had just returned from a visit to Washington's headquarters at Middlebrook, N.J. Washington, *Writings* (Fitzpatrick), 8:247–48. It is not known for what reason he made this trip.

[2] On June 10 Washington had requested Maj. Gen. Thomas Mifflin to forward these spears from Philadelphia, observing that they were "fit for Horse or light Foot." Ibid., p. 222.

[3] Washington responded to these questions on June 20. Ibid., p. 273.

Charles Carroll of Carrollton to Charles Carroll, Sr.

Dr Papa,   Monday P.M. 16th June 1777 Pha.
I have yours of the 11th instant covering your letter to Lewis, & one from him; the former of which I approve. I shall seal & send to the Priests as you direct, the latter I shall carefully keep.

I have heard of your letters to Chase.[1] You really give me great uneasiness. I wish you would never write or say anything more on the subject. What good do you propose to yourself? Will your invectives alter the law? May they not injure you much? For a wise man & of so much experience in the world, I think you have acted imprudently, as all men will, when they suffer their passions to get the better of their reason. The conduct, I should pursue, would be this: I would endeavour to make those who tendered the money, sensible of the injustice of their proceeding, tho' countenanced by law. If honor & justice will not restrain them, we must submit to the injurious act, & tamely submit to be plundered. I believe all the eloquence of Tully would be thrown away on a knave, who was determined to take advantage of the law. If you love me, you will persue this conduct. If you can place the money out at interest in Maryd. I should prefer that mode of getting rid of it to all others; if not, I believe you will not do better than by lending it to the Continent.

For the late movements in the Jersies I refer you to the inclosed prints. Whether the enemy intend to visit this city is uncertain; I think they will not till they find an opportunity of beating G. Washingon. I want my horses: do hire some careful trusty person to bring them up as soon as possible; no horses can be hired here, nor bought unless at a most extravagent rate: and I find I begin to want exercise. Direct the person to Mrs. Yard's in Second Street opposite the city Tavern. Send up Tartar, & Mrs. Darnall's horse. I have here my Saddle, my harness, & Sulkey, so the person who brings up the horses need bring only the saddle for the horse which must ride back again.

By advice from Canada given by a Spy we hear that Burgoyne & M'Lane arrived at Quebec the 10th May without any troops. The enemy have 7000 British & Germans in Canada. They lost last winter, in the Montreal district only, 1100. The Canadians will not inlist.

If you can find out a trusty person to bring up my horses, send me by him £150 in continental money. All the money you Sent me by Colo. Sim was Maryd. money.

Tuesday morning, 9 o'clock 17th June
You will not receive the newspapers by this day's post, as they will not come out till the evening. I therefore shall give you the substance of Arnold's letter dated Sunday evening 9 o'clock from Corriel's Ferry. "Enemy at Somerset court house, 7000 strong; have a line of com-

munication from thence to Brunswick. Sullivane at Fleming's town in the Jersies 12 miles distant from Corriel's ferry consequently near the enemy; his force supposed 5000. Arnold presses for reinforcements that he may join Sullivane & attack the enemy in front, while Washington attacks their rear. Arnold says the Jersey militia turn out very spiritedly & generally, hopes we shall have in a few days 20000 men in the Jersies." G. Washington writes on the 15th that he supposes the enemy had two motives in view when they marched out of Brunswick; 1st to cut off Sullivane, but this he prevented by moving his Station & making a rapid march so as to get before the enemy; 2d to draw Gen. Washington from his strong post. The General has sent for 4000 men from Peak's Kill under Gen. Putnam, who it is said has 8000 there; I wish he may have 6000. A letter from St. Eustatia dated 6th May advises that 8 sail of the line & several frigates had sailed from Brest for America; that war between France & Engd was inevitable: but who the letter writer is I know not nor how he gets his information. It is likewise rumoured that the discontent in Engd. are got to a great pitch & that they begin to see they will lose their colonies. My love to Molly & Mrs. Darnall. I am, yr. affectionate Son. Ch Carroll of Carrollton

RC (MdHi).
¹ For an extended discussion of the elder Carroll's controversy with Samuel Chase over Maryland's legal tender law, see Ronald Hoffman, *A Spirit of Dissension: Economics, Politics, and the Revolution in Maryland* (Baltimore: Johns Hopkins University Press, 1973), pp. 210–22.

William Ellery to Oliver Wolcott

Dear Sir,   Philadelphia June 16th 1777
    It hath been observed that this Scene should be considered as a Palæstra for the Exercise and Trial of human Virtue, if so it is not to be wonder'd at that even the Apostle Paul should have had Beasts at Ephesus to combat, nor ought it to be a matter of Amazement to Us that the uninspired Virtuous should have to conflict with the Vices and Follies of the World. Under this Idea may not this Stage of Existence be considered as a School of *Right*?
    I shall leave it to you to solve this Question, as well as to discover the Persons who were said to be suspected. I have endeavoured to plough with the Heifer, and to make the Discovery you want but have not been able to effect it. I should be glad to serve you in this or in any other Matter within my Power. I owe this to the Acquaintance I have with you and to the good Opinion I have been taught to entertain of your honorable Family. I expect to set out for our State in a few days, when I return I hope I shall have the pleasure of seeing you in Congress

when, if you should not have before obtained the Intelligence you wish, I will assist you in obtaining it.

Genl. Howe hath made a Move with his main Body. It was by the last Advice at Somerset, the Remainder are at Brunswick and on the Line of Communication between those two Places. If he should come forward he would meet with a severe Check. If he should remain where he is, but a short time, he may not be able to return. Things look well both at home and abroad. I am glad to hear that you are like to collect your Quotas. We shall have a fine Army and it will be by what I hear well officer'd. It is said that France & Spain are about to divide Portugal between them, that She hath called upon Britain for Assistance, and that Burgoyne is gone or going with some Troops to their Aid. Mynherr hath given a laconick Answer to Mr. York. In a Word John Bull is in poor Loaf. Tryon hath issued a Proclamation requiring *Benevolences* from the Tories in Kings & Richmond Counties &c. You will soon see the Proclamation with suitable Comments. It makes me laugh when I think of the Situation of the Tories. On one Side, of those who are with the Enemy Donations are asked by Howe, on the other Hand Sequestration and forfeiture of Estate are the Portion assigned them by the Whigs. I believe this same Proclamation will heartily sicken them and all the Tories.

A Duel hath been fought at Georgia between the late President Gwinnett and Genl. McIntosh.[1] The Assembly called upon the latter, as I am told, to know why an Expedition that was formed had not proceded. Gwinnet said it was owing to the General. He said it was a falsehood. Words ensued. A Challenge was given. They fought with Pistols. Both were wounded in the Thigh. Gwinnet died of his Wound. McIntosh hath not yet recovered. This World you will say again is the School of *Wrong*. We ought to be thankful to our Education and Climate that We are not forced out off Life in this Way. The People of New-England are not so prodigal of Life as the Southern People are. That you Sir may live long and happy is the sincere wish of, Yrs. Wm. Ellery

RC (CtHi). Addressed: "The Honble Oliver Wolcott Esq., Litchfield."

[1] This incident is discussed in George Walton to Lachlan McIntosh, April 18, 1777, note 2.

Rhode Island Delegates to the Rhode Island Governor and Assembly

Gentlemen   Philadelphia June 16th 1777

Congress sensible of the great Distress which Our army and the Inhabitants of these States must be reduced to, the Fall and Winter ensuing, for the Article of Salt, unless timely Provision be made, have passed the Resolves inclosed.[1] We doubt not, the most fixed and speedy Attention will be paid to Them; The last Resolve You will be pleased to communicate to the Continental Agent, and request him to communicate it to any Masters of Vessells fitting out of Our State on the Continental Account (if there are any such). The first Vollume of the Journals of Congress are printed, and twenty Copies are ordered for each State, but as yet we have no Opportunity of sending them.[2] A General Movement of Lord How's Army to attempt, as was by most People conceived, this City hath caused a general Alarm thro this State and the State of New Jersey. We have the Pleasure to inform You that the Militia in both States turn out with Spirit, And from every Information Congress hath received we entertain a hopefull Prospect of the Event. The Enemy we doubt not, are without the least Hopes of a Reinforcement of any Consequence this year. That the present Appearances may induce the States of New-England, with united Efforts and Spirit to extirpate the Vermin which have too long infested Our State, is the most ardent Wish of all; Beyond Expression must such an Event be to those who feel most for the Honor of New-England and the Peace, Welfare and Happiness of that State we have the Honor to represent. May that Event soon coincide with the Desires of, Gentlemen, your most Obedt, humble Servts.   William   Ellery

                                                  Hy. Marchant

P.S. I expect to set out for Providence in a few Days. W Ellery

RC (R–Ar). Written by Marchant and signed by Marchant and Ellery, with a postscript by Ellery. Addressed: "The Govr. & Compy. of the State of Rhode Island."
    [1] See *JCC,* 8:461–62.
    [2] On June 2 Congress had resolved that "twenty copies of the volume of journals be delivered to the delegates of each State, for the use of their respective States." *JCC,* 8:432.

Samuel Adams to Elizabeth Adams

My dear Betsy   Philade June 17, 1777
    I am disappointed in not receiving a Letter from you by yesterdays Post. The Fears you expressd in your last of the Arrival of Burgoin gave me Uneasiness. We receivd Advice from our Friends in France which gave us some Reason to apprehend the Intention of the Enemy was to attack Boston, and we thought it necessary to give timely Notice of it. I hope the People there will always be so much on their Guard as to prepare for the worst, but I think you will not be in Danger this Summer. This City has been given out as their Object.

Last Saturday General Howe with the main Body of his Army marched
from Brunswick to Somerset Court House about 8 Miles on the Road
to Cariel's Ferry with an Intention as it was thought to cross the Delaware there, but Genl Sullivan with about three thousand Regulars and
Militia got Possession of the post there. The Jersey Militia are coming
out with great Spirit and I think the progress of the Enemy in that way
is effectually stopped. Coll Whipple will set off tomorrow for Boston &
Portsmouth. If I can possibly get time I will write by him. I am now in
great Haste. I hope you duly receivd my last inclosing one to Henry
Gardner Esq.,[1] and that the Matter therein mentiond is settled to your
Advantage. Give my Love to my Daughter, Sister Polly &c. Write to
me by every Post. Adieu my dear & believe me to be most affectionately,
your,   SA

RC (NN).
   [1] Adams' letter to Henry Gardner, the treasurer of Massachusetts, has not
been found.

Elbridge Gerry to Thomas Gerry

Dear Brother   Philadelphia June 17 1777
   I wrote to You the 13th & 20th May,[1] & have since agreed with the
Quarter Master General to spare the Tents which I intended for Tyonderoga, for the use of the Troops in the Jersies, as the Others are
well supplyed. You will please to desire Mr Chase the Deputy Quarter
Master General, who resides in or near Boston, to receive & forward
them to General Washington without Delay; & I think it will be well to
take his duplicate receipt for the Duck, Ticklinbg., (Oznabrigs if any)
Wrapper, Twine & Needles, & let one be sent to me & the other retained for your own Security. This may be done, notwithstanding You
may have taken the Sailmakers Receipt for these Articles, as You can
endorse the latter to Mr Chase, & let him pay for making the Tents.
   With Respect to the Salt, if a Vessel cannot be procured to send it to
North Carolina, I wish You would order it to be stored or sold as shall
appear best; observing, that as it cannot be easily removed It will be
eligible to store it in a place not readily approached by Ships of Force,
but I hope a Vessel will be procured agreable to my former Letter. I
wish to be informed of the prices given by Mr Chase for the Articles
aforesd. & what are the prices of Salt & Blankets.
   I shall order a Remittance to be made for the Ballance of your Account as soon as known, or You may draw for the same if the Money is
immediately wanted.
   Mr. Howe is manæuvering in the Jersies, but our Army is on so respectable a Footing, that he has not yet ventured to attack them.

I find by a Letter from Doctor Jackson that the several Branches of our Family are individually in Health, which gives me great pleasure; I am as well as the Climate & Season will admit & wishing the Continuance of Health & Happiness to You all remain, with sincere Esteem your affectionate Friend,   E Gerry

[*P.S.*] My Complmts to the Doctr & other Friends.

RC (MHi).
¹ Gerry's May 20 letter has not been found.

Francis Lightfoot Lee to Richard Henry Lee

Dear Brother,   Philadelphia June 17. 1777
   On Friday last we received advice from Genl. Sullivan that the Enemy was advancing with their whole force, in two columns, one to Prince town, the other to Coryel's ferry. As we knew Genl. Howe had arrived at Brunswick with a considerable body of troops, It threw this City into great consternation, being in no state of defence, tho it has had so long warning. Sullivan with 1600 C[ontinental] troops & as many Jersey militia marched on Saturday to Coryel's ferry, secured his baggage, heavy Cannon & the boats; and on Sunday morning expected to be join'd by 2000 more J. militia, when he proposed to meet the Enemy, harrass them & retard their march. We learn since that it was only part of Howe's Army, and that they are encamped at Somerset Courthouse. Genl. Washington writes that he did not think it proper to follow them immediately as he supposed their principal intention was to draw him out of his strong camp into the plain being as yet much superior in numbers & their train, that he had endeavor'd to harrass them with light troops but with little effect, being too well guarded with Artillery.¹ Genl. Arnold, who is guarding the passes upon the River, wrote us yesterday, that the Jerseys are all in Arms; presses for the Militia of this State to be sent forward directly, for that if the party at Somerset shou'd escape, still Howe must be attacked while the spirit of the people is so high. Unhappily, tho the parties here have droped their dispute, yet things were left in such confusion by it, that it will be some time before they can be got into order. However as Genl. W. has order'd most of the troops at Peek's Kill to join him, we expect he will be strong enough with the assistance of Jersey to attack Howe. A Letter was recd. yesterday in this City, from a reputable person in Statia dated May 8th who says, he had just recd. a very late Bristol paper which said, the people of England were in the greatest consternation from the certainty of a French war, that there was the hotest press all over England, but very few seamen to be found, that they gave up America as lost, & were beyond measure confounded & distressed. We

have not yet heard from the Boston fleet. Genl. Gates arrived here yesterday. Every thing is in a very good way in the north. He is extreamly offended with our proceedings towards him, & will certainly leave the service. Your packet for France is not yet gone, & God knows when she will. I wish you wou'd have some measures fallen upon, to prevent the rascally tory Jew engrossers of this City & Baltimore from buying up the Salt & other necessaries imported into Virginia. None of the importations shou'd be allow'd to be exported, but by public agents of some State in distress & they shou'd purchase only under regulations made by the Governmt. Roman de Lyle talks of offering his services to Virginia, & depends upon you for an introduction When he arrives there. What troops shall hereafter come from Virginia, shou'd bring arms with them, for we are exhausted by the militia. My best complimts to the Govr & other friends. Yr. afft. bror. & friend,

Francis Lightfoot Lee

RC (PHi).

[1] Washington's June 13–15 letter is in PCC, item 152, 4:253–58, and Washington, *Writings* (Fitzpatrick), 8:239–44.

Marine Committee to Samuel Chew

Sir,   In Marine Committee Philadelphia June 17. 1777.

The good recommendations we have had of you as being well qualified for a command in our Navy, has induced us to appoint you a Captain therein, in full faith that it will be your chief duty to contribute all in your power to the Interest of the United States and the Honor of their Flag.[1]

We now think proper to direct that you repair directly to New London where you are to Take the Command of the Brigt Resistance lately purchased by Nath. Shaw jr Esqr our agent at that place. That Gentleman will assist you in fitting and manning that vessel, and we expect your best endeavors will be united with his, to have this done with all possible expedition.

We have directed our said Agent to make the necessary advances of the money that will be required in this business, and to put on Board sufficient provisions for a four month's cruize, therefore as soon as ready for the Sea, you are to proceed immediately on a cruize against the enemy choosing such stations as you think will be most likely to intercept their Merchant or Transport Ships, and you are to take, sink, Burn or destroy as many of their vessels of every Kind as may be in your power.

The prizes you may take you will send into the most convenient and safe Ports in these States addressed to the Continental Agents, and you may continue your cruize so long as your provisions will last and then return into the first safe Port you can make, advising us of your arrival when we will give you fresh orders.

You are to preserve strict discipline on board your vessel, using your people well; and you will treat any prisoners you may take with humanity; great care must be taken of the Brig, her materials and Stores, observing that you are to be accountable for every thing on Board, therefore you will take care that your officers keep proper accounts of the expenditures in their respective departments and see that no waste is made of any kind.

You must make monthly returns of the State of your Vessel while in Port, together with exact lists of every person on board, to the Navy Board at Boston or at this place and recommending strict attention to these orders we remain Sir, Your very humble Servants,

Roger Sherman	Robt Morris
Nichs. Van Dyke	H. F. Marchant
Phil Livingston	Abra Clark
	Thos Burke

P.S. We will send forward to Mr Deshon a sufficient number of Blank Commissions & Warrants to be filled up with the names of such Persons as he may think proper to appoint your officers.

P.S. Should you be tempted by any circumstances not known to us at present to continue your cruize untill your provisions & stores may be nearly expended you may procure further supplies at such Foreign Ports as may be convenient for the purpose and we shall punctually pay your drafts accot.

Robt Morris	Roger Sherman
Phil Livingston	Thos Burke
H. F. Marchant	Abra. Clark
	Nichs. Van Dyke

Tr (CtHi).

[1] Chew was a Connecticut sea captain who before the war had worked for Nathaniel Shaw, Jr., the Continental prize agent in that state, and later had been recommended by him for a Continental command. In March 1778 Chew was killed in an engagement with the British in the West Indies during his first cruise on the brigantine *Resistance*. William J. Morgan, *Captains to the Northward: The New England Captains in the Continental Navy* (Barre, Mass.: Barre Publishing Co., 1959), pp. 11–13, 118–19.

Marine Committee to John Deshon

Sir   June 17th. 1777

We have lately added to our Navy the Brigantine Resistance purchased by Nathaniel Shaw jr. Esquire our Agent at New London and have appointed Captain Samuel Chew to command her. We now inclose you some Blank Commissions which we must trouble you to fill up with the Names of such persons as you think proper for Lieutenants and Other Officers on board this Brigantine. In doing this we wish the preference to be given to the Officers that are in our Service at Rhode Island who may be unemployed or are deserving of promotion, this we leave to your discernment and requesting that you will transmit a List of the names of those you appoint, we remain Sir, Your very hble servants

P.S. We give you this trouble in consequence of your being Appointed a Member of the Navy Board of the Eastern Department.[1]

LB (DNA: PCC Miscellaneous Papers, Marine Committee Letter Book).

[1] John Deshon, a New London, Conn., merchant and sea captain who had extensive business dealings with Nathaniel Shaw, Jr., the Continental prize agent in Connecticut, had been appointed a member of the navy board in the eastern department on May 6. See *JCC*, 7:331; and Frances M. Caulkins, *History of New London, Connecticut. From the First Survey of the Coast in 1612, to 1852* (New London: Published by the author, 1860), pp. 505–6. For Deshon's dealings with Shaw, consult the indexes in Morgan, *Naval Documents*, vols. 4–7.

Marine Committee to Nathaniel Shaw, Jr.

Sir,   In Marine Committee, Philadelphia, June 17, 1777

We received by Captain Chew your letter of the 29th[1] ultimo advising your having purchased a Brig suitable for an armed Cruizer in our Navy.

On recuring to our letter to you of the 22d August last we find our orders were expressly that you should purchase & fit out the schooner taken by Commodore Hopkins in his return from the New Providence expedition and sent by his fleet into your Port. Our principal inducement in giving those orders was, that a vessel of that kind was then wanted for an expedition we had planned, & Commodore Hopkins recommended that schooner as suitable for our purpose. If on examination you found that vessel to be defective, you certainly did your duty to decline the purchase of her, but we cannot consider that you were authorized by the orders we gave you, to buy a Brig eight months after, without first having consulted us on that head. Commodore Hopkins has never been invested with any authority from us to order the purchase of vessels for our Navy, and we beg leave to recommend in future an observance of our orders only; advising us when you think any alteration of them will be of service to the publick.

From what we have thought proper to say on this subject, you will perceive that we do not consider ourselves bound to take this vessel; but as we think that the public service will be benefited thereby, we have concluded to take her, and have appointed Captain Samuel Chew to command her. We now request that you will assist him in getting said vessel ready for the sea with all possible expedition. You will please to put on board Provisions &c for a four months cruize, and make the necessary advances of money which will be wanted for manning & fitting her out, & recommend your doing everything in the most frugal manner.

Should you have any money belonging to the States in your hands for which you are to account with the Committee, you may apply it to this purpose, if not, you may draw on us, & your Bills shall be paid.

You will please furnish us in due time with accounts of the cost and outfitt of this vessel, with proper vouchers; and a list of the men on board at the time of sailing.

Recommending this business to your attention We remain Sir, Your very humble servants,   Robt Morris   Roger Sherman

Phil. Livingston   Abra. Clark

H. Marchant   Thos. Burke

Nichs Van Dyke

P.S. This brig is to be called the "*Resistance.*"

Reprinted from *Historical Magazine* 10 (October 1866): 306. LB (DNA: PCC Miscellaneous Papers, Marine Committee Letter Book).
    [1] "27th" in LB.

Robert Morris to Jonathan Hudson

Sir   Philada. June 17th 1777

I have your letter of the 2d & 6th Inst. from Williamsburg & duely note your transactions as therein described with which I am perfectly satisfied & hope they will end to our mutual advantage.[1]

Mr Benjn. Harrison writes me the 7th June that by express the day before you had called on him for £5500. In your letter of the 6th June you make no mention of it. Mr Braxton says he was to supply you with £2000 & you say nothing about it. The latter I suppose may be right but the former must certainly be some mistake which your next will no doubt clear up. I expect this will find you at Baltimore and I hope with part of your Goods safe arrived. I cannot by this Post give you the prices of Goods here but you shall have them by next post. This you may depend, every thing is scarce & dear, I believe Salt is 10 Dollers per bushl. Spirits if good 35/ to 40/ per Gall. West India Rum 25/ to 30/. However Sales are just now at a stand because Genl Howes movements in the Jersies last Week indicated a design on this place. The Militia were called out & business laid on side. I shall soon be able to tell you whether to send any thing here & what articles will answer best. I cannot write to Virginia about the Salt, but if they do stop it, I will interfere on a proper representation thereof from you. I hope the Pilot Boat you bought may answer expectation but I think with Mr Braxton that she has too many Owners. I hope you'l be able to furnish me with Goods or Money in time to pay the whole or greatest part of the bills drawn & to be drawn upon me for this concern & I am Sir Your obedt hble Servt. Robt Morris

RC (NHi).
[1] Morris had written a brief letter to Hudson two weeks earlier explaining that in order not to miss "good bargains for want of Money or Credit I agree to pay Your drafts on me to the extent of five or Six thousand Pounds this Curry. or even for one or Two Thousand pounds more provided you allow a reasonable time between the times of drawing so that I may not be put to inconvenience & as fast as you make purchases send up the Goods that I may be reimbursed soon as possible." Robert Morris to Jonathan Hudson, June 3, 1777, Fogg Collection, MeHi.

John Adams to Abigail Adams

Philadelphia June 18. 1777

We shall have all the Sages and Heroes of France here before long.

Mr. Du Coudray is here, who is esteemed the most learned Officer in France. He is an Artillery Officer.

Mr. De la Balme is here too, a great Writer upon Horsemanship and Cavalry. He has presented me with two Volumes written by himself upon these subjects, elegantly printed, bound and gilt.[1]

Mr. De Vallenais is with him, who speaks very good English.[2]

The inclosed Papers will give you all the News. You get Intelligence sooner and better than We.

We are under no more Apprehensions here than if the British Army was in the Crimea. Our Fabius will be slow, but sure.

Arnold, You see will have at them, if he can.

RC (MHi). Adams, *Family Correspondence* (Butterfield), 2:267–68.
[1] Augustin Mottin de La Balme (1736–80) had written *Essais sur l'equitation* (Amsterdam and Paris: 1773), and *Elemens de tactique pour la cavalerie* (Paris: 1776). Adams, *Family Correspondence* (Butterfield), 2:268n.1. On July 8 he was commissioned a colonel and inspector of cavalry. *JCC,* 8:539.
[2] On July 8 Joseph de Valnais was appointed an aide to Colonel de La Balme. *JCC,* 8:539.

Samuel Adams to James Warren

My dear Sir   Philade June 18 1777

This Letter will be deliverd to you by my worthy Friend Colo Whipple a Delegate of the State of New Hampshire. He is a Gentleman of Candor, and I wish he may have an opportunity of conversing freely with some one of Influence in the Massachusetts Bay upon Matters which concern that State particularly. I know of no one to whom I can recommend him on the Occasion with more Propriety than to yourself. He will be able to give you such Information of *Persons* & Things as one would not chuse to throw on Paper in this precarious Time, when an Accident might turn the Intelligence into a wrong Channel.

I observe by the Boston Papers last brought to us, that you are again plac'd in the Chair of the House of Representatives, with which I am well pleasd. Mr Pain Speaker pro Temp, Mr Hancock *first* Member of the Boston Seat and Mr T Cushing a Councellor *at large*. I have the Honor of knowing but few of your Members. I hope my Countrymen have been wise in their Elections, and I pray God to bless their Endeavors for the Establishment of publick Liberty, Virtue and Happiness.

You will hear before this will reach you of the Movements of the Enemy. It has been the general Opinion for some Months past that Philadelphia is their Object. Should they gain this Point, what will it avail them, unless they beat our Army? This I think they will not do. My Wish is that our Army may beat them, because it would, in my opinion, put a glorious End to the Campaign, & very probably the War. I confess I have always been so very wrong headed as not to be over well pleasd, with what is called the Fabian War in America. I conceive a great Difference between the Scituations of the Carthaginian and the British Generals. But I have no Judgment in Military Matters, and therefore will leave the Subject to be discussd, as it certainly will be, by those who are Masters of it.

I cannot conclude this Letter without thanking you for your Care in carrying a Matter in which I was interested through the General Assembly, of which I have been informd by our Friend Mr J A. I wish to hear from you.

Adieu my Friend,   S A

RC (MHi).

Thomas Burke to Richard Caswell

Dr Sir   Philadelphia June 18th 1777

Having just heard of an opportunity, I inclose you the Resolution of

Congress relative to Colonel Sheppard's Battalion.[1] I have written a letter which I left at my lodgings,[2] and have not now an opportunity of getting it, but I think it right to take advantage of the present conveyance for communicating to you the Resolution. You may expect the other by post. Mean time, having not one instant more time, I am with respect, Your obed. Sert, Thos Burke

Tr (Nc–Ar).
[1] See *JCC*, 8:475; and John Hancock to Washington, June 13, 1777, note 2.
[2] Not found.

Abraham Clark to James Caldwell

Dr. sir,[1]   Phila June 18h. 1777.

It was with pleasure I heard of the Enemys moving this way and am sorry they came no further. As matters are now Circumstanced I fear we shall have an Idle Summer—fighting is at this Time Necessary to keep up the spirit of the Forces—without it our Militia will be dispirited and not easily called out at another Time. Caution may forbid such a measure, Upon a supposition we can Support an army for years to come, but this I fear will not be easily Accomplished. The dearness of all the Necessaries of life makes the Support of An Army exceeding expensive, and their pay must be proportiona[lly. . . .] I take no pleasure in sheding blood, but at this time I think a little of it is requisite. Inactivity, if practised, will ruin our Army if not our Cause. We have many Spirited officers who I dare say wish for an Opportunity to Signalize themselves and I wish their Ardour may not be suffered to cool. We have no late News from Europe other than in the Papers. All seems to go on well for us there, and our Cause in the main may be said to appear prosperous. I take this opportunity by Mr. Arndt just to remind you, that if you have forgot, you are not forgotten by Dr Sir, your Humble Servt, Abra. Clark

RC (PHC).
[1] The endorsement on the verso of this letter—"From Abm. Clark Esqr, June 18"—appears to be in the hand of Rev. James Caldwell, one of Clark's regular correspondents. See also Clark to Caldwell, August 1, 1776, note 1.

Committee for Foreign Affairs to the
Commissioners at Paris

Philadelphia June 18th 1777

In this we send you an Account of the most Material Matters which have happened in the Military department.

Thomas Heyward, Jr.

The Enemy about ten weeks ago sent a large Party and destroyed some Continental Stores lodged at Peeks Kill the value not Great, and retreated immediately after. They afterwards made an Attempt to surprise M. Gen. Lincoln at Bound Brook which He vigilantly escaped with the loss of about 60 Men. Mr. Tryon who is made a Major Genl. was sent with about 2200 Men to destroy the Stores at Danbury in Connecticut. Notice was received time enough to remove the Most Valuable while Gens. Arnold and Woorster raised the Militia and attacked the Enemy in their Retreat with Good Success. The New-York Paper which may be Considered as Genl Howes Gazette makes their loss in Killed and Wounded 104, we may give them Credit for twice the Number. The loss we Sustained in Stores was chiefly in Salt Provisions and Rum and We had the Satisfaction of learning that the Cargoes of the Prizes brought in the same week amounted in the first Article to double the Quantity lost. Genl. Woorster who behaved Gallantly was mortally wounded and is since dead. Scarce a Week have passed without Skirmishing in which we have been very fortunate.

General Washington has removed from Morris Town to some advantageous Ground near Bound and Middle Brooks within eight Miles of Brunswick and the following is a Regular State of Intelligence received here since the 11th Inst.

June 11th

At a Meeting this day in the State House Yard Genl Mifflin dispatched for that Purpose from Genl. Washington informed the Inhabitants that from the late preparations of the Enemy, he had reason to believe their design was by a forced March to endeavour to possess themselves of Philadelphia, it was then Proposed and unanimously assented to, to turn out agreeable to the Militia Law.

12th

A Letter from Genl. Sullivan at Princeton received about 9 this Eveng informed that the Enemy at Brunswick had began to move the Preceeding Night but was prevented by the Rain.

13th

The Alarm Gun in this City fired at three this Morning answering the Alarm Guns up the River. Several letters by Express from Bristol mention the hearing Alarm Guns Towards Trenton and Princeton, but that no Express had arrived there from Genl Sullivan at Princeton.

14th

Express from Genl Arnold at Trenton informs, that the Enemy had moved in the Night from Brunswick; that Genl Sullivan had likewise moved from Princeton to some Part on Rocky Hill, with an Intention to harrass the March of the Enemy and thereby favor the approach of

Genl Washington on their Rear, and that of the Troops expected from Philadelphia.

15th

An Express from Genl Arnold dated *Trenton* 14th 6 OClock P.M. received here at half past 5 this Morning, says that He had waited six hours hoping to hear from Genl Sullivan, but had not. That he should set immediately off for Carryls Ferry, that the reports of the Country were that the Enemy were marching rapidly towards that place, and that Genl Sullivan was about two Miles ahead of them on the same Road.

NB Carryl's Ferry is the Place where our Boats are stationed sufficient in Number to Transport 3000 Men at a Time.

Another Letter from Genl Arnold dated *Carryls Ferry* 14th 9 OClock P.M. was received here at 9 this Morning, says, that Genl Sullivan arrived at that Place about 4 OClock and had with him 1600 Contl. Troops and about the same number of Jersey Militia making up the Number already there near 4000, that the Jersey Militia were turning out very Spiritedly, and that he expected to be about 5000 by the Next day, when He should march towards the Enemy who had encamped at Somerset Court House 8 Miles from Brunswick, that Genl Washington continued at his Quarters near Middle Brook 8 Miles in the Rear of the Enemy who were about 7000.

16th

The Above makes up the Chain of Intelligence to Genl Arnolds fourth Letter which was received here this Morning and is printed in the Papers of the 17 & 18th Inst to which we refer you.

17th No New Intelligence

From Various Quarters lately we have reports but none sufficient to depend on, that the Enemy will receive no Reinforcements from Europe, and likewise that a war with France is inevitable. Genl Burgoyne is said to be arrived at Canada without Troops. We have seen a Memorial Presented to the States General by Dr. Joseph York and two answers thereto, one, "that they had no account to render to him of their Conduct" the other, "there are no Gates to the Hague." [1]

18. No New Intelligence

We are Gentlemen, Your obt Hble Servts,

Benja. Harrison   Robt Morris

Jno Witherspoon   Thos Heyward Junr.

James Lovell

RC (PPAmP). In a clerical hand and signed by Harrison, Heyward, Lovell, Morris, and Witherspoon.

[1] For British Ambassador Yorke's memorial, see Charles Carroll of Carrollton to Charles Carroll, Sr., June 10, 1777, note.

William Duer to Philip Schuyler

My dear General,   Philadelphia June 18th. 1777

This Letter will be deliver'd to you by Mr. Archibald Stewart, who for some Time past has lived with me in the Capacity of a Clerk, and whose private and public Conduct has been unexceptionable. Genl. Mifflin at my Request has promised to appoint him Commissary of Forage in the Northern Department, provided the Appointment meets with your Approbation. I have therefore to request that you will kindly interpose in procuring this Appointment which I shall esteem as a Favor conferr'd on myself.[1]

Mr. Stewart will act conformably to your Directions and Advice should he be appointed to this Department, and I trust will execute it with Fidelity.

If you approve of this Gentleman be kind enough to signify it by Letter to Genl. Mifflin, as soon as possible.

I am Dear Genl., Very Affectly., Yours,   Wm. Duer

RC (NN).

[1] Congress appointed Stewart "deputy commissary general of issues" on August 6, but on August 11 Stewart declined to serve on the grounds of ill health. *JCC,* 8:617, 629.

Horatio Gates' Notes for a Speech to Congress

[June 18, 1777][1]

Unsought for and unsolicited this most Honorable Convention of the United States of America were pleased, for wise and prudential Reasons, to appoint me to the Command of the Northern Department.[2] In Obedience to their Orders I proceeded to Albany to execute the Functions of my Office. Upon my Arrival there I found every Thing in Disorder. The main Pass, Tyconderoga, in a manner destitute of a Garrison—the Goals of Albany full of Tories—Defection breaking out in all Quarters—and the Artillery Stores and Provisions, which should have been sent to Tyconderoga in the Winter, still in Albany, where only forty Soldiers of the Continental Army remained to guard them. Under these unpromising Circumstances I sent my Aids De Camp by different Routs with Dispatches to solicit the Neighbouring Eastern States to reinforce the Army, to supply the necessary Carriages to forward with all possible Expedition the stores upon the Road from Boston, & conjured them by the Love they bore their Country, and by that glorious Zeal, which they have ever displayed in its Defence, to reanimate the almost lifeless State of Public Affairs and by the Vigour of their Conduct convince our internal Foes that we meant to lose our

Freedom only with our Lives. To the Honorable the Convention of New York and the Committee of Albany I wrote and spoke in the same Strain, and am happy to declare I received their ready Assistance, and vigorous Cooperation in every Measure. And I do, only in Gratitude to them, declare how much they were pleased to signify their Approbation of my Proceedings. By the latter End of May Affairs wore a different Aspect. Tyconderoga was very considerably reinforced. The Posts upon both Communications were strengthened. Toryism was depressed. The Artillery Stores and Provisions were in Spite of bad Weather and worse Roads forwarded to Tyconderoga. The Indians of the six Nations were satisfied with the Spirit of our Conduct, & the warlike Appearance of our Defence. To sum up all the Faces of the Whigs shone with manly Confidence, while Despair and Disappointment clouded the Countenances of the Tories. But this is only a Recapitulation of my several Reports to this most Honorable Convention. Upon the
without any previous Reason Assigned—without any Cause of Offence given—without having lost one single Hour that could be usefully employed in the Service of the United States I recieved the following Resolve of Congress   [3]

My Rank, my Station, my Services entitled me to more Regard than such unceremonious Treatment, and I cannot be persuaded that the Despatches of Congress must have miscarried. For it is impossible that so wise, so honorable and so just an Assembly can have treated one of the first Officers in the American Army with such unmerited Contempt.

I have searched everywhere for a Shadow of a Reason for my being so disgraced, and can find but one. I am informed it has been asserted that I never meant to go to Tyconderoga, and that I conceived Albany the proper Post for the Commander in Chief of the Northern Army. Sir, I solemnly declare Nothing is more false. Nothing is more absurd. There is an Honorable Member[4] of this August Body in my Eye whom I saw upon the Road when I was going to Albany. As I had that Morning opened some Despatches from Tyconderoga I represented the wretched State of Affairs that Way. His Reply was "You will exert yourself to set Matters to Rights, which you cannot do, if you go and shut yourself up at Tyconderoga." [5] I was of Opinion with the Honorable Gentleman; but said Nothing more of Consequence upon the Subject. Had I wanted Advice upon a Point of Law there is no Gentleman in America to whose Opinion I would pay more Respect. But after serving so many Campaigns upon Hudson's & the Mohock Rivers I must have been an Idiot indeed to have wanted the best Advice that Gentleman was capable of giving me in my Profession.

I have in my Hand a Copy of a Letter to General Washington, of the 24 May ul[t]o., also a Copy of the Orders and Instructions which I gave the 7 May ulto. to certain French Officers whom I sent to the six Nations. These will shew that the Moment it was proper I meant to be at Tyconderoga. Had that Post been invested by the Enemy and I not there I should have expected to have been arrested with Disgrace, and broke with Infamy. My Experience, my Intelligence convinced me, that it was impossible for the Enemy's main Army to be at Tyconderoga before the Middle of July. Just as the Artillery, Ordnance Stores, and intrenching Tools had got over the Lake, a good Magazine of Provisions laid in, everything in a prosperous Train for the Summer's Supply, and my Affairs arranged for removing to the Defence of that important Pass, General Schuyler arrived with your Resolve depriving me of the Command, which two months before you placed in my Hands.

I beg Leave to assert that Tyconderoga is the proper and only Post for the Commander in Chief of the Northern Army, from the Middle of June, to the Middle of November; and if he is not there in that Term Tyconderoga is in Danger of being lost. I have the best Opinion of the Major General[6] now in Command there. He is a tried, and an approved good Soldier. But if he has it in his Power to play only half the Game, it is Odds but the Game is lost.

To explain this I need only inform you, Sir, that late in the Fall, last Year, General Schuyler sent me an Order to detach five of the best Regiments without Delay to Albany: being confidant from the Intelligence he had received that the Enemy were coming from Oswego by the Mohock River to attack that City. I scarcely had Time to consider this Order before the Fleet was defeated, and General Carlton landed at Crown Point. Had I obeyed the Order and detached the five Regiments I should have wanted Men to have maintained Mount Hope, a strong Point that commands the carrying Place from Lake George, which the Enemy might in that Case have been tempted to possess. My situation then may easily be known, when I acquaint this Honorable Congress, that I had only one Day's Provisions for the Garrison Army when the Enemy left Crown Point.

MS (NHi).

[1] On May 22 Congress appointed Gen. Philip Schuyler to command the northern department, which was to consist of "Albany, Ticonderoga, Fort Stanwix, and their dependencies." General Gates, the commander at Ticonderoga, thereupon went to Philadelphia to protest the apparent repeal of a March 25 resolve which he mistakenly believed had vested him with the entire command. Gates delivered his protest in a speech on the floor of Congress on June 18, which caused an uproar in that body and led Congress to explain that the March resolve had not placed him in command of the northern department. In order to avoid further conflict between the two generals, Congress ordered Gates on July 8 to repair to General Washington's headquarters and place himself under the direction of the general, but less than a month later, in reaction to the fall of Ticonderoga, the delegates finally appointed Gates to command the northern department. See *JCC*, 7:202, 8:375, 540, 603, as well as the letters of James Duane and William Duer to Schuyler dated June 19, 1777.

These letters of Duane and Duer clearly demonstrate that the present MS consists of the notes for the speech Gates delivered in Congress on June 18. At the same time, they also indicate that these surviving notes do not cover Gates' entire speech, for Duer informed Schuyler that Gates began with a recital of his *"Birth, Parentage and Education, Life, Character and Behavior,"* went on to describe his reasons for entering Continental service, and only then proceeded to discuss the northern command. As the extant notes start with a discussion of the disputed command, a page or more of introductory material has been lost.

For further information about the dispute between Schuyler and Gates, see John Hancock to Gates, March 25; and Schuyler's Memorial to Congress, May 6, 1777. Though Gates was never a delegate to Congress, his speech has been printed in this volume, not only because it was actually delivered in Congress but also because of the light it sheds on one of the more vexing issues the delegates had to face in 1777.

² In reality Congress had only ordered Gates on March 25 to "immediately repair to Ticonderoga, and take command of the army there." *JCC*, 7:202. Gates may be excused for thinking that this resolve was tantamount to making him commander of the northern department because in a letter transmitting it, President Hancock informed the general that he was "to repair to Ticonderoga immediately, and *take the Command* of the Army in that Department." See Hancock to Gates, March 25, 1777.

³ Here Gates left a large space in the MS to insert the May 22 resolves ordering Schuyler to take command of the northern department and placing Gates and Fort Ticonderoga within that command. *JCC*, 8:375.

⁴ James Duane.

⁵ According to the testimony of William Duer, it was just about at this point that James Duane rose to object to Gates' remarks and touched off a debate that forced the general to discontinue his speech and withdraw from Congress. He was instead ordered to state his grievances in a formal written memorial. See Duer to Schuyler, June 19, 1777.

⁶ Arthur St. Clair.

Marine Committee to John Paul Jones

Sir   June 18th 1777

Your Letter of the 26th May to the Secret Committee was laid before Congress and in consequence thereof the design of fitting the Mellish is laid aside and you are appointed to Command the Ranger Ship of war lately built at Portsmouth. Colo Whipple the Bearer of this carrys with him the Resolves of Congress appointing you to this Command and authorizing him, Colo Langdon & you to appoint the other Commissioned as well as the Warrant Officers necessary for this Ship and he has with him Blank Commissions & Warrants for this purpose.¹

It is our desire that you get the Ranger equipped, Officered and Manned as well and as soon as possible, and probably we may send you other Instructions before you are ready to Sail, however the design of the present is to prevent your waiting for such after you are ready for Service in every other respect and if that happens before the receipt of further orders from us you must then proceed on a Cruize against the enemies of these United States conforming to the Orders and regulations of Congress made for the Government of their Navy, and in conformity thereto Take, Sink, Burn or destroy all such of the enemies Ships, Vessels, goods and effects as you may be able. We shall not limit you to any particular Cruizing Station but leave you at large to Search for yourself where the greatest chance of Success presents. Your Prizes you will send into such safe Ports as they can reach in these United States, your Prisoners must also be sent in and we recommend them to kind treatment. Any useful intelligence that comes to your knowledge must be communicated to us whenever you have opportunity.

You are to preserve good order and discipline but use your People well. The Ship, her Materials & Stores must be taken good care of, and every officer to answer for any embezzelments that happen in his department. You are to make Monthly returns of your Officers, Men &c to the Navy Board. You are to be exceedingly attentive to the Cleanliness of your ship and preservation of the Peoples healths.

You are to afford Assistance and protection to the American Commerce whenever in your power & on your return from this Cruize lay Coppies of your Journal & Log Book before the Navy Board and inform us of the wants of your Voyage.

We are sir your hble servants

LB (DNA: PCC Miscellaneous Papers, Marine Committee Letter Book).
[1] See *JCC*, 8:465. The exploits of the *Ranger* under Jones' command are described at length in Samuel Eliot Morison, *John Paul Jones: A Sailor's Biography* (Boston: Little, Brown and Co., 1959), chaps. 7–9.

Marine Committee to John Paul Jones, John Langdon and William Whipple

Gentlemen   June 18th 1777

You will find herein Sundry Resolves of Congress passed the 14th instant the first relative to Captain John Roach and you'l be pleased to furnish him with a Copy thereof that he may do what is incumbent on him to do—another Copy will be sent to the Eastern Navy Board.

The second appoints John Paul Jones Esqr to Command the Ranger Ship of war. The Third empowers you Gentn. to appoint the Lieutenants and other Necessary Officers for this Ship and Colo. Whipple takes with him the Blank Commissions and Warrants which you are to fill up with the Names of those you appoint and make return thereof to the Navy Board Copy whereof be pleased to send us also.[1] We must also recommend that you make enquiry at Boston and other places in your neighbourhood, if there are any Young Officers who have served with reputation in our Navy that deserve promotion and give such the preference in your appointments, as it will be a great encouragement to all our officers when they find this practice is adopted and their merits attended to. We hope for your united endeavours to get the Ranger and Raleigh to Sea soon as possible and with much regard subscribe ourselves, Gentlemen, Your most obedt servants

LB (DNA: PCC Miscellaneous Papers, Marine Committee Letter Book).
[1] See *JCC*, 8:465. For the origin of the complaints which led Congress to "suspend" Capt. John Roche from command of the *Ranger*, see Executive Committee to John Hancock, January 25, 1777, note.

Robert Morris to John Langdon

Sir   Philada. June 18th. 1777

I am sorry to observe by yours of the 26 Ulto that your Embargo still subsists.[1] I had heard it was taken o[f]f & wonder at the Policy of it because nothing is more true than that all restraints & restrictions on Trade injure most the Country where they are laid. If you have a good opportunity to ship the Sugars by a handy fast sailing Vessell for this place, Maryland, Virginia or North Carolina I consent provided Insurance can be had on the Value in Boston at any premium not exceeding 25 per Cent as much less as you please & Underneath I will give you the Names of those they may go consigned to for Acct of Mr John M. Nesbitt & myself, you advising when they sail & where bound. If the French do not enter into this War I do think it may be a good plan to Order Goods out in French Ships to Miquelon & build a Couple of fast sailing Sloops or Schooners in your place to be imployed wholly in bringing the Goods to the Continent. Tell me your opinion & tell me if you & Colo. Whipple will be Concerned in such a plan. I am, Dr Sir, Your obed Servant,   Robt Morris

RC (Capt. J. G. M. Stone, Annapolis, Md., 1973).
[1] For the embargo imposed by the New Hampshire Assembly in December 1776, see William Whipple to Joseph Whipple, February 2, 1777, note 1.

Robert Morris to Captain LaRoche

Sir   Philada. June 18th. 1777

I have recd. your two Letters of 24th & 26th May advising of your Safe Arrival at Chas. Town So. Carolina with a valuable Cargo Shipped by Messrs Deane & Le Ray de Chaumont by the Ship Union under your command & very sincerely congratulate you on your fortunate escape from our Ennemies which are rather too numerous along this Coast. By a Letter from Mr. Deane dated Paris 5th Jany. last[1] I find he had Interested himself & me in this Cargo to the extent of £100000 which amot. he requests me to see remited back soon as

possible for his & my Acct. & his share of the Surplus arising on the
Sale of this Cargo he desires me to remit to his Wife & Son in Connecticut. Had you arrived in this Port this business might have been
adjusted with more ease than at this distance, however we must accomplish what is right soon as possible & the first Object in my opinion
is to send back the ship Union loaden with Rice on the same Acct. &
risque, & in the same proportions as the inward Cargo. I would advise
that you ship only Rice in the ship & not any Indico it is too dear.
Other means of remitting may be found out far more eligible & I shall
point them out to you & Mr. Bromfield in future Letters, at present I
have not time. I think you will do well to sell off only such parts of
your Cargo as obtains a good Price. Your whole Cargo of Cloths &
every thing else would have sold well here. I mean for enormous prices
but it was best that you went for Carolina as our Port is so closely
watched. This causes a great scarcity of Goods & People are flocking
from hence from Maryland & Virginia to Chas. Town to buy, therefore
you will soon find customers enough for all you have got but if they
do not offer you such prices as you like consult with Mr. Dorsius & Mr.
Bromfield about sending the Cloths & winter Goods this way by land.
The Carriage will to be sure come pretty high but the prices here will
richly defray it. I think his Excellny. Govr. Rutledge had a good Bargain of the Lead. It would have sold better here but that will not do to
bring by Land & I am not fond of risquing anything by Water. You
tell me you are ordered to carry the whole Remittances back with you,
if so it interferes with Mr. Deanes Views, for my own part I have no
objection provided the Remittances are made in such way as I approve
that is in Rice Tobo & such articles as will sell to advantage in France
but I will not be concerned in Shipping Indigo at a high price. I will
sooner pay you £50000 in good Bills of Exchange & receive that proportion of the Net Proceeds of the Sale you make & indeed I will do the
same for Mr. Deane sooner than let him be concerned in returns that
must sink Money. Therefore youll please to let me know your determination on this subject soon as possible but if you agree to remit totally
in Rice, Tobo. & such other ways as I shall hereafter point out I shall
agree that the whole net proceeds be invested in that way & returned
back to France where I shall be content to receive my proportion of
proffit or if the vessells are taken to pay my part of the loss. I wish to
have a Copy of your Invo. & a Copy of the Sales you make for my
Governmt & Satisfaction. You desire to know the State of military
Operations. Suffice it for the present to tell you the Campaign is just
opened & it is generally supposed the Ennemy look with longing Eyes
at this City but they will look (I hope) in vain. Genl. Washington is
watching their motions & you may depend he is a powerfull & dangerous Foe to them. The American Affairs look Better now than they
have ever done since the Commencement of the War. I do not dread

any Expedition against Chas. Town but think it likely they will station
some Cruizers of[f] the Port. I hope you will either write to France
for Insurance on what you ship or make it in Chas. Town. I wrote to
Mr Bromfield the 20th ulto. & hope he has recd. the Letter. My
Compts. to him & I am Sir, Your obedt. hble Servt.

P.S. Captn. Mason lives in the Country. Genl. Conway is with Genl.
Washington.

Tr (CtHi).
    [1] Undoubtedly Silas Deane's letter to Morris dated January 6, 1777, in *NYHS
Collections* 19 (1886): 448–49.

John Adams to James Warren

Dear sir   Philadelphia June 19. 1777
    Yours of the 5th inst. is before me.[1] It may be very true, that your
Regiments are as full as those of any other State, but none of yours
were so early in the Field—and We must not flatter ourselves with the
Reflections that ours are as full as others. When many Daughters do
virtuously we must excell them all. We are the most powerfull State.
We are so situated as to obtain the best Intelligence. We were first in
this Warfare, and therefore we must take the Lead, and set the Example the others will follow.
    The Armies at Ti and in the Jersies begin to be very respectable,
but not one half so numerous as they ought to be. We must not remit
our Exertions.
    You must not decline your Appointment to the Navy Board. If you
should, I know not who will succeed. Congress have passed no order
for a constant Residence at Boston. No doubt the most of your Time
will be taken up at Boston, but you need not renounce your Native
Town and County. It is a Board of very great Importance. I hope your
Commissions and Instructions will be soon forwarded. The Cause of
their delay so long is the same, I suppose, that has retarded all other
marine affairs. Causes, which it would be thought [injudicious?] to
explain.
    I am very sorry to see in the Papers, the appearance of Disunion
between the General Court and the Town of Boston, and to learn from
private Letters that there are Divisions between the Eastern and Western Part of our Commonwealth. I wish to know the Run of the Instructions from the Towns, on the subject of a Constitution, and
whether you are in a Way to frame one. Surely the longer this Measure
is delayed, the more difficult it will be to accomplish. The Rage of
Speculation, Improvement and Refinement is unbounded, and the
longer it is suffered to indulge itself the wilder it will grow.

I am much mortified that our State have neglected so long, to Number their Regiments, and to send Us a List of them and of all their officers. We loose one half the Reputation, that is due to Us, for want of a little Method and Regularity in Business.

We are much embarrassed here with foreign officers. We have three capital Characters here. Monsr. De Coudray, General Conway, and Monsr De la Balme. These are great and learned Men. Coudray is the most promising officer in France. Coudray is an officer of Artillery, Balme of Cavalry, and Conway of Infantry. Coudray has cost Us dear. His Terms are very high, but he has done Us such essential Service in France, and his Interest is so great and so near the Throne, that it would be impolitick not to avail ourselves of him.

I live here at an Expence that will astonish my Constituents, and expose me, I fear to Reflections. I Spend nothing myself. I keep no Company—and I live as Simply as any Member of your House, without Exception. But my Horses are eating their Heads off, and my own and servants Board are beyond any Thing you can conceive. I would have sold my Horses and sent home my Servant, but We have been every Moment in Expectation of the Enemy to this Town, which would oblige me to move, and in that Case such Confusion would take Place and Such a Demand for Horses to remove Families and Effects into the Country that I should not be able to obtain one to ride fifty miles for Love nor Money.

I have not made, and I cant make an exact Computation but I dont believe my bare Expences, here, if I should stay with my servant and Horses the whole year will amount to less than two Thousand Dollars. If my Constituents are startled at this, I can not help it, they must recall me.

We are in hourly Expection of momentous Intelligence, from every Quarter. Heaven grant it may be prosperous and pleasing.

RC (MHi). In Adams' hand, though not signed.
[1] Warren's June 5 letter to Adams is in *Warren-Adams Letters,* 1:326–27.

Board of War to George Washington

Sir   War Office June 19th. 1777[1]
I have endeavoured by Direction of the Board of War repeatedly to procure exact Accounts of the Receipt & Distribution of Military Stores, Arms &c received by the several Agents into their Custody on Continental Acct but have not yet been able to do it with any Degree of Precision. I intend however to persevere & when I have received Satisfaction on this Head shall transmitt to your Excellency exact Returns that you may be enabled to form your Measures as to ordering Supplies for the Army accordingly. The greatest Quantity of Ammuni-

tion & Stores will I apprehend be at Springfield whither I was directed to write for a Return but knew not to whom I should address my Letter, & must beg of your Excellency Information of the Commissary's Name or that you would write to Springfield & direct a Return of all Arms, Ammunition & Stores sent thither from the several Continental Agents who were directed by the Board of War to send hither all such Articles as they might have in their Possession to that Place. By our Account Mr Langdon Agent at Portsmouth must have sent on 9000 Stands of Arms so that if your Excellency should want Supplies of Arms it would be better to order them from Springfield as we have here scarcely sufficient to arm the Troops daily expected from the Southward.

I have the Honour of your Letter of the 20th instant & Directions are accordingly given on the Subject. I do myself the Honour to transmitt a Draft of the Pike or Spear as intended to be made that if any Alterations or Additions are thought necessary I may desire Col. Flower to attend to them. I fancy the Spears will weigh four Pounds each when completed. I am told they can not be lighter & strong.

Permitt me to congratulate your Excellency on the Enemy's Retreat which from the Manner & Precipitation with which it was effected (if it should be effected) was at least equal to half a Victory. The Spirits of our Troops will be raised to an high Pitch & those of the Enemy proportionably depress'd.

I have the Honour to be with the greatest Respect, your very obedt Servt,   Richard Peters Secy

P.S. I am directed to inform your Excellency of General De Haas's Resignation.[2]

RC (DLC).
[1] This letter did not reach Washington until July 7. See Washington, *Writings* (Fitzpatrick), 8:367.
[2] John Philip De Haas, who had been commander of the Second Pennsylvania Regiment, was appointed a Continental brigadier general by Congress on February 21, 1777. It is doubtful that he ever performed the new duties that this promotion would have entailed, however, and the reasons for his resignation remain a mystery. It should be noted, nevertheless, that this letter disproves the oft-repeated assertion that De Haas resigned his commission near the end of 1777. See *PMHB* 2 (1878): 345–47; Abram Hess, "The Life and Services of General John Philip de Haas, 1735–1786," *Lebanon County Historical Society Papers* 7 (February 1916): 71–124; and *DAB*. See also *JCC*, 7:141, 8:468; and Washington, *Writings* (Fitzpatrick), 8:34, 172, 244.

James Duane to Robert Livingston

My dear & honoured Sir: Philad 19th June 1777
I wrote you last[1] by favour of Major General Schuyler to whom I

referrd you for all the Intelligence of which Congress was possessed; and I hope you had the pleasure of an Interview with him.

We have since had the Prospect of an Invasion at this [place] from General Howe, but I own I never believd he coud have reachd so far had the Attempt been made. He was I believe of this Opinion for he never attempted it; detered, as I presume, from seeing the whole Country flying to arms to oppose him. In Jersey the militia it is said turnd out to a man; & the Pensylvanians laying aside their animosities, to defend their adord City, were preparing to follow the Example. And by these preparations, certain of meeting with powerful opposition in the front, and of being p[ressed] in the rear by a respectable Body of continental Troops, not inferior to the British Army in numbers, Appointment, or Courage, General Howe instead of advancing forward has intrenched himself on very strong ground at Millstone near Somerset Court house; and the two armies are contemplating each other with great Composure. In the mean time General Washington is drawing together a large Body of Eastern Troops to reinforce his Army, and several Battalions are daily expected from the Southward for the same purpose. Mr Howe is very civil giving the fullest Time & opportunity for the Slow movements of the new Levies who have all undergone the small Pox. Perhaps he scorns to take the Advantage, or wishes to make an End of America by one great and decisive Blow when all her strength shall be assembled, or perhaps he is not without Apprehensions of a Check which may prove fatal to him, and therefore waits the Arrival of Succours from Europe or Canada. Be this as it may People here seem universally easy holding the Enemy and their maneuvres cheaper than I wish they did; for to despise your Foes leads to Indolence & neglect, and often to Ruin. You may Judge of General Washington's Ideas from his mentioning in a Letter rec'd this day that he intended to discharge all the militia except 2000.[2] This will enable you to form a better Judgement of the two armies than any uncertain Conjecture of Mine.

Since our Arrival here things with respect to our State have taken a most favourable turn. General Schuyler is thro' our Exertions reinstated fully & honourably in his Command. The Commissary General's Department is reformd and establishd on a wise and salutary plan. Mr Jacob Cuyler is appointed Deputy Commissary General of purchases in the northern Department, notwithstanding all the opposition of our Eastern neighbours who being in possession strenuously endeavourd to maintain their ground. A Recommendation has passed from Congress to the united States to facilitate and encourage the supplying New York with Salt and other European and West India Commodities and which not only holds her up in a very honourable Point of Light, but reprobates in effect the commercial Regulations kindly passed by our Eastern Brethren to compleat our Calamities by effectually excluding us from all advantage of Impor[ta]tion & the Use of European & West India Goods. A Grant has also passed in our favour for 2000 Bushels of salt out of the publick Store at Plymouth in the Massachusetts with directions to the Commiss. general to exchange for it an equal Quantity nearer to our state if it can be done without prejudicing the publick Service.[3] Nor do we doubt but Congress will do [every]thing which can be asked consistent with Justice and the publick good respecting the Revolters from our state in the Northeastern Counties—a Business which will soon be determind!

We have therefore Reason to be satisfied with the Success of our Endeavours to promote the Honour & Interest of our state. Sorry we are to hear that it is like to be disgracd by internal Dissention. Alass is it worth while to greive for the Loaves and Fishes while they are surounded with burning flames? I hear Mr Scott is the Author of [these unreasonable Contentions.][4] Unhappy Gentleman will he never cease to fill his Country with Discord for the Gratification of his ambition! I am sure neither Uncle Philip[5] nor myself who we hear are talked as chief magistrates, among many others, desire to hold any office. We are Content with the Esteem of our Country, which will cancell all demands we can have for services or Losses in the cause of America. If others were as moderate and disinterested our internal Peace and Union woud not be endangerd by malicious slanders and intestine Divisions.

Be pleasd to present my dutiful Regards to Mamma & my affectionate compliments to every Branch of the Family. Accept them yourself, & believe me to be with unfeignd Regards, My dear & hond Sir, Your ever dutiful Son & Faithful servt,   Jas Duane

RC (NHi).
[1] No previous 1777 letters from Duane to his father-in-law have been found.
[2] Duane is referring to Washington's June 17 letter to Gen. Benedict Arnold, which Arnold forwarded to Congress. *JCC*, 8:480; and Washington, *Writings* (Fitzpatrick), 8:259–62.
[3] For the resolutions mentioned by Duane, see *JCC*, 8:375, 433–48, 465–66, 477.
[4] See Duane to Philip Schuyler, this date, note 3.
[5] New York delegate Philip Livingston was the uncle of Duane's wife.

James Duane to Philip Schuyler

My dear General   Philadelphia 19th June 1777
I set down to thank you for your friendly Letter to myself and Brethern in the Delegation and hope for a Continuance of your favours. I was not disappointed at the description of your Department the managemt of which requires *local* Experience, as well as military abilities, diligence and Activity. I waited with some Anxiety for the Close of the

period which made me quite easy as it assurd me that your perservance woud surmount every difficulty; and I knew Perseverance to be, if not your Fort, at least one of your strong Bulwarks.

General Gates arrivd here I think last   and immediately demanded an Audience of Congress. He was unfortunately for himself admitted. Discomposd, chagreend and Angry he recited all the great things he had effected at Albany; even the Suppression of Toryism he took to himself. He then pointedly called upon me and proceeded to a personal familiarity which was altogether unparliamentary. He was not very ungur ded in his Expressions (for what he deliverd was from a written paper)[1] but he shewd very plainly that he singled me out as the Author of his disgrace—for so he termd it. For this personal Address I called him to order; many members interposd, even to a Clamour and insisted that he shoud withdraw and he with marks of Reluctance was obligd to submit. After he retird he was censurd by several members very freely for his Personality and it was directed that he shoud be informd that it was the pleasure of Congress that if he had any thing to offer they expected to hear it by way of memorial only. I have no doubt but the General has heard very minutely what part I took with respect to him. I do not repent it. The Interest of the Continent, the Honour of Congress, & the dictates of Justice requird it; and I must put up with the General's displeasure, Which I find myself disposd to do with great Resignation and Philosophy. I have since been in his Company. We were civil, but rather reserved. He has heard from several candid Members that only one or two Justified his Claim to the Command and that the rest declard that there was no room for his supposing it ever had been invested in him. He ought to feel more pain and Resentment from this Circumstance than from any thing which fell from me. I am apt to think he does, for he has made no Representation to Congress, and instead of resigning talks of going to Genl Washington's Camp. If I might guess he expects that *you* will be elected Governour of New York, and resign your military Honours, and that then he will be reinstated in the possession of what he has much at Heart, the Command of the Northern Department.[2] I do not feel at all pleasd with the latter part of this Reflection: but I hate to anticipate disagreeable Events. There are several Ifs in the way—as *If* it shoud be attempted—*If* it can't be prevented &c. If I cant be reconcild to it &c &c, which renders it unnecessary to be at present much Concernd.

I feel with you for the weakness of my Country in falling into a party at this time. Scott I hear is much to blame. Unhappy Gentleman how often has he provd the Occasion of civil discord! I am informd he charges the Loss of his promotion in the Judicial Line upon Mr Livingston, Duer & myself in Concert with the Chancellor, Chief Justice & Mr Morris—whom he describes as a faction & tools to a Family Interest.[3] You know Sir how totally contrary this is to Truth; how entirely I disapprovd of these Appointments knowing the Envy & discontent they must encite; & how ardently I wished the instituting the Governmt might be deferred untill the End of the Campaign. When I left Kingston all this I fully expected and strenuously advised. This Calumny falls doubly hard on Mr Livingston who if he was elected Governour & accepted it, woud do it with a reluctant and aching Heart, and only for fear of injuring the common Cause by withdrawing from a conspicuous office in the Hour of Danger. These declarations are now too late I fear to appease the Spirit of faction & party; or I woud press you to communicate them with my Renunciation of all offices of Honour, Trust or Profit as far as I may be an Object of public Regard or Conversation. All I ask of my Country is its Esteem, which I will accept in full discharge of all my little Services and great Losses, since I had been honourd with Publick Confidence. Let the ambitious divide the rest among them so as they do not by contending for the Loaves & Fishes injure the Common Cause and loosen the Bans of Friendship & Union among those Virtuous Whiggs who when Terror overwhelmd many a noisy patriot stood firmly in the Defence of their Country without shrinking & wavering. But enough of this disagreeable Subject.

The Plan for regulating the Commissary's department is compleated. If out of the press I shall enclose it with these dispatches. You know in what Situation you left this affair. Trumbull is appointed Commissary General of Purchases, four Deputy Commissary Generals of purchases are elected. We had a delicate Card to play & which requird much Address to get this office into the hands of a fellow Citizen for the Northern Department. Our Eastern neighbours were in possession & worked hard to maintain their Ground: But it was of moment to our state who was to govern their markets & by the disposal of immense sums to influence their Policy; and it greatly concernd the Continent that prices shoud be Judiciously regulated & the Army well supplied. I therefore labourd assiduously & we were crownd with Success: our Friend Jacob Cuyler Esqr. obtaind the office, & I am persuaded will execute it with Integrity and Ability and do Honour to my Recommendation and that of my Colleagues.[4]

I enclose you another set of Resolutions with respect to our state which will give you pleasure as it proves the favourable Light we stand in here. You on recollecting the Commercial Regulations lately passed by our Eastern neighbours, so ungenerous & distressing to New York cannot but be pleasd with the Reprobation of their Conduct evidently implied in the first of those Resolutions: and you may wonder at our good fortune in getting it passed [without Cavil] or opposition. The stroke was too delicate & refined to be readily perceived on a Cursory reading; but I think it will be felt where I wish it to be fully understood.[5]

Present my respectful Compliments to Mr Secretary Lansing & let him know that I have not been unmindful of my promise to you & him,

Congress having at my request raisd his salary to 60 dollars a month.[6] Tell Him I am a little distressd in my mind on this Occasion as my Regard for him warped me to solicit a Salary which he himself will condemn as extravagant and I am not without Apprehensions that some honest members will yet get it reduced to 50 and expose my Partiality.

I thank you for your Attention to my Barn & Crop & hope in your next you will gratify my Curiosity by informing me of the state the former is in as I have not a Line from Jemmy Ellice.

I forgot to mention that I find some difficulty in getting leave for you to appoint a third Aid de Camp. The Example seems to be dreaded. You know my Rule is never to push a point till I am sure of Success; nor to loose sight of one which is worthy of pursuite; so that you must not conclude that it is unattainable, because it is not already accomplished.

I beg you'l make my respectful Compliments acceptable to Mrs. Schuyler & the young Ladies & to all the Albany Gentlemen who possess my Esteem & give me a place in theirs, and that yo'l beleive me to be, Dear Sir, with great Consideration & Regard, Your most obedient & very humble Servant,   Jas Duane

RC (NN).
    [1] See Horatio Gates' Notes for a Speech in Congress, June 18, 1777.
    [2] Schuyler was defeated by George Clinton in an election for governor of New York held at the end of June.
    [3] On May 3 the New York Convention had elected John Jay as chief justice and Robert R. Livingston as chancellor by margins of four and six votes respectively over New York radical leader John Morin Scott. *Journals of N.Y. Prov. Cong.*, 1:910.
    [4] See *JCC*, 8:434–48, 477.
    [5] See Congress' June 14 resolution on the supplying of salt to New York in *JCC*, 8:465–66.
    [6] See *JCC*, 8:475.

William Duer to the New York Council of Safety

Sir,   Philada. June 19th, 1777.
    When General Schuyler left this place, I requested the favour of him to apply in my name to the Honourable the Council of Safety for permission of absence for six weeks, and that they would be pleased to order Mr. Morris to attend in my place.

    As I have not yet received leave of absence, I am to impute it to Genl. Schuyler's neglect in making the application to the Council of Safety, which I requested him.

    I have therefore, sir, to request the favour of you to solicit the Council of Safety to grant me leave of absence for six weeks; as my presence is absolutely necessary not only to arrange my private affairs, which are

totally in disorder, but likewise to adjust several accounts with the State
of New-York, and the United States, which no one but myself can
properly adjust.

When the Council consider that I have been steadily engaged in the
public service, without intermission, for 14 months past, not having
once obtained leave of absence to visit my own home, I flatter myself
my request will not appear unreasonable.[1]

I have the honour to be, with great respect, Your most obedt. hble.
servt.   Wm. Duer.

Reprinted from *Journals of N.Y. Prov. Cong.,* 1:981.
   [1] On this point, see Duer to Robert R. Livingston, May 28, 1777, note 4.
Duer's fourteen months of "public service" included the time he spent attending
the New York Convention before his election as a delegate to Congress on
March 29, 1777.

William Duer to Philip Schuyler

My dear General,   Phia. June 19th. 1777
   I embrace the earliest Opportunity of returning my Part of Acknowledgment for your Letter of the 9th June to myself and Colleagues. I
had no Doubt when you left this Place but you would find Affairs in
your Quarter in a distracted Situation but I doubt not from your
Perservance and Attention you will be able to arrange them, and to
extricate yourself from the Difficulties which now Surround you.

   Yesterday Major Genl. Gates arrived in Town, and about 12 oClock
at Noon Mr. Sherman inform'd Congress that he was waiting at the
Door, and wish'd Admittance.

   Mr. Paca desir'd to know for what Purpose—to which *friend Roger*
replied to communicate Intelligence of Importance. He was accordingly
usher'd in, and after some Awkward Ceremony sat himself in a very
Easy Cavalier Posture in an Elbow Chair, and began to open his Budget.

   The Intelligence he communicated was that the Indians were Extremely friendly, much delighted with seeing French Officers in our
Service, and other common place Stuff which at present I cannot
recollect. Having thus gone through the Ostensible Part of the Plan, he
took out of his Pocket Some Scraps of Papers, containing a Narrative
of his *Birth, Parentage and Education, Life, Character and Behavior.*
He inform'd the House that he had quitted an easy and happy Life to
enter into their Service from a pure Zeal for the Liberties of America,
that he had Strenuously exerted himself in its Defence; that in some
Time in May [*i.e.* March][1] last he was appointed to a Command in the
Northern Department, and that a few days Since without having given
any Cause of Offence, without Accusation, without Trial, without hear-

ing, without Notice, he had received a Resolution by which he was in a most disgraceful Manner Superseded in his Command. Here his Oration became warm and contain'd many Reflections upon Congress, and malicious Insinuations against Mr Duane, whose Name he mentioned, and related some Conversation which he said had pass'd betwixt him and that Gentleman on his Way to Albany. Here Mr. Duane rose, and addressing himself to the President, hoped that the General would observe Order, and cease any Personal Applications, as he could not in Congress enter into any Controversy with him on the Subject of any former Conversation.

Mr. Paca caught the Fire, and immediately moved that the General might be ordered to withdraw; I seconded the Motion observing that the Conduct of the General was unbecoming the House to endure, and himself to be guilty of. Mr. Jerry Dysen,[2] Mr. Sherman, and some others of his Eastern Friends rose, and endeavour'd to palliate his Conduct, and to oppose his Withdrawing. On this Mr. Middleton, Mr. Burke, Colo. Harrison and two or three others arose, and there was a General Clamour in the House that he should immediately Withdraw. All this While General stood upon the Floor, and interposed several Times in the Debates which arose on this Subject. However the Clamour increasing he withdrew. A Debate then ensued concerning the Propriety of the General's Conduct, and that of the Members who contrary to the Rules of Parliament contended for the Propriety of his Staying after a Motion had been made and Seconded that he should withdraw.

The Want of Candor in Mr. Sherman who asked for his Admittance on the Pretence of his giving the House Intelligence was much inveigh'd against, but he bore it all with a true Connecticut Stoicism. Congress at length came to the Determination that Genl. Gates should not again be admitted on the Floor, but that he should be inform'd that Congress were ready and willing to hear by Way of Memorial any Greivances which he had to complain of. Here the Matter ended—not as you will observe to his Credit, or Advantage.

It is impossible for me to give you an Idea of the unhappy Figure which G.G. made on this Occasion. His Manner was ungracious, and Totally void of all Dignity, his Delivery incoherent and interrupted with frequent Chasms, in which he was poring over his Scatterd Notes, and the Tenor of his Discourse a Compound of Vanity, Folly, and Rudeness. I can assure you that notwithstanding his Conduct has been Such as to have eradicated from my Mind every Sentiment of Respect and Esteem for him, I felt for him as a Man—and for the Honor of human Nature wishd him withdraw before he had plunged himself into utter Contempt. You will perhaps think it was improper in me to second the Motion that he should be orderd to Withdraw, but I plainly saw that he was brought in with an Intention to brow beat the New York Members, whom he considers as his Mortal Enemies, and I was determin'd to let him see that it was indifferent to me whether I offended him or not.

Perhaps he may take it into his head to call me out, as he quitted the House with the utmost Indignation. Should this be the case I am determin'd not to She[l]ter myself under Priviledge, being convinced of the Necessity there is to act with Spirit, to enable me to discharge with Fidelity the Trust reposed in me.

On Saturday last a Body of the Enemys Troops (said at that Time to be about 7000 but since diminished to about 4000) under the Command of Lord Cornwallis moved towards Somerset Court House. Another Column took the Road towards Cranberry. Genl. Sullivan who was at Prince Town with about 1600 Continental Troops having Intimations of their Movement, and apprehending their design either to be to surround him with their two Columns, or to proceed to Coryells Ferry and destroy our Boats made a rapid March and threw himself betwixt the Enemy and the Ferry, being joined with about 1600 of the Jersey Militia who on the Alarm of the Enemy's immediately Joined him. On Saturday he sent all his Heavy Baggage over the Delawar, and on Sunday proceeded to Fleming Town with about 4000 Men, where he was by the last Accounts received. Genl. Washington being of Opinion that this Movement of the Enemy was made with a Design to draw him from his Strong Camp at Middle Brook, in order that they might fall on him in less advantageous Ground with the Main Body of the Army which was superior to his, and still at Brunswick, did not move. In about two or three Days he will be reinforced with about Five thousand Men from Peeks Kills, when it is not improbable that a pretty General Action will ensue, unless the Enemy retreat from Somerset Court House. In all probability an Attempt will be made to attack that Detachment of Howe's Army in Front and Rear, and as it can easily be supported by the Main body at Brunswick, with which a Communication is kept up the Conflict will in such Case be severe. I have the Pleasure to inform you that the Militia of the Jersies turn out with great Alacrity, and that the Parties have (at least for Time) subsided in this State and agree to stand forth in the Common Cause.

Genl. Mifflin taking Advantage of the Regress of the Enemy has again roused them from their Lethargy; and this City Militia will march in a Day or Two to the Number of about 1600 Men. So far from thinking that Philadelphia is in Danger (unless the Enemy should receive very large Reinforcements) I think there is a very great Prospect in the Space of three Weeks, that we shall give Mr. Howe a very Severe Drubbing, and oblige him to abandon the Jersies.

I am extremely sorry to hear that the Spirit of Electioneering has gone forth in our State. I dread the Consequences which may too probably ensue from that Soreness of Mind which is the natural Result of combated Elections. I am apprehensive that we shall never be able to exert as much Vigor during the War as we did under the Government of a Convention and Committees. Mr. Scot I am inform'd rails at an *Aristocratic Faction* which he pretends has form'd and Organised the new Government. His disappointed Ambition will lead him to make use of every Art however gross or Wicked which he thinks will serve to make himself popular. I flatter myself however that the Good Sense of the People and the Virtuous Exertions of those whom Mr. Scot considers as his Opponents will effectually counteract these wicked Insinuations, And that the Inhabitants in General of our State will be able to distinguish their Friends from their Foes.

I have asked for Leave by this Opportunity to return for a few Weeks to the State of New York. I expected that your Application would have obtained that favor for me.

I have the Pleasure to inform you that with some Difficulty we have counteracted the Arts of our Eastern Neighbors, and have got Mr Jacob Cuyler appointed Deputy Commissary Genl of Purchases in the Northern Department. As it is of infinite Consequence to the Wellfare of the Army under your Command, and to the Maintenance of the Credit of the Continental Money in our State, that a Person of Probity and Skill should exercise that Department, I hope he will not hesitate to accept this Appointment.

The Appointment is 150 Drs. per month and 6 or 4 Rations per Day (I forget which). As soon as the Commissary's Estabt. is printed I shall immediately forward it.

I beg you will tender my Affectionate Regards to him, Gansevort, Robt. Yates, and Genl. Tenbrook. Accept my sincere Wishes for the Health and Happiness of yourself, Mrs. S. and Family, and beleive me very Affectionately, Yours,   Wm. Duer

P.S. If the Department of Commissary of Forage should be promised by you (which I hope may not be the Case) I intreat the Favor to make some Provision for Mr. Stewart in some Line where he may benefit himself, and be advantageous to the Public.[3]

RC (NN).
[1] See John Hancock to Gates, March 25, 1777.
[2] Jeremiah Dyson (1722–76), an English civil servant and politician, was reputedly born the son of a tailor and rose to become clerk of the House of Commons, 1748–62, and member of Parliament, 1762–76. Early in his career Dyson was an ardent republican, but after the accession of George III he turned into a generally reliable supporter of the king. Although Dyson became the butt of humor because of his frequent interventions in parliamentary debates, he was otherwise regarded sympathetically by contemporaries. *DNB*. The identity of the delegate to whom Duer was comparing Dyson is not known, but James Lovell of Massachusetts seems to be a likely choice in view of his strong support for General Gates' interests.
[3] See Duer to Schuyler, June 18, 1777, note.

New York Delegates to the New York
Council of Safety

Honourable Gentlemen,   Philadelphia, 19th June, 1777.

In our last we informed you of the success of our efforts in vindication of General Schuyler, and it gives us great satisfaction to observe from your vote of thanks to Congress and other circumstances, that the honourable issue of this perplexed and delicate business has met with general approbation. Major-General Gates, a few days since, arrived in this city, greatly chagrined and enraged against your Delegates, to whom he ascribes what, without any solid reason, he is pleased to call his disgrace. As in this inquiry justice has been our view and truth our guide, we feel ourselves very indifferent about his resentment.

We have since assiduously laboured two points of great moment to the State which we have the honour to represent. The first, a recommendation of Congress to the United States respectfully to encourage and facilitate our being supplied with salt and other European and West India commodities. We have not only succeeded in this object, but with a testimonial highly to the honour of New-York, obtained the additional favour of a grant of near 2,000 bushels of the public salt in store at Plymouth, in the Massachusetts Bay, which for our more immediate relief, the Commissary-General is directed to exchange for an equal quantity nearer to our State if it can be done without injury to the service.[1]

When you reflect on some late regulations of our eastern neighbours, you will readily perceive the policy of the first of these resolutions, which evidently implies a reprobation of the ungenerous restraints which they have imposed upon a sister and confederated State whose misfortunes and distresses demanded a very different treatment, since they were drawn upon her only on account of her attachment to the common cause.

The secret committee, agreeably to the directions of Congress, have given us an order for the salt, and we shall endeavour to negociate the exchange with the Commissary-General, and by the first opportunity inform you of the results; the price will be that which is current at Plymouth. Several authenticated copies of the resolutions we enclose, conceiving you will have occasion to communicate them to some of the neighbouring States. To publish them we think would not be prudent, as by disclosing our distresses it would but too probably give a double keenness to the spirit of extortion which so shamefully prevails throughout the United States, and prevent your purchasing any necessaries but on the most exorbitant terms.

The other point which we had at heart, and which has employed much of our attention, was a regulation of the Commissary-General's department.

The abuses which had crept into it from the want of method and proper checks, the folly of the *purchasing* and the negligence of the *issuing* commissaries, to say nothing of fraud and embezzlement, called aloud for reformation; and the depreciation of our bills of credit, to which, more than any other cause, it contributed, made it a subject still more serious and important. A system is formed which, if properly carried into effect, will be productive of that economy which in all our affairs seems hitherto to have been but little practised; it is now in the press, and should it be published before these despatches are closed, we shall not fail to transmit it.[2]

When we observe how much depended upon a purchasing commissary, who from the vast sums at his disposal, commanded the market and had great influence on the internal affairs of a State, we thought it of great consequence to get this business as far as we were immediately concerned, conducted by one of our fellow citizens upon whose probity, capacity and patriotism a firm reliance could be placed. With this view we recommended Jacob Cuyler, Esqr. of Albany, as deputy commissary-general for the northern department, and though infinite pains were taken to disappoint us and continue the business in eastern hands, we finally prevailed.[3] This and other urgent affairs have put it out of our power to bring forward the instruction of our late Convention respecting the new Connecticut government attempted to be established within our jurisdiction. We have for some time, however, been paving the way for its success, and have reason to expect that every thing will be done for our State on this occasion which is consistent with justice and the public good. The beginning of next week is the time we have fixed upon for its introduction.

The expectations of a visit at this city from General Howe appeared last week, from the movements of his army, to be very probable. They now grow more and more remote. Intimidated by the spirit and vigour of the Jersey militia, who turned out to a man, and were ready to meet him in front while the Continental troops were in his rear; instead of pressing forward he is busily employed in entrenching his army on strong ground near Millston, as if resolved, for some time at least, to act on the defensive. General Washington's regular forces are much better appointed and in all respects superior to any he ever commanded. In courage they are equal to the enemy, in number exceed them, as well as in the goodness of their cause; besides they are daily gaining strength while the enemy are diminishing by desertion: so that every thing wears a smiling aspect, and with the blessing of Heaven, seems to promise a fortunate issue to this critical campaign.

We have the honour to be, with the utmost regard, honourable gentleman, Your most obedient humble servants,   Phil. Livingston

Jas. Duane,

Wm. Duer.

P.S. Be pleased to forward a copy of the resolution for making a present to Mr. Tilghman.[4]

Reprinted from *Journals of N.Y. Prov. Cong.,* 1:980–81.
   [1] See *JCC,* 8:465–66.
   [2] See *JCC,* 8:433–48.
   [3] See *JCC,* 8:477.
   [4] On March 26 the New York Convention had resolved to compensate Col. Tench Tilghman for a sum "not exceeding the value of eighty pounds, for his services in corresponding with a committee of this House, at their request, respecting the military operations last fall and winter." *Journals of N.Y. Prov. Cong.,* 1:851.

Charles Carroll of Carrollton to Charles Carroll, Sr.

Dear Papa,   P.M. 20th June 1777

The inclosed copy of G. Washington's letter[1] & sketch of the situation of both armies together with the newspapers will give you the best information respecting the late movements of the enemy. About 10 o'clock this morning an express arrived from Fourland Hills with an account that the enemy were retiring again into Brunswick; it was conjectured they had set Fire to Somerset & Middle Bush Villages by the smoak & fires that were seen at a great distance.

I imagine the enemy will next move up North River & attack our forts in the highlands. I wrote to you last Tuesday to send up my horses by some trusty person. I hope you have found out such a person, if so I desire you will send me £60 or £80 continental money. I want my horses much to ride out & take exercise, & I shall want them to return home, when I do next return; I have not yet fixed the time of my departure & while the weather continues so pleasant I think I shall remain in Congress.

                                                    21 June A.M. 8 o'clock

I have just recd a letter from Col. Fitzgerald dated yesterday evening containing very good news of which the following are extracts.

"You are pleased to ask my opinion of Gen. Conway. I assure you I think him a strict disciplinarian and an able & experienced officer & possessed of many requisites to render his Services very essential to us. Desertion has not of late been so prevalent amongst our troops. Our army grows in numbers and discipline, and will in a short time be able to bid defiance to Mr Howe on any ground; deserters come to us daily & by what we can understand, despondency & disaffection reign throughout the British army. I think this campaign must give a final cast to the complexion of public matters. By a letter from his Excellency to Congress you will see an account of the precipitate departure of their army yesterday to their old Post (Brunswick) where I think they are likely to remain for some time. Thus ended this glorious expedition which has been spoken of with so much confidence & assurance of success these many months past. The spirit and Unanimity of the Militia upon this occasion does them great honor, and deserves the highest commendation. They surpassed the expectations of the most sanguine amongst us & must convince G. Howe that a country where they prevail is not to be subdued. We this day have accounts from Boston from a gentleman of undoubted reputation, that two transports from England with Hessians on board are likely taken by one of our privateers, one of which with 82 prisoners is arrived at Por[t]smouth & the other hourly expected. The Hessians shewed the greatest joy, when our men boarded them, & offered their services as guards over their own officers. They sailed with 600, which is all the reinforcements to be expected from them, & as there were 3 of our Privateers together & the transports were but 6 days from land I expect a good account of the remainder. A ship from England to Quebec is also brought in, she had 4000 blanketts & a valuable cargo of other woollens on board. The General is in good health & spirits. I presented yr. compliments to him, & he desired his in return: He and all of us are exceedingly disappointed by the enemy not attempting Delaware."

I rejoice with you on this good news, and the bright prospect that begins to open our view. I shall dine this day with Mr. John Laurence at his mother's in the country where possibly I may spend this day & tomorrow. He has behaved remarkably polite to me I suppose on account of the civilities shewn him at my house & Elkridge. My love to Molly & Mrs. Darnall. With wishes for a continuance of yr. health I remain, yr. affectionate Son,   Ch. Carroll of Carrollton

RC (MdHi).
[1] Carroll enclosed an extract of Washington's June 17 letter to Benedict Arnold, which is in Washington, *Writings* (Fitzpatrick), 8:259–62.

John Hancock to George Washington

Sir,   Philada. June 20th. 1777.
The enclosed Resolves relative to the Army , and therefore necessary for your Information, I have the Honour of transmitting at this Time; and beg Leave to refer your Attention to them.[1]

The Congress have finished the Commissary's Department, and it is now in the Press. As soon as it is printed, I will forward sundry Copies for your Use.[2]

Your Favour of the 13th, 14th & 15th Inst., as also a Copy of your Letter to Genl. Arnold,[3] have been received, and are at this Time under the Consideration of a Committee. The Result shall be immediately transmitted. I have the Honour to be, with perfect Esteem and Respect, Sir, your most obed. & very hble Servt.   John Hancock Presidt

[*P.S.*] Genl Gates is here; I hope he will soon be establish'd in a Command equal to his Merits.

RC (DLC). In the hand of Jacob Rush, with signature and postscript by Hancock.

¹ These were resolves of June 16–18 on John De Haas, David Wooster, Abraham Sheppard, and the pardoning powers of general officers. See *JCC,* 8:468, 472, 475–77.

² Hancock subsequently enclosed John Dunlap broadsides of Congress' June 10 and 16 resolves concerning the commissary department in his June 24 letter to Washington.

³ These letters are in PCC, item 152, 4:253–58, and Washington, *Writings* (Fitzpatrick), 8:239–44, 259–62.

Robert Morris to William Bingham

Dear Sir   Philada. June 20th. 1777

You have herewith Copy of what I wrote you the 25th April & I have to grant receipt of your favours dated 1st & 15th April, Copy of 13th & original of the 29th May & will reply to such of their contents as require it in the order they occur.

You will probably have heard before this that Mr Webb was taken going into the Capes of Virginia & he is sensible now that had my plan for that Vessell been adhered to she would have been safe in No Carolina where the Tobo lyes this Moment that was intended for her Cargo.

I wonder much that the Gents in Guadaloupe shou'd detain so long as they have done the Net Proceeds of the ship & Cargo Mr Prejent was Concerned in. That ship was shamefully given away, if you had bought & sent her to Carolina she wou'd have made an Estate by one Voyage. You will see by the Acct Sales sent how the Wines turned out that you sent by the Betsey, Capt Stevens, but I am rather fearfull they are an Article that will frequently be overdone & they are apt to turn Sour. This however has not happened yet & you may venture on another parcell when a good opportunity presents itself. Capt Lockhart was taken & so is Capt Knox in that fine new Brigt of Mr McClenaghans. Your favour of the 1st April brought me Invoice & bill of Loadg for Sundry Medicines &c by the Sloop Independance Capt Young, who got safe into Sinepuxant from whence the Goods were Carted across the Country to Duck Creek and only part of them are yet brought hither. I have agreed for the Medicines at prices that will yeild us fine proffits but in future avoid Senna & Manna, there has been such large importations of these articles that the apothecarys are or will be overstocked with them. The other Goods will also sell well & the proffits on these adventures when they do arrive equal ones most sanguine wishes, but the danger of Capture is now greater than ever. I shall place to your credit half the Cost of Goods per the Independance the Amot. of what you supplied Capt Young & also Amot of what you shipped for Mr Hogeland But you dont mention what this last Sum is. It is well you did not get room for any Goods onbd. Mr McClenaghans Brigt as she is taken & carried into New York. I am very well satisfyed with my Brothers letter to you & with many he has wrote myself but still a little embarrassed about him. He has been very wild in Europe, but since he has had business to do it appears that he has been very attentive to it, the Captains lately arrived from Nantes assure me that he minds his business very steadily and every body agrees that he is exceedingly Capable. Others who I have some reason to believe rather envy his employment say he has such a taste for pleasure that he cannot apply closely to business. I am rather fearfull this may be the case & am Embarrassed between a desire to serve him & my doubts if he will serve himself and do honor to my recommendations of him. A little more time will convince me one way or other. We will quit all thoughts of further Connection with the very Cautious Mr Delap & apply to those that may be willing to risque a little for the chance of gaining a little. We must however remit Mr Cathalan & I shall point out the means of doing it, indeed I have bills by me that I wou'd remit but they Cost 300 per cent that is £300 Cury for £100 Stg. which is too high a rate to pay for these Goods in & for that reason I shall prefer Your remitting from Martinico.

I hope before long to receive the medicines & Muskets sent out by Mr Cathalan if you do but meet some good Conveyance for Sending them to the Inlets on the Coast but if You send 'em direct for this Port they have little chance. That same Mr Nichs Davis is a Rascall of the first Stamp and I wonder you wou'd run the Risque of trusting him or any other person with so much Money. It is not approved off. I will take care to have this passed in your Accounts but advise you to be extreamly cautious how you post with Public Money in future, or you may suffer loss of the money & be charged with want of discretion.

I expect Monsr Schwieghauser will have money of ours in hand to pay for our half of the Goods he ships to you, if some Tobo Consd. him arrives safe, but you had best remit him your half or perhaps the whole from Martinico when you can, as the Exchange we must charge if we pay for them is too high & disadvantageous. The same may be said of Mr. Limozin & all others in Europe from whom you import Goods.

It is a great pity the Hornet did not arrive safe as her Cargo wou'd have helped to relieve your Necessitys, we are horridly plagued to make remittances & the S. Commee. are now deeply indebted to you, to Mr. Curson at St. Eustatia & to Mr Ceronio at the Cape, have vessells loaden & ready to Sail but cannot get them out for if they run into the Lions Mouth it neither serves your purpose nor ours.

Theres no making a bargain with the Owners of the Rattlesnake, they talk of 100 per cent. Therefore it happens well that you settled with Capt McCullough. Your drafts in his favor are accepted & shall be punctually paid.

I was glad to learn by your favour of the 29th May that Cap Ord had sailed & was so well manned, he is an industrious, honest and I doubt not a brave Man, so my hopes of good success in that Concern seem to be well founded. I think if he had come towards Bermuda to intercept the Sugar Ships it would have been the best business at this time, but that is over before You get this letter and you must find the best employ you can for him.

I am sorry to hear of your meeting with so heavy a loss as that you mention but hope you may be insured as You suppose. I thank you for the intelligence of Captain Thompsons arrival at Point au Petre. Capt Luce left his vessell as he wrote you & she rode Quarantine for a long time on Account of the mate having the Small Pox, but I have not recd. any Remittance on her Account nor does Mr. Dorsius mention any such thing altho I have many letters from him lately.

I have sent to Mr Shaw by Colo Whipple to get his drafts for the Money he has in the West Indies. I expect Messrs Norton & Bealle have wrote you fully respecting the Powder & given you orders for replacing the parcells lost & that they have & will ship you Tobo to pay for it. You dont know how we are surrounded with these cursed Ships of War or you wou'd not be surprized that we do not send out Vessells to bring back the Stores &c. We wou'd gladly do it but cannot.

I charge you for our quarter Net proceeds of Indico per Capt Luce first Voyage & the acct shall be examined. I have already told you that your drafts to Capt McCullough are accepted & they shall be punctually paid. We have recd [£1519.3.11?] this Cury from Messrs McKim of Baltimore which is at your Credit and Mr James Warren of Boston advises that he has about £1300 Lawfull to remit us for net proceeds of some sulphur he sold on your Account. This shall be at your Credit when received & also any other Sums that come to our hands. I thank you for the Packet from Mr Limozin who is a very worthy man & an excellent Correspondent. You must Cherish him & Mr Cathalan; they deserve the utmost attention. As to Mr. Delap & Mr Schweighauser they discover such timidity & apprehension that I dont think it much worth while to trouble them, at least I wou'd never ask them for goods again untill they have the Money in hand to pay for them. Your favour of 24 May to the owners of the Brigt. Cornelia & Molly is with us, that Brigt is in New York but at your leisure we shall be glad to have Copy of the Invoice of her inward Cargo Acct of Disbursement & Acct Current with the owners. Messrs. Saml. Broome & Co. of Hartford in Connecticut

have returned Capt John McCleaves bills on them in your favr for
266 8/11th Spanish Dollars payable in Martinico, Accepted, they offer
to pay it to us but we shall decline that & require them to remit to
you its Amount. You will find herein all Sales of mercha. recd by the
Reprisal, Cap Wickes, in which the whole Goods you sent by that Conveyance are accounted for except 86 Swords which are very ordinary &
unsaleable your half net proceeds being £742.13.8 this Curry the same
is at your Credit. I find that Messrs Norton & Bealle have rather an
unpleasant affair on their hands with the Powder, for the Council of
Virginia with whom they must settle are not Merchants and Powder
being now pretty plenty, they complain of the price & instead of fullfill-
ing the Contract chearfully they give delay & throw all the obstacles
they can in the way, so that I have not received any money to this hour
on Acct of those parcells that have arrived. I intend writing you another letter by this Conveyance[1] & as the present was intended meerly in
reply to those letters I have received from you I shall now Conclude it
with assurance that I am, Dr sir, Your affectionate Friend & obedt hble
servant,   Robt Morris

RC (PHi).
[1] An FC of another letter to Bingham of this date, which Morris signed
"Willing, Morris & Co," is in the Bingham Papers, DLC. Morris also wrote a
business letter to Bingham on June 26, a Tr of which is in the Edmund C.
Burnett Papers, DLC, bearing the endorsement "Copied from the original then
in the possession of Mr. Stan. V. Henkels of Philadelphia."

Secret Committee to Thomas Mumford

Sir   In Secret Committee Philadelphia June 20th 1777
    Underneath you will find a Copy of a Resolve of Congress whereby
you will discover that the Cargo of Salt Imported by you in the
Schooner Polly to Plymouth is ordered to be sold to the State of New
York for the use of the Inhabitants.[1]
    In obediance to this Resolve, we now direct that you will deliver said
Cargo of Salt to the Delegates of that State or to their Order taking
Duplicate Receipts for the Same.
    You will take care to have it exactly measured and make out an
Account thereof; charging the Current price of Salt at the time of
delivery, which please to send forward to us with a Receipt. We are sir,
Your obedt. Servants,   Robt Morris, Chair Man

RC (Privately owned, 1974). In a clerical hand and signed by Morris.
[1] For the June 14 resolve that Morris enclosed in this letter, see *JCC*, 8:466.

John Adams to Abigail Adams

My dearest Friend   Philadelphia June 21. 1777
It would give Pleasure to every Body your Way but the few, unfeeling Tories, to see what a Spirit prevails here.

The Allarm which How was foolish enough to spread by his March out of Brunswick, raised the Militia of [the] Jersies universally, and in this City it united the Whiggs, to exert themselves under their new Militia Law, in such a Degree that nobody here was under any Apprehensions of danger from Hows March. It seemed to be the general Wish that he might persevere in his March that he might meet with certain Destruction.

But the poor Wretches have skulked back to Brunswick. This is a great Disgrace. It will be considered so in Europe. It is certainly thought so by our People, and it will be felt to be so by their own People—the poor Tories especially.

It will dispirit that Army in such a manner, that Desertions will become very numerous.

The Tories in this Town seem to be in absolute Despair. Chopfallen, in a most remarkable Manner. The Quakers begin to say they are not Tories—that their Principle of passive Obedience will not allow them to be Whiggs, but that they are as far from being Tories as the Presbyterians.

The true Secret of all this is, We have now got together a fine Army, and more are coming in every day. An Officer arrived from Virginia, this day, says he passed by Three Thousand continental Troops between Williamsbourg and this Town. I am with an Affection, that neither Time nor Place can abate, Yours, ever Yours.

RC (MHi). Adams, *Family Correspondence* (Butterfield), 2:268–69.

Samuel Adams to James Warren

My dear Sir   Philade June 23d 1777.
I wrote to you a few days ago by Colo Whipple with whom I hope you have had free Conversation. As he must have been not far from the Spot, he can give you a more particular Account than has yet been handed to us, of the late Scituation and Movements of the two Armies. The main Body of our Army were encamped at Middle brook and a considerable Force consisting of Continental Troops and Militia lay at a place called Sourland Hills within Six Miles of the Enemy who were posted at Somerset Court House Nine Miles on this Side of Brunswick. The Right of the Enemy was at Brunswick & their Left at Somerset.

They were well fortified on the Right & had the Rariton River in Front and Millstone River on the left. In this Scituation General Washington thought an Attack upon them would not be warranted by a sufficient Prospect of Success and might be attended with bad Consequences. His Design was to collect all the Forces that could possibly be drawn from other Quarters so as to reduce the Security of his Army to the greatest Certainty, and to be in a Condition to embrace any fair opportunity that might offer to make an Attack on advantageous Terms. In the meantime by light Bodies of Militia seconded and encouragd by a few Continental Troops to harrass & diminish their Numbers by continual Skirmishes. But the Enemy made a sudden Retreat to Brunswick & from thence with great Precipitation towards Amboy. All the Continental Troops at Peeks Kill except the Number necessary for the Security of the Post were ordered to hasten on to the Army in Jersey, and a Part of them had joynd. I am not disposd to ascribe great military Skill to General Howe, but if he designd to draw the whole of our Forces from the East to the West Side of Hudsons River in order to gain Advantage by suddenly crossing the River with his own Army, I cannot but hope they will be cut off and his Design frustrated. Great Credit is due to the Jersey Militia who have turnd out with Spirit & Alacrity. I congratulate you on the Success of our State Vessels of War.

Will you be so kind as to call on Mrs A. and let her know that you have receivd this letter, for she charges me with not writing to my Friend so often as she thinks I ought. The watchman tells me it is past twelve o'Clock.

Adieu my dear Friend, S A

RC (MHi).

Charles Carroll of Carrollton to Charles Carroll, Sr.

Dear Papa, Pha. 23d June 1777.

Yours with Molly's is before me. I am sorry to hear you are again confined with a sore leg. I hope rest & a course of medicines will carry off the scorbutic humor. I will endeavour to get the 4 yards of red shallon & 1 yard of scarlet Molly desires me to get, but I believe they are not to be had in this city. I do not know, nor can I fix the time of my departure from hence, it will depend on circumstances which I can not command. I wish Miss Molly Carroll all imaginable happiness, and I beg Molly to assure her these my wishes. If she regards the honor of her husband, she must not keep him from the field this campaign. I am surprised at Deards going in a privateer. I wish he may not repent this imprudent step. We are now upon the Confederacy. All seem to be desirous of confederating but the absurd claim to the back lands will not be given up—however I think it better to confederate even on these terms than not to confederate at all.

Our affairs at Tionderoga do not go on as well as in the Jersies. The garrison is weak, the militia going off, provisions scarce, & the works not compleated. The enemy are preparing to cross the lake with 10000, but I rather think 7000 under Burgoyne. If they should be delayed untill the middle of next month I hope that our northern army will be in a condition to oppose them & that provisions will be procured thro' the activity & influence of Schuyler, & the works at Tionderoga, if not entirely compleated, at least rendered very respectable. Gen. Washington has ordered 4 regiments to join Schuyler. The militia of N. York & the eastern States will turn out to save their own dwellings from fire & plunder, & their wives & daughters from dishonor; surely the noble ardor of the Jersies will communicate itself to those States. If we can support the expence, I have little doubt of success in the end, altho' we may meet with very severe rubs before we compel the enemy to give over their wicked project. I must again request you to be cautious with respect to the tender law—neither write nor speak agt it, but when business requires You to remonstrate with your fraudulent debtors, for such I esteem all those who will take advantage of an unjust & dishonorable law.

24 June 1777. 1/2 past 10 o'clock.

The inclosed copy of G. Washington's letter will give you the best intelligence. My love to Molly & Mrs. Darnall & complts to Mr. & Mrs. Ridout if with you. I am just going to Congress & have only time to assure you that I am, yr. affectionate Son,

Ch. Carroll of Carrollton

P.S. Please to forward the inclosed. It comes from Col. Fitzgerald, therefore give it a quick passage.

RC (MdHi).

Board of War to Elias Boudinot

Dr Sir,   War Office June 24th. 1777

I was duly favored with yours of the 20th instant on the Subject of Prisoners, & communicated the Contents to the Board, whose Feelings are in no small Degree roused by the Picture you give of the Sufferings of our unfortunate Friends in Captivity, who are not only smarting under the common Circumstances attendant on Persons in the Power of their Enemies & separated from their Friends, but oppressed with every Species of Insult & Cruelty their Captors, who are but too ingenious in Barbarity, can invent. Measures for their Relief would have been more early & more industriously attended to, but a Remembrance of what Britons once *were* lull'd us into an Inattention to what they *now are*. We saw their Prisoners with us, treated with every Degree of Humanity & Indulgence, & supposed ours with them equally well used.

By Order of the Board I inclose you several Resolves of Congress empowering you to open a Negotiation for the Relief of our Prisoners,[1] which you will no Doubt manage with the Address requisite to be used with an artful disengenuous Enemy. If they insist upon supplying their People in our Possession with Clothes, under an Idea of their being able (as they certainly are) to do it at a lower Rate than we can, you need not make a Point of it, but agree to their doing it. If you can bring about the Measures mentioned in the first resolve, it would be much the most eligible, but, rather than suffer our Fellow Citizens to remain longer in such deplorable Wretchedness, you will consent to the Plan contained in the last. This is giving in to the Arts & uncandid Demands of the Enemy; but the Necessity of the Case must plead in Excuse. Let it however be the last Resort.

Their Conduct would justify the severest Retaliation, but our People would in the mean Time have their Sufferings prolonged & that, if possible, with more poignant & diversified Cruelty. If we in this Instance yield to the unreasonable Demands of our Enemies it is because we have finer Feelings than those whose Inhumanity imposes the ungenerous Alternative of a Compliance with unwarrantable Requisitions or certain Destruction to many & the severest Distress & Want to all of our captivated Brethren. One Consolation of the *first Water* will however cheer us in this Business as well as in all our Transactions of a military Nature. Their Power to injure us is rapidly passing away & the Day is fast approaching when British Arrogance & Despotism will be levelled to the Ground & American Happiness & Independence rise & be firmly established upon their Ruins. As a Prelude to this enviable Period let me most heartily congratulate you upon their *Lexingtonian* Flight from Brunswick & to assure you that, I am with the greatest Regard, your very obed Servt,   Richard Peters Secy

RC (DLC).
[1] For these resolves, which Congress passed this day to guide Commissary of Prisoners Boudinot in his dealings with British officers, see *JCC*, 8:494–95.

James Duane to Robert R. Livingston

My dear Friend   Philadelphia 24t June 1777 Tuesday

I recd your obliging Letter with very great pleasure as it is a proof that I have one Friend left who thinks my Correspondence worth cultivating; for as to Mr Jay, Mr Morris and Mr Yates to whom in Conjunction with you I addressed two Letters, they have left me entirely unnoticed and my Attention to them at a time too when a variety of Cares being sufficiently heavy upon me, disregarded. I see plainly I shall be doomd once more to my former disagreable Situation; to be banished for a Season from my Family, and to be forgotten by my Friends. I wish you woud tell them my Feelings, not for any Gratification I can have in complaining; but to excite them to devote a small portion of their Time for our Information.

I shoud have written you a Letter by General Schuyler but he was so well acquainted with all my Connections and views, and so much master of Politics and military operations, and every minutia worth your notice that I esteemd it unnecessary.

From many Circumstances you may Judge that our State and it's Interest were at a very low Ebb in a certain Assembly. To add to our misfortune, several of our old Friends—Hooper, Hughes,[1] E Rutledge, Harrison, Reade, Stone, Chase &c &c—were absent and most of their seats filled with strangers. The affairs we had to conduct requird great Address as some of them were embarrassed with uncommon difficulties. My Brethern indulged me in the cautious and deliberate plan which I thought necessary; & in concealing even our Feelings. By Degrees we became acquainted with the new members to which the Hospitable and chearful manner we lived in contributed—for it was no time to consult Parsimony. We made it a Rule not to croud our complaints upon Congress which woud have fateagued and disgusted; but to confine our Attention to a single point till it was accomplished; Keeping every other Subject in the deepest Reserve.

We were told from several Quarters that it was too late to expect any Alteration with respect to Schuyler. Indeed Congress had gone very far to make their Embarassment inextricable. But that Integrity & love of Justice & Candour which ever distingushed this great Council when it consisted of a full Representation, in the End surmounted every obstacle: & the utmost of our wishes were answerd.

The Commissary's Department was our next object. The flagrant abuses which had crept into it called aloud for Reformation; & we esteemd it of the utmost moment that the purchasing Commissary who had our markets in his power shoud be a fellow Citizen of approvd abilities and Integrity. A Plan has accordingly been adopted; not altogether so perfect as coud be wished, but we shall not loose sight of its further Improvement. Our Friend Jacob Cuyler is appointed the purchasing commissary for the northern Department, which we esteem a publick Benefit.[2]

The illiberal Restraint put upon our Trade by our Eastern Brethren and a proper Reprobation of so unfriendly a proceeding from the only Authority which coud have weight, claimd a Share of our Attention. I think we have some merit in obtaining the Resolution of Congress upon this Subject which is already transmitted to the Council of Safety. It's operation, tho' obvious, was not perceived by those whom it most concernd and the House warmd by a pathetic description of our Distresses, our Perseverance, and our merit, were disposed to give us every possible Indulgence; of which the partial Grant of 2000 bushels of Salt when that Commodity is so very scarce and dear, is no contemptible Proof.[3] Indeed I flatter myself we shall be able to give an agreable account of every Business in which our State is immediately interested. The disposition of Congress is in my opinion strongly inclind to Honour, Justice and the publick good—I speak of the Body—and I am confident we shall never wish or ask any thing inconsistent with either.

Before this reaches you the Intelligence of General Howe's retreat must have undergone your Scrutiny. His motives, if any he had but the apprehension of Ruin, none can tell. But all seem fully persuaded that if he had perseverd in his Resolution to attack Philadelphia, his whole Army must inevitably have been destroyed. The Militia of New Jersey were ready for action; & the Pensylvanians suspending their civil Discord were preparing to Join them. Indeed if their Association had retaind it's former Vigour they might long since have supplied General Washington with 6000 militia, a Reinforcement which must have given him such a decisive Superiority that the British Troops coud not have escapd. General Washington thinks this a very brilliant and important Event for America; in common it is spoken of as a flight from Superior Skill, Courage, & Strength. But may not the Project of his joining the Canada Army be resum'd? May he not have rec'd Intelligence of Burgoine's preparations to pass the Lakes; & this have been the motive of his precipitate and disgraceful Retreat? If so the troubles of our state which I hope woud have been respited for this Campaign, will be renewed with double weight.[4]

RC (NHi).

[1] Joseph Hewes of North Carolina, whose failure to retain his seat in Congress is discussed in Hewes to Richard Caswell, March 30, 1777, note 2.

[2] See *JCC*, 8:477.

[3] See *JCC*, 8:465–66.

[4] For the continuation of this letter, see Duane to Livingston, June 26, 1777.

John Hancock to Joseph Trumbull

Sir,   Philada. June 24th 1777.

You will perceive from the Inclosures that Congress have compleated the Business of the Commissary's Department on a new and more accurate Establishment—and that you are appointed Commissary General of Purchases. I enclose you also a List of the Commissaries both of Purchases & Issues; and have only Time to refer your Attention to the whole of the enclosed Resolves, and to request your exact & punctual Compliance therewith.[1] I am with Respect, Sir, your most obed. & very hble Sevt.   J.H. Presid.

LB (DNA: PCC, item 12A).
  [1] See *JCC,* 8:433–48, 477. For an extended discussion of these new regulations, Trumbull's dissatisfaction with them, and his resignation as commissary general in August 1777, see Elbridge Gerry to Joseph Trumbull, April 19, 1777, note 1.

John Hancock to George Washington

Sir,   Philada. June 24th. 1777.
  Your Favour of the 23d,[1] containing the agreeable Intelligence that the Enemy had retreated from Brunswick, I had the Honour of receiving yesterday Afternoon, and shall, this Morning, with the greatest Pleasure, lay it before Congress. Give me Leave to congratulate you very sincerely upon this Event; as it must be principally ascribed to the Prudence and Wisdom of your Operations, which had so embarrassed the Enemy as to reduce them to the Necessity of acting in the Manner they have done. Should they be compelled finally to abandon the Jerseys (which I flatter myself will be the Case) it will be the most explicit Declaration to the whole World, that the Conquest of America is not only a very distant, but an unattainable Object. We have seen them, after penetrating some Miles into our Country, precipitately driven back; and in a Moment obliged to evacuate Towns after keeping Possession of them only a few Months.
  I do myself the Honour to enclose you the Resolves of Congress respecting the Commissary's Department, together with a List of the Persons appointed to carry it into Execution. I beg Leave to request your Attention to them, and to the other Resolves herewith transmitted.[2]
  Your Favour of the 20th Inst.[3] was duely received and immediately communicated to Congress. I have the Honour to be, with the greatest Esteem, Sir, your most obed. & very hble Servt.
                                        John Hancock Presidt.

RC (DLC). In the hand of Jacob Rush and signed by Hancock.
  [1] This letter is dated June 22 in PCC, item 152, 4:291–92, and Washington, *Writings* (Fitzpatrick), 8:281–83.
  [2] See Hancock to Washington, June 20, 1777, note 2. Hancock also enclosed resolves of June 18, 20, 23, and 24 on the appointment of commissary officers, the formation of an invalid corps, army supplies, and prisoners of war. *JCC,* 8:477, 485, 491–92, 494–95.
  [3] This letter is in PCC, item 152, 4:277–79, and Washington, *Writings* (Fitzpatrick), 8:269–72.

James Lovell to Joseph Trumbull

Dear sir   24 June 1777

I have recd. several of yours. The last brings nothing *unexpected*. I had prophesied it openly some days ago, on good grounds: and on the same, I ventured to assert that Genl. Howe would never be *able* to beat Genl. Washington in 20 years. Mind, I say beat not *fight*, for fear I should be charged with double Entendres. Will Posterity ever know what number of continental troops and militia were watching Genl. Howe's army in the Jersies on the 19th, 20th & 21st of June 1777 when the sd. Howe's Army was   thousands strong. Fill up the Blank when you tell the other number sought.

I imagine now the British General finds he cannot for the soul of him beat our army, he will only ravage the Colonies one after another; and leave our military to guard our Independence. I have heard some Gentlemen of the Army say our troops will probably be nicely disciplined by the *Fall*. This will open a fine prospect for us another year, if the enemy should not be able to get any reinforcements next spring, and should be very sickly in the winter and if our militia should turn out with spirit next summer, and we should catch the British troops then a good way from the Sea, without any Rivers upon their right, left or rear. How we shall maul them!!!

Indeed, my friend, I thought I was writing to the Muster Master Genl.[1] I owe him a letter and am so beat out with translating or answering letters from Boston that I must get you to show him this as the best reply I can make to his Sauciness about the States General of the United American Colonies. He will not allow *us* to be Fabii. He thinks that Gordian Knots are always to be treated alike. I beg we may have the chance of using tooth & nail, we are not Soldiers, we must unravel not cut. Adieu,   J L

[*P.S.*] After running my Eye over the inclosed I must pronounce it *confidential* & this without exception, to the 2d half sheet, beyond Ward. I did intend the 1st for Knox. I verily believe Du Coudray's treaty must be ratified.

I suppose you have heard thro the Genl. Schuylers ten thousand Complaints about the Qr. Mr. & Commy.

RC (CtHi). Addressed: "To Joseph Trumbull Esqr. Commissy. Genl Camp Jersies."

[1] Joseph Ward, who had been elected commissary general of musters on April 10, 1777. *JCC,* 7:252.

Robert Morris to Jonathan Hudson

Sir   Philada. June 24th 1777

I congratulate you on the safe arrival of your self & Goods at Baltimore & shall put at the foot of this letter a price Current [1] that you may judge if it will not be best to send most of the Articles here, as every thing is scarce & dear, and must Continue so whilst our Capes are so effectually blocked up. And it is with the greatest pleasure I can now assure you of the perfect Security of this City, for Genl. Washington has drove Mr Howe out of Brunswick & taken possession of it & our Troops were chasing Howe & his army out of New Jersey on Sunday they shamefully fled before our Troops with great precipitation. Therefore we may safely venture our property this way if the Market invites so to do, of which you'l judge by the prices. I note what you say relative to the affair of Money with Mr. B. Harrison, also the Sums you had taken up from Mr Braxton whose bills I shall pay for the whole or any part that he may draw on me.

I am glad to find your Voyage is likely to turn out so well & hope we shall have good luck with the fast sailing boat. I wish you may find an opportunity of buying out the Carolina Owners. I agree to your proposal of putting in £2500 Cury, you & Mr Braxton to do the same as a Stock to be employed in these Inland Speculations which if well attended to will produce more Certain & larger proffits than any other branch. You'l be carefull to keep the Accounts so clear & distinct that no confusion may arise. I am sorry to tell you I have received another of your bills on Woolridge & Kelly for £200 Stg protested & shou'd be glad you coud send me good Sterling bills for the amot of this & the other formerly mentioned to you, or if that cannot be done we must fix the Exchange & you must pay me in Curry. & you will dislike this at the high Exchange but still you must consider that the disadvantage is much greater to me than you for no damages can be equivalent to the advantages of having money in Europe at this time.

I am Sir, Your obedt hble servt.   Robt Morris

RC (PPRF).
[1] Not found.

John Hancock to John McKinly

Sir,   Philada. June 25th. 1777.

I have the Pleasure to inform you that Congress highly approve of the Zeal & Alacrity of the Militia of your State.

From the recent Alterations in the State of our Affairs, & the Reasons urged in your letter, the Congress have been induced to come into

the enclosed Resolve for the Discharge of your Militia.¹ I do myself
the Honour to forward a Warrant on your Loan Officer for 10,000
Dollars for their Pay, & am, with Respect, Sir, your most obed. & very
hble Servt.   J.H. Presid.

LB (DNA: PCC, item 12A). Addressed: "Mr. President McKinley at Wilmington in the State of Delaware."
    ¹ See *JCC*, 8:493. In a June 23 letter to Hancock, McKinly had requested the
discharge of these militiamen so that they could return home and tend to their
farms "as there are scarcely any Labourers to be hired, neither any indented
Servants & exceeding few Negroes." See PCC, item 70, fols. 615–17; and Delaware Public Archives Commission, *Delaware Archives,* 5 vols. (Wilmington,
1911–16), 3:1406–7.

John Penn to Richard Caswell

Dear Sir   Philada. June 25th 1777
    In my way to this place I was informed that Salt sold in Maryland
for 20 dollars a bushell. There are a considerable number of Merchts.
in this & that State that make it their business to buy up all the
Necessaries of life in order to fix what price they please afterwards.
    I suspect some of that tribe will be soon in No. Carolina to ingross
all our Salt & other things, would it not be proper to keep a look out
& prevent if possible such a pernicious practice.
    General Howe has left Brunswick in a very precipitate manner,
our Troops are in persuit of the fugitives & we are not without some
hopes that they will be able to prevent our enemies getting out of
the State of Jersey but with loss & disgrace.
    General Washington suspects that the willingness with which the
malitia turned out to oppose Howe was one reason for his wishing to
get back to New York.¹ The People here have agreed to postpone all
their private disputes about their form of Government &c &c untill
the enemies of America are subdued & it seems are now ready to
turn out, every thing near this looks well. I am with the greatest
esteem & respect, Dear Sir, Your very obt. Servt.   John Penn

RC (PHi). Addressed: "To His Excely. Richard Caswell Esqr., Governor &c of
the State of North Carolina."
    ¹ See Washington, *Writings* (Fitzpatrick), 8:270–71.

Samuel Adams to Richard Henry Lee

My dear Sir   Philade. June 26 1777.
    I intended to have written to you by the last Post, but being under a
Necessity of dispatching some Letters to Boston by the Eastern Post
which went off the same day I was prevented. When you left this City

you may remember the Enemy were at Brunswick and our Army at a place called Middle brook about 9 Miles North of Brunswick Since which General Howe who had joynd his Army marchd suddenly from thence with Design as it was generally believd to make a rapid Push for Philadelphia, but he disappointed the Hopes of some and the fears of others by halting at Somerset Court House about 9 miles on the Road leading to Caryels Ferry. General Sullivan who you know had been at Princeton made a quick March to cover our Boats at the ferry and by retarding Howes March to give an opportunity to our Army to come up & attack them. But the Enemy continuing at Somerset Sullivan advancd with a considerable Force consisting of continental Troops and Militia & posted troops at a place called Sourland hill within six Miles of Somerset Court house. The Enemy were very strongly posted, their Right at Brunswick & their Left at Somerset well fortified on the Right and having the Rariton in front and Millstone on the Left. In this Scituation Genl W did not think it prudent to attack them as it did not appear to him to be warranted by a sufficient prospect of success and he thought it might be attended with ruinous Consequences. His Design then was to reduce the Security of his Army to the greatest Certainty by collecting all the Forces that could be drawn from other Quarters, so as to be in a Condition of embracing any fair opportunity that might offer to make an Attack on Advantageous Terms, and in the mean-time by light Bodies of Militia seconded & encouraged by a few continental Troops to harrass & diminish their Numbers by continual Skirmishes. But the Enemy made an unexpected Retreat to Brunswick, and afterwards with great Precipitation to Amboy.[1]

RC (PPAmP).
[1] For the continuation of this letter, see Adams to Lee, June 29, 1777.

Charles Carroll of Carrollton to Charles Carroll, Sr.

Dear Papa,   26th June 1777. Pha.
    Johny arrived here yesterday evening & delivered me your letter of the 22d instant with its inclosures & £52.2.6. I return you the sundry letters which came under cover of your letter together with Mr. Lewis' letter. I really do think your correspondence with Chase was imprudent. What good did you propose to yourself by it? & why should you wish to be called before the assembly? To treat them as you have treated Chase you say: the consequence would be a commitment; perhaps, to Goal? Can you at your time of life bear such confinement? and would this conduct obtain a repeal of the law? Are you the only man injured by it? I have always thought it becoming a man to resent a private injury. I can not conceive that any individual is to turn Don

Quixote, or that the point of honor obliges him to combat whole bodies of men, particularly the Legislature of the State, which even when it errs, ought to be treated, at least, with complaisance, especially if it may be presumed that a majority has erred thro' well-meaning tho' mistaken principles: coarse language never yet corrected the folly or wickedness of man, or men—how honest would the British Parlt. have become, if the harshest epithets & the severest language could reform dishonesty? I intreat you to make yourself easy; fretting only hurts yourself & exposes you to the raillery or malice of your enemies. I have no apprehension of Wallace & Co. offering to discharge their balance due in England, in our paper money; if they were to make the offer I would reject it; they can not under the law compel us to receive that currency in payment. Johny tells me he thinks that neither yr. appetite or spirits are so good as they were when I left you. I suppose the chagrin occasioned by the unjust law above alluded to, & your confinement in consequence of your sore leg may occasion both—when the weather permits, I would advise you to use the exercise of your chair, and above all endeavour at a serenity of temper. If we succeed, & I have the strongest hope we shall, the money will be good in the end; it will & must suffer a temporary depreciation, which will not affect us very considerably. I am pleased to find a very considerable, nay a very great majority of Congress as anxious for a confederacy, as I am or you can be. The necessity of this measure is now obvious almost to every man, yet I fear the confederacy will not be formed on principles so mutually advantageous as it ought & might be: but in my opinion an imperfect & somewhat unequal Confederacy is better than none. We have not heared from Gen. Washington since the 22d nor do we know where abouts the enemy is encamped. General Arnold returned the day before yesterday to this house from Corryel's ferry, the enemy have abandoned in appearance all thoughts of marching thro' the Jersies to this city. I cannot think the piece signed Meanwell to be written by Chase—nor is there any thing contained in it to warrant the Major's suspicion, but I suppose he has better grounds for his conjecture.[1] I can not think Chase will attempt so undisguised a violation of our Bill of Rights as to move for such an appropriation as is mentioned by the Major. The Proprietary's Estate is somewhat differently circumstanced, and maybe in Jeopardy. The regalities most assuredly must be surrendered up. A purchase of his Q[uit] R[en]ts would be the most equitable manner of proceeding, but what is most equitable in such Convulsions as the present seldom takes place.

27th June

By the Evening post of yesterday you will learn the situation of the enemy. Gen. Washington writes they are too strongly posted to be attacked in their present situation, but that he has parties ready to take advantage of their movement.[2]

RC (MdHi).

[1] See Carroll to Charles Carroll, Sr., June 16, 1777, note.

[2] For the continuation of this letter, see Carroll to Charles Carroll, Sr., June 29, 1777.

Committee for Foreign Affairs to the Commissioners at Paris

In Committee of Congress for Foreign Affairs

Gentlemen   Philadelphia June 26th. 1777

Since our last of 18th Inst. in which you were informed of the Enemy being encamped at Somerset Court house eight miles from Brunswick we have the pleasure of acquainting you that on the 19th at Night they made a precipitate retreat therefrom to the last mentioned place, and on the morng of the 22d decamped again and wholly evacuated Brunswick and retreated to Amboy, for Particulars we refer you to General Washington's Letters to Congress printed in the News-Papers of the 25th Inst.[1]

We are unable to account for those movements of General Howe on any other Grounds than the following—That his march from Brunswick to Somerset afforded him an opportunity of trying the disposition of the States of New Jersey and Pennsylvania and on finding that the Militia of both States were turning vigorously out to Support our Army he might reasonably conclude therefrom that his Situation in the Jersies was too dangerous to be continued and therefore decamped to Amboy, from whence, he might, by his Bridge of Boats intended for the Deleware, throw himself into a Safe retreat on Staten Island. We give you Circumstances as they are, with such natural Inferences therefrom as our Situation and knowledge of things enable us to draw.

The Memorial presented by Sir Joseph York to the States General mentioned in ours of June 18th you will find in our newspapers of the 11th Inst. The said Memorial does not come Sufficiently authenticated to us to give you any particular instructions respecting your Conduct thereon, but as the progress of Friendship depends much on the improvement of accidents and little Circumstances we doubt not you will be attentive to the Conduct of the States General at all Times and whenever it appears to you that a Commissioner from Congress would be favourable received there, that you will give us information thereof.

We are Gentlemen, your Obt. Hble Servants,

Benja Harrison   Jno Witherspoon

Robt Morris   Thos Heyward Junr

James Lovell

RC (PPAmP). In a clerical hand and signed by Harrison, Heyward, Lovell, Morris, and Witherspoon.

[1] General Washington's letters conveying news of the British retreat from New Jersey are in Washington, *Writings* (Fitzpatrick), 8:269–72, 281–83.

James Duane to Robert R. Livingston

My dear Sir   June 26th [1777] Thursday

What preceeds has lain by me for want of a good Conveyance. This day came on before a Committee of the whole Congress the Case of our Revolters on which we were heard with great Attention.[1] Some of our Eastern Friends unluckily for them drew on the merits of our Title, tho' the Congress had only to do with the *Exercise* of Jurisdiction. Thus challengd I seizd the opportunity of explaining the Subject at large which I happen'd to understand much better than any of my Opponents tho' one of them boasted that he had expended two Quires of paper upon it.[2] I had the pleasure of observing that I made a suitable Impression, & out of the House rec'd the Compliments of several of the members for the light they were pleasd to say I had, with perspicuity and Candour thrown upon a dispute which to that time had remained in utter obscurity. This Explanation closd the debate: & the members of our state are desir'd to prepare for consideration such Resolutions as we think will be satisfactory to New York and become the Justice, Dignity and Impartiality of Congress. Unless an opportunity offers of sending forward these dispatches you will probably know the Event before they are clos'd.[3]

RC (NHi). A continuation of Duane to Livingston, June 24, 1777.

[1] According to the journals, Congress began to consider the controversy between New York and Vermont on June 25. *JCC*, 8:497. Congress' handling of this dispute is discussed in William Whipple to Josiah Bartlett, April 7, 1777, note 2.

[2] Duane's expert knowledge of this "subject" stemmed from the fact that he had received substantial land grants from the government of New York in the territory claimed by Vermont. See Edward P. Alexander, *A Revolutionary Conservative: James Duane of New York* (New York: Columbia University Press, 1938), chap. 5, and especially the map facing p. 70.

[3] For the continuation of this letter, see Duane to Livingston, June 28, 1777.

Marine Committee to the Eastern Navy Board

Gentln.   Philadelphia June 26th 1777

We have the pleasure to transmit you herein a Resolution of Congress appointing you A Navy Board in the Eastern Department to Conduct and manage the business of such part of the Continental Navy as may be Built, bought or fitted from Time to Time in the Four New England

States.[1] You are considered by this appointment as a Board of Assistants to the Marine Committee and subject to their Orders & directions in all such things as are not particularly provided for by Orders or Resolutions of Congress, and we have now under our consideration a Set of Instructions adapted to the Nature of your business, and the extent of the Powers you are to be Invested with.[2] In the mean time we desire you will meet together soon as Possible, fix on the most convenient place for opening your office, which we suppose will be at Boston, appoint your Clerk, and get all things so arranged as that you may be ready to enter on the Execution of your Duty without delay and *should* any business *Occur to you as necessary* to be done previous to the receipt of the intended instructions, we hereby Authorize you to do all such things in the Naval department as in your opinion will promote the Service and conduce to the true Interest of the United States of America; taking care however that you do nothing that is Contrary to, or inconsistent with the Rules, Regulations, Orders, or Resolves of Congress, which you are in all Instances and on all occasions invariably to pursue and Obey.

We are Gentln., Your Obedient Servts.

John Hancock	Geo. Frost
Robt Morris	Phil Livingston
Henry Marchant	Benj Harrison
Roger Sherman	George Walton

Tr (RNHi) Addressed: "To Wm Vernon, James Warren, Jno Deshon Esq., Navy Board, Eastern Department."

[1] Congress had created the Eastern Navy Board on April 19 and appointed John Deshon, James Warren, and William Venon as its commissioners on May 6. *JCC,* 7:281, 331. The origins, functions, and history of the board are described in Charles O. Paullin, *The Navy of the American Revolution: Its Administration, Its Policy and Its Achievements* (Chicago: Republican Printing Co., 1906), pp. 96–115. There is also much correspondence relating to the work of the three commissioners in "Papers of William Vernon and the Navy Board, 1776–1794," *Publications of the Rhode Island Historical Society,* 8 (January 1901): 197–277.

[2] For these instructions, see the Marine Committee's letter to the eastern board of July 10, 1777.

Marine Committee to Thomas Grenell
and John Hodges

Sir,[1]   In Marine Committee, Philadelphia, June 26, 1777.

As it is the opinion of the general officers, directed by his Excellency General Washington, to take the most effectual measures for securing the command of the North river, that the Continental frigates will be of essential service in defending the chain and obstructions in said river; and as by your letter of the 9th inst. we find you entertain a similar sense, we now think proper to direct that you have the frigate under your command put in as good a state of defence as can be admitted of, and follow such orders as may be given you by his Excellency the General or the commanding officer appointed to direct the operations in that quarter, using your best judgment in the execution of such orders as you may receive.

We now send forward, to the Council of Safety for the State of New-York, a sufficient number of blank commissions and warrants for your officers, who are to be appointed temporarily only, until such time as their characters and qualifications are sufficiently evinced and made known to us. Therefore, we wish you to join with the Council in having those commissions filled up with the names of men of merit, whom you can recommend freely for a permanent establishment.[2]

We recommend your taking great care of the frigate, her materials and stores, and keep us constantly advised of your proceedings. Being, sir, Your most h. servts.

(Signed)   John Hancock,   Geo. Groet [Frost],

              Robert Morris,   Phil. Livingston,

              Hy. Marchant,   Nichs. Van Dyke,

              Roger Sherman,   Benjamin Harrison,

                                     Geo. Wielton [Walton].

P.S. Congress have allowed pursers for their ships, whose pay dollars per month, and we send you herewith a pay list and the rules and regulations of the navy, for your government.

Reprinted from *Journals of N.Y. Prov. Cong.,* 2:512.

[1] Grenell and Hodges were captains respectively of the Continental frigates *Congress* and *Montgomery. JCC,* 6:861.

[2] Shortly after receiving this letter, Grenell and Hodges wrote to the New York Council of Safety, insisting that they alone had the right to appoint officers for their ships. They supported their contention by citing letters to Grenell of July 2 and August 22, 1776, from Francis Lewis, who was at that time a member of the Marine Committee. The council of safety referred this claim to the Marine Committee on July 25, but there is no evidence that the committee ever ruled on the matter. See *Journals of N.Y. Prov. Cong.,* 1:1015, 2:504; and the Marine Committee's letters to John Barry, July 2, note 3, and to Esek Hopkins, August 22, 1776, note 2.

Marine Committee to the New York Council of Safety

Gentlemen   In Marine Committee. Philadelphia June 26. 1777.

We are informed by a letter from the captains of the continental frigates in Hudson's river that the General officers sent by his Excellency General Washington to view the fortifications and obstructions in said river, were of opinion that the frigates would be serviceable in defending and covering the same, And we find by an extract from your minutes enclosed in said letter that you were of the same opinion. In consequence whereof we have now given orders to the said captains to have the frigates put in as good a state of defence as can be admitted, and to follow and obey such orders as they may receive from General Washington or the commanding officer who may direct the operations in that quarter.

We must beg your assistance in getting the ships fitted, and we now take the liberty to enclose a sufficient number of blank commissions and warrants for the lieutenants and other officers, who are to be appointed temporarily until such time as we are sufficiently informed that they are well qualified for the stations in which they may be put. Therefore you will please to fill up the commissions with this proviso: and we have required the captains to join with you in your researches for men of good character whom you can freely recommend for a permanent establishment in our navy, we must further beg leave to trouble you to send us a list of their names, stations and qualifications and have the honor to be, Gentlemen, your very obedient servants.

John Hancock	George Frost
Robt. Morris	Phil. Livingston
H. Z. Marchant	Nichs. Van Dyke
Roger Sherman	Benj. Harrison
	George Walton

Tr (DLC).

Thomas Burke to Richard Caswell

Dr Sir,   Philadelphia June 27th 1777

I have at present time to do little more than inclose you the paper which Contains a Letter from General Washington shewing the position of each army, and giving some particulars relative to the Enemy's retreat from Brunswick. I wrote to you last post and by a Man who went home last week Inclosed you all the Intelligence which occur'd since the Opening of the Campaign. I also inclosed the Resolution of Congress relative to Colo Shepherd, and I hope you have received them all. I sent a Duplicate of the resolution for fear of miscarriage—it's substance is that Colo. Sheperds Battalion is received on the Continental Establishment, on the Terms Stipulated by the assembly, and ordered, so soon as his three hundred privates are raised, to Join the General without delay, leaving proper officers to finish the recruiting.[1]

The Campaign has an Auspicious dawning, and I hope will set with great and happy Lustre. Give me leave Sir to Congratulate you thereon. Every Post shall be charged with such parts of the Progress [of] our arms as can be learned. At present Sir I must bid you Adieu, having the honor to be your Excellencys very obd Sert,   Tho Burke

July 3d 1777.

This goes by an Opportunity to Charleston. Enclosed are all the papers containing any Intelligence. By another Opportunity in a few days I will write again.

RC (MH–H).
[1] See John Hancock to Washington, June 13, 1777, note 2.

Jonathan Elmer to Ebenezer Elmer

Dr. Brother   Philadelphia 27th June 1777
Your Letter dated at Middle Brook Camp the 20th Instant with its inclosures came to hand this day. Since you wrote I learn that the Enemy have retreated from Brunswick to Amboy. I am sorry our Army had not a fair opportunity of giving them a genteel farewell on their leaving that place. I hope you will give them a good drubbing before they finally evacuate New Jersey.

If you know of any regiment that is not already supplied with a Surgeon & you have a mind for the place, upon your informing me of it I will endeavour to procure it for you. I hope you are careful to let no opportunity slip for improving yourself in the practice of Physic & surgery, particularly the latter.

I am, yours &c.   Jonathn. Elmer

RC (NjR).

Elbridge Gerry to John Wendell

My Dear Sir: Philadelphia, June 27, 1777.
I have for some time past, been deprived of the pleasure of writing

to my friends, by indisposition arising from the climate, & perhaps an attention to business, & am now to acknowledge the receipt of your several favors of March 26th, April 27th & May 5th which contain many articles of useful intelligence. Your suggestions, relative to the Friendship of France, are undoubtedly well grounded, & the policy of that Court induces her to avoid a declaration of War, as long as possible. Well knowing that whilst G. Britain is daily exhausting her resources, & growing feeble, France is encreasing in strength, & will be more able to give a severe blow. But her measures of late, have been so unreserved, that the British Court cannot avoid a declaration of War, If they possess but the shadow of that spirit, to which they have made such pretensions. Would this take place, Spain & Portugal will be inevitably engaged in the War, & the subduction of the latter, will be an object of great attention, with the house of Bourbon. The Porte & Russia, are already involved in a dispute, & probably will join in alliance with other powers, which will make the War general. This at present is but speculation, but the practice, has, for some time past, appeared to me, to be unavoidable.

The spirit shown by the Jersey Militia, upon the movement of General Howe, is a favorable circumstance to our affairs, & greatly tends to intimidate our enemies. He marched with but part of his army, to Somerset Court House, about ten miles from Brunswick, in hope of tempting our General to immediate action. But this being avoided, until a body of troops that were posted at Peeps Hill [Peekskill] could reinforce our Army & the Militia be collected, Wm. Howe, then thought it not for his interest, to risque a battle, but retired to Amboy.

Had General Washington left his post, to have attacked General Howe, the latter might have slowly retreated, towards Brunswick, until joined by the residue of his troops, & then the combat would have been nearly with equal numbers on each side, & might have been hazardous. But when reinforced, as before mentioned, I think General Washington had a promising prospect of defeating the enemy. An attack may be expected on Ticonderoga. I hope the New Hampshire battalions have their complement of men, or that their deficiency is applied with Militia, as the carrying that post may give spirit to the enemy, & bring the War nearer to our doors, although I really think, it would not be much injurious to our cause. A Navy board is established for the Eastern District, by which we may expect to see the difficulties relative to the Navy in some measure removed.

My compliments to friends & believe me to be, Sir, with esteem your friend & hum Servant.

(Signed)   E. Gerry.

MS not found; reprinted from *The Collector* 24 (June 1911): 87–88.

Board of War to George Washington

Sir   War Office June 28th. 1777
By Order of the Board I inclose you a Letter from Monsr De Coudray which is submitted to your Consideration.[1] The Board are of opinion that the whole of the Artillery imported in the Amphitrite should be together, with the Grand Army, & the Officers who came from France should accompany the Cannon that they may give the necessary Directions concerning them. But as your Excellency is the most capable of judging on the Matter the Board leave it entirely to your Discretion desiring that if you should not think the Order for the twelve Pieces from the Comr in Chief of the Northern Department a proper one, you will be pleased to order the whole of the Artillery immediately to Head Quarters.[2]
I have the Honour to be, your most obedt humble Servt

[*P.S.*] The enclosed Letter was taken from among the Papers of Lieut Cameron & tho' of no great Consequence I think it best to send it to your Excellency. Cameron broke his Parole & was taken in an Attempt to go on Board a Man of War at our Capes.

RC (DLC). In the hand of Richard Peters, though unsigned.
[1] Philippe Du Coudray's letter of this date to Washington, describing some difficulties which had arisen in connection with the disposition of cannon from the *Amphitrite,* is in Washington Papers, DLC. Washington's June 30 response is in Washington, *Writings* (Fitzpatrick), 8:323–24.
[2] Washington replied to this letter on June 30. Ibid., pp. 318–21.

Charles Carroll of Carrollton to Charles Carroll, Sr.

Dear Papa,   28th June 1777. Pha.
Johny got here last Wednesday with my horses; I should have ordered off the Friday following, but have been obliged to detain him here to wait on me. Poor Sam has been very ill these 8 or 10 days past and still continues so, occasioned by a violent cold. To day a blister will be put to his side, the seat of pain; he has been twice blooded. I do not apprehend any immediate danger, indeed I flatter myself he will be well enough in a few days to wait on me. I keep Johny to attend Sam, as much as to wait on myself. I am sorry that I am obliged to do it, as his detention here may probably prevent Molly from being at Miss Carroll's wedding. If Sam finds himself much better tomorrow, I will send off Johny tomorrow evening, he will be able to reach Elkridge time enough to drive his Mistress to Mellwood.
The Enemy by the last letter from Gen. Washington dated 25th instant from Quibble Town which is now our head quarters,[1] was strongly

posted at Amboy. They had sent off & were sending their baggage on board their transports which lie at the wartering place & Princes landing. If the express that carried orders to Gen. Maxwell to march to head the enemy had not been intercepted it is probable their rear would have been cut off. What the enemy intend doing next is uncertain: most people conjecture they intend going up north river to coopperate with Burgoyne, who may be expected at Tionderoga by the middle of July.

The Enemy are too strongly posted at Amboy to be attacked; they possibly may be there waiting for reinforcements, which when they receive, they may endeavour to penetrate again into the Jersies, & force Washington, if possible to a battle; this is certainly their interest; it is a desperate game, but their situation obliges them to run the risk. The same reasons which urge them to risk a battle dissuade us from venturing on one. Gen Washington will not hazard our cause by a battle, unless the odds are in our favor 100 to one.

I have seen extracts from the English prints as low as the 8th April. I do not find that any very considerable reinforcements are coming out. The critical situation of affairs in Europe, & the difficulties started by the German princes, have prevented the British Ministry from obtaining recruits, at least as many as they expected. I do not believe they will be able to send over this year more than 7000 at the outside: if I should be right in my conjecture, their army will not [be] near so formidable this year as the last, & ours on a much more respectable footing. Perhaps they hope to worry us out by the expence of the war. I hope your leg is better, & that you continue to enjoy your health. My love to Molly & Mrs. Darnall. I am, yr. affectionate Son,

Ch. Carroll of Carrollton

RC (MdHi).

[1] Washington's June 25 letter to President Hancock is in Washington, *Writings* (Fitzpatrick), 8:297–300.

James Duane to Robert R. Livingston

June 28th [1777] Saturday

Yesterday, tho' assigned for concluding the Business of our Revolters was taken up in other Cares, for we thought it impolitic to be too urgent for a preference tho it was a Right we might have maintaind. Experience has convincd me of the Propriety of such Condescensions at seasonable junctures. This morning the House In a Committee of the whole chearfully resumd the debate; and the Resolutions passed almost unanimously, for you'l observe they go upon general Principles highly interesting & important to every State which yet directly apply to our case. The only contest was on Young's address,[1] & that was ostensibly grounded on his death in the midst of the Debate; Compassion to his distressed family no doubt induced *some* of the Members to wish it to be passed over in silence. You will observe however that it was of great Consequence to us to have this wicked *production* censur'd and exposd, and this point was finally carried in our favour after a Sharp Conflict. The debate was spun out 'till after 4 'Clock and the Committee rose and agreed to finish it on Monday.

June 29th. Sunday

We have for several days been left in the utmost uncertainty concerning the Motions of the Enemy. From the Generals Letter which the President this Inst. called to shew us they carried their Retreat so far as to send part of their Army to Staten Island; but the same Evening they suddenly returnd with a Reinforcement of Marines; and by a Hasty march endeavourd to encompass Lord Sterling's division which had been employd in harrassing their Rear during the Retreat. Failing in this they attempted to gain the high grounds which General Washington had occupied at Middle brook; but that great and vigilant officer deprivd them of the Advantage by taking the Station himself. The Enemy by this account are at Spank Town; Skirmishes are frequent. We have lost but few men, and much less than they: which is an agreeable Circumstance considering the retreat which all thought as *Flight* was only a *Feint*. G. Washington's Circumspection and the disposition of his army on this occasion will do him the highest Honour. What the Enemy, who are compleatly disappointed in this fine maneuvre, will next Attempt is hard to conjecture. In my poor Judgment they coud not have chosen better ground for us than they now occupy, & there may they continue Till ashamd of their Instrumentality in support of the most cruel and unprovoked Persecution, and convincd of the Impracticability of subjugating to arbitrary Power a People who dare to be free; they shall in good Earnest fly away from these envied Regions never to return again. I presume General Washington will now draw to his Succour some of the Eastern Troops; and if he sees a prospect of considerable advantage the Jersey Militia and the Pensylvanians the latter of whom are arraying for Service tho' very slowly.

Fifteen hundred North Carolina Troops are passing thro' this Town under the Command of General Nash; & more both from thence and Virginia are expected. The Small pox which they have all taken by Innoculation has provd a vast Impediment, but from human appearances General Washington will soon be sufficiently powerful to disappoint if not to defeat his Enemies.

You who are acquainted with our former Connections here will be pleased to learn that perfect Harmony continues to subsist between us & the members of those States which formerly agreed with us in political opinions. Col. Harrison who by Artful Means was left out of the Virginia delegation, immediately on his Return home was reelected & to the great Satisfaction of every man of Candour has taken his Seat

again. On the other hand Col. Richd H. Lee is displaced.[2] Mr Hooper
has resignd, Mr Hughes was not reelected. From that State Doctor
Burck & Mr. Penn attend; Mr. Harnett is expected. From South Carolina Mr Middleton (an intimate Friend) and Mr Hayward. From
Georgia Col Walton with whom we stand on the best footing. From
Virginia Mr Francis Lee, Mr Page & our Friend Harrison. Maryland
our old Friend Paca & Mr Cariyl, the latter I believe you know to be
an amiable Gentleman & with whom we are very Sociable. From Delaware Mr Van Duyck with whom we have made an agreeable Ac-
quaintence. Pensylvania our Friends Morris & Wilson and Clymer: &
Mr Jona. B. Smith & Genl Roberdeau. We have not the pleasure of any
Intercourse with the Gent. from Jersey except Dr. Elmore who merits
particular Esteem. The other members are the revd Doctr. Witherspoon,
Mr Jona. Serjeant & Mr Clarke. The Gentlemen Eastward from New
York are your Neighbours & you know them: Except Mr Marchant
from Rhode Island who appears to be a Gentleman of good Sense and
Candour, and has hitherto sustain'd an independant Character, often
joining in Sentiments with your Delegates, and that even in the Business of the Revolt.

Please to have Patience & turn over once more.[3]

RC (NHi). A continuation of Duane to Livingston, June 26, 1777.

[1] Dr. Thomas Young's "address" is described in Duane to Certain Members
of the New York Convention, April 19, 1777, note 4.

[2] In reality Richard Henry Lee had also just been vindicated and reelected to
serve another term in Congress by the Virginia Assembly on June 24. See
Richard Henry Lee to Patrick Henry, May 26, 1777, note 1.

[3] For the continuation of this letter, see Duane to Livingston, July 1, 1777.

John Adams to Abigail Adams

My dearest Friend   Philadelphia June 29 1777

The enclosed Newspapers will communicate to you, all the News I
know.

The Weather here begins to be very hot. Poor Mortals pant and
sweat, under the burning Skies. Faint and feeble as children, We seem
as if We were dissolving away. Yet We live along.

The two Armies are now playing off their Arts. Each acts with great
Caution. Howe is as much afraid of putting any Thing to Hazard as
Washington. What would Britain do, surrounded with formidable
Powers in Europe just ready to strike her if Howes Army should meet
a Disaster? Where would she find another Army?

How are you? I hope very well. Let Mr. Thaxter write, let the
Children write, when you cannot. I am very anxious, but Anxiety at
400 Miles distance can do you no more good, than me. I long to hear

a certain Piece of News from Home, which will give me great Joy.[1]
Thank Mr. John for his kind Letter. I will answer him and all my little
Correspondents as soon as I can.

Tell Mr. John, that I am under no Apprehensions about his Pro-
ficiency in Learning. With his Capacity, and Opportunities, he can
not fail to acquire Knowledge. But let him know, that the moral Sentiments of his Heart, are more important than the Furniture of his Head.
Let him be sure that he possesses the great Virtues of Temperance,
Justice, Magnanimity, Honour and Generosity, and with these added to
his Parts he cannot fail to become a wise and great Man.

Does he read the Newspaper? The Events of this War, should not
pass unobserved by him at his Years.

As he reads History you should ask him, what Events strike him
most? What Characters he esteems and admires? which he hates and
abhors? which he despises?

No doubt he makes some Observations, young as he is.

Treachery, Perfidy, Cruelty, Hypocrisy, Avarice, &c. &c. should
be pointed out to him for his Contempt as well as Detestation.

My dear Daughters Education is near my Heart. She will suffer by
this War as well as her Brothers. But she is a modest, and discreet Child.
Has an excellent Disposition, as well as Understanding. Yet I wish it
was in my Power, to give her the Advantages of several Accomplishments, which it is not.

RC (MHi). Adams, *Family Correspondence* (Butterfield), 2:270–71.
   [1] Adams was waiting for news of the birth of their child. On July 11 Abigail
gave birth to a stillborn daughter. Ibid., p. 282.

Samuel Adams to Richard Henry Lee

June 29 [1777]

On Wednesday last the enemy reinforcd, as it is said, with Marines,
marchd from Amboy, through a Road between Brunswick and Elisabeth
Town [to] a place called Westfield about 10 Miles, with Design as it is
supposd to cut off our Light Troops and bring on a General Battle, or
to take Possession of the High Land back of Middlebrook, for which last
purpose Westfield was the most convenient Road and it was also a well
chosen Spot from whence to make a safe Retreat in Case he should fail
of gaining his Point. On this March they fell in with General Maxwell
who thought it prudent to retreat to our main Army then at Quibble town
from whence Genl W. made a hasty march to his former Station and
frustrated the supposd Design of the Enemy. I have given you a very
general narrative of the different Situations & Movements of the two
armies without descending to the particular, because we have not as
yet an Authentick Account, and one cannot depend upon the many

Stories that are told. I think I may assure you that our army is in high
Spirits and is daily growing more respectable in point of numbers.

We are going on within Doors with Tardiness enough—a Thousand
little matters too often thrust out greater ones. A kind of Fatality still
prevents our proceeding a Step in the important affair of Confederation.
Yesterday and the day before was wholly spent in passing Resolutions to
gratify N Y or as they say to prevent a civil war between that State and
the Green Mountain Men, A matter which it is not worth your while to
have explained to you.[1] Monsr D Coudrays affair is still unsettled. The
four French Engineers are arrivd. They are said to be very clever but
disdain to be commanded by Coudray.[2] Mr Comr. D——n continues
to send us French, German & Prussian officers with authenticated Conventions and strong recommendations. The military Science, for your
Comfort, will make rapid Progress in America. Our Sons and Nephews
will be provided for in the Army and a long and moderate war will be
their happy Portion. But who my Friend, would not wish for peace.
May I live to see the publick Liberty restored and the safety of our
dear Country secured. I should then think I had enjoyd enough and
bid this world Adieu. Yours,   S A

RC (PPAmP). A continuation of Adams to Lee, June 26, 1777.

[1] Congress debated the request of Vermont for recognition of its independence
in committee of the whole on June 25, 28, and 30, before rejecting the Vermont
petition. *JCC,* 8:497, 507, 509–13. See also William Whipple to Josiah Bartlett,
April 7, note 2; James Duane to Robert R. Livingston, June 26; and New York
Delegates to the New York Council of Safety, July 2, 1777.

[2] Only three French engineers, accompanied by a French lieutenant and a
sergeant, had arrived in Philadelphia. Lewis Le Bègue Du Portail, Obry Gouvion,
and Bailleul La Radière, bearing a February 13, 1777, contract signed by Benjamin Franklin and Silas Deane, were commissioned in the Continental Army
on July 8, 1777. The fourth engineer, M. de Laumoy, who had been delayed by
sickness in the West Indies, was appointed a lieutenant colonel in the Continental Army on October 2, 1777. See Wharton, *Diplomatic Correspondence,*
2:269–70; *N.C. State Records,* 11:486, 492–95; and *JCC,* 8:525–26, 538–39,
760.

Charles Carroll of Carrollton to Charles Carroll, Sr.

29th June [1777]

I wrote to you yesterday per post & informed you of my reason for
detaining Johny. Sam is this day much better. We have reports from
the army that the enemy had nearly on the 27th, by a secret march in
the night, surrounded Col. Morgan's regt. of riflemen. They were posted
at the edge of a swamp, which the enemy had Surrounded on two
sides, so that no retreat was left to our people but thro' the swamp,
which they effected with the loss only of 16 men missing. It is said that
we lost also 2 field pieces. The Enemy were discovered marching in a

long column up to the Scotch plains, which lie to the westward of Newark & under the mountains; this movemt. of theirs being timely perceived, General Washington marched to his old camp at Middle Brook. We have had no letter from the General Since the 25th. It is probable the Enemy are desirous of bringing on a general engagt. & it is my conjecture they retreated from Brunswick in order to draw G.W. nearer to the sea coast, that while he lay in that position, they might march a body of men round him so as to intercept his return to Middle Brook & the hilly country. If this was their intention, it is evident our cautious General has not given in to the trap, & they have missed their object. Gen. Washington will not risk a general action, unless the odds are greatly in his favor.

Monday 30th June

We had the greatest part of yesterday a fine gentle soaking rain, and this morning it began to rain at 7 o'clock, & has continued raining ever since to this hour (10 o'clock) and it seems as if it would rain the whole day. The inclosed copy of G. Washington's letter dated the 28th will best inform you of the late movements of the enemy & the present situation of both armies.[1] This day's post brought me yours of the 25th instant & one from Ashton which you will find among the inclosures herewith sent. What do you mean by putting off the persons who tender the Currency? If they make the tender, and your reasonings & expostulations with them will not prevent their so doing, to what purpose do you put them off to my return? This looks too like a subterfuge and they will insist on stoppage of interest from the time of the tender, & will involve us in disputes. I desire you will take the money when the debtors insist on tendering it in payment, notwithstanding the injustice done us. We are not the only Sufferers, and we must yield to the times. This measure my request, common prudence, & even necessity should induce you to take. I say *necessity,* for the law will have its course; nor ought any Individual to be above it. The letter of G.W. above referred to I shall forward to you in a letter tomorrow.[2]

RC (MdHi). A continuation of Carroll to Charles Carroll, Sr., June 26, 1777.

[1] General Washington's June 28 letter to President Hancock is in Washington, *Writings* (Fitzpatrick), 8:307–8.

[2] Washington's June 28 letter was actually enclosed in Carroll's other June 30, 1777, letter to his father. For the continuation of the present letter, see Carroll to Charles Carroll, Sr., July 4, 1777.

Robert Morris to Silas Deane

Dear Sir   Philada. June 29th 1777.

I have received by Monsr. duCoudray your letter of the 4th Decr.

addressed to me, but having met with an accident was delivered open.[1] Your letter of the 5th Jany addressed to my House W. M. & Co. arrived only about ten days since being forwarded from Charles Town South Carolina by Captn. Roche.

These are the only private letters come to my hands but there are several recommendatory ones in favour of the many Officers come out under your auspices. I will reply to the Contents of the two first.

The many letters I have written to you must have been exceedingly unfortunate in their passages to you, as well as yours to me, or you wou'd have had little cause to complain for want of intelligence as I never let a month pass all last Fall & Winter without writing, & sometimes wrote twice or thrice within the month, but feeling the difficulties you were exposed to, you seem to have attributed them to a wrong cause, Silence, on our part, instead of those accidents, to which our letters are exposed after written. Sure I am that all the Congress together, nor any one Man in America has been at the pains to give you intelligence that I have & sorry I am that my letters have not had better success. With respect to my Brother I shall deal very candidly with you, by declaring to you that I never was more shocked & hurt by any incident of my Life, than at the manner in which you Gentn Commissioners at the Court of France have been pleased to mention him in Public letters that you knew must be laid before Congress.[2] These letters arrived long before I had a single Scrip of a pen from you on the Subject. It occurred to me instantly that I had unbosomed myself to you respecting him, that I had solicited your Friendship in his favour and asked you to inform me fully & freely of his Conduct, that to all this I never had one word in answer & found your name at the bottom of letters blasting his character in the most Public manner & exposing me to Feelings the most poignant I ever knew. It also occurred to me that I had solicited Doctr. Franklin to admonish & advise him if he found it necessary & to shew him Countenance if he proved deserving. From these Circumstances I really did expect that any complaints he merited, wou'd have been made to myself in private letters giving me Account of his Conduct and if it was necessary to remove him from his employment, I cou'd have done that so as to prevent any the least disservice to the Public or his being unnecessarily exposed. You will see that these sentiments were strong in my mind when I wrote the Commissioners on the 1st April,[3] and they made so Strong an impression on me at the time Your letters were read in Congress that I got up instantly, gave my Brother his true Character, complained of his being so publickly exposed, told what my desires & expectations from you respecting him were & added that by my letters to you per Capt Bell I had put him in your power, either to be confirmed in his employment or dismissed from it as his Conduct might require.[4] I think the letter I wrote you by Capt Bell respecting him must have Convinced you that I did not wish him employed in the Public Service if he did not deserve it, it must also convince you that a Public letter to Congress on that Subject was not necessary to procure his removal if his Conduct was not right for you found me as ready to displace him as you cou'd wish & I begin to fear that I was rather too forward in it. From what I now write you will naturally conclude I do not think my self in the least degree beholden to Doctr Franklin or you for your Conduct towards this Young Man & in plain truth I do not. However, I do not cherish resentment and hope my passions may be always subdued by Reason & my reason influenced by good principles; therefore I mean nothing more than to let you know, that I think those Public letters were Cruel to my Brother & extreamly unfriendly to myself. I shall inform him of them & if he has Spirit to resent them I hope he will also have judgement to do it properly. Perhaps I have flattered myself with the expectation of more Friendship from the Doctor & you than I had a right to & shall therefore correct the error in future. Thus much for what you say of him in Public. As to what you write me of him in these letters of the 4th Decr. & 5th Jany now before me, I thank you most sincerely for it, and shou'd do so, had the Account of him been ten times more disagreable. It is bad enough God knows, and what is worse, I believe he deserves every tittle of it. Had these letters of yours reached me before the Public letters I shou'd in some degree have been prepared & probably shou'd not have said anything about him in Congress but even in that case, I shou'd have thought in the same way of your Public letters because I think it was totally unnecessary to mention him there. You refer me to Mr. Bromfield for further particulars & anecdotes respecting this Youth & Mr. Bromfield has kindly referred me to all the Gentn from Virginia where he landed, to South Carolina where he is gone by land, & had industriously communicated these particulars & anecdotes to every body he met with. I must now in turn inform you of some particulars & anecdotes that Gentn from Nantes have lately informed me of.

They say that since Toms arrival there he has applied himself most assiduously & closely to business. This appears to be true, because he has done his business well & given a most clear & satisfactory account of it. I laid his letters before Congress, in order that they might judge for themselves and assure you that many Members differ from the Honorable Commissioners & did not seem to think that he ought to be *Immediately removed from his Commercial employment.* These Same Gentn from Nantes inform me, that that employment is sought for by others whom the Commissioners wish to gratify at his Expense. That Mr. Williams & others envie him & that Relatives & Interested motives are united to remove my Brother to make way, for a Nephew, a Couzin & a Partner. I am not fond of believing these storys and yet there are many Circumstances related with them, that stagger my want of faith. However the principal foundation for me to Act upon is wanting. If my Brothers conduct had been such as to inspire me with perfect Confidence, all the Commissioners at Paris shou'd not remove him. But as he has not done that, I had rather any mans Nephew, Couzin or Partner had the Employment, than that my Brother shou'd give just cause for a single complaint. Therefore if you have removed him I shall acquiesce & trouble you nor myself any farther about the matter, and having no views or designs but what I can justify you see I dont hide from you my Sentiments on any one point, but you will enter into the distinction I make, & think yourself justly entitled to my thanks for the accounts given to myself of this same Troublesome Brother of mine & I shall ever acknowledge that favour. I anxiously wish to hear what you did with him in consequence of my letter by Capt Bell for untill I know that or learn what has been his line of Conduct since that time, I am & shall be much embarrassed how to direct the affairs that have been Committed to his management.

I wou'd wish to indulge the Fond hope that he will see his Folly with an Eye of judgement and take up another Conduct that will give him Character & Consequence in the World, on these terms & no other do I wish to serve him, and I do assure you upon my honor if your letters respecting him had been confined to myself, instead of being offended, you wou'd have experienced the most unbounded acknowledgements & the most gratefull returns for your Candour & even now I shall not suffer the feelings occasioned by the Public letters to stifle what is due to You for the pains you did take to put him right. And now for the Commercial affairs depending between us. I am not surprized that my Brothers Conduct in London shou'd have hurt the reputation & Credit of our House because a good deal of pains had been taken & even ministerial influences used (as I am well informed) to do that previous to his arrival & there is no doubt but his irregularities furnished fresh materials. However I disregard all this as I shall honorably fullfill all my engagements in that Country & wish I cou'd say that every one there had done so by me. But probably the day may come when some that rank high in the Commercial World may blush at the Recital of their Conduct. You say the American Credit, both Public & private was in a most Wretched state. I doubt it not in the least, indeed I always expected it wou'd be so, and am now as well as then convinced that General Washington must be the Great Banker to establish our Credit with the Banks & Bankers of Europe and this I believe he will be able to do, at least appearances are more favourable now than ever and I have not despaired at any time.

You tell me you have engaged on your & my Account One hundred thousand Livers interest in the Cargo by the Union, Capt. L. Roche, Consigned to Mr Bromfield for which remittances must be punctually made. This Vessell is arrived safe at Charles Town in South Carolina where the Captain was selling the Cargo at a considerable advance. Mr Bromfield left that Ship at Cape Francois & came to Virginia in a small Sloop from whence he set out by Land for Carolina. You seem to rely much on this Gentlemans prudence but I have Conceived a very indifferent opinion of it, for he has not only done what I have already mentioned respecting my Brother, but he has told to every body the Concern you & I had in the Union Cargo with many circumstances that I know little about. Colo Harrison who happened to be in Virginia when he arrived says all the People in that Country are acquainted with the whole Concern & from hence it is not improbable but they may conjecture by & by that private gain is more our pursuit than public good, for such unworthy suspicions are frequently taken upon less grounds. However I shall continue to discharge my duty faithfully to the Public & pursue my private Fortune by all such honorable & fair means as the times will admit of and I dare say you will do the Same, but we are not much indebted to Mr Bromfields discretion. Neither can I think myself under any great obligation for a Credit so limited & guarded as this Cargo by the Union seems to be. Capt. La Roche writes for my opinion & advice but takes care to let me know, he is to remit the entire Net proceeds to his owner Monsr La Ray du Chaumont. Now altho I have no real objection to his doing so, yet it carries an air of distrust that I dislike. Enclosed you will find copies of what I wrote to Mr Bromfield in answer to his letter from Virginia before I knew how very communicative he was, also Copy of which I wrote Capt La Roche by which you'l see I offer to pay him for your & my part the Cost of the Cargo in Good Bills of Exchange and receive our share of the Net Proceeds, rather than consent to his shipping back Indico on our account.[5] That article is very dear & I know must entail a heavy loss on us, whereas if the remittances are confined to Rice, Tobacco, Furrs, Skins, Flour &c a handsome proffit will result from what does arrive safe and if he will wait to make returns in these articles I have no objection to the whole going back as I have no inclination on occasion to finger any of the money arising from the sales of this Cargo, therefore it was quite unnecessary to be so guarded against its coming into my hands. In short I shall rest satisfyed with this Concern because I have run my share of the Risque but there is a certain degree of Indignity in the terms that I will not submit to again, to hold an Interest in a Cargo addressed to a Captain & Super Cargo with orders for them to have the sole Management, receive the commission & remit the entire Net Proceeds back, so that had they come here I must have had the trouble, been their adviser & looked on whilst she carried back any share to France altho' I was ready to pay down the Cost.

This will never do, and I desire not any further Concern on such terms, therefore I will not give you any more trouble about interesting me in Commercial matters, in what is done on our joint account previous to the receipt of this letter I hold myself bound and will make good my part of the engagements but I suppose this Cargo by the Union will be the only one shipped. If Capt Roche accepts my offer & delivers up your proportions & mine of the Net proceeds on my paying him Good bills for Livres 100,000 I will comply with it & in that case the surplus or Proffit on your share shall be remitted to Mrs. Deane as you direct. On the Contrary if the entire returns for this Cargo are made to France you will see the Final Settlement of the account and I beg that my share of the Proffits may be paid to Mr John Ross of this City, now in Europe whose address you will be acquainted with no doubt & shou'd the remittances from America be taken or fail of making entire payment for the first Cost of the Union Cargo I will desire Mr Ross in such case to pay whatever ballance may become due on the proportion of Livres 50,000.

Notwithstanding what I have said above respecting future concerns, I shou'd have no objection provided they were to come on such a footing as is consistant with that Credit and Character I am entitled to but on no other. The Cargoes shou'd be consigned to me or my order & the Captains be directed to get into the first safe Port they can make. I have the best Correspondants at every port on this Continent who can sell the Cargoes & make remittances to much better advantage than any Super Cargoes for these always do much mischief to Trade in general as well as to their own particular Voyages. Goods continue in great demand & if Insurances cou'd be obtained in Europe great Fortunes might be made with Certainty. On the above terms I am willing to be further concerned but not on any others.

Your letter of the 3d Decr. to Messrs. Alsop, Livingston, Lewis & myself[6] came also by Monsr. duCoudray, & I need only tell you in answer that many Vessells were taken of those loaded for acct of that Contract & General Washington unloaded several that were loaden in New York for the same purpose. Therefore it appeared evidently you never cou'd receive the remittance of £40,000 Stg from the Money's allotted to make you that remittance & for this reason the ballance that remained was thrown back into the Secret Committee & they gave orders to the Commercial Agents to supply you with what you fell short of the £40,000 Stg after you had received all the remittances the Contractors had made you. This was putting you on the surest footing because the Committee keep Constantly Shipping & the Contractors cou'd only have gone to the end of the money advanced one half of which had been stopped early by Friends & Foes as already mentioned.

We are so Cursedly hampered with their Numerous Cruizers along our Coast, that remittances are precarious & very difficult to be got out. Therefore I hope you will negotiate Loans of Money in Europe on such terms as will give us time to look around & make Remittances to the best advantage & with the greatest security that can be. However I must refer you to public letters for this & other Subjects being Dr sir, Your Obedt hble servt.   Robt Morris

RC (CtHi).

¹ Deane's December 4 letter to Morris is in *NYHS Collections* 19 (1886): 399–402.

² See Wharton, *Diplomatic Correspondence,* 2:248.

³ Not found.

⁴ For the steps Morris had taken to put his brother Thomas in Deane's "power," see Morris' letters to Silas Deane, to Thomas Morris, and to John Ross, January 31, 1777. See also Morris to William Smith, December 17, 1777.

⁵ See Morris to Captain LaRoche, June 18, 1777. For his most recently dated extant letter to Bromfield, see Morris to Thomas Bromfield, May 20, 1777.

⁶ Not found, but for Deane's December 3 letter to the Committee of Secret Correspondence, which also discusses problems encountered in making remittances from France, see *NYHS Collections* 19 (1886): 392–95.

Samuel Adams to James Warren

Dear Sir   Philade June 30 1777.

I have the pleasure of receiving your friendly Letter of the 16th Instant,¹ and have little more than time enough barely to acknowledge it. There is an unaccountable Uncertainty in the conducting the Post office. About a month ago I remonstrated to the Post Master General that the Time allowd the Eastern Delegates to answer the Letters they receivd (being on the Monday between the Hours of 9 & 2) was altogether spent in Congress, and requested that we might have one Evening for the purpose. He granted it and the Post has been since detaind till Tuesday Morning. But I am now informed that the former Regulation is revivd, for what Reason I know not, and our Letters must be ready at two o'Clock. I do assure you I should hardly forgive my self, if I could reflect upon my having once neglected to write to so valuable a Friend as you.

You wish to hear "how our Confederation goes on." I do not wonder at your Anxiety to have it completed, for it appears to me to be a Matter of very great Importance. We every now and then take it into Consideration, but such a Variety of Affairs have demanded the Attention of Congress, that it has been impracticable hitherto to get it through. There are but two or three things which in my opinion will be the Subjects of further Debate, and upon these I believe most if not all the Members have already made up their Minds. One is, what Share of Votes each of the States which differ so much in Wealth and Numbers shall have in determining all Questions. Much has been said upon this weighty Subject, upon the Decision of which depends the Union of the States and the Security of the Liberty of the whole. Perhaps it would be more easy for a disinterested Foreigner to see, than for the

united States to fix upon the Principles on which this Question ought
in Equity to be decided. The Sentiments in Congress are not various,
but, as you will easily conceive, opposite. The Question was very largely
debated a few days ago, and I am apt to think it will be tomorrow
determind that each State shall have one Vote, but that certain great
and very interesting Questions shall have the concurrent Votes of nine
States for a Decision. Whether this Composition will go near towards
the Preservation of a due Ballance, I wish you to consider, for if your
Life and Health is spared to your Country *you* will have a great Share
in the Determination of it hereafter.

You have Advices from abroad later than ours. Our last Intelligence
I gave you pretty minutely in a Letter which I sent & suppose was
deliverd to you by Cap Collins.[2]

I find by the Newspapers that the General Assembly under the De-
nomination of a Convention are forming a new Constitution. This is a
momentous Business; I pray God to direct you! Shall I be favord with
your own and others Sentiments upon it. I am greatly afflicted to find
that angry Disputes have arisen among my dear Countrymen, at a time
especially when perfect good Harmony should subsist and every Heart
and Tongue and Hand shd unite in promoting the Establishment of
publick Liberty and securing the future Safety and Happiness of our
Country. I am sure you will cultivate Harmony among those who love
the Country in Sincerity. With Regard to *others,* I will say in the Aposto-
lick Language "I would they were all cut off" (banishd at least) "who
trouble you."

Will it too much infringe upon your precious Time, to acquaint Mrs
A that I am in good Health and Spirits; and have not opportunity to
write to her by this Post. I am with the most friendly Regards to your
Lady & Family, very affectionately, yr Freind,   S A

RC (MHi).
[1] Warren's June 16 letter to Adams is in *Warren-Adams Letters,* 2:449.
[2] See Samuel Adams to James Warren, June 23, 1777.

Charles Carroll of Carrollton to Charles Carroll, Sr.

Dear Papa   30th June 1777.
I just write to inclose you a copy of Gen. Washington's last letter to
Congress & acknowledge the receipt of yr. letter of the 25th past, which
I shall answer more fully by Johny, whom if Sam continues to mend, I
shall send off in 3 or 4 days from this day. Sam is out of all danger, but
not well enough to wait upon me yet. I hope Molly will excuse my detaining him here, tho it may possibly prevent her going to Miss Carroll's
wedding. I refer you to the inclosed newspaper for eastern news. It

gives me great pleasure to hear that your leg is healing. I hope it will soon be perfectly healed that you may take your evening's walk as usual.

1st July

Upwards of 4,000 stand of muskets have lately arrived at an eastern port on Account of the Massachusetts State & on continental acct the following articles vizt. 285 pieces of shirting, 54 do of Duck, 52 Tons of cordage & 16 large anchors. Commodore Manly has taken a Snow bound from London to N.Y. with cordage, duck, &c. A transport has been taken by a privateer bound for Quebec with 32 recruits, a captain & Lieutenant. A transport has been taken by one of our sloops of war after 9 glasses fight with 70 soldiers bound for N. York. I mention these articles of news least the newspaper should not be out in time to go by this post. My love to Molly & Mrs. Darnnall. Sam rested well last night & continues to mend. I hope I shall be able to send Johny off Thursday or Friday next. Wishing you a long continuance of health I remain, yr. affectionate Son, Ch. Carroll of Carrollton

P.S. Not being able to get the Pena. packet I send you the last Boston paper brought by yesterday's post. We have no news from the General since his last letter which you have inclosed. I write this in Congress at 10 o'clock.

RC (MdHi).

Elbridge Gerry to James Warren

My dear sir   Philadelphia June 30th 1777

Your agreable Favours of the 10th, 15th & 19th of June with the Inclosures are at Hand,[1] & the Goods shipped by Messrs Gardoqui onboard the Charlotte, Capt St Clair, & the Alexander, Capt John Williamson, & consigned to you for my Acct are the property of the Continent; in Consequence of which I shall desire the Secret Committee to take the Charge thereof to order payment of the Freight prem[iu]m & other Expences by you incurred, & for your services herein.

Messrs Gardoquis mentioned in their Letter a parcell of Duck which they for some Time before had shipped by Capt Hodges for my private Acct., it being now appropriated to answer an Order which they have recd from the Hona Mr Lee in behalf of the united States. I am much at a Loss to understand their Intention, or to know upon what principles or Misconception they have made the proposal. You may remember that I purchasd in Novr last 3 Cargoes of Fish to import military stores & intended that the Contt or the State of Massa Bay should have the Benefit thereof & take the *Cargoes* on their own Acct.[2] As the latter had been greatly drained of Arms & other Stores, & could not so easily

come at Imports as the Commissioners employed by Congress to purchase for the Continent, I thot it necessary to offer *them* to the Board
of War, & finally concluded to risque with the Board half the Cargoes
on my own Acct. They enquired into the quality of the Cargoes &
finding them inferior declined to be concerned, & before I was apprized
thereof, I recd Advises that one of the vessels wch afterwards proved to
have been captured by the Enemy, was a long time out & not arrived
at Bilbao. In Consequence of this I declined offering the Cargoes to
the Continent or any Individual as it would be in Fact an unequal
proposal, & therefore risqued the whole in my own Acct. Two of the
Cargoes arrived & Mess Gardoquis not being able to procure Fire
arms, Lead & Flints, without breaking the strictest Injunctions of the
Court of Madrid, procured 16 Bales of Duck which they mention &
shipped them by Capt Hodges who was altogether in my Service,
specifying particularly that the Reason of their doing this was that he
could not procure for me the other Articles mentioned. The first cost
of the Fish which he recd of mine was abt £2200 ster. & bad as the
Quality was it must neat near 3/4 of that Sum. The Whole Amo[unt]
of what he has shippd for my Acct including the 16 or 17 Bales of
Duck is abt £700 sterl., so that he must Now have about 9 or 1000£
sterl. of mine in his Hands, therefore it was not from want of Interest
of mine that he proposed to make the new Appropriation. In addition
to this, the Vessel had sailed from Bilbao near one Month, all which
Time the risque was mine, before he made the proposal, & had she been
taken & carryed in to any port of France or Spain It must have been
known & the loss would have been mine. She is also arrived & the
Goods disposed off for my acct without the most distant Expectations of
any Embarrassment in the affair. I have been thus particular, that You
may hereafter if occasion should require explain the Matter, as I
prefer any Loss to the least Misunderstanding with the public relative to
Interest; & altho I shall not neat above one half in Bilbao of what the
3 Cargoes cost here without charging any Insurance, yet I will consent
to lose the Duck including the Cost of it, should it be desired by any
public Authority whatever.

I shall probably have occasion to obtain the Notary's Seal to some
papers for recoverg abt £250 strg which Messrs Gardoquis inform me
another House in Bilbao Messrs Lynch & Co who owe me the Money
refuse to pay because I sent back Bills of Exchange for the Money
here, which they sent after I had ordered my Interest to be there kept
& invested in produce. This is something extra in the commercial
World, & I shall probably trouble you for the purposes mentioned &
to teach these merchants that they are in an Error.

FC (MHi).
[1] Warren's June 10, 15, and 19 letters to Gerry are in C. Harvey Gardiner, ed.,

A Study in Dissent: The Warren-Gerry Correspondence, 1776–1792 (Carbondale: Southern Illinois University Press, 1968), pp. 63–65, 67–71.
[2] See Gerry to Warren, November 26, 1776.

James Lovell to Joseph Trumbull

My dear Sir   30th June [1777]
Yours of 27th I have just recd. Being quite ill I can only say I will communicate, what is proper, to others who are as anxious as I to have your present perplexing Situation altered by sending others to Head Quarters to take a Share off yr. hands. I am told you have stood at the Scales yourself lately. These Frenchmen have used me up quite.
Yr. Friend & h[umble] S——t.   J L

[*P.S.*] Gates is in Virginia.

RC (CtHi). Addressed: "To Joseph Trumbull Esqr. Commissy. Genl. Head Quarters Jersies."

James Lovell to William Whipple

Dear Sir   June 30th. 1777.
I had intended to write a letter to you on this day somewhat minutely about our in-door political turns & twists, but I am too ill. 4 Engineers having arrived on a Treaty with Messrs Franklin & Deane find the former one made between Deane and Du Coudray intirely inconsistent with their Honor; and they have made it appear that D—— was only a Child in the hands of Du Coudray, who has united, as under one direction, the Engineers & Artillerists; and made a Jews bargain for himself, and all the officers with him.[1]
These contending endless talkers and writers have entirely destroyed me. I suspect a settled fit of sickness will be [*the*] end of my present confinement. If I am mistaken, you shall soon hear again from, Yr. real Friend & humble Servt.   JL.

Tr (MH–H).
[1] For further information on the French engineers, see Samuel Adams to Richard Henry Lee, June 29, 1777, note 2.

Henry Marchant to Nicholas Cooke

Honord Sir,   Philadelphia June 30th. 1777
I have nothing to communicate, save my Wishes That the Order of

the Genl. Assembly may be duely complyd with, which appointed a Committee to correspond with Their Delegates, & to transmit immediately after every Session of the General Assembly Abstracts of their Proceedings, and a General State of their Affairs. I should be glad to know the Numbers of the Contl. Troops raised, and how many are sent forward, The Numbers of Militia in the Field, The Force and Shiping of the Enemy. I could wish That Our State may if possible early take Measures to import next fall cloths, Linnens, Hats, & Stockings, at least sufficient for Our Proportion of Continental Troops, & such as we may think necessary to keep in the Field for Our own immediate Defence. For altho' Congress take every Measure in their power for clothing the whole, yet if we do it ourselves, we shall then have the Satisfaction of knowing That our Troops are provided for, and we shall have their Blessings. I could wish that Our State would see it Their Interest to fit out one or two State Brigs. The Expence might most probably be doubly paid to Them in One Cruise. I cannot think The Hazard of Loosing them ought to discourage the Attempt, if They could be got out of the River when fitted. Might They not be ventured out only in a set of Ballast with a few Hands and sent round to Bedford and fitted out from thence?

I venture Sir at Suggestion from an Attachment to the Honor, Interest & Happiness of the State—Should they not meet with Approbation I know their Candour will excuse. Relying upon that upon all occasions I shall unremittingly endeavour to convince Them of my Zeal for their Service, And you Sir, that I am with great Truth & Sincerity, your most obed, humble Servt,   H Marchant

RC (R–Ar).

Eliphalet Dyer to Joseph Trumbull

Sir   Philadelphia June   1777[1]

Recieved your kind favour of the 22nd Instant. Had then but just arrived in Town put up at the Indian King while we could look out for Lodgings which I find dificult to find such as is agreable but have now concluded to take chambers at the same house I Used to live in kept by Mrs. House in Lodge Alley but now kept by Mrs Sword, Coll Williams & Mr. Low [Law] with me. I desired Mr Root to Inform you very particularly that Mrs Trumbull is well, the rest of the family as usual.[2] Coll Thos.[3] has for some few days before I left home been a little regaining as to his health was determined to set off for the Army soon. Of your New Appointment I have been Informed by Mr. Sherman, and of the salary or Wages allowd you. I think you will have much less Trouble more leisure or rather time to Visit your Friends than when at the head of the Issuing part, how far your Wages will as now fixed answer or exceed your Expences I cannot determine, but am rather of Opinion and so is Coll Williams, Mr Low & Mr Sherman that unless you must by serving fall in the rear you had better Accept your Appointment.[4] We think the Country requires your service & the cause may suffer by your refusal, we therefore rather advise you on the whole to accept. I am very Solicitous for Mr Root, not to serve him, but my Country by his service. I may possibly be prejudiced in his favour, but I really think he will make one of the most distinguished Officers from Connecticut, after a little more experience even as a Genl Officer. There is a Vacancy of a Coll in late Coll Huntingtons Regt. & Douglass one of which Vacancys he ought to fill if the real good of the service & the Country is Attended to.[5] At first it will be dissagreable to some & so it will if any other Gentn. whoever shall be Appointed but matters will soon quieted and all reconciled. Root has an Excellent Talent that way, the Regiments & Officers will soon respect & Esteem him. I know the best Gentn. in the Colony & whose Judgment is most to be depended upon wish him to fill one of those Vacancys. I dare say he would have been appointed by Govr & Councill of Safety (before the New Election) but no official Account of Coll Huntingtons advancement had arrived till too late. Part of the Regiment was Marched forward & it was then doubted whether we had Authority to fill up the Vacancy, but rather concluded it belonged to Genll Washington. If that is the Case how shall Genll Washington be Acquainted with what is really best for the publick service. I know he would make the greatest good his Motive Am sure & he may depend upon it, Coll Root will be preferable to any other appointment, which is the least probable may be made from that State. I only wish Genll Washington to know it. I dare pawn all my honor & Judgment upon it. I wish Genll Washington to know what can be known & doubt not of the Wisdome & rectitude of his decision. I do not my self love to trouble him with a letter, I know his cares, his Attention, & burthens in some measure, he has doubtless many Applications. Perhaps he may know my Sentiments from you or by reading him a few lines from this letter as am loath to Trouble him with one but if you think best will write him on the Subject.

Many New faces in Congress tho but about half or little more of their full Numbers. Let me hear from you as often as Convenient & am sincerely yours,   Elipht Dyer

[P.S.] I had forgot to Mention to you the affair of son Oliver. He had set out with John Fitch for Fishkill or there about before I receivd your letter. Am at a loss what is best to be done with him. If you can find any place for him which will suit should be glad you would & let me hear.

Mr. Low & Coll Williams present their regards to you.

E D

RC (CtHi). Endorsed by Trumbull: "needs no Answr."

¹ Dyer had arrived in Philadelphia with his colleagues Richard Law and William Williams on June 24 and undoubtedly wrote this letter just a few days after he took his seat in Congress on the 25th. See *JCC,* 8:496; Williams to Jonathan Trumbull, July 5, 1777; and "The Expenses of a Congressman in 1777," *The Connecticut Magazine* 10 (January-March 1906): 28-32.

² Joseph Trumbull had married Dyer's daughter Amelia in March 1777. *DAB.*

³ Dyer's son Thomas.

⁴ Trumbull had been appointed commissary general of purchases under the reorganization of the commissary department on June 18. In his July 19 letter to Hancock, which is in PCC, item 78, 22:265-67, Trumbull declined the position, explaining that he would not have sufficient authority to meet his responsibilities for supplying the army. See *JCC,* 8:477, 598, 620.

⁵ These vacancies had already been filled, and Dyer's friend Jesse Root continued to serve as a Connecticut militia officer until he took his seat in Congress in December 1778. *DAB.*

John Adams to Abigail Adams

Philadelphia July 1. 1777

We have no News: a long, cold, raw, northeast Storm has chilled our Blood, for two days past. It is unusual, to have a storm from that Point, in June and July. It is an Omen no doubt. Pray what can it mean?

I have so little Ingenuity, at interpreting the Auspices, that I am unable to say whether it bodes Evil to Howe, or to Us.

I rather think it augurs a fine Crop of Wheat, Rye, Barley, Corn, Spelts, Buckwheat, and Grass. It is a Presage of Plenty. Therefore let the Land rejoice. Flax and Cotton will grow, the better for this Weather.

July 2d.

The News Papers, inclosed, with this, will tell you all, that I know concerning the military operations in N. Jersey.

We have a Letter from Arthur Lee, from Spain, giving Us comfortable Assurances of Friendship and Commerce. We may trade to the Havannah and to New Orleans, as well as to Old Spain.¹

RC (MHi). Adams, *Family Correspondence* (Butterfield), 2:271–72.

¹ Arthur Lee's March 18, 1777, letter to the Committee of Secret Correspondence was read in Congress this day. See *JCC,* 8:514; and Wharton, *Diplomatic Correspondence,* 2:292–96.

James Duane to Robert R. Livingston

July 1 [1777] Tuesday

Yesterday the Committee of the whole House finished their Proceedings concerning our Revolters and reported them to the House. An unexpected Field of Debate was open'd and some of our neighbors (R.S.[1] in particular) discoverd an Earnestness and Sollicitude that did not belong to a Judge between a State and it's discontented members. But it was of little avail to object to what had been agreed to by the Committee of the whole House on the most solemn Argument and Debate of which I have been witness. The enclosd Resolutions were finally agreed to by Congress. The two first unanimously, all the rest by a considerable Majority. What was most keenly oppos'd is the last Resolution respecting Young's address; because it brought all the preceeding home more pointedly to the Case of New York.[2]

This appears to us to be a happy Decision for our State which if not neglected must produce very salutary Consequences. I shoud think it ought to be instantly circulated by handbills throughout every part of the State; and that Commissioners shoud be sent into the three Counties to announce the Resolutions and induce the People to conform to the new Government and avail themselves of its Blessings. We did not think it necessary to press for a Recommendation of Congress to these people to submit to our Jurisdiction; nor for the dismission of Warner's Regiment. We thought we had obtained what was sufficient for the present. It will depend on the Impression these important Decisions may make on that Regiment & the disaffected at large, whether the former shall be dischargd; & the latter enjoind more directly to a peaceble Conduct. If either shoud be turbulent and be guilty of Acts of Violence or Hostility I presume on proper Application Congress will interpose. A motion came from the southward that the power of the Continent shoud be employd to suppress these Insergents. Another from the same Quarter that Warner's Regiment shoud be dismissed: but it woud not have been wise to hazard either of them; & a spirit of candour & moderation, which on this occasion distinguishd your Delegates, was of no little Service in the other Points which after the first Debate we saw the finest prospect of obtaining. As I said before these Requisitions are kept in Reserve for a proper Season if they shoud become essential. I beleive the fine Politicians who have workt up this System of Independance have quite enough to digest. It was offensive to Congress in the highest Degree. If I have time I will send you a Copy of these Resolutions by this Conveyance: they go to the Council of Safety.

This is a very incorrect Letter. I wish it was transcribed; but have no Leisure to attempt it. If you think any part of it worth communicating shew it to Jay, Yates, Morris or any other of our Friends; and particularly to my Father in Law whom I hope you sometimes visit.

My Compliments to all I ought to respect, particularly to your Lady, Mamma and Sisters, and believe me to be, with the utmost Regard, Dear Sir, Your affectionate Friend & most Obed Servant,

Jas. Duane

July 2d. Wednesday

I have still an opportunity before I close this Letter to inform you that by the latest Intelligence from General Washington the Enemy again appear to be retiring from New Jersey; whether with Intention to embark for the Delaware or for Hudson's River, or on any other Enterprize, is so uncertain that the General himself does not hazard a Conjecture, & considering what has passed within the time I began this Letter you will allow that it is no easy matter to measure the Depths of Genl Howe's maneuvres. If he means to draw half our Army into an Engagement against the whole of his, he must be disappointed, for General Washington is not to be deluded by these thin disguises; & I am perswaded never will give up the Advantage of his strong Ground 'till he is convincd of Success from the Superiority of his Forces, or other very favourable Circumstances.

We have now finished every thing in Congress which immediately concerns our State, & I own I feel no small satisfaction in contemplating our Success. I wish our Countrymen may be as well pleased; & I shall have for a great deal of pains and Labour & anxiety a full Reward. I ought to have excepted as an unfinished business our publick accounts with the united States. To this my attention shall now be directed. Adieu! J.D.

Once more Verte.[3]

RC (NHi). A continuation of Duane to Livingston, June 28–29, 1777.

[1] Roger Sherman. See New York Delegates to the New York Council of Safety, July 2, 1777.

[2] See *JCC*, 8:509–13.

[3] For the continuation of this letter, see Duane to Livingston, July 8, 1777.

Unknown to Samuel Chase?

Extract of a Letter from Philada. July 1st 11 OClock A.M. [1777]

The enclosed Copy of Genl. Washingtons Letter, of the 28th will inform You of the Transactions in the Jersies since my last to You.[1] We do not exactly know the Enemies Strength in the Jersies. They have called in all their Outposts & have left but weak Garrisons in N York & Long Island. I apprehend Howe may have in all about 15,000, but these will moulder away by daily Skirmishes, desertion & fatigue, unless he can force our General to a Battle, & Should come off Conqueror. I fear the Loss of our three field pieces was owing to Surprise. Was it not shameful to be surprised when the Enemy were within 8 Miles? Nothing but Severity will introduce Discipline into our Armies, and dear bought Experience only can convince our officers & Men of its Utility, nay of its absolute Necessity. Mr. Duer a Delegate from N York informs Me that an intelligent person arrived yesterday in Town from Peaks Kill acquainted him, that the obstructions in the High Lands are in great forwardness & that the Enemy should they attempt that passage, will meet with a most vigorous Resistance. I wish our Situation at Ty. may be as respectable; I expect great Matters from the Influence, Conduct & Activity of Schuyler, and from the military Knowledge of St. Clair, who commands at that post. Four French Engineers arrived here last Week engaged by our Agents in France by the Direction of Congress. They refuse to serve under de Coudray. The Terms on which these Gentlemen engaged are modest & moderate. A Lieut. Colo. in the French Service is to be a Colonel in ours, a Major a Lieutt Colonel & a Lieutenant a Captain.

Extract of a Letter from Philada. 1/2 after 12 oClock July 1st 1777.

By a Letter from Gen. Washington dated the 29th,[2] & just now received in Congress, We are informed that the Enemy have all returned again to Amboy, and from Appearances are pressing for a general Embarkation. The General inclosed a Letter from Lord Sterling which mentions several Circumstances inducing him to think the Enemy in the late Skirmish lost a General officer, & that Lord Howes Son was dangerously wounded. We took 13 prisoners, & have lost about as many, with 3 field pieces.

Tr (PPAmP). In the hand of Samuel Chase. Although the author and recipient of these letters are not known, a plausible conjecture is that they were directed to Samuel Chase, who made the extracts printed here and sent them to Richard Henry Lee. These conclusions rest simply upon the facts that the document was written by Chase and is now located in the Lee Papers at PPAmP. Chase had not attended Congress since its departure from Baltimore in February, and Lee had returned to Virginia from Philadelphia on June 15.

[1] Washington's June 28 letter to President Hancock is in Washington, *Writings* (Fitzpatrick), 8:307–8.

[2] Ibid., pp. 308–10.

Committee for Foreign Affairs to the
Commissioners in Paris

No. 6th. In Committee for Foreign Affairs

Gentlemen   Philadelphia July 2d. 1777

Since our last No 5th of the 26 Ult which mentions the Enemy being retreated to Amboy we have to inform you that General Washington dismissed the Militia except about 2000 and likewise countermanded the reinforcements of 3000 Men from General Putnams Camp at Peeks Kill. We suppose Genl Howe to be apprised of those Circumstances as he immediately after returned with his whole force from Amboy and made an attempt to cut off a Division of our Army under Genl Sterling but without Success. For particulars we refer you to Genl Washington's Letters in the News papers of the 2d Inst.

A Letter from Genl Washington just received informs that the Enemy have totally evacuated the Jersies and are retreated to their last years Quarters on Staten Island.[1]

We enclose to you commissions and Instructions for Ralf Izard and William Lee Esqrs., the first appointed Commissioner for the Court of Tuscany and the other for the Courts of Vienna and Berlin. Their Instructions are so intimately connected with yours that we have thought proper to send them open to your Confidential Care, that you may give information to the Gentlemen and take every due Step to forward the Execution of the Intentions of Congress.[2]

We are Gentlemen, yr Most Obt. Humble Servts,

Benja Harrison	Thos. Heyward Jun
Robt Morris	James Lovell

RC (PPAmP). In a clerical hand, and signed by Harrison, Heyward, Lovell, and Morris.

[1] The British retreat from Amboy was reported in Washington's July 1 letter to Hancock, which was read in Congress on July 3. *JCC,* 8:527; and Washington, *Writings* (Fitzpatrick), 8:324.

Richard Henry Lee, a member of the Committee for Foreign Affairs, wrote to the committee's secretary Thomas Paine from his home in Virginia on July 12, urging him to transmit this news to the commissioners at Paris. "It appears to me of much consequence that an early transmission of Gen. Howes motions, thus far, should be made to our Commissioners in France & Spain. The procrastinating genius of the Committee will, I fear, greatly injure our affairs in Europe, and produces a wish that you would, officially, transmit the papers containing the Congress publications of these wants to Dr. Franklin & Dr. Lee. By sending them to a trusty hand in Massachusetts or N. Hampshire concerning which you may be advised by Mr. Adams or Colo. Whipple, the frequent opportunities from the Eastward will furnish speedy & safe conveyances. I know that some adventurous Politicians think, or affect to think, that it were better for America, Foreign interference should not take place until we had evidenced our ability to work out our own salvation. Whether a state of obligation be the best, I will not undertake to destmine [determine?], but I incline to think, that the reception of favors when they can be returned, serve to bind Men more strongly together in friendly union. But whilst I feel myself compelled to consider American Independence as the greatest good, and a return to the domination of G.B. after what has happened, as the greatest evil, I am willing to embrace every measure that tends to secure the one, and guard against the other. I am alarmed for our funds, and I am not quite free from apprehension, whilst our enemies whole force, both of Arms and Arts, is employed against us. I wish therefore that France & Spain may come forward without much longer delay, and by so doing, render secure our best and surest good. Both France & Spain doubt our strength, and fear our return to the former connection. The unremitting care of the Court of London hath been to cherish and support this way of thinking. It is our business to counteract their plan, by the most frequent & most authentic transmissions of our State & of events here. The first of August I hope to see you in Philadelphia." Lee, *Letters* (Ballagh), 1:310–11.

[2] On July 1 Congress approved commissions and instructions for William Lee as commissioner to the king of Prussia and the emperor of Germany and for Ralph Izard as commissioner to the grand duke of Tuscany. *JCC*, 8:518–22.

Jonathan Elmer to George Washington

Sir   Philadelphia, 2d July 1777

I am extremely sorry that the circumstance of affairs & Gen Howe's unreasonable demands have hitherto prevented the final settlement of the Cartel for a general exchange of prisoners. I flattered myself when I had the honour of waiting upon your Excellency in March last at Morris Town, on account of my Brother-in-Law John Gibbon, who has long been a prisoner of war in New York, that this matter would, before now, have been fairly compromised, & our prisoners released from their barbarous confinement. At present I see no prospect of so desirable an event taking place. I am therefore, at the earnest request of Mr. Gibbon's wife, under the necessity of mentioning his name once more to you, & of earnestly solliciting your Excellency, if possible, to procure his exchange or releasement upon parole. If no favourable opportunity is like to offer for accomplishing either of these ends, would it be inconvenient for you to admit his wife & some one of his friends to go to New York to see him, & carry him cloaths & other necessaries? He must undoubtedly stand in great need of them as he has been a prisoner upwards of six months.

If Mr. Gibbon cannot be released upon any other terms, his wife begs me to acquaint you that she has engaged a man to go & remain a prisoner in his room, until an exchange can be effected. This to me is a new expedient, of which I can form no Judgment at present. If your Excellency conceives it probable that such a thing could take place, or any other more eligible mode of relief adopted, Should esteem it a singular favour to be speedily informed of it.

I have the honour to be, Your Excellency's most obedient & very Hble Servant,   Jonathn. Elmer

RC (DLC). Washington evidently forwarded this letter to Elias Boudinot, the commissary of prisoners, because it is now part of the Boudinot Papers at DLC.

New York Delegates to the New York
Council of Safety

Honourable Gentlemen,   Philadelphia, 2d July, 1777.

Since our last we have applied to Commissary Trumbull to exchange in the manner directed by Congress the 2,000 bushels of salt which they were pleased to grant for the relief of our State; as soon as we receive his answer you shall know the result. We are endeavouring to purchase further quantities of this necessary article for the use of our fellow citizens, and have a prospect of succeeding.

The manufacturing of salt in the interior parts of our own State is certainly an object most worthy of the attention of the public. The Indians far from being averse to it, seem heartily disposed to favour the design, and by being made partakers of the advantages, might become warmly engaged for its success.

If the war should be prolonged, it is far from being improbable that we may be deprived of all foreign supplies. How necessary then may this expedient prove to our comfortable subsistence and to our internal union and repose?

We hope to hear that the experiments which were directed before we left Kingston have proved favourable, as well as that good progress has been made in the manufacture of lead and flints, and the refining of sulphur. A certain prospect of internal supply of these important articles would give Congress singular satisfaction; and if derived from your researches and exertions, would add highly to the reputation of the State.

We were yesterday honoured with your favour of the   and immediately took the necessary steps to procure an account of the State prisoners sent to Philadelphia by our late Convention, and of the manner of their discharge.[1] It shall be transmitted to you by this conveyance, with the reasons which induced the Council of Safety of this Commonwealth to use so little ceremony in a business which had been represented to them as of a very serious nature.

Congress, between this and the 26th of June, have spent the greatest part of four days in considering the claim of some of the inhabitants of our State to a new government, independent of the community, and the letters and remonstrances of our late Convention and your Honourable Council, on that interesting subject. The principles upon which this ambitious project was granted, were admitted to be of universal concern to the general confederacy; and they were considered as particularly odious, from the attempt to confirm them by the grossest misrepresentation of the resolutions of Congress. No debate was ever conducted with more deliberation and solemnity, and the decision was such as, in our judgment, ought, for the present, to be satisfactory; it does not, it is true, come up to the requisition of our State, "that the insurgents should be recommended to a peaceable submission to its jurisdiction by the authority of Congress, and that Warner's regiment should be discharged." But by totally reprobating the idea that a minority can establish an independence of the community of which they are members, by proclaiming the duty of Congress to secure and defend the several communities of which it is composed:

By censuring the supposition that Congress could do, recommend or countenance any thing injurious to the rights and jurisdictions of those communities:

By declaring expressly that the independent government attempted to be established by those misguided people, can derive no countenance or justification from the particular resolution on which it is pretended to be founded, or from any other act or proceeding of Congress:

By the contemptuous rejection of their petition to be received and ranked as a free State, and to be represented by their own Delegates in Congress:

By the apology to the State of New-York for raising Warner's regiment, implied in the explanation of the motives which gave rise to it, and by the severe censure of Doct. Young's address, encouraging those people to persevere in their defection:

By all these different resolutions, we think a substantial foundation, on general and undeniable principles, is laid, either for reclaiming our fellow citizens to their duty and a submission to the laws, by the force of reason and persuasion, and the fears of offending a whole continent; or should they obstinately persevere in their revolt, for a future requisition of the aid of Congress, to be administered in such manner as the opposition of the disaffected, and our own circumstances, may render expedient.

We flatter ourselves, therefore, that we shall meet with your approbation, and that our country will be pleased and benefitted by the measures adopted on this occasion. May we be permitted to suggest the propriety of despatching commissioners, without delay, to explain and enforce, among our too aspiring countrymen, these resolutions of Congress, and to seize the advantage which the first impression of unexpected disappointment and condemnation from the only tribunal they fear, may make on their minds, in order to induce them to a submission of your jurisdiction.

This appears to us to be the more necessary, as Mr. Roger Sherman, of Connecticut, who brought in the petition for these people to Congress, and has all along acted openly as their advocate and patron, and in the last debate plead their cause with a zeal and passion which he never discovered in any other instance, and which, in a judge, between a State and some of its own members, was far from being commendable. This gentleman, we say, immediately on passing the resolutions,[2] procured copies, and having obtained leave of absence, is already set out on his journey to the eastward. What may be his views with respect to our dispute, we know not, but to his enmity and officiousness you ought not to be strangers.

We have the honour to be, with the greatest respect, honourable gentlemen, Your most obedient humble servants,

Phil. Livingston,

Jas. Duane,

Wm. Duer.

Reprinted from *Journals of N.Y. Prov. Cong.*, 1:998.

[1] The council of safety had requested an account of these prisoners in a June 19 letter to the New York delegates. See *Journals of N.Y. Prov. Cong.*, 1:968, 970; and New York Delegates to the New York Council of Safety, July 8, 1777.

[2] The June 30 resolves on the dispute between New York and Vermont. *JCC*, 8:509–11.

New York Delegates to Joseph Trumbull

Sir,   Philadelphia, July 2d, 1777.

The Congress have been pleased in consideration of the peculiar situation and distress of our State, to favour us with the grant at the current price of about 2000 bushels of the public salt, which is stored at Plymouth, in the Massachusetts government, and is under the care of Thomas Mumford, Esqr. of Groton, Connecticut. The more effectually to relieve our suffering fellow citizens, they have been pleased to direct you, if it can be done without injuring the public service, to exchange for that salt an equal quantity nearer to the borders of our State.

This we flatter ourselves will be in your power; and in that case, we beg that you will be so obliging as to forward without delay, an order to the Council of Safety of our State, to authorize them to receive the salt; and in return they will give you an order on Mr. Mumford, to vest in you the property of the salt in his possession.[1]

The President has wrote to you on this subject. We beg to be informed of your resolution.

And are, sir, your most obedt. servants.

Reprinted from *Journals of N.Y. Prov. Cong.*, 1:1000–1001. Addressed: "To Joseph Trumbull Junr. Esqr., Commissary-General."

[1] On this point, see John Hancock to Joseph Trumbull, July 5, 1777, note 2.

James Wilson to Arthur St. Clair

My dear General   Philada. 3d July 1777

Doctor McKenzie sets out for Ticonderoga. I embrace, with Pleasure, the Opportunity of writing to you by him.

Some Time ago, the Enemy advanced from Brunswick as far as Somerset Court House. It is probable that their Design was to push for Philadelphia. This, at least, was believed; and the Belief produced the best Effects. The Militia of New Jersey turned out with the greatest Rapidity; and to a Man The Citizens of Philadelphia agreed to suspend their Disputes about the Constitution and to join unanimously in every Measure proper for repelling the Enemy and defending the State. General Washington kept his strong Encampment at Middle Brook. The Body under General Sullivan, consisting of Militia and Reinforcements of Continental Troops from the Southward, was increasing very fast at Correll's Ferry. General Howe thought it proper to retire from Somerset to Brunswick, from Brunswick to Amboy; and lately from Amboy to Staten Island. These different Movements have produced frequent Skirmishes, with the Advantage generally on our Side; once on that of the Enemy, so far as gaining three Field Pieces from us and losing, according to the best Accounts, a much greater Number of Men than we lost, can be called an Advantage. Concerning the future Views of the Enemy, the Sentiments expressed here are very different. Some think they mean to push up the North River; others, that they will make an Irruption into New-England; others, that they will come round by Sea to Delaware; others, that they know not what to do. Indeed I think it probable that their Plan for the Campaign, if they had a Plan, is very considerably deranged. We hear of no Reinforcements worth mentioning being arrived from Europe.

As to the Politics of Pennsylvania—they are not in the Situation I would wish. If a regular System were formed between General Howe and the Friends of our Constitution, his Motions could not have been better timed for them than they have been in two different Instances. When an Opposition has been twice set on Foot; and has twice proceeded so far as to become formidable; He has twice by his Marches towards Delaware procured a Cessation. The Assembly have twice taken Advantage of it to promote *their own* Purposes. Though those in the Opposition generously, and like true Patriots, suspended it while the Approaches of the Enemy were dreaded; the Assembly, just before their Adjournment, and just after this laudable Instance of Conduct was exhibited, have branded them, in a public Address to the People, with carrying on their Opposition in a Manner improper under *any* Government. They have agreed, however, at last, to take the Sentiments of the People with Regard to a Convention. What will be the Event, I am uncertain. They have *one* useful Quality. It would be a Virtue if exerted for a good Purpose. I mean Industry. This is much wanted on the other Side. As the Sense of the People will not be taken till after the next Election, I have some Expectation that their Eyes may be opened to see their true Interest by that Time.

I long much to hear from you. What I intimated to you long ago has happened. I hope you will be happy. I know you will be useful, at Ticonderoga. A good correspondence, I have every Reason to believe, will subsist between General Schuyler and you. If he is at Ticonderoga, please to present my Compliments to him. I am, Dear Sir, Yours very sincerely,   James Wilson

RC (OHi).

Samuel Adams to Arthur Lee

My dear Friend   Philade July 4 1777
I did myself the Honor to write to you on the 2d of Jany past since which your favor of the 21st of the same Month from Paris came to my Hand.[1] You have supposd that this Campaign would put General Howe, after the Junction with Burgoyne in Possession of the States of New York, New Jersey, Pennsylvania & the Delaware with Rhode Island as his Center of Attack upon the States of New England; you have even considerd such a situation of things as almost certain. But I have now the satisfaction of informing you that General Howe has found it necessary to withdraw all his Troops from New Jersey, and I am of opinion that it is impracticable for him to distribute his Troops among the States you have mentioned in sufficient Numbers to keep possession of them and afford enough to attack the New England States with the least Prospect of subduing them. I have thought that the Impression which the Enemy made the last Winter in the State of New Jersey was owing to favorable Circumstances which then took place, and was not in pursuance of the original Plan. The Time for which our Troops were inlisted had expired, our Army was reduced to a mere handful and General Howe had flatterd himself that the middle States were so generally disaffected to our Cause as to render their total Submission practicable & easy. He therefore made a vigorous push in the Depth of Winter as far as Trenton upon Delaware, and there cantond his Troops with a Design probably of availing himself of this City early in the Spring before we should be able to collect a force sufficient to prevent it. But General Washington, having gaind a signal Advantage by an attack as you have heard obligd him to retreat and make his remaining Winter Quarters in Brunswick; since which the Vigilance & Activity of the people of Jersey who by frequent Skirmishes have lessend his Army, has given him Reason to alter his opinion of their disposition & his removing from

thence has I think afforded sufficient Proof that he has not been able by Arts or Arms to conquer even one of our smaller States. What his next step will be is uncertain, perhaps he may embark his troops for Philadelphia, or more probably he may attempt a Junction with Burgoyne. If the first, has he to expect more Laurels or better Success than he gaind in Jersey? or, if the latter should be his Choice judge what must be his Prospect. Burgoyne who it is said can not muster more than 7 or 8 thousand will be oppos'd by our Northern Army & I hope overwhelm'd before they approach Albany. How will be follow'd close by the Army under the immediate Command of G W, at present more than equal in number, in high Spirits, full of the Idea of Victory and daily increasing. Under these unpromising circumstances should he ever complete a Junction, he will then have to begin an attempt of the most arduous Business of conquering the whole Army of the united States together with the numerous, hardy & stubborn Militia of New England. These are my Views of the present State of our military affairs and I am perswaded, when I reflect on the Spirit & Valor discover'd in my Countrymen of Georgia, So & No Carolina, Virginia & Jersey to say nothing of Lexington & Bunker Hill in my own dear native State, Great Britain will ever show herself feeble in her Efforts to conquer America. I beg you to write to me full as often as you can find Leisure, and for my own part I feel a disposition almost to persecute you with my letters but I must conclude with congratulating you on the first Anniversary of American Independence and assuring you that I am unfeignedly and very affectionately, your Friend,   S A

FC (NN).
[1] See Samuel Adams to Elizabeth Adams, April 1, 1777.

Charles Carroll of Carrollton to Charles Carroll, Sr.

4th July A.M. 7 o'clock.
We had yesterday advices from Gen. St. Clair, who commands at Tionderoga, as low down as the 26th ultimo.[1] The Enemy were approaching: their fleet was on the lake, part of it at Crown Point, but uncertain whether they had landed any forces there. They had landed Some on Chimney point opposite to Crown Point. They had an encampment at Gilliland's Creek 45 miles below Crown Point: several of our People have been killed or taken by small parties of Indians within a very small distance of our lines at Tionderoga. Our garrison is weak, not exceeding 2500 effectives: however if they defend themselves well, time may be given to collect a force sufficient to prevent the place from falling into the enemy's hands, but the garrison is badly armed & cloathed. If the Enemy [waste?] away their time & delay their attack

to the middle of this month, I have hopes we shall keep possession of Tionderoga, at least of Mount Independance. This day the Congress dine at Smith's Tavern. You will see by the inclosed paper it is to be celebrated as the anniversary of Independance. When Sam gets well enough to travel, I believe I shall return home as our State will be represented without me.[2] But I am anxious before I leave this place to see what sort of confederation will be formed & on which side G. Howe will begin his operations. Give my love to Molly & Mrs. Darnall. I shall write to you again by next Tuesday's post. I am, yr affectionate Son,

Ch. Carroll of Carrollton

RC (MdHi). A continuation of Carroll to Charles Carroll, Sr., June 29, 1777.

[1] Arthur St. Clair's June 25 letter to President Hancock was read in Congress and referred to the Board of War on July 5. *JCC*, 8:531.

[2] Doubtless a reference to the recent return to Philadelphia of William Smith, for apparently Carroll had been the sole Maryland delegate in Philadelphia since William Paca's departure from the city about June 29. The exact date of Smith's arrival is not known, but he had been considering a possible return for some time. Addressing James Wilson from Baltimore on June 7, he wrote the following brief letter about his business interests and efforts to avoid returning. "A plan is forming here for a trading Co. to France & Holland, to consist of Twenty or Twenty five, one of which I am one. Each partner is to put in £5000, to be Under the management of directors chosen by the Compy. I intend to mention your name as a Share. Youll therefore plan to let me hear from you by return of the post, if you dont choose a whole Share perhaps you may choose to Adventure one or Two thousand. I intend to write Mr. Donnaldson on this Subject, & would be glad he could be persuaded to go out, as I think him a fit person. As our assembly meets next week I intend to try to be excused from any further attendance in Congress by having a better man Sent in my place, if this cannot be done I suppose I will see you in Philada. a week or Two hence. If have any news from France or elsewhere interesting I'll thank you for a line on that Subject. We have a Confused report that Genl Washington has forced the enemys lines & gave them a Sound drubing. I pray God it may prove true, but I fear it is premature." Gratz Collection, PHi.

James Lovell to Benjamin Franklin

Hond. and dear Sir   [ante July 4, 1777][1]

I catch up my pen in haste: but, it is not that circumstance which makes me omit prefatorial apology, in this attempt to draw You into a literary correspondence. Difference of age and other differences vastly more important vanish, when I consider our relationship as "Friends to America." And, I am conscious that the service of these United States is the only motive prompting me at this time to an act, otherwise, egregiously vain.

Letters to Congress have been too often cast into the sea by the bearers of them, when in danger of being taken by the Enemy, in consequence of directions given by the Writers. The last unfortunate instance was where Mr. McCreary was bearer for the Honble. Mr. Deane. I think the great ingenuity of that young Gentleman could have found means to preserve a packet in the chase & his after captivity, if he had been emboldened by any consideration to make tryal, under contrary orders. I wish to lessen the necessity of such directions as have been heretofore given on like occasions.

You have practised modes of secret correspondence. I submit the annexed plan to your judgment. Having gained it by accident, I am satisfied myself that it is sufficiently inscrutable to warrant the attempt of preserving packets of importance thro' the risques of captivity.[2]

Should this letter arrive unbroken in its seal; we may draw advantage from the Thistle.[3] Should it arrive under dubious circumstances, you may use the Alphabet, and, by one of your ten thousand ready devices, may communicate to me a new Key-Word.

The secret Committee doubtless give you all proper history. I am too young in my present service to know the just limits of communicating those subjects which are most interesting to your Heart.

I am, With great & sincere Esteem, Your very humble Servant

James Lovell

ENCLOSURE

```
1 a b c d e f g h i j k l m 1 n o p q r s t u v w x y z & 1     1
2 b c d e f g h i j k l m n 2 o                                 2     2
3 c d e f g h i j k l m n o 3 p                                 3     3
4 d                         4                                   4
5 e                         5                                   5
6 f                         6                                   6
7 g                         7                                   7
8 h
```

9 i   Three lines of figures help the eye in making angular
10 j   reference.
11 k

12 l   By continuing till the square shall be compleat, each letter
13 m   of the Alphabet will be referable to every figure of the 27.
14 n
15 o

16 p   Example
17 q   chardo n char
18 r   Powder & Ball are already sent to the amt. ordered,
19 s   doncha   rdo
20 t   and Cannon as directed will be shipped by May.
21 u
22 v

23 w   14.8.23.14.2.4.14.27.21.12.2. are sent to the amt. ordered,
24 x   and 27.14.1.12.8.14 as directed will be shipped by 23.25.11.

25 y
26 z
27 &

RC (PPAmP).

¹ The precise date of this letter cannot be determined, but it was clearly written after Lovell's April 17 appointment to the Committee for Foreign Affairs and apparently before July 4. Franklin explained when he acknowledged the receipt of this letter: "I received your letter (without a date) communicating a method of secret writing, for which I am obliged to you. I have since received yours of July 4." Wharton, *Diplomatic Correspondence*, 2:411.

² Lovell employed variations of this cipher, which was based on a columnar table of alphabets built upon a key word, throughout his career as a member of the Committee for Foreign Affairs. Although his system appears to be a simple one, many of his correspondents repeatedly had difficulty in deciphering his letters and Franklin eventually abandoned the attempt to use Lovell's ciphers. For years Lovell used a similar cipher based on the key "Cranch" in his correspondence with John and Abigail Adams, but they too experienced great frustration in attempting to decipher his coded passages. For a more elaborate explanation of Lovell's codes and explicit examples of difficulties encountered in using them, see Adams, *Family Correspondence* (Butterfield), 4:viii–ix, 188, 393–99. For a general discussion of the use of ciphers by delegates during the revolution, see Edmund C. Burnett, "Ciphers of the Revolutionary Period," *American Historical Review* 22 (January 1917): 329–34.

³ Although Lovell appears to be transmitting the key word "Thistle" to Franklin, experimentation with *thistle* as the key for the examples contained in his enclosure has not been successful.

James Lovell to Benjamin Franklin

Sr   Philada. July 4th 1777

I think it my duty as an Individual to communicate some Information to you which you may not perhaps receive in a more formal or authorative way. The Contracts made with the Chevalr. De Borre, Mr. Du Coudray and several more have given infinite trouble, being inconsistent with each other, and all of them, except the one You signed with 4 Engineers, inconsistent with the honor of our American Officers, who, tho' not formed in regular standing Armies, have the most just claims from their services since the war began. It is not to be doubted but that a multitude of foreign Officers, by no means deficient of merit, are willing to come over & supersede such of ours as have been constantly in the field, and have borne innumerable hardships, when our poverty in Arms & Amunition would have terrified the stoutest European who had been accustomed to systematic Campaigns. Though we have now a standing Army for 3 Years or during the War, yet the Genius of the people of these United States is far from relishing this monarchical production: So far, at least, as not to be willing, for the sake of Theory, to have Foreigners placed in the highest trusts.

The Merit of Br. Genl. Knox is great, and he is beloved by his Corps. How then could it be conceived that Mr. Du Coudrays treaty should not create the greatest confusion among our Officers of Artillery? But these are not the only ones disgusted. Numbers of our Major Generals are injured by an antidate. The 4 Engineers who have arrived this Week disavow in the most preremptory manner being under the Command of Mr. Du Coudray who is not of the royal Corps of Engineers. Nor is it usual or convenient that those two Parties should be under the same Guidance.

Mr. De la Balme may be *Inspector* Genl of Cavalry without umbrage given to any of that Corps.

B. Genl Conway resigns upon finding De Borre ranking above him. The first might be ten thousand times more useful to us than the last. Mr. Holzendorf is a fresh Embarrassment in all respects.

I much fear that an Instruction, formerly passed in Congress respecting Foreigners who do not understand our language will be construed as a patent for those who do. It was not intended for that end I assure you. Nothing is more dreaded than such a Construction.[1]

I will not multiply words, but conclude by assuring you of my most sincere Esteem as, Sr., Your Friend & very humble Servant,

James Lovell

RC (PPAmP).

[1] Lovell was referring to Congress' March 13, 1777, resolution directing the Committee of Secret Correspondence "to write to all their ministers and agents abroad, to discourage all gentlemen from coming to America with expectation of employment in the service, unless they are masters of our language, and have the best recommendations." *JCC,* 7:174. Franklin's October 7, 1777, reply to Lovell is in Franklin, *Writings* (Smyth), 8:65–67.

John Adams to Abigail Adams 2d

My dear Daughter   Philadelphia, July 5th, 1777

Yesterday, being the anniversary of American Independence, was celebrated here with a festivity and ceremony becoming the occasion.

I am too old to delight in pretty descriptions, if I had a talent for them, otherwise a picture might be drawn, which would please the fancy of a Whig, at least.

The thought of taking any notice of this day, was not conceived, until the second of this month, and it was not mentioned until the third. It was too late to have a sermon, as every one wished, so this must be deferred another year.

Congress determined to adjourn over that day, and to dine together. The general officers and others in town were invited, after the President and Council, and Board of War of this State.

In the morning the Delaware frigate, several large gallies, and other continental armed vessels, the Pennsylvania ship and row gallies and guard boats, were all hawled off in the river, and several of them beautifully dressed in the colours of all nations, displayed about upon the masts, yards, and rigging.

At one o'clock the ships were all manned, that is, the men were all ordered aloft, and arranged upon the tops, yards, and shrowds, making a striking appearance—of companies of men drawn up in order, in the air.

Then I went on board the Delaware, with the President and several gentlemen of the Marine Committee, soon after which we were saluted with a discharge of thirteen guns, which was followed by thirteen others, from each other armed vessel in the river; then the gallies followed the fire, and after them the guard boats. Then the President and company returned in the barge to the shore, and were saluted with three cheers, from every ship, galley, and boat in the river. The wharves and shores, were lined with a vast concourse of people, all shouting and huzzaing, in a manner which gave great joy to every friend to this country, and the utmost terror and dismay to every lurking tory.

At three we went to dinner, and were very agreeably entertained with excellent company, good cheer, fine music from the band of Hessians taken at Trenton, and continual vollies between every toast, from a company of soldiers drawn up in Second-street before the city tavern, where we dined. The toasts were in honour of our country, and the heroes who have fallen in their pious efforts to defend her. After this, two troops of light-horse, raised in Maryland, accidentally here in their way to camp, were paraded through Second-street, after them a train of artillery, and then about a thousand infantry, now in this city on their march to camp, from North Carolina. All these marched into the common, where they went through their firings and manœuvres; but I did not follow them. In the evening, I was walking about the streets for a little fresh air and exercise, and was surprised to find the whole city lighting up their candles at the windows. I walked most of the evening, and I think it was the most splendid illumination I ever saw; a few surly houses were dark; but the lights were very universal. Considering the lateness of the design and the suddenness of the execution, I was amazed at the universal joy and alacrity that was discovered, and at the brilliancy and splendour of every part of this joyful exhibition. I had forgot the ringing of bells all day and evening, and the bonfires in the streets, and the fireworks played off.

Had General Howe been here in disguise, or his master, this show would have given them the heart-ache. I am your affectionate father,

John Adams

MS not found; reprinted from Adams, *Family Correspondence* (Butterfield), 2:274–75.

Thomas Burke to Richard Caswell

Dr Sir   Philadelphia July 5th 1777

Your several favours of 10th & 11th ulto have come to hand,[1] and you may rely on my best attention to all your commands.

Mr Penn is arrived, and has brought the papers necessary for obtaining the money, but the Treasury being very nearly exhausted of all former emissions I fear we must wait some time before we can procure a sum from one lately voted adequate to the demand. We have however obtained an order of Treasury for three hundred thousand dollars to be delivered at Baltimore where the press and Signers are, and the Board of War are properly instructed to forward it without delay.[2]

I observe the Resolve of the Assembly directs the Delegates to send forward 250,000 dollars and the residue of the 500,000 not drawn for under this Resolve, or previous thereto.

Two difficulties occur. Are the 250,000 to be considered as part of the 500,000, or are they to be an additional demand? Are the Delegates to send this money at the risque of the State, and not in the usual way under the direction of the Board of War? The latter I can not think to have been intended by the Assembly, and therefore I have ventured to advise its being sent at the risque of the Continent in the usual way. In this Mr Penn concurs with me. The former question I can not decide upon, but until it is more clearly expressed must suppose it is intended as part of the 500,000 dollars.

We know not what sums have been drawn for by the Treasurers. Mr Johnston did indeed always advise me of his draughts, but Mr Ash did not, and want of information on this head obliges me to retain two hundred thousand dollars to be applied in payment of all the bills drawn heretofore by the treasurers.

I perceive Mr Penn had a bill from Mr Ash in his own favor for sixty odd thousand dollars, on what account this is, I know not, or under what authority Mr Ash has drawn it. But I shall take no notice of it as a public transaction until I see some Resolution of the Assembly which gave rise to it. Your bill in favor of Mr Ellis has been paid, the others are not yet arrived.

Nothing material has happened since I wrote you last, except the celebration of the fourth of July (the Anniversary of the declaration of Independence). You will see it at large in the enclosed paper, but one thing is remarkable, this day, and the 28th of June, memorable for the defence of Sullivan's Island, were both celebrated here, and at both a Hessian band of music which were taken at Princetown performed very delightfully, the pleasure being not a little heightened by the reflection that they were hired by the British Court for purposes very different from those to which they were applied.[3]

Tr (Nc–Ar).

¹ These letters are in *N.C. State Records,* 11:494–95.

² On July 8 Congress ordered Continental treasurer Michael Hillegas to forward to North Carolina $300,000 of the $500,000 that was supposed to be paid to the state under the terms of a resolution passed on February 5, 1777. *JCC,* 7:92, 8:538. Unless one concludes that this letter is misdated—an unlikely hypothesis in view of the July 7 postscript—Congress' July 8 order must simply have been a confirmation of the "order of treasury" mentioned here by Burke.

³ For the continuation of this letter, see Burke to Caswell, July 7, 1777.

John Hancock to Joseph Trumbull

Sir,   Philada. July 5th. 1777.

The enclosed Resolves of Congress respecting the Commissary Genl.¹ I have the Pleasure of transmitting for your Information and the Direction of your Conduct in the Department committed to your Care, and am, with Respect, Sir, your most obed. & very hble Sert.

J.H. Presid.

[*P.S.*] I must also request your particular Attention to the Resolve concerning the Salt; which Congress are desirous, from the peculiar Situation of the State of New York at this Juncture, they should be supplied with in the Manner therein mentioned, if it can be done consistent with the publc Interest.²

Inclos'd you have a Warrant on John Lawrence Esqr. Commissioner of the Loan Office in Connecticutt for One hundred thousand Dollars for the use of your department, to be accounted for.

LB (DNA: PCC, item 12A). Addressed: "Jos. Trumbull Esqr., Commissy. Genl. of Purchases."

¹ See the June 23 and July 2 resolves on the mode of supplying the army, travel expenses for assistant commissaries, and the commission for commissaries of purchases in *JCC,* 8:491, 523–24.

² Trumbull wrote to Hancock on July 7 and explained why he could not comply with the June 14 resolve of Congress requesting him to provide supplies of salt to New York. See *JCC,* 8:466; and PCC, item 78, 22:251.

John Hancock to George Washington

Sir,   Philada. July 5th. 1777.

Since I had the Honour of addressing you on the 24th of June, I have been favoured with the Receipt of your several Letters of the 25th, 28th, 29th, and 30th of that Month, and the 1st and 2d instant; all which were immediately laid before Congress.¹

Having Nothing in Charge at this Time but to transmit the enclosed Resolves,² I beg Leave to request your Attention to them; and have the

Honour to be, with the utmost Esteem and Respect, Sir, your most obed. & very hble Servt.   John Hancock Prest

[*P.S.*] A large Supply of Money is on the way.[3] I will Reply to your several Letters as soon as Congress have Determin'd upon them.

RC (DLC). In the hand of Jacob Rush, with signature and postscript by Hancock.

[1] These letters are in PCC, item 152, 4:295–97, 305–6, 309–11, 313, 317–21, and Washington, *Writings,* (Fitzpatrick), 8:297–300, 307–8, 324, 328–31. The letter of June 30 is actually a postscript to that of June 29.

[2] These were resolves of July 1 and 2 on a Virginia artillery regiment, the election of a deputy commissary as well as a physician general for the middle department, a Connecticut request for arms, and traveling expenses for deputy commissaries. *JCC,* 8:516–18, 523–25.

[3] On this day Congress ordered transmission of $524,000 to the paymaster general for army pay. *JCC,* 8:533.

Henry Marchant to the Rhode Island
Governor and Assembly

Gentlemen   Philadelphia July 5th. 1777.
    I recd. a Letter from the Honorable William Greene Esqr. Speaker of the lower House signed at the Request, and in Behalf of, the General Assembly (the Govr. being absent) of the 22d & 24th of June last, directed to Mr. Ellery and myself.[1] Mr. Ellery having some Time before sat out on his Return Home, I instantly, on the same Day I received your Letter, being the third of this Instant July, moved Congress for the Sum requested, being sixty Thousand Pounds (meaning I presumed lawful Money) or two hundred Thousand Dollars. Congress were much surprised that so large a Sum should be requested so soon after the large Sum granted the State of Rhode-Island &c. The Gentlemen of the Treasury Board would hardly allow it possible You should have expended such very considerable Sums on Continental Account, and moved that the Sum of sixty Thousand Dollars only should be now granted, especially as it was very probable the Continent would soon have Occasion for large Drafts upon the Eastern Loan Offices, if the Enemy's Movements should be into New-England, or up the North-River, the latter of which from Genl. Washington's Letters that Day received, seemed, and still appears most probable.
    I did not fail to state and urge, in the strongest Manner I was capable of, the Necessity and Expediency of this Supply, the absolute Necessity you would otherwise be under of emitting a large Sum, the destructive Consequences of which we are all awakened to. I further suggested, what I fully imagine to be the Case, that a very great Part

Henry Marchant

of this Sum would go into the Loan office by Way of Discount with the State, that it could not be expected so large a Sum would in Fact be thrown into that Office. After a considerable Debate, the Consideration thereof was submitted to the Treasury Board. I applied there this Morning and inforced my Application with every additional Argument in my Power, and was very happy in obtaining a Report agreable to my Wishes, and upon which the inclosed Resolves passed Congress.[2] I inclose You also an Order from the President in Consequence of One of said Resolves, on Jos. Clarke Esqr. Comr. of the Loan Office State of Rhode-Island, for One hundred and Ninety Thousand Dollars. As by the Speakers Letter your Delegates were required to accept of the Bills which might be drawn on them by Messrs. Saml. Purviance and Company for a Load of Flower &c, and as you had not directed your Delegates where the Bills were to be paid, and as I could not tell what Sum the Bills might amount to, I obtained the other Resolve inclosed for the remaining ten Thousand Dollars to be advanced your Delegates out of the Treasury here. If the Bills should not be forwarded to me for Acceptance and Payment, I can at your Request procure an Order of Congress for the same to be paid you out of the Loan office in Our State. Whatever Directions herein I may receive, I shall endeavour to comply with, and hope what is done will meet with your approbation. I should be glad that an Account of the Expenditures on the Continental Account comprehending the Account last Spring sent forward, and the Amount of the whole Sums advanced by the State on Continental Account from the first Advances, and the whole Sum at various Times received and placed to Continental Credit might be sent me, for my own Information, that I may be the better able to state to Congress or the Treasury Board the Propriety of your Applications in Future.

Such has been the great Demand for Loan Office Certifficates that the Treasurer has not been able to forward them from Maryland (where he now is) as fast as called for. The Treasury Board are in Daily Expectations of receiving a large Supply, and will immediately send a proper Number to the State of Rhode Island &c. I have the Honor to be, Gentlemen, your most obedient, humble Servant,

Henry Marchant

RC (R–Ar). Addressed: "The Honorable The Governor and Company of the State of Rhode Island &c."

[1] Letters to the Rhode Island delegates of these dates and apparently dealing with the same issues are attributed to Gov. Nicholas Cooke in William R. Staples, *Rhode Island in the Continental Congress, 1765-1790* (Providence: Providence Press Co., 1870), pp. 141–42.

[2] These resolves ordered the payment of a total of $200,000 to Rhode Island. *JCC*, 8:533.

Marine Committee to John Young

Sir　　　　　　　　　　　　　　　　　　　　July 5th. 1777

It is expected that the Continental Sloop Independence under your command is now ready to proceed to France agreeable to the directions sent you a few days since.[1] You will receive herewith sundry dispatches from the Committee of Foreign Affairs and Secret Committee[2] respecting which you will obey such orders as they may give. You are to proceed in Said Sloop from Senepuxent for the Port of Nantes in France where you must apply to William Lee and Thomas Morris Esquires Commercial Agents of the United States and they will supply you with Money to defray the expences of your Journay from thence to Paris and back. Whilst you are on that journay your Lieutenant must employ the Crew in heaving down, Cleaning and refitting the Sloop, and in getting all such things done to her as may be necessary. The Agents will supply the Money and other articles proper on this Occasion for amount whereof you must grant them receipts. You must give directions also to your Lieutenant and other Officers to engage as many Seamen as possible that you may return full manned—the more the better only taking care to lay in a Stock of Provisions proportioned to the number of men you get. You are to receive from the Honorable Docter Franklin and the other Commissioners at Paris all Letters and dispatches they have to Send, and to wait any time they may think proper to detain you.

You are to receive from the Commercial Agents any goods they have to send out by the Sloop and bring from [them] also all Letters and Packets they have to send. Should the Honorable Commissioners think it necessary to detain you any time for their dispatches, it may probably be an eligible plan for you to make a Cruize on our enemies Trade from which you may return at an appointed Time for their dispatches & then also take in such goods as may be ready. This you may propose to the Commissioners and to the Agents.

If you are fortunate enough to take any Prizes you will send them to Address of said Agents, who will receive the Continental Share and divide the other as it ought.

When you are dispatched from France you must make the best of your way for this Coast and get into the first safe port you can, immediately bringing to us all the dispatches and Letters, which both going & Coming have always ready Slung to a weight sufficient to Sink them, and if you perceive an inevitable misfortune put them into the Sea for they must not on any Account fall into the enemies hands.

You must duely observe the Instructions of the Navy Board, preserve strict discipline but use your Officers & men well that they may be fond of the service—treat Prisoners with humanity and in All things

act the part becoming an active good Officer which will recommend you
to, Sir, your hble servants

LB (DNA: PCC Miscellaneous Papers, Marine Committee Letter Book).
¹ Not found.
² For the former, see Committee for Foreign Affairs to the Commissioners at
Paris, July 2, 1777; but no such Secret Committee dispatches have been found.

William Williams to Jonathan Trumbull, Sr.

Hond Sir   Philadelphia July 5. 1777
    The current News all the road as We came, was that the Enemy were
pushing to this City & had made considerable Progress, that Ships
were up the river as high as Kings Ferry, that the Boats were taken up
by Genl Washington &c which determined our rout by the Way of
Fish Kill, Easton & Bethlehem, which made our Journey long & tedious,
so that we did not arrive here 'till Tuseday the 24th ulto, thro the good
Hand of God, in Health & Safety.¹ Our Intelligence from the Armys
was vague & uncertain on the road & even here. What has happened
since, the partial Battle & the evacuation of the Jerseys, & it is now
reported of Staten Island, &c you will have heard by Mr. Sherman &
otherwise, I dare Say, eer this can reach you & more perfectly than I
can give it. There is great reason to believe the Enemy are bound to
the nothern quarter or to New England, & if reports are true They
have sailed & their Designs are known before this. Our Letters from
Genl. Sinclair who commands at Tya. indicate his full Expectation of
being attacked by Genl. Carlton, & I wish I cod say of his readiness to
receive Them, but not so, & if They go to New England it will thro
my dear Country into great Distress but I shod hope our army will be
able to meet them before They can make any great Progress. Our Sins
are so great that We have reason to expect severe Correction. O that
this People were wise, but there is no appearance of it. God will accomplish his own Designs & what He does is, & will be right & as You
piously observe, "future Events are in the safe hand of the all wise &
most merciful Director." The Enemy have left Jersey in Desolation &
ruins where They had been & marked their way with merciless rage &
Brutality. May the God of Heaven look on & pity the Sufferings of his
People & save Us from the further Effects of their Brutal Rage. The
Accos. you had recd. of the raising & joining of the southern Troops
were certainly not just. I will not say how untrue, for obvious reasons.
    The Jersey militia turn'd out most spiritedly on the last occasion. To
their active zeal & exertions, it may in good measure (under God) be
ascribed that the Enemy proceeded no further. I find Congress much
as I left it, in every respect, some new Members; their Time mostly

taken up by daily Incidents & occurrances, very little progress made in the Confederation. It had passd the Comte of the whole House before I left, has been a good while before Congress & few important questions yet determined, the capital ones of the weight of each Colony in deciding Questions, & Taxation & many others undetermined. The first respecting the Vote of Each has been entered on, & it is most strenuously contended in behalf of the larger ones that their vote shall be proportionate to their population which is forcably opposed. I trust & hope it will be carried in favor of the equal Footing it has been, & without it, the smaller Colonies will be in effect swallow'd up & annihilated.

Your Letter to the Presidt & its inclosures are recd,[2] the papers not read in the House, but committed. I cant say what will be done. Nothing but what is originated in this Batch of ——— Politicians seems to make any great impression. Mr. Erkelens seems to be vanished, we can find He has been here, but no Body knows who or where he is, tho I believe by enquiry he is in Town, but have not been able yet to find him. I suspect he is chagrined at the cool reception he has met with, & keeps retired.[3]

We have applied for the Arms you wrote by Us for, but find exceeding Difficulty in obtaining Them. I believe not a man southward or in the middle Department is supplied with an Arm but by the Continent. We have done it thro zeal & strong attachmt to the Cause, & yet They will not seem to know, believe or care any thing about it. There is indeed such a thing as being righteous overmuch, & yet I can hardly expect that we have in such Instances fallen into this Error, but shod N. E. be attacked & unarmed we shod have reason. The matter is however referd to Genl Washington,[4] & Mr Sherman is to negotiate the Affair with him on his return (he set out the 2d Inst).[5] More than all the Arms We have are wanted, which must be allowed as some excuse for their lothness to comply.

We have a very extra[ordinar]y Contract now lying before Congress entered in Sepr. last by Mr. D.— with Monsr Du Coudray (after a long list of pre nomens) who is present, making him Genel & Commander in Chief of the whole Choir of Artillery, with power to fill every vacant office now & in future, & to be subject to no Controul but by the Congress & the Comander in Chief of the whole Army, & with the rank of Maj General & his pay as in a separate Department, to be on pay from the 1st of Augt. last, & a large Train of under officers of various ranks who are with him, for whom also he has made appointments, & to Monsr. & all he had has advanced a half years pay for expences of preparation & Passage, not to be accounted for, & with Pensions for Life equal to half their Pay annually &c &c. The Contract has had several Assignments but is not yet taken up. I do not expect it will be ratified in full.[6] I forebear to say many things. The City swarms with French Men.

I dont know but I transgress the Rules We all sign in divulging any Matters sub Judice & unfinished in Congress, but I cant refrain from mentioning important matters to one who has so good a right to know & to whom I & even the Continent are subject to great Obligations but Sr. you will not make them to be publick nor known as from me especially.

The Prices of every thing here are most alarmingly extravagant, much owing to the malicious Cunning of our worst Enemys, the Torys, & coinciding with the boundless avarice of the Merchants, whose Gain is the summum Bonum, & all the God they seem to know, in these parts. Nothing to be done by Congress, because, forsooth, it will be interfering with the internal Police of this grand State, in this respect the mother of Harlots &c. The principle properly applied is however very important. Congress seems to be chaind to this place, & the longer they stay, the stronger a multitude of offices & officers are established & employed in this City, & some of the worst men in some of them.

Yesterday was in my opinion poorly spent in celebrating the anniversary of the Declaration of Independance, but to avoid singularity & Reflection upon my dear Colony, I thot it my Duty to attend the public Entertainment. A great Expenditure of Liquor, Powder &c took up the Day, & of Candles thro the City, good part of the night, I suppose. I conclude much Tory unilluminated Glass will want replacing &c.

Dr. Young died lately of a Fever caught in attending the Congress Hospitals in the City, & was buried the day we came into Town. Poor man He now knows the reality of Things, he lately disputed & disbelieved. Can find out very little of his last Ideas but believe he died just as he lived, expecting if there was a future State that a man of his Benevolence must be happy.

Am extreamly sorry I can not write my hond & worthy Friend, Genl Huntington, & Mr. Hosmer whose Letters I have recd. & shall acknowledge soon as possible. My apology will be I dare say in their opinion sufficient. The Rhumatic Pain that had for long afflicted my right Arm, has a few days since suddenly fallen into my wrist, which is much swolen, has been in great Pain day & night, feels as hot & looks like the Skin of a roasted Pig. It is with much pain I write this, & were it not better than yesterday, it wod have been impossible. They will accept my best Compliments.

I had also a Letter from my most dear Mrs. Williams, it is peculiarly serious I cant write her, please to remember me to her with most tender Affection, & my other dear Friends. May God in infinite Mercy save this People from their Sins & remove his Judgments. I am with all possible esteem, affection & Respect, your most dutiful obedient, Son & Servant,   W. Williams

[*P.S.*] Our Lodgings are at present inconvenient, but excessive dear &c.

RC (NN).

[1] Williams' account with Connecticut listed his services as a delegate from June 12 and Richard Law's listed his from June 14, but these dates obviously signified their respective departures from home and their travel time was understandably increased by the circuitous route they took to avoid the British. The two accounts are located in the Emmet Collection, NN; and Revolutionary War Collection, Ct.

[2] See *JCC*, 8:497.

[3] Congress had paid a large sum of money to Gosuinus Erkelens on April 18. *JCC*, 7:276.

[4] For Washington's explanation of why he could not honor Trumbull's request for arms, see his July 2 and 7 letters to Trumbull in Washington, *Writings* (Fitzpatrick), 8:333–36, 367–69.

[5] Sherman had been granted a leave of absence on June 30. *JCC*, 8:508. His accounts with Connecticut indicate charges for services through July 6 (Sherman Papers, DLC), but according to his July 11 letter to Samuel Adams he did not arrive in New Haven until the evening of the seventh (Samuel Adams Papers, NN). Sherman did not return to Congress in 1777.

[6] See John Adams to Nathanael Greene, July 7, 1777, note.

John Penn to Richard Caswell

Dear Sir   Philada July 6th 1777

It is with great concern that I inform you we have not been able to send off the money for our State yet. Doctor Burke and myself have done every thing we could to procure it, knowing what pressing demands you have, and the necessity there is for using dispatch; there was very little money in the Treasury when I got here, and one or the other of us has been almost every day at the Treasury Board. I am in hopes we shall be able to dispatch 300,000 dollars in two or three days, you may depend that nothing on our part will be wanting. The money is chiefly raised in this and the Eastern States by way of the Loan Offices.

General Howe after having made a variety of manouvres and finding that Gen. Washington would not give up his strong post, went over to Staten Island, and soon after sailed with his troops towards New York. It is supposed that he intends by way of the No River to form a junction with Burgoyne if possible.

General Washington did not incline to risque a battle on equal terms, nor was Gen. Howe willing to attack our army on the hills, or to march far this way, & have our Troops behind him. It is not of my power to tell you how many soldiers are in either army, ours is said to be increasing. The Brigades sent after the enemy had frequent skirmishes, tho' nothing of great consequence was done.

We have nothing new from Europe lately. Mr Lee one of the Embassadors is gone to Madrid.

I informed you some time ago, how dear salt was in Maryland and this State, owing to a few persons purchasing it up, and that I suspected endeavours would be made by some of them to engage all that useful article with us, in order that your Excellency might if possible put a stop to such a mischievous practice, should it be attempted. I mention it again for fear the letter may have miscarried. I am with the greatest respect, Your Excellency's obt Serv't, John Penn

Tr (Nc–Ar).

John Adams to Nathanael Greene

My dear Sir, Philadelphia July 7. 1777

I never before took hold of a Pen to write to my Friend General Green, without Pleasure, but I think myself obliged to do it now upon a Subject that gives me a great deal of Pain.

The Three Letters from the Generals Sullivan, Green and Knox, have interrupted the Deliberations of Congress, and given many of the Members of it much Uneasiness.[1] They thought themselves bound in Honour and Justice to the great Body of People whom they represent, to pass the Resolutions which before this Letter reaches you, will be communicated to you by General Washington.

The Contract between Mr Deane and Monsr Du Coudray, is not yet decided upon. It is in Truth one of the most delicate and perplexing Transactions that has ever fallen in our Way: but those three Letters instead of relieving Us has only increased our Mortification.

Many great Questions ride upon that Contract. Such as these, whether Mr Deane had Authority to make it? If he had not, how far it is consistent with Sound Policy to confirm it. What Merit Monsr Du Coudray has in procuring Cannon, Arms, Ammunition and other Things for our Use. What Interest the French Court may take in our Complyance with the Contract? What Monsr Du Coudrays Abilities to serve Us really are? How far we may comply, consistently with Justice to our own officers? and how far Such a Trust may be confided to a foreign officer with safety to the public interest? &c &c &c. In the Midst of these Deliberations, the Three Letters are received, threatening that if we fullfill the Contract, Three officers, on whom We have depended, will resign in the Midst of the Campaign when the Attention of every officer ought to be wholly taken up in penetrating the Designs of the Enemy and in Efforts to defeat them.

If We dissagree to that Contract what will our Constituents say? What will foreign Nations say? Our Journals upon which the Three Letters must appear, will be read by both. Will not foreign Nations say, that the Ambition and Turbulence of three of our best officers necessitated us to violate our public Faith?

What Confidence will any Nation have in our Promises, if they think that our Authority is so feeble, among our own Ranks and even among our own officers, that We cannot perform our Covenants for fear of disobliging them?

What will our Constituents Say? You have lost the Friendship of foreign Powers, you have broken a Covenant with one of the best officers in Europe, and why? because your own officers would not permit you to perserve your own Honour.

It is impossible now for Congress even to determine that Deane had no authority to make the Bargain, without exposing themselves to the Reflection that their own officers intimidated them into it.

I must be careful my Friend in Saying, that if you or the other Generals Sullivan and Knox, had seriously considered the Nature of a free Constitution, and the Necessity of preserving the Authority of the Civil Powers above the military, you never would have written such Letters.

The Right of an officer to resign I shall not dispute, and he must judge for himself, what Causes will justify him—but surely you ought to have waited, till Monsr Du Coudray had appeard in Camp and assumed the command, before you resigned, or at least untill you had seen an attested Copy of our Journals in which he was appointed to supercede you.

I must needs freely say, that there is more of Rashness, Passion and even Wantonness in this Proceeding than I ever expected to see in my Friend Green and Knox in whose Judgment and Discretion I had the Utmost Confidence. If the Letters had been written to individual Members of Congress, in private Confidence, desiring to be informed what Congress had done, and conveying the Same sentiments, it would have been attended with no evil Consequences, but Letters addressed to Congress, which must be recorded in the Journals and published for the Inspection of all the World, are exposed to the Reflections of all the World, and one Instance of the Kind passing with Impunity establishes a Preceedent for all future officers, and one stride after another will be taken, one Breach of the Priviledge of Congress after another will be made, and one Contempt of its authority after another will be offered, untill the officers of the Army will do as most others have done, wrest all authority out of civil Hands and set up a Tyrant of their own.

I hope these Letters will have no Influence upon Congress in determining Du Coudray's Pretensions, but of this I am sure, they will not induce them to grant him less Rank and Emoluments, than they would otherwise have undertaken.

Nothing in this affair gives me more Pain than the Necessity you have laid Us under of passing a Resolution, which will lessen your Characters and diminish the Confidence which the good People of America have in your Judgment, and attachment to the Principles of

Liberty. But there was not one Member of Congress who dared to justify the Letters, very few who could say a Word in Mitigation or Excuse. It was universally considered as betraying the Liberties of the People to pass them by unanswered. Some were more for dismissing all three of you instantly from the service, others for ordering you to Philadelphia, under arrest to answer for this offence.

The Resolution expresses an Expectation that some Acknowledgment or Apology will be made. I sincerely hope it will, for I think that in a cool Reconsideration of those Letters, the Impropriety and Danger of them must be manifest.

I would be far from dictating to you, or giving Advice unasked, but I really think, that a Declaration that you had no Intention to influence Congress, to contemn its authority or infringe the Liberties of the People or the Priviledges of Congress, a Declaration that you have the fullest Confidence in the Justice of Congress and their Deliberations for the public Good, is the best that you can do, provided you can do this with Truth and sincerity, if not I think you ought to leave the service.

LB (MHi).

[1] Letters to Congress from Greene and Henry Knox, who threatened to resign if Du Coudray's contract was honored, were read in Congress on July 5. Congress had already received a similar letter from Gen. John Sullivan on July 3 and immediately resolved to accept his resignation if it were formally tendered, condemning his letter as an unwarranted attempt to "control" Congress, but as this entry has been deleted from the journals it seems apparent that Congress decided against treating Sullivan's case separately and reopened it when the letters from Greene and Knox arrived. *JCC,* 8:527–28, 531; PCC, item 155, 1:35 and item 78, 13:439; and Sullivan, *Letters* (Hammond), 1:403.

On July 7 Congress forcefully denounced the three generals' threats to resign as "an attempt to influence their decisions, and an invasion of the liberties of the people, and indicating a want of confidence in the justice of Congress." *JCC,* 8:537. See also Eliphalet Dyer to Joseph Trumbull, and James Lovell to William Whipple, this date; and James Lovell to General Washington, July 25, 1777.

Du Coudray was ultimately authorized to serve as a volunteer with the Continental Army, but before he could assume his duties he drowned in the Schuylkill River on September 15, 1777. *JCC,* 8:740, 751, 845. According to James Lovell, Du Coudray had only been appointed a brevet captain. Lovell to William Whipple, September 17, 1777.

For a subsequent summary view of the problem of foreign officers, see Committee for Foreign Affairs to the American Commissioners at Paris, December 1, 1777.

John Adams to James Warren

My dear Sir   Philadelphia July 7. 1777

Yours of June 22d recd only to day. We have no Thoughts of leaving

Philadelphia. I believe Howe has no Thoughts of attempting it—but if he has We are determined to keep it. Our Army, with the assistance of the Militia, will be sufficient to defend it.

Why our Army fills up no faster I cant conceive. The Massachusetts Regiments at Ti are not one Third full. And We cannot learn from Peeks Kill, that Putnam ever had above six Thousand Men, in all, from Mass., Rhode Island, Connecticutt and New York. You must have been deceived in the Numbers inlisted.

There is a loud Complaint here, about Arms. Eighteen Thousand Arms have arrived at Portsmouth and We know not what becomes of them. Other Arms have arrived in Mass. but We know not where they are, and it is Said the Game Cock carried Six Thousand into Dartmouth. Where are they?

I wish you Joy of your Employment in making a Constitution. Hope you will make a good one. I hope to Sit quietly under it, altho I shall have no hand in forming it.[1] Do you intend to make every Man of 21 a Voter for the Council? I have nothing to Say, but I fear you will find a Fountain of Corruption, in making so many Voters.

The Bill for freeing the Negroes, I hope will sleep for a Time. We have Causes enough of Jealousy, Discord & Division, and this Bill will certainly add to the Number.[2]

I am weary enough of Complaints, concerning Navy Matters. I do all I can in public and private to Stimulate but all in vain. The Commissions were never sent untill 4 or 5 days ago by Mr Sherman. The Instructions are not Sent yet. Who is in Fault, I dont say.[3] It is enough for me to answer for my own Faults.

Is a certain elevated Citizen[4] to put his Hand upon the Pommell of one Chair, and leap into another, at 370 Miles Distance?

For my own Part I wish to see Gravity, Wisdom, Constancy and Fortitude in every Chair upon the Continent. My Hopes were placed upon Mr B.[5] but his Retirement, has damped if not extinguished them. My next Expectations were from the Philosopher[6]—But I doubt whether the popular Breath will blow that Way. My Wishes and Judgment are entirely for another.[7] But I know not the Chance.

I Should be more anxious about the Chair, if I were to be near it. But I pant and sigh for private Life and rural Felicity. Here all my Wishes terminate—and the sooner I reach it, with an eternal Renunciation of all concerns with the public, the better for me. An Idol in the Chair that I cannot and will not worship, will only facilitate my Progress to that Condition in human Life, where alone I can be happy or even comfortable.

RC (MHi). In Adams' hand, though not signed.

[1] Adams proved to be a poor prophet. Efforts to form and ratify a new Massachusetts constitution at this time failed, and subsequently Adams was one

of the principal architects of the new state constitution that was finally adopted in 1780.

[2] An antislavery bill had been read in the Massachusetts House on June 9, but its consideration was postponed until June 13. On that day the bill was read a second time, debated, and ordered to "lie upon the Table" while Congress was to be consulted "on the Subject thereof." Thereupon a committee was appointed, which included Warren, "to prepare a Letter to Congress accordingly," but when it submitted a report the following day the report was merely read and ordered to lie on the table. Journals of the Massachusetts House, DLC(ESR). Warren had provided the following information in his June 22 letter to Adams. "We have had a Bill before us for freeing the Negroes, which is ordered to lie, least if passed into an Act it should have a bad effect on the Union of the Colonies. A letter to Congress on that subject was proposed and reported, but I endeavoured to divert that, supposeing it would embarrass and perhaps be attended with worse consequences than passing the Act." *Warren-Adams Letters*, 1:335.

Not until the 1780s, when the state Supreme Judicial Court simply declared slavery unenforceable under the commonwealth's new constitution did slavery end in Massachusetts. Donald L. Robinson, *Slavery in the Structure of American Politics, 1765-1820* (New York: Harcourt Brace Jovanovich, Inc., 1971), pp. 24–29.

[3] Approximately two lines following this sentence were inked out in the MS. For the instructions to the naval commissioners, see Marine Committee to the Eastern Navy Board, July 10, 1777.

[4] John Hancock.

[5] James Bowdoin.

[6] John Winthrop.

[7] James Warren.

Samuel Adams to Samuel Hewes

My dear Sir,   Philadela. July 7 1777

I intreat you to ascribe my not having yet acknowledgd the Receipt of your favor[1] to the true Cause, a perpetual Hurry of affairs. I have not been unmindful of its Contents. Major Ward, as you have heard, is appointed Commissary General of Musters with the Rank and Pay of a Colonel.[2] I have long known him a Man of Sense and a zealous and steady Patriot, in Times less promising than the present; and the Part he took on the ever memorable 19th of April 75, together with the Experience he has gaind by constant Application ever since in the military Line, intitles him to particular Notice. I will bear in my memory the Hint given in the Close of your Letter. If at any Time I may have it in my power to render benefit to a Friend by puting him in the Way of serving our Country, it will afford me double Satisfaction. You will have heard before this reaches you that General Howe has at length drawn all his Forces from the State of Jersey to New York. It is the Business of General Washington to penetrate his future Design. This City has been threatened for some Months past; if he ever had such an Intention, it is probable he has now laid it aside, and that he will attempt to force a Junction with Burgoyne and subdue the Eastern States. [Bu]t why should I hazard a Conjecture of this kind who profess no Skill in military affairs? I hope my Country men are prepared to give the Enemy a proper Reception whenever they may be attackd!

I have written you a friendly letter though a short one—Short for want of time to write more. I have twenty things to say to you but at present must conclude with most respectful Compts to your lady, Family & Connections.[3] Very cordially your friend,   S A

FC (NN). Addressed: "Saml. Hewes Esqr. Boston."

[1] A letter to Adams of March 25, 1777, from Samuel Hewes (1728?–93), is in the Adams Papers, NN.

[2] Joseph Ward was appointed commissary general of musters on April 10, 1777. *JCC*, 7:252.

[3] The next day Adams wrote the following brief letter to John Pitts. "I do not recollect to have receivd a Letter from a later Date than the 21 of Decr last, although I have been since writing to you as often as I cod find Leisure. I do not know that I have by any thing I have written given you just Cause of offence. If you think otherwise pray let me know it, and I will make as full Atonement as I am able, for I do assure you I wish to continue a friendly epistolary Correspondence with you. Be so kind as to write me by the very next Post and assure yourself that I am unfeignedly and most cordially, Yr Friend, S.A." Adams Papers, NN.

Thomas Burke to Richard Caswell

July 7th. [1777]

This moment I received yours of 17th ulto. by post inclosing the Resolution of Assembly, and a letter to Captain Caswell.[1] Our troops are encamped within a mile of this City, and General Nash lodges in the same house with me. I have not seen Captain Caswell, nor did I know until I received yours, that he was in the Army. I shall immediately send to him, and hope to have the pleasure of his company tomorrow to dinner. Be assured, Sir, it will give me the greatest pleasure to attend to him, & render him every service in my power. I shall, Sir, observe your commands relative to him with a friendly solicitude. The Resolution of the assembly shall be laid before Congress, and you shall know the result. I thank you, Sir, for your attention to my private inconveniences manifested in the permission you give me to return to my family. I shall avail myself thereof as soon as I can assure myself that it can be done without injury to the public business. I shall write you again by the next post, or opportunity, and meantime have the honor to be with the greatest respect and esteem, Your Excellency's most obedt Servt,   Thos Burke

[*P.S.*] I take the liberty of inclosing you two letters,[2] which I beg the favor of you to forward.

Tr (Nc–Ar). A continuation of Burke to Caswell, July 5, 1777.
¹ Governor Caswell's June 17 letter to Burke is in *N.C. State Records*, 11:500–501. Enclosed in it was a resolve of the North Carolina Assembly asking that the state's artillery company be taken in Continental service, which request Congress granted on July 19. *JCC*, 8:544, 567.
² If these letters were written by Burke, they have not been found.

Committee on Publishing a Bible to Sundry Philadelphia Printers

[ca. July 7, 1777]¹

The Congress desire to have a bible printed under their care & by their encouragement, & request you to inform them

1. How many thousand pounds of Types would be sufficient to set, or Compose a whole bible of the common sort; and what they would cost?

2. In how long time such a bible could be set & Printed?

3. What it could be sold for, as well bound, as our common bibles?

4. Whether Paper fit for the purpose, & a sufficient quantity of it could be had in this country, so as to carry on the work with expedition?

5. How Long the Types when set would continue good, and fit for this purpose of casting off a new edition from time to time?

6. What would be expected from the Congress to carry on this work, that it might be well done & sold nearly as cheap as common school bibles?

An answer to these queries is requested against Friday at 6 o clock in the afternoon—to be given to the Committee of the Congress at the state house in this City.

RC (DNA: PCC, item 46). In an unidentified hand. Addressed: "To Mr. Henry Miller Printer." The same letter was also sent to Robert Aitken, Thomas Bradford, John Dunlap, and William Sellers. Another, nearly identical copy of the committee's letter, in the same unidentified hand but addressed "To Mr. Sellers Printer," is in ibid., fol. 175.
¹ Three Philadelphia Presbyterian clergymen—Francis Alison, John Ewing, and William Marshall—this day submitted a petition to Congress praying that "unless timely care be used to prevent it, we shall not have bibles for our Schools, & families, & for the publick Worship of God in our Churches." "We therefore," they continued, "think it our Duty to our Country & to the Churches of Christ to lay this design before this honourable house, humbly requesting that under your care, & by your encouragement, a Copy of the holy Bible may be printed, so as to be sold nearly as cheap as the Common Bibles, formerly imported from Britain & Ireland, were sold." See *JCC*, 8:536; and PCC, item 42, 1:35.
The petition was referred to a committee consisting of John Adams, Daniel Roberdeau, and Jonathan Bayard Smith, who promptly submitted the queries contained in this document to several Philadelphia printers to determine the

feasibility of the petitioners' request. For the printers' responses, one of which is dated July 10, 1777, see PCC, item 46, 1:155–73.

The committee eventually reported against the petitioners' recommendation because of the expense and difficulties involved in procuring the proper types and paper for such an edition of the Bible, and Congress instead adopted the committee's recommendation to "order the Committee of Commerce to import 20,000 Bibles from Holland, Scotland, or elsewhere." *JCC*, 8:733–35. As this decision was not reached until September 11, the day of the battle of Brandywine and only one week before Congress was forced to flee from Philadelphia, no action was taken to implement this order.

Another document related to the committee's work in the summer of 1777, bearing the heading "Regulations proposed for the Printing of a Bible for common Use under the Direction & by the Authority of Congress," is also located in PCC. See item 46, 1:163–64. It consists of 15 articles pertaining to the production of an American edition of the Bible to be carried out under the "Inspection" of Congress and essentially endorses the proposals embodied in the petitioners' memorial. Indeed it may have been drafted as the committee's original report, although the report finally read in Congress on September 11 rejected the practicality of executing such an American edition and recommended instead importing 20,000 Bibles. It has been printed in William H. Gaines, Jr., "The Continental Congress Considers the Publication of a Bible, 1777," *Studies in Bibliography* 3 (1950–51): 275–76, where it has been misidentified as the petition of the Presbyterian ministers.

It was not until 1782 that the first English language American edition of the Old and New Testaments finally appeared. For information on the circumstances that led to the publication of Robert Aitken's edition of the Bible, which appeared with an official congressional endorsement of September 12, 1782, see Margaret T. Hills, "The First American Bible, as Published by Robert Aitken," *Bible Society Record* 113 (January 1968): 2–5; and *JCC*, 19:91, 23:572–74.

Eliphalet Dyer to Joseph Trumbull

Dear Sir   Philadelphia July the 7th 1777

I wrote you a few days agoe by Coll. Stewart which hope you have Recievd. We have in the Course of a few days recieved some Very Unpolite letters from two or three Gentn of high rank & Esteem in the Army Viz Genlls Green, Sullivan & Knox. If they had prudently wrote the same Matter to any particular friend Member of Congress & he had divulged it to his brethren no offence would have been taken & it might have Answered every valuable purpose, but to write to Congress as a Body while they had a matter under consideration (I mean the affair of the Command of Monsr. de Coudre) to dictate to or Influence their Conduct is looked upon by many as the highest Insult and Indignity & which they cannot pass by without the severest Censure, or Otherwise must give up their own dignity & superiority to a few Gentn of the Army, & who will Assume for the future to dictate & Influence all their measures, or if Congress do not at once Yield they will resign their Commissions, break up the Army & leave their Country to the total desolation & Subjection of the Enemy. This is the Construction many put on their Conduct. There is a Number of us endeavour to palliate matters to soften the Asperity of others, tho all Condemn the manner of those Gentns letters & the timeing of them. Indeed they will have a bad effect on the Matter Under Consideration. I believe there would have been great caution & prudence in that affair. We readily felt for those Gentn & the Indignity it might at least be Construed to be to place Monsr. de Coudre in a rank superior to them. It would have been opposed, & believe never would have taken place, but these Gentn before the matter was so much as debated in Congress have thrown in their threats to them as a body that if they do this &c they will immediately leave the Army. It embarrasses every free Step both in debate and Conclusion, for if they now refuse which I dare say they before would have done to give de Coudre a Superior Command instead of being Imputed to their Justice & prudence, it will be entirely attributed to their fear occasioned by the threats of those Gentn and the Consequence will be, in every matter for the future. We must be either Dictated to or threatned by the Army or if we do not do this, or that, or just what they please, they will give up the cause or goe over to the Enemie, Sacrifice their Country, &c.

They will easily see the Impropriety, & I believe they were in no danger before. Am extremely sorry it has happened, how severe the conclusions will be I know not, Some threaten hard, others Indeavour to moderate; the times are truly Critical & I think those Gentn. would not wish to lessen the Authority, Esteem or dignity of Congress, as their own & Countrys honor, Safety & Liberty so much at present depends upon its being preserved & whatever may be the result I hope they will take it patiently consider themselves as Imprudently (at least) giving an Occasion. A few reflections will be for their honour and all may be set right. They must Consider their Country at Stake which I hope they preferr above everything else even their own particular honor, or life, I mean in the manner in which it may be effected in Compromising this matter which I hope would establish, instead of wounding it in the least. As they threaten to resign, it is a wonder if Congress dont tell them they may just when they please but I hope these Gentn love their Country too well. This is a most unhappy affair & our old Friend D—an has been in more Instances than one, Imprudent to the last degree, he has brot us into the most unhappy Dilemma in several of his Contracts & Stipulations with Gentn sending over Sworms of Commanders, Pensioners &c &c. I dare say no more at present upon the Subject & trust you will Improve what is said with caution and prudence, if these Gentn. knew how Congress were embarrassed & plagued with D——n's Imprudence & his ——— they would rather pity than Insult. I did not think it best to write to either of the Gentn. directly, but to you that you might deal out to them or either, any part you think proper that they may be prepared. Numbers in C——ss will Meliorate and Soften down as far as possible & hope those Gentn. will not be averse to some reasonable Concessions or at least if they are told as they threaten they may give up their Commissions as soon as they please. The Congress is ready to receive them Yet they will persist to serve their Country, & preferr Jerusalem above their Chief Joy. I write this with the Utmost Friendly disposition & design towards them. Hope all will be properly settled but the General Cause must not Suffer. Make the best of this letter for a few days, then burn it. Hope you will see the Gentn as soon as possible if in your Neighbourhood or some of them & let them know the friendly hints you have had from a Member of Congress &c. Can say no more. Am Sincerely Yours,   Elipht Dyer

[*P.S.*] Hope to hear from you as often as leisure will permit a few lines or more as the Subject offers or time will afford. I hear Root is returned home. Wish he might Succeed to some good place in the Army. E.D.[1]

Please to accept the kind Compliments of your cordial Friend & Bror.
                                                    W Williams

RC (CtHi).
[1] Remainder of letter in the hand of William Williams.

George Frost to Josiah Bartlett

Dear Sir   Philadelphia July 7th. 1777
    I Recd. Your favour of the 14th Ulto. Inclosg. a coppy of a letter from our Cols at Ticonda. and laid it before Congress who gave orders for a Supploy of Cloathing to be forwarded with all dispatch to Ticonderoga for the trups there;[1] I should have backed the aforesaid letter by laying Yours also before congress but could not without dishonour to my selfe not to say with som Reflection on My Worthy frind Col. Bartlet (as the manner of his addres was to Col. Whipple and in his absence to Geo. Frost thereby treeting me as a spare topmast). Sr. I trust it was not out of any disregard.
    You say the State is about to make application to Congress for Money to redeam our paper bills. I wish I could give you any incoragement of Succes; the Treasure here is so low that it takes all the money for the army. I wrote you in my last[2] Col. Whipple Recd. an Order on the loan office for 100,000 Dollars. If you are in Cash at Sd. office perhaps you may git a further Order on it. I am sorry for the distress you seem to be in on Account of our moneys being counterfited. I hope the State wont be wanting in Duty to themselves in not haveing a proper Spirit to Inflict a proper punishment on those (without Distinction) who are the authers of so heanious a crime of countifiting our Money. I shall give you som parragraphs of a letter from a gentleman of distin-

tion in Spain (you'l see it was not Intended it should be made public)
dated March 18th 1777.[3] "As for an Immediate declaration in your
favour they say this is not the moment & for Reasons which if I might
venture to Commit them on this paper I think you woud deem satisfactory. The same Reason render an explicet acknoligement of Your
Independency & a treaty of Alliance With you inadmissible at present
but am desired to assure you of their taking a sincere & Zealous part in
the Establishment of Your liberties which they will promote in every
way consistent with their own Situation. I cannot help thinking that the
postponing a treaty is happy for us since our present situation woud
raise demands and perhaps enforce Concessions of which we might
sorely Repent hereafter. I am sensible that in Consequence we shall be
Obliged to make greater exertions & to serch deeper for resources
within our selves but this must in the end be highly benifical to a Young
People. It was in this manner the Roman Republic was so deeply rooted
and then the liberty which are hardly earned will be highly prized &
long preserved. I mentioned in my last that the Germans intended to be
sent the latter end of this month thro Holland were to consist of Seven
thousand recruits but from the Best Accounts I can git they will neither
be so forward nor so numerous as was Intended. To retard them the
more I have proposed to the Commissioners at Paris to Remostrate with
the States General against granting them a passage which is to ex-
pediate their embarkation & I have written to Holland to have the Account of the Captivity of their Countrymen and the refusel to Exchange
them, settle a Cartel distributed among the troops in German before
they Embark. If they are not very beasts indeed this will rouse a spirit
of Indignation against their Buyers & Sellers." You'l please to give my
Best Respects to the Honoble. Councel and Remain Sr., Your most obt.,
Humble Sevt.   Geo. Frost

RC (PHi).
  [1] For further information on supplies for the northern department, see Board
of War to George Washington, July 8, 1777; and *JCC*, 8:535. On blankets for
the troops at Ticonderoga, see John Hancock to the New York Council of Safety,
July 8, 1777.
  [2] Not found.
  [3] Frost copied extracts from Arthur Lee's March 18 letter to the Committee
of Secret Correspondence in this and in his July 12 letter to Bartlett. Quotation
marks have been supplied editorially.

James Lovell to William Whipple

Dear Sir,   7th July 1777
    As you seemed particularly to wish when you left Philadelphia to be
made acquainted with the proceedings in the Commercial and Foreign

Committees, I would inform you that last Saturday Mr Geary, Mr. W. Smith & Mr Heywood were joined to Messrs. Morris and Livingston, to the no small mortification of H———n.[1] Geary pleaded hard to be excused but we would not allow of it till a proper opportunity. This day we have the pleasure of knowing we shall soon have that opportunity to the double mortification of said H———; for we this day find that Col R H Lee has not only rec'd the most honorable testimonies of approbation for his past conduct but was elected anew on the 24th ulto. Old H——— has whispered it all along on the road that Col Lee has ordered his overseer to demand produce or bullion for rent, but this was proved to be false by the fullest declaration of the overseer and other evidence.[2] I feel exceedingly glad on this event, and should be completely secure against the prevalence of a certain set, if a certain late resolute member of the Marine Committee was about to return speedily from Portsmouth,[3] one, who though quite as honest as his neighbors, yet did not confess ten times a day "I dont know what the question is Mr President" like good honest I, for be sure I mean myself.

We of the other Committee have sent an armed sloop to France.[4] The Commissioners [i.e. Commissions of] Wm. Lee and Izzard do not promise ratification of whatever they may transact, but their proceedings on commercial treaties at Vienna, Berlin and Tuscany are to receive our approbation and only to continue 12 years, though a treaty of friendship may be made outright for a longer period.[5]

I will aim to send you the issue of a plaguy altercation upon bringing on afresh the affair of the New Hampshire Grants. I was unfortunately confined to my bed and G divided against S.A. on the two last resolves as did Elmore against Serjeant, the others of the two States being absent. You must know that Jimmy D. has got E———re fast.[6] I do not however think that New York has much to boast of. It is still a mootpoint whether the people of the Grants belong to Massachusetts, New Hampshire or New York.

I forgot to mention that we have a good opportunity to send duplicates of all our papers by Mr McCreary who is going to settle at Nantz for some time.

Du Coudray's treaty is not yet determined upon; but I think there will be few advocates for confirming it. The 4 Engineers who were the only persons absolutely sent for, are arrived; and though modest men, upon a very modest treaty, yet possitively refuse to be under the command of Du C———y who has duped Deane to make him Commander in Chief of all the artillery and engineering through the States. But this is only a part of our present distraction. For 1st Sullivan sends to know whether the report is true that Congress has ratified De C———y's claim, because if it is, he desires leave to resign. Two days after Green and Knox proceed in the same style. This is judged to be a military attempt to influence our free deliberations. For it is certain, they know we had not settled the matter or General Washington would have rec'd the Resolves. If they chose to take it for a thing done why did they not ask leave to retire without any *ifs*. There is as much pulling and hauling, about rank and pay, as if we had been accustomed to a military establishment here 150 years.

That same Mr Nicholas Davis who got the money of our Commissioners and then drew a Bill of Exchange upon them in France, and afterwards imposed upon Bingham, is now here. He turned an evidence against the Seine to condemn her; and yet has had the impudence to come hither. He is a meagre, smooth tongued, sly chap and I believe will go unpunished for he has nothing but dress; and to make him rot in jail will not regain the money.

I have much to scrawl in the morning both public and private, and it is now past one o'clock as a noisy chap tells me from the street. But I will not take his hint till I have presented my affectionate compliments to your Lady, your brothers and sisters, and any others who love you and do not hate me; further you need not go, for you know I never pretended to the sublime pitch of loving my enemies.

Tell thy African I miss him and his many willing services. I reckon his full joy at getting away from Philadelphia may have intoxicated his former philosophic resolutions, so far as to make him risk becoming the author of a *Slave* in the early hours of his return to Portsmouth.

Messrs Dyer, Williams and Law have been here 10 days, so that father Sherman is by this time, like your Honor, vigorously serving his country in connection with his nearest dearest friend. Good night, say morning,   J.L.

Tr (DLC).

[1] Benjamin Harrison was not named to the Committee of Commerce when it was reconstituted as the successor of the Secret Committee on July 5, 1777. *JCC*, 8:533–34.

[2] For a discussion of the complaints against Richard Henry Lee, see Richard Henry Lee to Patrick Henry, May 26, 1777.

[3] Lovell is simply alluding to his correspondent William Whipple.

[4] The Committee for Foreign Affairs dispatched the sloop *Independence*. See Committee for Foreign Affairs to Arthur Lee, August 8, 1777.

[5] See Committee for Foreign Affairs to Commissioners at Paris, July 2, 1777.

[6] The references are to Elbridge Gerry and Samuel Adams, James Duane and Jonathan Elmer.

John Adams to Abigail Adams

Philadelphia July 8. 1777 Tuesday
Yours of June 23d have received. I believe there is no Danger of an Invasion your Way, but the Designs of the Enemy are uncertain and

their Motions a little misterious. Before this Letter is sealed, which will not be till Sunday next, I hope I shall be able to inform you better.

I rejoice at your fine Season, and at my Brother Cranches Attention to Husbandry. Am very glad he bought the Farm, and that he likes it so well.

I pant for domestic Life, and rural Felicity like his.

I am better than I have been. But I dread the Heats, which are coming on.

This Day compleats Six Months since I left you. I am wasted and exhausted in Mind and Body, with incessant Application to Business, but if I can possibly endure it, will hold out the Year. It is nonsense to dance backwards and forwards. After this Year I shall take my Leave.

Our Affairs are in a fine prosperous Train, and if they continue so, I can leave this Station with Honour.

Next Month compleats Three Years, that I have been devoted to the Servitude of Liberty. A slavery it has been to me, whatever the World may think of it.

To a Man, whose Attachments to his Family, are as strong as mine, Absence alone from such a Wife and such Children, would be a great sacrifice. But in Addition to this Seperation, what have I not done? What have I not suffered? What have I not hazarded? These are Questions that I may ask you, but I will ask such Questions of none else. Let the Cymballs of Popularity tinckle still. Let the Butterflies of Fame glitter with their Wings. I shall envy neither their Musick nor their Colours.

The Loss of Property affects me little. All other hard Things I despize, but the Loss of your Company and that of my dear Babes for so long a Time, I consider as a Loss of so much solid Happiness.

The tender social Feelings of my Heart, which have distressed me beyond all Utterance, in my most busy, active scænes, as well as in the numerous Hours of melancholly solitude, are known only to God and my own soul.

How often have I seen my dearest Friend a Widow and her Charming Prattlers Orphans, exposed to all the Insolence of unfeeling impious Tyrants! Yet, I can appeal to my final Judge, the horrid Vision has never for one Moment shaken the Resolution of my Heart.

RC (MHi). Adams, *Family Correspondence* (Butterfield), 2:276–77.

Board of War to George Washington

Sir   War Office July 8th 1777

The Generals & Officers in the Northern Department complain

heavily of a great Want of Arms & Cloathing for the Troops under their Command. The Field Officers of the New Hampshire Regiments have represented the Matter in the strongest Terms, & yet the greatest Quantities of both Arms & Clothes have arrived in their State. Mr Langdon, the Agent for the States at Portsmouth, gives himself credit for the Delivery of 2,100 Stands of Arms to the New Hampshire Forces, 4,000 Stands to those of Massachusetts & 3,000 to the Troops of Connecticut. The Return of the N. Hampshire Troops at Tyconderoga amounts to 1063 & I am satisfied they cannot have in their 4 Regiments more Men than they have received Arms. These Matters are inexplicable, but all Accounts agree that whatever might have been their Supplies they are now in Want. The Board have directed a thousand Suits of Clothes to be sent as soon as the Clothier General can possibly get them ready, & have directed me to request your Excellency will take Measures for sending forward a Supply of as many Arms as you think can be spared; but how the Number wanted will be ascertained is not known here, for altho' a general Complaint has been made by the Officers they have not been attentive enough to reduce to any kind of Certainty, what Arms, Clothes or Necessaries will answer their Exigencies. The Board never receive Returns but of the Numbers of the Troops. In the British Returns Clothes, Arms & Necessaries (for which they have 3 Columns *"Good," "bad," "wanting"*) are always included. Many of our Soldiers have been detected in selling their Necessaries; & Practices of this Sort it is apprehended are but too common amongst them. In the British Service the Serjeants & Corporals are made responsible for the Mens Necessaries of which they return a weekly Account & if any wanting & not lost in actual Service the Men are punished. It is submitted to your Excellency whether Regulations of this kind would not be proper to be introduced into our Army. But unfortunately our Serjeants & Corporals are as raw & want as much Regulation as the privates, whereas in the Enemy's Army much Dependance is placed on their Non Comd. Officers who are in general more acquainted with & attentive to Service than their Superiors.

I have the Honour of your Excellency's Letter of the 7th inst[1] & am surprized at the Delay of mine of the 19th. The Commissary at Springfield has made a Return deficient in every Article according to the Expectations of the Board; but perhaps the Residue was on the Road from Boston when Mr Cheevers made his Return. There certainly ought to be at least nine thousand Stands of Arms at Springfield altho' Mr Cheevers returns only 3320. The Spears are in Hand & I shall urge their speedy Completion. The Cannisters have been sent on some time & I am surprized General Knox has not received them. I endeavoured to have them filled with Cartridges but had not Interest *enough* with the Officer employed in the Business to have it done.

The enclosed Letter from Monsr. De Coudray I was directed by the Board, to transmitt to your Excellency.[2]

I have the Honour to be, with the greatest Respect, your very obedt hble Servt,   Richard Peters Secy

P.S. Monsr. De Coudray has sent on his Letter by the Officer mentioned in it & only desires that it may be mentioned to your Excellency that the Board had perused the Letter.[3]

RC (DLC).

[1] For Washington's July 7 letter, in which he requested the dispatch of spears and cartridge cannisters, as well as his July 12 reply to this letter, see Washington, *Writings* (Fitzpatrick), 8:376, 387–89.

[2] Du Coudray's July 4 letter in which he volunteered observations concerning the cannon at Springfield and recommended Captain De Goy for an artillery command is in the Washington Papers, DLC. For Washington's July 13 reply, see Washington, *Writings* (Fitzpatrick), 8:396–99.

[3] On July 10 Peters sent Washington another letter in which he discussed replacing arms lost by soldiers. "Arms & Necessaries lost in actual Service should beyond a Doubt be replaced," he explained, "but if any Neglect has happened on the Part of the Officers & the Soldiers have sold or wantonly lost their Arms or Clothes & the Officer has taken no Pains to recover them or enquire into the Causes of their Loss it ought to fall upon the Captains of the Companies or other officers in Fault & be deducted out of their Pay." Washington Papers, DLC. For Washington's July 16 response, see Washington, *Writings* (Fitzpatrick), 8:416–17.

James Duane to Robert R. Livingston

July 8t 1777

This Journal (for it is too much for a Letter) I have kept by me several days waiting the departure of Capt Chadd, who has been strangely delayed. General Howe's motions are narrowly watched by General Washington. The first lies with his main army along the north side of Staten Island, & the new Levies sketchd along from the Blazing Star on the South side. General Washington occupies his first Encampment at Morris Town; one Division under Sullivan having marched towards Peeks Kill. If Howe proceeds up the North River he will instantly be followd by the American Army who are in fine order & high Spirits.

I have mentiond in what preceeds the Propriety of instantly communicating the Acts of Congress respecting our Revolters—perhaps the situation of our Affairs to the Northward may make it prudent to delay it for a while. Remember however that Mr Sherman has taken with him to New England a Copy of the Resolutions and no doubt will make them publick.

Adieu and believe me most sincerely, Your Friend,

Jas. Duane

[*P.S.*] I forgot to mention that General Gates remains in this City. He is pleasd to charge me as the author of his Disgrace and to pay me Compliments which I do not deserve. We have had an Exploration on this subject *over a Bottle!* He ought to be pleasd with my Candour for I did not conceal from him the least Tittle of what I had said or thought of his last Claim to the Command of the Northern Department. He is clearly of opinion that Ticonderoga and indeed our whole State will be lost by his Removal!

I hope you will favour me with some account of your late polticial maneuvres. We are as much strangers to the affairs of our own State as if we liv'd in Siberia!

RC (NHi). A continuation of Duane to Livingston, July 1–2, 1777.

Eliphalet Dyer to Joseph Trumbull

Sir   Philadelphia July 8th 1777, 10 oClock
   I recieved yours of the 7th this moment by express. I wrote you by Brown yesterday but he has not yet left Town waiting for Mr. Hancocks dispatches. Am very sorry you have not recievd my first which I sent by a Young Southern Officer who promised particular care in delivering it.[1] I remember I therein on the whole advised you to Accept, with the Advice of Mr Law & Coll Williams, but I then had no Idea of the plague & Trouble you had to goe through but hope it will not be of long duration. The ground of my advice was principally the publick good. Am Sensible many Inconveniences & much Confusion will arise on this New Regulation but hope it may not be of long duration & it must be Supposed if a person of your experience should leave the Army it most probably would be much Worse. Youll find by Mr Stewart that the Wages of the Dept. & sub Commissys are somewhat raised, your Clerk from 40 to 50 dolls. per month, tho am persuaded it is insufficient Considering his residence must be in Philadelphia but dare say it will soon be raised as believe the other will if on Tryal it is found Insufficient.[2] It is a general Observation in Congress that there is room to rise but no way to fall. I hope Mr Stewards Arrival may give you some relief. Coll Champion & Dunham must not resign. They must Consider the large Profits they have made in years past & goe on in expectation that there wages will be raised when it appears reasonable. You have the power to make an Additional allowance for expences as you find occasion not exceeding one dollr & one third per diem. They will consider there Wages of 4 dolls per day goe on every day & there are many days when they are not in Actual service & yet their 4 dolls per day goes on & that their expences are not so high in New England as this way & that all Cost of & expence of drovers &

persons employed to collect & drive the Cattle &c is allowd beside. These New regulations were all come into before my Arrival. I have since procured some Addition to the Wages but it will take some time before the Subject can be taken up again without being Troublesome & a thousand Other matters Crouding. It is impossible for me to Judge for you in this matter as I cannot be fully acquainted with the Troubles & difficulties you have to encountre. Your letter to Congress seems to carry with it an acceptance but suppose if you should find on Tryal that the embarrassments are too great to Struggle with, you may on giving seasonable Notice no doubt resign. It has been several times mentioned in Congress that there is a large quantity of flower up at Lancaster & that was purchased by Walton & in danger of spoiling. I just mention it that you may take that care which belongs to you.

I am much concerned for my son Thos, fear he will not be Able to join the Army & Indeed whether he will survive this sickness. He is very Careless Inattentive to his health and pays but little regard to the Advice of his Physitions. If you should hear further from him should be glad you would Inform me.

Am with sincere regards,   E Dyer

[*P.S.*] The Congress will Insist on some retractions from those Genll officers Who have wrote the letters I mentioned in my last. I hope they may be Induced to make them in some proper manner & soon; as they esteem their honour so much concerned as I fear, the consequences will be serious if not done.

RC (CtHi).
[1] See Dyer to Joseph Trumbull, June 1777.
[2] The increase in the clerk's salary was not formally approved until August 7. *JCC,* 8:621.

Elbridge Gerry to Joseph Trumbull

Dear Sir   Philadelphia 8th July 1777

I recd your Favour of yesterday, & am glad to hear that Mr Stewart & Mr Hoop are at the Camp.[1] Mr Buchannan is altogether under your Direction.[2] True it is, the Commissary General of purchases can only appoint a Clerk, but it is also true, that he is exempted from Blame on account of the Misconduct of Officers not of his appointment. If the Salary is not Sufficient for your Clerk, who certainly ought to be a reputable person, Congress will undoubtedly make the necessary Addition. Your Memorandam shall be revived as soon as I can attend the Treasury Board, which will probably be to Morrow. With respect to the Salt which I have in the Massachusetts, if a Vessel can be obtained, it will be sent to the Southward, but I wanted to know whether it can be well spared to New York, if it cannot be sent to N Carolina. If you think it necessary to take it for the Continent, I Will Charge You therewith, & shall be glad to have the Vessel discharged without Delay. The risk must belong to the United States as the Vessel is made the Store Room for the Salt. The Salt at Hartford is not to be delivered, unless You can consent thereto Without Injury to the Service; Therefore I Suppose it will not be desired, or delivered, as your opinion appears to be against it.

Nothing new occurs, but from the Movements of the Enemy, they intend to proceed up the North River, to the Delaware, or Some part of N England.[3]

I remain Sir yours with Esteem,   E Gerry

[*P.S.*] Pray mention in your next the Date of your last Letters & by whom sent.

RC (CtHi).

[1] Charles Stewart was commissary general of issues and Robert Hoops was deputy commissary general of issues. *JCC*, 8:477, 517.

[2] William Buchanan of Maryland was elected deputy commissary general of purchases on June 18; on August 5 he was appointed Joseph Trumbull's successor as commissary general of purchases. *JCC*, 8:477, 607.

[3] According to the brief description of a letter appearing in an autograph catalog, Gerry had written the day before to an unidentified recipient concerning "the danger threatening Ticonderoga, and the importance of additional forces there to repel the enemy." *C. F. Libbie Co., Catalog*, January 6–10, 1891, item 1277, p. 133.

John Hancock to the New York Council of Safety

Gentlemen,   Philada. July 8th. 1777.

The distressed Situation of the Troops at Ticonderoga for Want of Blankets, and the Sickness consequent thereupon, have induced the Congress to pass the enclosed Resolve, directing me to request you will exert yourselves to collect and forward to that Post fifteen Hundred Blankets with all possible Expedition.[1]

The Congress engage to replace the same Number of Blankets out of the first that shall be imported into any Part of the United States on Account of the Continent.

I have the Honour to be, Gentlemen, your most obed. Servt.

John Hancock Presidt

RC (PHC). In the hand of Jacob Rush and signed by Hancock.
[1] See *JCC*, 8:537.

John Hancock to Joseph Trumbull

Sir,   Philada. July 8th. 1777.[1]
I inclose to you sundry Commissions for Officers in your Department, which I must request you will please to deliver to them.

The Congress being informed, that the Price of Cattle in this State is very exorbitant, think it adviseable that as few should be purchased therein as may be; and have come to the enclosed Resolve, directing you to give your Agents Instructions to govern themselves accordingly.[2]

Your Favour of the 7th I duely received and laid before Congress.[3]

I am, with Respect, Sir, your most obedt Servt.
                                                    John Hancock Presidt.

RC (Ct).
[1] Trumbull also received yet another letter written by a delegate this date. The following brief note from James Lovell is in the Joseph Trumbull Papers, CtHi. "I have yours of the 5th. The order is certainly forwarded. Mr. Bates disappointed both the president and Coll. Dyer by his sudden departure. You will see by the Dates of my scrawls, that I *do* write. Tho' as I depend on others to forward, I suppose you find some of them mouldy. I will be longer by the post."
[2] This resolve had been passed on June 27. *JCC*, 8:504–5.
[3] See Hancock to Joseph Trumbull, July 5, 1777, note 2.

John Hancock to George Washington

Sir,   Philada. July 8th. 1777.
I have the Honour to transmit at this Time Copies of three Letters from Generals Sullivan, Green, and Knox, to Congress, the Receipt of which, as the Contents were highly derogatory to the Honour and Justice of Congress, could not fail to be extremely displeasing. They have therefore come to the enclosed Resolve on the Subject,[1] to which, as it clearly expresses their Sense of the Impropriety of the Conduct of those Officers, I beg Leave to refer your Attention, and to request you will make them acquainted therewith.

Your Favour of the 7th Instant I this Morning received, and in a few Minutes shall lay it before Congress.[2]

I have the Honour to be, with the greatest Respect, Sir, Your most obed. & very hble Servt.   John Hancock Presidt

P.S. 5 O'Clock P.M. Since writing the foregoing, the enclosed Resolutions of this Day have been passed,[3] which I transmit for your Information.

RC (DLC). In the hand of Jacob Rush and signed by Hancock.
[1] For a discussion of this resolution, which reprobated the threats of Generals Greene, Knox, and Sullivan to resign in protest against Philippe Du Coudray's

contract and ordered their offending letters to be sent to Washington, see John Adams to Nathanael Greene, July 7, 1777.

[2] This letter is in PCC, item 152, 4:327-28, and Washington, *Writings* (Fitzpatrick), 8:366-67.

[3] These resolves pertained to Delaware River defenses, the appointment of certain French officers, and Gen. Horatio Gates. *JCC*, 8:538–40. For the resolve pertaining to the use of Virginia and North Carolina troops on the defensive works at Billingsport, which was initiated at the request of the Pennsylvania delegates on instruction from the Pennsylvania Council, see also *Pa. Council Minutes*, 11:236, 242.

New York Delegates to the New York Council of Safety

Honourable Gentlemen,   Philadelphia, 8th July, 1777.

Since our last letter of the 4th instant,[1] the President, at our request, has written to Commissary Trumbull, on the subject of the exchange of the salt appropriated to our State, and we hope this formality will give weight to our own solicitations.

We transmit you the secret committee's order in our favour, on Mr. Mumford, their agent for the salt at Plymouth, and our transfer to you. A copy of our letter to Commissary Trumbull,[2] we also enclose, from which last you will be pleased to observe, that for the sake of despatch, we have requested him to correspond on the subject immediately with yourselves.

Salt continues to be very scarce here and to the southward, the coast being closely watched by the enemy's ships. Mr. Lewis writes from Baltimore the 23rd of June, that two small vessels had arrived there with that article from Virginia, purchased by a private trader, who asked for it no less than £5 a bushel. As we cannot at present expect to get it delivered at this place for a less price, we must request your directions, whether we shall proceed to purchase, and what quantity?

With these despatches we forward a calendar, returned to us by the jailer, of the prisoners sent from our State to Philadelphia, and the time and manner of their discharge.[3] Sutton, whose name you will not observe, never was committed to prison, but left at large, and finally released on his parol at General Morris's intercession, who, it seems, entertained an opinion of him much too favourable.

Finding that our constitution was published on very mean paper, without any marginal notes of the contents, we thought it would not be disagreeable to our State to have an impression struck off here, and we took the same opportunity to have printed the resolutions of Congress respecting the independent government attempted to be established within our jurisdiction; we now forward them to be disposed of as you shall direct.[4]

If our State is likely to be pressed both from the north and the south, which, however rash and desperate, is an enterprise which the enemy once seriously contemplated, and now seems at least as practicable as the conquest of Pennsylvania, you will have but little time to apply to domestic concerns, however urgent; and this may possibly induce you to wish that the publication of the decision of Congress respecting our revolted subjects, may for some time be deferred. From these considerations, we shall refrain from communicating a single copy; but it must be remembered that Mr. Roger Sherman, who is gone to the eastward, was furnished with one, and there is too much room to apprehend that he may forward it to his friends in New-Connecticut.

We have taken the liberty to retain your letter to Congress, of the 17th of June, and the several enclosures. Already have we employed so much of their time on the affairs of our State, that good policy strongly urges us to give them some respite; and as the subject matter of those despatches though of some moment to our State, requires no immediate decision, we flatter ourselves that you will not be displeased with our reserve. The reasons you assign to show that the defence of Hudson's river ought to be a Continental charge, appears to us to be very cogent; and they must always have great weight; and we therefore make no scruple in recommending that all the expenses be charged to the account of the Continent, comprehending even such as may accrue subsequent to the late resolutions of Congress pointing out a discrimination; for, had the transaction been fully explained, we cannot think those resolutions would have passed.[5]

We have the honour to be, with great respect, Honl. gentlemen, Your most obedient humble servants,   Phil. Livingston,

                                                              Jas. Duane,

                                                              Wm. Duer.

Reprinted from *Journals of N.Y. Prov. Cong.*, 1:999–1000.
[1] Not found.
[2] See New York Delegates to Joseph Trumbull, July 2, 1777.
[3] This item is printed in *Journals of N.Y. Prov. Cong.*, 1:1000, under the heading "A List of the York Tories lately confined in the State Prison, Philadephia."
[4] Full bibliographical information about these two publications is given in Evans, *Am. Bibliography,* nos. 15474, 15673.
[5] The council of safety's June 17 request for congressional funding for the defense of the Hudson is discussed more fully in New York Delegates to the New York Council of Safety, May 31, 1777, note 3.

North Carolina Delegates to Richard Caswell

Sir   Philadelphia July 8th 1777
We have obtained an order of Congress to the Treasurer, who has

been at Baltimore since the time the Congress sat there, directing him to send to your State three hundred thousand dollars.[1]

This sum is as much as can now be spared from the Treasury, and we hope will answer the present exigencies.

We will transmit you a State of the Treasury debit against our State in a few days after this. At present we think it not expedient to detain the messenger, especially since your occasions for money are so pressing.

We know not the amount of the bills drawn by Mr Ash, and wish your Excellency would direct him to transmit us an account thereof.

We have the honor to be, Your Excellency's obedient Servants,

Thos Burke

John Penn

Tr (Nc–Ar).
[1] See *JCC,* 8:538.

William Duer to Robert R. Livingston

My dear Friend,   Philadelphia July 9th. 1777

That I may not give you Reason to think that your Pardon is bestowed on an Ingrate, I steal a Few Moments from urgent Business to acknowledge the Receipt of yours of the   Inst.

I have the Pleasure to inform you that Congress have adopted Sundry Resolutions respecting the Insurgents in the Counties of Gloucester, Cumberland, and Charlotte, which, if our New Legislature acts with Spirit, and Wisdom, will I think be attended with happy Effects. We transmit them by this Opportunity to the Council of Safety.

I beleive no Matter has ever been more solemnly argued in Congress than this. The House were in Committee for three Days, and very Warm Opposition was given by some of our Eastern Freinds against the Resolution for dismissing the Petition of Jonas Fay &ca and that censuring Dr. Youngs Incendiary Production. Mr. Sherman was quite thrown off his Bias, and betrayd a Warmth not usually learnt within the Walls of Yale Colledge. I think it is of the utmost Consequence that these Resolu[tio]ns should be generally throughout the revolted Counties, and that means should be speedily devised by the Legislature of doing Right to such as have really Cause of Complaint from the Iniquities of the old Government. Their Number I think is not many.[1]

I am sorry to inform you that Colo. R. H. Lee is returning to Congress Crownd with Laurels.[2] His Smooth Discourse, and Art of Cabal have blunted the Edge of his Countrymens Resentment, and they have lauded him Encomiums on his Patriotism and Attention to Business, which he modestly says, he is Anxious of deserving. For particulars I refer you to the Pensilvania Papers. I suppose he will return here more rivitted than ever to his Eastern Friends; I assure you they lost in him no Contemptable Ally.

You tell that you hope I have given over Thoughts of returning for some Time. I assure you that I can not with Justice to myself, or indeed with others in our State with whom I have Transactions in Business, stay here long. Since my Letter to you I have made a formal Application to the Council of Safety for Leave of Absence, which I hope will be granted.[3] I entreat your Influence to prevent any Procrastination in this Matter.

At present there are no very great Matters in which our State is particularly interested before Congress; and indeed if they were, Mr. Morris[4] can supply my Place with great Advantage to the Reputation of the State, as well as his own. His Coolness of Temper, and happy Vein of Irony are Qualifications, which would render him a very powerful Antagonist to Mr. R. H. Lee.

I hope you will give him a Hint not to neglect this great *Orator*. You may depend upon it, he will advance his own Reputation, and be of Advantage to the Public in making the *Person* appear in that Contemptable Point of View which he really deserves.

In Case I have not Time to write to Mr. Jay, I beg you to remember me to him and to Mr Morris. I am very affectionately, Yours,

W. Duer.

RC (NHi). Addressed: "To R. Rt. Livingston, Esq., Chancellor of the State of New York, Kingston."

[1] See also James Duane to Robert R. Livingston, July 1; and New York Delegates to the New York Council of Safety, July 2, 1777.

[2] See Richard Henry Lee to Patrick Henry, May 26, 1777, note 1.

[3] See Duer to the New York Council of Safety, June 19, 1777.

[4] Gouverneur Morris, who had been elected a delegate in May 1777 but did not attend until January 1778.

Elbridge Gerry to Joseph Trumbull

Dear Sir   Philadelphia July 9th 1777

Your Petition of November last has been this Day revived at the Board of Treasury,[1] & It appeared to be the Desire of the Board that You Should be present & heard, previous to their considering the prayer & reporting thereon. This will probably occasion no great Delay, & may be the Means of producing a Decision that will be agreable on all Sides.

I remain sir yours with Esteem,   E Gerry

RC (CtHi).

[1] See Gerry to Trumbull, October 22, 1776, note 4, and April 19, 1777, note 1.

James Lovell to Benjamin Franklin

Sir   July 9th. 1777

Since the former date of this sheet[1] Congress has confirmed the treaty made by you on the 13th of Febry. but the Engineers are altogether discontented, upon a comparitive view of their rank. I hope we shall some time or other see an End of such pretensions. I almost dread to hear of the arrival of a foreign vessel on this particular foundation.

With Truth, Sir, Your most obedt. huml Servt,   James Lovell

RC (PPAmP).

[1] This letter was appended to one of the multiple copies of Lovell's July 4 letter to Franklin.

New York Delegates to the New York Council of Safety

Honourable Gentlemen,   Philadelphia, 9th July, 1777.

Since we addressed you yesterday, the President has received a letter from Commissary Trumbull, declining to exchange the salt, as he says the public have been at the expense of removing what he has, nearer to our State from the Massachusetts Bay. This will reduce you to the necessity of sending for the salt which has been granted to us by Congress, to Plymouth, in the Massachusetts Bay, after obtaining an order from Mr. Mumford of Groton, in Connecticut.[1]

We conceive no time is to be lost; salt may rise, it may become scarce, and the country through which it passes, averse to its transportation.

We have the honour to be, With great respect, honourl. gentlemen, Your most obdt. humb. servts.   Phil Livingston,

Jas. Duane,

Wm. Duer.

Reprinted from *Journals of N.Y. Prov. Cong.*, 1:1001.
[1] See John Hancock to Joseph Trumbull, July 5, 1777, note 2.

John Adams to Abigail Adams

Philadelphia July 10. 1777. Thursday

My Mind is again Anxious, and my Heart in Pain for my dearest Friend. . . .[1]

Three Times have I felt the most distressing Sympathy with my

Partner, without being able to afford her any Kind of Solace, or Assistance.

When the Family was sick of the Dissentery, and so many of our Friends died of it.

When you all had the small Pox.

And now I think I feel as anxious as ever. Oh that I could be near, to say a few kind Words, or shew a few Kind Looks, or do a few kind Actions. Oh that I could take from my dearest, a share of her Distress, or relieve her of the whole.

Before this shall reach you I hope you will be happy in the Embraces of a Daughter, as fair, and good, and wise, and virtuous as the Mother, or if it is a son I hope it will still resemble the Mother in Person, Mind and Heart.

RC (MHi). Adams, *Family Correspondence* (Butterfield), 2:278.
[1] Suspension points in MS.

James Duane to the New York Council of Safety

Philad. 10th July 1777

Since our Letter of Yesterday the Connecticut Courant of the 30th of June last has made it's appearance in this City. It contains a new and extraordinary Declaration from a part of our State which is attempted to be wrested out of our Jurisdiction and which is dubbed *The State of Vermont:* a name hatched for it in Philadelphia. Indeed it is evident that the plan has been laid here under the direction of Doctor Young (and too probably of some others of more Consequence) and that his Letters have pushed the People to this last Extremity. The more effectually to impose upon the publick they have subjoind a List of their Complaints against the late Government of New York, and have not even spared the late Convention. Such a Train of Falsehoods and misrepresentations does but little Credit to this meek Convention which will very probably proceed to elect Delegates for Congress, and once more press for their admission. Be this as it may confident we are that they will meet with the utmost discouragement.[1]

One of the Printers who has been requested to publish this production called upon us with it, and proposd, himself, that it shoud be preceeded or followed by the Resolutions of Congress of the 30t of June. It is probable we shall consent to it to prevent any bad Impression which it might otherwise occasion; and for the same Reason we have thoughts of making some Observations on the ostensible Causes which are assignd in Support of the Project of a seperate Government; that the matter may appear in it's true Light.[2]

We have the Honour to be, with great Respect, your most Obedient huml Servants,   Jas. Duane

P.S. Mr. Livingston and Mr. Duer are attending Congress, and Mr. Child going off, which prevents their subscribing this letter.

RC (MeHi). Journals of N.Y. Prov. Cong., 1:1000. RC damaged; dateline and postscript supplied from Tr.

[1] This "new and extraordinary Declaration," approved on June 4 by the "General Convention" of the "State of Vermont," is in E. P. Walton, ed., Records of the Governor and Council of Vermont, 7 vols. (Montpelier, Vt.: J. & J.M. Poland, 1873–80), 1:54–57.

[2] Congress' June 30 resolves on Vermont appeared in the Pennsylvania Evening Post on August 7 and in other Philadelphia newspapers during the following week. The Vermont Convention's June 4 declaration was not printed in any Philadelphia newspaper, nor have any "Observations" on it by Duane or the New York delegates been found. See JCC, 8:508–11.

John Hancock to the Massachusetts Assembly

Gentlemen,   Philada. July 10th. 1777.

I do myself the Honour to enclose to you Copies of sundry Papers, transmitted to Congress by the State of North Carolina, accompanied with the Resolution of Congress founded thereon. From this you will learn, that a Brig belonging to two Gentlemen of that State, Mr. Smith and Mr. Hewes, was some Time ago captured by a certain Brazilla Smith Commander of the Privateer Eagle, said to be owned by Mr. Elijah Freeman Payne of the Town of Boston. The Congress therefore have recommended it to the State of Massachusetts Bay, to enquire into the Matter, and unless the Master and Owner can shew sufficient Cause to the contrary, to order full Restitution to be made, and the Offenders to be punished. I beg Leave to refer your Attention to the Resolve and also to the Papers.[1]

Mr. Hewes, who is the Bearer hereof, and one of the Owners of the Brig, was a Member of Congress for a considerable Length of Time in the Representation from the State of North Carolina. From the enclosed Memorial you will perceive, the Sense his Constituents entertain of his Merit—to which I shall only add, that his Conduct as an inflexible Patriot, and his Liberality as a Gentleman, justly entitle him not only to their Protection, but to the Notice and Protection of every good Citizen, and Friend of America.

I have the Honour to be, with great Respect, Gentlemen, your most obed. & very hble Servt.   John Hancock Presidt

RC (M–Ar). In the hand of Jacob Rush and signed by Hancock.

[1] For a fuller discussion of the case of the Joseph, see William Hooper to Joseph Hewes, January 1, 1777.

Marine Committee to the Eastern Navy Board

In Marine Committee Philadelphia 10 July, 1777

Whereas by a Resolve of Congress the Nineteenth day of April 1777 You were appointed a Board of Assistants to the Marine Committee to Reside at or in the Neighborhood of Boston, in the State of Massachusetts Bay, with Power to adjourn to any Part of New England, and to have the Superintendance of all Naval and Marine Affairs of the United States of America within the four Eastern States under the direction of the Marine Committee.[1]

You are immediately to repair to Boston and having there met appoint a Clerk properly Qualified and of undoubted attachment to the Interest and Independence of the United States of America.

You are to superintend and direct whatever relates to the building, Manning and fitting for Sea all Armed Vessels of the United States built or ordered by the Congress to build in the Eastern Department, and to provide all materials and Stores necessary for that purpose, subject to such Orders as you may from Time to Time receive from Congress or the Marine Committee.

You are to collect in due season all fit and necessary materials of every kind, for the above purposes and such materials as you may not be able to provide and Shall Judge necessary to be imported. You are timely to report to the Marine Committee the Kinds and Quality of each and how and upon what terms they may be imported by you or any Persons you may be authorized to appoint within your District. You are to receive and settle all accounts relative to the above business and also all such Accounts as Shall be refered to you by the Marine Committee.

You are to keep an exact Register of all the Officers, Sailors and Marines in the Continental Navy fitted and Manned within your District and the same transmit to the Marine Committee.

You are to require all Captains or Commanders of Continental Arm'd Vessels coming into any port within your District to make return to you of the Officers, Sailors and Marines on Board their Vessels and of the State and Condition of their Vessels and Stores, and you are to transmit Duplicates thereof to the Marine Committee. You are to apply to the Marine Committee from Time to Time for such sums of Money as may be necessary in your Department.

You will cause your Clerk duely to Register every Continental Vessel that hath been, or shall be Built within your district, which Register Shall contain the Name, Dimentions, Burthen, Number of Guns, Tackle, Apparel and Furniture of the said Vessels and transmit a Copy thereof to the Marine Committee.

You will direct the Oconomy of all Continental Vessels and ascertain the Modes in which their Accounts shall be kept on board and how returns shall be made, not contrary to any that may be, or have been directed by Congress or the Marine Committee you are hereby required to keep fair books of all expenditures of Publick Moneys for the Navy within your department which Books shall at all Times be subject to the Inspection & examination of Congress and the Marine Committee or of such Persons as they may Authorize and appoint for that Purpose and you are to render Accounts of your disbursements Annually or Oftener if required.

You are hereby empower'd to order Courts Martial in all Cases where the Commanding officers shall refuse, or neglect the same and it shall appear to you requisite; and (in the absence of the Commander in Chief) in all cases where the Commander in chief only is Authorized thereto by the Resolutions of Congress. When any Continental Ships of War comes into any port within your District, you are immediately to give Notice to the Marine Committee of her Arrival and the time it will require to fit and equip her for Sea again in Order that Instructions may be sent by said Committee for such Ships future destination.

By order of the Marine Board,   John Hancock Presidt.

Tr (RNHi). Addressed: "To William Vernon, James Warren, & John Deshon Esqrs."

[1] See Marine Committee to the Eastern Navy Board, June 26, 1777, note 1.

Robert Morris to John Langdon

Sir   Philada. July 10th. 1777

I have your favour of the 16th Ulto. and find Ships have got up beyond their Value with you as well as in other places therefore must wait for a better time to execute my plan,[1] but whenever you see an opportunity of buying a good Vessell fit to carry a Cargo of Rice from Georgia to Europe, and can get her on reasonable terms I request you will do it and send her to Mr Wereat as mentioned in my letter of the 20th May,[2] and I also confirm what is said in mine of the 18th Ulto. respecting the Sugars. With respect to the plan of Importing Goods from France in French bottoms as you propose there is but one objection, & that is, You must load the Vessell & thereby make the Concern too Valuable (unless you take in a good many partners) and by experience I know that it is difficult to Charter Vessells in France on reasonable terms, for I have made the attempt without Success. Now if you can find in any of the Ports of France Ships really bound to Miquelon that will take in freight, we might order more or less Goods out as shou'd best suit us, and that wou'd depend a good deal on the Remittances we might get safe to Europe for I wou'd not wish any Goods out but what we paid ready Money for. If you & Colo. Whipple will mention what Sum you will embark in this business I will engage an equal Sum for Mr Nesbitt & my self and set about the execution of it immediately. My Compts. to Colo. Whipple. I shall be glad to hear from him & am, D sir, Your Obedt hbl servt.   Robt Morris

RC (Capt. J. G. M. Stone, Annapolis, Md., 1974).
[1] See Morris to John Langdon, June 18, 1777.
[2] Not found.

John Adams to Abigail Adams

Philadelphia July 11. 1777
This Letter will go by the Hand of the Honourable Samuel Hewes Esqr.,[1] one of the Delegates in Congress from North Carolina, from the Month of September 1774, untill 1777.

I had the Honour to serve with him upon the naval Committee, who laid the first Foundations, the Corner Stone of an American navy, by fitting to Sea the Alfred, Columbus, Cabott, Andrew Doria, Providence, and several others. An Honour, that I make it a Rule to boast of, upon all Occasions, and I hope my Posterity will have Reason to boast. . . .[2] Hewes has a sharp Eye and keen, penetrating Sense, but what is of much more Value is a Man of Honour and Integrity. If he should call upon you, and you should be about, I hope you will treat him with all the Complaisance that is due to his Character. I almost envy him his Journey, altho he travells for his Health, which at present is infirm. I am yours, yours, yours,   John Adams

My dearest Friend
We have had no News from Camp for 3 or 4 days. Mr. How, by the last Advices, was maneuvring his Fleet and Army in such a Manner, as [to] give Us Expectations of an Expedition, some where. But whether to Rhode Island, Hallifax, up the North River or the Delaware, is left to Conjecture. I am much in doubt whether he knows his own Intentions.

A Faculty of penetrating into the Designs of an Enemy is said to be the first Quality of a General. But it is impossible to discover the Designs of an Enemy who has no Design at all. An Intention that has no Existence, a Plan that is not laid, cannot be divined. Be his Intentions what they may, you have nothing to fear from him—He has not force to penetrate the Country any where.

RC (MHi). Adams, *Family Correspondence* (Butterfield), 2:280.
[1] That is, Joseph Hewes.
[2] Suspension points in MS.

James Lovell to Joseph Trumbull

Dear sir   July 11th [1777]
   Yours of the 9th & 10th are come to hand. Mr. Aylet's letter was
read, and Several of yours also. As the Committee you mentioned is appointed, it is needless for me to say any thing about your Department.
I hope Brother Geary will be disposed to do every thing proper to make
those regulations practically useful about which he has already had a
vast deal of perplexity.[1] I shall be very sorry if you can not have the aid
of two such men as Aylet & Wadsworth. You know how little I like the
slow manner of conducting business in large popular assemblies. I do
not better like the short way in which the Depy. Issuers have managed
their matters: if the army was not in such a very critical state just at
this time I should rejoice to have every man, heretofore employed in
that way, dropped, and others found to whom I would give 10 per Cent
rather than retain the old ones at the lowest Salary.
   Mr. Hoops is an example to them which they ought to follow. He
will take up *at present,* tho' he does not think to continue. He accompanies the Committee, so that I hope you will have some Leisure to
mend a bad scheme.
   If Bucannan should not accept I hope yr. old friend[2] here will find it
worth his pains. I am sure it may be made so, to the public advantage.
   Yr Friend & humble Servant,   J. Lovell

RC (CtHi).
   [1] Acting on the request of Joseph Trumbull, who had the support of General
Washington, Congress appointed a committee this day to go to army headquarters and "make a diligent enquiry into the state of the army, particularly
into the causes of the complaints in the commissary's department." Elbridge
Gerry, Philip Livingston, and George Clymer were appointed to the committee, whose work is discussed in Committee of Congress to George Washington,
July 16, 1777, note 2.
   [2] Perhaps Ephraim Blaine of Pennsylvania, who was appointed deputy commissary general of purchases on August 6, 1777, to succeed William Buchanan.
JCC, 8:617.

Marine Committee to the Eastern Navy Board

Gentln   In Marine Committee. Philadelphia July 11th 1777
   As there are now lying within your Department several Continental
Vessils of War which if at Sea might do essential service[1] we are exceedingly anxious to have them out fore these desirable purposes and
have strong hopes from your exertions that they will not remain long
inactive. We know of no better way they can be employed than in
Cruizing, and now direct and Authorize you to send them out as fast
as they can be got ready directing the Commanders to such Lattitudes

as you shall think there will be the greatest chance of success in intercepting the Enemies Transports and Merchant Ships and they are to Take, burn, Sink or destroy as many of their Vessils of every kind as may be in their Power. The Prizes they may take are to be sent into the most convenient and safe Ports in these States addressed to the Continental Agents.

We shall leave you to judge of the Time for which each Vessil is to Cruize and when they return into Port, you must again dispatch them with all possible expedition on fresh Cruizes, always advising us of their Arrival and the Time you think they will be ready for Sea, but They are not to [be] detained for any further Orders from us.

You are to Instruct the Commanders that they are to be careful of the Ships their Stores and Materials, that they Support strict discipline on board their Vessils, but treat their People well. Prisoners are to be treated with humanity and that they are to be accountable to you for the expenditure of everything on board their Ships recommending to them a strict observance of frugallity and Œconomy. We remain, Gentlemen, Your very Obed Servts. By Order Marine Board.

John Hancock Presidt.

Tr (RNHi). Addressed: "Wm Vernon James Warren & John Deshon Esqrs." LB (DNA: PCC Miscellaneous Papers, Marine Committee Letter Book).

[1] At this point in LB is the following: "to the States and much injury to our enemies."

North Carolina Delegates to John Allen

Lieutenant John Allen   Philadelphia July 11th. 1777.

You are forthwith to repair to Baltimore and deliver the paquet herewith delivered to you to Michael Hillegas Esquire Continental Treasurer. He will put under your Care three hundred thousand Dollars and furnish you with proper Carriage & Escort.[1] With them you are to proceed by the nearest, safest and best rout to the Governor of North Carolina and then observe his further Directions.

You are to be very attentive to this Service, taking great care that the packages where the Money is be never without a proper Watch over them in the day, and that you have them in the Appartment where you sleep every Night using also such other cautions as you shall find necessary for the great Security of your Charge.

We rely much on your attention and Fidelity in Discharging this Duty, and hope your Country will have Just Cause to Approve your performance thereof.

We wish you well home, and your hum Serts.   Tho Burke

John Penn

Tr (DLC). Copied for Edmund C. Burnett "from the original then in the possession of Mr. Stan V. Henkels of Philadelphia."

[1] See *JCC*, 8:538. On December 4, 1777, Congress ordered the payment of "90 60/90 dollars" to Lt. John Allen for "the balance of his expences to and from North Carolina with 300,000 dollars to that State in July last." *JCC*, 9:1003.

George Frost to Josiah Bartlett

Dear Sir   Philadelphia July 12th. 1777

In My last I wrote you some parragrafts of a letter from Spain. The post went so sudden I had not time to finish 'm and would now continu. them.[1] "We are Assured by Both France and Spain that such a Disposition of their fleets & forces will be made as ought to perswade England that she cannot Sustain the war against you as she has planned. Your Wisdom will direct you how fer to trust to those assurances or their expected consequences when our stake is so presious that the most ardent & Unremitting exertions cannot be too great, not that I suspect the Sincerity of those Assurances but the effects they are to produce. From Germaney they have little more to hope to Raise Recrutes. To Russia alone they may apply if the Cloud that is rising from Constantinople should blow over without which it is Impossible they should have any aid from thence, but if this should happen it will be our endeavour & I hope we shall succead in rasing the Opposition of Other European powers to that measure. I mean to propose on my Return to Paris the Sounding both the Emperour & the King of Prussia (to which Courts we (the Congress) have sent Commissioners to anounce our Independency and Settle a treaty of frindship and Commerce) on this Subject. The one wishes to promote the port of Ostend the other of Emden & by those we may perhaps work them up to our wishes. It is upon this View of things that I found my hopes of the next Campaign being the last Struggle of any Importance the Enemy can make against us. The Dutch on whom Britian so much depend withold their money as fer as they can find Spanish paper to vest it in. The degree of their alarm from France & Spain may be seen from the Embodying of the Militia & their Expences. I belive their divisions at home are apparent from the suspension of the Habus Corpus Act which will proberly [realize?] their apprehensions of Domistic troubles. The measure of their iniquity is now full when they have put the liberty of every Subject in the power of the most merciless & Unprincipled Tyrent that ever disgraced a throne." The State of Europe is such as to Render it morally certain that a war in Europe will relive you from extraordinary exertions befor a year has passed away. Sr., You'l see the desine of this letter from our frind in Spain was not to be maid public but I have taken the liberty to send Such parts as I thought would be agreeable to you and the Rest of my

Good frinds at Court to know, after all that the Courts of France & Spain have said our security and welfare is within our selves with the Blessing of our Good and Gracious God on the Means he has put in our power which I trust You and every lover of his Country will exert to the Utmost of his power and If we support our Independency this Year the Day will be our owne.

How has quited the Jerseys and is gone to New York but where he is going is Uncertain (he found it Impractable to penatrate througe the Jerseys [to] Phila.) Some says to New England, others Suppose he is going Up the North or to the Southern States. On the whole it is soposed he dont know what to do himselfe at present and it is said by some that came out from New York [only?] that the first in Command of the Hessions is much disgusted and is gone home. I fear things dont go well with our Armey at Ticondaraga, but we are in good Spirits here. Am, Sir, Your Most Obt. Humble Sert.   Geo. Frost

PS After you and my good frinds at Court (to whom please to present my Sincear Regards) have read the papers please to let my Frind Esqr. Thomson have 'm that my frinds at Durham may see them.

RC (NhD).
[1] In his July 7 letter to Bartlett, Frost had extracted material from Arthur Lee's March 18 letter to the Committee of Secret Correspondence. Quotation marks have been supplied editorially.

John Hancock to Benedict Arnold

Sir,   Philada. July 12th. 1777.
I have the Honour to inclose you an Extract of a Letter from Genl. Washington from which you will perceive the General is of Opinion "a brave, active and judicious officer" [1] should be immediately employed in collecting the Militia to check the Progress of Genl. Burgoyne, as very disagreeable Consequences may be apprehended if the most vigorous Measures are not taken to oppose him.

The Congress therefore concurring in opinion with General Washington who has strongly recommended you for this Purpose, have directed You to repair immediately to Head Quarters to follow such Orders as you may receive from him on the Subject.[2] I have the Honour to be, with Respect, Sir, your most obedt. Serv.   J.H. Presid.

LB (DNA: PCC, item 12A). Addressed: "Honble Major Genl Arnold, Philada."
[1] Washington had used these very words to describe Arnold in a July 10 letter recommending his employment in the northern department in consequence of the British capture of Ticonderoga. "His presence and activity," Washington told Hancock, "will animate the Militia greatly, and spur them on to a becoming conduct." Washington, *Writings* (Fitzpatrick), 8:377.
[2] See *JCC*, 8:545.

John Penn to Richard Caswell

Dear Sir,   Philada. July 12th 1777

Having been informed that the Troops belonging to our State could not part with the money they brought with them, but at a very great loss, Doctor Burke and myself thought it reasonable to exchange with the Men, by giving them an equal number of Continental dollars, which Mr. Blunt at our request did, amounting in the whole to 2485 1/2 dollars agreeable to the inclosed list—we hope the money will be of use with you, indeed it was lost to the Soldiers here.

We have Imployed Lieut. John Allen to Conduct the money from Baltimore and have requested Mr. Helligrass to dispatch him as soon as possibly he can. You will receive the above quantity of dollars besides the 300,000 sent by the Congress, the whole is to be Conducted at the expence of the Continent.

It is still uncertain what General Howe means to do as he remains between Staten Island & New York. Genl. Burgoyne is in the Neighborhood of Ticonderoga, his force is not known. I am afraid we shall not be able to keep that Fort.

Your son is very well, our Troops are near this City waiting for Genl. Howe's movement. With great respect, I am, Dear Sir, Your ob. Serv.

John Penn

[*P.S.*] Doct. Burke was out of the way so could not sign this letter.

MS not found; reprinted from *N.C. State Records,* 11:736.

John Adams to Abigail Adams

My dearest Friend   Philadelphia July 13. 1777

We have a confused Account, from the Northward, of Something Unlucky, at Ticonderoga, but cannot certainly tell what it is.[1]

I am much afraid, We shall loose that Post, as We did Forts Washington and Lee, and indeed, I believe We shall if the Enemy surround it. But it will prove no Benefit to them. I begin to Wish there was not a Fort upon the Continent. Discipline and Disposition, are our Resources.

It is our Policy to draw the Enemy into the Country, where We can avail ourselves of Hills, Woods, Walls, Rivers, Defiles &c. untill our Soldiers are more inured to War.

How and Burgoine will not be able to meet, this Year, and if they were met, it would only be better for Us, for We should draw all our Forces to a Point too.

If they were met, they could not cutt off the Communication, between the Northern and Southern States. But if the Communication was cutt off for a Time, it would be no Misfortune, for New England would defend itself, and the Southern States would defend themselves. Coll. Miles is come out of N. York on his Parol. His account is, as I am informed, that Mr. Howes Projects are all deranged. His Army has gone round the Circle and is now encamped on the very Spot where he was a Year ago. The Spirits of the Tories are sunk to a great Degree, and those of the Army too. The Tories have been elated with Prospects of coming to this City, and tryumphing, but are miserably disappointed. The Hessians are disgusted, and their General De Heister gone home, in a Miff.[2]

RC (MHi). Adams, *Family Correspondence* (Butterfield), 2:281.
    [1] On July 5–6 Gen. Arthur St. Clair evacuated Fort Ticonderoga after Gen. John Burgoyne's maneuvers had rendered its defense untenable. Don Higginbotham, *The War of American Independence* (New York: Macmillan Co., 1971), pp. 189–90. See also John Hancock to Philip Schuyler, July 14, 1777.
    [2] The recall of Lt. Gen. Leopold Philipp, Freiherr von Heister, commander of the Hessian troops in Sir William Howe's army, was apparently arranged by Howe after the 1776 New York campaign, although von Heister did not leave the army until June 22, 1777. Edward J. Lowell, *The Hessians and the Other German Auxiliaries of Great Britain in the Revolutionary War* (Williamstown, Mass.: Corner House Publishers, 1970, reprint ed.), pp. 113–15.

Henry Marchant to Nicholas Cooke

Honored Sir,   Philadelphia July 13th. 1777
    I wrote the Governor and Company by the last Post and enclosed Them an Order of Congress upon the Loan Office State of Rhode Island &c for 190,000 Dollars which I hope will come to Hand.
    I now enclose Your Honor the Resolves of the Marine Comee. passed March the 25th 1777,[1] respecting the Contracts made by some of the Officers &c of Commodore Hopkins's Fleet when in Deleware River. As the Complaints in Consequence of that Contract have still continued notwithstanding those Resolves were forwarded long ago to the Continental Agents; by order of the Marine Comee I sent a Copy of them to the Agent Mr. Tillinghast by the last Post, supposing it possible They might have miscarried before.[2] And as I never heard of Them before I left the State, for that Reason I have enclosed them to your Honor.
    Our Accounts from the Northward are very unfavourable, but at the same Time so confused that no certainty can be collected. Yet we are very apprehensive that Ti is in the Hands of the Enemy, with all the Cannon & Stores, if not the Garrison. To what Causes this Misfortune must have arisen Time only can unfold. If the Case is so, We are not to dispond but rise with new Vigour and manly Fortitude. Let *New England* now shew Her Prowess, Her Vigilance and Her every Virtue. Let

us rise at Once, as tho' collected into One Soul. Let us meet the Enemy where their Ships cannot avail Them—upon equal Ground, and by the Blessing of Heaven Success, Victory and Honor must attend us. Let not the Jersey Militia have the only Honor of riding Their Country of the Enemies of Mankind by a United, brave Effort. I only wish New-England may maintain that Character She hath hitherto entitled Herself to.

I have the Honor to subscribe myself your Honors most Obedient, humble Servant,   Hy Marchant

RC (R–Ar).
[1] For these resolves, see Marine Committee Examination of John Grannis, March 25, 1777, note 8.
[2] No letter from Marchant to Daniel Tillinghast has been found.

John Hancock to Certain States

Gentlemen,   Philada. July 14th. 1777.
The enclosed Resolve of Congress recommending it to your State to send such Reinforcements of Militia to the Armies under Generals Washington or Schuyler, as may be requested, comes with such peculiar Force at this Juncture, that I am persuaded any Arguments to induce you to comply with it will be unnecessary.[1] From the Continental Battalions not being compleated agreeably to the original Plan, there is indeed an absolute Necessity for adopting the Measure in our present Situation. Give me Leave therefore most earnestly to request your Compliance with this Requisition of Congress as the only effectual Mode of checking the Progress of our enraged & cruel Enemies.

I have the Honour to be, Gentlemen, your most obed. & very hble Servt.   J.H. Presid.

LB (DNA: PCC, item 12A). Addressed to the convention of New York and the assemblies of Connecticut, Massachusetts, New Hampshire, and Rhode Island.
[1] See JCC, 8:549. The passage of this resolve was precipitated by the arrival of a July 10 letter from Washington enclosing a July 7 letter from General Schuyler containing the first news of the evacuation of Ticonderoga. PCC, item 152, 4:337–39, item 153, 3:222; and Washington, Writings (Fitzpatrick), 8:376–78.

John Hancock to Philip Schuyler

Sir   Philada. July 14th. 1777.
I have the Honor to transmit you sundry Resolves, to which I beg Leave to refer your Attention.
The Congress have strongly recommended it to the State of New

York and the Eastern States to send such Reinforcements of Militia to your Assistance and also to the Assistance of General Washington, as may from Time to Time be requested and I have accordingly addressed them on the Subject.

Your several Favors of the 8th & 9th, 14 and 25th of June and 5th Instant have been duly received in the order of their Dates. Last Night I was honored with Copies of your two Letters of 7th & 9th Inst. to Genl. Washington.[1] Their interesting Contents shall be immediately laid before Congress.

I have the Honour to be, with the greatest Respect Sir, Your most obedt & very humble Servant,   John Hancock Presdt.

[P.S.] As soon as Congress have come to a Determination on your last Letters you shall be acquainted with the Result. I have paid the Bearer for his Detention here.

Tr (NN).
  [1] With the exception of the last, these letters are in PCC, item 153, 3:144–224. The one of July 9 to Washington is in Washington Papers, DLC, and PCC, item 152, 4:345–46. Only the letters to Washington deal with the American evacuation of Ticonderoga.

John Hancock to George Washington

Sir,   Philada. July 14th. 1777.
    You will perceive from the enclosed Resolve that there are at present about fourteen Hundred Men at Philada. and Billingsport who are ready to march, and wait only for your Orders.[1]

The Congress have recommended it to the State of New York and to the Eastern States to send such Reinforcements of their Militia to your Assistance, and also to the Assistance of Genl. Schuyler as may, from Time to Time be requested; and I have accordingly addressed them on the Subject.

P.S. 6 O'Clock P.M. Since writing the foregoing, your Favour of the 12th Inst came to Hand, and Congress have issued Orders to Genl. Nash to march immediately to Head Quarters with all the Carolina and Virginia Troops under his Command. Similar Orders have likewise been issued to Colo. Proctor to March with his Regiment of Artillery, which was raised for the State of Pennsylvania, but has been since taken into Continental Service.[2]

I have the Honour to be, with the greatest Respect, Sir, your most obed. & very hble Servt.   John Hancock Presidt

[P.S.] A Comme. of Congress are Sent to Head Quarters to Consult respectg the Commissary's Departmt.[3]

RC (DLC). In the hand of Jacob Rush, with signature and second postscript by Hancock.

[1] See *JCC*, 8:549.

[2] See PCC, item 152, 4:341–44; and Washington, *Writings* (Fitzpatrick), 8:551.

[3] See Committee of Congress to Washington, July 16, 1777.

Samuel Adams to Samuel Cooper

My dear sir   Philade July 15 1777

Before this reaches you, it is probable you will have heard of the untoward Turn our Affairs have taken at the Northward. I confess it is not more than I expected when Genl Schu[yle]r was again intrusted with the Command there. But it was thought by some Gentlemen that as he had a great Interest & large Connections in that Part of the Country, he could more readily avail himself of Supplys for an Army there as well as Reinforcements if wanted upon an Emergency, than any other Man. You have the Account in the inclosed Paper, which leaves us to guess what is become of the Garrison.[1] There is something droll enough in a Generals not knowing where to find the main Body of his Army. Gates is the Man I should have chosen. He is honest and true, & has the Art of gaining the Love of his Soldiers, principally because he is always present and shares with them in Fatigue & Danger. We are hourly expecting to be relievd from a disagreeable State of Uncertainty by a particular Relation of Facts. This Account, as you are told, is related upon *Memory*, & therefore some Circumstances may be *omitted*, others *misapprehended*. But the Post is just going, & I have time only to acknowledge the Receipt of your favor of the 12 of June & beg you would write to me often.[2]

I am affectionately, your freind,   S A

FC (NN).

[1] Probably the July 15 issue of the *Pennsylvania Packet* containing extracts from Gen. Philip Schuyler's July 7 letter to Washington announcing the retreat of the American army from Fort Ticonderoga.

[2] Cooper's June 12 letter to Adams is in the Adams Papers, NN.

Samuel Adams to Richard Henry Lee

My dear Freind   Philade July 15 1777

I wrote to you a Fortnight ago in so great Haste that I had not time to transcribe or correct it, and relied on your Candor to overlook the slovenly dress in which it was sent to you. You have since heard that

our Friends in Jersey have at length got rid of as vindictive and cruel
an Enemy as ever invaded any Country. It was the opinion of General
Gates that Howes advancing to Somerset Court House was a Feint to
cover the Retreat of his Battering Train, ordinance, Stores and heavy
Baggage to Amboy. I confes I cannot help yet feeling myself chagrind,
that no more has been done to diminish his paltry Army in that State.
If their Militia, among whom so great an Animation prevaild, had been
let loose upon the Enemy, who knows but that they wod. have destroyd their Army, or at least so far have weakend it as to have put a
glorious End to this Campaign, and perhaps the War! I will acknowledge that my Temper is rather sanguine. I am apt to be displeasd when
I think our Progress in War and in Politics is Slow. I wish to see more
of an enterprizing Spirit in the Senate and the Feild, without which I
fear our Country will not speedily enjoy the Fruits of the present Conflict—an established Independence and Peace. I cannot applaud the
Prudence of the Step, when the People of Jersey were collected, and
inspired with Confidence in themselves & each other, to dismiss them
as not being immediately wanted, that they might go home in good
Humour and be willing to turn out again in any *other* Emergency. I
profess not the least Degree of Knowledge in military Matters, & therefore hazzard no opinion. I recollect however that Shakespeare tells us,
there is a Tide in human Affairs, an Opportunity which wise Men carefully watch for and improve, and I will never forget because it exactly
coincides with my religious opinion and I think it warranted by holy
Writ, that "God helps those who help themselves."

We have letters from General Schuyler, in the Northern Department,
giving us an Account of untoward Situation of our Affairs in that
Quarter. I confess it is no more than I expected, when he was again
intrusted with the Command there. You remember it was urged by some
That as he had a large Interest and powerful Connections in that Part
of the Country, no one could so readily avail himself of Supplys for an
Army there than he. A most Substantial Reason, I think, why he should
have been appointed a Quartermaster or a Commissary. But it seems
to have been the prevailing Motive to appoint him to the Cheif Command! You have his Account in the inclosed News paper, which leaves
us to *guess* what is become of the *Garrison*. It is indeed droll enough
to see a General not knowing where to find the main Body of his Army.
Gates is the Man of my choice; He is *honest* and *true,* & has the Art of
gaining the love of his Soldiers principally because he is *always present*
and shares with them in *Fatigue* & *Danger*. But Gates has been disgusted! We are however waiting to be releivd from this disagreeable
State of uncertainty, by a particular Account of Facts from some
Person who *was near* the Army who trusts not to *Memory* altogether,
but some Circumstances may be *omitted* while others are *misapprehended.*

I rejoyce in the Honors your Country has done you. Pray hasten your Journy hither.[1]

Your very affectionate,   S Adams

RC (NN).

[1] For Lee's July 27 response to this letter, see Lee, *Letters* (Ballagh), 1:313-14.

Board of War to George Washington

Sir   War Office July 15th. 1777

I have the Honour of your Letter of the 12th instant which I have communicated to the Board.[1]

General Sullivan has written concerning an Hudson Burr condemned at Sourland by a Court Martial as a Spy but says your Excellcy would not ratify the Proceedings desiring that the Man might be sent to Philada. where he is now under Confinement, that the Board might discharge him if they knew Nothing against him; but as they are not certified properly of the Proceedings of the Court Martial they cannot with Propriety take Notice of the Matter. Mean Time the Man is suffering in Prison & therefore I am to request that your Excellency will be pleased to write them on the Subject[2] that Burr may be discharged on Security being given for his good Behavior & the public be eased of the Care of him, as his Friends here who are numerous are constantly applying to see him in Prison & solliciting for his Release. His Connexions are among the Quakers & *so far wrong,* but he is not capable if ever he intended it to do much Harm.

I have the Honour to be, Your Excellency's very obed Servt,

Richard Peters Secy

[*P.S.*] I have the Honor of transmitting the enclosed Return of Tents furnished by the Quarter Master General for your Excellency's Inspection with a Request from the Board that if you can spare any Tents you will order a Number to General Schuyler.[3]

RC (DLC).

[1] See Washington, *Writings* (Fitzpatrick), 8:387-89.

[2] For Washington's response to this request, see ibid., pp. 494-95.

[3] On the following day Peters wrote a brief note to Washington introducing Mr. Dupre, an armorer with a North Carolina brigade, and requesting on behalf of the board that Washington "give Orders for Mr. Dupre's being employed as Superintendent of the Armoury attending the Camp, or in any other manner you may think proper, as his Abilities will render him exceedingly useful." Washington Papers, DLC.

Eliphalet Dyer to Joseph Trumbull

Dear Sir   Philadelphia July 15th 1777

Recievd your favr. of the 9th Instant, yours to Congress was recievd at the same time and the Matter Immediately taken up in Congress. There is so many fond of their New plan that it is difficult to make them attend to the Objections against and cannot bare so soon to throw up What they have entertained so great a fondness of but however they soon agreed to send a Comtee of Congress to goe to the Army and see and hear and report.[1] The Congress is very thin and most Gentn. had a Very great Aversion to goe on this business. Except Mr Gerry I think there could scarce been one more unsuitable. Mr Livingston was chose one principally because he was gone that way before and would be in the way. I much fear the Consequence arising from this New Regulation but hope for the best. Every thing must be Endured before the Army must fail. It is said in Congress by some that you must goe on your Old way till the New one gets into a proper regulation and employe purchasers as formerly. I know not what or how to advise you only in General to do the Utmost in your power to advance and promote the general good and service.[2] Am sure I should at once advise you to quit if I did not apprehend the worst Consequences would follow and if you do not it may possibly be as bad unless Congress should place the purchasing Commissy. business in the same line as formerly. If the Comtee should report favorably that way it may possibly be done. If you had the appointment of your Depty Commiss of purchasers and to allow Wages according to their Merrit I see no difficulty in carrying on your part but fear it will be hard to bring them back to that mode unless the Genll. and Comtee should recommend it.

The News we have recievd from Ticonderoga is truly Alarming. Fear it will throw the New England States into the greatest Consternation. Expect the Enemies ships are all along the sea coast giving the alarm there to divert them from giving aid to other parts where they may be wanted. Expect every hour to hear Genll. How has pushd up the North river. God grant he may meet with a repulse there. I fear the late success of the Enemy will again oblidge us to call of Our Militia as last summer and now in this most Critical season. There ar about 15 hundrd. or two thousand Southern Troops now forwarding from this place to join Genll. Washington. I want much to hear from our Country if you have Any Accounts from there, especially of our family you will be so kind as to let me hear.

I Am with sincere regards, Yrs   Elipht Dyer.

RC (CtHi). Burnett, *Letters,* 2:414–15.

[1] For the work of this committee, see Committee of Congress to George Washington, July 16, 1777, note 2. Trumbull's July 9 letter to Hancock and his July 22 letter to the committee are in PCC, item 78, 22:255, 273.

2 A list of Trumbull's reasons for declining to serve as commissary general of purchases, which he apparently submitted to the committee, is in PCC, item 78, 22:275–76. For details on his refusal to serve under the new commissary regulations, see Elbridge Gerry to Trumbull, April 19, note 1; and Dyer to Trumbull, June 1777, note 4.

James Lovell to Joseph Trumbull

Dear Sir   July 15th. [1777]
    I wrote a few days ago under the idea of sending by my very worthy colleague Mr. Geary, who is doubtless with you.[1] Tho' I cannot expect you can pay any present attention to the inclosed, yet I wish you may in future for mutual Benefit of yourself & the staunch Whig who writes it. I say in future—for I will not think you will throw up the Commissariate since it is so far advanced into a Probability of success. I do not suppose you yourself would have balloted for Envoys just as others have done on this occasion but I hope you have a Ball[an]ce to yr. Liking. I hope to hear from you by Mr. G as to your own & the matters of Ty in the *Northern Department.*
    Yrs. affectionately,   J L

RC (CtHi).
[1] See Lovell to Joseph Trumbull, July 11, 1777.

John Adams to Abigail Adams

My dearest Friend   Wednesday July 16. 1777
    Your Favour of the 2d instant reached me on the 14th.
    The last Letters from me which you had received, were of the 2d. 4th. and 8th June. Here were 24 days between the 8th of June and the 2d July the date of yours. How this could happen I know not. I have inclosed you the Newspapers and written you a Line, every Week, for several Months past. If there is one Week passes without bringing you a Letter from me, it is because the Post does not its Duty.
    After another Week, you will probably write me no more Letters for some Days. But I hope you will make Mr. Thaxter, or somebody write. Miss Nabby or Mr. John may write.
    We have another Fort Washington and Fort Lee affair at Ticonderoga. I hope at last We shall learn Wisdom. I wished that Post evacuated Three Months ago. We are Fools if We attempt at present to maintain Posts, near navigable Water.
    As to the Tories, I think our General Court would do well to imitate the Policy of Pensilvania, who have enjoyned an Oath to be taken by all the People, which has had an amazing Effect.

The Tories have been tolerated, even to long Suffering. Beings so unfeeling, unnatural, ungratefull, as to join an Enemy of their Country so unprincipled, unmerciless[1] and blood thirsty, deserve a Punishment much severer than Banishment.

But you should establish an Oath, and outlaw all who will not take it—that is suffer them to hold no Office, to vote no where for any Thing, to bring no Action, to take out no Execution.

I am grieved to hear that our Fruit is injured by the Frost because as Wine and Rum will wholly fail, from the stoppages of Trade, Cyder will be our only Resource.

However We must drink Water, and Milk, and We should live better, be healthier, and fight bolder than We do with our poisonous Luxuries.

RC (MHi). Adams, *Family Correspondence* (Butterfield), 2:283–84.

[1] Adams apparently wrote "merciless" and then inserted the prefix "un" in the MS. But he clearly meant either unmerciful or merciless.

Committee of Congress to George Washington

Wednesday Eveng [July 16, 1777][1]

Messrs. Livingston, Clymer, & Gerry present their Complimts to his Excellency General Washington, & beg Leave to inclose him a Copy of the Resolution of Congress appointing them a Committee to repair to the Camp & enquire into the State of the Army. As they have not Time to wait upon his Excellency this Evening, they propose to be at Head Quarters in the Morning at ten oClock, & shall be glad to know the State of the Army in General as well as the several Departments thereof, with his opinion on the Measures necessary to releive it from any Inconveniences that have or are likely to take place.[2]

RC (DLC). In Elbridge Gerry's hand, though not signed. At the bottom of the page Gerry copied the July 11 resolution of Congress creating the committee.

[1] There can be no doubt that the committee wrote this letter on the 16th, the first Wednesday after its appointment on July 11. See, for example, Washington's July 19 letter to the committee in Washington, *Writings* (Fitzpatrick), 8:439–45.

[2] On July 11, after reading letters of the 9th from Washington and Commissary General Joseph Trumbull complaining about the set of regulations for the commissariat adopted on June 10, Congress appointed a committee consisting of George Clymer, Elbridge Gerry, and Philip Livingston "to make a diligent enquiry into the state of the army, particularly into the causes of the complaints in the commissary's department, and to make such provision as the exigency and importance of the case demands." The committee subsequently met with Washington at his headquarters in Clove, N.J., and with Gen. Israel Putnam at Peekskill, N.Y. On July 24 Livingston submitted to Congress a July 19 letter from Washington to the committee that described at length many of the army's more pressing needs. Congress approved most of Washington's

George Clymer

suggestions with respect to supplying the army, encouraging recruits, and apprehending deserters in a series of resolves passed on July 25 and 31. On August 5 Congress also received a comprehensive report from the committee that dealt with the shortcomings of the commissariat and made numerous proposals for reform. Action was taken on many of these proposals during the same month. See *JCC*, 8:434–48, 546, 577, 580–81, 593–95, 608–13; PCC, item 152, 4:331–34; and Washington, *Writings* (Fitzpatrick), 8:373–74, 439–45.

Robert Morris to William Patterson

Sir[1]   Philada. July 16th. 1777
   Your favr. of 10th June with Copy of 19th May came safe by the last Maryland Post but the Original of the 19th of May has not yet found its way hither. What you write of the Schooner Tryal, Captn. Keeling, & Sloop Cristiana, Captn. White, is bad news for me who have a considerable Share in each of those Vessels. By the Miscarriage of your Letter of 19th May we are deprived of the Acct. Sales & Acct. Currt. for Brigt. Rodger's Cargo. The Letter that is come you have marked 2d Copy & shoud the others not arrive we must give you the trouble to send us other Copies of those Accts.[2] In the mean time we duely note the remittances you have made to Messr. Geo. Clifford & Teysett of Amsterdam on our Acct.
   I hope the Dutch Vessells you mention to be carried into Antigua may not be condemned for it will have bad consequences to our Trade, but if they are it may serve to embroil G.B. the more with European Nations if they have spirit enough to protect themselves. I believe your Vessell arrived safe with Messr. Norton & Bealle as they recd. one parcell of Cordage, Sail Cloth &ca. I wish you Success at Martinique & shall be glad of Opportunities to contribute thereto, being, Sir, Your Obedt. hble Servt. (Copy)

Tr (MdHi).
   [1] This letter was enclosed in a letter of October 31, 1777, which Morris addressed "To Mr. William Patterson, Merchant in St. Eustatia" and described as a "copy of my last."
   [2] In his October 31 letter to Patterson, Morris reported that "as I have not received the accounts respecting the Brige Rodgers must beg the favour of a Copy thereof." William Patterson Papers, MdHi.

John Adams to Abigail Adams

                                                    Fryday July 18, 1777
   The Papers inclosed will inform you, of the Loss of Ticonderoga, with all its Circumstances of Incapacity and Pusillanimity. Dont you pitty me to be wasting away my Life, in laborious Exertions, to procure

Cannon, Ammunition, Stores, Baggage, Cloathing &c. &c. &c. &c., for Armies, who give them all away to the Enemy, without firing a Gun.

Notwithstanding the Mortification arising from such Considerations, yet I can truly say that this Event is a Relief to my Mind, for I have a long Time expected this Catastrophe, and that it would be aggravated by the Loss of the Garrison, which it seems has been happily saved. My only Hope of holding that Post, has been a long Time founded in a Doubt whether the Enemy had Force enough in Canada, to attempt it.

The Design of the Enemy, is now no doubt to attack poor New England on all sides, from Rhode Island, New York and Ticonderoga.

But I believe their Progress will be stopped, for our Army is pretty numerous, and Discipline, upon which alone We must finally depend, under Providence, for Success, is advancing.

Howes Army is in a miserable Condition, by the best Accounts We can obtain.

My Mind runs upon my Family, as much as upon our public Concerns. I long to hear of the Safety and the Health of my dearest Friend. May Heaven grant her every Blessing she desires.

Tell my Brother Farmer, I long to study Agriculture with him, and to see the Progress of his Corn and Grass. Sister too, does she make as a good dairy Woman as your Ladyship?

RC (MHi). Adams, *Family Correspondence* (Butterfield), 2:284–85.

James Duane to Elias Boudinot

Dear Sir   Philad Treasury Office 18 July 1777

You'l observe by the enclosed Memorandum[1] from a Member of Congress that a difficulty arises at the Treasury board in ascertaining the pay due to Prisoners both Officers & Soldiers, living and dead. It woud be an Act of equal Justice and Humanity if the several Commanding officers who are Prisoners coud by proper payrolls ascertain the money due to their Captive Corps; and the Board of Treasury recommend this Business to your Consideration and that it may receive all possible Dispatch.

I am, Sir, your most huml servt,   Jas. Duane

RC (DLC).
[1] Not found.

John Hancock to the Delaware and
Virginia Assemblies

Gentlemen,   Philada. July 18th 1777.
I have it in Charge most earnestly to entreat you will immediately
send a sufficient Number of Members to represent your State in Congress.[1] The Advantages resulting from a full and constant Representation of every State, by giving Weight to the Councils of America and
promoting Union and good Correspondence thro' the United States,
are extremely obvious—but a full Representation is more especially
requisite at this Juncture, as the Congress for Want of it, are under a
Necessity of putting off the Consideration of several important Matters,
and particularly the Confederation of the States, one of the grandest
Objects that ever came before a Human Assembly for Discussion. The
United Wisdom of America should be collected on this Point, in order
that the most firm and permanent Foundations may be laid for the
future Glory and Happiness of our Country. I flatter myself therefore
you will immediately comply with this Requisition of Congress.[2]
I have the Honour to be, Gentlemen, your most obed. Serv.
                                              J.H. Presid.

LB (DNA: PCC, item 12A).
[1] See *JCC*, 8:559.
[2] After several false starts, Congress finally resumed sustained consideration of
the Articles of Confederation on October 7, 1777. *JCC*, 8:760, 9:778.

John Hancock to Philip Schuyler

Sir   Philada. July 18t. 1777.
I have Nothing in Charge from Congress at this Time, but to transmit the inclosed Resolves for your Information and Direction, to which
I beg Leave to refer your Attention.[1]
The Loss of Ticonderoga still remains a very mysterious Affair for
Want of proper Information nor have we as yet received any Account
of the Fate of the Garrison under the Command of General St. Clair,
only from Report, which is of such a Nature as to increase our apprehensions without removing our Suspence. I am therefore to request
you will favor us as soon as possible with the best Intelligence you can
procure, as Congress are extremely anxious to hear the Event, together
with the particulars.

P.S. July 22d. Since writing the foregoing, Congress have received a
Letter from General St. Clair of the 14t Instant inclosing a Copy of
the proceedings of a Council of War, with the Reasons for evacuating

Tyconderoga & Mount Independence. They have also received a Copy of your's to General Washington dated at Fort Edward the 14t Instant.[2]

I enclose to you an order on the Commissioners of the Loan Office of the State of New York in Favor of Mr. Jonathan Trumbull, which I must request you will please to deliver to him.[3] Your very humble Servant,   John Hancock Presidt.

Tr (NN).

[1] Probably the resolves pertaining to Schuyler's command passed by Congress on July 17. See *JCC,* 8:561–62.

[2] See James Lovell to William Whipple, July 21, 1777, note 1.

[3] Congress had issued this order on June 27. *JCC,* 8:505.

John Hancock to Joseph Spencer

Sir,   Philada. July 18th. 1777.

I am particularly instructed to inform you in Answer to your Favour of the 20th May last, that Congress Confirm the Appointment of William Peck Esqr as Deputy Adjutant General to the Militia, and State-Troops of Rhode Island that are in Continental Pay, and that you are to apply for Money to pay the said Troops to Ebenezer Hancock Esqr at Boston Deputy Paymaster General to the Troops in the Eastern Department.[1] The Quarter Master General having the Appointment of all his Deputies, the Application must be to him for the Appointment of a Deputy Quarter Master general to the Troops under his Command.

I have the Honour to be, with Respect, Sir, Your most obed Serv.

                                                    J.H. Presid

LB (DNA: PCC, item 12A). Addressed: "Honble Major Genl. Spencer at Rhode Island."

[1] See *JCC,* 8:497, 561. General Spencer's May 20 letter to Hancock, which was read in Congress on June 25, is in PCC, item 78, 20:107–9.

John Hancock to Joseph Trumbull

Sir,   Philada. July 18th. 1777.

The great Scarcity of Salt, and the Necessity of procuring a Supply for the Use of the Army, have induced the Congress to direct the Committee of Commerce to take Measures for importing large Quantities of that Article: and I have it in Charge to transmit the enclosed Order to inform you thereof.[1]

I am, Sir, your most obedt. & very hble Servt.

                                                    J.H. Presidt.

[*P.S.*] The Congress direct that the Flour which is stored at Lancaster & other Places & in Danger of spoiling, should be immediately baked into Biscuit, for which you will give orders.[2]

LB (DNA: PCC, item 12A).
    [1] See *JCC,* 8:560–62.
    [2] Hancock may have added this postscript on July 23, when Congress passed the resolve described in it. *JCC,* 8:574–75.

John Adams to Abigail Adams

Phila. July 20th. 1777

The little masterly Expedition to Rhode Island has given Us, some Spirits, amidst our Mournings for the Loss of Ti. Barton conducted his Expedition with infinite Address and Gallantry, as Sir. Wm. has it. Meigs and Barton must be rewarded.[1]

Although so much Time has elapsed since our Misfortune at Ti, We have no particular Account from General Schuyler or Sinclair. People here are open mouthed, about the Disgrace and Disaster in that Quarter, and are much disposed to Censure. For my Part I suspend my Judgment, until I know the Facts. I hope the People with you will not be too much dejected at the Loss. Burgoine is a wild Man, and will rush into some inconsiderate Measures, which will put him in our Power, but if not, his Career will be stopped.

The Loss of so many Stores is more provoking than that of the Post.

Before this reaches you, I hope you will be happy in the Embraces of a little female Beauty. God bless her. Pray let me continue to hear from you, every Week. When you cant write, make some other Pen do the Duty.

We have had here a few hot days, when Fahrenheits Mercury was at 88, but the Weather has in general been very cool. Such a July was scarcely ever known, which is a fortunate Circumstance for the Health of our Army.

We have The four Months of August, September, October and November, before Us, for the Armies to Act in. There is Time enough to do a great deal of Business. I hope, that the Enemy will not do so much Mischief as last Year, altho their Exploits then have not done them much Good, nor the united States as a Community, much harm.

The Examples of Meigs, and Barton, will be followed I hope, by Numbers. The Sub[t]lety, the Ingenuity, the Activity, the Bravery, the Prudence, with which those Excursions were conducted, are greatly and justly admired.

Connecticutt has the Honour of one, Rhode Island of the other. Will Mass. be outdone?

RC (MHi). Adams, *Family Correspondence* (Butterfield), 2:285–86.
¹ For the exploits of Cols. William Barton of Rhode Island and Return Jonathan Meigs of Connecticut, see John Hancock's letters to Barton and Meigs, July 26, 1777.

Cornelius Harnett to William Wilkinson

Dear Sir¹   Philadelphia July 20. 1777
   I was Inoculated at Port Tobacco & had the Disorder very favourably. My Arm Continues very Sore & inflamed indeed so bad that I can not wear a Coat, & has prevented my Attending Congress tho' I arrived here the 18th. Inclosed is a Letter for Mrs. Harnett² which I must beg the favour of you to have well smoked with Brimstone as she is very fearful of the small Pox. I put all my Letters in the Sun for an hour before I seal them and am very Certain the infection can not be conveyed in a letter so far but it is best to be Cautious. All kinds of goods are selling here at the most extravagant prices. I shall send you the Prices Current in my next. I am afraid you are fooling away your rum, Whiskey was selling at Tarborough as I passed through at 20/ per Gall by the barrell. I hope you will make the most of the rum on hand, I cant buy a Linnen Jacket & breeches under £10 this Currency, Bro Cloth 9 & £10 per yd, a Common Dinner & Club if you drink any wine 20/. I hope you have managed to exchange the [Co's.?] money in hand for Continental Currency as Mr. Clayton offered to have it done for us. Remember me to all friends. I shall write Cap Forster & Mr. Quince very soon. The Lottery will be drawn soon. For News I refer you to the Paper inclosed. I sent the Numbers of the Tickets³ purchased by me for sundry persons. On the Other side You have them again lest my Letters should not have come to hand. You will please make them known to the Concerned. I shall write you more fully in my next. I am, Dr Sir, Your sincr friend & hu Sert,
                                                          Cornl Harnett

Tickets purchased for Mr. Day
No. 18m918 (10 in all)
    18m919
    18m920
    18m921
    18m922   For Quince & Co. 5 Tickets, Viz
    18m923   Richd. Quince   No. 19m786
    18m924   Corns. Harnett   19m787
    18m925   Willm. Wilkinson   19m788
    18m926   Forster & Brice   19m789
    18m927   Thos. Craike   19m790

1 Ticket Mr. Erasms. Hanson
No. 19m783

2 Tickets for Majr. Caleb Grainger
No. 19m784
   19m785

Cap Forsters 2 Tickets on his own private Account delivered by him to me, Viz
No. 18m973 and No. 18m990.

I had it not in my Power to procure any other Paper but the Evening Post.

RC (NcU).
¹ William Wilkinson and Harnett were partners in a mercantile firm in Wilmington, N.C. David T. Morgan, "Cornelius Harnett: Revolutionary Leader and Delegate to the Continental Congress," *North Carolina Historical Review* 44 (July 1972): 239–40.
² Not found.
³ Continental lottery tickets.

John Adams to Abigail Adams

My best Friend   Philadelphia July 21. 1777
   I have long sought for a compleat History of the Revolution in the low Countries, when the Seven united Provinces seperated from the Kingdom of Spain, but without the Success that I wished, untill a few days ago.
   Sir William Temples Account is elegant and entertaining, but very brief and general.¹
   Puffendorfs, I have not yet seen. Grotius's I have seen, and read in Part, but it is in Latin, and I had it not in my Possession long enough, to make myself master of the whole.
   A few days ago, I heard for the first Time, of an History of the Wars in Flanders, written in Italian by Cardinal Bentivoglio, and translated into English by the Earl of Monmouth. The Cardinal was a Spaniard and a Tory, and his History has about as much Candor towards the Flemish and their Leaders as Clarendon has towards Pym and Hampden, and Cromwell. The Book is in Folio, and is embellished with a Map of the Country and with the Portraits of about Thirty of the Principal Characters.
   Mr. Ingersol, who lent me the Book, told me, that in the Year 1765 or 6, being in England, he was invited together with Dr. Franklin to spend a Week in the Country with a Mr. Steel a Gentleman of Fortune, at present an eloquent Speaker in the Society of Arts, descended from Sir Richard Steel.² Upon that Visit Mr. Steel told them that the

Quarrell which was now begun by the Stamp Act would never be reconciled, but would terminate in a Separation between the two Countries. Ingersol was surprized at the Prædiction and asked why and how? I cant tell you how says he, but if you want to know why, when you return to London, enquire at the Booksellers for Bentivoglios History of the Wars in Flanders, read it through, and you will be convinced that such Quarrells cannot be made up.

He bought the Book accordingly and has now lent it to me. It is very similar to the American Quarrell in the Rise and Progress, and will be so in the Conclusion.

RC (MHi). Adams, *Family Correspondence* (Butterfield), 2:286-87.

[1] For citations to this work and to editions of works mentioned below which were a part of Adams' personal library, see ibid., p. 287, nn.1–4.

[2] Joshua Steele (1700–91), a member of the Irish gentry and friend and correspondent of Benjamin Franklin. *DNB.*

James Lovell to William Whipple

Dear Sir,   Philadelphia July 21st 1777

I shall only acknowledge the receipt of your pleasing favor of the 8th and enclose you a newspaper. I am not at leisure, and scarcely in a temper, to make reflexions upon the vile situation of our affairs at the Northward, which before this reaches you will be the main topic of conversation. Believe me this is the first day that we have had any thing from St Clair. We had a line from Schuyler of the 9th, a scrawl without head or tail, and an artful one of the 14th rec'd this day.[1] Busy as we are this matter must be searched to the bottom. A most uncommon composure has appeared in Jemmy Du—— and his colleague D.[2] Uncle Phil[3] is at Camp with Geary and Clyman [Clymer] to try to patch the Commissary's department, as the issuers will have their own price & customs.

An attempt will be made to throw the whole fault in the Northern Department upon the New England States, whose Delegates ought to be furnished with the exact quota of our troops sent forward prior to the disaster. Genl Folsom arriving yesterday may possibly give a true history of your part.[4]

I find by a line from Dr Gardner that he had not the pleasure of seeing you in Town. I wish Mr[s] L——[5] had been made happy by a second visit, though I might consequently have been a sufferer by your rogueries.

You will see I did not wait to hear of your being at Portsmouth before I took occasion to give you assurances of my esteem. I will not be backward to add proofs, whenever I think I can do it agreeably by furnishing you with any interesting intelligence.

By a letter from Col. Brigr Lee to day I have the hope of seeing him in August early.[6] We sent to get a full representation that we may if possible confederate. Har——n[7] obstinately pushed to lay it aside in indulgence to his State's want of a vote at present, Page being gone home. I called a hornet's nest about my ears by *soberly* asserting that Schuyler was beloved by the Eastern States, especially by the officers from thence, that he was the key to the Militia of Albany County, and that the Indians called him father. I asserted that I was told so six weeks ago by gentlemen of intelligence, veracity and honor. The ungrateful curs said I was *satirizing* and Middleton joined them.

Tr (DLC).

[1] Philip Schuyler's and Arthur St. Clair's letters of July 14, "with a copy of the proceedings of a council of war for evacuating Ticonderoga and Mount Independence," were read in Congress this day. *JCC,* 8:569.

[2] That is, James Duane and William Duer.

[3] Philip Livingston.

[4] Nathaniel Folsom took his seat as a New Hampshire delegate in Congress this day. *JCC,* 8:568.

[5] Lovell's wife Mary.

[6] Undoubtedly a reference to Richard Henry Lee, who resumed his seat in Congress on August 12, 1777. See *JCC,* 8:631; and Lovell to Lee, July 22, 1777.

[7] Benjamin Harrison.

Charles Thomson to George Washington

Dear Sir,   Summerville, July 21. 1777

Having lately met with an Ordinance of the King of France, passed last December, for establishing the corps of engineers I made a hasty translation of it, from which I apprehend some useful hints may be taken for establishing such a corps in this country. And as I know of no better hands into which it may be put for this purpose, I have taken the liberty to send you a copy.[1]

You are doubtless informed of the four engineers sent over by Doct. Franklin & Mr Deane, three of whom are arrived & taken into the service of the continent, the first as colonel, the second as lieutenant colonel & the third as major of engineers.[2] What probability there is of their being men of experience you will see by the enclosed ordinance and the rank they held in the royal corps of engineers. Whether their being taken into the service as Colonel &c of engineers will give them rank of those heretofore engaged simply as engineers with similar ranks will I presume be left to your determination agreeably to the r[ules] of the army.

I congratulate you on the capture of [genl] Prescot, & hope soon to hear of the release [of] genl Lee. The haughty instrument of tyranny will I trust abate his insolence, at least [to ad]mit the propriety of *now* insisting on genl Lee's release *"when you have an officer of equal rank to offer in exchange."* Though I must confess, I should be very glad before any exchange even now took place, that a cartel was settled on such plain and equal principles as to remove all grounds of cavil. The board of war have had the cartel, settled between the French & English in the year 1759, lately reprinted, which you have undoubtedly seen.

I cannot forbear thinking that the posts held in the army ought to be attended as much if not more than nominal rank. Without this our enemy will have greatly the advantage. Their general officers have all regiments, so that there are but few colonels. Ought not therefore lieut colonels or even majors when they command regiments to be estimated as colonels.[3]

But I am transgressing my line and I fear trespassing on your time.

I am, Sir, Your obedient humble Servt.   Chas Thomson

RC (MH–H).

[1] Thomson's enclosure has not been found, but it was undoubtedly extracted from the "Ordonnance concernant le corps royal du génie et le service des places" of December 31, 1776, for which see *Recueil général des Anciennes Lois Françaises, depuis l'an 420 jusq' à la révolution de 1789,* 29 vols. (Paris: Plon Frères, 1821-33), 24:295–323.

[2] See Samuel Adams to Richard Henry Lee, June 29, 1777, note 2.

[3] For Washington's July 28 response to this letter, which is erroneously identified as a letter to James Lovell, see Washington, *Writings* (Fitzpatrick), 8:488–89.

Samuel Adams to Richard Henry Lee

My dear sir   Philada July 22 1777

Your very acceptable Letter of the 12th came to my hand yesterday. The Confederation is most certainly an important Object, and ought to be attended to & finishd speedily.[1] I moved the other Day and urged that it might then be brought on; but your Colleague Col H[2] opposed and prevented it, Virginia not being represented. It is put off till you shall arrive; you see therefore the Necessity of your hastening to Congress.[3]

We have still further & still confused Accounts from the Northward. Schuylers Letters are rueful indeed! even to a great Degree and with such an awkward Mixture as would excite one to laugh in the Midst of Calamity. He seems to contemplate his own Happiness in not having had much or indeed any Hand in the unhappy Disaster. He throws Blame on St Clare in his Letter of July 9th. "What adds to my Distress is that a Report prevails that I had given orders for the Evacuation of Tyonderoga, whereas not the most distant Hint of any such Intention

can be drawn from any of my Letters to General Sinclare or any
other Person whatever." He adds "What could induce the General
Officers to a step that has ruind our Affairs in that Quarter, God only
knows." And indeed Sinclares own Letter of the 30th of June dated
at Ty. would induce one to be of the same opinion, for he there says
"My People are in the best Disposition possible and I have no Doubt
about giving a good Account of the Enemy should they think proper
to attack us." Other Parts of his Letter are written in the same spirited
Stile. The General officers blame N E for not furnishing their Quota
of Troops. It is natural for Parties to shift the Fault from one to the
other; and your Friend General Steven, who seems desirous of clearing
his Countryman from all Blame, in a Letter to your Brother says "Eight
thousand Men were thought adequate to the Purpose. They (N E)
furnishd about three thousand, for Want of the Quota the Place is lost
& they stand answerable for the consequences." The General forgets
that five of the ten Regiments orderd from Mass. Bay were countermanded and are now at Peeks Kill. I will give you an Abstract of the
Forces at Ty & Mount Independence the 25th of June taken from the
Mustermaster General Colo Varicks Return.

Fit for Duty of the 9 Continental Regiments Commissiond & Noncommissiond & Staff Officers included	2738
Colo Wellss & Leonards Regiments of Militia [their time expired the 6th of July]	637
Colo Longs Regimt of Militia [engagd to 1st of Augt]	199
Major Stephens Corps of Artillery	151
5 Companies of Artificers	178
Whitcombs, Aldrichs & Lees Rangers	70
	3973
Men at Out Posts not included in the Above	218
Sick in Camp and Barracks	342
	4533

Besides a Number of Recruits belonging to the Continental Regiments
arrivd at Ty. between the 18th & 29th of June, that are not included in
the above Abstract, General Schuyler in his Letter of the 9th of July
says, "I am informd *from undoubted Authority* that the Garrison was
reinforced with twelve Hundred Men *at least,* two days before the
Evacuation." When the Commander in chief writes in so positive Terms,
one would presume upon his certain knowledge of Facts; *but as he was
not present with his Army,* let us suppose (though it does not seem
probable by the general gloomy Cast of his Letters) that he has over-
rated the Numbers, and set down 967 and it would complete the
Number of 5500. Deduct the sick 342, and I am willing also to deduct
the two "licentious and disorderly" Regiments from Massachusetts who
left Sinclare, though he acknowledges they kept with him two days upon

the March, and there remaind near five thousand. Mentioning this yesterday in a publick Assembly, I was referrd to the Generals Information to his Council of War, who says "the whole of our Force consisted of two thousand & Eighty nine effective Rank & file." But allowing this to be the Case, Is an Army the worse for having more than one half of its Combatants Officers?

Notwithstanding Nothing is said of it in the publick Letters Genl Sinclair writes to his private Friend that the Enemy came up with the Rear of the retreating Army, & a hot Engagement ensued, other Accounts say that many were killed on both sides, that our Troops beat off the Enemy & that Colo Francis of the Massachusetts & some of his officers were among the slain.[4]

I shall not write you any more Letters for I hope to see you soon. Adieu my Friend. SA

FC (NN).

[1] In his July 12 letter to Adams, Lee had expressed particular concern for forming a confederation, the work of the commissioners in Europe, and the instructions to his brother, William, as commissioner to Prussia and Vienna. "A proper attention being paid to the means of rendering this Campaign successful," Lee explained, "the next great object is certainly the *Confederation*. This great bond of Union, will more effectually than any thing else, produce present strength, credit, and success; and secure future peace and safety. Nor can any human plan more conclusively establish American Independence. I incline to think that this last effect of Confederation is clearly discerned by the friends of Dependence, because it is obvious, that those generally, who were marked foes to the declaration of independence are the men that now thwart and delay Confederation, altho they are obliged to act with more reserve and cautious concealment of their true motives. These considerations should urge the friends of America to a firm and persevering union, to finish this all important business quickly as possible. Let the days appointed for this purpose be *devoted* to that alone, and let the Green Mountain, and its Boys too, be sunk in the red Sea, rather than be the occasion of calling you off from the accomplishment of this momentous, and greatest of all earthly considerations. But what occasion can there be my friend, for such an infinity of criticism and care, about that, which is to undergo revision by our Masters before it becomes authentic? I grant it should be well considered, and digested with judgement; but such excessive refinement, and pedantic affectation of discerning future ills in necessary, innocent, and indeed proper establishments, I cannot hear with patience.

Hitherto Congress has been greatly wanting in not giving quick intelligence to their Commissioners in Europe of events here. You know how heavily they, and our other friends, have complained of this neglect. If the proper Committee does it not, I think Congress should take measures therein. The late movements of Gen. Howe and their consequences, appear to me sufficiently important to be notified immediately. Slow moving France may have its pace quickned by shewing the weakness of G.B., and removing from her yet smarting apprehensions, the dread of British power. If Howe has been obliged to change his situation from Continental to Insular, it will be a striking proof of this weakness. My friend Mr. Lovell informs me that these words are to be inserted in the latter Commissions, 'agreeable to instructions now *and hereafter to be sent.*' I am utterly at a loss to know what good can result from this insertion. Are the instructions to be publickly produced, or is any business to be done? The former is without example, and the latter is fraught with most pernicious consequences. Indicision, doubt, and perhaps fraudulent intentions may be charged upon such a mode of procedure; nor can I think that any sensible Man will be found to undertake a business, that must necessarily expose him to contempt, if not to worse consequences. I incline to think that if you wish to have this business done with propriety and effect, it will be better to agree on a P——n Agent, and one for Vi——na—less exposed to the envy & hatred of a certain sett than your friend the A—-d—r—. I hope to be with you early in August." Lee's letter is in the Samuel Adams Papers, NN, and Lee, *Letters* (Ballagh), 1:307–9.

  [2] Benjamin Harrison.

  [3] On August 16, four days after Richard Henry Lee returned to his seat, Congress resolved to take up the Articles of Confederation on August 18. But there is no evidence in the journals that Congress formally resumed debate on them before October 7, 1777. *JCC*, 8:631, 648, 776, 779–82.

  [4] In a letter directed to James Warren, Adams this day repeated most of the information pertaining to Ticonderoga that he discussed here with Lee. See *Warren-Adams Letters*, 1:343.

Thomas Burke to Richard Caswell

D Sir   Philadelphia July 22d. 1777

I waited some time for the Inteligence from Ticonderoga which you will find in the inclosed paper, and I declined writing until I could give you particulars because I did not chuse to put you on disagreeable Speculation.

Many of us have long expected that Ticonderoga would be evacuated at the Approach of an Enemy because we had no hopes of having a force there competent to its defense. We have mistaken much, in my Opinion, our Line of conduct in these matters. We have relied too much on Fortifications without sufficient force or discipline to defend them. Our Troops in general make no resistance when they are cooped up within Lines and assailed on all sides, and experience has Convinced the World that even Veteran Troops prove unequal to such a Trial. To wait firm and determined to Sustain the Shock of an Enemy charging from all sides is an Effort of Fortitude that very few armies have ever been found equal to, and it Seems to me not very wise to expect it in our raw and undisciplined Armies. Our own Experience too is Sufficient to Instruct us in avoiding this kind of battle, for therein the Enemy is always superior to us and in desultary war we are always superior to them. We shall now dispute the Country with the Enemy, and I hope with more Success than we defend fortifications.

General How is still inactive at New York and Staten Island, and General Washington with a superior army is ready to oppose him whichever way he moves.

Mr Harnett arrived here on Friday night last but has not yet been able to go into Congress. I shall use the permission you are pleased to give me of returning home, as soon as I can do it without danger of Injury to public Service.

I shall at present trouble you with nothing more but to wish you all possible Happiness.

I have the honor to be, Your most Obdt. hum Serv, Tho Burke

[*P.S.*] Captn Caswell is with his regiment at Trenton; I have not heard from him Since his Departure from this City.

RC (NcU).

James Lovell to Richard Henry Lee

Dear sir   Philada. July 22d. 1777

The honour you did me at Chantilly the 12th came yesterday to my knowledge. Your just reflections served to recall a chagrin which I had sensibly felt at the time of debating the Commissions refered to.[1] Those, like the Confederation, are martyred to the change in Delegation which takes place between the periods of second and third distant discussions upon the same point. The obstinate Vanity of N[or]th C[arolina] and the persevering Design of N.Y. have been reinforced by the ill timed Bodings & Frosty Caution of C[onnecticu]t.

I will not say much upon the Events in the northern department. Your well founded prophesies six weeks ago will have tended to blount the edge of this cutting misfortune.

As Mr. Adams & your worthy Brother will have the opportunity of getting minute facts from papers at the board of war, I presume their letters at this time will be lengthy.

I find the N England States are to be pointed out as the sole cause of the retreat from Ty.

I shall put my Friends in Boston upon a thorough scrutiny for their own honour. Though Genl. Stevens makes a number of very alleviating remarks to your *Brother* as to the Consequences of this Loss, yet he is full as to the Cause of it against *my* Country.

"That Post was esteemed of interesting consequence to the States of *N. England.* It was, therefore, given in charge to *their* troops. *8,000* were thought *adequate* to the purpose, *they* furnished about *3,000.* For *want of the Quota* the place is lost, and, if the war is protracted by it, *they* stand answerable for the consequences."

It is a curious way of estimating the strength of a Garison to omit counting the Officers for any thing; and it is also droll to think that militia would go away when a fort was surrounded on every side, probably because their time expired during the Seige. But such Curosities as these are visable in the Letters & returns.

I shall hope to have the pleasure of seing you here sooner than you intended when you favoured me, as before acknowledged.

Affectionate & respectful Compliments to your Lady from, Your obliged humb. Servt.   James Lovell

RC (ViU).

[1] In his July 12 letter to Samuel Adams, Lee had alluded to Lovell's role in the debate over the commission and instructions for American agents abroad, among whom were Richard Henry's brothers Arthur and William. See Samuel Adams to Richard Henry Lee, this date, note 1.

Robert Morris to Jonathan Hudson

Sir   Philada. July 22d. 1777

I have yours of the 19th whereby observe you are acquainted with what has passed in Virginia respecting the Salt and I shall not enlarge on that Subject,[1] & as you intend this way with the Goods ordered to the Head of Elk I shall have the pleasure of seeing you & need not take up your or my time on that Article. If Capt Wilson you mention is in the Continental service & has Acted the part you mention it may be in my power to make him but then I must be well ascertained of the man & of his Conduct. I cannot say any thing about the Cable you mention; indeed I thought you had made the needfull enquiries on that Score when here. You shou'd not write to me in private letters on any Public business you want done, but address the Marine Committee respecting the Brigt you are building & her Captain for I cannot attend to it. I will render Mr. Barney the service you desire if I can.

I am Sir, Your Obedt hble servt,   Robt Morris

[P.S.] Pork[2] from £14 to £15 per bbl.

RC (OClWHi). Addressed: "To Mr. Jona. Hudson, Mercht. at Baltimore."

[1] Hudson's July 19 letter to Morris "Respecting the Mob taking our Salt" is in the Robert Morris Papers, DLC.

[2] Remainder of postscript added in a clerical hand. Hudson had asked Morris for advice on the price of pork.

William Williams to Mary Williams

My dear Love   Philadelphia 22d July 1777, in the morning

I received yours of the 26 June by Brown. It gave me not a little Satisfaction to hear of your Welfare, that of our dear Children & Connections. God grant this may find you all in health & safety. It was impossible for me to write you; my right arm which you know has been affected with the Rheumatism has been tenfold worse than ever, the pain at first fell suddenly into my wrist, sweld & became exceedingly painful, & after some Time returnd back to my Elbow & was worse than before & my whole arm was inexpressibly sore & painful from my Shoulder to my hand so that I cod not dress, undress nor sleep for some time, but by the mercy of God, & his blessing, it is much better but not perfectly well, & I fear it may return. Am able to write, tho have nothing very material to say. We are at present in the same Lodgings which Col Dyer used when He was formerly here, tho not occupied by the same Family. The House swarms with French men, part of the seventy odd Mr Dean has sent over &c tho we have very little to do with them save at Breakfast Time, we keep our Chambers pretty much & are Company for Selves, tho Mr Law is obligd to sleep in a lower bedroom, & at suppers. I have nothing to do & we dine by our Selves, abt 4 or 5 oClock. The swearing & Wickedness that abounds in this City is truly shocking to chaste Ears & alarming in a moral View, the Judgments of God don't seem to have any Effect, unless the most awful one, of rendering us worse. I tremble to think so, but I really fear it is true, will he that made us, shew mercy to such a People? His Mercy is boundless, & infinite. I will yet hope in it nor Limit the Holy one of Israel. O, that Wickedness was confined to this City. Alass I fear 'tis as great in N. England & thro the Country. When I was here last Summer & heard of the Defeats at N York, the Northward &c I thot it was impossible but it shod alarm our Countrymen & awaken them to turn to him that smote Them but I found it far otherwise. Alass, the Chastisements of his Providence will have good Effect without the inward teaching of his Spirit, but God is pleased to withhold those Influences, the most sore & distressing of all Calamities. O, that every Soul who has an Interest in Heaven wod cry day & night with ceaseless & unfailing ardor, that God wod pour out his blessed Spirit to awaken & bring the Country to Repentance. Too few I fear think of the infinite importance of that Blessing even without any regard to our present Calamities. But what can I say or Do. God will work as pleaseth Him.

Among the other Sins that prevail here extortion & oppression is not the least, & it is by the wicked Arts of our internal Enemys here brot to such a pass, tis hardly possible to tell the price of their Shop Goods. There are many Goods here & yet They keep the Prices at the most extravagent sums. I believe Linnens I used to sell at abt 2/ are 20/ & more, Tea £8, the pound, dirty base brown Sugar 5/ & more, Loaf 10/, rum 45/ the lowest the Gallon, Molasses, my drink with Water 6/ a quart, butter in market 5/ & 6/ the pound, beaf 2/6 & every thing in proportion, & daily rising, & will rise, unless our affairs in infinite mercy shod take another turn. I believe tis not best to mention these things lest it shod still add to our own distresses of the same kind, but be very careful of what little stores We have. It will be too late or I shod ask you to be careful of rum to Mowers &c. Surely They shod be content with very little &c.

I regret my absence & long to be with my dear Wife, Children & Friends, but there is no peace there, & I must stand in my Lot & wait the Will of God, & his appointed Time. If He shall ever bring me home again in Peace, I hope I shall not forget Jacobs Vow. May God be gracious to you & the dear Children, little do They know what I feel for Them. I wish to hear from you of every thing even the least Incidents. The last We heard from the army They were at Clove, abt 12 or more miles from Morris Town toward Peekskill, to be as ready as They can to move up the river or to this Place as the designs of the Enemy shod appear. It is very uncertain whether they do not intend to have this City, & many things look much like it. If They shod I hope We shall find a place of Safety, & that it will prove a trap & Snare to them & trust it will. It is very surprizing We hear no more from Schuyler. Have nothing but the confused Acco. That Ty. is gone & all the Stores &c &c. I dare say your Father[1] has better Intelligence. This is another sad Token of Gods anger but We dont lay it to heart. It is reported that a large reinforcement is arrived at N. York but we have not the certainty.

(Afternoon)

O sad, it this moment comes to my mind I have got no Cap for Sally & Timithy. The Times are such I think little of such things. If I can will send them but fear I shant have a Chance to obtain them.

May God have mercy on & spare you & all my dear Friends, remember me tenderly to them all. With strong Affection I am tenderly yours,

W. Williams

RC (CSmH).
[1] Gov. Jonathan Trumbull.

Board of War to George Washington

Sir,   War Office July 23d 1777

As no precise Account had ever been transmitted of the Strength & Situation of the Division under General Putnam I had it in Direction to write to him for Returns of the Numbers of Men & the Situation of their Arms & Clothing, their Supplies & their Wants. I have the Honour of enclosing the Answer I received which is by no Means satisfactory to the Board who expected General Putnam would have complied with their Request altho' not in a separate Department, being too of Opinion that no regular Returns were made to your Excellency or they would have been transmitted to Congress. The Board have transmitted the enclosed Resolve of Congress to Genl. Putnam & again desired his Returns, but if there be more Propriety in their coming thro' your Hands, you will be pleased to give the necessary Orders concerning the Matter.[1]

General Knox informs me your Excellency has not received the Resolves of Congress relative to the Invalid Corps. I thought I had sent them. But least I should not have done it, I enclose them. Your Excellency will excuse their being sent in a News Paper as we are much hurried.[2]

I have the Honour to be, with the greatest Respect, your very obed Servt.   Richard Peters Secretary

[*P.S.*] Colonel Lewis Nicola is appointed to the Command of the Invalid Regiment.[3]

RC (DLC).

[1] Israel Putnam's July 16 letter to the board which was enclosed with this letter along with the July 19 resolve requesting his returns, is in Washington Papers, DLC. For Washington's response, see Washington, *Writings* (Fitzpatrick), 8:495.

[2] For the resolves respecting a corps of invalids of June 20 and July 16, the latter of which had been published in *Dunlap's Pennsylvania Packet* on July 22, see *JCC*, 8:485, 554–56.

[3] Three days later Peters sent Washington a brief letter pertaining to $200,000 "for the Use of the Northern Department." "But as the State of the Country is not certainly known," Peters explained, "it is thought safest to direct Robert Dinwiddie, who accompanies it, to call on your Excellency for Advice & if necessary Assistance. The Money is guarded by a Party under the Command of Lieut. ――― who it is supposed cannot proceed to Albany & therefore that your Excellency will furnish another Guard if you shall think proper." Washington Papers, DLC; and see *JCC*, 8:572.

James Lovell to George Washington

Sir,   Philadelphia 24th July [1777]
So long ago as Decr. 2d 1775 direction was given by Congress to the committee of secret correspondence to procure from Europe four good Engineers. This was not however accomplished till the 13th of last Febry., when the bearer the Chevalier du Portail, with Mr. La Radiere, Mr. Gouvion and one other Officer who is left sick in the West indies, was engaged by Doctor Franklin & Mr. Deane to come over to America.[1]

I beg your Excellency to observe well that these are the only Officers, of any species, who have been procured from abroad by express direction of Congress. And this I do because I am about to furnish you with several circumstances peculiarly within my knowledge relative to a point of equity well worthy of your Excellency's attention. The corps of Engineers is very honorable in France; and officers from it are sought by different European Powers. These Gentlemen who are come over into our service made an agreement with our Commissioners to rise one degree from the rank they held at home, upon a supposition that the practice of Europe had been regarded here. But, when they arrived, they found instances very different with respect to officers in all other corps. It was their mishap also to see a Major of artillery affecting to be exalted four ranks, as a Chief in his proper line and theirs also. They made a representation of these circumstances & appealed to the Equity of Congress. But, they had arrived at a time when the Infatuation of some here and the wild conduct of one abroad had rendered a spirit of reformation absolutely necessary as to the point of rank. The Ingenuous, however, must own that there is singular hardship in the case of these gentlemen. The only officers ever sent for by us—procured by the *real* political agents of Congress—coming out with the good wishes of the French Ministry—being of undoubted rank & ability in their profession, find themselves in the Dilemma of becoming the first examples of our new reforming Spirit, or else of going home during a Campaign, which their high sense of honor will not allow. But, tho' the Chevalier du Portail was not made a Brigadier, yet it appeared too gross to expose him to be directed in his peculiar line by such as will readily acknowledge his pretensions by regular education & discipline to be greatly superior to their own. His commission prevents this, and enables him so to distribute, in work, the others who came with him, as to prevent them, who have been within a few months as long in service as himself, from being interfered with by such as never belonged to the royal corps of Engineers in France or perhaps but a very short time to any other. Your Excellency cannot but wonder at the strange manner of wording the commission. I shall explain it with the greatest freedom. Mr. Du Coudray being employed as a good artillery officer to examine the arsenals in France to see what cannon &c could be spared from them acted with great Industry in that employment and much seeming regard to America. In the course of his transactions between the Ct. de St. Germain & Mr. Deane, he was not blind to perceive that he might take occasion to serve himself. Besides being paid for his trouble & Expenses in France he procured an agreement from Mr. Deane wch has already been shown to yr. Excellency, and has affected you, doubtless, with the same surprize & indignation which it has excited in others, almost without a single exception. I shall omit any remarks upon that treaty, or a long too-ingenious memorial presented to Congress with it, except such as are strictly connected with the occasion of this letter. Mr. Du C. having erected himself to the Command of Artillery *and* Engineers persuaded Mr. Dean that it will be impossible to get any from the *military* corps of Engineers now called *royal* because their Demands would be so exorbitant; and that it would be also unnecessary, because we ought not to build fortified Places in America to serve as secure Holds to our Enemy when once taken from us; and that therefore, a few *Bridge & Causeway-makers* would answer all the ends of military Engineers.

Such he brought with him; who were quite ready to fall under the command of an *artillery* direction; when not the lowest officer of the royal corps of Engineers would have submitted to such a novel pretension. It is needless to enquire whether it be true that Mr. Deane acknowledged he had been surprised into his uncouth compact. It is sufficient that Doctr. Franklin made an after one, which Mr. Deane also signed. Is not this in fact tantamount to a disavowal of the first treaty so far as relates to the orders of Congress? For, if those orders were fullfilled by the first, why was a second treaty made? The Agents show that there had been a deception; or that there had not been any attempt to follow the instructions of congress as to Engineers, in all the train attending Mr. Du C——. Another remark may not be impertinent here. As these four Engineers showed their treaty to the Count de St. Germain to whom they have also written from hence, it cannot be supposed that he would have permitted a Lt. Collo. of the royal corps of Engineers & two old Majors of the same to come over hither, to be under the immediate command of a young Major of Artillery. It is not to be conceived. From whence, I conclude that Mr. Du C—— never let his exorbitant & whimsical treaty be known to that Minister of the War-Department, who must have been shocked at the confusion of corps in the principles of the contract. Excuse me, dear General, I will not again wander from the points which I said I would explain. Mr. DuC—— has given full scope to *his* species of Ingenuity here as in the Neighbourhood of Mr. Deane. I have been told that he has said, if he could not be employed himself he would bring it about that these others should not. This may be an absolute Falsehood. But, I will own it comes the nearest of any thing, which I can conceive of, to explain the delays which have taken place in regard to these Engineers, who ought to have been sent to your Excellency long ago. They have remained subject to the crucifying expences of this city, because their employment seemed to interfere with Mr. DuCoudray's Pretensions, tho' those very Pretensions had been rejected. Your Excellency would doubtless smile if you should ever hear that even a number of *Peasants* disputed 3 days about the difference between the consequences of a man's being Colonel in Chief, or First Colonel, or Colonel to take rank & Command of all heretofore appointed, or Colonel *Commandant* of Engineers. Would not a Brigadier or Major General of Engineers alike annul the supremacy of the differently worded commissions? Or rather, do not the 4 different modes give like command? I shall pass from rank to pay. These Gentlemen not only far from the prophesied exorbitancy in demand of rank, never received one shilling in France as Gratification tho' others who were *not sent for* received large sums and claim pay from their embarkation and even pensions for life. But Doctr. Franklin, supposing it would be less trouble to himself and more agreeable to the Engineer to see to their own passages, stipulated their pay from the 13th.

of Febry. As no Regulations have yet been made in regard to Cavalry or Engineers, these Gentlemen have received 5 months pay as Infantry; which will not refund the expense of their voyage. I am really uneasy when I find manly honourable Intentions do not meet with at least equal emoluments with artful suspicious tricking contractors. If these Officers do not walk to camp, it is not because they were furnished by the Board of war with horses upon my application for them. And yet the nature of their Profession demands a provission of this Kind. Are they suddenly to reconnoitre a Camp, a River, a Shoar, or a whole neighbouring country thro' which an army is to march, and to make the speediest returns to the Generals, on foot? I trust your Excellency when asking for Engineers had Ideas of something beyond what the sinister views of an ambitious foreigner has sought to inspire us with here; which is forming a causeway or cutting a ditch or planking a bridge. And I shall consequently rest satisfied that you will receive the Officers now presenting themselves to you, and secure to them such honours and emoluments as you shall find them to merit from their education & abilities *exemplified under your command.*

No one has been more backward then I in desiring to see foreigners in our service, to the slight of my countrymen. And, except Engineers, I could not admit the thought of our wanting any military strangers other than one or two veteran adjutants or Majors, who knew our language well, and could serve as instructors-at-large to our spirited and well attached young American Officers.

I wish these Engineers could speak English better than they do; but they can receive orders & give them in English, and will speedily learn to speak.

I hope your Excellency will not think amiss of the freedom I have taken at this time both as to the matter of my letter & the interruptive length of it. I do not write officially, as of the Committee on foreign Applications. In that capacity I have more than once communicated to you the proceedings of Congress in a stile which might lead you to misconjecture my individual opinion. I write as a Friend to my Country and the Reputation of it's Congress its Army & its Agents abroad. I write as being well acquainted with your Excellency, or, in other words, as thinking I know you. In short, I write because I had determined it to be my Duty so to write. *That* path once determined, I never ask myself whether there may not be a Lion in the way.

After the important kindnesses which your Excellency has done me, I so far forgive the late injury of your apologizing for a *short* answer written by one of your hurried family, as not to revenge myself, by intreating you to excuse my *rough uncopied* sheets to a violent headache.

Aliquando dormitat did not appear an unnatural charge against Homer. Nimium vigilat would have appeared so against Scipio or

Marlbrough, and yet I am led by you to think they might have given provocation for it.[2]

With truest vows for your prosperity, I am, Your Excellency's Obliged Friend & humble Servant, James Lovell

RC (DLC).

[1] See *JCC*, 3:400–401; Wharton, *Diplomatic Correspondence*, 2:269–70; and Samuel Adams to Richard Henry Lee, June 29, 1777, note 2.

[2] Lovell's meaning in juxtaposing the vigilance of Scipio or Marlborough with the occasional "nod" or lapse to which even Homer sometimes succumbed is obscure. The reference to Homer is derived from Horace *Ars Poetica* 359.

Charles Thomson's Notes of Debates

Report of the board of War *10 July*[1]   July 24. 1777

Mr. Harrison for it. 1. Because it will injure the enemy in their trade, in their connexions with the indians. in their fame. 2. It will benefit the states by supplies gained from it &c. 3. It will be agreeable to the Spaniards.

Mr. Duane agst. it. 1. Because we want men. 2. Money. 3. Cannot retain it, if we succeed.

Mr. Burk on the same side. Addit. reason. Too late to undertake it this ensuing fall & winter.

Mr. Duer for it. Answered the Objections.

Mr. Burk spoke again, said nothing new.

Mr. Wilson for it. Points out more at large the advantages of undertaking it. Much to be gained; tho' no attempts made agst. Mobille and Pensacola. The importance of the settlements on Mississippi & of taking post at Messhack.[2] What sort of men shd. be employed? 2 reg[iment]s & 400 militia. Great proba[bi]lity of succeeding; no great ill consequences, because of safe retreat

Mr. Clarke declares for it but wants farther time to consider. Mentions the many objections agst. it. The danger of delaying, on account of the rapid encrease of inhabitants.

Mr. Morris for it. States the force of the enemy at present not more than 300. Requires little advances of money to procure provisions or military stores. Explains the nature of the country. Now is the time. Danger of delay.

Mr. Duer spoke again. Another argumt. This country may be made to contribute greatly to the expence of the war.

Mr. Harrison spoke again. Enlarged on the reasons he first offered, obviated the objections.

Mr. Middleton moved to put of[f] the determination.

Mr. Duane seconded the motion to postpone & strengthened his first

Objection with this consideration that it cannot be undertaken without gold & silver.

Question put. Carried to postpone till to Morrow.[3]

MS (DLC). In the hand of Charles Thomson.

[1] This report consisted of two parts, the second of which was the subject of a resolve Congress had adopted on July 19. The first section of the report, which was the subject of debate on July 24 and 25, reads as follows: "That an Expedition be undertaken against Pensacola & Mobille in West Florida, to facilitate which, that Colonel George Morgan be sent to New Orleans with Power to negotiate with the Governor of that Place, and endeavour to gain his Interest & assistance in the Business; and, that One thousand Men will be necessary for this Service, & the Command of the Expedition be given to General Hand." For the board's report and supporting papers from George Morgan and Benedict Arnold, see PCC, item 147, 1:251–71.

The proposed West Florida expedition attracted considerable support at the outset, but the arguments of its critics, especially Henry Laurens, quickly eroded support for the plan. The journals indicate only that after debate of the report on July 25, its "farther consideration" was postponed and immediately thereafter Congress resolved "That a committee of five be appointed to take into consideration the state of Georgia." See JCC, 8:566–67, 578–79; and Henry Laurens' letters to Lachlan McIntosh and to John Rutledge, August 11 and 12, 1777.

Although Congress temporarily dropped consideration of an expedition against West Florida at this time, the idea was subsequently revived and implemented in the "raid" conducted by James Willing in the Natchez district on the Mississippi in 1778. See John Caughey, "Willing's Expedition down the Mississippi, 1778," Louisiana Historical Quarterly 15 (January 1932): 5–36; and Robert V. Haynes, "James Willing and the Planters of Natchez: The American Revolution Comes to the Southwest," Journal of Mississippi History 37 (February 1975): 1–40.

[2] Apparently Fort Massac, located near the mouth of the Tennessee River.

[3] See Charles Thomson's Notes of Debate, July 25, 1777.

Henry Laurens to John Lewis Gervais

Dear Sir[1]   Philadelphia 25 July 1777.

The inclosed News papers contain all the Public Intelligence known in this Place except that Genl. Washington was three days ago at a Place call'd Clove where he had march'd to watch the motions of the Enemy. The Sailing of the Fleet will put him also in motion, but in what Direction? is the important Question. Conjectures are as upon all such occasions various. Some look towards the Capes of Delaware and others say New England is to be attacked on all sides. Chesapeak Bay is talk'd of, and there are [those] who think Carolina or Georgia as likely to be an Object notwithstanding the Season of the Year, as any Place. Be that as it may, when so important an Armament is on the March I think every State shd be alarm'd and therefore I proposed yesterday morning to my Colleagues to send an express Messenger for that purpose to Charles Town but they were not of my opinion.

I catch this opportunity by mere accident, pray present my Compliments to the President, to Mr & Mrs Manigault, to Mrs Gervais and to every body you think proper. I arrived here the 20th. J. Laurens will begin his Journey to the Army this morning. J. Ball, his Man and my George were innoculated for Small Pox the 21st. Pray communicate this with my Respects to his Father and Brother. I shall in two or three days have another opportunity of assuring you &c.

I should have excepted of Public Intelligence that our Fleet of Zebeques and Galleys lie ready in the River for a concerted Expedition below, upon which they wd have sail'd before this time but for an improper Demand of Increase of Wages made by the Lieutenants 12 in number. The Congress orderd them immediately to be dismiss'd the Service under a Resolution rendring them incapable of serving in any of the States in any Capacity, civil or Military. This Resolution produced humble Petitions from the whole. They are now reinstated and I suppose Business will go forward again.[2] A Combination of Sargeons in the fleet treated in the same manner.[3]

LB (ScHi).

[1] John Lewis Gervais (1741–95), a Huguenot who emigrated to South Carolina in 1764 and became a successful planter and merchant, had once been Laurens' business agent in the South Carolina backcountry and was now looking after some of the delegate's affairs during his term in Congress. Raymond Starr, ed., "Letters from John Lewis Gervais to Henry Laurens," *South Carolina Historical Magazine* 66 (January 1965): 15–17.

[2] On May 15 Congress had referred to the Marine Committee a petition from twelve Continental naval lieutenants asking for the same pay and allowance as Continental military captains. After waiting in vain for Congress to act on this petition, the officers informed Capt. John Barry on July 21 that they would not perform their naval duties until their grievances had been redressed. Upon learning of this news, Congress dismissed them from office on July 23 and sought to prevent them from engaging in any further state or Continental service. In the face of these harsh measures, however, the naval officers relented and therefore Congress restored them to duty on July 28, which was probably when Laurens added the foregoing paragraph to this letter. See *JCC,* 8:573–74, 578, 584; and PCC, item 42, 4:114–16, 146.

[3] Congress' only recorded action on naval surgeons in 1777 was a July 16 resolve raising their pay and subsistence to the same levels as those "of the lieutenants of the vessels to which they shall respectively serve." *JCC,* 8:554. This was hardly comparable to the treatment accorded the twelve naval lieutenants, and as it took place before Laurens arrived in Congress, perhaps he simply misunderstood its import.

Charles Thomson's Notes of Debates

Resumed the consideration of report.   July 25. 1777

Sergeant. Desires to know whether the country thro wch. the troops are to pass is healthy. Till he knows this cannot give his voice.

Chase. Desires to know to whom the country will belong, if it succeeds. Unless it is first determined that it is to belong to the united States generally, he will be agst. it.

Middleton. Against it. It will draw the attention of the enemy to the southern states, & endanger them, particularly S. Carolina.

Williams. Desires it may be postponed for a day or two till the enemy's intention is better known.

Sergeant. Against it. Because he thinks there is great w[eigh]t in the observation that it will turn the attention of the enemy agst. the S. States he thinks we shod. oppose the enemy here.

Duer. It will save the Southern States, & divert the enemy from immediately attacking them. It will save N Y & the middle states from the incursions of Indians

Laurens. 1000 or 1200 too few. Situation of the country much changed since 1771. The banks of the Mis. lined with inhabitants, many of them enemies to these states. Many have gone & are going from the U. S. who are enemies & discontented. We cannot keep it a secret, they will be ready to oppose our troops & there are sundry advantagious posts can be taken, where they & the regulars can oppose our passage. Besides two enemys to oppose not mentioned. 1. The Ague & fever 2. Choctaws. If we have troops to spare, They shd. be applied to defend Georgia, which is in a defenseless state and in wch. they have made inroads and carried off [. . .][1] tken 50. & The plan not well concerted. That part respecting frigates particularly. First we have no[2] frig. If we hd they[3] cd. be betr. employg. 1. Force inadequate. 2. The enemy have[4] more strength than we can oppose wth. 3. If we had force to spare they cd. be better employed. Has no objection to send person to N.O.[5] Thinks it wd. be proper & prudent.

Burke. Agst. it. We shd. bend our whole force agst. the enemy's army. Exp. & preparation will be great. We must set off wth full supplies of Arms, Amm. & provs. for 6 Mo. We cannot depend on the inhab. on the banks for provs. They have none to spare. They do not raise prov. (here Mr Morris beg leave to set him right in that matter. He has imported from thence cargoes of rice & exported from thence to the W.I. cargoes of indian Corn.) *B.* continues. This informa. does not satisfy him that they have *now* provisions to spare. But if they had we have not money to purchase it. Impracticable to keep poss. of the river. Ought to be given up, because disagreeable to southern states, who will not suffer that country to be possd. By Spain as it is necessary for their own safety.

Harrison. Answers the objection abt. it being divulged. The fever & Ague. All accts. agree the country on the Miss. healthy tho' Mobille unhealthy. Ind. cant become enemies by our going down. Want of money answered. Obj. abt. frig & Georgia answd.

Wilson. Draws an argumt. for undertaking it *now* from the Obj. that a number have gone & are going to settle there who are enemies or discontented with the governments of these states. We shd. get poss. of that country to prevent such from fixg themselves where they will undoubtedly be dangerous & troublesome even tho we shd. defeat the enemy here. The gaing. poss. will open a new trade, wch. the poss. of Aug.[6] will not & this can be secured tho Pensac. or Mob. are not attacked. As it must sometime be undertaken, as it can never be undert[ake]n at any future time with a greater probability of success than the present, he is for the present Exp.

Burke. The Argumt. of encrease of settlers not of w[eigh]t because they are freemen not slaves & however they may differ in sentimts. they retain & their posterity will in a higher degree retain a love of it. And hopes for a Union wth. the inhab. wch. will be better than a conquest.

Moved to postpone. Carried to postpone.

MS (DLC). A continuation of Thomson's Notes of Debates, July 24, 1777.
  [1] At this point Thomson resorted to a form of personal shorthand; approximately six characters undeciphered. See also notes 2, 3, and 4 below.
  [2] "Have no" deciphered from Thomson's shorthand.
  [3] "They" deciphered.
  [4] "Have" deciphered.
  [5] New Orleans.
  [6] St. Augustine.

John Adams to Abigail Adams

My dearest Friend   Philadelphia July 26. 1777 Saturday
  At this Moment, I hope you are abed and happy. I am anxious to hear, and the more so because I had no Letter, from you, nor concerning you by the last Post. I wait with Impatience for Monday Morning, when the Post is to arrive.

  I am more Anxious, now, than ever, on another Account. The Enemy's Fleet has sailed—But to what Place, they are destined, is unknown. Some conjecture Philadelphia, some Rhode Island, and some, that they mean only a Feint and intend soon to return to the North River. If they go to Rhode Island, I suppose they will not remain inactive there, which will throw you and your Neighbourhood into Distress.

  Poor, unhappy I! who have never an opportunity to share with my Family, their Distresses, nor to contribute in the least degree to relieve them! I suffer more in solitary silence, than I should if I were with them.

RC (MHi). Adams, *Family Correspondence* (Butterfield), 2:289.

Samuel Chase to Joseph Trumbull

Dear Sir,   Philadelphia. July 26th. 1777.[1]
Mr. Robert Cummins a Gentlemen of Maryland has involved himself
in a very considerable purchase of Cattle for the Supply of the army.
He is now afraid that he has given too great a Price, and wrote to Me
to advise him of the expected Demand, and what Price may be expected from the Commissary General. It is said here, that the whole
Army can be supplied with Beef from New England. I have a particular
Esteem for Mr. Cummins, and therefore take the Liberty to solicit your
advice to him, I am anxious for his Interest, and hope You will excuse
this trouble. I shall always be ready to render You any Service in my
Power, and am, Sir, Your Obedt. Servant,   Saml. Chase

RC (Ct).
   [1] The preceding day Chase wrote the following brief letter to "The Honorable
Caesar Rodney Esquire, near Dover, Delaware State." "About four Months ago
a Negro Man ran away from my Plantation, near Annapolis, in Company with a
Slave of Governor Johnson. I am informed they were seen a few Weeks ago at
the back of one John Potter's Plantation, Sussex County. My Negroe is
named Joe, Six foot high, deep black in Complexion, with remarkable thick
Legs, as if in the Dropsy. He reads well, and is very cunning. I am not acquainted
with Mr. Johnsons Fellow. As I am entirely unacquainted with any one in that
County, I beg the favor of You to employ some Person to make Search after
them. A Reward of £10 is advertised for each.
   "We have no News, but what You will see in the public Papers." Gratz Collection, PHi.

Nathaniel Folsom to Meshech Weare

Sir   Philadelphia July 26th. 1777
   I arrived here in good Health the 20th being stopt two days on the
Road by foul wather.[1] I Performed the journey in 12 Days. On my
joining the Congress I found them wourid with Petitions from a grate
Number of French gentlemen for commissions to serve in our army—to
be made generals & none less then colonels & that our agents in France
& General Washington in the camp were not less troubled with them.
   The first oppurtunity we had we presented the Petition of Mr. Phillbrook & that of our State to the Consideration of Congress which was
referred to the treasury board & this morning we arre to have a hearing before them. By what we Can learn from the Members & the
exhausted State of the Treasury, at this Time we despair of Success on
the Petition of the State, tho it seems to be the wish of Congress that
the same thing which is asked by us might be done with each of the
thirteen united States. However if we should fail now we Shall embrace

the first favourable oppurtunity to try them again & do every thing in our Power to accomplish so desirable an end.

I am not without hopes of obtaining a grant for Mr. Phillbrook as at Present I have heard no objection to it.[2]

The Loss of Ticonderoga considerably alarmed Congress as they were informed but a Little Time before by General St. Clair that it wase in a good State of defence. An Enquiry into that affair is thought necessary. By Intelligence from ouer Guards near New York, we learn that Lord & General Howe Sailed from that place with the most of the army on Wensday the 23d Inst., it is generaly thought fore Some part of New England. I am Sir, with the greatest Respect, yr. most obedt. huml. Servnt.   Nathel. Folsom

RC (MeHi).
[1] Folsom took his seat in Congress on Monday, July 21. *JCC,* 8:568.
[2] The petition of Joseph Philbrick was read in Congress on July 24 and referred to the Board of Treasury. *JCC,* 8:577; and PCC, item 42, 6:166. Philbrick's house had burned, consuming 538 Continental and 130 state dollars. The petition asked for the replacement of the money on the grounds that its destruction was equivalent to saving the treasury an equal sum. The New Hampshire government had already agreed to compensate Philbrick for the New Hampshire money. *N.H. State Papers,* 8:600.

John Hancock to William Barton

Sir,   Philada. July 26th. 1777.

It is with the greatest Pleasure I transmit the enclosed Resolve of Congress, expressing the Sense of that Body, on your successful and hazardous Enterprize agt. Genl. Prescot; and I must request you will be pleased to communicate to the Officers & Men under your Command this distinguished Mark of the Approbation of their Country.[1]

As an Acknowledgmt. of your Services on this Occasion, the Commissary General of Military Stores is ordered to present you with an elegant Sword in the Name and on Behalf of the United States of America.[2]

I am, Sir, your most obed Ser.   J.H. Presid.

LB (DNA: PCC, item 12A). Addressed: "Lieut Colo. Barton, Rhode Island Govt."
[1] On July 10 Lt. Col. William Barton of the Rhode Island militia led a small raiding party that seized Brig. Gen. Richard Prescott just outside Newport. Washington learned of this daring coup on the 16th and immediately conveyed the news to Congress. At the same time he decided to arrange an exchange of Prescott for Gen. Charles Lee, who, Americans feared, was about to be sent back to England and tried for treason. Congress subsequently approved Washington's decision, but not until April 1778 was he able to complete this exchange and secure Lee's release. See *JCC,* 8:565, 579–80, 9:1050–51; PCC, item

78, 20:129–30, item 152, 4:355–60; Washington, *Writings* (Fitzpatrick), 8:416, 419; Frederick Mackenzie, *Diary of Frederick Mackenzie,* 2 vols. (Cambridge: Harvard University Press, 1930), 1:150–51; and John R. Alden, *General Charles Lee: Traitor or Patriot?* (Baton Rouge: Louisiana State University Press, 1951), chap. 12. Alden cites no evidence for his assertion that Barton undertook this raid in order to exchange Prescott for Lee, and in fact this seems to be nothing more than the historian's conjecture. Washington's correspondence indicates that he originated the idea for this exchange.

   ² Here the LB contains the following deleted paragraph: "Altho the intrinsic Value of a Sword is not an object of Consideration, yet the Manner of acquiring it, may make it highly esteemable; for Nothing can be so proper for a free People to give, or more honorable for a brave Man to receive, than this unsolicited Testimony of his Bravery and good Conduct."

John Hancock to Return Jonathan Meigs

Sir,   Philada. July 26th. 1777
   I have the Pleasure to enclose you a Copy of a Resolution of Congress in which you will perceive they express their Sense of your Bravery & good Conduct on your late Expedition to Long-Island, and likewise of the Officers & Men under your Command; to whom I must request you will be pleased to communicate this distinguishing Mark of the Approbation of their Country.

   As an Acknowledgment of your Services on that Occasion, the Commissary General of Military Stores is ordered to present you with an elegant Sword on Behalf of the United States of America.¹

   I am, Sir, your most obed & very hble Serv.   J.H. Presid.

LB (DNA: PCC, item 12A).
   ¹ Lt. Col. Return Jonathan Meigs had led an expeditionary force from Connecticut to Sag Harbor, L.I., which on May 24 killed six British soldiers, captured ninety, and destroyed numerous boats and supplies. Washington informed Congress of this welcome news in a May 31 letter that the delegates referred to the Board of War on June 2. In response to a report from the board, Congress resolved on July 25 to thank Meigs and his men for their "prudence, activity, enterprize and valour" and to give Meigs "an elegant sword." See *JCC,* 8:409–10, 565, 579; and Washington, *Writings* (Fitzpatrick), 8:139–40, 143, 150–51, 158.

John Hancock to Thomas Mifflin

Sir,   Philada. July 26th. 1777
   I have it in Charge to transmit the enclosed Memorial from a Committee of the Trustees of the College of New Jersey, with the Resolve of Congress founded thereon; & to direct that you immediately give such Orders in the Matters therein mentioned as for the future may

prevent any just Cause of Complaint.[1] I have the Honour to be, with great Respect, Sir, Your most obedt & very hbl Sert.

J.H. Presid.

LB (DNA: PCC, item 12A).

[1] On July 15 three trustees of the College of New Jersey—Elihu Spencer, Richard Stockton, and John Witherspoon—signed a memorial to Congress protesting the use of Nassau Hall, the college's main building, as a barracks for Continental troops and asking for the appointment of a special quartermaster at the college to provide alternative housing for them. In response, Congress decided on July 19 to send a copy of this memorial to Quartermaster General Thomas Mifflin with a resolve directing him "to give such orders . . . as may, for the future, prevent any just cause of complaint." Whether or not Mifflin complied with this resolve is unknown, but shortly afterward Congress apparently considered the following resolve on this issue: "That a Person be elected at Princeton to act as an Occasional Quarter Master & Commissary for forage with Directions to hire empty houses & otherwise with the Assistance of the Magistrates to provide quarters for any troops that may be passing through that Place so that none may be suffered to quarter in the College unless one or more magistrates find it absolutely necessary and in that Case said quarter master shall take effectual Care that no Damage be done." This resolve, which is in the hand of Witherspoon, is located in PCC but is not recorded in the journals. At the foot of it Witherspoon listed two nominees for this office, and on August 6 Congress named one of them, John McComb of Princeton, to the post. See JCC, 8:566, 615–16; PCC, item 41, 7:5–7; and Varnum L. Collins, President Witherspoon: A Biography, 2 vols. (Princeton: Princeton University Press, 1925), 2:97–99. In 1779 the college collected $19,357 from Congress for damage done by Continental troops. Thomas J. Wertenbaker, Princeton 1746–1896 (Princeton: Princeton University Press, 1946), p. 63.

John Hancock to George Washington

Sir,   Philada. July 26th. 1777.

I have the Honour to transmit sundry Resolves of Congress[1] for your Information and Direction, to which I beg Leave to refer your Attention.

Lieutenant Colonels Meigs and Barton having distinguished themselves by their Enterprizes against the Enemy, the Congress, as an Acknowledgment of their Bravery and good Conduct, have ordered an elegant Sword to be presented to each of them.

The Congress having empowered you to appoint Mr. Robert Erskine (a very ingenious Gentleman) or any other Person you may think proper, Geographer and Surveyor of the Roads, you will be pleased to carry the Resolve into Execution agreeably to the Terms of it.[2]

Your several Favours to the 22d instant have been duly received and laid before Congress.

We have not yet heard any Thing of the British Fleet since it sailed from Sandy Hook.[3]

I have the Honour to be, with the greatest Respect, Sir, Your most obed. & very hble Sevt.   John Hancock Presidt.

11 O'Clock A.M. P.S. I have just received your Favour of the 25th. which shall be laid before Congress ⟨on *Monday with the Inclosures*⟩.[4]

RC (DLC). In the hand of Jacob Rush and signed by Hancock.

[1] In addition to those mentioned in the text of the letter, Hancock also sent Washington resolves of the 25th concerning army accounts and supplies. *JCC*, 8:580.

[2] See *JCC*, 8:580; and Washington, *Writings* (Fitzpatrick), 8:443, 495–96.

[3] Pursuant to Washington's expressed concern for intelligence about the location and intentions of the British fleet, the Board of War met with the Pennsylvania Council on July 24 to consult "on the means of procuring the earliest intelligence of the approach of the Enemies' Fleet on our Coast." See Washington, *Writings* (Fitzpatrick), 8:453–54; and *Pa. Council Minutes,* 11:251.

[4] This letter and enclosures are in PCC, item 152, 4:391–99, and Washington, *Writings* (Fitzpatrick), 8:470–73. See also *JCC*, 8:582.

James Lovell to Henry Knox

Dear Sir,   July 26th 1777, Philada.

I suppose you among others have been led, from my being Chairman of the Committee on foreign Applications, to dub me Patron of the whole Rank-mad Tribe. I am so far from thinking it proper to disavow that Title, under the present Circumstances of Things, that I rather confirm it by recommending to your notice the Bearer the Chevalr. Du Portail, or, D'erford,[1] as he chuses to be named. His Talents have such Relations to your Department that I could not refrain from thus announcing him to You, tho you have omitted to direct a private Line of friendly Correspondence to me on more [. . .] Occasions.

His manners will, I hope, prove agreable to you. More than 14 years in the royal Corps of Engineers. I think he must be an Acquisition to us in that Branch. I wish his Confidence in the Good Sense & Equity of the People of the United States may be more Use to *him* than the Cunning & Distrust of some of his Countrymen has proved to *them*. I doubt not it will as I have given an Explanation to our admirable General.

A happy Campaign, notwithstanding present appearances! We must not flinch even at plaguy *great* Trifles. Allow the Expression from Your Friend & h Sert.   James Lovell

RC (MHi).

[1] Lewis LeBegue Duportail (Chevalier Derford) was one of the authorized engineers contracted for by Benjamin Franklin and Silas Deane. Congress refused his request to be ranked higher than his contracted rank of colonel of engineers but on July 22 authorized him to "take rank and command of all engineers heretofore appointed." *JCC*, 8:539, 558–59, 571; and Lovell to Washington, July 24, 1777.

han the present. he is for ye propose ...

Burke. The regim. of e increase ... these things of w.ch because they ... free men & however they may ... differ in sentim.ts they retain ... their post & will in a higher de- gree retain a love of it. And hopes for a union &c the inhab. w.ch will be better than a conquest. — moved to postpone Carried to postpone. —

July 26. 1777

Mr. Serg. move to send G.G. to com. in the North.n departm. Mr. Rob.- reasons adduced. G.S. is unpopular milit. have not confid. in him. G. popular &

Harrison think the this is delicate ... Our affairs critical. However unpop. may be elsewhere always understood ... was very pop. in his own country & move him. you disoblige that whole country & risque the entire ... of it. Has no object.n to an inquiry into the cond. of senec.t - who ... if is on enquiry found in- volv.d has no object - But why remove

8663

one off. because another behav.d amiss or is unfortunate. ... J. Adm.s in fav.r of mot.n is for reas.ns adduced. Knows his pop. in last N. thinks he is pop in N.Y. grds. belf on advise of convn of N.Y.

Chase. ag.t it. It lost not thro fault of genls but for want men. En.d 7000 men but 2000 - not suff.to d find post. they not well arm.d. It wd disgr. officer with just found. disgr. congs, who lately send leh to y.r cmrs.

Wilson. seconds mot. for inqy oppose the other from motiv. policy justice&publ utility.

To arg. unpop. A man may be unpop. because virt.

Serg. support. his mot. spoke long- al. arg. ag.t pop. thos. drawn for justice policy. delicacy. paints the prf.t what adduc.d G.leh's letters in proof. A change can't hurt. it may do good.

Dyer. All not qualf. for all posts. thinks him endow.d o m.y val. qual.t but not disting. for milit.y abilities. he has not talents for govern.g an army & therefore unpop. It is no crime not to have talents. It is no support of a

Charles Thomson's Notes of Congressional Debates

Charles Thomson's Notes of Debates

July 26. 1777

Mr. Serg[eant][1] move to send G[eneral] G[ates] to Comd. in the Northn departmt. Seconded by Mr. Rob[erdea]u. Reasons adduced. G[eneral] S[chuyler] is unpopular. Milit. have not confid in him. G—— popular &

Harrison thinks this is delicate ground. Our Affrs. critical. However unpop. S. may be elsewhere, always understood he was very pop. in his own Country. Remove him, you disoblige that whole country & risque the entire loss of it. Has no objectn. to an inquiry into the cond. of Sinclair who lost Ti. If S is on enquiry found involved, has no object[ion.] But why remove one Off. because another behavd. amiss or is unfortunate.

S. Adams. In favr. of motn. with an amendmt. & for the reasns. adducd. Knows G. is pop. in Eastern st.[2] Thinks he is pop. in N Y. Grounds belief on adrss of Cnvn of N.Y.

Chase. Agst it. Ti. lost not thro fault of gnrls, but for want men. Enemy's 7000, Sinclair's but 2000—not suff. to dfnd post. These not well armd. It will disgr[ace] officers without just foundation. Disgr. Congr, who lately sent Sch to that commd.

Wilson. Seconds mot. for inqy. Opposes the other from motiv policy, justice & publ utility. To arg. unpop. A man may be unpop because virt.

Serg[eant]. Supports his mot. Spoke long. Ansr arg. agst pop. Those drawn from justice, policy, delicacy. Paints the prest. situation. Adduced G. Sch's letters in proof. A change cant hurt. It may do good.

Dyer. All not qualfd. for all posts. Thinks Sch. endowed of many val quals, but not distingd. for mility. abilities. He has not talents for governg. an army & therefore unpop. It is no crime not to have talents. It is no supposit. of a crime to remove one who is unfortunate, or unqualified. Pitt recalled many officers last war witht impeaching them. The quitting Ti. unpop. Smallness of gar[riso]n and numb. of Enemy not a suff. justification in opinn. of people. Abercromby with 16000 was defeated at same place by 3000. But suppose abil. & integry. & admit a genl. unfortun. it wd. be proper to change him.

Burke. Thot. this inconsid. motn. wd. not have been deemd worthy debate. Evy membr. must kno the Genls. have been guilty of no fault. It it fruitless to debate it farther. A majority of the house must see the impropriety of it & that no good & much ill must arise from it & therefore desires the question.

Folsom. 3 regemts. from N.H. well armed. Declares that from his Knowledge & he had great opport. to know Sch is not pop. with either off. or soldiers who served last year; nay what is worse, he hopes witht good grnds, they have not confidence in him.

Williams. Confirms the want of Sch pop. in Conn.: mentions the joy of the people on Gates appmt., their apprehensions when Sch came to Cong., their grief when replaced.

Marchant. This congr. depends upon the genl. Opin. of the people. Without attending to this we cannot support this cause. Has a grt. Opin. of the Judgmt. of the people. It is genly. pure, uncorrupt and well founded. Sch unpop in his State & the Neighbg. states This Opin. not lately taken upon. Strongly rivetted ever since last war. Mila. will not serve under him. The Enemy can only be opposed by the East. Mil[itia], hence the necessity of recallg. him & placing at the head of the Northn. a man in whom that Milia. can have confid.

Lovel. Is for.

Duer. An army of the enemy with Ind[ians] at Oswego the frontier of Tryon from whence great part of the mil. come. Ti an important frontr. on the other side given up. Three counties have revolted. A weak army ill provided, ill disciplined to defend him. A well appointed victorious army entered the State. Under these circumstances can it be supposed the Mil. wd. turn out. It is therefore owing to circumstances not to want of inf[luence] or popularity in Sch. With regrd to Indns. it is well known Success influences them.

Burke. Went into the conduct of Sch & G to each other & of Cong. towrds. them. Has no objectn. to inquiry, but to recalling them.

Clarke. For the motion with a small amendment.

J. Adams. Gave an accot. of the diff. in the northn. depart. & the steps taken to heal those diff. but without effect. As to his unpopularity, knows it to be great in the eastern States: thinks he is not so ⟨great⟩ popular as represented even in his own state. A late instance proves, when ⟨*he was out voted*⟩ another carried an election agst.[3] notwithstanding all the pains Cong have taken by res. to splice his chrctr. The evil genius of N[orthern] D[epartment].

Motion made & seconded to postpone. Question put. Carried in the affirmative.[4]

MS (DLC). In the hand of Charles Thomson.

[1] Jonathan Dickinson Sergeant's motion to replace Philip Schuyler with Horatio Gates, the latest episode in the protracted struggle between the supporters of the two generals in Congress, was occasioned by the news that Fort Ticonderoga had been evacuated on July 5–6. In the journals of Congress there is no mention of the debates of Saturday the 26th and Monday the 28th which Thomson's notes detail, but on the 29th Congress resolved "that an enquiry be made into the reasons of the evacuation of Ticonderoga and Mount Independence, and into the conduct of the general officers who were in the northern department at the time of the evacuation," and on the following day "That Major General St. Clair, who commanded at Ticonderoga and Mount Independence, be, and he is hereby directed forthwith to repair to head quarters." *JCC*, 8:585, 590.

See also Nathaniel Folsom to Meshech Weare, July 26; William Duer to Philip Schuyler, July 29; New York Delegates to the New York Council of Safety, July 29, 1777; and *JCC*, 8:727n.

2 "CM" appears here above the line, perhaps signifying that Gates was especially popular in Connecticut and Massachusetts.

3 A reference to Schuyler's defeat by George Clinton in New York's recent June 1777 gubernatorial election.

4 Continued July 28, 1777.

John Adams to John Quincy Adams

My dear Son   Philadelphia July 27. 1777

If it should be the Design of Providence that you should live to grow up, you will naturally feel a Curiosity to learn the History of the Causes which have produced the late Revolution of our Government. No Study in which you can engage will be more worthy of you.

It will become you to make yourself Master of all the considerable Characters, which have figured upon the Stage of civil, political or military Life. This you ought to do with the Utmost Candour, Benevolence and Impartiality, and if you should now and then meet with an Incident, which shall throw some Light upon your Fathers Character, I charge you to consider it with an Attention only to Truth.

It will also be an entertaining and instructive Amusement, to compare our American Revolution with others that Resemble it. The whole Period of English History, from the Accession of James the first, to the Accession of William the third, will deserve your most critical Attention.

The History of the Revolutions in Portugal, Sweeden and Rome by the Abbot de Vertot, is well worth your Reading.[1]

The Seperation of the Helvetic Confederacy from the Dominion of the House of Austria, is also an illustrious Event, that particularly resembles our American Struggle with Great Britain.

But above all others, I would recommend to your study, the History of the Flemish Confederacy, by which the seven united Provinces of the Netherlands, emancipated themselves from the Domination of Spain.

There are several good Histories of this great Revolution. Sir William Temples is short but elegant, and entertaining. Another Account of this Period was written by Puffendorf, and another by Grotius.

But the most full and compleat History, that I have seen, is one that I am now engaged in Reading. It is intituled "The History of the Wars of Flanders, written in Italian by that learned and famous Cardinal Bentivoglio, englished by the Right Honourable Henry Earl of Monmouth, the whole Work illustrated, with a Map of the seventeen Provinces and above twenty Figures of the chief Personages mentioned in the History."

Bentivoglio, like Clarendon, was a Courtier, and on the side of Monarchy and the Hierarchy. But Allowances must be made for that.

The first Cut is of Guido, S.R.E. Cardinalis Bentivolus.

2. The Emperor Charles the 5th. Prince of the low Countries.

3. Phillip the 2d. King of Spain, Prince of the low Countries.

4. William of Nassau, Prince of Orange.

5. Margarett Dutchesse of Parma and Piacenza, Daughter to Charles the 5th. Governesse of the low Countries.

6. Elizabeth Queen of England, France and Ireland.

7. Anthony Perenott Cardinal Granvel, Councillor of state to Margarett of Parma.

8. Peter Ernest Count Mansfeldt Governor of Luxemburg.

9. William Lodowic Count Nassau, Governor of Frisland.

10. John Lignius, Count Aremberg, Governor of Frisland, General at the Battle of Hilligal.

11. Ferdinand of Toledo Duke of Alva, Governor of the Low Countries.

12. Sancho Avila Governor of the Fort, at Antwerp, General at the Battle of Mooch.

13. Chiapino Vitelli Marquiss of Cetona, Camp Master General.

14. Robert Lord Dudley Earl of Leicester, Governor of the united Provinces.

15. Maximillian Hennin Count Bossu, Governor of Holland and Utrecht.

16. Lodovico Requesenes, Great Commandador of Castile, Governor of the Low Countries.

17. Phillip Croy Duke of Areschot, Knight of the golden Fleece, Governor of Flanders.

18. Don John of Austria, son to Charles 5th. Governor of the Low Countries.

19. Mathias, Archduke of Austria, Duke of Burgundy and Governor of the united Provinces.

20. Alexander Farnese, Prince of Parma, Governor of the low Countries.

21. Francis Hercules De Valois, Duke of Anjou, Alencon, Brabant and Protector of the Netherlands.

22. Phillip Count Holach, Baron of Langenberg, first General of the united Provinces.

23. Maurice of Nassau, Prince of Orange, Count Nassau, Governor of the united Provinces.

24. Adolphus Solm Count de Meurs, Governor of Gelderland and Utrecht.

There are three most memorable Seiges described in this History, those of Haerlem, Leyden, and Antwerp.

You will wonder, my dear son, at my writing to you at your tender Age, such dry Things as these: but if you keep this Letter you will in some future Period, thank your Father for writing it. I am my dear son, with the Utmost Affection to your Sister and Brothers as well as to you, your Father,   John Adams

RC (MHi). Adams, *Family Correspondence* (Butterfield), 2:289–91.
  [1] For citations to the editions of these works in the personal library of John Adams, see ibid., p. 292n.1.

John Adams to Abigail Adams

My dearest Friend   Philadelphia July 28. 1777
  Never in my whole Life, was my Heart affected with such Emotions and Sensations, as were this Day occasioned by your Letters of the 9, 10, 11, and 16 of July.[1] Devoutly do I return Thanks to God, whose kind Providence has preserved to me a Life that is dearer to me than all other Blessings in this World. Most fervently do I pray, for a Continuance of his Goodness in the compleat Restoration of my best Friend to perfect Health.
  Is it not unaccountable, that one should feel so strong an Affection for an Infant, that one has never seen, nor shall see? Yet I must confess to you, the Loss of this sweet little Girl, has most tenderly and sensibly affected me. I feel a Grief and Mortification, that is heightened tho it is not wholly occasioned, by my Sympathy with the Mother. My dear little Nabbys Tears are sweetly becoming her generous Tenderness and sensibility of Nature. They are Arguments too of her good sense and Discretion.

RC (MHi). Adams, *Family Correspondence* (Butterfield), 2:292.
  [1] On July 11, Abigail had given birth to a stillborn daughter. See ibid., p. 282.

Samuel Adams to Paul Revere

My dear sir   Philade July 28 1777
  I receiv'd your favor of the 26th of June and also one from Col Crafts of the same Date.[1] I wrote to him by the Return of the Post & desired him to communicate the Contents to you.[2] I conversd with Mr. J A upon the Subject of your Letter, and we venturd, both of us, to step out of the Line of strict order in a debate in Congress, the other day, to bring your Regiment of Artillery into View. It occasiond a Conversation in the House in which we had an opportunity of acquainting the Members of the long Standing of that Regiment & the Seniority of its Officers. But still it was considerd as a Regiment raisd by a State & not by the Continent. And though we caused the Merit of it to be well understood &

it was acknowledgd in the House the Difficulty of altering the Regulations you refer to appeard so evidently in the Minds of the gentlemen, that we waved making any Motion at that time, because we apprehended that the Issue would be unfavorable. Indeed I am of Opinion that Congress will not be induced to make the Alteration you wish for, until it shall become a Continental Regiment. In that Case, I am apt to think there would be no Difficulty with Regard to the Seniority of other Regiments which have been raisd since, over yours. But till that is done, it is feared that an Alteration in this Instance would cause Discontent in other States, where it is said there are Instances similar. A Regiment of Artillery rais'd in this State under Command of Colo Procter was lately taken into Continental Service and the Commissions were dated at the time they were raisd. It was upon this Occasion that Colo Craft's Regiment was mentiond; and I suppose that Regiment wd be admitted on the same terms.[3] But I think I foresee an insuperable Obstacle in that Case. If any thing can be done consistently with the general Service, to shew Honor, but especially to do Justice to the Regiment of Artillery in Boston, I shall not fail to push it as far as I may have Influence. My fellow Citizens well know that I have never been indifferent *to them*. I am thought here in a great Degree partial in their Favour. I have in particular a Predilection for that Regiment. But my Friend, let me intreat you and the Gentlemen of your Core, above all other feelings to cherish those of the virtuous Citizen. I will allow that the Ambition of the Soldier is laudable. At such a Crisis as this it is necessary. But may it not be indulgd to Excess! This War we hope will be of short Duration. We are contending not for Glory, but for the Liberty, Safety & Happiness of our Country. The Soldiers should not lose the Sentiments of the Patriot; and the Pride of military Rank as well as civil Promotion should for ever give way to the publick Good. Be assured that I am very cordially, your Friend

                                                              S A

FC (NN).

[1] Thomas Crafts, colonel of the Massachusetts artillery regiment, and Paul Revere, lieutenant colonel of the same regiment, wanted Congress to give militia officers on active duty equality in precedence of rank and command with Continental Army officers. Revere's letter to Samuel Adams is in the Adams Papers, NN, and Crafts' letter to John Adams is in the Adams Papers, MHi.

[2] Not found.

[3] This debate occurred on July 15 and 19, but Crafts' and Revere's regiment is not mentioned in the journals. *JCC,* 8:552, 564.

John Hancock to George Washington

Sir   In Congress, Philada July 28. 1777
This morning I laid before Congress your letter of the 25 with that

inclosed from Mr W Franklin & have the honour to enclose you the result of their deliberations thereon.[1]

Time will not admit my Enlarging farther than to inform you I have recd. your letter from Cross roads.[2]

I am, Sir, Your very hume Servt.   John Hancock Presidt

RC (CSmH). In the hand of Charles Thomson and signed by Hancock.

[1] These letters are in PCC, item 152, 4:381–88, and Washington, *Writings* (Fitzpatrick), 8:474. Congress rejected former New Jersey governor William Franklin's request to visit his sick wife in New York City because of his recent violation of his parole in Connecticut. See *JCC*, 8:583–84; and Hancock to Jonathan Trumbull, Sr., April 23, 1777, note 1.

[2] This was Washington's July 27 letter to President Hancock, only the postscript of which was written at "Cross Roads 16 Miles West of Morris Town." PCC, item 152, 4:401–3; and Washington, *Writings* (Fitzpatrick), 8:486–88.

Charles Thomson's Notes of Debates

[July 28, 1777.]

Monday question resumed.

Duane. Before this question is decided, all the reso. of Con[gress], the lettrs. from the Genls. should be read. Light wanted. A fault somewhere. Enq[uir]y shd. be made to see whether pt. of the fault is not here. Before any censure is passed on the genls it shod be preceded by a res. that Con have done everything that ou[gh]t to be done. This an unusual attack more alarmg as formed by a combination of 4 States. *Apprehends* arises from resentmt or private views.

S. Ad[ams.] Set memb. ri[gh]t with respect to combination. The 4 St. did not move it &c; he ⟨desired⟩ moved an Am[endmen]t.

Rob[erdea]u disclaimed combinations. Laments divisions. Has no view to injure any character. But thinks it necessary to recal the 2 off. but is willing it be done in the easiest manr & most agreeable to them & th[ei]r frds.

Williams. Disclaimed combinations. Believes the assertions of member from N.Y. that he is not influenced by resentmt or partial, private motives, & thinks he shd. give like credit to others. Declares he has no resentmt., no private views. Acknowledge 4 States have not conf[idence]. Thinks regard shd. be paid to their joint desire of a change in the Off[icers].

Gerry. Has not heard the argumts. but thinks it proper. Everything in disorder. Can only be put right by change. Gates has shewn what he can do. Collected shattered remains of army last year under every disadvantg. Reduced it to order. Repulsed the enemy.

Wilson. Against the motion. Thinks it unjust. Acknowledges fault somewhere. The genls., part[icularly] Sch. not to blame. Fault in East.

S[tates]. Attack of Quebec beging of misf. owing to the troops refusing to continue after time expired This common to troops of all the states. The sending 3 reg. from Cambridge opposed by Del. from East. states & troops ordered not sent forward in time, hence misfort. continued. The levies for this campn. not raised in time nor properly armed cause of present misf. The want of popularity an ill timed object[ion] agst Sch. Shod have been urged before he was last sent up.

Sergeant. Provoked at being accused of combing. Scorns the charge. Speaks & acts his own sentimts. Reit[erates] his object. ag. Sch. Enumerates complnts agst. him. Is interrupted by Duer, on mentiong Sch's keeping a store of goods at Alby. Proceeds. Repeats what he has heard. Thinks it propr. these Accusa. whether true or false shd. be known. The Opin[ion] of off[icers] & sol[diers] respectg his abil. as genl. The genl. Answr. Good Q[uarte]r M[aste]r &c.

Postponed till to morrow.[1]

Question resumed.

MS (DLC). A continuation of Thomson's Notes of Debates, July 26, 1777.

[1] A line drawn across the MS at this point setting off the following two words suggests that debate on the issue was probably resumed the next day, but no other explicit evidence for this conjecture has been found.

William Duer to Philip Schuyler

My dear Friend: [Philadelphia] 29th July 1777

I have experienced extreme uneasiness in not hearing from you since the loss of Ticonderoga, and hardly know how to account for your silence. Your enemies in this quarter are leaving no means unessayed to blast your character, and impute to your appointment in that Department, a loss which, when rightly investigated can be imputed to very different causes. The friends to truth find an extreme difficulty to stem the torrent of a calumny.

Be not surprised if you should be desired to attend Congress to give an account of the loss of Ticonderoga. With respect to the result of an enquiry I am under no apprehensions. Like gold tried in the fire, I trust that you my dear Friend will be found more pure, and bright than ever.

There is but one thing for you to do, to *establish your Character on such a basis that* even *suspicion* itself *shall be silent,* and in doing this, you will I am concious follow the impulse of your own heart. From the nature of your Department, and other unavoidable causes you have not during the course of this war had an opportunity of evincing that spirit which *I* and your more intimate friends know you to possess. Of this circumstance prejudice takes a cruel advantage, and malice lends an easy ear to her dictates. A hint on this subject is sufficient. You will not I am sure see this place till your conduct gives the lie to this insinuation, as it has done before to every other which your enemies have so industriously circulated. Genl. Washington has lately transmitted to Congress a late letter of yours to him.[1] I know the strong coloring used in it was done with a design to induce him to reinforce you with Continental troops, the only sure dependence in opposing the enemy's army. You know *Congress like an hysteric woman want cordials.* Write truths, without making any reflections of your own. When you call to mind what conversation has passed betwixt you and Mr. Duane on this subject, you will understand what I mean without my enlarging further.

My dear Schuyler, if you knew how warm an interest your friends have in whatever concerns your reputation and happiness you would spare time to write them fully and frequently. I entreat you by the ties of our long acquaintance not to be silent, at least to *myself.* May heaven preserve you, and may I shortly see you crowned with Laurels, or may I have an opportunity (should fate decide for the worse) to rescue your memory from the cruel assasinations of wicked men, who are endeavoring by every artifice in their power to raise the popular clamor against you, and your friends, in order to divert the public attention from the true source of our misfortunes in your quarter. I am, very affectionately yours,   Wm. Duer.

Tr (NN).
[1] Probably Schuyler's July 22 letter to Washington, which was read in Congress on July 26 and touched off a vigorous debate on the command of the northern department. PCC, item 152, 4:393–94.

James Lovell to Joseph Whipple

My dear sir   July 29th. 1777.
Perhaps it is from my attachment to N England that I do not give into the Determination that How is certainly coming into the Delaware with his Fleet wch. has appeared off the Capes, but I still imagine he has other Designs. I hope the Alarm List in the Eastern States will be ready to give amusement & opposition to him if he should take a turn that way, till they shall be joined by continental Troops. For tho we have not near the Army voted to be in the field, yet you may be assured we have a fine body, in good Spirits and giving signs of the best Discipline, as our Committee just returned from Camp affirm, among friends, for it is thought best to say little yet. There were in the Jersies and at Peaks Kill 18,000 besides Cavalry & many troops which were not in the Rolls but wch. we know have since gone or are at work on this River making upwards of 20,000. I think just at present this should

not be public. If Howe is coming here it is under circumstances more in favour of Philada. than will again happen. The brave Jersey Militia who have been baulked of fighting at home as much as they wish will be as good or better here than continental; the last fight from duty, the first from a spirit of revenge.

The States General of Holland made a too humble reply to York's saucy remonstrance, and Lord Suffolk was sarcastic to Count Welderen in a responsive letter of the 10th of April in which he tells the Count that his Majesty's *Expectations* are fulfilled by the *Recall* of De Graaf & a *disavowal* of the insult complained of.[1] People in Holland & elsewhere are dissatisfied with the *Humility* of their *High* Mightinesses.

From the report of an English pacquet being taken & carried to France, we are wishing to hear from our Commissioners more than usually. It cannot be long I think before we shall have a vessel from France. The southern Coast is too much used; our eastern Country affords more certain ports. I shall be punctual in letting yr. Brother know of any interesting arrival, tho I may not always accompany my letters to him by a distinct written Proof of my Love and Esteem of You & your Lady as now.

Yr. h St.

James Lovell

RC (MHi).
[1] On February 21, 1777, Sir Joseph Yorke, the British ambassador at The Hague, submitted a harsh memorial to the States General in which he demanded the recall of Johannes de Graff, the governor of St. Eustatia, for returning the salute of an American warship and permitting "an illicit commerce" between that island and America. Count Welderen, the Dutch ambassador in London, informed the British government on March 26 that de Graff was being recalled for consultation, that the Dutch government had no intention of recognizing American independence, and that Dutch authorities in the West Indies had been ordered to observe the restrictions on trade with America. See Daniel A. Miller, *Sir Joseph Yorke and Anglo-Dutch Relations 1774–1780* (The Hague: Mouton & Co., 1970), pp. 51–55.

James Lovell to William Whipple

My Dear Sir,   July 29th 1777

With most hearty wishes for the health and happiness of you and your's, I acknowledge the receipt of a kind proof of your remembrance of me dated the 15th. Your ideas about Ticonderoga you will find by my letters of last Tuesday are similar to those which we had here.[1] But will you believe that the same obstinacy which withstood the sending Schuyler to Head Quarters in the Jersies 7 weeks ago, now also withstands calling him hither to give an account of our affairs in the Northern Department and of the causes of the relinquishment of Inde-

392 JULY 29, 1777

pendence, to say nothing of the Western part. He writes that the Tories will all join Burgoyne and the timid Whigs and Six Nations of Indians and that the Eastern Militia will not stay with him; yet we are not to send a more fighting popular General in his place. Just such contradictory letters as you and your brother mention, we received here. If the Eastern States do not muster all possible proofs that they have done as well at least as others, a number in Congress with the Northern Council of War and Schuyler, and more than *one* in the Jersies, will cry out "New England *alone* is to blame."

In addition to the perplexities which I have before mentioned to you about French Treaties made by Deane we have a fresh quantity from the arrival of 2 Majors General, two Brigadiers, 2 Lt Cols, 2 Majors, 3 Captains and two Lts created and ranked 7th Nov last and 1st of Decr to whom have been advanced 16,000 livs 1/2 gratuity & half pay.[2] Ought not this weak or *roguish* man to be recalled;[3] if as a corresponding Agent he did thus, what will not he think himself entitled to do as a Commissioner! General Washington is coming this way with his forces some of which are actually in this City already. Howe's fleet are off the Capes 250 sail. I should not wonder if he tried to draw the General even to Virginia and then pushed for New England, that great object of Ministerial malice. I expect he will do this or make a quick return up North river. I shall not believe he will *now* come here; he must attempt it before he leaves America, but he may watch much better opportunities than the present. I think he ought now to alarm your Sea-coast, while Burgoyne is on the Frontiers. Two or three days will determine the matter.

Tr (DLC).

[1] See Lovell to Whipple, July 21, 1777.

[2] Marie Joseph Paul Yves Roch Gilbert du Motier, marquis de Lafayette (1757–1834), arrived in Philadelphia on July 27 after an arduous journey from France via Charleston, S.C. The Baron Johann De Kalb and 11 other French officers accompanied him. When Lafayette and his party, all bearing contracts and letters of introduction from Silas Deane, reached Philadelphia they at first received a brusque reception from Congress and Lovell, who as the French-speaking chairman of the Committee on Foreign Applications usually interviewed newly arrived French officers.

Congress, still in the midst of the controversy surrounding Philippe du Coudray's claims to preferment, was in an ill mood to receive applications from additional French officers. Moreover, De Kalb had already applied to Congress by letter for a commission and his offer had been refused on March 19, 1777. See Robert Morris to John Hancock, February 17, 1777, notes 2 and 3; and John Adams to Nathanael Greene, July 7, 1777, note.

Despite the initial unfavorable reaction of Congress, Lafayette's court connections and his willingness to forfeit many of the favorable terms specified in his contract gained him a commission as major general in the Continental Army, though he was given no assigned post. De Kalb was not granted a commission as major general until September 16. The remainder of Lafayette's suite, including Charles Louis de Mauroy and Louis Cloquet de Vrigny, formally petitioned

Congress for commissions. When these were not forthcoming they asked for funds to return to France, which Congress authorized on September 14, 1777. See Lovell to Vicomte de Mauroy, September 8, 1777; Louis Gottschalk, *Lafayette Joins the American Army* (Chicago: University of Chicago Press, 1937), pp. 1–48; *JCC*, 8:592–93, 628, 634, 637–38, 651, 673, 721, 733, 738, 743–44, 747, 9:870; and Chevalier Dubuysson's Memoir, in Lafayette, *Papers* (Idzerda), 1:72–87. For a discussion of the nature of Lafayette's commission, see also Benjamin Harrison to George Washington, August 20, 1777.

³ The subject of Deane's recall surfaced at about this time in the context of the debate over his contract with du Coudray and several other foreign officers, which stirred Congress intermittently from early July to early September 1777. A motion for his recall was offered on August 5, according to Charles Thomson's endorsement on the document, which appears to be in the hand of Richard Law. See PCC, item 19, 2:133; and *JCC*, 8:605n.2. Another version of the motion, undated and without endorsements that might facilitate identification, is in Lovell's hand and may have been written at about the time he wrote this letter to Whipple, to judge from a letter William Williams wrote to Jonathan Trumbull, Sr., on November 28, 1777. "On Fryd, the 21," Williams explained, "the Motion made last July was revivd for recalling Mr Deane, was again taken up & carried without a dissenting Voice." The charges against Deane are contained in the opening paragraph of Lovell's motion. "Whereas Silas Deane Esqr., when agent under the Committee of Secret Correspondence entered into Conventions with several foreign Officers, which Congress have declared themselves not bound to ratify, and which in the present Situation of Affairs, they could not comply with without deranging the Army, and thereby injuring, at this critical juncture, the American Cause; And, whereas the Credit, Reputation and Usefulness of Silas Deane Esqr., now one of the American Commissioners in France, will be greatly impaired by the Consequences of his Indiscretion in having entered into such Conventions, his Recall becomes necessary for the Interest of these United States." See *JCC*, 8:605n.2.

New York Delegates to the New York Council of Safety

Honourl. Gentlemen   Philad. 29th July 1777
We have the Honour of Your favour of the 17th Instant with the several Enclosures, to which we shall pay all due Attention.¹

We had flatterd ourselves that having happily accomplished the various matters given us in Charge by our late honourable Convention, our Anxiety relating to our own internal affairs woud have been for some time at least relievd. But the misfortunes in the Northern Department, and the fresh attack which is made upon General Schuyler in consequence of them, renew our Difficulties. The Eastern States openly affirm that their Troops have no Confidence in General Schuyler and assign this as the Reason that they have not marched to his Assistance. They therefore insist that he as well as Genl. St. Clair shall be recalled and General Gates again appointed to the Command: or that Congress must Take upon themselves all the Consequences which

may attend a Refusal of this Proposition. You see Gentlemen the
Delicacy of our Situation. If the Eastern Delegates carry their point
the World is left to conclude not only that General Schuyler is unworthy
of the Command; but that if the late changes had not taken place,
Ticonderoga, by the abilities of Genl Gates, might still have been preserved.

In what Light your Delegates & the State by whose Authority they
interposd will be represented, on this View of the Case, is sufficiently
obvious. But supposing General Schuyler, after this warm application
for his Removal, shoud be continued in the Command, and the Eastern
States be backward in supplying their militia, and the calamities of the
Country in that Quarter encrease, Would there under these circumstances, be any End to Clamour and Reproach?

It is not easy to determine the Line of Conduct we ought to pursue
especially as we cannot be assisted by your Advice nor strengthend by
your Authority.

We shall take the first opportunity to inform you of the Event. And
in the mean time assure you that we are most respectfully, Honourl
Gentlemen, Your most Obedient, humble Servants,

Phil. Livingston

Jas. Duane

Wm. Duer

RC (N). Written by Duane and signed by Duane, Duer, and Livingston.
Journals of N.Y. Prov. Cong., 2:500–501. RC damaged; missing words supplied
from Tr.

[1] Apparently a reference to the council's July 18 letter to the New York
delegates, as no letter of the 17th appears in its printed journals. *Journals of
N.Y. Prov. Cong.*, 1:1003–4.

John Adams to Abigail Adams

My dearest Friend   Philadelphia July 30. 1777
I am sorry to find by your late Letter what indeed I expected to
hear, that my Farm wants manure. I fear by your Expressions that
your Crop of Hay falls short.

But, there has been an Error in our Husbandry in which We have
been very inconsiderate and extravagant, that is in pasturing the Mow-
ing Ground. This will ruin any Farm.

The true Maxim of profitable Husbandry is to contrive every Means
for the Maintenance of Stock. Increase your Cattle and inrich your
Farm. We bestow too much manure upon Corn—too little upon Grass.
Make Manure, make food for Cattle, increase your stock—this is the
Method.

Howes Fleet has been at Sea, these 8 days. We know not where he is gone. We are puzzling ourselves in vain, to conjecture his Intention. Some guess he is gone to Cheasapeak, to land near Susquehanna and cross over Land to Albany to meet Burgoine. But they might as well imagine them gone round Cape horn into the South Seas to land at California, and march across the Continent to attack our back settlements.

Others think them gone to Rhode Island, others think they mean only a Deception and to return to the North River. A few days will reveal their Scheme....[1]

We have now before Us, the Months of August, September, October and November, for the Operations of the Campaign. Time enough for Mischief.

G Washington is so near this City, that if the Enemy come into Delaware Bay, he will meet them before they can come near this City.

RC (MHi). Adams, *Family Correspondence* (Butterfield), 2:296–97.
[1] Suspension points in MS.

Thomas Burke to Richard Caswell

Dr Sir   Philadelphia July 30th 1777

Altho. I expected by this time a very active Eventful scene yet I have scarcely anything to communicate to you worth your attention; for near a week past the enemy have been expected here, and preparations are made for effectively opposing them, but there is yet no appearance of them. What gives rise to the apprehension is that a fleet of Men of War and Transports amounting to upwards of two hundred sail departed from Sandy Hook on Tuesday Last, and steered southeast, having on board Troops, horses, artillery &c in great quantity. This appearance has convinced all who deemed this City their peculiar object, that their destination was for the River Delaware, and even such as have always thought otherwise feel their opinions now wavering: they can see no other probable object, and are therefore constrained to admit that it must be Philadelphia. For my own part, I am still of opinion that they will co-operate with their Forces from Canada in endeavouring to effect a junction and establishing a line of communication between the sea and the Lakes, so as to divide the Continent, and bar all succours from one part to the other, while their operations are carried on against either. But why should I trouble you with my conjectures? Time alone can discover what they intend; and as neither we nor they can govern events, there is no foreseeing what they will do.

No new accounts have arrived from the Northern Department since my last. Our affairs there give us great uneasiness. The loss was certainly occasioned by the want of sufficient well appointed force, and as the Eastern States were to supply the Troops for that station, they are very solicitous that it should be thought the fault of the officers, who in reality could not have done more than they did with the force in their hands. They are unwilling that it should be thought they have not the force they have always pretended to; and altho' it must be and is admitted they have exerted themselves as much as any States, yet they are very unwilling to admit that any of our misfortunes has happened through a weakness which they only share in common with the rest. The result I suppose will be that the Officers must be unjustly disgraced. Upon the whole of our affairs, they bear rather a promising aspect, and could we, by general taxing, or any other means, establish the credit of our money, every campaign would give us more command of the war. I shall not trouble you, Sir, with any more at present. I have the honor to be, with the greatest respect & esteem, Your obt Sert.

                                                            Thos Burke

Tr (Nc–Ar).

Samuel Adams to James Warren

My dear Sir   Philade July 31 1777
    It is a long time since I had the pleasure of a Letter from you. I have not heard your opinion of the Evacuation of Tionderoga.[1] You are doubtless as much chagrind as I am. It is ascribd to different Causes. Congress is determind that the true Reasons shall be enquired into, & the Conduct of the General officers. Schuylers Freinds are endeavoring to clear him from all Blame, because, say they, *he was not there*. This is true. And as it was well known he had never been used to keep his own Person near his Army, perhaps it may be pertinently asked, Why *he* was pitchd upon to take the Command. *Your* Delegates, I can assure you, were utterly against it. And, notwithstanding it was publishd in one of the Boston News papers, said to be warrented by a *Letter from this City,* that General Schuyler had the entire Confidence of Congress, there were five only of Eleven States present, in favor of it. The Paper I think was of the 5th of June.[2] I wish I could know who gave the Letter to the Printer. In order, I suppose, to give Credit to that Letter, there was another Publication in the Papers here, informing the World, that when he set off to the Northern Department, he was accompanied by the President and other Members of Congress, which I take for granted is true. These are trifling political Manœvres similar to those which we have formerly seen practicd in the Massachusetts Bay, when a Prop was wanted for a sinking Character. You may think them not worth your

Notice; Excuse my troubling you with them. Cunning Politicians often make use of the Names of *Persons,* & sometimes of *the Persons themselves,* who have not the least Suspicion of it, to serve their own designs. When I mentioned five out of Eleven I should have explaind my self. There were five States for the Measure, four against and two divided.[3] Had not the State of Rhode Island been at that Juncture accidentally unrepresented, there would have been an equal Division, and the Measure would have been prevented. The most important Events may sometimes depend upon small Circumstances. Some Gentlemen of the State of N Y are exceedingly attachd to G Schuyler. They represent him as Instar Omnium in the Northern Department. After all that has been said, I concieve of him, as I have for a long time, excellently well qualified for a Commissary or Quartermaster. The N E Delegates were (perhaps one excepted) to a Man against his having the Command of that Army. But of this I will write particularly in another Letter.

I am not willing to prejudge, but I must say, it is difficult to reconcile the sudden Evacuation of Ty. with the previous flattering Letters of General St Clare. In one of his Letters written but a few days before he says "My People are in the best Disposition possible and I have no Doubt about giving a good Account of the Enemy if they shall think proper to attack us." He has been esteemd here a good officer and in his Letter he bespeaks the Candor of the Publick till he can be heard. Pains will be taken to lay the Blame upon the N E States, for not furnishing their Quota of Men. I wish therefore you would procure for me an authentick Account of the Number of Men, both regular and Militia sent to the Northward from our State, and how they were cloathd and armd. You may remember that Congress recommended to the Eastern States, some time I think in December last, to send a Reinforcement of Militia to Tionderoga to remain there till they could be replacd by Continental Troops then raising. I have never been informd of the Effect of that Recommendation, or if I have I do not recollect it.[4] Pray put it in our Power to state Facts precisely as far as they regard our State. It is agreed on all sides that a Fault lies some where. I hope the Truth will be thoroughly investigated, & to use the homely Proverb, the Saddle laid on the right Horse.

We are looking every moment for the Arrival of the Enemy in this River. Two hundred & 55 Sail were seen on Wednesday last steering from the Hook South East. Seventy Sail were seen from the Shore near Egg Harbour about 20 Leagues from these Capes on Saturday last steering the same Course. The Wind against them. They could not come here at a better time. Genl W. is drawing his Troops into this Neighborhood. Some of them are arrivd. But as the Enemy has the Advantage of us by Sea, it is too easy for them to oblige us to harrass our Troops by long and fruitless Marches, and I should not wonder to hear that they have tackd about and gone Eastward. I hope my Countrymen are prepared. *Let brotherly Love continue.* Adieu. Pay my friendly Respects to your Lady & family.

[*P.S.*] Write particularly in another Letter.

RC (MHi). In Adams' hand, though not signed.
[1] See Warren's August 7 response to this letter in *Warren-Adams Letters,* 2:450–51.
[2] On June 12 the *Independent Chronicle* carried an extract from a letter dated May 27, 1777: "General Schuyler will return to the Northern Department, possessed of the full Confidence of Congress, his Conduct has been fully enquired into, and the Congress have given very honorable Proofs of their good opinion of him."
[3] For a similar breakdown of this vote, see James Lovell to Horatio Gates, May 22, 1777.
[4] Adams is probably referring to Congress' December 24, 1776, resolve. *JCC,* 6:1038. In response to President Hancock's earlier December 18 letter requesting additional troops for Fort Ticonderoga, James Bowdoin stated in a January 13, 1777, letter to Hancock that the Massachusetts General Court had ordered more troops to Ticonderoga. PCC, item 65, fols. 179–81.

Samuel Chase to Thomas Johnson?

Philada. July 31st. 1777.
Dear Sir,[1]   Thursday morning 9 oClock
Inclosed is a copy of the intelligence received this morning from Dover.[2] I doubt not congress will request at least one thousd. men from our state. Mr Hollingsworth leaves this City immediately, and I take the first chance of giving you notice of the designs of the enemy.

Gen. Washington was expected with the first division (they march in three) at Caryals [Coryell's] ferry last night.

This state is called on for 4500 of their militia, Jersey for 2000, and Delaware for 700.

If you can venture to spare our Artillery, it will be, I believe, necessary to furnish them with field-pieces. You have some Iron ones. There is an universal complaint for arms from every state, and yet 35000 have been imported within the last six months.

Your affectionate and obt. servant.   S.C.

Tr (MdHi).
[1] Although the recipient of this letter is not identified, Chase clearly seems to have been addressing Maryland's Gov. Thomas Johnson. This Tr is part of a document that contains not only Chase's enclosure (a July 30 Caesar Rodney letter) but also two other Chase letters (see under the dates August 12 and 19 below) that were directed to Governor Johnson.
[2] For Caesar Rodney's July 30 letter to President Hancock reporting the sighting of a British fleet at the capes of the Delaware, see Hancock to Washington, July 31, 1777, note.

John Hancock to William Alexander

Sir,   July 31t. 1777 5 O'Clock A.M.
Last Night I recd. a Letter from Genl. Washington requesting that any Advice of the Enemy appearing in Delaware Bay, shd. be immediately communicated by Express both to himself and to the Commanding Officer at Trenton:[1] In Consequence of which I have forwarded a Copy of the enclosed to him, and now do myself the Honour to enclose you a Copy of the same.[2] You will therefore agreeably to the General's Request to me, advance immediately with all the Troops under your Command. I have the Honour to be, Sir, your most obed Ser.   J.H. Presid.

LB (DNA: PCC, item 12A). Addressed: "The Right Honble Lord Stirling, or commanding officer at Trenton."
[1] See Washington, *Writings* (Fitzpatrick), 8:501–2.
[2] See Hancock to Washington, this date, note.

John Hancock to Certain States

Gentlemen,   Philada. July 31st. 1777.
The Congress have this Day received Intelligence that the Fleet of the Enemy consisting of two Hundred and twenty eight Ships have arrived at the offing in the Capes of Delaware, and are standing in for the Bay with a fair Wind.[1] No Doubt therefore can remain that the City of Philada. is the object of their Distination & Attack.

Upon this Occasion there is no Necessity to use Arguments to animate you. It is sufficient to mention the Importance of this City to all America, and that the Preservation of it will be attended with the most extensive Consequences in Favour of our Country. I must therefore most ardently entreat you to call out your Militia with the utmost Expedition, that they may be in Readiness to repel any Invasion of your State, or to assist in the Defence of the State of Pennsylvania, which is immediately threatned with an Attack from the Enemy.[2] I beg Leave to request your Attention to the enclosed Resolve of Congress on the Subject, and your Compliance with it, and have the Honour to be, Gentlemen, your most obed & very hble Sert.   J.H. Presid.

LB (DNA: PCC, item 12A). Addressed to the assemblies of Delaware, Maryland, and New Jersey.
[1] See *JCC*, 8:591.
[2] See *JCC*, 8:592.

John Hancock to George Washington

Sir   Philada. July 31t. 1777. 5 O'Clock A.M.

An Express this Moment arrivd with a Letter from Genl. Rodney a Copy of which I enclose agreeably to your Request in your Favour of yesterday which came to Hand last Night.[1] The Enemy by this Intelligence are in the offing of the Capes, and the Wind was fair yesterday for their coming up this Bay. I shall send likewise to Lord Sterling a Copy of the enclosed immediately.

I am, Sir, with the greatest Respect, your most obd Set.

J.H. Presid.

[*P.S.*] The enclosed I just recd. from Genl. Mifflin.

LB (DNA: PCC, item 12A).
  [1] This enclosure was a July 30 letter from Caesar Rodney to Hancock, which was written at Dover, Del., and stated that "two hundred and twenty Eight of the Enemies Ships have appeared in the offing." PCC, item 78, 19:101; and Rodney, *Letters* (Ryden), pp. 201–2. This letter was endorsed by Rodney "Per Thomas North Express who must be furnished with a Horse wherever he stands in need" and by Gen. Thomas Mifflin "Received at 10 Minutes after 3 O Clock at Chester and forwarded at 30 Minutes after Three."

John Adams to Abigail Adams

My best Friend   Philadelphia August 1. 1777

The Fleet is in Delaware Bay, 228 of them were seen, in the Offing, from Cape Henlopen, the day before yesterday. They come in but slowly.

G Washington, and the light Horse came into Town last Night. His Army will be in, this day—that is the two or three first Divisions of it —Greens, Sterlings and Stevensons [Stephen's].

The rest is following on, as fast as possible. General Nash with about 1500 North Carolina Forces, has taken Post on the Heights of Chester, about 15 miles below this City on the River. The Fire Ships &c. are ready.

I really think that Providence has ordered this Country to be the Theatre of this Summers Campaign, in Favour to Us, for many Reasons. 1. It will make an entire and final Seperation of the Wheat from the Chaff, the Ore from the Dross, the Whiggs from the Tories. 2. It will give a little Breath to you in N. England. 3. If they should fail in their Attempt upon Philadelphia, it will give Lustre to our Arms and Disgrace to theirs, but if they succeed, it will cutt off this corrupted City, from the Body of the Country, and it will take all their Force to maintain it.

RC (MHi). Adams, *Family Correspondence* (Butterfield), 2:297–98.

Samuel Adams to James Warren

Dear sir   Philad Augt 1. 77

I wrote to you on the 30 Ulto. by Mr Bruce, who did not leave the City on that day as I expected. His Stay gives me the oppty of acquainting you that an Express who left the Capes yesterday informs us that the Enemies Ships all went out to Sea in the morning steering ENE supposd to be going to Hudsons River, Rh Island or Boston. Mr Bruce will give you as particular an Acct as I can, I therefore refer you to him. This is what I expected. I trust you are upon your Guard.

Congress have orderd that an Enquiry be made into the Reasons of the Evacuation of Tyonderoga and Mount Independence & into the Conduct of the General officers who were in the Northn Departmt at the time of the Evacuation. That Schuyler, St Clair, Poor, Patterson & Roche de Fermoy repair to Head Quarters & that Genl Washington order such Genl officer as he shall think proper immediately to repair to the Northern Department to releive Schuyler in his Command there. A Come is appointed to digest and report the Mode of conducting the Enquiry.[1]

It appears to me difficult to account for the Evacuation of those Posts even upon the Principle of Cowardice. The whole Conduct seems to carry the evident Marks of Deliberation & Design. My utmost Endeavors shall not be wanting to have the Matter searchd to the Bottom.

If we are vigilant, active, spirited & decisive, I yet flatter my self, notwithstanding the present vexatious Situation of our Affairs at the Northwd, we shall humble our Enemies this Campaign. I am truly mortified at their leaving this place, because I think we were fully prepared for them, and I believe the cowardly Rascals knew it. May Heaven prosper our righteous Cause.

Adieu.   S.A.

RC (MHi).

[1] Congress voted on July 29 to conduct an inquiry into the evacuation of Ticonderoga and Mount Independence, and the next day recalled Gen. Arthur St. Clair. On August 1, Congress appointed a committee to report a method of conducting the inquiry, recalled the three other brigadier generals involved, and ordered Washington to appoint a replacement for Gen. Philip Schuyler. See JCC, 8:585, 590, 596; and Hancock to St. Clair and Schuyler, August 5, 1777, note.

The following day, several New England delegates also wrote to Washington urging him to appoint Gen. Horatio Gates to replace Schuyler, but Washington asked to be excused from making the appointment, whereupon Congress proceeded to appoint Gates to command the northern army. See New England Delegates to Washington, August 2, 1777; Washington, Writings (Fitzpatrick), 9:8; and JCC, 8:600–601, 603–4.

John Hancock to George Washington

Sir,   Philada. 1 Augst. 1777. 7 oClock PM
An Express having this moment Arriv'd from Cape May with a
Letter, Copy of which I have the honour to Inclose you, by which it
appears that the Fleet which was suppos'd to be destin'd for the Dela-
ware had stood off & Steer'd to the Eastward.[1] I thought proper to
Transmit this Intelligence to you by Express, & will not detain him
further than to assure you that I am with the utmost Respect, Sir,
Your most Obedt hum set,   John Hancock Presidt

RC (DLC).
[1] The enclosed letter was written by John Hun at Cape May on July 31.
Washington Papers, DLC.

James Lovell to William Whipple

My Dear Sir,   (In confidence)   Friday August 1st 1777.
You will easily guess that some of your friends here have had a task
indeed to get so much justice done to the public as to call Schuyler and
St Clair, Poor, Patterson and Fermoy to Head Quarters, and direct
General W—— to send a proper officer to command in the Northern
Department—hot work from last Saturday.
These recalls were prefaced the 29th of July by a Resolve that an
enquiry be made into the reasons of the evacuation of Tyconderoga
and Mount Independence and into the conduct of the General Officers
who were in the Northern Department at the time of the evacuation.
Committee to digest and report a mode of conducting the enquiry—
Col Lawrence, South Carolina, a worthy member, J Adams, Col Dyer,
General Roberdeau and General Fulsom.
I doubt not Gates will be sent, and I hope the militias of New England will do justice to our labors, by turning out and behaving well. The
unpopularity of the Northern Commander has been declared a bar to
our hopes—therefore the change.[1]
Before this reaches you, it will be fully decided whether the enemy
intend for Philadelphia. General Washington seemed this morning not
to doubt it. I found him in good health and much relieved by finding
repeated proofs of what he has for a long time been most inclined to
believe were the views of Howe.
I am your friend and Servant,   J.L.

                                                      10 at night
Since writing the foregoing, we are told the enemy's fleet has left the
Capes, and steered Eastward. You cannot think I am pleased with this,

because I had prophesied it. No indeed, I wished them to come here, though I declared I would not believe they were coming till they had landed some of their artillery.

They will kill our army by a march to New England in this cruel hot season. All are baulked much both Whigs and Tories.

We had recommended to the Council of State here to seize all such Crown & Proprietary officers and other persons as are suspected to be disaffected or dangerous to the public cause; but should not be mentioned as it may be now laid aside as unnecessary.

Tr (DLC).
[1] See Samuel Adams to James Warren, this date, note.

John Adams to Abigail Adams

My best Friend   Philadelphia August 2. 1777 Saturday
By an express last night from Cape May, We learn that the Fleet went out of the Bay, the Morning before, i.e. on Thursday Morning and put to Sea, and went out of Sight.

What this Man is after, no Wisdom can discover.

Aug. 3

Last night another Express says the Fleet appeared off the Capes again, i.e. part of it, upwards of one hundred Sail.

After all these Feints and Maneuvres, it is most likely he designs to run up the North River, by and by.

The hot weather grows burthensome. And our Business thickens, and presses. I feel as if I could hardly get along through this Month and the next. But must see it out as well as I can.

We have News from France, from our Embassadors.[1] The French will not declare War, as yet. They tell the English they neither desire War nor fear it. But they will lend Us Money, and they have sold Us Eighty thousand Stands of Arms, and will aid Us in every indirect Way. So will Spain.

I hope by this Time you are in perfect Health. Tomorrows Post, I hope will confirm the most agreable Account, in the last I received from you, of your being in a good Way. My Health and Spirits and Life are bound up in yours. May Heaven preserve my dearest Friend, and make her happy.

Never was Wretch, more weary of Misery than I am of the Life I lead, condemned to the dullest servitude and Drudgery, seperated from all that I love, and wedded to all that I hate.

Digging in a Potato Yard upon my own Garden and living in my own Family would be to me Paradise. The next Time I come home, shall be for a long Time.

RC (MHi). Adams, *Family Correspondence* (Butterfield), 2:298–99.
1 See William Williams' second August 2 letter to Jonathan Trumbull, Sr.

Samuel Adams to Elizabeth Adams

My dear Betsy   Philad. 2d Augt. 1777
     Mr Bruces tarrying in this City longer than I expected affords me
an opportunity of giving you a second short Letter by him. The Enemies Fleet have left these Capes & it is supposd they are gone either to
N York or N England. Secure a Place in the Country to which you may
retreat in Case there shd be a Necessity for it. Preserve your usual
Steadiness of Mind. Take the Advice of those who are your and my
Friends with Regard to removing. I hope there will be no Necessity
for it. I am truly sorry the [enemy] have not made this City their
Object, as they [have] long threatned. I think we were fully prepared
to receive them. Perhaps Providence designs that N England shall have
the Honor of giving them the decisive Blow. May Heaven prosper our
righteous Cause, in such Way and by such Instruments as to his infinite
Wisdom shall seem meet. I am in good Health and Spirits. Adieu my
dear,   SA.

RC (NN).

John Hancock to William Heath

Sir,   Philada. August 2d. 1777.
     You will perceive from the enclosed Resolve, that your Letter of the
27th [*i.e.* 17th] of May ulto. was duely received, and laid before Congress; and that they have directed you, to make Enquiry into the Fact
set forth by the Committee of Salem with Respect to Fry's Insanity—
not because Congress have any Doubt of their having represented the
Matter as it appeared to the Committee, but because the Crime is the
most atrocious and detestable, and should never on any Account or
Pretence whatever pass with Impunity, where the Person committing
it has the proper Exercise of his Faculties.1
     I beg Leave to refer your Attention to the Resolve as the Rule of
your Conduct, and have the Honour to be, Sir, your most obedt. & very
hble Servt.   John Hancock Presid

[*P.S.*] I imagin'd the Board of war had forwarded you the Resolve, or
you should earlier had it from me.2

RC (MHi). In the hand of Jacob Rush, with signature and postscript by
Hancock.

[1] In his May 17 letter to President Hancock, General Heath had reported that Private Peter Pickman Frye of the Tenth Massachusetts Regiment had been convicted of desertion and sentenced to be executed but that the day of execution had been postponed to give "some principal Gentlemen" in Massachusetts time to petition Congress for mercy. PCC, item 157, fols. 13–15. Eight days later the Salem Committee of Correspondence petitioned Congress to pardon Frye or mitigate his sentence on the grounds that "he is a Person . . . not possessed of a common share of understanding: and . . . is really incapable of committing a Crime, maliciously and with design, deserving so severe a Punishment, as that to which he is now Sentenced." PCC, item 42, 3:25–26. In consequence Congress authorized Heath on June 20 to pardon Frye only if he appeared to be "of unsound mind" and not "on account of friends or connexions, who should never be considered when public justice demands vicious men to suffer." *JCC,* 8:410, 428, 483–84. Accordingly, Frye was granted a pardon on September 11, 1777. George F. Dow, ed., *The Holyoke Diaries, 1709–1856* (Salem, Mass.: Newcomb & Gauss, 1911), p. 96.

[2] This day Hancock also wrote a brief letter to Washington, enclosing some recent resolves on the northern department. Washington Papers, DLC; and *JCC,* 7:585, 590, 596. See also Samuel Adams to James Warren, August 1, 1777, note.

New England Delegates to George Washington

Sir   Philadelphia Augt. 2d 1777
As Congress have authorized your Excellency to send a proper Officer to take the Command in the northern Department, We take the Liberty to signifie to your Excellency that in our Opinion, no Man will be more likely to restore Harmony, order & Discipline, & retrieve our affairs in that Quarter, than Majr. Genl. Gates. He has on Experience acquired the Confidence, & stands high in the Esteem of the eastern States & Troops. With Confidence in your Wisdom We chearfully submit it to you Excellency's Consideration.[1]

Have taken this method to communicate our Sentiments, judging it wold give you Less Trouble, than a Personal Application.

We are with great Esteem your Excellencys most obedient & most humble Servants,

Delegates for	John Adams	Elbridge Gerry
Massachusetts	Nathel. Folsom	Elipht Dyer
N. Hampshire		
R. Island	Samel Adams	Wm. Williams
Connecticut	Hy Marchant	

RC (DLC). In the hand of William Williams and signed by Williams, John Adams, Samuel Adams, Dyer, Folsom, Gerry, and Marchant.

[1] Congress had directed Washington to name a replacement for Gen. Philip Schuyler, but after he demurred Congress named Gen. Horatio Gates. See Samuel Adams to James Warren, August 1, 1777, note.

George Walton to George Washington

Sir,   Philadelphia 2d. Augt. 1777.

Despairing of an opportunity of personally communicating a piece of business, in your present perplexing situation, I beg leave to take this method of doing it.

The exposed state of Georgia calls aloud for a pretty formidable force to defend it; for this reason congress have not forbid Col White recruiting deserters from the British Army. I have been informed that there are a considerable number now in the grand army; and [these?] I conceive might be more safely and better employed at a distance from the army from which they deserted. I would then submit it, whether it would not be eligible to turn them over to White, he refunding to the officer the bounty?[1]

It is not necessary to adduce reasons to a Gentleman of your discernment, to prove what ought to be done; but I would only observe, that I have no view in making the proposition but the public service.

It may be objected, that, if deserters are refractory, or willing to return, in the face of the grand Army, they would more probably be worse in a distant weak state. Against which I would say, that Discipline is much severer there—they might be incorporated into other regiments, & kept in Garrisons and upon the Indian line to awe the Savages.

I have the happiness to be your Excellency's most Obedient Servant,

                                            Geo Walton.

N.B. I have desired Colonel White to wait upon & deliver this to you, of whom you may satisfy yourself as to any particulars.

RC (DLC).

[1] There is no evidence that Washington responded directly to Walton's request that British deserters serving in the American army be transferred to the Georgia battalion, but Col. John White's recruiting activities were examined by a board of general officers on August 12 and White was cleared of charges that he had been recruiting men for the Fourth Georgia Regiment from other Continental regiments. Washington, *Writings* (Fitzpatrick), 9:64.

William Williams to Jonathan Trumbull, Sr.

Sr.   2 Aug. [1777]

Since Sealing my Letters & [coming] to Congress, I found an oppertun[ity to] extract the Votes respecting the Nothern Affairs &c while the members are loitering,[1] which [. . .] you be willing to see. They are mangled, & garbled, from wha[t was] the original Plan, & with great difficulty we avoided, the order to Shuyler, from standing, that He repair to Congress, to give an Acco of the State of Affairs in his department, instead of repairing to Head Quarters.

It may be very possible, if Howe has left us in good Earnest, That He may go to N England, instead of the N River, but tis impossible to say. They are in the Hands of God almighty & all gracious, & in Him alone may we trust.

Your most dutiful & obedt Son & Servt,   W. Williams

RC (CtHi). Endorsed by Williams: "Per Mr Hunt. 2d Letter." No earlier August 2 letter from Williams has been found.

[1] Williams enclosed copies of the resolves of July 29 and 30 and August 1, ordering an investigation of the conduct of the general officers in the evacuation of Ticonderoga and Mount Independence and directing Schuyler and St. Clair to report to headquarters. See *JCC,* 8 : 585, 590, 596.

William Williams to Jonathan Trumbull, Sr.

Hond Sir   Ph. 2d Aug. p.m. 1777, (3d Letter)

Congress have this Day recd. a number & very large Letters from Dr Franklin, Mr Lee & Dean, with a great variety of Papers, the Letters from 12 Mar. to abt. the 26 May.[1] Tis vain for me to attempt any particular Acco. of their Contents. They have purchased 6 ships, 80,000 stand of Arms, & Pistols, Swords & accoutremts very many & Cloathing, Blankets &c &c &c. They meet with every Encouragemt They can wish in a secret Way, but Fr. & Sp. are not ready yet for an open rupture & save appearances as much as possible, & the King forbids in pompous Terms many of the Things he immediately promises in private & any Money in France & Spain may be had that is needed. 2,000,000 Livres have been lent them from the K's Treasure, with an Injunction, They keep it secret, & call it private Loans &c which They have inviolably done, save telling it to Congress &c. The only thing They fail of is the Ships they were to obtain. They alledge if They go into a War, they shall want Their Ships. If They Do not they want them to awe Engld. & shall keep just as many more English Ships at home, which is equally advantagious to Us &c & our Embassadors are building 2 or 3 Ships more equal to 60 Gun Ships on a new Construction tho not of equal Cost by much. All Europe wish us well & will support as far as They cleverly can & Call our Cause the Cause of Mankind. In Short there is no room to entertain a doubt, if the Enemy dont get a signal & almost decisive Advantage against us this Campaign, it will be out of their power to open another.

For the Sake of all that's near & dear then, & let our Country men be roused this once & I hope all will be saved, & repent & God will certainly be on our Side. Let Them not fear nor be dismayened.

Schuyler I dare say is removed forever. You will improve these broken hints, to the greatest Advantage.

Have wrote so much, I must Cease once more. Your most affectit. Dutiful Son & Servt.   W Williams

RC (CtHi). Endorsed by Williams: "Per Mr Hunt. 3d Letter, 2d inclosed."

[1] Benjamin Franklin and Silas Deane wrote five joint letters between March 12 and May 26, 1777, only three of which arrived in Philadelphia at this time—those of March 12, May 25, and May 26, with several enclosures including an agreement with Leray de Chaumont for monthly packet service and an account of the arms purchased at Nantes. The commissioners' letters of March 14 and April 9, which are mentioned in their letter of May 25, still had not arrived several months later, according to a marginal note made by James Lovell in March 1778. PCC, Item 85, fols. 33–64; Wharton, *Diplomatic Correspondence,* 2:283–96, 319–27; and *JCC,* 8:599, 601, 607.

For evidence that there were other letters in the packet, see James Duane to John Jay, August 3; and Committee for Foreign Affairs to Charles Dumas and to Arthur Lee, August 8, 1777.

Board of War to George Washington

Sir   War office Augt. 3d 1777

The Officers of Regiments & Companies are separately & constantly applying for Arms & Necessaries. A few have produced the Ajut. Generals Signature to their Returns of Deficiencies. The Demands are so great that there are not a sufficient Number in the Store to supply them. Each is anxious to get the whole of his Demand & let others shift as well as they can. There should be some Plan fallen upon either to apportion what we have among the whole or to let those have them who most want them. I shall be obliged to your Excellency for Information what is proper to be done. Shall an Order issue to Col Flower to deliver to such Officers as have the Ajut. Generals Approbation of their Returns such Arms & Necessaries as they want & to receive from them all defective Arms? Or would it be most proper for the Ajudt Genl to collect the whole of the Demands & then order the Commissary Genl to proportion his Stock of Arms &c among them according to the Numbers wanted by the respective Regiments? Twelve thousand Arms have been delivered out of the Store in this City within these four Months & yet the Troops, tho not equal in Number already have large Demands. Where the Carelessness or Peculation lies I cannot tell, but fancy the Inattention of many of the Officers give great Latitude to the Soldiers.

I have the Honour to be with the greatest Respect, your very obed Servt.   Richard Peters Secy

P.S. I have told the Officers you disapprove of the Mode of their Applications, & many of them say it is in Orders that they should apply in this Way. I do not know whether they said the Orders were from you or the Commanders of Divisions. But if any such were issued the Generals could not have known your Excellency's Opinion.

RC (DLC).

[1] Anticipating Washington's response, the board sent a brief note to Commissary Benjamin Flower on the fourth, requesting him "to deliver to His Excellency Genl. Washington's Order, or that of such Persons as he shall appoint, all Arms, Accoutrements & all Millitary Stores the Army may or do require." And on the fifth Peters informed Washington that "the Board have given Orders to the Commissary General to make a Return to your Excellency of every Thing in his Department as they have put all Arms Acoutrements & military Stores under your immediate Direction. All Arms repaired are under the Care of Col. Flower, but Orders for the Reparation of Arms must issue to Mr Thomas Butler, Chief Armourer, who has also Directions to put himself & his Workmen under your Excellency's Command or that of such Person as you shall appoint." Washington Papers, DLC. For Washington's response to the board's letters of the third and fifth, see Washington, *Writings* (Fitzpatrick), 9:18–20.

James Daune to John Jay

Dear Sir   Philad 3d Augt. 1777

I enclose you a Letter from France for yourself[1] and another to Mr Platt which last you'l be pleased to forward with my respectful Compliments.

General Howe and his grand fleet to the utter astonishment and vexation of the People here have disappeard as every necessary preparation for his reception was made. He has left us to guess at his next attempt.

General Schuyler to humour the Eastern people who declare that their militia will not fight under his command is recalled. As is St Clair for surrendering Ticonderoga &c in order to take his trial which he has demanded. Congress have left it to General Washington to name the Commander of the northern Department. On whom that arduous Task will fall is yet unknown? [2]

Is it possible, my dear Sir, that Burgoine at the head of not more than 6000 men can dare to penetrate into the Country in defiance of the numberless Enemies he must have to encounter? Two years ago such an attempt would have been thought fortunate for America and now it terrifies. Oh New England are thou so fallen, so lost to publick Virtue!

The Accounts from France are flattering. Our Ambassadors have negotiated very considerable Loans of money and Supplies of Ammunition and Goods; & assure us that all Europe except England are our Friends.

I have no time to add—to say the Truth I can hardly perswade myself to write this much, Since two long Letters to you & Mr Livingston &c remain totally disregarded. Present my respectful Compts to Mrs Jay and believe me to be with great Respect, Dear Sir, your most Obed. & very huml Sert.   Jas Duane

RC (NNC).
[1] Perhaps the letter to Jay from the American commissioners at Paris, dated June 2, 1777, in Wharton, *Diplomatic Correspondence*, 2:329. Although William Williams wote on August 2 that Congress had just received letters from the commissioners "from 12 Mar. to abt. the 26 May," Henry Laurens reported on the fifth that he had "seen & read . . . Letters from France as late as June." See William Williams' second letter to Jonathan Trumbull, Sr., August 2; and Henry Laurens to John Lewis Gervais, August 5, 1777. It should be noted, however, that in their June 2 letter the commissioners mentioned a May 26 letter to Jay that is not in Wharton.
[2] See *JCC*, 8:585, 590, 596; and New England Delegates to Washington, August 2, 1777.

John Hancock to the States

Gentlemen,   (Circular) Philada. Augt. 3d. 1777.
While the American War continues, & our cruel Enemies manifest a Disposition to persevere in their Views of reducing us by Force of Arms to submit to their Dominion & Government, it becomes the United States to pursue every Step in their Power to oppose them. The American Army, from the Events of War, and other Losses unavoidable in Camps, must necessarily suffer a considerable Diminution. To supply this continual Waste, as well as to encrease our Army, and to fill up the Regiments which were to be raised by the respective States, must certainly be an object of the utmost Importance. The Congress therefore in Hopes of accomplishing their Views in this particular, and rendering the Army of the United States sufficiently strong to vanquish our Enemies, have come to the enclosed Resolves, which are extremely well calculated to answer those Purposes, and if adopted by the States, cannot, I flatter myself, fail of Success. I beg Leave to request your particular attention to them, and also Compliance therewith.[1] I have the Honour to be, Gent., Your most obedt. Set.
                                      J.H. Presid.

LB (DNA: PCC, item 12A).
[1] Although this letter was meant to accompany some July 31 resolves on the encouragement of recruits for and the apprehension of deserters from the army, it was crossed out in the president's letter book and never sent. Instead Washington, who was then in Philadelphia, wrote a circular letter on August 4 to every state but North Carolina, South Carolina, and Georgia, urging compliance with these resolves, and Hancock merely dispatched copies of them to the states. Evidently the delegates felt that an appeal from their president would carry

less weight with the states than one from the commander-in-chief. See *JCC*, 8:593–95; and Washington, *Writings* (Fitzpatrick), 9:10–11. The genesis of these resolves is discussed in Committee of Congress to Washington, July 16, 1777, note.

Hancock also wrote a brief letter to Washington on the third, transmitting some resolutions of that date about the northern department. Washington Papers, DLC; and *JCC*, 8:600–601.

John Adams to Abigail Adams

My dearest Friend   Philadelphia August 4. 1777

Your kind Favour of July 23, came by the Post, this Morning. It revives me, to hear of your Health, and Welfare, altho I shall be, and am disappointed of a Blessing, which I hoped to enjoy. But this is the Result of Wisdom superiour to ours and must be submitted to with chearfull Resignation.

The Loss of Ti. has occasioned as loud Complaints and as keen Resentment in Philadelphia as in Boston. And Congress have determined that an Inquiry shall be made, and have ordered the Major Generals Schuyler and St. Clair, to Head Quarters and ordered M.G. Gates to relieve M.G. Schuyler.[1] Lincoln and Arnold are there. These three I believe will restore our Affairs in that Department.

We have Letters from France, Spain and the West Indies, which shew that our Ground in Europe is firm, and that a War is brewing.

We have all the English Papers, till the latter End of May, which shew that Britain is in a wretched Condition indeed—their East India Affairs in Distraction, their Affrican Trade ruined and their West Indian Concerns in the Utmost Distress. Almost all their West India Planters have left the Kingdom in Despair.

Their Scavengers of the Streets of Germany have been able to rake together, but a little Filth.

Where How is going No Astroleger can determine. He has left the Capes of Delaware and where he is gone no one can tell. We expect to hear from him at the North River, or at Rhode Island, but cant tell when.

I, for my Part am very homesick, but I will not leave the Field untill the Campaign is ended—unless I should fall sick. This horrid Hot Weather melts my Marrow within my Bones, and makes me faint away almost. I have no other Way to keep alive, but by Abstinence from Eating and drinking. I should not live a Month if I did not starve myself. When I come home I shall be an Epicure.

Tell Tom, I would give a Guinea to have him climb upon my shoulder, and another to chase him into his Jail. My Love to all the rest. I will write them as soon as I can. I wrote Mr. Thaxter inclosing Letters to the Court and Bar. Has he received them?[2]

RC (MHi). Adams, *Family Correspondence* (Butterfield), 2:299–300.

¹ Adams was a member of the committee appointed on August 1 "to digest and report the mode of conducting the enquiry into the reasons of the evacuation of Ticonderoga and Fort Independence;" and on August 28 he was named to the committee to conduct the inquiry. *JCC*, 8:596, 688. See Hancock to St. Clair and Schuyler, August 5, 1777, note.

² Not found, but see Adams, *Family Correspondence* (Butterfield), 2:257n.3, 300n.3.

John Hancock to George Washington

Sir,   Philad. August 4th. 1777.

I have it in Charge from Congress to inform you that they have this Day appointed General Gates to the Command of the Army in the Northern Department, and to direct, that you immediately order him to repair to that Post.¹ Any Instructions that may be necessary, shall be sent after him with the utmost Expedition.

I have the Honour to be, with the greatest Respect, Sir, your most obed. & very hble Servt.   John Hancock Presidt

RC (DLC). In the hand of Jacob Rush and signed by Hancock.

¹ See *JCC*, 8:603–4. Washington, whose headquarters was temporarily at Philadelphia, sent a copy of this letter to Gates this day. Washington, *Writings* (Fitzpatrick), 9:11–12.

James Lovell to William Whipple

Dear Sir,   August 4th 1777

The paper of Dunlap will show you how we go on both as to *Ty* and Europe. New York pushed for a reference to General W—— as to the successor of Schuyler, intending and attempting to prevent G—— from being sent, but it was referred back to us and we were 11 to 1 which is far from 5 to 4 and 2 divided.

As the Courts of France and Spain will not ceremoniously adopt our Independence till they declare war, Congress ought not to let Britain see facts under it's vouching, except such a notorious matter as Storment's saucy reply to Franklin and Deane.¹

The *establishment* of our Currency is a matter for your *own* knowledge. Spain is unbounded in manly friendship.

I must to bed being galled to death almost this morning to see Col Trumbull at Germantown. He has resigned and I suppose Buchanan will be in his place.² This owing to you know what—I am plaguily chagrined at it. I fear we shall feel the sad effects of it in about 4 months. I will be a little more particular by Mr Bass, the express in a day or two.

You will see by my past letters that I did not expect Howe here.

I have rec'd the Bill of Exchange paying only 2/6 for the notification. I shall send a Loan certificate to the Proprietor by Mr Bass.

Your friend & humble servt, with love and compliments as usual,

J.L.

Tr (DLC).

¹ Lord Stormont, the British ambassador to France, on receiving Benjamin Franklin's and Silas Deane's April 2, 1777, letter concerning an exchange of prisoners, had refused to open the letter and returned it with an unsigned note: "The king's ambassador receives no letters from rebels, except when they come to ask mercy." On August 3 Congress ordered publication of the commissioners' letter and Stormont's haughty reply and both appeared in the August 5 issue of the *Pennsylvania Evening Post.* They were widely reprinted in other American newspapers. *JCC,* 8:601.

² William Buchanan was elected to replace Joseph Trumbull as commissary general of purchases on August 5. *JCC,* 8:607.

Samuel Adams to Samuel Freeman

My dear sir   Philade Augt 5 1777

I have had the Pleasure of receiving several Letters from you and I thank you for the Intelligence therein communicated to me. I beg you to continue your favors although it may not be in my Power to balance the Account.

Our Affairs are now in a very critical Situation. There is strong Reason however to promise ourselves a favorable Issue. Men of Virtue throughout Europe heartily wish well to our Cause. They look upon it, as indeed it is, the Cause of Mankind. Liberty seems to be driven from every other Part of the Globe. The Prospect of our affording for its Friends an Asylum in this new World, gives them universal Joy. France & Spain are in reality, though not yet openly, yeilding us Aid. Nevertheless, it is my opinion that it would be more for the future Safety, as well as the Honor of the united States of America, if they could establish their Liberty and Independence, with as little foreign Aid as possible. If we can Struggle thro' our Difficulties alone and establish ourselves, we shall value our Liberties, so dearly bought, the more, and be less obligd, and consequently the more independent on others. Much depends on the Efforts of this Year. Let us therefore lay aside the Consideration of every Subject which may tend to a Disunion. The Reasons of the late Conduct of our General Officers at Tyconderoga must endure a strict Scrutiny. Congress have orderd an Inquiry, and for this Purpose Genl. Schuyler & St. Clair are orderd to Head Quarters. Gates immediately takes the Command of the Northern Army. He gains the Esteem of the soldiers, and his Success in restoring the Army there the last year, from a State of Confusion & Sickness to Health & good order affords a flattering Prospect. In my opinion he is an honest and able officer. Bad as our Affairs in that Quarter appear to be, they are not ruinous. Reinforcements of regular Troops are already gone, & I hope the brave N. England Militia will joyn in sufficient Numbers to damp the Spirits of Burgoyne. One grand Effort now may put an End to the Conflict. I am, Yr affectionate Friend,   Samuel Adams

RC (MeHi).

Thomas Burke to Richard Caswell

Dr Sir   Philadelphia August 5th 1777
    Yesterday your favor of 15th ulto came to Hand inclosing a Letter for Captain Caswell which shall be Immediately forwarded to him, and you may be assured that every possible attention will be paid to him by me, and with the greatest pleasure.[1] I have written to you on every Subject which you Suggest in your Letter, by many Opportunities, and am much Concerned to find they had not reached your Hands before the Date of your last. I hope however you have received them long before this, and you will perceive by them that I have paid the most early and dilligent attention to your Commands. The Business relative to Collo. Shepherds Battalion, and the Artilary Company underwent no delay except what was absolutely Necessary for the several references and reports Incident to the War Department. The result on Both was, the Battalion was taken into Continental pay as one of the 16 (the Stipulations of the Assembly being observed), the Company also taken into pay (but not annexed to any Battallion), and both are ordered to Join the Grand army without delay. The resolutions relative to these were transmitted to you both by the Board of War and by me, and Inclosed duplicates of that relative to the Battalion.[2]
    I am much Concerned that the money has met with such unexpected delay, but I assure you that so soon as I heared of the Determination of the Assembly I took the only step then in my Power to expedite the Transmission of it, which was to give Notice to the Treasury that I daily expected to demand of them the Ballance of the 500,000 Dollars, but the Constant and pressing Demands render this precaution Ineffectual, because the Military Service would admit of no delay, and the Treasury were obliged to pay out what was reserved for our State, and not having the Resolve of the Assembly, I could not Interfere to prevent it. When Mr Penn arrived the Treasury here was exhausted, and we were obliged to apply for an Order on the Treasurer at Baltimore. This Occasioned very great delay and Difficulty. The ordinary mode of Transmission by the Board of War could not take place, and

we were obliged to apply to General Nash for an Officer to take Charge
of the money when delivered by the Treasurer. The officer received
from us his Instructions on the 11th July and we have Since heared
nothing more of him but presume he has before this arrived in your
State with three hundred thousand Dollars and some proclamation
which Mr Penn charged him with.[3] From Mr Penn's having with him
the resolve, and from some other Circumstances, I concluded he was
chiefly Expected to transact this Business. This however did not prevent
me from giving the most dilligent attention to it, and I can assure you
that no unnecessary delay happened after his arrival here, for altho he
undertook to do that part of the Business which respected the Treasury,
and I what respected the Board of War, yet I gave the strictest attention to Both, nor did I perceive him in the least remiss. In short Sir if
you knew how heavily money Business proceeds here you would not
wonder at the delay.

As the Post is Just going out I have not time to add any thing more
to this letter, except that we have been for some days under Expectation of an Invasion of this State. The Enemys Fleet Sailed from New
York, as you will see by my last and they soon appeared off the Capes
of Delaware. After hovering there several days they steered away but it
is not agreed what Course. General Washington is here and great part
the army Encamped in the Neighborhood. The Movements of the
Enemy have disappointed both whigs and Tories. The latter wished for
them in order to their Subduing us, and the whigs wish for them in
full Confidence that we should give them a very warm reception, and
an Effectual Check. It is now pretty generally thought that they have
no design on this City, and that their principle object is to Establish a
Communication by way of Hudsons River, between the Sea and the
Northern Leaks.

A Gloom still hangs over our affairs in the Northern Department,
and we are using our best Endeavours to remove it. Nothing Interesting
has transpired thence since my last.

You shall have the earliest Intelligence of every thing that is worth
your attention.

I have the honor to be, your Excellency's very obedt Servt.

Thos Burke

RC (Nc–Ar).

[1] Governor Caswell's July 15 letter to Burke is in *N.C. State Records*,
11:737–39.

[2] See *JCC*, 8:450, 475, 544, 567; John Hancock to Washington, June 13,
note 2; and Burke to Caswell, July 7, 1777, note 1.

[3] See Burke to Caswell, July 5, note 2; and North Carolina Delegates to
John Allen, July 11, 1777.

Nathaniel Folsom to Josiah Bartlett

Philadelphia Agust 5th. 1777

I arrived here in good Health the 20th of July. On my joining the Congress. I found them worried with Petitions from a Great Number of French gentlemen for Commissions to Serve in our Army and Continue to Plague us to this day.

Saterday Mr. Bass Came to Congress from Portsmouth and brought Letters from ouer agents in France up to the 26th of May, by which We aire informed that ouer Effaires bair a feavourable aspect all over Europe, that a fund is Establishing in France and Spaine Suffishant to Support the Cradit & Pay the intrest of ouer Continental money—and that if We Can hold ouer owne this year a War will most Sertainly take Place before the Comemencement of annother; and we aire further informd by them that it is the opinion of the ministers of the Last menshoned Corts that thay Can be at Present of more Servise to us then thay Could be if thay ware to Declare war against Briton. The Loss of Ticonderoga hes given grate unEasyness. Generall Schyler and Sant Caire aire orderd to head Qurters in order for an inquirey, into thaire Conduckt. The other Generals that Sat in Councel aire to Stay at thaire Departments till General Washington thinks thay Can be Recald with out hurting the Servise. General Gates is orderd to take the Comemand in the northen Department. Congress have Past a Resolve that New Hampshier, Massachussetts, Connecticut, New Jersey and New York & Pennsylvania Raise & march as many of the militia to Serve in the northen Department till the fifteenth of November as General Gates Shall think Suffishent for the Defence of that Part of the Cuntrey. You will See by the Paper Inclosed that the Enemys fleet have been hovering abought the Capes of the Delleware amounteing to 228 Saill Till Fryday Last & have Since Disapeaird. It is Prity Generaly thought thay aire bound up the North River or to Rhode Island. General Washington is incampt at Garmantown with abought foure Thausend troops but I beleive will in a day or two march to wards the North River.

I am with Respect your Humbl. Servent,   Nathll. Folsom

RC (NhD).

John Hancock to Philip Schuyler and Arthur St. Clair

Sir,   Philada. Augt. 5th. 1777.

The Congress haveing come to a Determination to enquire into the Reasons of the Evacuation of Ticonderoga & Mount Independence, as well as into the Conduct of the general officers who were in the Northern Department at the Time of the Evacuation, I have it in Charge to transmit you the enclosed Resolve, and to direct that you repair to Head Quarters for this Purpose.[1] I have the Honour to be, Sir, your most obedt. & very hble Servt.

J.H. Presid.

LB (DNA: PCC, item 12A).

[1] On August 1 Congress appointed a committee of five to report on the mode of investigating the evacuation of Ticonderoga and Fort Independence. After considering the committee's report at some length, Congress decided on August 27 to appoint another committee to collect the facts about this episode and transmit them to Washington so that he could "appoint a court martial for the trial of the general officers who were in the northern department, when Ticonderoga and Mount Independence were evacuated, agreeable to the rules and articles of war." Then on the following day John Adams, Richard Henry Lee, and Henry Laurens were chosen to make up this committee.

These three delegates proved to be unfortunate choices for this task. Adams returned to Massachusetts early in November and later that month was selected to replace Silas Deane as a commissioner in Paris. Laurens succeeded John Hancock as president of Congress on November 1, thereby making it difficult for him to attend to committee business, and Lee returned to Virginia early in December, further disrupting the committee's work. In order to expedite the investigation, Congress added five new members to the committee between December 26, 1777, and January 27, 1778—Francis Dana, William Ellery, James Lovell, James Smith, and John Witherspoon—and ordered them on January 20 to submit a report on the 26th. The committee failed to meet this deadline, but on February 5 it submitted "a variety of evidence," which Congress promptly forwarded to Washington with instructions "to appoint a court martial for the trial of the general officers who were in the northern department when Ticonderoga and Mount Independence were evacuated."

Congress soon learned that the committee's work had been seriously deficient in one crucial respect, however, for Washington wrote to Congress on February 27 that he was unable to convene a court-martial because of the committee's failure to make "any particular charges against the Officers who are to be the objects of trial." Consequently Congress appointed a new committee on April 29 to reexamine the evidence and specify charges against the officers responsible for the loss of Ticonderoga and Fort Independence. This committee, consisting of Francis Dana, William Henry Drayton, and Roger Sherman, submitted a lengthy report to Congress on June 12, summarizing the evidence about the evacuation of these two posts and recommending that General St. Clair be tried on five counts involving charges of "neglect of duty . . . cowardice . . . treachery . . . incapacity as a general . . . inattention to the progress of the enemy . . . shamefully abandoning the posts of Tyconderoga and Mount Independance" and that General Schuyler be tried on one count for "neglect of duty in not being present at Ticonderoga to discharge the functions of his command." Congress approved this report and ordered a copy of it to be sent to Washington on June 20 so that he could hold trials for St. Clair and Schuyler.

As a result, St. Clair and Schuyler were court-martialed separately in September and October and acquitted "with the highest honour" of all charges against them. Congress confirmed their acquittals on December 3 and 16, 1778.

See *JCC*, 8:596, 653, 668–70, 674–75, 681–86, 688, 9:786–87, 901, 1053, 10:66, 92–93, 125, 238–39, 403, 11:593–603, 628, 12:1186, 1225; Washington,

Writings (Fitzpatrick), 10:518–19, 11:195, 391, 476, 12:201, 321, 352, 354, 406, 495, 526, 13:6, 9, 15, 41, 429, 449–50; and Martin H. Bush, *Revolutionary Enigma: A Re-Appraisal of General Philip Schuyler of New York* (Port Washington, N.Y.: Ira J. Friedman, Inc., 1969), chap. 11. The proceedings of St. Clair's and Schuyler's court-martials are in *NYHS Collections*, 12–13 (1879–80): 1–211, 1–171. See also Henry Laurens' Heads of Inquiry about the Northern Army, August 27; and Committee of Congress to Meshech Weare, September 4, 1777.

Henry Laurens to John Lewis Gervais

Dr Sir,   Philada. 5th August 1777
   I wrote to you the 25th Ulto by Capt Budd of the Georgia Troops. Every day since my Arrival in this place has produced something new from the Theatre of War, you will find the principal occurrences in the News Papers which I shall send you.
   The Loss of Ticonderoga has raised universal Complaint, an inquiry has been demanded by the Voice of the People and is now orderd by their Representatives. To say all that I think upon that Subject founded upon his own Letters might bear too hard upon the Commanding Officer, but 'tis easy to perceive great Propriety in the advice of the General Officers for evacuating the Fortress at the time their Opinions were ask'd, and a criminal Deficiency on the Commanders Part in not calling for them while there was opportunity for saving the Cannon, stores and some Lives. Be that as it may, Genl. Fermoy disclaims the merit of abandoning the whole to have been consistent with his Sentiments before a proper Resistance had been made.[1] General Schuyler is not a little blamed for absence from his Post, nor on the other hand does he want Advocates who hesitate not to cast part of the Fault upon Congress. These are the Ebullitions of Party. A Court of Inquiry will develop Truth and give the Public better Information. In the mean time Genl. Gates by the unanimous Vote of Congress is orderd to take Command of the Northern Department, tis said he is an excellent officer and exceedingly popular in N. England, whence we hope to derive such Aid from the Militia as will at least check Mr Bourgoynes Progress. I am sorry to say he seems at present to be bearing down all before him.
   The late Motions of Lord and Genl Howe have puzzled every body on our Side of the Question. After we had learn'd of Bourgoynes Successes I uniformly maintain'd that the Fleets appearance even off the Capes of Delaware was no more than a Feint calculated to draw Genl Washington into fatiguing Marches and remarches through Jersey. It seems the General was so strongly persuaded of that Fact he would not cross Delaware until he had received Orders from Congress in consequence of an erroneous Information that 60 of the Fleet had certainly anchor'd within the Bay, and the Remainder were pouring in with a fair Wind. So strongly had this false Intelligence been impress'd

upon our minds that orders were dispatch'd for driving off Cattle, removing Waggons, Horses &ca &ca from the borders of the Bay and River.[2] Five Ships were equipp'd and the best inform'd had mark'd the very day for landing the Enemys Troops. All parties were disappointed—the cursed Tories who abound in and about this City, because they had expected their Friends—the Friends of freedom, because they had wished to give a decisive Blow to those British Buccaniers. These finally disappear'd about four days ago, and whither they are now wandering we know not, probably they may have re-enter'd North River, possibly landed at Rhode Island and part of the Fleet may be gone to bombard Boston which we know to be one Line in the general Plan. Our Troops are encamp'd within a few Miles of this City, by the time they have recover'd from the fatigue of the late severe Marches we shall learn more certainly the Destiny of the Strollers. Part of them must have shar'd fatigues with our People. Their Horses & many of their Men had been a full Month on Shipboard, when we Last heard from them. Mischief they may do—tis all they can hope to do. Conquest they cannot expect, even if they should work our Destruction, in that Case they will only have enabled their Rival Neighbours to reap the Harvest of their own Ruin. To console us in some measure we are told and it is believed that our Eastern Friends have in a second Attempt actually taken Fort Cumberland in St Johns.[3] To morrows Paper which I shall have time to inclose with this will shew you the fate of brave Manly, whose fall I think more glorious than all his Feats.[4] He was announced at N. York as a Pirate but it will behove his Keepers to treat him like a Gentleman if they have any regard for the late Commander of the Fox. We have heard nothing late from General Lee. The Capture of Major Genl Prescott will be another Bar against further ill Usage to him and when the heat of present Enterprizes has a little subsided an Exchange will probably be effected.[5]

The repeated Instances of British cruelty exercised upon American Prisoners particularly those produced in Doctor Franklins letter to Lord Stormont and others this very day by a Master of a Vessel escaped from N York have raised a Spirit which will soon appear with the Label of Retaliation. When the Question is brought I will oppose it in part. I abhor the practice of Cruelty and will never in our circumstances consent to make Returns except in cases where good effects may be expected. Circumstanced as we are a general and rigid Retaliation wd be impolitic. The common people of England are our Friends. I believe their infamous Leaders have strove to extort Cruelty to prisoners on our part in order to enrage and unite them against us. Nothing less will make them our Enemies. To imprison closely and if occasion require to hang a Prescot and a Barrington for Injuries done to Lee will not displease but rather be applauded by those common people. Such

Strokes I have no Objection to. With the lower Class of Soldiers and Seamen I would contrast American Humanity against British Ferocity, but if a Douglas or a Jordan could be handled some Atonement should be made for the Blood of Burke and others who have sufferd under their Barbarian Hands.

It does not appear that Genl Howe has received any considerable Reinforcement the present Year, perhaps a few hundred, at most 2000 chiefly Anspachers. These we are well inform'd refused to march and by a Letter from a Friend at Rotterdam[6] we are assured that most of them were sent down the Maes tied Neck and Heels. The foreign Troops on the Spot are much disgusted and among Bourgoynes a Mutiny lately happend in which eighty Lives were lost.

We are assured from good Authority that this City is the grand Object of the Campaign. It might have been so while Reinforcements were expected, but the late Movements of the Brothers mark the Imbecillity of the Generals Army which we think cannot exceed 8000 & General Washington seems to be certain that Bourgoyne has not above 6000. To them some recruits may have been added from among the mal Contents on his late rapid inroad. You will see in the News papers we have taken the Liberty to hang two of General Howes recruiting Officers on North River. If those Generals can form a junction, no doubt an attempt will be made to penetrate the Country & we may hear of them in front & Rear before October. On the other hand Spirited measures under General Gates who will go out this day (the 6th) to Command the Northern Department will keep them asunder & may prove the ruin of their Campaign.

General Putnam commands at Peeks Kill. He will have his hands full & if not Speedily & well supported we shall lose our frigates on North River, the Country will be laid open & Thousands of Tories & property Men join the Enemy. Exposed to Similar dangers I find we are at Providence, where we have also two Frigates & much other Valuable Shipping. These the Enemy are at this time attempting to destroy to complete the Conquest of Rhode Island Government & open an easy passage to Boston. Not one of these projects could be executed if the people were anxious to defeat them, but there seems to be an universal langour, except in the article of Money. Zeal & animation to make as much of that as possible & by all possible ways & means are very visible among all Classes. While this Spirit Governs nothing more can be expected than base defensive action, but tis clear if we were united & would act with vigour only three Months no British Troops would remain on this side the Lakes but such as were protected by Men of War or confined by prison Walls. The New Yorkers & some others blame New England, the Yankees retort & upon a fair hearing it appears that the latter have given more Men in proportion than any other State. But Say the Southern States they are able to do more, they are attentive only to privateering & making Money. New England replies we furnish our quota ascertained by your Selves, we have a large frontier to defend both by Land & Sea, our Country is barren & affords bare Subsistence in return for hard Labour. Ye enjoy fertile fields, live in Luxury Without the Labour of your own hands, Ye are Rich in Money & Products & can better afford to pay. I believe New England is at this time, unless the British Army is actually gone there, in happier circumstances than any Southern State, but we should remember three things. They bore the first & Severest attack—what they now enjoy they have gained by their address & their industry— their gains have greatly distressed the common Enemy & in so far we participated I may add, they are still the grand object of British revenge.

We have the best assurance that the port of Havanna is open to American Vessels, that the Caribs in the Island of St Vincents have reasserted their rights, obtained Supplies of Arms & ammunition from Martinico, made Several Successful inroads upon the planters, taken many of their Negroes, destroyed vast fields of Cane & Grain, that the Governor at the head of the Militia had marched against them. If I remember right seven British Regiments were fully employed to bring those half armed Savages to a treaty & a drawn game in 1773. Lord North has now cut out work enough to employ Seventy Regiments.[7]

The late flood of French Men rushed in upon us under argeements with Mr. Deane has reduced Congress to a painful dilemma. If we employ with all his unwarranted Contracts, many of our best Generals will be grosly affronted; if we do not, the United States will be exposed to the reproach & probably resentment of Men who have been deceived & ill used. Some of them have been very clamorous & we shall be obliged to make pecuniary Satisfaction for their disappointment of Rank, Some of them by the by prove to be rank Cheats, nevertheless they have Credentials from our agent Deane & must be provided for in Some way. Holzendorf being a long time upon hand, I interposed on his behalf, obtained his Commission of Lt. Colonel according to agreement, but he is not employed.[8] This so far looks well as it Shows these people we are not altogether dependent upon Frenchmen. The Chevalier Faliat [Failly] who in his passage from Charles Town to Virginia had been taken by the Daptine M.W. [H.M.S. *Daphne*] arrived here a few days ago. The recommendation of Doctor Franklin Seconded by that of Monsieur de Coudrie has ensured him a Majority, a Commission only but no employment at present.[9]

A Commission of Major General is granted to the Marqui de la Fayette the young nobleman who lately came from Charles Town. He required no pension, no Special Command; the honour of fighting

near General Washington & having rank in the Army was all he
coveted except opportunities to shew his Zeal for the glorious cause of
American Freedom either in the Field, or at Court when it shall be
judged he can be more Servicable at Versailles. This illustrious Stranger
whose address & manner bespeak his birth will Serve a short Campaign
& then probably return to France & Secure to us the powerful Interest
of his high & extensive connexions.[10]

General Howe has published by proclamation an extraordinary
regulation of Trade in New York, calculated as they pretend to Starve
the Rebels.[11] Except the necessary article of Salt we abound in good
things although we pay abundantly for them. Salt is excessively dear,
16 Dollars per bushel. Nevertheless the Enemy's men who are purchased & fed at much dearer rate will be all defunct or banished before our whole Stock of Salt is exhausted. From the Same quarter we
learn that the Inhabitants of that City & its environs are very unhappy
infinitely more so than their old friends whom they infamously forsook.
I have seen & read English News papers up to the 13 May & Letters
from France late as June. England is truely distressed on all hands.
She has Suffered by Captures made by the Americans & Frenchmen
Americanized far beyond my former apprehensions. The number of
Privateers Maned by Frenchmen under English Captains & Congress
Commissions is astonishing. These have destroyed the English West
India & African Trade & are daily making prizes in the Channel from
Scilly to the German Sea. To such insults do the British Ministry
Tamely Submit—while on the other hand they meanly threaten Hol-
land only for having connived at illicit Trade with us. You have seen
Sir Joseph Yorkes memorial presented at the Hague, I will Send you
the Dutch Envoy's humble answer & we learn from undoubted authority that a Mr. Vanbibber our Commissioner or Agent was lately
imprisoned at St. Eustatia for having caused an English Vessel to be
taken in Sight of the Island.[12] Tis however Said this is the effect of
policy. I will not take upon me to comment but you may depend upon
it we have now a Vessel for War building in Amsterdam which will be
equal or is intended to be, to an English 64 Gun Ship & that the States
of Holland are as anxiously concerned to establish our Independence as
the French are, & that in order to be ready for defense they are
augmenting their Navy.

Our Agents in France have contracted with proper persons to dispatch an advice Boat together with 30 Tons of Merchandize if required once a Month to Congress. The first arrived at Portsmouth
a few days ago & brought us the accounts which the News papers &
This have retailed to you together with Some of a more private nature.
The Second Sailed as I suppose the latter end of June or beginning
of July & on this Instant learn she was taken within Six hours of her

leaving port—Stratagem which must be guarded against in future time.

Mr Lee (Arthur) had been at Madrid where he had been well received as a private Agent for the American States, but the Court would not recognize him in any higher Character. From thence we have obtained Strong assurances of friendship. The ports of Spain in Europe & that of Havanna in America are open to our Ships Warlike & Commercial & every desirable encouragement held out to us. Content with this Since no more was to be gained, Mr Lee turned his face to the Court of Berlin.[13] I long to know his reception & Success there.

I shall send to the President Copy of a Letter from a very intelligent writer at Paris which he will probably give Wells to print,[14] the Gentleman to whom it was addressed assures me we may depend upon his correspondents veracity. Indeed tis no more than consonant with advices which we have received from our Commissioners. You will learn there how much all the States in Europe, Portugal excepted, Interest themselves in our Cause, it is said that even the Empress of Russia wishes our Establishment & we are assured we shall not be troubled with Troops from her dominions. Our greatest Enemies are within ourselves & not among those Men who oppose us by Arms or who honestly & openly profess themselves averse from our measures & politics. You would be astonished were you here to see the number & influence of the property Men. I call them so because almost every Man of them were the most Vigorous in opposing the measures of the British Ministry until they perceived *that* opposition, proceeding to a serious War, then fear of the Loss of Life & Estate shocked their faith, they wished to remain neuter, they still acknowledged that America had been greatly aggrieved but withdrew from the Councils & Society of their former Colleagues under pretences, some that Independence had been declared too soon, others that it had never been their design to be Independent. A few such we have in Carolina, observe them, they are Men of property called sensible & good Sort of Men. They are cunning Men, & their cunning is exceedingly baneful to a cause which in their hearts they wish well. If we lose that Cause it will be the effect of their timidity & their pernicious examples. Whether their wishes to enjoy their Estates in quiet will succeed I know not—I rather beleive they will drag a few years of life through painful reproaches & reflections— but I say, Such Men in this State & that of New York abound—& unless the progress of Burgoyne & his junction with Sir William Howe is Speedily prevented they will have room to expand to join the Enemy & to reduce the friends of Freedom to the utmost hazards & difficulties.

The amazing scarcity & high prices of articles formerly imported from Europe & the West Indies have influenced the rates of every necessary of Life. Fire Wood delivered at a House not 1/4 Miles from the Wharf at £20 Carolina Currency per Chord, Butter at this Season the best a Dollar a pound, Beef 6/3, Mutton & other small Meat 7/6, Rum £12, Wine £13, Brown Sugar 25/, Horses at Stable a Dollar & upwards per day—for a Living Room, a Bed Chamber & the use of a Kitchen, where I find my own Fire & my own food of every kind, my Cook also, I pay 14 2/3ds Dollars per Week, & so in proportion for every thing else. These extraordinary circumstances hurt a few people, I am one among the hurt, but they by no means threaten immediate ruin to America, yet from them these property Men denounce our destruction & are very industrious to impress the minds of weak people with the most direful apprehensions. Some Steps have been taken by the Executive power to remove such Men from the Capital, weak & feeble attempts & hitherto without any good effect. We are not yet Sufficiently distressed to make us Sufficiently in earnest. An old friend of mine now a rigid Tory, complained to me of the friends of Liberty who had on the 4 July broke the Glass Windows of such quiet people as had refused to illuminate their Houses upon that anniversary. In reply I expressed my concern for the ill timed destruction of Glass and added for his consolation, that he might depend upon this as a type of broken bones to that Glass unless they soon reformed or removed out of the Country. I have dwelt too long perhaps upon a Subject which you are well acquainted with, but although you are well acquainted with the Subject in general, you had no Idea when I left Charles Town of the number & influence of the Tories in these parts.

7th August. Your obliging Letters of 4th & 5th July by Colo C C Pinckney just came to hand & I thank you for all the trouble you have taken for me. More particular replies may appear in the sequel of this or in a future Letter.[15]

LB (ScHi).
[1] See Brig. Gen. Roche de Fermoy's July 25 letter to President Hancock in PCC, item 78, 9:107–12.
[2] See *JCC*, 8:588–89.
[3] This information was false.
[4] The capture of Capt. John Manley and the Continental frigate *Hancock* by H.M.S. *Rainbow* on July 8 is described in William J. Morgan, *Captains to the Northward: The New England Captains in the Continental Navy* (Barre, Mass.: Barre Publishing Co., 1959), pp. 89–91.
[5] See John Hancock to William Barton, July 26, 1777, note 1.
[6] See Wharton, *Diplomatic Correspondence*, 2:288.
[7] There is a brief discussion of the Carib Revolt of 1772–73 in Sir Alan Burns, *History of the British West Indies* (Norwich, England: Jarrold & Sons Ltd., 1954), pp. 505–6. The report of a new Carib uprising on St. Vincents was untrue.
[8] This statement is puzzling. Congress agreed to make Baron de Holtzendorf a Continental lieutenant colonel, in accordance with his agreement with Silas Deane, on July 17—five days before Laurens took his seat as a delegate. Perhaps

Laurens means that there was some delay in carrying out the July 17 resolution and he helped to clear it up. *JCC,* 8:559–60.

[9] Congress was even more impressed with the chevalier de Failly than Laurens supposed, for on August 21 it appointed him a lieutenant colonel and assigned him to the northern department. *JCC,* 8:638, 663.

[10] There is much original material pertaining to the marquis de Lafayette's July 31 appointment in Lafayette, *Papers* (Idzerda), 1:3–88.

[11] This proclamation, dated July 17, appeared in the *New-York Gazette: and the Weekly Mercury,* July 21, 1777.

[12] For the Anglo-Dutch confrontation Laurens mentions here, see James Lovell to Joseph Whipple, July 29, 1777, note. For the case of Abraham Van Bibber, see Friedrich Edler, *The Dutch Republic and American Independence* (Baltimore: Johns Hopkins Press, 1911), pp. 56–58.

[13] See Wharton, *Diplomatic Correspondence,* 2:292–96, 319–20.

[14] John Wells, publisher of the *South-Carolina and American Gazette.*

[15] For the continuation of this letter, see Laurens to Gervais, August 9, 1777.

Richard Law to Nathaniel Shaw, Jr.

Sir   Philadelphia Augt 5t. 1777

The foregoeing is a Copy of Mr Mifflins Petition.[1] When I arrived here Mr Mifflin was not in Town for sometime, when he came I gave him your Letter. He sayd he was immediately going out again & should return in about a fortnight when he would confer with me further upon the Matter but have not seen him since. I beleive they have not got the papers from admiralty Court relative thereto. However Sir as soon as I can get them to attend on it you shall hear further from me on the Subject. In the mean time youll see how far the Petition states the Facts aright & let me hear from you thereon.

I have taken up one hundred pounds L[awful] m[one]y of Mr Whartons & given a Draught on you therefore shall send you a Draught for sd Sum on the Treasury or pay Table.

As to News youll see all there is in the public Papers. We have for sometime been expecting an Attack upon this City, but the Fleet has now left our Capes & tis probable are gone with a Design to penetrate the North River. Genll How by this Manouvre has drawn Gen. Washingtons army this way, which leis en[camp]ed about 7 mile from hence. The great Advantage our Enemies have by their water Movements, put it in their power to harrass our Army by sudden & long Marches. We were in hopes that How would have pursued his attempt up this River as it is imagined we might have received them here to as great Advantage as any Where Else. Our Accounts from France look favourable and have reason to think a war in Europe cant be far Distant. We have many Frenchmen over, applying for Commissions &c bringing most exorbitant Contracts, which Congress have been obliged to disanull. However some have been taken into our Service, where our Interest & Policy made it necessary.

Scyler & St Clair are ordered down to head Quarters in order that
an Enquiery be made into the Conduct of the northern Department.
General Gates is ordered to take the Command there & to call on the
neighbouring States for Militia. Have not time to add but that I am,
Your humble Servt,   Rich Law

RC (CtNlHi). Addressed: "Mr. Nathel Shaw junr, Mercht, New London,
Connecticut." Law began this letter to Shaw at the foot of a copy he had made
of Samuel Mifflin's petition to Congress.
   ¹ Mifflin's May 8 petition requested the assistance of Congress in prosecuting
an appeal against the capture and condemnation of his brig *Sally* at New Bern,
N.C. A second petition which he submitted to Congress on December 24, 1777,
a draft resolve recommending that Mifflin appeal to the North Carolina assembly
for a new trial, and Mifflin's May 8 petition are in PCC, item 42, 5:59–62, 65,
67–68.

James Lovell to William Whipple?

My Dear Sir   [August 5, 1777]
   Matters remain here much as when I wrote you last, except some
alarms caused by a report that a very large fleet appeared off Cape
Ann on the 31st Ulto. The time agreed very well with the accots we
previously had of the fleets sailing from N.Y. As we supposed The
Town was the Enemies object, all hands were preparing to go thither
when on a sudden the Fleet vanished in a fogg & we have heard nothing of it since, but its still a matter of great speculation where this
invincible Armada is Bound. It is reported as Gen'l Washingtons
opinion that Virginia is the object but those who have not the most
favorable opinion of that Climate think they know better than to go
there, that this is only a finesse and that they will return immediately
& push up Hudsons River. Others will have it that they are certainly
coming this way. The last opinion I endeavor to support, not because
I realize it, but because I wo'd have everybody in readiness if that
sho'd be the case. The enemies ships are so thick on the coast that it
is almost impossible to escape them, one of them chased a ship on
shore a few days ago within 6 or 7 miles of this. She proved to be
a West India man which had been taken by a Connecticut Privateer
but unfortunately for the captors the tide was rising & the enemy soon
took her off with them. It was reported yesterday that we had gained
great advantages in a Battle on Wood Creek & that the Enemy had
left Skeenborough & Castleton but we have no acco'ts from that way
that can be depended on. I wish I co'd Know from the fountain of
intelligence how matters stand with the Northern Army and to what
the late extraordinary disaster is owing. Here the general Cry is treachery and some go so far as to name the sum given, however these re-

flections are always to be expected on such occasions. If you meet with any plans of that country I wish you wo'd send me sketches that I may form some Idea of their movements. Can nothing be done with the officers that are loitering about.

I am told Boston is full of them, I suppose they pretend on the Recruiting service but if that is their business it must be for the next war for by the means they seem to use the recruits they raise cannot be fit for service under 17 or 18 years.

Tr (PHi). Endorsed: "James Lovell Esqr. Aug't 5 1777."

Henry Marchant to Nicholas Cooke

Honored Sir,   Philadelphia Augt. 5th. 1777
The large Fleet which sailed from New-York, and hath since been seen off and on the Capes of Deleware, have not been seen or heard of since last Thursday at sunset. A few there are, who still beleive they are yet intending an Attack upon this City—some there are, who suppose them gone still more South-ward, to Maryland, Virginia or So. Carolina —but the most general Opinion is, that they have either returned to New-York to push up the North River, or have gone to Rhode-Island. By this Faint, they have drawn Our Army at too great a Distance to give immediate assistance to the Eastern States; besides that Our Men must be greatly fatigued by such long Marches. Our Army is however in great Spirits & good Health. They are indeed much disappointed in not meeting with Mr. How, but will not murmur at making a much longer March than their last; If They can but releive their Brothers, and cut off our *Amphibious* Enemies from their Sea Retreat. I hope the New England States have been in such Suspicions of the Intentions of Mr. How, as to have put them upon every necessary Measure of Opposition. This I expect will be a trying Day to New-England. Her own future Happiness or Misery, and Her Fame amongst the Nations of the World, depend upon Her Firmness, Fortitude and Patriotism at this critical Moment. Threatned and invaded on all Sides, may She rise with Strength and Dignity, striking Terror and dismay upon the Hearts of Her Enemies, exciting Envy even from Her Friends, and securing thereby Glory & Honor to Herself & Peace and Happiness to Millions yet unborn.

Ticonderoga! I know what the Public must expect! I hope their Ardour has not been damped. I hope the Conduct of Congress will give Spirit & Vigour to Our Arms in the Northern Department. Genls. Sc——r and Sin——r are ordered to Head-Quarters, Genl. Gates is ordered immediately to repair to the Northern Departmt. A Thorough

Examination must and will be made. Meanwhile Our noble Exertions may restore Our Honor & secure Our Country.

The Treasury have not yet procured the Loan Office Certificates from Maryland; They expect them in a Day or two, when they will be immediately forwarded. I have heard nothing yet of the Arrival of your Vessell at Maryland for Flower &c.

Some few Days past upon an Application of One of the Southern States for Money, it was moved that a Carriage and a Guard might be procured at the Expence of the States.[1] And it appeared it had been granted several Times, this was somewhat surprising, as the New England States have ever risked their own Money & been at the sole Expence of conveying it. It was said those Charges would be allowed, I therefore advise you of it, that the proper Charges may be brought forward in your next Account.

Before I left the State a Committee was appointed to correspond with your Delegates, but I have never had a Line from that Committee. Perhaps Sir, there is not a State in the Union, that has so little Correspondance with its Delegates, upon Measures which respect the States in general, and their own State in particular.

Our Advices yesterday recd. from France are equal to Our most sanguine Expectations. An immediate Publication of them might frustrate Our Own Wishes, as well as the Efforts of Our Friends to serve us. By a Letter yesterday recd. from Martinico, we are justly lead soon to expect a War between France & England. Our Advices also from France strengthen those Expectations. It is agreed by all that if we support Ourselves but this year, the Day is, by the Blessing of Heaven, Our Own. And We must all agree that the present Strength of Our Enemies in America, is nothing to Our real Strength, if unanimously and vigorously exerted. With my best Wishes for the Honor, Peace & Happiness of Our Country and the Deliverance of Our State from the Invasions of Our Enemies, and the present threatning Appearances against it, and for Your personal Health & long Continuance in the Affection, Esteem & Honor of your Country I am, Honored Sir, yr. most obdt. & humble Servt.   Hy Marchant

P.S. I submit it to the wisdom of the Genl. assembly, whether it is not essentially necessary to empower their Delegates in Congress to Act untill others shall be chosen in their Stead, and take Their Seats in Congress. Their appointment for the year, to the contrary, notwithstanding.[2] Mr. Ellery can more fully explain to you the necessity of this measure.

I enclose you certain Resolves of Congress, least you should not otherwise receive Them timely, as they require the immediate Consideration of the Genl. Assembly.[3]

RC (R–Ar).

[1] Although this issue is not mentioned in the journals, the state in question

was probably North Carolina. See North Carolina Delegates to John Allen, July 11, 1777.

[2] The Rhode Island Assembly adopted Marchant's proposal during its August 1777 session. John R. Bartlett, ed., *Records of the State of Rhode Island and Providence Plantations in New England*, vols. 8–10 (Providence: Cooke, Jackson & Co., 1863–65), 8:290–91.

[3] These were July 31 resolves on Continental Army recruits and deserters. See ibid., pp. 298–300; and *JCC*, 8:593–95. President Hancock also sent a copy of them to Governor Cooke in a brief letter written on August 6: "I am just now so much Engaged that I have only time to Cover you a resolution of Congress for promoting the Recruiting Service to which I beg leave to Refer your Attention." American Manuscripts, RPJCB.

Robert Morris to John Langdon

Dear Sir   Philada. August 5th. 1777

I have yours of the 21st July and am sorry to find every part of this poor Continent so exceedingly fettered in their Trade and convulsed about their Constitutions & Governments. We must have patience & let things take their Course. I will not at this time give any orders about the Sugars but if the Enemies Fleet which lately paraded to our Capes & back shou'd go your way I depend that you will do the need-full to secure my property & remain Dr sir Your Obedt hble Servt.

                                                                                  Robt Morris

P.S. The bearer has been detained longer than was agreable to him, but the Committees have not time to dispatch business as fast as they coud wish. I pray you to put the letters enclosed herewith into the mail & give the Captain of the Packet strict orders to throw the Mail over if needfull, as no Public dispatches shou'd fall into the Enemies hands if it can be avoided. I am always yours &c,[1]   RM

RC (Capt. J. G. M. Stone, Annapolis, Md., 1974).

[1] This day Morris also wrote the following brief letter to St. George Tucker at Williamsburg, Va., on behalf of Willing, Morris & Co. "Your favour of the 25th Ulto. came by the Post yesterday & we are sorry to tell You that soon after the Commencement of the present War with Great Britain the Underwriters in this City declined the business & that it never has been taken up again so that all the Commerce carried out from this port is at the sole & entire risque of the adventurers. We shou'd have been very happy to serve You on this occasion as we shall also if future opportunities puts it in our power." Tucker-Coleman Papers, ViW.

New York Delegates to George Clinton

Sir   Philad 5 Aug 1777

We wrote to your Excellency Yesterday[1] and have now only to observe that General Washington declind nominating a Successor to General Schuyler. Congress therefore thought fit to appoint General Gates; who we suppose will soon proceed to the northern department.

We remain, with very great Respect, Sir, your Excellency's most Obed. humble Servs.   Jas. Duane for Self & Colleagues

RC (PHi). Endorsed: "Letters of 4 & 5 August from Representatives of the State in Continental Congress."
[1] Not found.

John Penn to Richard Caswell

Sir   Philada Augt. 5th 1777
I this day received your favour of the 15th July but as you take no notice of a letter I wrote you dated June 21st[1] I suppose it miscarried. In order therefore to answer some questions you put to me, Inform you that I was detained about two weeks occasioned by my horses geting hurt, and not being able to purchase others sooner.

I arrived here the 19th and Immediately con[ferred with] Doctor Burke on the most expeditious method of sending away the money agreeable to the direction of our Assembly. We accordingly went to the Treasury Board, the Gentn. promised to furnish us with 300,000 Dollars in a week at farthest. We could have sent off 100,000 which was the largest sum in the office for a long time but as we looked upon that sum as too trifling and were made to believe that we should be supplied from the loan office we waited. At length finding that the money was received in small sums and the Treasury board was so pressed, we obtained an order of Congress on Michl Hiligass esqr. for 300,000 Dollars. He was at Baltimore superintending the press, with direction to send that sum to Newbern as soon as he possibly could under a proper guard. We were obliged to appoint a person to receive the money tho' it went at the risque of the United States and at their expence.

Lieutenant Allen was recommended by Mr. Blunt & Genl. Nash for that purpose. Our Troops were in possession of some No. Carolina dollars wch would not pass here and as every necessary of life was so exceedingly dear I thought it but Justice to exchange with the Soldiers and give them Continental money. I accordingly recd. 2485 1/2 dollars which sum was sent by Mr Allen with a list, made out by Mr. Blunt of the different parcels. This with the other money I hope you have received before this.

I assure you it was not in my power or Mr. Burke's to send off the money sooner. I knew the pressing demand you had for it and the very frequent applications made by us to Congress on that subject, will excuse us from the charge of inattention or negligence to that buisness. The reason I did not mention any thing relative to the money in my letter of the 25th was owing to my having wrote fully on that subject a few days before.

Inclosed I send you a resolve of Congress relative to the recruiting business & apprehending deserters.

General Howe three weeks ago was supposed to have the greatest part of his Army on board with his horse. Upwards of 220 ships sailed from New York, part of them was seen near Egharbour, this induced Genl. Washington to march 8, or 10,000 men near this City. The Fleet appeared at the mouth of the Delaware for three days and then went off in the night. We have not been informed what course they went.

We have some accounts from France & Spain that are agreeable. Those powers are disposed to supplie us with all sorts of military stores, and to give our paper money a credit.

The Marques de Fiette a young Nobleman of the first Family in France and Nephew to their Embassador now in England, has la[tely?] got here. His desire was to obtain rank in [our] army without pay or command. His request [has] been Complied with. I send you some News papers. I am with due respect, Sir, Your most obt. Servt.

John Penn

RC (InU).
[1] Not found.

George Walton to George Washington

Sir,   Philadelphia, August 5, 1777.

I moved Congress a few days ago, to order Brigadier General Mc.Intosh from his station in Georgia to join the grand Army; and it was objected to, because it was feared it might derange the Army, or that you would have no command for him. The cause of my having made this proposition was that he had lately fought a Duel with Governor Gwinnett, in which the latter had fallen; and I was afraid the friends of the deceased, made sore by the loss of their principal, would again blow up the embers of party & dissention, and disturb the harmony & vigour of the Civil & military authorities.

I have since received a letter from Georgia, proving that my conjectures were too well founded. I therefore take the liberty of requesting to know, whether it will be convenient and agreeable to you that he should be ordered to join the grand Army.[1]

He is a man of sense and judgment, with a great experience of the world; and, in point of bravery, he is fit to fight under the banners of General Washington.

I have the happiness to be, Sir, your Excellency's most obedient
Servant,   Geo Walton

N.B. As I intend to send off an Express to Georgia tomorrow I should
be obliged by an answer to day.

RC (DLC).
    [1] On August 1 Congress had directed Robert Howe to relieve Lachlan Mc-
Intosh of his Georgia command and assign him to other duties. After learning
of Washington's favorable response to Walton's request, Congress immediately
directed Howe to order McIntosh to headquarters at once. See *JCC,* 8:597,
616. Washington's August 6 letter to Walton is in Washington, *Writings* (Fitzpatrick), 9:25–26.

John Adams to Abigail Adams

Philadelphia Aug. 6. 1777 Wednesday
Price current. Oak Wood £4:15s:od. Per Cord. Bad Beer, not so
good as your Small Beer, 15d: Per Quart. Butter one Dollar Per Pound.
Beef 2s:6d. Coffee a dollar a Pound. Bohea 8 dollars. Souchong £4:10s.
Hyson £6. Mean brown sugar 6s. 6d. a pound. Loaf sugar 18s. a pound.
Rum 45s. a Gallon. Wine 2 dollars a Bottle.[1]
    The Hounds are all still at a Fault. Where the game is gone, is the
Question. The Scent is quite lost.
    Sullivan Thinks the Fleet is gone to Portsmouth—Green to New-
port—Parsons, up the North River—Mifflin to Philadelphia. Thus each
one secures his Reputation among his Townsmen for Penetration and
Foresight, in Case the Enemy should go against his Town.
    Some Conjecture Charlestown S.C.—others, Georgia—others Cheasa-
peak Bay.
    For my Part, I have formed an Opinion, in which I am as clear and
positive as ever I was in my Life. I think I can adduce Arguments
enough to convince any impartial, cool Mind, that I am in the Right.
    My Opinion is, that four Months Time will discover where the
Fleet is gone—perhaps less Time than that.
    Some begin to be whimsical, and guess them gone to the West
Indies. But this is impossible. Some surmise Hallifax—some old England. But these are too flattering Conjectures.[2]

RC (MHi). Adams, *Family Correspondence* (Butterfield), 2:302.
    [1] For no apparent reason, Adams left the next half page blank in the MS.
    [2] Adams continued in much this same vein in his brief letter to Abigail the
next day. "We have not yet the least Intimation of Howes Design. He is wasting
away the Time. Let him aim at what Object he will, he will have scarcely Time
to secure that, and will have none left to pursue his Advantage, if he gains any.
    "Burgoine I hope will be checked, and driven back. I hope the New England-

men will now exert themselves, for it has cost Us, severe Conflicts, to get Affairs in that Department, in the Order they are. Gates cost Us a great deal of Pains." Adams, *Family Correspondence* (Butterfield), 2:303.

John Hancock to Certain States

Gentlemen,   Philada. Aug. 6th. 1777
The Congress having ordered Generals Schuyler & St. Clair to Head Quarters that an Enquiry may be made into their Conduct and the Reasons of the Evacuation of Ticonderoga, they have directed Genl. Gates to take the Command in that Department and to repair thither with the utmost Expedition.

In the present critical State of our Affairs in that Quarter, it is absolutely necessary that some vigorous and decisive Measures should be taken to stop the Progress of the Enemy. These Steps should be taken as early as possible, as the Consequences of Delay may be extremely disagreeable. From the great Advantage our Enemies have over us in the Facility with which their Troops may be transported by Sea to any Part of America, they will always have it in their Power to make a Descent before the Continental Army can possibly arrive to oppose them. The Militia therefore whenever this happens must be depended upon, and their Exertions I trust will never be wanting when called on, either to defend their own Country, or to join with the Army of the United States to oppose the Common Enemy. I am therefore most earnestly to entreat you will order such Part of your Militia to reinforce the Army under Gen. Gates as he may judge sufficient, & that you will exert yourselves to comply with the Enclosed Requisition of Congress[1] without the least Delay.

I have the Honour to be, Gentlemen, your most obed & hble Set.

J.H. Presid.

P.S. I must request your Attention to the other Resolves herewith transmitted as recommending the most effectual Way to fill up the Regiments, and to supply the continual Waste of Men Occasioned by the Events of War, & other Losses unavoidable in an Army.[2]

LB (DNA: PCC, item 12A). Addressed to the assemblies of New Hampshire, Massachusetts, Connecticut, New York, New Jersey, and Pennsylvania.

[1] See *JCC*, 8:600–601. Congress took this step as a result of a suggestion Washington made to a committee of delegates that had been ordered to confer with him in Philadelphia on August 2. See *JCC*, 8:599; and Washington, *Writings* (Fitzpatrick), 9:9.

[2] See *JCC*, 8:593–95. This day Hancock also wrote a brief letter to James Bleeker informing him "that Congress have this Day appointed you Deputy Commissary General of Issues for the Northern Department, and Inclos'd I Send your Commission. You have also herewith the Regulations for the Com-

missary's Department. I hope it will be agreeable to you to undertake the Business." Horatio Gates Papers, NHi. Bleeker replaced Elisha Avery, who was appointed to this office on June 18 but declined to serve. *JCC,* 8:477, 601, 617.

William Williams to Jonathan Trumbull, Sr.

Hond Sir   Philadelphia Aug. 6 1777

I can do very little more than inclose You a Newspaper, as I am & have been several Days exceedingly unwell, a heavy constant Head Ach, from it habit, weakness & faintness &c. I have before me a Vomit I am going to take.

The Enemys Ships have disappeard again now for a number of Days. They had returnd after once going out. Where They are going we cannot tell, probably up N. River. Genl Washington remains here, & his Army at & ab[out] German Town, 6 Miles distant. Genl Washington yesterday sent in a Letter beging Congress to excuse him from appointing the officer to the Comand of the Nothern army, assigning plausible Reasons, upon which Congress took it up & appointed Gen Gates. It was strenuously opposed by N. York, & supported by N England, & was carried by almost every Vote. The truth is Duane &c had earnestly remonstrated agst Him to the Genl & told him it wod greatly disgust their Convention &c (The fact is Schuyler hates him) & N. Engld Delegates had written to the Genl in favr of his appointmt & so I conclude He was embarrasd & chose to get rid of it, & it has turned out well.

I hope N England will take their own measure & drive Burgoyne into the Lakes, without waiting for Congress, no not a moment. Their resolves you will see in the Paper. Can it be that N E will be long driven & distresd by 6000 men, surely we can eat them up at a Meal. O That They wod rouse in earnest, the work wod be short & easy. I trust they will, & the more for the late shamefull Conduct to say no more, of St Clair &c.

I cannot add but my best Regards to my dear Friends & that I am with the greatest Respect & dutiful Regard, your most Obed. & most H Servt,   W. Williams

[*P.S.*] I hope my illness will go off, & beg no Body to give themselves any Pain on my Acco.

RC (PHi).

Samuel Adams to John Langdon

My dear Sir,   Philade August 7. 1777
   Major Bass will be kind enough to deliver to you this Letter. He brought me a very friendly Message from you for which I return you my hearty Thanks. If I had Inclination or Leisure to write a Letter of Complement, I am sure you would not be pleasd with it. The Times are very serious; our Affairs are in a critical Situation. The Enemy, after long promising a Visit to this City, made an Appearance last Week near the Capes of Delaware. But they have not been seen these six days past. The Hounds are in fault and have lost Scent of them. We shall hear where they are gone, I dare say, before long. It belongs to the military Gentlemen to penetrate their Design. I think they could not have come here in a better time, because we were well prepared for them. General Washington had drawn his Forces into the Neighborhood of this Place and I verily believe the people here, divided and distracted as they are about their internal Government, would have joynd in sufficient Numbers to have given a good Account of them.
   The shameful Defeat of our Forces at Ticonderoga is not more distressing to us than it is vexatious. A thorough Scrutiny into the Causes of it must and will be made. For this Purpose Schuyler and St Clair are ordered to Head Quarters. I confess I cannot at present account for it even upon the Principle of Cowardice. There seems to me to be the evident Marks of Design. Bad as our Affairs are in that Quarter they are not desperate. Gates is gone to take the Command. He is an honest and able officer; always belovd by his Soldiers because he always shares with them in Fatigue and Danger. This has not been said of his immediate Predecessor. I hope the N. England States will once more make a generous Exertion, and if they do I am deceivd if Burgoyns Prosperity does not soon prove his Ruin.
   Our Intelligence from Europe is very flattering to us. The virtuous and sensible there universally wish well to our Cause. They say we are fighting for the Liberty and Happiness of Mankind. We are at least, contending for the Liberty & Happiness of our own Country and Posterity. It is a glorious Contest. We shall succeed if we are virtuous. I am infinitely more apprehensive of the Contagion of Vice than the Power of all other Enemies. It is the Disgrace of human Nature that in most Countries the People are so debauchd, as to be utterly unable to defend or enjoy their Liberty.
   Pay my respects to Colo Whipple. He promisd to write to me. I hope he will soon have Leisure to fulfill his promise. A letter from you would oblige me much. Adieu.

FC (NN). Addressed: "To J Langdon Esqr Portsmo N H."

Committee for Foreign Affairs to the
Commissioners at Paris

No. 7   In Committee for Foreign Affairs

Gentlemen   Philadelphia Augt 7. 1777

Inclosed are duplicates of Commissions and Instructions for Willm. Lee and Ralf Izard Esqrs. and Triplicates of Letters No 1, 2, 3, 4, 5, 6.

Since our last No. 6[1] a variety of Circumstances in the Military department have happened, many of which are so intricate and unfinished as not to enable us to draw any just Conclusion therefrom.

Immediately after the unsuccessful attempt made by Genl Howe to cut off a division of our Army under Lord Sterling as mentioned in No. 6 The whole Body of the Enemy retreated to Staten Island, embarked on board their fleet and on the 23 of July put to Sea. On the 27th they were off the Capes of Deleware. Genl Washington with the Army arrived at German Town the 29th. The 31st the Enemy's fleet stood out again to Sea. They made a Second appearance at the Capes, but did not attempt to come in, since which we have heard no Account of them. As this Packet goes from the Eastward you will probably be furnished with something from that Quarter before she sails.

Our Worst News is, we have lost Ticonderoga; whether by Neglect or necessity, Cowardice or good Conduct will appear afterwards. Congress have ordered Genl Gates to that Department and have directed that Genls Schuyler and St Clair appear at Head Qrs. that enquiry be made into their Conduct of this Mysterious Affair. In the Philadelphia News Papers of July 16th & 23 and Augst 5th & 6th you will see Genls. Schuyler's & St. Clair's Letters, and the resolves of Congress.

We have been fortunate enough to take and unfortunate enough to lose again the Fox Frigate, she was made a Prize of by Capts Manly and McNeal but a 40 and 64 being in Sight when she struck she was afterwards retaken by them.

Major Genl Prescot who Commanded the Enemy's forces at Rhode Island was seized and made Prisoner of by a Small Party under Lt Col Barton, see Genl Washington's Letter to Congress in a Philadelphia News Paper July 23d. Congress have presented the Col with a Sword, and Likewise Lt Col Meigs with another who performed a Gallant exploit on L Island bringing off near an hundred Prisoners and destroying a Large Quantity of forage.

Were it not for the Ticonderoga Affair we should have nothing but good News to write, and even that may in the End be as lucky a Circumstance to the general Cause as their attempting to march thro' the Jersies last Winter. We have a fine healthy Army anxious for nothing so much as to meet the Enemy. Surely! it must appear a ridiculous thing in Europe that Genl Howe should be thus shunning the Army he came to conquer, and wasting his time on running up and down the Coast with his whole fleet at this hot season of the year, when the ministry in England and perhaps Ld Stormont at Paris have given out that he has penetrated an hundred Miles or more up the Country.

We are with the greatest Respect, Gentlemen, yr. most Obt humble Servants,   Benja Harrison

Robt Morris

James Lovell

P.S. Please to forward the Letters directed to Arthur Lee Esqr and M. Dumas, paragraphs of which relate to you.[2]

RC (PPAmP). "Duplicate" copy in a clerical hand.

[1] That is, Committee for Foreign Affairs to the Commissioners at Paris, July 2, 1777.

[2] Probably the committee's August 8 letters to Arthur Lee and Charles W. F. Dumas.

James Lovell to William Whipple

Dear Sir   August 7th 1777

By the delay of Mr Bass here without any good purpose being answered, you will find things go much after the old sort. Indeed, I do not think if he had been earlier dismissed, any thing could be sent by the packet boat which brought the dispatches from France for she must have sailed before he got here.

I still think General W's march to this City will give Howe and Burgoyne full swing in New England and New York. There seems to be no more moving here than if there was no other spot in America where it could be expected the British army could be tempted to land.

I ought to own to you that General Gates is quite of opinion that the enemy will make themselves Masters of Chesapeake and Delaware Bays for it—then will come up this river to attack the Cheveaux making Wilmington head quarters. I do not know whether I tell his story right for I did not believe what he said enough to fix it in my memory. My greatest anxiety is, to have him gone to stop Burgoyne's army which we hear is at Saratoga.

Mr Du Coudray has put in a memorial and petition wherein he requests that I may be dismissed from any Committee relative to his affairs and that no attention may be paid to any thing I may have said relative to his treaty with Mr Deane. Even his most enamored advocates did not think proper to support his petition. It was dismissed.[1]

I hope Gates' name will produce a willingness to turn out in the Militia of New England. He will have some excellent French officers with him who may induce the Canadians to keep back at least with the Indians if not desert over to us.

We promised great spirit for our countrymen, if they could only have a brave Commander instead of one whom they thought the contrary and some of them even thought to have been traitorous.

General Fermoy writes like one crazy with chagrin. Though he voted for evacuating the posts, yet he meant to have sold them very dear. He says there never was so ill conducted a retreat made by man before. You see by Jay's publication that St Clair excuses Schuyler altogether.

I need not Scrawl any more as Mr Bass can tell you all the chat-history of this city and I have no secret informations beyond what I have before mentioned.

Your affectionate friend,   J.L.

Tr (DLC).

[1] For Du Coudray's August 5 memorial asking that Lovell be excluded from any committees dealing with his contract with Silas Deane, see PCC, item 41, 2:19–23. In it, Du Coudray incorporated both a July 29 letter he had written to Lovell explaining his views and Lovell's curt July 30 reply. "Your letter of yesterday," Lovell responded, "was this hour Delivered to me by Mr. Defleury. The manner implied in the motive mentioned to induce me to give an *immediate* answer puts it out of my power to give any further than that, I am JL." Congress voted to dismiss the memorial by a vote of 7 to 4 on August 6. *JCC,* 8:615.

John Witherspoon to David Witherspoon

Dear David,   Philadelphia, August 7, 1777.

I received your last and Mr. Smith's two weeks ago at least, and I am sorry that I have not been, nor am at present, able to write you fully. You will have heard with pleasure that the enemy did not get so far as Princeton on their last excursion, which was very happy for us. They have lately appeared at Delaware Capes, but they are now gone from thence, and have not been seen since Thursday last.

I am glad to see that you are thinking of determining your profession for life. I have not time to write upon this subject, but shall do it fully in a few days. You know what my desire and ambition is upon that subject; but I am of all things most concerned that you should fear God. I want much to hear that you have renewed your baptismal engagements in the Lord's Supper. Your absence and distance have hindered me from many opportunities of speaking to you upon that subject. Your friends here are all well—James at the camp at German-

town, and John at Trenton. I go this morning to Princeton, and shall
return next week. My kind love to Mr. and Mrs. Smith and all friends.
I am, dear David, Your affectionate father,

Jno. Witherspoon.

MS not found; reprinted from *Christian Advocate* 2 (October 1824) : 445.

John Adams to Abigail Adams

Philadelphia August 8. 1777

I have concluded to run the Risque of sending Turner Home. It
will save me the Expence of his Board and Horse.

The Moment he arrives, I hope you will send his Horse to Boston
to be sold at Vendue. If he rides the Horse let him be sold immediately.
If he rides the Mare, you may keep her if you chuse to do so and sell
the old Horse, provided the Mare will go in a Carriage which must be
tried, because I dont know that she ever was in one.

We have heard nothing from the Enemys Fleet, since they left the
Capes of Delaware. They may intend for Philadelphia yet, which makes
me a little irresolute about sending away my Man and Horse without
which I should be puzzled to get away from this Place, if it should
be invaded. I believe I shall delay his Journey for a few days. Perhaps
We shall hear more within that Time.

This day compleats Seven Months, since I left all that I delight in.
When shall I return? Not untill the Year is out, provided I can keep
myself tolerably well.

Our Accounts from the Northward are still gloomy. Gates is gone,
and I hope will restore some degree of Spirits and Confidence there.
Burgoigne is laying himself open to destruction, in that Quarter, every
day. It is strange that no Check is given him.

These vile Panicks, that seize People and Soldiers too, are very
difficult to get over. But at last they turn to Vigour, Fury and Des-
peration, as they did in the Jerseys. I suppose a few Tories in New
York, in the Grants and in Berkshire and Hampshire will join Burgoigne, but they will soon repent their rash Folly, and be sick of their
Masters. For indeed they will find that neither Burgoigne nor Howe,
nor their Master are kind Masters.

The longer We live, the more clearly We see, that nothing will serve
our Purpose, but discipline and Experience. Discipline—Discipline, is
wanting and must be introduced. The Affair of Ti. will introduce it.
The Public calls for Justice, and will have it. This Demand does Honour to the People and is a sure Omen of future Success and Prosperity.

RC (MHi). Adams, *Family Correspondence* (Butterfield), 2:303–4.

Samuel Adams to Elizabeth Adams

Dear Betsy   Philada. Augt 8 1777
    I have lately written to you by every opportunity and am determined
to omit none for the future, till I shall have the Pleasure of seeing
you, which I Intend some time in the Fall. We have heard Nothing of
the Enemies Fleet since this Day Week. General Gates is gone to take
the Command of the Northern Army in the Room of Schuyler. Gates
has always been belovd by his Soldiers & I hope will restore our Affairs
there; for although they are in a Situation bad enough I do not think
them desperate. He is empowerd to call on the N England Militia, who
I hope will once more make a generous Effort. If they do, I am mistaken if Burgoyne's present Success does not [prove his ruin]. A Change
of officers, I dare say, will give new Spirit to the Men. But I forget that
I am writing to a female upon the Subject of War. I know your whole
Soul is engagd in the great Cause. May Heaven prosper it! Adieu my
dear.   S A

[*P.S.*] My Regards to my Family & Friends.

RC (NN).

Committee for Foreign Affairs to
Charles W. F. Dumas

Sir   Philadelphia Augst. 8th. 1777
    We have received your several Favours to the 1st of May, and shall
always have a grateful Memory of your Sentiments and Exertions in
our Cause:[1] But, as we have now Commissioners settled in France, we
think it will be needless that you should be at the Trouble of making
and of forwarding to us from Time to Time that Collection of Papers
which we formerly mentioned to you. We shall inform our Friends at
Paris of our Opinion on this Head, and shall leave it to them to point
out the Ways in which your Zeal for Liberty may be most useful to
them & us with the least Degree of Trouble to yourself and Injury
to your domestick Interests. The part you have taken in Regard to
the Legacy of Daniel Schomacker & his Heirs does Honour to you as
a Man & a Christian. At present we are at a Loss about the District
from which you say he dated his Letter four years ago.[2] We shall make
publick what you have furnished us with, and we hope you will continue your laudable Efforts to procure the longest Period possible in
Favour of the Heirs.
    Our Affairs are not in so good a State as we know you earnestly
wish them to be; nor are they so injured as the great Preparations of

England may have led you & other Friends at a Distance to fear they would be at this Period of the 3d Campaign.

Genl. Burgoynes Advances over the Lakes are Disadvantages which will be greatly magnified by him: And General Howe will most probably gain some Ground, at first, wherever he is gone. But be assured, Sir, we have firm Hopes of final Success to that Cause which you have espoused as the Cause not only of America but of Mankind at large— the Cause of Liberty.

The Humility of the Count de Welderon's Memorial seems to have been followed by some positive Orders to our Disadvantage in the West Indies.[3] We doubt not you will give our Commissioners the fullest Information on all such Points, from whom we shall consequently obtain it.

We are with real Truth, Sir, your most humble Servts.

> Benja. Harrison
> Robt Morris
> James Lovell

RC (DLC). "Triplicate" copy in a clerical hand.

[1] Most of Dumas' letters to Congress are in PCC, item 93. Fortunately, Dumas also maintained a voluminous letterbook that contains even more of his dispatches to Congress as well as those to the American commissioners and agents in Europe, so that an almost complete file of his letters relating to the United States survives. The letterbook includes a brief account of the origins of Dumas' correspondence with the Committee of Secret Correspondence and summaries of the first two letters he wrote in response to the committee's letter to him of December 12, 1775. Thereafter Dumas identified each dispatch to the committee with a letter of the alphabet. Those acknowledged here "to the 1st of May" probably consisted of dispatches through "F" dated April 30, May 14, June 30, and September 1, 1776, and April 12 and May 1, 1777. PCC, item 93, fols. 18–64; and C.W.F. Dumas Letterbook, Inventaris I, Dumas Collection, Algemeen Ryksarchief, The Hague (DLC microfilm). Dumas' letters of April 30, May 14, and September 1, 1776, and April 12, 1777, are also in Wharton, *Diplomatic Correspondence*, 2:85–92, 134–36, 305–6.

[2] The copyist wrote the following note in the margin of the MS, which he keyed to this sentence and apparently intended as a reference to the unknown "district" mentioned: "found the next Week, and the papers delivered to the identical person."

[3] See James Lovell to Joseph Whipple, July 29, 1777, note.

Committee for Foreign Affairs to Arthur Lee

Sir   No. 1. In Committee. Philadelphia Aug 8. 1777

We have to acknowledge yours of the 18th of March from Victoria in Spain, and another of May 13th from Paris.[1] The first falls particularly under the Notice of the Committee of Commerce to whom it has been refered.

You could not at the time of writing, have been certified of the arrival of some interesting despatches from Congress to your Colleagues in France on the 10th of that Month, which might have occassioned a very considerable alteration in the Politics of the Court of Versailles, which would consequently influence those of the Court of Madrid.

The intelligence contained in your last is a most pleasing confirmation of the hopes which you had given us, of pecuniary aid from Spain. Whatever tends to establish the value of our paper currency is most highly important to us. Congress will immediately go into a Consideration of the several hints for this purpose given by you and Messrs Franklin & Deane. The unpleasing events in the Nothern Department has so far engaged the attention of all public bodies, that it has been impossible for Congress to write upon the Subjects mentioned to them by you early enough for us to forward their determinations by the present opportunity.[2]

By our several Letters dispatched in the armed Sloop Independence, from hence, or by Duplicates and Gazettes sent by Mr McCreary from Baltimore, you will know by way of Paris, the history of our Military affairs in a regular detail. We are at this time altogether uncertain as to Mr Howes destination, his Fleet not having been seen since the first of this month. Indeed we shall leave you for the most part to get information of our opperations from the gentlemen at Paris, to whom we shall have the most direct opportunities of conveyance. We wish you Success on the Embassy you are now engaged in, and we are pleased that you are so agreably connected with Mr Sayer, whose attachment to the cause of Liberty and this Country has been Manifisted. We are with much regard Sir your Friends & hum. Servts,

Signed—   Benj Harrison

                                                     Rob Morris

                                                     James Lovell

FC (DNA: PCC, item 79).

[1] Arthur Lee's March 18 and May 13 letters to the committee are in Wharton, *Diplomatic Correspondence,* 2:292–96, 319–20.

[2] For the actions taken by Congress in response to the commissioners' advice that money was available in Europe, see Elbridge Gerry to Unknown, September 10, 1777, note; and Henry Laurens to John Rutledge, September 10, 1777, note 5.

John Hancock to George Washington

Sir,   Philadelphia August 8th. 1777

Your favour of yesterday's Date, with its Inclosures from General Schuyler I duly Rec'd, & laid before Congress:[1]

We have no kind of News, nor have I any thing in Charge from

Congress to communicate further than to Inclose you several Resolutions of Congress,[2] to which I Beg leave to Refer you, and am with the utmost Esteem, Sir, your very huml Servt,

John Hancock Presidt

RC (DLC).

[1] Washington's letter is in PCC, item 152, 4:443, and Washington, *Writings* (Fitzpatrick), 9:35. General Schuyler's August 1 letter to Washington and enclosures, describing the dismal military situation in the northern department, are in PCC, item 152, 4:447–51. Congress ordered copies of all these to be sent to General Gates, Schuyler's successor in that department. *JCC*, 8:621.

[2] These were resolves of August 1, 6, and 7 on a Georgia post, the northern department, commissaries, Lachlan McIntosh, Joseph Trumbull's resignation, and a prisoner exchange. *JCC*, 8:597–98, 616–17, 619, 621.

James Lovell to William Whipple

Sir,   August 8th 1777

Though Mr Bass has been needlessly delayed till this time, I cannot make any addition to what the enclosed contains. I only take up my pen now to desire you to enclose one or two of the latest Gazettes to Dr Franklin and to give him at the same time any circumstance which may have been able to obtain respecting either Burgoyne's or Howe beyond what *our* newspapers contain.

I am your affectionate,   J.L.

[*P.S.*] Walton wrote Arnold that he was not likely to have his old date of rank as the Eastern States were particularly against it.[1] But he "*excused*" Rhode Island and Connecticut. Upon a new motion to restore his rank, two days have been spent, and finally it was carried in the negative when poor Mass. was the only New England State *faulty*. We put the yeas and Nays of each member in the Journals if any Delegate desires it. N.H., Con., R.I., Georgia Yea—Mass., York, Jersey, Penn., Del., Mar., N.C. Nay. It was really a question between Monarchical and Republican principles put at a most critical time.

Tr (DLC).

[1] Walton's letter has not been found. For the motions and votes denying the request to give Benedict Arnold the rank of major general "from the nineteenth day of February last," see *JCC*, 8:623–24.

Henry Laurens to John Lewis Gervais

[August 9, 1777]

9th. Yesterday was Spent at a review of that part of our Army immediately under General Washington. It seems the General had directed this general Muster of Horse & foot in order to get Men & Officers together & immediately Marched them off the Ground towards Trent Town where they will be halted until we learn somewhat certain of the late Coasting Admiral & General having heard nothing of them Since they left the Capes of Delaware & taken as proof of their having gone beyond North River.

This Morning Mr. John Laurens who made one in the Cavalcade yesterday joined General Washington at head Quarters near German Town as one of his family. My heart was too full at parting & would not allow me to enquire into particulars. To tell you truly my Sense of this matter—although I believe the Young Man will acquit himself well any where, yet I am persuaded he has made an indiscreet choice for his outset in life. His Talents & his diligence would have enabled him to have been much more extensively & essentially useful to his Country in a different line at the same time to have been the Cement of mine & the builder of a new family. As a Soldier One Man can act only as one (very few Cases excepted) & in point of real usefulness will often be excelled by Men of moderate abilities & better Nerves. From this persuasion you will know that I am not perfectly happy under this event, but tis Man's part to bear disappointment with patience.

I have intimated above the high prices of articles in this Market. Let me add, that in consequence of your order I enquired this Morning the price of a Copper Still of 40 Gallons & was informed two hundred Dollars, this enormous 5 fold demand together with the impossibility of getting one to you for the use of your present Crop of Peaches induces me to Suspend a purchase until I hear from you again. Observe, while the Men of War lie in our Bay we can have no Water Carriage, such Vessels as now & then drop into Charles Town with Letters from Philadelphia go from the Sea Coast of Jersey & I believe the land Trade by Waggons is pretty well over.

Some of our Smaller Men of War are now upon an attempt to clear one of the Channels from Delaware to Sea by means of Fire Wrafts— tis said two Frigates lie in Cape May Channel, those are the objects of the present enterprize. We have no Sanguine hopes of a Success.

We have just received dispatches from General Schuyler informing that Mr. Burgoyne was within 25 miles of Albany, & giving Some hopes of cutting off his retreat if the New England forces are alert in coming to his aid.[1] Burgoyne has a numerous train of Indians with him, the Militia it Seems are panic Struck by these Savages, 50 of whom as General Schuyler writes lately put 300 of our people to most infamous flight. I wish our friend Williamson & his Ninety Six Regiment were here.

The packet Boat which I said was taken, was one which had Sailed from hence not one of the late Contract. I am afraid the Capt of the Fox Frigate was prisoner to Manly when he was taken, if so, we shall be at a loss for means to ransom that brave man.

General Howe's proclamation for restricting the Trade & Commerce & Gen. Morgan's regulating the police in New York mark out very Strongly that Governor Tryon is only a Cypher. Indeed when the Inhabitants who are called his Majesty's Loyal & faithful Subjects are threatned with Military Execution for breach of orders as they are in Major General Jones's Proclamation I cannot conceive what part's left for Governor Tryon to act. Comfortable Specimen of Military Government.² I perceived by the numerous advertisements in the Royal Gazette of New York that there have been vast importations of every Species of Merchandize into that City & when I tell you the Jews of all denominations in this, give 16 paper Dollars for a Guinea & in proportion for other Gold & Silver & Bills upon London, you will agree that Some of those Goods find a Safe passage hither notwithstanding the prohibitions of General & Major General. As Mr. Desaussan had arrived safely at Nantz I shall have Balance in the hands of [. . .] & Co. which I have desired them to remit in Blankets for my Negroes, but my Letter may Still be in Charles Town in Doctor Gordons hands. If so, I beg you to forward it & write by Some future opportunity as I will endeavor to do from hence. Pressing the Subject it may be possible to get a Supply from that quarter before Christmas. The prices you quote at the prize Sale are enormous; nevertheless I will rather Strip my Pocket naked than suffer my Negroes to be so in a Winter's Night. Therefore my good friend if any Blankets are to be had toward October or November buy a few which with the number I left at home may with prudent management of the Overseers serve the ensuing Winter.

I will not trouble you on my Plantation or Town affairs more particularly than I have done. I know you will do as much for me as your own will permit. I am here at an amazing expence in my Country's Service. If I can render it such as will deserve their acceptance I shall chearfully Submit to such Losses of Estate as will unavoidably be the consequence of my absence. Be so good as to tell me how long that is to be according to the Rule of your House of Assembly are we delegated for one or two Years & recollect that by the nomination to Vice Presidentship my Seat in the House was vacated & by my absence from the State I am no longer Vice president. Be assured I do not remark merely on my own account for tis my inmost wish & will be my utmost endeavour when I return, also to retire from public business, but because it is a flaw in the Constitution which had not been foreseen, tho' by the by I think it a greater that one man should represent the people of Charles Town in Assembly & the State of So. Carolina in General Congress at the Same time according to your present practice except in the event which I have premised.

Possibly to morrow may produce important intelligence from the Eastward. In that case you will [be] troubled with a postscript to a Letter already enormously long, & may prove much ado about nothing as you will probably have heard all its contents before it reaches you. Be that as it may, you will acknowledge I have laboured to say some thing. I will conclude with what I always repeat with pleasure, my best wishes to you, to Mrs. Gervais & the Children.

LB (ScHi). A continuation of Laurens to Gervais, August 5, 1777.

[1] General Schuyler's August 4 letter to President Hancock, which was read in Congress on the 11th, is in PCC, item 153, 2:230–32.

[2] Maj. Gen. Valentine Jones, the British commandant of New York City, issued a proclamation on July 23 forbidding, on pain of death, any travel from the city to New Jersey between sunset and sunrise. *New-York Gazette: and the Weekly Mercury*, July 28, 1777.

Henry Laurens to Robert Howe

Dear General   Philadelphia 9th August 1777.

About the 22d July I had the honour of delivering Severally your Letters to Congress & to the New England Delegates. The former was instantly committed to the Board of War & their Report followed by a confirmation of your appointment to Colo. Eveleigh & Mr. Purcel, but for your fine polite Commercial story which must have cost you Some labor to learn & given you much pleasure to relate no more notice was taken than of the particular kind of paper upon which the tale was told. I am sure I thought it a very clever thing when I read it at Mepkin & Sealed it up so nicely.[1] What sort of writing in this World goes for nothing. In that class your other Letter touching Rank may possibly be found, & it will if one may judge from our determination two days ago upon an application from an old & valuable Servant M[ajo]r Genl Arnold whose prayer to be restored to his rank was rejected notwithstanding the acquiescence of Officers whose dates are, as they admit, improperly prior to his.[2] But good General draw no hasty conclusions. Another unexpected vote may turn up & be in your favour.[3] When I am a little older in Congress I'll try hard at a reformation in that article of Rank, persevering in the present mode which is arbitrary & often Subject to caprice will not promote the welfare of our Army.

The evacuation of Ticonderoga & concommitant circumstances have excited public clamour & resentment. Burgoynes advance & Schuyler's retreat to the very threshold of Albany fills the minds of some with the most direful apprehensions, others say he will be checked & his retreat cut off. Everybody wonders what is become of your name sake Sir

William who abandoned his Jersey garrison early in July, embarked his Troops, Horse & foot about the middle, paraded with 228 Sail off the Capes of Delaware the latter end & vanished the 1st August. The Second maneuver drew great Washington [. . .] to this City by a fatiguing Countermarch of upwards 120 Miles, his Letters regularly intimated his opinion that the whole was a calculated feint. We shall probably soon hear of Ld. Howe's appearance at Rhode Island or farther eastward, he cannot be so mad as to leave Burgoyne to Struggle with the united force of New York & New England. We have received most shocking accounts of scalping & mangling by Burgoyne's Indians. He carries fire, Sword & terror with him. The Six Nations are heartily disposed to be our friends, or it appears so by a Talk which they lately Sent in & those who know best say they certainly will be, if our people will fight & give them prospect of conquest. Generals Schyler & St Clair are ordered to head quarters. General Gates gone to take the command of the Northern department. 'Tis agreed the New England Men will chearfully follow him, although they had abandoned Schuyler in whom, rumour reported, they had no confidence. General Fermoy one of the subscribing Council of War at Ticonderoga has written a Letter to Congress disclaiming any part of merit arising from the Surrender of the Fortress without an attempt to repel the Enemy or to Save the Stores. I have seen added in a Letter from a Man of Character that one hundred head of fat Cattle were driven & left within the lines the very morning the fort was evacuated. A deep & impartial enquiry will bring out the truth. Till that event I will neither join those who censure nor those who condemn Mr. St. Claire. The principal charge against Schuyler in the public mouth is his residence at & attention to his own Estate, which ought to have but which never had been at the head of his Troops in Garrison. A few days before the Surrender General St. Clair expressed as you will read in one of the News papers strong hopes of making such a defence as would, if not destroy the Enemy, at least cripple him & Spoil his Campaign. The question anxiously asked by those who have a right to demand, is, what happened between that date & the Surrender & Shameful flight? Shameful no doubt, when Mr. Schyler himself writes that our people were panic struck. 300 of them had fled from a party of fifty Indians.

If we learn any thing farther of the British Fleet or from Albany you will be troubled with a postscript.

General Washington lay last night at Correls Ferry or Trent Town, he means as I am informed to encamp on the old ground in Morris Town & await events. Possibly in the enemy's absence he may attempt another Christmas Coup.

Intelligence from our Agents in France is much in our favour—but we have got a Thousand difficulties to Struggle against, if we persevere we shall break smooth ground for our Successors.

Adieu, I am &c

LB (ScHi). Endorsed by Laurens: "Sent News Papers."
  [1] The letter of June 8 from Brig. Gen. Robert Howe, the commander of the southern department, to President Hancock is in PCC, item 160, fols. 360–64. On July 23 the Board of War reported in favor of approving Howe's appointments of Nicholas Eveleigh as deputy adjutant general for South Carolina and Georgia and Henry Purcell as judge advocate general for the same states, but, contrary to Laurens' statement, Congress did not actually approve this report until February 17, 1778. *JCC*, 8:575n.2. Howe's "polite Commercial story" was the long description in his letter of southern trade. Mepkin was one of Laurens' plantations in South Carolina.
  [2] See *JCC*, 8:623–24.
  [3] Howe was promoted to major general on October 20, 1777. *JCC*, 9:823.

Henry Laurens to John Loveday

Sir[1]   Philadelphia 9th August 1777.
  I have received your favour of the 6th July by Colo. Cotesworth Pinckney together with the News papers & thank you for the management of my affairs as you have described. My present time will not permit me to write much but I shall soon have another opportunity.
  If Mrs. Wooley is a bad neighbor you must hire the House she lives in to Some body else & at a better rent. Mr. Henry must be ejected. You will See that his Rent was raised as a Step to that purpose & if necessary you will apply to a Lawyer under counsel from Mr. Gervais. Sammy Debat must be held with a tight rein, he is connected now with a very idle family & indulgence will ruin them & him.
  I thought I had given orders to send as much of the Hams & Bacon to Mr. Gervais as he thot to take & to sell the rest, it was my intention to have done so, if Mr. Gervais does not want it now, sell it for the most it will yield. Poor Geofry, I am afraid his malady is beyond the Skill of the Baron. If the Baron will cure him I will give him half the Boy is worth for his trouble, but it would be mean to Sell him. If he Still lives consult Doctor Garden & Mr. Gervais & give him proper Cloths.
  The Letter you mention for Mr. White did not come to hand.
  Doctor Garden Should be consulted on the use of Betty & perhaps it may be necessary to take her into your Kitchen or to Send her into the Country.
  Cato was working for the public at Braughton's Battery, my Accot. delivered in will shew to what day his Wages had been paid & you will remember my direction for him to Sleep at home & that you Should Send him in the Country if he attempted to play tricks. Mr. Gervais has an Accot. of my Brothers Rents & Negroes & probably you have before this time a Copy.
  Public affairs here are in an unpleasant train. General Howe, tired with looking at General Washington without power to fight him quitted the Jerseys the beginning of July, about the middle embarked his Troops

Horse & foot Sailed out of Sandy Hook & made a parade with 228 Sail of vessels off the Capes of Delaware. From thence he disappeared about the 1st Inst. & may now be in the Moon for aught we know, but he is probably gone to New England & will Strive to join General Burgoine who found Ticonderoga evacuated & the Road clear for him down to Albany. Perhaps he may receive a check there; otherwise we shall be in a troublesome situation. Articles of every kind are exceedingly dear here. A Breast of Veal 55/ to 65/ our Currency. Butter 22/6 to a Dollar— meaning our Currency. Fire Wood when laid in the Cellar upwards of £22 a Chord. Horse feeding & Standing at Stable upwards a Dollar per day & every thing in proportion. It will cost me more to maintain 3 people here than it did to keep House & entertain Company at Anson- burgh. I hope we shall make something at home to ease this enormous weight. I fear all that my plantations will make will not support it. I thank Mrs. Loveday for her remembrance & desire my Compliments & good wishes to her & am &ca.

LB (ScHi).
[1] John Loveday (d. 1804) was a Charleston merchant who was helping John Lewis Gervais care for Laurens' business affairs during his service as delegate to Congress. Raymond Starr, ed., "Letters from John Lewis Gervais to Henry Laurens, 1777–1778," *South Carolina Historical Magazine* 66 (January 1965): 17n.2.

John Hancock to George Washington

Sir   Philadelphia August 10th [1777]. 5 oClock P.M.
    I was this moment called out of Church by the arrival of an Express, with a letter informing of a large fleets being seen off Sinapuxen.[1] Copy of the letter I enclose you per Express, should I hear any thing further I shall immediately advise you of it. I have the honour to be, with sincere respect & esteem, Your most obedt. & very hble Servt.
                                              John Hancock Presidt

RC (DLC). In a clerical hand and signed by Hancock.
[1] A contemporary copy of Zadoc Purcell's August 7 letter stating that "this afternoon there appear'd off the bar of Sinapuxon a large fleet of shiping to the amount of two-hundred & some odd sail, all bearing to the southward with the wind about South East which it is imagined that their intention is for the Cape of Virginia," is in the Washington Papers, DLC.

John Adams to Abigail Adams

                                                   Aug. 11. 1777
    Your kind Favour of July 30 and 31 was handed me, just now from the Post office.

I have regularly received a Letter from you every Week excepting one, for a long Time past, and as regularly send a Line to you inclosing Papers. My Letters are scarcely worth sending. Indeed I dont choose to indulge much Speculation, lest a Letter should miscarry, and free Sentiments upon public Affairs intercepted, from me, might do much hurt.

Where the Scourge of God, and the Plague of Mankind is gone, no one can guess. An Express from Sinnepuxent, a Place between the Capes of Delaware and the Capes of Cheasapeak, informs that a fleet of 100 sail was seen off that Place last Thursday. But whether this is Fishermens News like that from Cape Ann, I know not.

The Time spends and the Campaign wears away and Howe makes no great Figure yet. How many Men and Horses will he cripple by this strange Coasting Vo[y]age of 5 Weeks.

We have given N. Englandmen what they will think a compleat Tryumph in the Removal of Generals from the Northward and sending Gates there. I hope every Part of New England will now exert itself, to its Utmost Efforts. Never was a more glorious Opportunity than Burgoine has given Us of destroying him, by marching down so far towards Albany. Let New England turn out and cutt off his Retreat.

Pray continue to write me every Week. You have made me merry with the female Frolic, with the Miser. But I hope the Females will leave off their Attachment to Coffee.[1] I assure you, the best Families in this Place have left off in a great Measure the Use of West India Goods. We must bring ourselves to live upon the Produce of our own Country. What would I give for some of your Cyder?

Milk has become the Breakfast of many of the wealthiest and genteelest Families here.

Fenno put me into a Kind of Frenzy to go home, by the Description he gave me last night of the Fertility of the Season, the Plenty of Fish, &c. &c. &c. in Boston and about it. I am condemned to this Place a miserable Exile from every Thing that is agreable to me. God will my Banishment shall not last long.

RC (MHi). Adams, *Family Correspondence* (Butterfield), 2:305–6.

[1] In her July 30 letter, Abigail had described how more than a hundred women had manhandled Boston merchant Thomas Boylston and forced him to sell them a hogshead of coffee from his warehouse. Ibid., pp. 295–96.

John Adams to Abigail Adams

My dearest Friend   Phila. Aug. 11. 1777

I think I have sometimes observed to you in Conversation, that upon examining the Biography of illustrious Men, you will generally find some Female about them in the Relation of Mother or Wife or Sister, to whose Instigation, a great Part of their Merit is to be ascribed.

You will find a curious Example of this, in the Case of Aspasia, the Wife of Pericles. She was a Woman of the greatest Beauty and the first Genius. She taught him, it is said, his refined Maxims of Policy, his lofty imperial Eloquence; nay, even composed the Speeches, on which so great a Share of his Reputation was founded. The best Men in Athens frequented her House, and brought their Wives to receive Lessons from her of Œconomy and right Deportment. Socrates himself was her Pupil in Eloquence and gives her the Honour of that funeral oration which he delivers in the Menexenus of Plato. Aristophanes indeed abuses this famous Lady but Socrates does her Honour.

I wish some of our great Men had such Wives. By the Account in your last Letter, it seems the Women in Boston begin to think themselves able to serve their Country. What a Pity it is that our Generals in the Northern District had not Aspasias to their Wives!

I believe, the two Howes have not very great Women for Wives. If they had We should suffer more from their Exertions than We do. This is our good Fortune. A Woman of good Sense would not let her Husband spend five Weeks at Sea, in such a season of the Year. A smart Wife would have put Howe in Possession of Philadelphia, a long Time ago.[1]

RC (MHi). Adams, *Family Correspondence* (Butterfield), 2:306.

[1] Adams wrote a third letter to Abigail this day, informing her that he was sending his servant John Turner, a "very intemperate fellow," back to Braintree. Ibid., p. 304.

John Adams to John Quincy Adams

My dear Son   Philadelphia August 11. 1777

As the War in which your Country is engaged will probably hereafter attract your Attention, more than it does at this Time, and as the future Circumstances of your Country, may require other Wars, as well as Councils and Negotiations, similar to those which are now in Agitation, I wish to turn your Thoughts early to such Studies, as will afford you the most solid Instruction and Improvement for the Part which may be allotted you to act on the Stage of Life.

There is no History, perhaps, better adapted to this usefull Purpose than that of Thucidides, an Author, of whom I hope you will make yourself perfect Master, in original Language, which is Greek, the most perfect of all human Languages. In order to understand him fully in his own Tongue, you must however take Advantage, of every Help you can procure and particularly of Translations of him into your own Mother Tongue.

You will find in your Fathers Library, the Works of Mr. Hobbes, in which among a great deal of mischievous Philosophy, you will find a learned and exact Translation of Thucidides, which will be usefull to you.

But there is another Translation of him, much more elegant, intituled "The History of the Peloponnesian War, translated from the Greek of Thucidides in two Volumes Quarto, by William Smith A.M. Rector of the Parish of the holy Trinity in Chester, and Chaplain to the Right Honourable the Earl of Derby."

If you preserve this Letter, it may hereafter remind you, to procure the Book.

You will find it full of Instruction to the Orator, the Statesman, the General, as well as to the Historian and the Philosopher.[1] You may find Something of the Peloponnesian War, in Rollin.

I am with much Affection your Father,   John Adams

RC (MHi). Adams, *Family Correspondence* (Butterfield), 2:307.
[1] For a list of some of the various editions of Thucydides' works still surviving in the Adams libraries, see ibid., p. 307n.

Samuel Adams to Roger Sherman

Dear Sir   Philada. Augt 11. 1777

I duly receivd your obliging Letter of the 11 July by the Post.[1] I thank you for the favor and beg you to continue to write to me as often as your Leisure may permit. The Rumor you mentioned has since appeared to be a serious Fact. We have lost Ticonderoga and as far as I can yet judge shamefully. I was going to add vilainously, for indeed I am not able to account for it but upon the worst of Principles. The whole appears to me to carry the evident Mark of Design. But I hope & believe it will undergo the strictest Scrutiny. The People at large will not, they ought not to be satisfyed until a thorough Enquiry is made into the Causes of an Event in which their Honor & Safety is so deeply interested. The only Letter receivd by Congress from St Clair you have seen publishd under their Sanction. Schuyler has written a series of weak & contemptible *Things,* in such a Stile of Despondence which alone is, I think, sufficient for his removal from that Command. For if his Pen expresses His true feelings of his Heart it cannot be expected that the bravest Veterans would fight under such a General, admitting they had no Jealousy of Treachery. In a Letter recd this Day,[2] dated the 4th Inst at Stillwater he writes in a Tone of perfect Despair. He seems to have no Confidence in his Troops nor the States from whence Reinforcements are to be drawn. A third part of his Continental Troops he tells us, consists "of Boys, Negroes & aged Men not fit for the field or any other Service." "A very great Part of the Army naked—without Blankets—ill armed & very deficient in accoutremts without a prospect of relief."

"Many, too many of the officers wd be a disgrace to the most contemptible Troops that ever were collected." The Exertions of others of them of a different Character "counteracted by the worthless." "General Burgoyne is bending his Force this way—he will probably be here in Eight days, and unless we are well reinforced" (which he despairs of) "as much farther as he pleases to go." Was ever any poor General more mortified? But he has by this time receivd his Quietus. Gates takes the Command there agreably to what you tell me is the Wish of the People, and I trust our affairs in that Quarter will soon wear a more promising Aspect.

The Enemies Ships upwards of 200 Sail after having been out of sight Six days were discovered on Thursday last off Sinepuxint 15 Leagues from the Capes of Delaware steering towards Chessapeak Bay. Your Friends here are well except Colo Williams who has been confind a few Days but is growing better. I have a Thousand things to say to you but must defer it to other opportunities & conclude in haste with Friendly Regards to your family. Affectionately yours,   S A

FC (NN). Adams, *Writings* (Cushing), 3:404–6.
  [1] Sherman's July 11 letter to Adams is in the Adams Papers, NN.
  [2] See *JCC,* 8:628.

Cornelius Harnett to Richard Caswell

Sir   Philadelphia 11 August 1777
    I have been honor'd with your Excellency's favour of the 15 July for which you will be pleased to accept my Acknowlegments. I took the Small pox by Inoculation at Port Tobacco in Maryland which detained me three weeks at that place tho' I had it in a very favourable manner. I did not lie down one Minute for it.
    The money Your Excellency is so Anxious about Mr. Penn tells me has been sent long ago. An Officer went off to take Charge of it. I do not find however whether it is certainly gone or Not as the Treasurer has not yet acquainted Mr. Pen with it. We expect every hour to hear from Baltimore about it.
    I should have wrote you sooner had I not been waiting to give you a certain Account of the destination of the British fleet which sailed upwards of three weeks ago from Sandy Hook with Genl Howes Army on board. Every body believed their Intention was against this City, which was also General Washingtons Opinion by the movements in our Grand Army under his Command which has been some time Incamped at German Town. Yesterday Morning Our Army begun their March towards N. York Government. The evacuation of Ticonderoga & the Successes of Genl Burgoin since that event Has thrown the People &

army in that State into great Consternation which they have not as yet recovered from. This, together with the Tardiness of the New England Militia make our affairs rather wear a gloomy aspect in that Quarter. Genl. Gates is gone to take the Command of Our Army in the Northern department, & we have great expectation from that Gentlemans Military abilities that an immediate change will take place as the N England People have a high esteem for him. The uncertainty of Genl. Hows Intentions has hurt Our affairs accordingly by Harrassing our Army by unnecessary Marches. The No. Carolina Troops are in High Spirit. I have seen some of the Officers. I inquired particularly after Cap Caswell who is in good health & Spirits. Genl. Nash with his Brigade is stationed for the present at Trent Town.

Mr. Burke talks of returning home the beginning of the next Month. I tell him he will not be suffered to stay Long in No. Carolina which indeed is my wish. I am Sorry he is under the Necessity of going. I beg Your Excellency will be pleased to present my most respectful Compliments to the Gentlemen of your Council. I shall keep this letter Open until the setting off of the Post, & shall Communicate to you any further Intelligence which may be received Concerning Genls. Burgoin & Howes Operations. I am with the greatest respect, Sir, Your Excellencys Most Obedient & very huml Servant. Cornl. Harnett

[*P.S.*] For further News yr. Excely. is refer'd to the papers Inclosed.

RC (NNPM).

Cornelius Harnett to William Wilkinson

Dear Sir Philadelphia 11th August 1777

Your favour of the 16 July only came to hand a few days, I am exceedingly anxious to hear from Cape Fear & am obliged to you for the Information in regard to my family. I sincierly regret the death of our worthy friend Forster. He has a Brother living in One of the Counties in the Deleware State, pray inform me whether he made a Will & how he has left his affairs.

The Northern Department have been much alarmed by the Loss of Ticonderoga. Genl. Gates is appointed by Congress to Command the Army in that Quarter & the Genl. Officers who commanded there before, are ordered to repair to head Quarters to have their Conduct inquired into. We have had no certain account of the Destination of the fleet which sailed from Sandy Hook upwards of three weeks ago with Gen. Howes Army on board, which has kept Genl. Washington in great suspence as you see by the News Papers Inclosed. Mr. Mallet who arrived here a few days ago informs me there has been a Terrible Mortality among the Slaves at Cape Fear; I am sorry to hear it. I beg you will inclose me the So & No Carolina papers by every Post or Other Oppertunity; you know there is no danger of paying Postage. At foot I send you the Prices Current of sundry articles here and should you have Occasion for any of them at those prices I desire you will send the money, as I have spent all I brought with me & my £800 per an. will not maintain me. Present my Compliments to Mr. Brice & desire him to send me the Acco. Sales of all the Prizes sent in by the Continental Ships of war as I am obliged to Settle with the Bord of Treasury. I write Mr. Hooper &c by this Opportunity[1] but I desire you will tell them I expect Letters from them in return or I shall stop my hand. Remember me kindly to all my friends & be Assured that I am, Dr Sir, Your sincr. Friend & hu Servt,

                                                    Cornl. Harnett

Prices Current Pensilva Curry.
West India rum 40/ to 45 per Gall
Noward rum 30/–35/
Lo Sugar 15/ per pound
Bro Sugar 7/6 Do
1 quart punch 10/
Board by the week £10 to £12
Beef 2/6 per lb
Chickens 3/9 & 2/6
a water mellon 7/6
1 Night Stablege & feeding 1 horse 10/ to 11/
Shirting Linnen 40/ to 45/
And indeed every Other Species of Goods & Provisions in proportion
Tea £6 per lb, Wine £3 to £4 per Gall
Dinner & Club at a Tavern from 20/ to 35/

RC (NcU).
[1] The only other Harnett letter of this date that has been found is the preceding entry.

Joseph Jones to George Washington

Dr. Sr.   Phila. 11th Augt. 1777.
    Capt. Monroe[1] leaveing Town this evening I cannot avoid informing you by him that as far as his conduct has fallen under my observation and I have not been unattentive to it, he has been diligent in endeavouring to raise men but such is the present disposition of the people in Virginia neither Capt. Monroe or any other Officer preserving the Character a Gent. ought to support can recruit men. Some men have indeed been raised but by methods I could not recommend and I shod. be sorry he should practice. The enlisting Men for the usual bounty is

now and will I expect be for some time impractical if at any time it shod mend, on acct of the high bounty given by the Militia exempts, a mode of raising Men very hurtfull I conceive to the recruiting Business. I wish Capt Monroe could have made up his Company on his own accot. as well as that of the Public but I am satisfied any further Prosecution of the attempt will be equelly unsuccessful with his past endeavours. It is probable I may have the gratification of seeing you in this City as I cannot think the Enemy mean to carry on their operations to the Southward—a few days will I expect open their design. Very respectfully I am, Dr Sr yr aff. Sev.   Jos. Jones

RC (DLC).
1 Undoubtedly Jones' nephew James Monroe.

Henry Laurens to Lachlan McIntosh

Dear Sir,   Philadelphia 11th August 1777.
    Some where on my journey hither your favour of the 30th May overtook me, at my arrival I put it into the hands of Colonel Walton. The very Morning after I reached this City I took my Seat in Congress where I had intended to have remained a silent auditor at least until I should have perused the Journals for some Months back, gained a clue to business & an acquaintance with Members & their manners, but I was soon provoked to break through the prescribed bounds & to oppose a random scheme for a Western enterprize which had been proposed to the House as equally practicable & advantageous & which to my amazement the whole House appeared to have adopted, nothing remained to do on their part but to vote Men & Money.[1] I saw in that business destruction of a number of honest fellows whom we want exceedingly for better employment, disgrace to our Arms & a vast increase to our general debt already swelled to an alarming heigth & felt that I should rise a criminal if I forbore to say every thing in my power which might tend to avert such evils. I delivered my sentiments & was successful, the question had scarcely an affirmative. I took occasion to report the value & at the same time the precarious & dangerous state to which Georgia was reduced, wished if so many Men as had been talked of could be spared from this quarter, they might be immediately ordered to that Colony, as well for its protection as for laying the foundation of an enterprize nearer home which at a proper time might be carried into execution with success & which would work half the Conquest of the other place without marching a foot towards it. Before I sat down I moved for a Committee to consider the State of Georgia or wished to second the Delegate from thence in a motion to that effect. In consequence of these suggestions a Committee was appointed whose report

favorable to Georgia & I hope very agreeable to my friend Mr Clay & yourself you will receive from Colonel Walton.[2] I think it does not go far enough, if we might have raised a certain number of Men for an intended service full of perils & almost certain shame & loss, the same number might have been added for the security of Georgia worth ten thousand times more, estimating property, than the other would have been if we had conquered, & for conquering a good barrier & removing very dangerous Neighbors. These matters are not enjoined in secrecy but the less said upon what we had intended or do intend the better, let our Enemies apprehend by our silence, we sleep. I have been driven too to a necessity of giving my old freind McIntosh a Character in open Congress in opposition to the insinuations of some of his back freinds who I suppose had industriously transmitted the poison to a few Members, I did not find a difficult task in that part, the Labour was pleasant & Gentlemen generally disposed to think favorable of him, even those who had "seen" or perhaps received "Letters," retreated as soon as they were better informed. Colo. Walton will be more particular.[3] I shall on this head only add, that I expect you will give me notice of your approach to Philadelphia & an opportunity of meeting you if possible at some Miles distance. Come by way of Camden through Hallifax, every Body says that is the best Road, all are bad enough. In a word favour me with a hint of your intentions by the first opportunity & add if you please a state of your public affairs in Georgia.

The loss of Ticonderoga is a subject of discontent to all the friends of Liberty. It has opened a Passage to Mr. Burgoine who with his motly Troops of Britons, Germans, Canadians & Indian Savages had penetrated by our last Accounts within 25 Miles of Albany, our Generals Schuyler & St. Clair having regularly retreated as he advanced, where the stand which has been much talked of will be made is uncertain. 'Tis said & I beleive with truth, that the Militia are so prejudiced against those Generals they will not fight under them. I hope by this day General Gates who is more beloved is at their head & that the Enemy will not only receive a check but be stopped from retreating. This however will be an arduous work if the Army from Quebec & that which lately made a parade near the Capes of Delaware should unite. Indeed tis rather to be feared a complete conquest of New York will be made, that our Ships at Providence will be destroyed & that this City will be the aim of a large detachment before Winter sets in. If such calamities betide us we shall owe as much to the Languor & Luxury of Whigs as to the malice & artifice of Tories, a Class abounding in this & the next northerly State.

Gen Putnam is at Peeks Kill with about 7000 Men who have hard duty & may be soon brought between two fires.

Our brave Commodore Manly after having fought with & taken the Fox Frigate of 28 Guns lost his prize to a Ship of 60 Guns & was taken himself by one of 40 & is carried in great triumph prisoner to New York. His own Ship was so Shattered she could scarcely swim. What is worse than all, the Captain of the Frigate tis said is retaken in Manly's Vessel & we have not an adequate to offer for the ransom of our Hero.

If tomorrow produces any further important Accounts you will be informed by a Postscript. At present I conclude with Compliments to Mrs McIntosh & to the young Gentlemen & assurances of remaining with great regard, Dear General, Your most obedient servant,

Henry Laurens

RC (MHi).

[1] See Charles Thomson's Notes of Debates, July 24 and 25, 1777.

[2] For Congress' August 1 resolves on Georgia, see *JCC*, 8:596–98.

[3] See George Walton to Washington, August 5, 1777.

James Lovell to William Whipple

Dear Sir,   Philadelphia 11th Aug 1777

Your double favor of the 28th reached me this day. I have laid it by with several other papers that will deserve particular reading when the Northern Commanders shall come this way. You will find various accounts in the Gazettes. There is one better in particular under the Hartford Head which seems to make all mighty well, and calls for *gratitude* to the General who brought off the Troops so nicely.

I hope Gates will reach the hiding spot of Schuyler before the Militia get quite disgusted. A most whining history dated the 4th is come to hand from the matchless leader.[1] But the Deputy Pay Master General gives a good account of numbers and only wishes that Gates' Yankies had a spirited Commander.

I have wrote you that 11 Colonies in 12 sent Gates, and the 12th only made objection that he had addressed the Committees of the Grants by the same title as they had used in their letters to him— miserable objection!

Jemmy D——[2] promised me a printed copy of the resolves of Congress of the 30th of June which the New York Delegates got struck off but he did not perform his promise, though I told him, I wanted it *only* for you.[3] However Town has given them to the world at large to praise or condemn as shall seem best.[4] It was scarcely rub and go by the absence of a Jersey member. The expressions are no encouragement to New York though the petition of the Grant-men was not allowed.

Commissary Trumbull has at last got free. Arnold too is at liberty to quit. He conducted almost without blemish in resigning, if a man may be said to do so, who leaves a patriotic exertion because self love was injured in a fanciful right incompatible with the general interest of the

Union. Georgia[5] wrote that he could not expect his claimed rank would be restored, as the Eastern States were set against it though he owned he had made an exception of Con. and Rh. Isl. If any member demands it the yeas and nays of every member are voted. It was demanded on this mighty occasion, the vote against restoration being 7 to 4; 3 of which 4 were N.E. and Georgia the 4th happening all to be single voices, one of your's being unwell and two of Connecticut also sick. They intend to have Mass. hanged on a tree we being all 4 of a mind, as were all the rest except General R——[6] among the Pennsylvanians. This registering is childish for if I am at a loss in any other question, I can defend this against a crowd.[7]

We have found Howe again; I thought he was lost in the Gulph stream.

I will not say a word about Manly—read the Halifax account. I wish Thompson better success, nor do I doubt his prudence will have it.[8]

Love & compliments from yours,   J.L.

Tr (DLC).

[1] Gen. Philip Schuyler's August 4 letter to President Hancock was read in Congress this day. See Samuel Adams to Roger Sherman, this date.

[2] James Duane.

[3] These were the resolves dismissing the petition of Vermont for recognition as an independent state. *JCC,* 8:509–13.

[4] Benjamin Towne was the publisher of the *Pennsylvania Evening Post,* which printed the June 30 resolutions pertaining to the New Hampshire Grants in its August 7 issue.

[5] That is, George Walton. See Lovell to Whipple, August 8, 1777.

[6] That is, Daniel Roberdeau. See *JCC,* 8:624.

[7] When Henry Marchant demanded, on August 8, 1777, that the yeas and nays be recorded when the delegates voted on the issue of the date of Benedict Arnold's commission as major general, Congress inaugurated the practice of recording roll call votes at the request of any delegation. See *JCC,* 8:599, 624. For convenient summaries and lists of the roll call votes accompanied by maps illustrating the breakdown of each vote state by state that Secretary Thomson recorded in the journals from this date until the Articles of Confederation were implemented in 1781, see Clifford L. Lord, ed., *The Atlas of Congressional Roll Calls for the Continental Congresses, 1777–1781* (Cooperstown, N.Y.: New York State Historical Association, 1943).

[8] See Henry Laurens to John Lewis Gervais, August 5, 1777, note 4.

Robert Morris to Jonathan Hudson

Sir   Philada. August 11th. 1777

You begin yours of the 8th Inst. with saying a letter is enclosed for the marine Committee but that was not the case, however I will soon as I can find time get some orders for you respecting that Brigt and in the mean time you had best employ the Captain you recommend to look after & see her finished. I fancy the prices of Goods here must be full as high as they ought and if yours come up you will be satisfyed with what you get for them. Our people shall give any assistance wanted from me or them on the occasion and whatever comes shall be taken care of. I am glad you have got your Iron again & that things will go on as they ought and it is well that Mr. Vashons Goods are to be disposed of by others, if they are put into good hands, it is not much matter who the persons are, they will get high prices. I will send your advertizement to the press & am ready to do you any service therein that I can. I have told Mr Braxton that I was content he should execute the plan proposed by Mr. Dorsius as long as he found it wou'd answer but I think we shou'd attend carefully to avoid confusion in Accounts by mixing them & extending our Con[. . .] too far or letting them run too long without settling accounts and I cou'd wish for this reason that the Accounts of your Voyage shou'd be settled soon as possible. I am sir, Your Obedt hble servt.   Robt Morris

RC (PHarH).

John Adams to James Warren

Dear Sir   Phila. Aug. 12. 1777
I see by the Papers, our assembly is called, and conclude it is now Sitting.

The Letters we receive from G. Schuyler, are enough to frighten any Body who does not know him. G.W. Says that all the Regiments from N.H. & M.B. are at the Northward and yet, Schuyler tells Us he has not above 4000 Men. I hope this Matter will be investigated. I believe Gates will find greater Numbers. If not I hope they will be sent him.[1]

Burgoyne is treading dangerous Ground, and proper Exertions will ruin him. Those I hope will not be wanting. I rejoice to see such a Spirit arise upon the Loss of Ti. and such determined Calls for Inquiry. The Facts must be stated from the Returns and other Evidence, and the innocent will be I hope acquitted—the guilty meet their Deserts. I see no Medium, I confess, between an honourable Acquittal and capital Punishment.

What is become of Howe? The Jersies are very happy, relieved from an heavy Burthen. What Fears were propagated in Boston last January, that the Jersies were lost. Not a Single Village has revolted.

We have still Accounts of part of Howes Fleet, coasting between the Capes of Delaware and those of Cheasapeak. What this Mans design is, can not be conjectured. It is very deep or very shallow.

Washington has been here with a noble Army, very obedient, and orderly.

Our News from France, is agreable. Trade, Friendship, Assistance underhand, and Loans of Money for the present—other Things by and by. I am &c

RC (MHi). In Adams' hand, though not signed.

[1] The second session of the Massachusetts General Court began on August 5, one month earlier than scheduled. The session lasted only until August 16, but the general court acted strongly to reinforce the northern army with men and equipment. *The Acts and Resolves, Public and Private, of the Province of the Massachusetts Bay* . . . *1777–1778* (Boston: Wright & Potter Printing Co., 1918), pp. 85–109.

Samuel Adams to James Warren

My dear Sir   Philadelphia Augt 12 1777
   The inclosd is an attested Copy of General Schuylers Letter to the President of the Congress.[1] It needs no Comment. How far the Massachusetts State deserves the Strictures therein made, you can tell. I send it to you for the Perusal of the Members of your Honbl House. If they have sent into the Army, Boys, Negroes & Men too aged to be fit for any Service, they will lay their Hands on their Mouths. If not, I hope some decent but *keen* Pen will vindicate them from that & other Aspersions. This, like all his other Letters, is written in such a desponding Stile, that it is no wonder that Soldiers decline fighting under him, though they may be under no Apprehension of Treachery. But he has by this time receivd his Quietus, at least till he can give a good Account of his Conduct. Gates has gone to take the Command and our Affairs in that Quarter, I dare say, will soon wear another Face.
   The Enemies Fleet have been again seen, 200 Sail, off Sinipuxin about 15 Leagues South of the Capes of Delaware. I think I have now a just Demand upon you for a Letter. I shall be disappointed if I do not receive one by the next Post. Adieu my Friend.   S A

RC (MHi).

[1] The enclosed August 4 Schuyler letter to Hancock is in *Warren-Adams Letters*, 1:352–53.

Charles Carroll of Carrollton to Benjamin Franklin

Douhoragen,[1] *Anne Arundel County, 12th August 1777.* Encloses letter to William Carmichael, left open for Franklin's perusal "as it relates principally to public concerns. When you have read it, please to seal it. No doubt the Secret Committee will give you a full & true account of the present situation of our affairs, & of our wants; they may not, perhaps, enter into the causes of our miscarriages on lake Champlain: the loss of the posts of Tionderoga & Mount Independance, and of our stores must be imputed to the dilatoriness of the New England States in not sending sufficient forces to defend the lines: to an unhappy difference between Generals Schuyler & Gates, the foundation of which was laid before you left Congress, & lastly to the improvidence of Congress in not giving positive orders for evacuating those posts, and the removal of the stores before the arrival of the enemy at Crown point. The campaign hitherto has been inactive: Gen. Howe must have been weaker than we imagined, or must have wanted some essentials, otherwise his remaining cooped up at Brunswick all the Spring must appear to every military man a strange piece of conduct: the temperature of the weather at that Season, and the weakness of G. Washington's army were strong incentitives, one would think, to action: it is their interest to be active & enterprising in order to finish the war with the utmost expedition; it is ours, to procrastinate & avoid a general battle. Perhaps the Enemy mean to worry us into slavery by a lingering & expensive war, and despair of succeeding by open force, viribus et lacertis. The Enemy will probably direct their whole force this fall against the State of New York with a view to reduce it entirely, others open a communication with Canada, and render difficult & hazardous the communication between the eastern & middle States: whether they will Succeed in this plan, time must discover; the chances, I think, are against them, if the eastern & middle States exert themselves, and as their own preservation depends on speedy & vigorous exertions, we may hope the Enemy will be baffled in their attempt. I flatter myself, our struggles for Independence will in the end be crowned with success, but we must suffer much in the mean time, and unless we continue to receive powerful assistance in arms, ammunition, & cloathing & other warlike Stores, and supplies of cash, or a credit in Europe equivalent thereto, we must sink under the efforts of a rich & inveterate Enemy, mistress of the Ocean, and determined, it seems, to run every hazard in subduing these States to unconditional Submission. My greatest apprehensions arise from the depreciation of our paper money; if we emit more bills of credit, they will fall to nothing; we cannot tax to the amount of the charges of the war, and of our civil establishments; we must then raise money by lotteries, & by borrowing; but the adventures in lotteries will be few, and the monied men will not part with their money without a prospect of having their interest paid punctually & in some thing that deserves the name of money & will serve the uses of it: if the annual interest of the Sums borrowed could be paid in gold & sylver, it would be a great inducement to monied men to lend their money to Congress; where one pound is now lent, forty pounds would then be lent. If bills of Exchange drawn by Congress on some house in France would be accepted to a certain amount, considerable sums proportionable to the obtained credit, might be speedily raised by the sale of such bills, particularly if advantage were taken by the Public of the Exchange. . . .

"We have not yet confederated, but almost every member of Congress is anxious for a Confederacy, being sensible, that a Confederacy formed in a rational Plan will certainly add much weight & consequence to the united States, collectively give great Security to each individually, and a a credit also to our paper money: but I despair of such a confederacy, as ought, & would take place, if little & partial interests could be laid aside: very few, & immaterial, alterations will be made in the report of the Committee of the whole house; this is only my opinion, for we have made but very little progress in the house in that important affair; immediate & more pressing exigencies having from time to time postponed the consideration of it to this day, when, I am informed, it is to be again resumed. If this war should be of any considerable duration, we shall want men to recruit our armies: could we engage 5 or 6 thousand men, Germans, Swiss or the Irish Brigade? I have mentioned this matter to several members of Congress, but they did not seem to relish the introduction of foreign mercenaries; I own it ought to be avoided, if possible. Handycraftsmen would be very Serviceable to us, such as black Smiths, nailors, Shoemakers, weavers & persons skilled in the management of Hemp & flax. One of the greatest distresses we have yet felt is the want of salt, but, I hope, we shall not be in so great want of that essential article for the future, as we have been: a bushel of salt some months ago was sold at Baltimore Town for £9. Necessity is said to be the mother of Invention, it surely is of industry among a civilized People. Many private persons on our Seacoasts & Bays are now making salt to supply themselves & neighbours; these private, and the public salt works together will in a few months, I hope, yield a tolerable supply to our People and at pretty reasonable rates compared with those, which have obtained for some time past: perhaps the private Saltmakers may afford to sell salt at 30s. per bushel; the undertakers of the public salt works in this State are under contract to sell what salt they make at 5s. We are casting salt pans: but they cost £100 per Ton, and are subject to cracks: when our plating mills get in full works, it will be better to make the pans of plate iron, altho' they will come considerably higher: a large importation at this time from Europe of salt pans would be very serviceable: they would sell high. The necessaries of life, except wheat flour, are risen to an amazing *nominal* price, owing to an encreased demand, & great depreciation of our currencies: wheat sells at 6/6 in this part of the country; the market for flour is very dull at present; the price of live stock of all kinds is prodigiously advanced; a cow, for instance, which a year ago would have sold for £6 only, would now sell for £18, or 20: cloths, linnens & woollens are excessive high; I have a coat on, the cloth of which is not worth more than 10s. a yard & would not have cost more 18 months ago, which lately cost me £4.10.0 a yard. Rye sells as high as 10s. per bushel; the distillers give that price to distill it into whisky; stills are set up in every corner of the country; I fear they will have a pernicious effect on the morals & health of our people. The months of June & July were pleasant & seasonable; the spring was very cold & dry with late frosts: we had a frost here the 28th May which destroyed our European grape vines & apples: the crops of flax through-out this State are bad: the crops of wheat & rye in general good. The 1st instant the weather set in very hot, and has continued so ever since; yesterday was the hottest day I ever felt; this is almost as bad."

RC (PPAmP).
¹ Apparently Carroll had left Philadelphia when Samuel Chase returned to take his seat in Congress on July 21. It is not known how long Carroll remained at his father's Douhoragen estate, but shortly after news arrived in Maryland that Lord Howe's fleet had arrived in the Chesapeake, Carroll set out on a trip lasting about four weeks that eventually took him back to Congress at Lancaster and York, Pa., where Congress reconvened at the end of September following the evacuation of Philadelphia. Carroll's August 22 letter to Gov. Thomas Johnson, which was probably written from Douhoragen and not from Philadelphia as indicated by Rowland, is in the Etting Collection, PHi, and Kate Mason Rowland, *The Life of Charles Carroll of Carrollton, 1737–1832, with His Correspondence and Public Papers*, 2 vols. (New York: G.P. Putnam's Sons, 1898), 1:212–14. Letters to his father of September 8, 11, and 18, written from "Swan Creek," "Johnson's Ferry on Susquahanna, Cecil County," and "Reading Furnace," are in the Carroll Papers, MdHi.

Samuel Chase to Thomas Johnson

Dear Sir,   Philada. Augst. 12. 1777. Tuesday
    I am honoured with your favor of the 8th Ult., and will pay every attention in my Power to the Remarks of Mr. Coudray, but I despair of ever introducing Œconomy into either our civil or military Department. My assistance will not be wanting to obtain so desirable an Event.
    By Letters from Sinepuxent of Fryday last by Express we are informed, that on Thursday a fleet of between 200 & 250 Sail passed by steering to the Southward, & on Fryday, they were seen off the same Place steering North. Genl. Washington is now with the main Body of his army about 16 or 20 Miles from this City, on the Road to Coryels ferry.
    I expect to see the Credit of our Money established in a very little Time. Our Commissioners have advised Congress to draw Bills, at par, on them, to the amount, if they choose, of twenty Million of Dollars, that they will accept them, payable with an Interest of 5 per Cent, from the Day of Payment till discharged.¹ To support the Credit of the Bills, they will [be] accepted by some of the first Bankers in France—in a word the Nation of France will be our Security for the Payment of the Interest—Spain will do the same.

Our army has retreated from Saratoga to Still-Water, about 25 Miles above Albany. We have about 3,000 Regulars & about 1,000 or 1200 Militia. Burgoyne has about 6,000 Regulars, & 400 Indians & 200 Canadians. The Savages butcher & scalp whole Families. I gave Gab. Duvall a Copy of a Letter to Me which is more particular.

Major Jenifer Adams applied to Me for his Commission. He was appointed a Lieutt. Colonel, by the Council of Safety 10 Jany last. He was appointed a Major in April by the Assembly. I offered him a Commo. bearing Date the 10th of April, agreeable to the Directions of the Assembly, & offered to indorse that he was appointed a Lieut. Colo. 10 Jany, to intitle to pay from that Time. He thought such an Indorsement would reflect Disgrace on his Character. He would not receive his Commo. dated the 10th of April. I promised to inform you and Council of this Difficulty.

I expected to hear from you relative to our Militia. If Genl. Howe should still attempt to execute his Design agt. this City, Gen. W. is very desirous that a Body of Militia should hang upon his Rear. He proposes to encamp a little beyond Darby. Chester, New Castle and Wilmington will be excellent Quarters for Howe. If a respectable Body could be collected at Wilmington, it would be of infinite Service.

I shall give you every Intelligence.

I beg my Compliments to the Gentlemen of the Council. Your affectionate & obedt. Servt.   S Chase

RC (PPRF).
¹ This information was contained in the commissioners' letter to the Committee of Secret Correspondence of March 12, 1777. See Wharton, *Diplomatic Correspondence,* 2:286.

Nathaniel Folsom to Josiah Bartlett

Dear Sir   Philadelphia Agust. the 12th. 1777
I Recd. your Kind feavouer of the first Instant in which you have Represented the Effect and Consequences that have taken Place, with the People at Large by the Loss of that important fortrise Tyconderoga—and I find them the Same, that wase Expected by all the Newengland Dellegates, and made use of in thaire arguements in Congress, for the Recalling of the Generals Schyler & Sat. Clare and for an inquirey into thaire Conduct for three Days togather abought Eighteen Days agoe, which wase most voilently aposed by the New York & Some of the Southern members—but at last Carried by a Large majority, and a Committe appointed in Congress to Report the mode of inquerey. General Gates is apinted to take the Comand in the northen Department & went off Last Thursday. As to the newes by the Packet from France it is taken

up in a general way that ouer affairs baire a feaverable aspect tho no probelety of a war this year, yet thay aire makeing every Preperation in thaire Power both in France & Spaine and that all Europe aire Plesed with ouer independence.

That funds will be Established by ouer agents for Paying the intrest and Part of the Prinsible of the Continental money.

The ministers of France Continue to tell ouer agents that they Can be of more Servise to the united Staes than thay Could be if thay ware to Declare war with Briton that thay aire not yet Rady alltho thay say a war will sertainly take Place when thay aire.

Some of the Leters which Came by the Packet aire Publisht which you will See before you recive this.

Hows fleet waire seen Last Thursday forty five miles Southward of the Capes of the Deleware which wase the Last Congress had heard of them. His Differant menovers have Puseld us all. Genl. Washington is now at Coraels feray with the bigest half of the armey waiteing the moshon of the Enemy. The Congress wood be glad Mr. How wood Come up the Deleware all most to a man because it Give you an oppertunity to Scurge those Sons of murder in the north. The wather here is exceding Hot. The Post is waiting. I am with Grate Respect your Humbl Servent.

Nathl Folsom

RC (NhD).

Henry Laurens to John Rutledge

Dear Sir   Philadelphia 12th of August 1777.

I reached this City the 21 July & next Morning took my Seat in Congress where I found upon the tapis a subject not well understood & which was to be agitated within eight & forty hours—an expedition to West Florida projected by persons out of doors & recommended upon vague & indigested plans & propositions, adopted by a few within & apparently acquiesced in by a great majority. The delegates from So Carolina are to be excepted.[1]

1000 or 1200 Men were to be immediately raised & embarked in Battoes on the Ohio[2] & proceed down the Stream to rely for assistance on the friendly disposition of the Inhabitants on the Banks of Mississippi "who were chiefly emigrants from the United States," upon the Governor of New Orleans for supplies of Money, Cannon & Artillery, Stores, upon the Strength of "friendly assurances received from the Spaniards." The troops were to lie perdue in a certain Cove or Bay near the mouth of the River till intelligence should be received of the arrival of 3 or 4 Frigates in the Bay[3] of Pensacola, these were to attack in front & aid the efforts which were to be made on the land side. The Frigates indeed were to rendezvous at Havanna from whence they were to Sail when advice Should be given of the arrival of the Troops near Orleans.

The intended operation to be kept a profound Secret & the whole coup to be accomplished between the middle of October & Christmas.

The Strength of the Enemy Supposed to be about 800 Men on Shore & one Frigate or two Sloops of War.

Benefits expected.

an acquisition of vast Stores of Merchandize & other valuables.[4]

destruction of a rising trade from W. Florida to Great Britain & the English West Indies.

a 14th State if we should resolve to receive it into our confederacy.

Lustre reflected upon the Arms of the United States.

In answer to these fine things it was Said.

The projectors should have been present, their answers to many questions which were necessary to put to them would prove they had not fully considered the Subject & that the scheme was impracticable upon their principles.[5]

If 1000 or 1200 Men could be so suddenly raised they were extremely wanted to act against the British Troops in this quarter & more as auxiliaries in the sothern States now held by a tenure very little better than the will of the Enemy. The power against which they were to act in West Florida was confessedly unknown & the junction of Army & Frigates admitting these to exist precarious in the highest degree. But where were the Frigates? If we had "3 or 4" to spare upon foreign exploits they could not be better directed than by orders to scour the Coast from E. Florida to Cape Fear whence in all probability we should derive additional Strength to our Navy & open the passage to Charles Town now become the envy of British Cruisers & the emporium of at least one half the States. Emigrants from these States had in general abandoned us & our Cause in search of Trade, of free Imports & Exports—from Such Men we could expect neither assistance nor secrecy. On the contrary they would join with numerous tribes of Indians who had not been thought of in the scheme of attack, in order to repel our Troops as the most dangerous invaders whose design was to plunder their present Stock & to cut off the means of future Supplies.

The Governor of Orleans would entertain no high estimation of our political forecast should we embark 1200 Men in dependence upon him at 1000 Miles distance for the very essentials of our expedition before treaty or even consultation & what would be the consequences if we should then fail of success.

If our Frigates found harbour at Havana we Should remember that Jamaica afforded safe anchorage to a large Squadron of British Ships of War & that the vulgar Spaniard for a little Gold would convey intelligence in a very few hours.

1000 or 1200 Men just taken from the Mountain Air & Water sent in the latter end of October & November to lie in any Cove of brackish Water & near Salt Marshes would Sicken & die very fast. Even upon the fresh Rivers where such men were exposed to night dews huddled together & lived upon Salt food, the list of dead & non affectives would increase every day. It was vain to hope for Secrecy of an enterprize which had been often talked of in different States & long Suspected by the Enemy.

Finally that vast expence of money & Men & further disgrace on our Arms would be the result of so mad an enterprize, into which it seemed Gentlemen had been hastening merely because they could not see their way.

Your Excellency will not be displeased with the detail of this affair if you think the termination without a serious question, a fortunate event & that if the Expedition had been attempted & failed as most undoubtedly it would, that our Enemies would have been furnished with strong arguments for moving the Creek & other Indians to act offensively against So Carolina & Georgia.

From the above circumstance & Sorry I am to Say, more than a few others which I have been witness to in short three Weeks I can hardly forbear concluding that a great Assembly is in its dotage & that happily for us our Enemy is at the Same time very infirm.

I came here with great reluctance diffident of my abilities to serve my Country effectualy—from the same apprehensions heightened by what I have already Seen I wish ten thousand times more I had never come as a delegate. Mr. Middleton tells me he is to leave us in October & Mr. Heyward expects soon to follow him. Your Excellency will perceive the necessity for pressing the House of Assembly to Send as able Men in their Stead & to fill up immediately the number of our delegacy.

General Howe's movements from New York, his parade in Sight of the Jersey Shore off the Capes of Delaware, pretences of coming within the Bay, then vanishing & now appearing again on the Coast of Maryland are all enigmatical & give rise to various guesses & conjectures. A few Men celebrated for penetration & Sound judgement persist in their opinions that this City will be his first object—granting so much as I will praise him for being even more indulgent than Sir Peter Parker,[6] had he come up the River immediately after his appearance off the Bay what was there to have withstood him. Billings Port was in no preparation for defence nor Fort Island & all the work which has been Since bestowed on the former is now to pass for nothing—General Washington having in person made a survey of the River & adjacent Lands & by advice of a Council of Engineers & able Navigators recommended to abandon the former for the present & to make Fort Island our Hope.[7] Our Fire Ships & wrafts are numerous but the effect of such engines always uncertain, in a word our Safety if we are even now safe rests in the weakness & distraction of the Enemy.

General Washington after a most fatiguing Countermarch contrary to his own opinion encamped his Troops near German Town from whence two days ago he Marched them again to Shamony where he means to wait for intelligence of Sir William who will probably be heard of from some part of New England & we shall then know that their Ships have been Coasting a fortnight or 3 Weeks for amusement.

My Son is now of the General's family & has I presume acknowledged his obligation to your Excellency in the Letter which will accompany this. I wish he had made a choice for his outset in Life in a sphere in which he might have been more extensively useful to his Country, the mark of your Excellency's good will to one so nearly connected with me nevertheless demands & will ever have my grateful thanks.

General Burgoyne who made a most extraordinary form of a proclamation[8] the Harbinger of his Entrance into the territories of the United States Seems to bear down all before him or more properly to be marching on without opposition. A Letter the 4th Inst. from General Schuyler depicts our circumstances in that quarter in the most gloomy colours. The Public Voice is clamorous against that Officer & more so if possible against his Sub. General St. Clair. These are remanded to headquarters & orders given for an enquiry into their conduct. General Gates is gone to take the Command of the Northern department, now the immediate post of honour & 'tis generally expected that his popularity in New England will recollect those of the Militia who had by thousands forsaken his precedessor as well as bring in thousands more & that he will soon be in a condition to give Mr. Burgoyne a Check & many hope, to cut off his retreat.

From the tenor of a Proclamation issued by Sir Wm. Howe at New York restricting & regulating Imports & exports & the whole commercial department, & of another Proclamation issued by Major General Jones Commandt. of that City arranging the police & threatning Military execution upon offenders, one would think the power & authority of Mr. Tryon very slender emanations from our late King's despotic Representatives & that the Tory inhabitants lead the Comfortable Life of Camp followers.

A late determination in Congress relative to the rank of a good old Servant General Arnold will probably deprive us of that Officer & may be attended by further ill effects in the Army.[9] The reasoning upon this occasion was disgusting. He was refused not because he was deficient in merit or that his demand was not well founded but because he asked for it & that granting at such instance would be derogatory to the honour of Congress. It would be tedious to relate all the particulars but a curious anecdote will arise from them. Our proceedings have also been injudicious toward many of the French & other foreign Officers too hastily chartered & flooded upon us by Mr. Deane. Some of these have addressed very riotous Letters to Congress & tis too certain that some of them have Solid ground for Complaint. I have no doubt but that besides disparaging reports of Congress at the Court of France Actions will be brought against Mr. Deane for breach of Covenants. He has certainly Stretched his Commission if not beyond the Letter far beyond all bounds of discretion, it seems as if he could not say nay to any Frenchman who called himself Count or Chevalier.

This day's paper will show Your Excellency the fate of brave Manly in the Hancock Frigate but a very different & truer Account of his defence will soon be laid before the public. The Royal New York Gazette says the Hancock was so shattered she could not swim to New York & was therefore sent to Hallifax—& our Accounts say the Flora had struck to Manly before the Rainbow came up.

The Executive Council of Pensylvania by recommendation from Congress had formed a parole to be signed by the late Officers of King George. Governor Penn & Mr. Chief Justice Chew to whom it was tendered having in the most indignant terms refused to comply, were taken into Custody this Morning & Congress have recommended to send them under guard to Virginia to be there held in confinement. It will be no misfortune if every other King's Officer & other suspected persons who are also included should follow the example of these leaders.[10]

The price of every article of traffic is most enormously advanced & very suddenly. Judge Sir of Beef 1/6 to 2/ per pd. Butter 6/ to 7/6. Fire Wood on the Wharf £4.10/ to £5 per Chord. Salt £6 per bushel. Horses at Livery 8/ per day. Brown Sugar 7/ per pd. Rum 55/ & Madeira Wine £3 per Galln. A Labourer two Dollars per day. A yard of coarse brown Linen 15/ a ps. of Coarse Thread Hair 25/. A pair of Coarse common Shoes 26/, fine shoes 35/ & other articles in proportion, in so much that a Stranger living decently tho' sparingly will find himself at the end of £1500 Stg when the year expires without having made any addition in the mean time to his Wardrobe. I have ordered a Beaver hat & must pay £9 for it. All this is owing, in our present circumstances, to the Stoppage of foreign Trade & not to combination as some people ignorantly assert. Every House on the Road between this place & Carolina is a manufactory of Linen & most of them of Woolen also but they produce very little more than enough for their own consumption. The Farmer & Labourer will have prices in return for their commodities & Labour nearly adequate to the rates which they are obliged to pay for articles which they Stand in need of. I say nearly because the Farmer Still Sells his produce at a lower price comparatively than he formerly received. For instance a pound of Beef was formerly the exchange for a pound of Sugar, now 4 lb Beef is given for a pound of Sugar. A Chord of Fire Wood at 20/ would have purchased 10 or 15 bushels of Salt, at present the price of one bushel is a Chord & a half. The resource there-

fore of the Farmer & labourer must be in frugality. Nothing but great
frugality can save the Suspended Merchant & Money lender from ruin,
& your poor distressed Delegates must fly to economy or be conducted
to Gaol. These advanced prices do not arise I say from combination but
are genuinely the offspring of necessity. I will prove this by an observation founded in fact & which I think will contain an answer to all that
ever has been & all that ever can be said to the contrary. I had occasion
lately to purchase a Gold Watch for a young friend. The article had
cost in London 25 Guineas. The Merchant here demanded 300 Dollars
not a farthing less. I asked how many golden Guineas will you take—
answer 19. In the first case near 3 times the original price was demanded, in the latter the Commodity was offered at 25 per Cent less
than prime Cost. Square Dollars would have borne only their nominal
value in the purchase of domestic articles. Guineas will slide to a post
where Advertisements of Just imported fill Columns of the News paper
& purchase articles there which may be returned here & establish the
price of the Watch at 500 Dollars. For a pipe of Madeira Wine was
demanded of Mr. Heyward & Self £320—£180 Stlg ordinary per—yet
my Bill upon London for £54 will pay for the Wine. The power only
that can stop Delaware may attempt to stop the Channels of Exchange
& Commerce among a free people, but these are at this time serious &
alarming considerations & cry aloud for our utmost exertions to open a
foreign Trade which is not so impossible as the next alternative the Suppression of Idleness & Luxury. Tis true our advices from our public
Agents in France & at Martinique are very flattering but 'tis equally
true that nothing they have Said in consequence of French promises
can be depended upon & we ought to be & continue jealous of the
French & Spaniard until they recognize the Independance of the States
& enter into a formal Treaty. Every thing short of that point awakens
my apprehensions that the original plan of partition & mutual guarantee
may be revived.[11] The very loan which is made to us is insidious. The
French under all their pretensions to kindness have the best Security in
the World. They may receive their Capital with large Interest at the
Bank of England when they please, or may compel us to pay it upon
worse terms than their pitiful offer of a Livre per Acre for 300 Miles
Square or 57,600,000 Acres.

I have not the least doubt of the good wishes of all the Trading &
other people in the middle Life that our Independence may be established, tis probable they hold themselves Interested in the event & that
many thousands already anticipate happiness in a Land of Liberty. The
more this Spirit appears or is even suspected, the more artfully will the
movements respecting us be conducted at Versailles. One of our Agents,[12]
I mean no offence, has not discovered competency to the immense work
in hand. The other[13] is on the verge of Life & judging from the ordinary
course of nature must soon drop. I have urged Congress to appoint a

proper person to repair to France in order to act as a Co-adjutator to Doctor Franklin while he lives, & in his Stead, in case of Sudden death. A precaution like this, a wise Man would take where the Interest of a Distant Rice & Indigo Plantation was concerned and by Heavens Sir we wont feel for the Salvation of thirteen plantations 1700 Miles long at a distance of a thousand Leagues. With submission I think our Treaties have been prematurely offered. Proposals should have commenced on the other side or if on ours not plumply by a schedule of all we would yield. The subtle French of whom we should ever be jealous have now an amazing advantage over us, nor can it be doubted but that our terms will be made a proper use of & held up for higher bidding. Already the British Ministry waving all resentment for the innumerable insults which have been offered to their Flag & their Trade have proposed a largess in the Newfoundland Fishery to the French Court & we are now a hostage.[14]

LB (ScHi). Laurens' letterbook also contains a partial draft of this letter dated August 11 that includes significant variations, which are cited in the notes below.

[1] See Charles Thomson's Notes of Debates, July 24 and 25, 1777.

[2] In place of the last three words, Laurens wrote "at Fort Pitt" in the August 11 draft.

[3] In the August 11 draft, the remainder of this sentence reads: "in order to Second the efforts on the Land side of Pensacola where vast Magazines of Merchandize, Warlike Stores & other valuables were to be Seized, the Town & fortifications to be destroyed or reserved according to circumstances."

[4] The equivalent of this line in the August 11 draft reads: "an acquisition of necessary articles for our Troops & Indian Trade & of other effects."

[5] In place of this paragraph, Laurens wrote in the August 11 draft: "I listened with patience to the reasonings on these points till I found the House hastening into the measure not because they saw the way but rather because they did not & had relied implicitly upon papers sent in by the out of door projectors who ought to have been examined pointedly at the Bar of the House. My objections were partly to the utility in our present circumstances but principally against the practicability."

[6] The British naval commander at the battle of Sullivan's Island in June 1776.

[7] See Washington, *Writings* (Fitzpatrick), 9:45–53.

[8] See Laurens to John Lewis Gervais, August 17, 1777, note 5.

[9] See *JCC*, 8:623–24; and James Lovell to William Whipple, August 8, 1777.

[10] See *JCC*, 8:591–92, 633–34. On August 14 former Gov. John Penn and former Chief Justice Benjamin Chew informed Congress that they were now willing to take a parole, whereupon Congress ordered the Board of War to administer one to them and reversed the order for their removal to Virginia. With the approach of the British toward Philadelphia, however, Congress changed its mind again and on August 28 instructed the board to remove Penn and Chew from Pennsylvania. See *JCC*, 8:641–42, 695; and PCC, item 41, 2:27, item 78, 18:147.

[11] On this point, see Richard Henry Lee to Patrick Henry, April 20, 1776, note 3.

[12] Silas Deane.

[13] Benjamin Franklin.

[14] For the continuation of this letter, see Laurens to Rutledge, August 15, 1777.

John Adams to Abigail Adams

My dearest Friend   Phila. Aug. 13. 1777

We have been sweltering here, for a great Number of days together, under the scalding Wrath of the Dog Star. So severe a Spell of Heat has scarcely been known these twenty Years. The Air of the City has been like the fierce Breath of an hot oven. Every Body has been running to the Pumps all day long. There has been no finding a Place of Comfort—the shade, and the very Entrys of Houses where they have the best Draughts of Air, have been scarcely tolerable. This season always affects me, deeply. It exhausts my Spirits, and takes away all my Strength of Mind and Body. I have never lived here in Dog days, without becoming so enfeebled, and irritated, as to be unable to sleep soundly and regularly and to be still more reduced by Night Sweats. If I can avoid these Inconveniences, this year, I shall be happy. But I have experienced something of it, already, altho not in any great Degree.

When the Weather is so extream, the Fatigue of even holding a Pen to write a Letter, is distressing.

We have no News from the Fleet since last Thursday when about 200 of them were seen off of Synepuxent.

What will our People do with Burgoigne? He has put himself in the Power of the People in that Quarter, and if they do not make him repent his Folly, they will be to blame. It is a Shame that such an handfull should ravage in a Country so populous.

You will see by the Papers that Manly is taken. What a Disappointment to Us! Yet We might have expected it. What rational Creatures could order two thirty Gun Frigates to cruise on the American Coast, for the Protection of Trade. They should have been ordered to some other Seas—to France, to Spaign, to the Baltic, the Mediterranean—any where but where they were.

The Ship and Men are a Loss, but We must build more.

RC (MHi). Adams, *Family Correspondence* (Butterfield), 2:310.

Samuel Adams to William Heath

My dear sir,   Philade Augt 13th 1777

The Surrender of Tyconderoga has deeply wounded our Cause. The Grounds of it must be thoroughly inquired into. The People at large have a Right to demand it. They do demand it and Congress have orderd an Inquiry to be made. This Matter must be conducted with Impartiality. The Troops orderd for the Defence of that Post were cheifly from New England. It is said there was a great Deficiency in Numbers and General Schuyler tells us that a third Part of the Army there were Boys, Negroes and aged Men not fit for the Field or indeed any other Service. That a great Part of them were naked, without Blanketts, ill armed & very deficient in Accoutrements. Such is the Picture he draws. I wish to know as soon as possible, how many Men actually marchd for that Place from N.E. & particularly from Massachusetts Bay. What Quantity of Cloathing was sent for them & under whose Care, and how they were furnishd with Arms & Accoutrements. In short I am desirous of being informd by you as minutely as possible, of the Part taken by Muster Masters, Quartermasters, Cloathiers & their Agents and all other Persons employed in making and providing for the Army in the Northern Department, as far as it has properly fallen under your Notice & Direction.[1] Excuse me for giving you this Trouble & be assured that I am very cordially, your Freind,   Samuel Adams

RC (MHi).
[1] General Heath's August 27 response to Adams included this evaluation of the quality of the Massachusetts troops. "As to the ability of body of the men I can not fully determine. The greater part that I saw appeared able, but it is more than probable that there were some men advanc'd in life, and some lads, and a number of negroes (the latter were generally able bodied, but for my own part I must confess I am never pleased to see them mixed with white men)." *Collections of the Massachusetts Historical Society*, 7th ser. 4 (1904): 147–50.

Elbridge Gerry to the Massachusetts Board of War

Gentlemen   Philadelphia August 13. 1777
    The Bearer Doctor Cutting is Apothecary General of the middle District, & sent by the Director General to purchase Medicine in your State, who has desired a Line to your Board in Favour of the Doctor for assistance herein if required.[1] As You are well apprized of the Usefulness of military Hospitals, & the Reputation which they give to the Service when rendered successful, I have no Doubt that the Director General would have received your assistance upon the application of himself or any of his officers; I shall only say, that his Character is high with every Gentleman who has the pleasure of his Acquaintance & that You may depend upon an honorable Compliance with the Engagements made by him or any of the Officers employed by his Direction. I am with much Esteem, Gentlemen your very hum serv,   E Gerry

RC (M–Ar).
[1] Dr. John Brown Cutting also carried with him to Boston an August 14 letter of recommendation from President Hancock to Gen. William Heath, who was asked to "afford him any Assistance he may require towards dispatching the Business he has in View." Heath Papers, MHi.

Henry Laurens to Christopher Zahn

Dear Sir,[1]   Philadelphia 13th August 1777.
My journey to this place was in general very pleasant & after I had
left the Moravian Settlement where I found it necessary to halt two days
for a Waggon we travelled very fast often 40 & sometimes 44 Miles a
day. I found the air so Cool in the Mountains from the 2d July as to
require a buttoned Coat & Wastcoat till the Sun had mounted an hour
high. I took what is called the upper Road near 300 Miles from the Sea
& to my astonishment found it upon the back of Virginia & Maryland
particularly more fully inhabited than the Road between your House &
Charles Town. The Farms are delightful & almost without exception
abundant Crops of grain. Every Man has his patch of Flax & hemp &
almost everyone a few Sheep, the Spinning Wheel & Loom to be Seen in
every House & Scarce one with less than 8 Children. Thus circumstanced
these people complain of want in no other article but that of Salt. They
make a good Spirit from Peaches & from Barley & other grain, & Substitute honey for Sugar. The Water & Air two grand proofs of the human
frame are excellent, bread the Staff of Life abundant, fine pasture, good
Horses, black Cattle, Sheep, Hogs & Fowl of all kinds, & I am in hopes
their complaints were rather from a fear of wanting than from absolute
want of Salt although It was very scarce & every Man had his stock. In
time, conquer the Country who may, that Land will become the seat of
health, wealth, Arts & Science & in a very few Ages of peace be covered
by Inhabitants a thousand Miles back, the prospect is unbounded.
    The weather in this City has been the last fortnight day & night very
hot, Some days & nights more disagreeable so than ever I found it in
Charlestown. This may be from the Same cause to which we ascribe the
intolerable Cold Sometimes felt in that warmer Climate, the Sudden &
extreme change of the Air. My health is as good as ever.
    Mr. Ball & the two Negro Boys have passed Safely & with very little
inconvenience through the Small Pox.
    Mr. White is at home in this City & has not yet put on his War hat.
    My Son John is in the family of General Washington who is now en-
camped about 35 Miles from hence waiting to learn the destination of
Sir William Howe who has been amusing us with inexplicable movements for near a Month past. About the middle of July he embarked
Horses & Troops in the Bay of New York & in a few days a pompous
fleet of 250 Sail in two divisions passed Sandy Hook to Sea, in a few
days more one half of them were so near in the Jersey Shoar as to be
Seen distinctly, next apparently the whole fleet paraded near the Capes
of Delaware & 228 Sail counted by our Look out & the shew of coming
in was so much in earnest that the Officer at the look out advised that
about 40 or 60 Sail were at Anchor within the Bay & the rest of the
fleet moving in fast. Next Morning they were at Sea again & about the

1st Augt were Standing with a Southerly Wind E.N.E. By that time they must have been informed that General Washington had Marched his Troops to the banks of Delaware in order to meet Sir William below this City. Here we concluded the fleet after the Commanders had by so deep a feint effected their purpose of drawing off General Washington from North River & Sufficiently harrassed his Troops by long Countermarches had now Sailed again for North River in order to effect a junction with General Burgoyne who had found an easy, too easy, a passage into the territories of the Eastern States. But to our amazement twelve days are past, we learn nothing of Sir William, but of his fleet we have assurance that near an hundred Sail have been seen on the Coast of Maryland & tis the opinion of our deepest politicians that this place is still their object. If so I will not allow Sir William Howe & his Council to be deep politicians. We must have patience, a day or two more will unfold this riddle.

The loss of Ticonderoga has raised universal complaints against General Schuyler & General St. Clair, the former who was Commander in Cheif for neglect of duty by absence from his post—the latter for abandoning the post & immense Stores without an attempt to Save either. They are both remanded in order to answer to an enquiry into their conduct. In this State 'tis but generous to forbear censure. General Gates is gone to take upon him the Command of that department, 'tis now the very post of Honour, he is a great favorite of the Eastern people who will join him with alacrity. If he gives a Check to Burgoyne his name & his memory will be ever dear, indeed upon his efforts & success all that Country & I may say the Cause of America depends. Burgoyne announced his Entry by the herald of a pompous proclamation in which he is equally lavish in friendly promises to Tories & faint Hearts & in threats of the severest punishment to all those who dare to oppose him. There is no doubt if he had it in his power of his keeping Strictly up to the letter, but unhappily for those who trusted him he has failed of his promises to his friends. His Indian Allies have indiscriminately butchered Men but chiefly Women & Children who had in obedience to his mandate remained quietly at home. Such Scenes of Carnage as he has exhibited are shocking to the last degree. We hope his progress will be stopped by General Gates & Men who know the Country say his retreat may be cut off. The News papers which I inclose with this will give you many particulars.

Intelligence from our Agents in France & at Martinico is very flattering. The French Court have lent us a pretty large Sum of Money & have given assurances of continuing to supply us with Merchandize & Warlike Stores & that all their ports shall be open to our Ships, but go no further. They will not yet recognize our Independence nor enter into Treaty with us as a free & distinct people. Until they do both I will have no dependence upon French promises. They have the best Security in the

World for this Money which they may receive with large Interest when they please at the Bank of England, or may compel us to pay four fold in Land which they Seem to aim at but touch the Subject cautiously. The British Ministry in order to tempt them to abandon us have already made one concession by an offer to enlarge their bounds of Fishery on the banks of New Foundland, probably they wait to hear what further offer those abandoned wretches will make, & at length when both Britain & the United States are nearly exhausted to carve for themselves. Our Cause is good, I am Satisfied we shall under all disadvantages support it. Our Harbours in these middle States having been long locked up by British Cruizers every Specie of foreign Goods is become Scarce & the prices greatly enhanced. The Farmers & Labourers have enhanced their demands nearly but not altogether in proportion—consequently those who have no Trade, or farm are greatly oppressed. I am one in that Class & you will judge of the vast expence I [am] at to live even Sparingly from the following Specimen:

Butter 5/to a Dollar per pound. Beef & other Butchery 1/6 to 2/. Fire Wood 13 to 14 Dollars a Chord. Brown Sugar one, & Loaf Sugar three dollars a pound. A pair coarse thread stockings 4 1/2 Dollar to 6 Dollars. Shoes 4 to 5 Dollars a pair. Rum 7 1/2 dollars & Wine 9 Dollars a Gallon. A Fish not sufficient for one Man's meal a Dollar & upward. Coarse brown Linen 3 to 4 Dollars a Yard. A Beaver Hat 20 to 24 Dollars. Eggs a Doz 1/2 of a Dollar & upward. These extravagancies hurt a few but do not tend to ruin the Country as many people erroneously assert.

We are overrun with French Men, Marquis's, Counts, Barons & Chevaliers in Search of Commissions & the honour of fighting in the cause of Liberty are living here at a very dear rate & we have no employment equal to their expectations.

I say nothing of my affairs at Sante under your protection. I have nothing to say because I am confident you will do all for me that is necessary. I beg you will assure Mr McCullogh of my desire to be his friend & also to Burnet & Martin. I expect you will favour me with a Line of intelligence when occasions require & I beg you will beleive that I continue with great regard

LB (ScHi).

¹ Christopher Zahn, South Carolina assemblyman and planter, was one of several South Carolinians keeping watch over Laurens' manifold business affairs during his service in Congress. Raymond Starr, ed., "Letters from John Lewis Gervais to Henry Laurens, 1777–1778," *South Carolina Historical Magazine* 66 (January 1965): 26.

Francis Lightfoot Lee to Landon Carter

My dear Colonel,   Philadelphia Aug. 13. 1777
    I have the pleasure at last of sending you some directions for making sugar; which I hope will be usefull.
    You have my sincere thanks for your agreeable Letter by R.H.L. I am well pleased to find no abatement in your usual flow of good spirits. In spite of the cholic, I hope you will live long enough to see the down fall of this excessive fondness for popularity. It cannot long exist, in any great degree, where there are not many lucrative Offices in the gift of the people, and in Popular Governmts. I think the error is generally on the side of Parsimony. We are kept in great anxiety by the extraordinary manoevre of Genl. Howe, his going to sea with his Army; we can as yet only guess at his intentions. He was seen Last Fryday, about 50 miles to the southward of these capes, & perhaps may be in Chesapeak by the time you receive this, tho we think if he has any wisdom left he shoud go to the northward to cooperate with Burgoyne, whose genius, at present, seems to have the ascendency in his department. Our people there are still in a panic & Burgoyne's thoughtless activity is well calculated to keep it up. Our only comfort is, that the further he penetrates, the more surely he may be ruined; when they recover their senses. The Enemy have taken one of our finest frigates from us; but I believe we have one of theirs in return.
    I have not yet had an opportunity of delivering your present to Doctr. Shippen. I am sure he will make every gratefull return in his power. You may be sure of your Sickles. It is so excessive hot & biting flies so plenty that I can scarce write. Mrs. Lee sends her best respects & wishes to God she coud comply wth. yr. kind invitation, in wch. she is join'd by yr. afft.
                                        F.L. Lee

RC (ViHi).

John Adams to Abigail Adams

                              Philadelphia August 14. 1777
My dearest Friend   Thursday
    We are still parching under the fierce Heats of Dog days. It is agreed, by most People, that so long and so intense a Heat has scarcely been known. The Day before Yesterday, Dr. Ewing an eminent Philosopher as well as Mathematician, and Divine told me, the Spirit in his Glass, was at 91 in his cool Room, and from thence he concludes that it was above an hundred abroad in the Shade, because he says it is generally ten degrees lower, in his cool Room, than it is in the Shade out of Doors. Yesterday, it was at 94, abroad in the Shade. He placed his

Thermometer, against a Post which had been heated by the Sun, and the Spirit arose to an 100, but removing it to another Place, and suspending it at a distance from any warm Object and the Spirit subsided and settled at 94. How we shall live through these Heats I dont know.

If Howes Army is at Sea, his Men between Decks will suffer, beyond Expression. Persons, here, who have been at Sea, upon this Coast, at this Season of the Year, say, the Heat is more intollerable, on Shipboard than on Land. There is no Comfort to be had any where, and the Reflection of the Sun Rays from the Deck, are insufferable.

I wish this Wiseacre may continue to coast about untill an equinoctial Storm shall overtake him. Such a Thing would make fine Sport for his Fleet.

The Summer is consuming, and there is not Time enough left, for accomplishing many Things. If he should land tomorrow, it would take him three Weeks to reach Philadelphia. On the Jersey Side of the Delaware, is an ugly Road for him—many Rivers, Bridges, Causeys, Morasses, by breaking up of which, a Measure which is intended, and for which Preparations are made, his Army might be obstructed, puzzled and confounded in their March. His Army cannot proceed without many Horses, Waggons, and Cannon with their Carriages, for the Passage of which he must make new Bridges and Causeys, which would consume much Time, besides that he would be exposed, to the Militia and to the regular Army. On the other side the River there are several Streams and one large River to cross—the Schuylkill. And We have many fine Fire ships to annoy his Fleet. It would be happy for Us if he should aim at this Place, Because it would give Us an Opportunity of exerting the whole Force of the Continent against him. The Militia of the Jerseys, Pensilvania, Delaware and Maryland, would cooperate with Washington here—those of N.Y. and N. England with Gates.

Writing this Letter, at Six o Clock in the Morning in my cool Chamber has thrown me into a profuse and universal sweat.[1]

RC (MHi). Adams, *Family Correspondence* (Butterfield), 2:315–16.

[1] In his next letter to Abigail the following day, Adams resumed discussing the consequences of the heat in Philadelphia but in a postscript ecstatically reported the arrival of thundershowers giving relief. Ibid., pp. 316–17.

John Hancock to Horatio Gates

Sir   Philada August 14th 1777

The enclosed Resolve, which I have the Pleasure of transmitting, I hope, will find you safely arrived, at the Head of the Army, in the Department committed to your Care.

From the Want of Discipline, and other Disorders, too apt to prevail in a retreating Army, the Congress have been induced to pass a Resolve, empowering you to remedy those Evils as far as possible—and have for this Purpose, authorized you, for the limited Time of four Months, to suspend any Officers for Misconduct; not doubting that before the Expiration of that Period, you will be able to introduce that Order and Subordination, so necessary in the military Line. You will be pleased to forward Congress, with as much Dispatch as possible, the Names of those you may suspend, with the Reasons of their Suspension.[1]

Your Zeal and Success in the American Cause, have hitherto been so distinguished, that it is impossible for me not to flatter myself with the Expectation that we shall ere long have the most agreeable Accounts from the Department, where you command. I beg you will be pleased to transmit every important Intelligence, as early as the Situation of Affairs will admit. All such Resolves, as relate to your Department, shall be forwarded without Delay. At present, I have only to request your Attention to *that* herewith transmitted.

I have the Honour to be, with the greatest Respect, Sir, your most obedt. & very hble Servt.   John Hancock Presidt.

RC (NHi). In the hand of Jacob Rush and signed by Hancock.
    [1] See *JCC,* 8:642.

Henry Laurens to William Brisbane

Dear Sir[1]   14th August 1777
My journey to this yet fine City was in general pleasant the air rather hot till I reached the Mountains in the back of No Carolina about the 2d July where I found the Mornings so very cool as to require buttoned Coat & Wastcoat till the Sun mounted an hour or two & the whole day like our fine air in November, below. I travelled the upper Road 300 Miles from the Sea where to my equal Surprize & pleasure I found the Country more fully inhabited than even is between Purysburgh & Charles Town. The Landskapes are delightful, fine Farms & almost without exception abounding with Crops of Grain, Cotton, Flax & Sheep. The Spinning Wheel & Loom are seen on every farm & very few with less than Eight Children, that number seemed almost to be the Standard. What an increase will an Age or two of peace make. Water & Air are excellent. Bread the Staff of Life abundant. Fine pastures & Meadows consequently good Horses, black Cattle, Sheep, Hogs & Fowl of every kind. Thus circumstanced almost the sole complaint of these people was the want of Salt which had been very scarce & dear & so continued. They make good Spirit from Peaches, Barley & other grain & Substitute Honey for Sugar, in the Winter they brew good Ale & Beer & generally are well provided with Cyder but this year the Cold Spring destroyed the growth

of Apples. Conquer the Country who may, it will in time become the Scene of Health, wealth, Arts & Sciences & extend thousands of Miles back. The prospect is unbounded. The Envy of our Older Brethren in England has fooled them to attempt to check & restrain this growth, had they any knowledge of the Subject they would see the impossibility of success, they would be convinced that their Labours for that purpose will be as fruitless as an attempt to build a Bridge from Plymouth to Philadelphia. The work which they have taken in hand may be compared to that of building a Babel & it will have Similar effects, the builders will be confounded, will leave off the work & be scattered upon the face of the Earth, already many hundreds amounting to thousands have deserted their work & become good Americans. In the mean time it cannot be denied that we the faithful representatives of posterity feel many a hard Stroke from their rude & sorry am I to Say it, barbarian hands—Cursed by those who have borne false witness against us & encouraged this unjust persecution & all those who now from avarice & Interested motives look at our distresses with pleasure & the cruel hope of seeing our burthens increased.

My Son John [is] in the family of General Washington who is now encamped on the Northern Road, waiting to learn the grand design of Sir William Howe who has been amusing us with movements as yet inexplicable for a whole Month past. About the middle of July we received certain advice of the embarkation of his Horse soon after of the Infantry & upon the 23d a Fleet of 250 Sail in three divisions Shot Sandy Hook & Stood to Sea about SE. The 2d or 3d day after this invincible Armada was seen from the Jersey Shoar near the Cape, next it appeared off the Capes 228 Sail distinctly counted from our look out & so much in earnest did the conductors seem to be to enter the Delaware that about 40 or 60 Sail came actually within the Bay & the rest made a show of following as fast as circumstances would admit. After all their parade they stood to Sea again & on the 1st August were seen Steering E.N.E. with a strong southerly Wind which would have brought the whole fleet into this River in a few hours if Philadelphia had been their object. 'Tis to be supposed that some of the Rascally Tories had by this time informed General Howe of General Washington's arrival with his army near this City. Most people apprehend that to have been the thing he wished for & concluded that the fleet had Sailed to the Eastward, that the Troops would debark in some part of New England, that Country be attacked on all sides & a junction secured with the Army under Mr. Burgoyne. While we were in this suspense we received certain intelligence about 3 days ago of the Fleet or a Fleet of upwards of 200 Sail which must be the Same Seen off Sinnepuxent on the Maryland Shore & the same intelligence has been repeated. In the mean time we learn not a Syllable of Sir Wms. Army appearing any where to the Northward or Eastward. This riddle gives rise to a thousand conjectures. Every politician forms

AUGUST 14, 1777

& retails his own opinion. Some who pretend to be deepest say Phyladelphia is certainly the object in view. I reply, if it is, Sir Willm. Howe is more indulgent than ever Sir Peter Parker. In order to be quite right in my guess I declare I know not where they are gone nor whither bound. A few days probably hours will inform us. The evacuation of Ticonderoga has raised universal complaints against Generals Schuyler & St Clair who are both remanded in order to answer an Enquiry which will be made into their conduct respectively. General Gates is gone to relieve Mr Schuyler & to assume the Command of the Northern department which is now the very post of Honour. Tis said the Eastern people who detested his successor[2] adore him & will join him with alacrity. In this view me thinks he is in a delicate Situation. I wish him Success; upon that I may Say almost depends the Cause of America. If he gives Burgoyne an effectual Check the British Campaign will be over & Gates will Stand next to Washington; this will ever have the lead in America & an illustrious character in future history.

General Burgoyne announced his Entry upon the territory of the United States by a pompous proclamation in which in very affected language he is lavish of friendly promises to Tories & property men & not less profuse in denunciations against those who dare treat him as Junius did set him at Defiance.[3] Unhappily already for many who had confided in his promises of protection, they have fallen a Sacrifice to the ferocity of his gentle Allies the barbarian Indians. These even in presence of the British Savages have murdered & scalped some men & many women & Children who in obedience to the proclamation had remained quietly at home & removed none of their effects. Innocent young girls whose parents thought them in perfect safety & indeed under the protection of the British Commander have been taken as they were amusing themselves in the fields & inhumanely Butchered.

I hope General Gates will stop their progress. Gentlemen who are better acquainted with the Country than I am, say if the New England Militia are in earnest Mr. Burgoyne may not only be checked but his retreat cut off. In the meantime the number of auxiliaries which he may have collected from among Tories is altogether uncertain.

We have lately received very flattering intelligence from our Agents at Paris & in the West Indies. The French Court have lent us a round Sum of Money at an easy Interest, have reiterated assurances of keeping their ports open to our Ships, Commercial & Warlike, but are extremely shy with respect to recognizing our Independence & entering into a formal Treaty. Until they do both I will have no confidence in them. Every thing else is consistent with their own Interest & may be calculated & made use of hereafter to our further distress. For the Money lent they have the best security in the World & may raise the amount with large Interest at the Bank of England whenever they please, or may compel us to pay four fold in Land, which by one of their movements though cautiously made they seem to aim at. In order to draw them from their seeming attachment to our Cause have made one Concession by offering them a large share of the Newfoundland Fishery.[4] The awful Frenchman waits no doubt to learn the highest bidding before he will explain. In the meantime he is certainly by Suffering his subjects to cruize upon the British Trade under Congress Commissions which at an hundred Sail at least so, offering poor old England such Insults as she has never been accustomed to Submit to.

Chesapeak Bay, Delaware, New York, Rhode Island having been long blocked up by British Men of War every article of foreign goods is become scarce & extravagantly dear. Hence the Farmer & Labourer have enhanced their several demands. Consequently those who have neither Merchandize nor Farms to live by & who give their Labours to the public are greatly oppressed. I am one in that Class & you will judge of the vast expence I am put to even for a Scanty decent living from the inclosed accot of prices—exclusive of Cloths I dont think I can live half so well as I had at home & maintain only two instead of a dozen Servants for £1500 Sterling a year.

French Marquisses, Counts, Barons & Chevaliers in pursuit of Commissions & of the honour of fighting for what is a mere *phantom* in their Country, "*Liberty*," overrun Philadelphia, living at a very dear rate, four Dollars for a warm dinner & as they have been accustomed to get for half an one many of these are truly to be pitied. For although Liberty is visionary in their Native clime, they are not ignorant of its estimate. From many accounts which I have seen from France, however artful the Court may be, the people in general wish us success & seem to feel themselves Interested in our Cause. If we attain to our wishes of confirming Independence I have no doubt but that in a few years there will be an addition to our number of some hundred thousands from the Continent of Europe. This very circumstance may possibly weigh with proud Kings & prevent their giving us all that assistance which otherwise they would.

The loss of Manly & the fine Frigate he Commanded is not a trifle, however he fought more bravely than his Captor is pleased to declare. Another Account in the Royal Gazette of New York says his Ship was so much Shattered she would not have swam to New York; she was therefore sent to Halifax. His fall was glorious, nor did he fall before he had convinced the World that the British Flag might be Struck to the American. The taking of the Fox of 32 Guns was a great act, according to English estimation she should have been an overmatch for Cap Manly's. I believe the Fox is retaken & what is equally unfortunate the Commander of her was on board the Hancock, which deprives us of the means for Exchanging our brave Captain. Every day now teems with important events. This Campaign will, whether successful or not, spin the Web of British power to a fineness which will expose it to extreme danger from foreign blasts. Granting Britain should acquire a

farther extent of Sea Coast unless she conquers the hearts of half a
million of Men determined not to submit to her the Conquest will but
accelerate her down-fall. The more I see into the Subsisting dispute the
more confirmed am I in the opinion which I have often declared to you
—whatever may be the State of us the friends of America & whatever
may be the Issue of our Contest, America is lost to Britain. There is but
one way to regain all the advantages which she can hope for from Commerce with this Country, a Treaty. This 'tis probable would soon be
attempted if the parties knew each others mind.

I shall not at present trouble you on the Subject of my own affairs;
the confidence which I place in your friendship renders it unnecessary.
You will save me if possible from farther illegal & unjust Strokes. I find
that was *one* which was made under the authority of Mr. Dillon to
which I must for a while Submit. I will beg of you to deliver the enclosed to Mr. Baillie half an hour. Present my Compliments to Mr
Patterson & believe me to be with the most friendly regard & esteem &ca.

LB (ScHi).
1 William Brisbane (1740–78), a South Carolina planter, was acting as one
of Laurens' business agents in that state. E. Haviland Hillman, "The Brisbanes,"
South Carolina Historical and Genealogical Magazine 14 (July 1913): 127.
2 Laurens apparently meant to write "his predecessor," a reference to Philip
Schuyler.
3 Junius was the pseudonym of the still unidentified author of a series of
letters bitterly criticizing the British government that appeared in England
between 1769 and 1772. Burgoyne was the object of Junius' wrath in a letter
dated December 12, 1769. *The Letters of Junius* (Dublin: Thomas Ewing, 1777),
pp. 211–14. See also Laurens to John Lewis Gervais, August 17, 1777, note 5.
4 According to Laurens' August 12 letter to John Rutledge, Great Britain made
this offer to France.

James Lovell to Elias Boudinot

Sir   Philada. Augst 14th. [1777]
I beg you would endeavour to find out the real Situation of Charles
Hughes a Swiss who speaks several Languages besides the English, and
who left Philada. in Febry. 1776 for France and was taken in his Home
voyage. He was said to be on Board the Rainbow about 5 Months ago,
and is now on Board the Preston either as a Prisoner or Volunteer. He
has a distressed Wife & sick Infant in this City on whose account I wish
you to make this Enquiry about his *real* Situation.

I am, sir, your humb Servt.   James Lovell

RC (PHi). Addressed: "Elias Boudinot Esqr. Commissary Genl. of Prisoners at
Head Quarters."

Henry Laurens to Gabriel Manigault

Dear Sir,[1]   15th August 1777

I arrived within half a mile of this City the 20th July where I halted
for a night in order to adjust a plan for innoculating three persons who
had travelled with me, Mr John Ball, his Black Boy & one of mine.
Thank God they have passed very happily through the small Pox, neither
of them were confined by the disorder 24 hours.

My journey although it would Seem long to count from the 7 June to
20 July was travelled in less than thirty days. I came the upper Road &
when I had reached the Mountains about the 2d July I found the air
extremely pleasant so cool in the Evenings & mornings as to make it
necessary to button a Coat over the Wastcoat & so it continued until I
approached this City. Here it is warm enough. The last fortnight has
been intensely hot, I am now writing in an open room & striped to my
Shirt, yet I am so moistened as to oblige me to use a paper under my
hand & the nights are worse. I fear my friends in Charles Town must
suffer more, but perhaps not, you may there have refreshing breezes
from the Sea, here we are Shut up from all breezes.

On my journey I found every where plentiful Crops of Grain together
with Cotton, Flax & Hemp, almost every House with Looms for Linen
& Woolen & few with less than eight Children. The Country is delightful
& no heavy complaints but for the want of Salt. Many other articles are
Scarce & dear but the people can either do without or find Some substitute for such. I believe they have Scarcely Salt enough to Serve for the
ensuing Winter's provision. Nevertheless they seem in general contented
to bear inconveniencies in preference to British Taxes. For you scarcely
find a Tory or a disaffected person to our righteous Cause among the
Back Settled people in that part of the Country.

When Sir William Howe had been obliged to abandon New Jersey
& to take Some new Step to distress us, he embarked his Troops, Horse
& foot near New York between the 5th & 21st July & on the 23d sailed
from Sandy Hook with a fleet of about 250 Sail great & Small in three
divisions & stood to Sea about a South East course. Great care was
taken to make a Show of the Fleet as it sailed along the Jersey Shore,
the latter end of July 228 Sail were counted from our look out near
the Capes of Delaware & every appearance was made of a design to
come up this River, about 60 Sail came within the Bay & the remainder affected to be Standing in. These movements brought General
Washington by very fatiguing Countermarches from the Clove about
120 Miles distance to the environs of this City. On the 1st August the
fleet stood to Sea again Steered E.N.E. with a fresh Southerly breeze.
It then became the general opinion they were bound for New England
& had made a feint in order to draw General Washington this way &
to harrass his Troops. After waiting Several days in uneasy Suspence,

to our great Surprize we learned that the Same fleet was seen off Sinnepuxent on the Coast of Maryland. This advice has been confirmed by different Expresses, the last added that they had been seen steering Southerly with a Wind about South East. General Washington has marched his Army & is encamped about 21 Miles hence on the North Road where I suppose he will wait for further intelligence. 'Tis true Soldiers march quicker on Ships than we can on Shoar, but those various movements clearly demonstrate the difficulties which the British Generals have to encounter in their present dispute.

The loss of Ticonderoga has occasioned an universal clamour. General Schuyler & St. Clair are remanded in order to answer at a Court of Enquiry & General Gates sent by Congress to the Command of that department. He is said to be a favorite with the people of New England & that thousands who had abandoned Mr. Schuyler will immediately join him.

General Burgoyne who sent a very pompous proclamation as his forerunner towards Albany had met with very little opposition & had advanced within 25 or 30 Miles of that City the 4th Inst. He had marked his progress with the blood of many Innocent people chiefly Women who had been butchered & scalped by his Indians in Sight of British Troops, these unhappy people had remained quietly on their Lands in obediance to Mr. Burgoyne's proclamation. Every body hopes his cruel progress will be Stopped by General Gates & those who are well acquainted with the Country say his retreat will be cut off. He is a bold enterprizing Officer inclined rather to be rash, if he is as foolish in his Marching as he is in his writing I have no doubt but he will soon meet with a Check. Time must show the event. This Month will be marked with blood.

Our Accounts from France are all very flattering but methinks I perceive great artifice in the whole behaviour of that Court. We have in my opinion been much too forward in our offers of Treaty. The British Court on the other hand has made a proposition to them of some concession in the New Foundland Fishery. They are waiting to see who will bid most or possibly where they can make most, in the meantime benefiting by our trade & insulting the Flag & Commerce of poor old England in a degree which must gall that high Spirited nation.

Tis very true France has lent us a large Sum of Money but I do not pass that to the Credit of friendship. She has the best Security in the World for principal & Interest & may raise both at the Bank of England whenever she pleases, or may compel us to repay upon her own terms.

The midle rank of people & many of higher degree are panting for our Success in full prospect of participating Liberty. Nothing more natural than this, but how the King & his Court enjoy the prospect of losing thousands of their Subjects is a question which time must Solve. Upon the whole I have no confidence in France that she will take one Step for us but such as lead to her own Interest & Security. This would lead me into an hours conversation.

The Consequence of having all our ports blocked up is scarcity of such articles as were wont to be imported from abroad & advanced prices. These are met by advances nearly equal on the part of the Farmer & Labourer—a schedule of which I will inclose. People therefore who are not concerned in Merchandize or Farming & hold no profitable Office under Government bear the weight of this extraordinary charge. I find myself in this Class, if I live half as well as I have been accustomed to at home fifteen hundred pounds Sterling will not pay one years expences exclusive of Clothing.

My Son John is now one of General Washington's family. I have no doubt of his being very happy there & am persuaded he will be very useful to the General. Our Seperation at the hour of parting weighed down my Spirits more than I had suspected it would. I felt it as the greatest disappointment I had ever Suffered nor could I forbear the intimation to himself. I wish he had made a choice for his outset in Life where he might have been more extensively useful to his Country where he might have been the long expected Support to mine & the builder of his own family. If I had suspected the contrary I should have—what should I have done—whatever is best, because nothing is but by the direction of Supreme wisdom & goodness. 'Tis the Duty of Man to bear Seeming misfortune & reason himself into conviction that there is no real misfortune & ever to be Thankful for the good which he has enjoyed.

Adieu My dear sir. My good wishes are ever with you & yours. I beg you to present my respectful Compliments to Mrs. Mannigault, Mr Joseph & the young Ladies & to accept the repeated assurance of being, your much obliged humble Servant

LB (ScHi).
[1] Gabriel Manigault (1704–81), wealthy South Carolina merchant and planter and occasional business associate of Laurens, was noted for the fact that he lent more money to the revolutionary government of his state than any other South Carolinian. Walter B. Edgar et al., eds., *Biographical Directory of the South Carolina House of Representatives* (Columbia: University of South Carolina Press, 1974–), 2:428–31.

Henry Laurens to John Rutledge

[August 15, 1777]

15th. Mr. Penn & Mr. Chew have been introduced by motion in

Congress from a Member as willing now to give their parole. The mode was objected to & after seven hours one day & four another wasted in debate a Letter from the former & a Memorial from the other Gentleman conceived in terms which offer a gross affront, "*I despise the Authority*," would not have been admitted as satisfactory by a private Gentleman, have gained their point. Congress accepts their parol without concurrence of the Executive Council whose authority derived if not from a certain Law from recommendation of Congress had been contemned. Private conversation between a Member of Congress & Secretary of Council is received for good evidence & is even entered upon the Journal altho contradicted by other members who had conversed with Members of the Council.[1] Judge Sir from this specimen of our ability to keep the mighty Machine in its proper direction. My Colleagues see & own the justness of my Complaints & are anxious to get away. What am I to do. I will do everything in my power for the service of the particular state which I represent, nor do I apprehend (from the giving & granting spirit of the times) I shall meet difficulty in obtaining every proper consideration toward my Constituents but alas Sir what will this avail, unless by wiser management than I have yet been witness to, we conserve the whole system.

Some of these intimations appear to me to be important & to merit the consideration of every Man embarked in the great Cause of American Liberty. Your Excellency will excuse what are not so & courteously accept the whole intended as a mark of the Esteem & respect with which I have the honour to be &ca.

LB (ScHi). A continuation of Laurens to Rutledge, August 12, 1777.

[1] On this point, see Laurens to Rutledge, August 12, 1777, note 10. The phrase "*I despise the Authority*" does not appear either in the letter or memorial former Gov. John Penn and former Chief Justice Benjamin Chew submitted to Congress on August 14. PCC, item 41, 2:27, item 78, 18:147. Laurens had voted for an unsuccessful motion on the 14th to accept the paroles of these two proprietary officials "with the concurrence of the executive council of Pennsylvania." *JCC*, 8:661.

Thomas Burke to Francis Nash

Dr Sir[1]   Philadelphia Augst. 16th. 1777

Yesterday Lieutenant Colo. Patten delivered me a paper Signed by the Field Officers of Your Corps. It relates to the promotion of Colo. (now General) Hand and has in it the following Paragraph. "The Merit of General Hand, for what we know, may be very great, and Justly intitle him to the favor of Congress; but we believe him almost unknown to every person in North Carolina except to Doctor Burke—and Such partiality for a Country man as we are informed, in preference to the Officers of the State he represented, whose prior claim to preferment from their Long and many Services we humbly think from Duty Demanded his support we feel not only as a wound to ourselves, but consider it a reflection on that State, which appointed us, and a Stab to Military honor throughout the Continent in general." [2] Coll. Patten on delivering it declared it had your approbation and as it Contains a Scandalous charge of Partiality in the discharge of my Duty, I can not prevail on my self to pass it over without particular Notice, and Considering the Terms on which we have always stood with each other, the knowledge you have of my private as well as public Character, I cannot be persuaded you would give Sanction to an aspersion so injurious and dishonorable, and which you cannot believe to be Just. I think no man better knows than you, that Partialities have never found place with me. I must therefore desire to know from yourself, whether Coll Patten's declaration was right, or not?

Among the Names to this paper I am surprised to find, Sumner, Polk, Hogun, Clark, Patten and Lyttle, Gentlemen of whom, from my knowledge of them I had conceived an Opinion particularly favorable. Their Behavior in this Instance has determined me to forego all particular attention to them. I hope they will so distinguish themselves that their merit alone will be sufficient for their Promotion, without Standing in need of any assistance which I could give. I shall be glad of your answer as soon as possible, and am &c.

FC (Nc–Ar). Endorsed: "Copy to Genl Nash."

[1] Francis Nash (ca. 1742–77), a North Carolina lawyer and merchant who had been appointed a Continental brigadier general by Congress on February 5, 1777, was currently commander of the North Carolina troops with the Continental Army in New Jersey. Nash was fatally wounded at the battle of Germantown and died on October 7, 1777. *DAB.*

[2] This quotation comes from an August 14 protest to the North Carolina delegates, signed by sixteen North Carolina officers then stationed in Trenton, N.J., against a "Report" that Burke had brought about the appointment of Gen. Edward Hand of Pennsylvania as commander of North Carolina's Continental troops. *N.C. State Records,* 10:750-51. Hand never received such an appointment; and it is not known how the rumor that Burke favored it originated.

Henry Laurens to William Manning

My Dear Sir[1]   16th August 1777

Having just heard of an opportunity to France I sit down to write you half a Line. Some of your family are Interested in the welfare of Some of mine. God grant they were once more happily United. The Step which J.L.[2] has taken is not the most likely to effect that desirable purpose. I wish however my three Daughters & grand Daughter were here or at the Town which I lately left. I would endeavour to make them all happy. The presence of one of them however might tend to lead that Gentleman into a way in which he might be more extensively useful to his Country, be the promised Support of mine & the builder of his own family. I am to presume he consulted you no more than he had Studied my inclinations. He was determined & therefore 'tis to be Supposed he would not hazard a question. Indeed I thought it incumbent upon me to intimate my Sentiments, he heard them & persued the dictates of his own mind. Let us hope, my Dear Sir, that the measure which he is pursuing will have happy effects.

He is in Gen. W's family, I am persuaded he will be very useful to that good & great Man & that he will be as happy as circumstances in that course of Life will Admit of.

Believe me we are happier here than you can conceive. If Some great Men had known this Country, this vast beautiful populous Country as well as I did, my advice in the Years 1773 & 1774[3] would have Saved a Nation which I dearly Love & therefore am Sorry to fight against immense Sums of Money & Streams of Blood the Loss of which they carefully conceal from you, would have Saved her from disgrace perhaps from ruin. Nothing was wanting on their part but knowledge. They abandoned themselves to lying imposters who deceived them & they their Master. If they had been capable of receiving the truth we should have been in union a happy people for Ages to come. The time is past for union. Treaty may yet make us happy friends. God grant Wisdom to some on your Side to propose terms which we on this, dare accept. As terms hitherto, depend upon it, have been offered truth on this important point has likewise been concealed from you.[4]

LB (ScHi). Endorsed: "Per Mr. Morris to be forwarded from Sinepuxent, had not time to proceed as I had intended nor even to sign the Letter."

[1] William Manning, a London merchant who often served as Laurens' banker, was also the father-in-law of Laurens' son John. David D. Wallace, *The Life of Henry Laurens* (New York: G.P. Putnam's Sons, 1915), pp. 464–67.

[2] John Laurens.

[3] Laurens had lived in England during these years.

[4] This day Laurens also wrote a letter to Philip Minis of Savannah, Ga., the only part of which that has been found is the postscript Laurens entered in his letter book: "Your Petition is before the Board of Treasury. I hope to get your prayer granted & your demand paid out of Money voted to be sent to Mr. Clay now Deputy Pay Master General in that district." Laurens Papers, ScHi. Congress finally resolved on October 28, 1778, to pay $6,919 to Minis, "it being so much advanced by him to the late Mr. Kennon, deceased, acting pay master and commissary to the Virginia and North Carolina troops in the State of Georgia." *JCC*, 8:630, 12:1071–72.

Robert Morris to George Washington

Dear sir,   Philadelphia August 16. 1777

Agreeable to your Excellencys desire in your favour of the 14th Current, I have taken from the Minutes of the Committee of Congress who resided here last winter an account of the Silver sent you to Trenton as underneath.[1] I must assure you that it affords me true pleasure to be favoured with your Commands and that my best wishes are constantly for your health and prosperity being most respectfully Dr sir, Your affte. and Obedient hble servant,   Robt Morris

December 31. 1776 sent per John Hay an Express

410	Spanish Milled Dollars		at 7/6	153.15.0
2	En.	Crowns	7/6	15.0
½	French	Do	3/9	3.9
10½	En.	Shillings	1/6	15.9
		Penna Curry.		£155. 9.6
		deduct 1/5th		31. 1.10
		Lawful		£124. 7.8

RC (DLC).

[1] See Morris to Washington, December 30, 1776, note 2. Washington's brief August 14 letter to Morris is in Washington, *Writings* (Fitzpatrick), 9:65.

John Adams to Abigail Adams

Philadelphia August 17. 1777

My dearest Friend   Sunday

Yesterday We had a cool Day, the Wind Easterly and cloudy, this Morning there is a brisk northeast Wind and cool Rain, which restores Us, to some Comfort. A Number of People died here with excessive Heat, besides others, who fell Sacrifices to their own Imprudence in drinking cold Water.

This Wind will oblige the Knight Errant and his Fleet, to go some where or other. We have had no Intelligence of it, since last Thursday week.

We have a Letter from G Schuyler, in which he "is not insensible of the Indignity of being call'd away, when an Action must soon take Place." But I hope, the People will not resent this Indignity, so as not to turn out. G Gates I hope, will be able to find Men, who will stand by him. Never was there a fairer opportunity, than now presents of ruining Burgoigne. By the same Letter, We have confused Hints, that an Attack has been made upon Fort Schuyler, and the Enemy repulsed.[1]

The Letter seems to suppose, that he had written a fuller Account of it before. But no such Account has reached Us.

The Enemy at Niagara and Detroit, are endeavouring to seduce the Indians, to take up the Hatchet, but as yet, with little success. They seem determined to maintain their Neutrality.

I read a Letter last Evening directed to Mr. Serjeant, and in his Absence to me from Mr. Clark a Delegate from N. Jersey who is gone Home to Elizabeth Town for his Health, giving a particular Account of Howes Army, in their late precipitate Retreat from Westfield. They were seized with the Utmost Terror, and thrown into the Utmost Confusion. They were so weak and sickly, and had gorged themselves so with fresh Meat, that they fell down in the Roads, many died, and were half buried, &c. &c. &c.

We have many new Members of Congress, among whom are Mr. Vandyke of Delaware, Mr. Jones of Virginia, and Mr. Lawrence of S. Carolina. This last Gentleman is a great acquisition—of the first Rank in his State, Lt. Governor, of ample Fortune, of great Experience, having been 20 Years in their assembly, of a clear Head and a firm Temper, of extensive Knowledge, and much Travel. He has hitherto appeared as good a Member, as any We ever had in Congress. I wish that all the States would imitate this Example and send their best Men. Vandyke is a Lawyer, and a very worthy Man, his Abilities very good and his Intensions very sincere. Mr. Jones also is a Lawyer, but has so lately come in that We have seen as yet no Exhibitions of him.

RC (MHi). Adams, *Family Correspondence* (Butterfield), 2:317–18.
[1] In his August 10 letter to President Hancock, which was read in Congress on August 16, Gen. Philip Schuyler briefly reported on the August 6 battle of Oriskany near Fort Schuyler. PCC, item 153, 3:242; *JCC*, 8:647.

John Hancock to George Washington

Sir,   Philada. August 17th. 1777. Sunday Morning.

The Complaints of the Want of Men to the Northward, are so great & urgent, that Congress, with a View of affording them some Assistance, have come to the enclosed Resolve; by which you will perceive, it is their Desire that five Hundred Rifle-men, under the Command of an active Officer, should be immediately sent into that Department, to oppose the Incursions of the Indians.[1]

Your Favour of the 16th Inst. I was last Night honoured with containing sundry Inclosures, which shall be communicated to Congress tomorrow.[2]

The Plan you have adopted and recommended for the Defence of the River Delaware, is ordered to be carried into Execution.[3]

As soon as Congress shall come into any Resolve on the Subjects of your several Letters, the Result shall be immediately transmitted. I have the Honour to be, with the greatest Esteem, Sir, your most obed. & very hble Servt,   John Hancock Presidt[4]

RC (DLC). In the hand of Jacob Rush and signed by Hancock.

[1] See *JCC*, 8:649.

[2] This letter is in PCC, item 152, 4:485–88, and Washington, *Writings* (Fitzpatrick), 9:72–75. For a list of the enclosures, see ibid., p. 75.

[3] Washington set forth this "Plan" in his August 10 letter to President Hancock, and on the following day Congress ordered the Board of War to put it into effect "with all possible despatch." *JCC*, 8:630; PCC, item 152, 4:469–75; and Washington, *Writings* (Fitzpatrick), 9:45–53.

[4] On August 16 Hancock had written a letter to Gen. William Heath in Boston, asking him to forward the baggage belonging to Philippe Du Coudray "& his officers." Heath Papers, MHi.

Henry Laurens to Elias Ball

Dear Sir[1]   17th August 1777

The News paper which I shall Send with this will give you a pretty distinct Account of the State of the War in this quarter. I may add that we have begun to give General Burgoyne's Savage Allies a Check. An attack was made on Fort Schuyler by a detachment from Burgoyne's main body aided by Tories & Indians. Colonel Gansevor Commander of the Fort made a Sally from within & took 4 pieces of Cannon & 2 Royals. General Harkimer of New York Militia had an engagement with them, in which he suffered considerably but kept the field & counted after the Action 50 Indians lying dead. This will give that Tribe some kind of check & we hope a more effectual one will Soon to be given to the head Savage Burgoyne himself. Who can forbear calling him Savage when he boasts of Sending them to Murder Innocent Women & Children, which they have done to a shocking extent & even to many who had taken Shelter under his proclamation. The last Account we heard of the Grand New York Fleet was their Steering southerly from the Coast of Maryland. The Season of the year would seem to forbid it but I am not without apprehensions of a sudden attack on the land side upon Sullivants Island—where else but there or Georgia can that fleet be destined. I am not free from deep feelings for you all.

Your Brother John lodges at Doctor Bond's for the benefit he says of taking advice & Medicine for a pain in his Side, he went happily through the Small Pox & left on about the 11th Inst. in a manner not Satisfactory to me, I had taken as much care of him as if he had been my Son & had intended him some essential Service if he had continued longer under my protection.[2]

Present me in cordial terms to your Father & Sister. Let me hear from you when you have leisure & believe me with great regard &ca.

[*P.S.*] I forward by Colo. Sumpter the bearer of this a packet from your Brother.

LB (ScHi).

[1] Elias Ball of Limerick (1752-1810) was a South Carolina planter who was related to Laurens' wife, Eleanor Ball Laurens. Anne S. Deas, *Recollections of the Deas Family of South Carolina and the Comingtee Plantation* (n.p.: 1909), pp. 113–27, 184–85.

[2] John Ball (1760–1817), who had accompanied Laurens to Philadelphia, wrote to his older brother Elias on August 21: "Mr. Laurens hires two or three rooms in a House and keeps his own Table. I staid with him whilst I had the small-pox, but after I was well I thought it not proper to be living at his expense when I had money enough to support myself." Ibid., p. 129.

Henry Laurens to John Lewis Gervais

Dear Sir   17th August 1777

I refer to my last Letter of the 5th Inst & 16th Inst.[1] by the hand of a Georgia Officer dispatched by Colo. Walton. This will be delivered or forwarded to you by Colo. Sumpter who gives me very short warning of his design to leave Philadelphia to morrow morning. I am just going to attend a Committee[2] where I shall be detained till tis very late. Excuse me therefore for crowding together as much as I can in a few minutes.

We have heard from the Northern department by a Letter from Gen Schuyler the 10th Inst.[3] Fort Schuyler had been attacked by the Enemy, Colo Gansevort Commandant of the Fort by a timely sortie had taken 4 feild pieces & two royals. General Harkimer in the field near the Fort had engaged them, had suffered some loss but kept the ground, drove them off & counted after the action 50 Indians lying dead on the Field, many wounded were carried off. That number in one affair will appear considerable to the Surviving Indians & I am in hopes will incline them to go home as their custom is after much blood in order to take breath.

As Mr. Burgoyne had made no impossible from the 4th to the 10th we hope General Gates who must have been at the head of the Army about the 12th will put a stop to his further progress. 500 Rifle Men under a Select Commander are ordered by Congress to join General Gates immediately.[4] He cannot yet learn what is become of the Fleet which Sailed from New York the 23d Inst., appeared off the Capes of Delaware the 28th to the 1st August, then vanished, appeared again upon the Coast of Maryland the 7 & 8th Inst. & was last day seen Standing Sotherly. If we do not hear to morrow of their arrival in Cheasapeek Bay many people notwithstanding the forbidding Season of the year will be anxious for Carolina & Georgia.

General Burgoyne according to the menace in his extraordinary proclamation has given Stretch to his Savage friends.[5] We received advices yesterday from Colo. Morgan of many murders committed by Indians on the western frontiers of Virginia & Pensylvania, with these Butchers a few Canadians & British are joined. Where they murder they leave Proclamations from the General & say all the Savages on the frontiers of the United Colonies are to attack in that Side while 100000 British Troops are to enter Pensylvania, Virginia, Charles Town & Georgia from the Sea Side.

General Hand who Commands at Fort Pitt & Colo. Morgan seem to be under no apprehension of being routed. They intimate that Britain will have the Glory of Murdering many helpless Innocent Men, Women & Children & bring on the destruction of their friends. In preparation for this purpose they recommend to carry the War directly into their own Country & the most Speedy measures are adopted for that purpose.[6]

If any thing above mentioned will be acceptable to Mr. Wells please to give it him or to Mr. Timothy if his Gazette is to come first out. I need not Say I dont wish to appear as a News Correspondent. I never write News without good grounds apparently & I believe now every word I have written to be true but to morrow may contradict or vary all that does not proceed from authority.

I beleive that nothing less than the mode of a parliamentary enquiry into the Conduct of the Officers in the Northern department will content the people. For the purpose of answering Gen Schuyler will be in or near this City in a few days. We hear not a word from Genl. St. Clair nor do we know where he is—probably with the advanced Army.

My Compliments to Mrs Gervais & all friends & believe me with great affection & regard &ca.

LB (ScHi).

[1] Laurens' August 16 letter to Gervais has not been found.

[2] Doubtless the committee to consider a method for investigating the evacuation of Ticonderoga, which submitted a report to Congress on August 19. JCC, 8:596, 653, 659.

[3] This letter is in PCC, item 153, 3:242–43.

[4] See JCC, 8:649.

[5] In a proclamation dated June 20, General Burgoyne had called upon Americans to submit to royal authority and warned them not to take any comfort in being remote from his army because "I have but to give stretch to the Indian forces under my direction (and they amount to thousands) to overtake the hardened enemies of Great Britain and America." Paul Lewis, The Man

Who Lost America: A Biography of Gentleman Johnny Burgoyne (New York: Dial Press, 1973), p. 144.

⁶ On August 16, in response to letters from Gen. Edward Hand, Indian Commissioner George Morgan, and Gen. Philip Schuyler, Congress appointed a committee to consider "the state of the western frontiers, and the northern department." In addition to approving recommendations of this committee on August 16 and 20 to send reinforcements to the northern department, Congress on its own initiative requested Pennsylvania authorities to send General Hand such militia forces as he required. See *JCC,* 8:648–49, 659; and PCC, item 153, 3:242–43, item 163, fols. 277–80.

Henry Laurens to John Rutledge

Dear Sir   17th August 1777

I have before me a Letter which I intend to trouble your Excellency with by the hand of a special Messenger from Colo. Walton to morrow who will probably be in Charles Town before Colonel Sumpter the bearer of this.

The News paper inclosed with this will shew we have begun to give Mr. Burgoynes Savage Allies a Check, & as General Gates must have been already to look him in the face Some days ago we expect soon to hear that Mr. Burgoyne himself has been stopped in his Career. He has indeed given "Stretch" to his Indians, large bodies of these headed by a few British & Canadian Soldiers have butchered many an Innocent Woman, Girl & Child upon the Frontiers of Virginia & Pensylvania. We received yesterday an Account of their Murders from General Hand & Colo. Morgan at Fort Pit. General Hand recommends to carry the War directly into their own Towns & every measure for that purpose will be expeditiously pursued.

Congress have now before them a plan for borrowing ten Millions Dollars. I hope the Carolina Delegates will oppose the mode much favoured by particular persons & Succeed. The Interest of all the States is concerned.[1]

As the destination of the grand Fleet from New York remains to us a Secret & that our last Report from Maryland was their being Seen Steering Southerly with the Wind at So. So.E. I am not free from apprehensions of an attack upon South Carolina—aware at the same time of the hazard from autumnal distempers & Tempests—but we are exposed to them as much as they are—a Sudden debarkation upon Sullivant's Island would put as much greater hazard on our Side & certain other movements give us cause to wish we had employed our Engineers, Carpenters & Labourers to good purposes during twelve past Months. We have heard from General Schuyler as late as the 11th Inst & about the 11th from Peek's Kill. General Howe had not made his appearance on North River & if his Army had been by a

Seperate fleet transported to Rhode Island or even as far as Boston we must have heard of it before this day. &ca.

LB (ScHi).
[1] Laurens objected to a proposal to raise this money by drawing bills of exchange on the American commissioners at Paris. See also William Duer to Robert R. Livingston, May 28, 1777, note 3.

Henry Laurens to William Thomson

Dear Colonel[1]   17th August 1777.

I made my journey pleasant enough by taking the Mountain Road which furnished Cool Air, fine Water & plenty of provision for Man & Horse. I reached this place the 21st July.

Your application for leave to arm half your Regiment with Smooth bores & bayonets lies before the board of War—where a multiplicity of business may keep back a report many days. In the mean time I am well assured Congress will have no objection to your arming agreeable to your desire provided His Excellency the president shall judge the variation to be for the good of the Service. Make your application here or possibly with propriety to the General Commanding in the Southern department. From thence also you must expect to be supplied with Arms. There has been I am informed great waste made in this quarter & there is now an universal Cry for Muskets for the Militia.[2]

I have employed a proper person to enquire for a Bolting Cloth for you—the article is become very scarce & the price at least four times doubled of the former rate. I mean such as I have yet discovered, if I can find none cheaper I must Send you one by next opportunity. Tis an article which I suppose you cannot dispence with.

News as in Mr. Gervais's last Letter dated 17th Inst.[3]

The time is teeming with some grand event. The British Forces in this quarter Seem to be Struggling their last. If they do not conquer tis probable they will withdraw but tis hardly possible they should do so without one more attempt upon Sullivants Island if they make it suddenly by Land. I think more than is necessary to be Said to you on that Subject; you know what must follow.

This River is blocked up by four Men of War, every article of Life is amazingly dear. My Compliments to Mrs Thomson & the young Ladies & be assured I am with great regard &ca.

LB (ScHi).
[1] William Thomson (1727-96), a South Carolina planter, military officer, and political leader, was currently serving as colonel of the Third South Carolina Regiment. Walter B. Edgar et al., eds., *Biographical Directory of the South*

Carolina House of Representatives (Columbia: University of South Carolina Press, 1974–), 2:669–71.

[2] There is no mention of Thomson's "application" in the journals.

[3] A shorthand description of what Laurens apparently wrote in the RC of this letter.

Richard Henry Lee to John Page

My dear Sir,   Philadelphia, 17th Aug. 1777.

Were it not for the very disgraceful evacuation of Ticonderoga and the loss of our Stores there, we should have little but good to relate of this Campaign as far as it has gone. The Generals Schuyler and St. Clair are ordered down to Head Quarters, where an enquiry will be instituted, and the public fully acquainted with the whole of that business. Gen. Gates is reappointed to the command of the Northern Army and by this time has joined it. The Militia is turning out to join that army, and now that they have the General they love and can confide in, I hope our affairs in that quarter will soon wear a better countenance. Already Gen. Hackerman of the N. York Militia has beaten a part of the enemies forces and slain 50 Indians.[1] Gen. Howes fleet was seen off the Eastern Shore of Maryland on the 7th instant, stearing southward, but it is somewhat doubtful whether his troops are on board now or not, and if they are, it is surely the strangest Manœuvre that was ever before put in practice—For, is it not wonderful, that whilst Burgoyne is pushing into the Country on one quarter, Howe should quit it on another? Time will explain this, at present, inexplicable movement. In the meantime Gen. Washingtons forces are so placed as to be ready to meet Mr. Howes visitation if it happens any where but on the two extremes of the United States. Our information from Europe does not promise us immediate war, but we are sure of very substantial aid from thence, whilst the powerful Armaments quickly preparing by France and Spain denote approaching war and certainly will check the British violence against [us?] by the necessity it creates of watching their powerful and dangerous Neighbors. The spirit of France rises with the increase of its Fleet, since we learn that when the British Ambassador lately told the Ministry that if N. America continued to be supplied from France, that the Peace could not long continue—He was answered 'Nous ne desiron pas la guérre, et nous ne le craignon pas.'[2] Dr. Lee is returned from Spain, and set out in May for the Court of Prussia. Gen. Lee is removed on board the Centurion, but we are not certain whether the ship remains at York or is gone with the Fleet. We hear that a Speech of Lord Chathams in the house of Lords lately has come to N. York, but they will not publish it, in which his Lordship advises them to make peace with America immediately on *Any terms*, assuring them they have no more chance to conquer this Country with the force they have or can get, than he to conquer Britain with his Crutch, and that the longer they contend the more certain will be their ruin and disgrace.[3] The good old Man, instead of being dead as was reported, is, it seems, recovered to better health and revived powers.

Pray my dear Sir urge on our Works near the Falls of James River, we want heavy cannon extremely—And it would be greatly to our advantage if Copper and Calamine could be found in quantity sufficient to furnish us with Brass. My compliment to Mrs. Page.

Farewell dear Sir Affectionately yours.

P.S. If Government was now and then to stimulate the Managers of the Salt Works, might we not hope for a supply of that necessary. I fear Howe is gone to Charles Town in South Carolina. If so, against such a Land and Sea force no effectual resistance can be made—curse on his Canvas Wings.

MS not found; reprinted from Lee, *Letters* (Ballagh), 1:315–17.

[1] Brig. Gen. Nicholas Herkimer of the New York militia had been mortally wounded at Oriskany on August 6 while attempting to relieve Fort Schuyler. *DAB.*

[2] This information was contained in a March 12 letter from the commissioners at Paris, one of several letters from the commissioners that Congress had received earlier in August and was still considering. See William Williams' second letter to Jonathan Trumbull of August 2, 1777.

[3] For Chatham's remarks on May 30 introducing his motion to stop hostilities in America, see *The Parliamentary History of England, from the Earliest Period to the Year 1803*, 36 vols. (London: T. C. Hansard, 1806–20), 19:316–20.

Richard Henry Lee to Mann Page

My dear Sir,   Philadelphia 17th Augt. 1777

We are not able yet to give you any account of the wandering Howe and his fleet, save that they were seen on the 7th instant off Sinapuxen stearing Southward. Our accounts from France say that George depends much on the "desperate efforts that Howe & Cornwallis must make to redeem their Bankrupt honor."[1] His present Manœuvre seems the effort of a *despairing* Bankrupt. For what good can result from having multitudes of Men & Horses confined on board Ships at this season of the year, exposed to the torrid hell that beams upon their heads? Gen. Washingtons forces are well placed to meet Gen. Howes return, unless he should visit either extreme of the United States. The main body is about 20 miles from hence on the road to Coryells ferry on both sides of which the Carolina Troops & other Corps (about 2000) are stationed. Sullivan with 2000 more is in the Neighborhood of Morris Town, & Gen.

Putnam with about 5000 occupies the Heights at Peekskill. I lately visited the Army here. It realy makes a fine appearance. Health, discipline, and good spirits, prevail thro the whole. I wish things lookt as well in the North, however I hope they will soon mend in that quarter. Gen. Gates is reappointed to the command there, and the Militia are turning out. Already Gen. Hackerman of the N. York Militia has had an engagement with a part of the enemy and beaten them, having killed 50 Indians on the spot. Congress has ordered 500 Riflemen from this Army to be sent up there immediately to check and chastise the Barbarian Auxiliaries that Burgoyne has brought with him and who are murdering & scalping all before them, Men, Women, & Children; without sparing those who have taken protection & sworn allegiance to the Tyrant. Even inveterate Tories feel the keen edge of the Scalping Knife, and the barbarous butchery of the Tomahawk. Gens. Schuyler & St. Clair are ordered to Head Quarters that an enquiry may be had into the loss of Ticonderoga and its valuable Stores. Tis a shocking affair and cannot, at present, be accounted for. Our accounts from France, late in May, do not promise immediate war, but *substantial aid* most certainly. Both France & Spain are arming powerfully and with great rapidity. The spirit of the former rises as its Fleet grows stronger, since we understand that the Minister lately replied to Lord Stormont, when he said the peace could not long continue if N. America continued to draw supplies from France, "Nous ne desiron pas la guerre, et nous ne le craignon pas." We neither desire War, nor fear it. The potent armaments of two such dangerous Neighbors must infallibly check the efforts of G. Britain against us, by putting her under a necessity of watching them, and being prepared to defend herself. Doctr. Lee is returned from Spain and gone to the Court of Prussia. I suppose William will soon take his place. Lord Chatham is not dead as report made him, but it seems is better in health than usual, and we understand a late speech of his is arrived at N. York, in which he advises the Lords "that Peace be made with N. America immediately and on *any terms,* assuring them they had no more chance to conquer this Continent with the force they had or could get than he would have to conquer Britain with his Crutch and that the longer they carried on the War the more certain would be their ruin, and the greater their disgrace." Wise and good Old Man, what pity is it that if Kings will be allowed, they cannot be directed by such Men!

I believe Manly is certainly taken & the Fox retaken.[2] They were greatly overpowered by superior force. My best wishes attend the family at Mansfield.

Farewell dear Sir, Affectionately yours,   Richard Henry Lee

[*P.S.*] Colo. Lee & Lady are well.

P.S. Since neither the Northern or Southern posts of this day bring us any account of Howes fleet I am almost sure that he is gone to Charles

Town South Carolina, which, in its present state, against such a great
Land & Sea force, cannot stand. It must fall. Curse on his Canvass
Wings. Tis an unfair advantage they take of us.   R.H. Lee

RC (MdAN). Addressed: "Man Page Junr. esquire at Mansfield near Fredericksburg in Virginia."
    [1] A similar phrase was included in Arthur Lee's May 13, 1777, letter to the
Committee for Foreign Affairs, which is in Wharton, *Diplomatic Correspondence,*
2:319–20.
    [2] See Henry Laurens to John Lewis Gervais, August 5, 1777, note 4.

John Adams to James Warren

Aug. 18, 1777

My Dear sir, The inclosed Copies, you will see must not be made
public.[1] You will communicate them in Confidence to such Friends as
have Discretion. When you have made such prudent Use of them as you
shall judge proper, be pleased to send them to the Foot of Pens Hill,
because I have no other Copies and should be glad to preserve them.

It is in vain for me to write any Thing of the Northern Department,
because you have all the Intelligence from thence, sooner than We have.
The G. W. has ordered Morgan's Rifle men and two or three more
Regiments there. There has been a smart Action near Fort Schuyler,
in which our People were successfull, but with a severe Loss.

I hope the Mass. will exert itself now, for the support of Gates and
the Humiliation of the blustering Burgoine. It is of vast importance
to our Cause that the Mass. should be exemplary upon this occasion.

Howe's Fleet and Army are still incognito. When or where We shall
hear of them, know not.

We are in deep Contemplation upon the state of our Currency. We
shall promise Payment in the Loan offices of the Interest in Bills of
Exchange on our Ministers in France. But Taxation, My dear Sir,
Taxation, and Œconomy, are our only effectual Resources. The People
this way are convinced of it and are setting about it with spirit.

RC (MHi). In Adams' hand, though not signed.
    [1] Adams enclosed copies he had made of Arthur Lee's February 11, 1777,
letter to the Committee of Secret Correspondence and January 31 and February
3 letters from an unidentified friend of Lee's in London. These enclosures are
in *Warren-Adams Letters,* 1:360–63. At the end of the January 31 enclosure
Adams appended this note: "If I had two or three Aid de Camps and a
Secretary, as the great Men of the Age have, I would present you with a
fairer Copy. But We Small Folks are obliged to do our own Drudgery, and We
have so much of it to do, that We must do it in Haste." Warren-Adams Papers,
MHi.

James Lovell to William Whipple

My Dear Sir   August 18th 1777.
I have nothing material to inform you of beyond what the Gazette contains, except in confidence, that it is a disputed point whether we shall go upon the scheme of drawing Bills of Exchange on France to carry interest after a certain day if not paid, hoping that bankers and merchants will discharge them upon the plighted faith of these States, or whether we shall only draw from the interest due on our Loan certificates to be paid out of a fund already visible and of most probable increase. Should the first plan take place, the mercantile part here would immediately run mad after the Bills, and so sink the Loan Office supply; whereas the certainty of dollar for dollar interest would encourage the Loan business, would induce the merchant to pay off widow's and orphan's dues to them, increase his claim of interest to be paid by Bills of Exchange at the offices and would give credit to our tickets in France where they will be bought up at par or a trifling discount. In the mean time we may tax very considerably to lessen the quantity of current paper by burning Colonial. Honesty and justice are for the last, fear and cunning are for the first. I will give you early intelligence of the decision; I only add that the last is the opinion also of our Commissioners, who have hinted a further plan for laying out land on the Mississippi as an object of a Subscription in France. This is much more honest than selling Bills without a known fund.
Schuyler has heard of the changes of command in the Northern Department, and is very angry but doubts not he shall receive the thanks of his country. As to the recruiting service which you mention in yours of the 5th measures have been taken which have gone to the General in Resolves and to the States. I will scratch a part of the only Northern Map I have if Monsieur A.B.C. &c will permit.
Your friend,   J.L.

[P.S.] In the name of the Union what orders have you given to Stark?[1] He had better have tarried at home, than have marched so far as he has to refuse Continental regulations. He knew them before he set out. Maryland will not let her militia be under Continental Articles of War, but then she does not send her men out of the State till this is consented to. *Secret* and scandalous.
I do not know the merits of Stark's case but he makes great confusion. Your Colleague opened the enclosed according to your orders.

Tr (DLC).
[1] See George Frost to Josiah Bartlett, August 19, 1777.

Henry Marchant to Nicholas Cooke

Honored Sir,   Philadelphia Augt. 17th [*i.e.* 18th] 1777[1]
I have done myself the Honor of writing frequently to the Govr.
and Company of the State I have the Honor to represent in Congress;
The Contents of some of those Letters I apprehend were of Consequence; yet I have not been so happy as to receive an Answer to any
one of Them. Nor have I had a Line from the Come. appointed to
correspond with Their Delegates. Congress this Day received the
Resolutions of the Committee of the Eastern States, transmitted to
Them by the Honb Stephen Hopkins Esqr. President of that Committee; those Resolutions have been read, but not yet considered.[2] I
now Sir enclose you a Resolve of Congress of the 15th Instant requesting you to transmit to Congress Accounts of all Monies advanced
and Expences incured by Prisoners of War &c. The Resolve points out
to you the Necessity of an immediate Attention thereto.[3] An Expectation of a general Exchange of Prisoners soon to take Place occasioned
that Resolve, As without those Accounts an Exchange cannot well be
made.
We have no certain account of the Fleet since they were seen off
Maryland. It is strongly suspected They are gone either to Virginia or
So. Carolina. The latter is rather in my Judgment the Place of Their
Destination. Now then is the Time for New-England to exert Themselves, by sending forth a formidable Body of Militia to the Northward;
and by making a Desent upon Rhode Island. Our State in sundry Instances have of late done much Honor to Themselves. I hope they will
continue on, and with the assistance of Their neighbour Sisters will fix
their Character for Fortitude and Bravery to be transmitted as *unequaled*
to the latest Posterity. I have the Honor to be Honored Sir, Yours and
the States, most obedient and humble Servant,   Hy. Marchant

RC (R–Ar).
[1] Congress read the "Resolutions . . . transmitted . . . by . . . Stephen Hopkins,"
which Marchant mentions below, on August 18 and did not meet on the
17th, a Sunday.
[2] In response to a proposal by Massachusetts, representatives from that state,
New Hampshire, Rhode Island, Connecticut, and New York met at Springfield
to discuss measures to deal with the problems of currency depreciation, price
inflation, and military supplies. At this meeting, which lasted from August 1 to 6,
the conferees agreed to urge all state legislatures to redeem most of the paper
money in circulation and pay for the war by taxation instead, to curb inflation
by regulating prices, to prevent engrossing and provide military supplies to
soldiers at reasonable prices, and to remove most restrictions on interstate commerce. In order to add force to their appeal, they also decided to ask Congress
to express its approval of these recommendations to the states. PCC, item 78,
11:207–22.
Congress read the proceedings of this meeting, together with Stephen Hopkins' August 6 covering letter, on August 18 and referred the issue to a com-

mittee consisting of Joseph Jones, Henry Laurens, and John Witherspoon. On September 10 Congress added five more members to this committee—Eliphalet Dyer, James Duane, Elbridge Gerry, Henry Marchant, and Robert Morris—and instructed it "to prepare an earnest recommendation to the several states to proceed to taxation." The committee submitted a report written by Gerry on October 27, which urged the states to levy taxes, curb emissions of paper money, subscribe to loan office certificates, regulate prices, procure military supplies, and confiscate the property of Loyalists. Congress then approved the report in stages on November 22, 26, and 27, 1777. *JCC,* 8:650, 731, 9:841, 953–58, 968–71.

³ See *JCC,* 8:643.

John Adams to Abigail Adams

My best Friend   Aug. 19, 1777 Tuesday

Your obliging Favour of the 5th came by Yesterdays Post, and I intended to have answered it by this Mornings Post, but was delayed by many Matters, untill he gave me the slip.

I am sorry that you and the People of Boston were put to so much Trouble, but glad to hear that such Numbers determined to fly. The Prices for Carting which were demanded, were detestable. I wish your Fatigue and Anxiety may not have injured your Health.

Dont be anxious, for my Safety. If Howe comes here I shall run away, I suppose with the rest. We are too brittle ware you know to stand the Dashing of Balls and Bombs. I wonder upon what Principle the Roman Senators refused to fly from the Gauls and determind to sit, with their Ivory Staves and hoary Beards in the Porticoes of their Houses untill the Enemy entered the City, and altho they confessed they resembled the Gods, put them to the Sword.

I should not choose to indulge this sort of Dignity, but I confess I feel myself so much injured by these barbarean Britains, that I have a strong Inclination to meet them in the Field. This is not Revenge I believe, but there is something sweet and delicious in the Contemplation of it. There is in our Hearts, an Indignation against Wrong, that is righteous and benevolent, and he who is destitute of it, is defective in the Ballance of his Affections and in his moral Character.

As long as there is a Conscience in our Breasts, a moral Sense which distinguishes between Right and Wrong, approving, esteeming, loving the former, and condemning and detesting the other, We must feel a Pleasure in the Punishment, of so eminent a Contemner of all that is Right and good and just, as Howe is. They are virtuous and pious Passions that prompt Us to desire his Destruction, and to lament and deplore his success and Prosperity.

The Desire of assisting towards his Disgrace, is an honest Wish.

It is too late in Life, my Constitution is too much debilitated by

Speculation, and indeed it is too late a Period in the War, for me to think of girding on a sword: But if I had the last four Years to run over again, I certainly would.

RC (MHi). Adams, *Family Correspondence* (Butterfield), 2:318–19.

John Adams to Abigail Adams

My best Friend   Philadelphia August 19. 1777 Tuesday
    The Weather still continues cloudy and cool and the Wind Easterly.
    Howe's Fleet and Army is still incognito. The Gentlemen from South Carolina, begin to tremble for Charlestown.
    If Howe is under a judicial Blindness, he may be gone there. But what will be the Fate of a scorbutic Army cooped up in a Fleet for Six, Seven or Eight Weeks in such intemperate Weather, as We have had.
    What will be their Condition landing, on a burning shore abounding with Agues and Musquetos, in the most unwholesome Season of the whole Year?
    If he should get Charlestown, or indeed the whole State, what Progress will this make towards the Conquest of America? He will stop the Trade of Rice and Indigo, but what then? Besides he will get some ugly Knocks. They are honest, sincere and brave and will make his Life uncomfortable.
    I feel a strong Affection for S. Carolina, for several Reasons. 1. I think them as stanch Patriots as any in America. 2. I think them as brave. 3. They are the only People in America, who have maintained a Post and defended a Fort. 4. They have sent Us a new Delegate, whom I greatly admire, Mr. Lawrence, their Lt. Governor, a Gentleman of great Fortune, great Abilities, Modesty and Integrity—and great Experience too. If all the States would send Us such Men, it would be a Pleasure to be here.
    In the Northern Department they begin to fight. The Family of Johnson, the black part of it as well as the white, are pretty well thinned. Rascals! they deserve Extermination. I presume Gates will be so supported that Burgoingne will be obliged to retreat. He will stop at Ticonderoga I suppose for they can maintain Posts, altho We can not.
    I think We shall never defend a Post, untill We shoot a General. After that We shall defend Posts, and this Event in my Opinion is not far off. No other Fort will ever be evacuated without an Enquiry, nor any Officer come off without a Court Martial. We must trifle no more. We have suffered too many Disgraces to pass unexpiated. Every Disgrace must be wiped off.
    We have been several Days, hammering upon Money. We are con-

triving every Way We can, to redress the Evils We feel and fear, from too great a Quantity of Paper. Taxation, as deep as possible, is the only radical Cure. I hope you will pay every Tax that is brought you, if you sell my Books, or Cloaths, or oxen or your Cows to pay it.

RC (MHi). Adams, *Family Correspondence* (Butterfield), 2:319–20.

Samuel Adams to Elizabeth Adams

My dear Betsy   Philade Augt 19 1777
    I was favord with yours of the 2d of this Month by yesterdays Post. I am much obligd to you for writing to me so often, and hope you will not omit any future opportunity. One or another of my Boston Friends write to me by every Post, [so] that I think I should be informd if any extraordinary Accident should happen to my Family, but I am never so well satisfied as when I receive one from you. I am in continual Anxiety for your Safety, but am happy in committing you to the Protection of all gracious Heaven. May He be your Refuge in every Time of Distress! I had before heard that the Enemies Fleet was seen off Cape Ann. We had an Account of it by an Express from General Heath, who contradicted it the [same] Day by another Express. Indeed I did not give Credit to [the] News for the British Ships were seen off the Maryland Shore on the first of August, the very day on which they were reported to have been seen off Cape Ann. Having the Command of the Sea, they have it in their Power to give frequent Alarms to our Seaport Towns. We have not heard of them since, and it is the opinion of some that they are gone to South Carolina, but as it is altogether uncertain when they will go, it is prudent to be ready to receive them in every Place. It is a Question with me whether they have any Plan upon which they can depend themselves. I pray God that [their] Councils may be confounded.
    I earnestly hope with you, my Dear, that our [. . .] Life is not always to live at this Distance from each o[ther] but that we shall see the happy Day when Tyranny s[hall] be subdued and the Liberty of our Country shall be settled upon a permanent Foundation. If this is not to be accomplishd in our Day, May we hereafter meet our virtuous Friends in that blessed Region, where the wicked shall cease from troubling.
    My Love to my dear Daughter, Sister Polly & the rest of my Family & Friends. Tell my Servants I thank them for their kind Remembrance of me. I am, my dear, ever yours,   S.A.

[*P.S.*] I have sent the Letter to Capt. M. inclosd in one to Dr F.

RC (NN).

Board of War to George Washington

Sir   War Office Augt 19th. 1777
   There are about 80 Men with Officers for three Troops of Horse of
thirty Men each now at Philadelphia. They came from North Carolina
with General Nash's Brigade & have been here for a considerable Time
their Horses being sold as they were unfit for Service & the Board were
so embarrass'd with the high Price of Horses & other Necessaries for
sending them into the Field that they had determined to order them
back to N. Carolina. They were induced to do this too from the Men
having refused to enlist during the War & they have only from 12 to
18 Months to serve. But it has been represented that they are all
Americans & therefore the more to be depended upon & that many
of the Regiments of Cavalry either from the Misbehaviour of the Men
or Accidents have many Horses more than Men. The Board have therefore thought it best to represent the Matter to your Excellency for your
Opinion upon it & desire to know how these Men could be employed &
mounted. It seems they object to being drafted into the Regiments without their Officers but are willing to be annexed with them to any Regiment of Horse. Col Baylors would be most agreeable to them & it is
said he has Horses & cannot get Men equal to the Number of Horses.
The Board would be happy to receive a speedy Answer as the Business
has been too long delayed & the Men are kept here at a great Expence.[1]
I have the Honour to be, your very obed Servt,
                                              Richard Peters Secy.

RC (DLC).
   [1] For Washington's August 22 reply, see Washington, *Writings* (Fitzpatrick),
9:117–18.

Samuel Chase to Thomas Johnson

My Dear Sir,   Philada. Augt. 19th. 1777
   I yesterday received your letter of the 14 ult. We have been pretty
distressed here with the heat, several have died in the streets. I beleive
our army under Gen. W. are well, they lie at their ease near Caryels
ferry. We have not one word about the Enemies fleet, it is now ex-
pected, tho' with little credibility, that Howes army are on Long
Island.
   We have no intelligence from the North, except what you see in the
Packett. Two New York Battalions, about 600, and Morgans Rifle
Battalion, 500, are ordered to reinforce our army in that quarter. I

shall take care of the shoes &c and send them to our Troops. I will
apply to Congress for an order for 4 twelve pounders, as you request.
I rejoice at a prospect of obtaing Salt, & if we can be suppling with
that necessity article, agreeable to your wishes, I doubt not we shall
be, amply furnished. I am so strongly impressed with the necessity of
obtaing Salt, that I would eagerly seize every means, if any the least
probability of success.[1]

I beg my compliments to the Gentlemen of the Council. Your
affectionate friend,   S. Chase

Tr (MdHi).
[1] In the journal and correspondence of the Maryland Council for the period
of mid-August 1777, there is no mention of the shoes, twelve-pounders, and salt
that Chase discussed in this paragraph. See *Md. Archives,* 16:332ff.

Connecticut Delegates to Jonathan Trumbull, Sr.

Sir,   Philadelphia Augt 19. 1777

Your Favour of the 7th instant have received, which is the only one
that has come to hand since our arrival here. We have wrote two
official Letters,[1] in the last of which we acquainted, that Congress had
ordered an Enquiery to be made into the Losses sustaind in the northern
Department, and that General Gates was appointed to take the Command there, and Genl. Scuyler & St. Clair orderd to repair to head
Quarters. General Gates must have arrived eer now, and we cant but
have great reason to hope that our Affairs in that Quarter will soon
put on another Face, for if Burgoin Elated with his late Successes
should push down much farther, he must leave such an opening that
it will be in our power to throw such a body in his Front & Reer, that
he must enevitably be cut off—especially if our People do but turn out
and act with Spirit on this occasion, as we trust they will now their
Confidence in their Commanders is restored.

We are still at a Loss what is become of Hows Fleet! The last we
heard any thing about them, was that on the 8t instant they were off
Sinepucscent Bar standing to the Southward.

General Washington with his Army is now encamp'd about 20 miles
from hence, near Corels Ferry, waiting the movements of this Fleet—
an oppertune Season now for an Attempt on New York. Congress have
order'd 500 Rifle Men to the northern army.[2]

Yesterday the Report of the Convention of the Eastern States came
to hand and was laid before Congress and a Comtee is appointed to
take the Matter up.[3]

It seems to be universally allowed that it will not do to emit any more
Bills, and how to restore our *Finances* and to keep up the Credit of our

Money is the present great Object under the Consideration of Congress. However we are in hopes a Plan may be devised and come into that will in some measure answer those important purposes and as soon as agreed on shall communicate.

As we have now a full Representation of the States the Affair of Confederation, which was put off on that account will be now again resumed.[4]

The Season for a Fornight past has been extreem hot, more so than has been ever here Known. Numbers have dropd down dead in the Streets occasioned by the imprudence of drinking cold Water.

We have the honor to remain with due Regard, Your Excellencys most Obedt, humble Servants,   Elipht Dyer

Richd Law

Wm Williams

RC (MA). Written by Law and signed by Law, Dyer, and Williams.
[1] Not found, but see Williams to Trumbull, August 6, 1777.
[2] See the resolve of August 16. *JCC*, 8:649.
[3] See Henry Marchant to Nicholas Cooke, August 18, 1777, note 2.
[4] Transcripts of Law's draft of this letter in the Law Papers, CtHi and DLC, are dated August 18 and end at this point.

George Frost to Josiah Bartlett

Dear Sir,   Philadelphia Augst. 19th. 1777
    I Recd. Yours of the 25th Ulto. (it came to hand after the post was gonn). You Say the Appointment of Genl. Schoyler to the Command at the Northward gave great uneasiness to New Hampshire and I'l add to many other States also and that very justly. The Deligate from the Eastern States told Congress that the People in those States had no confidence in Sd. Genl. but the Influence of Said Man and the Deligates of New York (Dewane & Duer In my opinion is no better then their Genl.) had more wait in Congress at that time then all the Deligates from the Eastern States and Obtained a majority of one Vote in his favour, they now see the Ill Consequence of that Appointmt and have order'd Genl. Gates to Supersead him in that Command and sopose he is at that post if well before this time. Schoyler and St. Clear is orderd to head quarters in order for tryeul. I hope you'l furnish the Court of Inquiry with all the proofs Relating to the Situation that post was in and in what manner the troops was furnished. Schoyler & St. Clear writes to Congress and says most of the troops was old men, Boys, & negros and unfit for garison duty, their Armes very bad & but one bayinet to ten men, that many of the officers mutinous and a disgrace to an Armey, that he (Schoyler) wants power from Congress to Suspend

them.[1] Thanks be to praise they are Suspended themselves. I Rejoice to here that our brave Countrimen are marching with Spirit & Viger to opose their Enemi. May the God of Armies go forth with 'm. Our Commissioners at the Courts of France and Spain have Established a loan for the payment of the Interest that is or may arrise on our money Issued by congress which we may draw from time to time on sd. Commissrs. at Paris at the Rate of five livers money of France for every Dollar which will we trust give our Loan office certificates as great if not greater Credit In Europe then the Bank notes of Great Britian as they carrey larger Interest and Incorage every Monied man with us to put his money in sd. office as they may be sure to Receive the Interest in Dollars as aforesaid and that these Courts have particuler strong Reasons for keeping out of the war as long as they can, besides the general one that on both sides the nation attacking losses the Claim which when attacked it has for aid from its allies and we have these advantages in their keeping out of the war ⟨as long as they can⟩ that they are better able to afford us private assistance that by holding them selves in Rediness to invade Britain they keep more of her forces at home and that they leave to our Armed Vessels the whole harvest of Prizes made upon her Commerce. The Commissioners have purchasd. 80,000 muskets, a number of pistols &c at second hand that if but one half arives safe they will be Cheep, all Europ is for us, the articles of Confediration and the Seperate Constiutions of the several States are published in France which affords abundance of Speculation to the Politicions of Europ and it is a very general Opinion that if we succeed in establishing our liberties we shall as soon as peace is restored receive an immence addition of numbers and welth from Europe. Those who love liberty gives general Joy and our Cause is Esteamed the cause of all mankind. Glorious is it for the Mericans to be called by providence to this post of Honour. Cursed and Detested will every one be that deserts or betrays it. The Congress is about setting the mode for drawing bills for the Interest of our money and it should be made publick that we now have a fund in France for the payment of the Interest [on?] our bills of Credit, which knolidge coming to the public [may] conduce them to put their money in to the loan Office, thereby we sopose may have a sufficient to carrey on the war without Emiting any more bills. Am with much Esteam, Sr. Your most obt. Sevt.   Geo. Frost

P.S. Inclosed you have a Copey of a letter from Genl. Lincoln to Genl. Schoyler.[2]

RC (MeHi).

[1] Gen. Philip Schuyler made these charges in his August 4 letter to Hancock, which was read in Congress on August 12. *JCC*, 8:628; and Samuel Adams to James Warren, August 12, 1777.

[2] Gen. Benjamin Lincoln's August 8 letter to Schuyler was forwarded by him to Congress, where it was read on August 18. Lincoln reported that Gen. John

Stark, who had resigned from the Continental Army when Enoch Poor was promoted to brigadier general, told him that "by his Instructions from that State, it is at his option to act in conjunction with the Continental Army or not" and that he did not intend to join the Continental Army unless he was restored to his position of seniority in the army.

As a result, Congress resolved on the next day to transmit a copy of Lincoln's letter to the New Hampshire government with the admonition that "the instructions which General Stark says he has received from them, are destructive of military subordination, and highly prejudicial to the common cause at this crisis; and therefore that they be desired to instruct General Stark to conform himself to the same rules which other general officers of the militia are subject to, whenever they are called out at the expence of the United States."

The New Hampshire delegates sent a copy to Meshech Weare with their August 22 letter. Frost, however, sent Bartlett a separate copy with these comments: "The foregoing letter was sent by Genl. Lincoln to Genl. Schuyler and by P. Schuyler to Congress which is very alarming to Congress. Genl. Starkes should take occasion to Resent any supposed affrunt by Congress to him when his Country lays at stake. At the same time woud take notis that we shall loos the benifet of our troops being put in the Continentall pay Except the measures are alterd, and woud also observe he dont refuse to put him self under Genl. Schuyler who is Recarled from that Command and Congress has given the Command of that Armey to Genl. Gates, wch I suppose Gl. Starke knew not of at that time, as to the promotion of officers in the armey the Congress went on a new plan agreed on in Baltimore (at the Raising the as it called standing armey) that Every state should in some measure have their propotion of Genl. officers according to the Troops they Raised by which Reason som officers was superseeded or as they call afronted." Bartlett Papers, NhD.

But before any of these actions could take effect, General Stark had already led the New Hampshire, Massachusetts, and Vermont militia forces to victory at Bennington on August 16. When news of Stark's victory arrived on August 21 criticism of him all but disappeared, and on October 4, 1777, Congress voted its thanks to Stark and the New Hampshire militia and appointed him a brigadier general in the Continental Army. See *JCC,* 8:649, 656–57, 9:770–71; *N.H. State Papers,* 8:662–64; New Hampshire Delegates to Meshech Weare, August 22; and John Hancock to the New Hampshire Assembly, August 25, 1777.

Henry Laurens to John Rutledge

Dear Sir, 19th August 1777.

I had the honor of writing to your Excellency besides the enclosed of the 12th, the 17th Inst. by Colo. Sumpter with News papers & I now add one of this date.

Congress has on the Table a plan for negotiating a Loan for Ten Millions of Dollars, if they go no further it may not quite ruin us.

I am as averse from this measure as I was from that of the Western expedition[1] but have no hopes of Succeeding against a confirmed Majority. The mischief will be done but not without a modest dissent on my part.

General Howes appearance in this quarter & the sotherly Course

steered by the Fleet the 8th Inst. has raised an uncommon anxiety in
my mind for the Safety of my Country & my friends if an attack is
made there, the interposition of Heaven may save them & give your
Excellency Glory & happiness. I sincerely wish it being with great
esteem & regard &ca.

LB (ScHi).
[1] See Charles Thomson's Notes of Debates, July 24 and 25, 1777.

Henry Laurens to John Wells

Dear Sir,[1]   19th August 1777
The day before yesterday I wrote to you by Colo. Sumpter.[2] Tis
probable you will know more of the Coasting Fleet than I shall when
this reaches you. I begin to be confirmed in my opinion founded upon
their leaving Synnepaxent that a Coup was intended at Sullivants &
James Island & I know if successful what must follow if this conjecture
be right we are indebted to the abjuration Act & to Major General
Grant who knows better than to be discouraged from a great Stroke
by common opinions of the Season of the year. In this prospect I feel
an anxiety for my Country & my friends which never finds a place in
my mind from appearances or small circumstances.

The News papers which I shall Send to Colo. Gervais or you will
shew you how affairs generally stand in the Northern department.

Than followed English News & Concluded as follows

Nothing of this may be News to you as I see (not by advice from
you) a Brigt from London has been taken about 20 July by Capt
Seymour & carried into George Town. Be that as it may you will
accept the Labour & endeavour of &ca.

LB (ScHi).
[1] John Wells, the publisher of the *South-Carolina and American Gazette*.
During the British occupation of Charleston Wells became a loyalist and was
forced to flee to the Bahamas when the British left the city in 1782. Arthur M.
Schlesinger, *Prelude to Independence: The Newspaper War on Britain 1764–
1776* (New York: Alfred A. Knopf, 1958), pp. 238, 290.
[2] In his letter book, Laurens simply noted that on August 17 he had written
a "Letter Containing Sundry News &ca" to Wells. Laurens Papers, ScHi. The
letter has not been found.

Richard Henry Lee to Landon Carter?

My dear Sir,[1]   Philadelphia 19th Augt. 1777
As it is always with pleasure that I obey your commands, so it is per-

fectly agreable to me to make use of the opportunity offered by Mr. Butler of furnishing you with the present state of our affairs as well as I am able. Gen. Howe has thrown us all into the field of conjecture by his late embarkation, and various have been the opinions touching his destination. At present however, Many reasons concur to induce belief that he is gone to Charles Town in South Carolina, where unhappily for that place & for the Union in general, he may succeed. They are strong towards the sea, but all their fortifications are weak on the land side, and may be attacked with success in reverse. In fact, it does not seem likely that they can resist the great Land & Sea force that Mr. Howe has with him. It is not absolutely certain that he is gone to Charles Town, and therefore Gen. Washingtons army is obliged to remain inactive, a mere army of observation. This, added to a variety of other causes, gives Burgoyne an opportunity of figuring away in the North, and he uses the opportunity as might be expected from the abandoned servant of an abandoned Master. First he prevails with the people to remain with their Stocks on their plantations and [gives] protections to quiet their fears, immediately follow bands of Indians, some Canadians & Regulars, who scalp and murder all before them, neither age, sex, nor political character makes any difference. Men, women, children, whig, Tory, and Protectiontaker, all promiscuously feel the keen scalping knife and the murdering Tomahawk. This Burgoyne is a true Type of the Court he comes from; Howe & Carleton have *some* humanity. Very soon I hope his career will be stopt. Schuyler & St. Clair are ordered down to Head Quarters that an enquiry may be had into the loss of Ticonderoga &c. Gen. Gates by this time has joined the Northern Army as Commander of it. Gates is able, and he is beloved in the Eastern Countries. The Men will now turn out. Morgans Corps, with some other Troops are sent up to check and chastise the inhuman Butchers of bloody Burgoyne. An affair has lately happened in that Quarter on the Mohock river that gives spirits to the people. Near Fort Stanwix a body of the enemy intending to beseige that place, were attackt by a party of Tryon County Militia under command of a General Hackerman. The General was wounded but bravely kept the ground & encouraged his men, several valuable gentlemen of that County were slain, but their enemies were totally defeated with great loss both of officers, men, & baggage. In the meantime the Commander of the Fort sallied out and did considerable execution upon 200 Regulars who made head against him. He brought off some artillery from the enemy, and a good deal of baggage.

I went the other day to see the Army, the main body of which is about 20 miles from this City. 2000 men are at Coryells ferry & Sullivan with 2000 more is placed at Morris Town. Old Putnam with 5000 occupies the heights of Peeks Kill on Hudsons river. This disposition was taken, to be in readiness to turn northward, or to defend this place, as Gen. Howes visit might render necessary. I think the Army is a gallant one, well disciplined, clothed, armed (for they have all bayonets now) and sound in every respect—The Soldiers in good health and spirits, and every thing looks tout en Militaire. Among other curiosities there, I saw the young Marquis de la Fayette, a Nobleman of the first fortune and family in France, the favorite of Court and Country. He left behind him a most beautiful young wife, and all the soft enjoyments that such a situation, with an immense fortune in a polished Country can furnish to fight in American wilderness for American Liberty! After this can there be a Tory in the World? He has rank of Major General in the Continental Army & fights without pay. He is thirsty for glory but the Commissioners at Paris wish the General may restrain the arder of youth and not suffer his exposure but on some signal occasion. He is sensible, polite, and goodnatured. How this example ought to gall the worthless Nobility & Gentry of England, who meanly creap into the Tyrants service to destroy that liberty which a generous Frenchman quits every delight to defend thro every difficulty! Our intelligence from France is late in May, and tho we are not to expect immediate war in Europe, yet we shall assuredly receive *substantial aid* from thence. Both France & Spain are powerfully and rapidly arming, whilst the necessary attention to security agst such powerful neighbors, obliges England to incur great expences and prevents her efforts against us. The better opinion is, that the peace of Europe cannot continue a year. With their Fleet, the French spirit rises, for we yearn that when Lord Stormont lately said to the Minister of France "The peace cannot long continue, if America continues to draw supplies from France," he was answered "Nous ne desiron pas la guerre, et nous ne le *craignon* pas." The truth is, that both France & Spain are most heartily our friends and will give us every substantial aid, but directly going into the war, for which they are not yet ready. Dr. Price told a Gentleman in London the other day, that the Custom House books began to shew great deficiencies in point of duties, and a Ministerial Man said that nothing but the interposition of Providence could save G. Britain from destruction. But the Tyrant relies we hear, upon the *desperate* efforts that Howe and Cornwallis must make to redeem their "*Bankrupt Honor.*" The Court of London, for purposes very obvious, encourages every kind of amusement and dissipation throout England. By royal Authority Theatres are licenced in the formerly busy Manufacturing Towns of Birmingham, Sheffield &c &c.

Lord Chatham is not dead, as was reported, but lives with better health than usual. He has been figuring lately in the House of Lords, where he advised an immediate peace with America, on *any terms*; assuring his Hearers, they had no more chance to conquer this Continent with the Forces they had, or could get, than he would have to conquer England with his Crutch. He said they might create distress along the Sea Cost, and seize the Towns there, but the longer they carried on the war the greater would be their disgrace, and the more certain their ruin. Good old Man. If Kings will be suffered in the World, why is it not *insisted on* that they shall attend to Wise and good counsellors!

I hope our friend Parker will soon be about salt making, and I further hope you will find time to assist him in the art of seperating and preparing the Purging Salt.

I have trespassed sufficiently on your time, and the little liesure that business allows me, begging therefore [my love?] to Doctor Steptoe I bid you heartily farewell,   Richard Henry Lee

[*P.S.*] Poor Manly is certainly taken, and there is too much reason to fear the Fox is also retaken. They are yet much too powerful for us on the Sea. Manlys Frigate was very little superior in force to the Fox, but he made her strike. He could not immediately fight a 44 gun ship. Remember me to all friends.

RC (DLC).
[1] Landon Carter was probably the recipient of this letter, since Richard Parker and Dr. George Steptoe (mentioned near the close of this letter) were mutual friends of Lee's and Carter's, and Carter (like Parker) was actively involved in manufacturing salt. See Landon Carter, *The Diary of Colonel Landon Carter of Sabine Hall, 1752–1778,* ed. Jack P. Greene, 2 vols. (Charlottesville: University Press of Virginia, 1965), 2:1098, 1105, 1111, 1128.

Maryland Delegates to George Washington

Sir   Phila. Aug. 19. 1777
We are just now honoured with your Letter respecting the Arrest of Lieut. McNair of the Artillery and shall immediately enclose it to Governor Johnson to take such measures on the Subject as the Law will warrant him.[1] We wish the Artillery Corps and the 16th Regiment had been apportioned on the States that our State knowing its Proportion might have pursued the same means for raising it as it has taken to fill up its Quota of the 88 Battalions. Had this been done by Congress the present act of our State would not have occasioned the Difficulties objected. We doubt not Gover. Johnson will do every Thing in his Power for the Discharge of Lieut. McNair & wishing you every Success & Happiness, We have the Honour to be with the greatest Respect, Sir, yr. most Obd. hble Servts.   W. Paca

Saml. Chase

RC (DLC). Written by Paca and signed by Paca and Chase.
[1] Washington's August 17 letter to the Maryland delegates, complaining of the arrest of Lt. James McNair for recruiting Marylanders for a Continental artillery regiment, is in Washington, *Writings* (Fitzpatrick). 9:84–85.

Robert Morris to Jonathan Hudson

Sir   Philada. August 19th. 1777
    Yours of the 16th is with me and I will deliver the list of Cordage
&c to the Navy Board here, but whether they can supply you or not
I really do not know. I believe this Brigt must be put under their direction untill compleated. I have not heard any thing of the mobs
you mention at the Head of Elk & having lately had some Goods up
from thence I hope you have been misinformed. It is well you will be
so clear & distinct in your Accounts, we have therefore nothing to do
but make money fast as we can & wishing your honest endeavours may
be crowned with success I am sir, Your Obedt hble servt,
                                                    Robt Morris

RC (PHi).

William Paca to Thomas Johnson

Dr. Sir,   Phila. 19 Aug. 1777
    I enclose you Genl. Washingtons Letter and doubt not you will make
a proper Enquiry into the Arrest he complains of.[1] I wish the Artillery
Corp & the 16 Regts. had been apportioned on the States that each
State might have known what was it's Quota and the present difficulties
in filling up those Corps prevented.
    We have no Intelligence of Howe's Fleet. The Army we know for a
Certainty is embarked. We begin to be apprehensive they have gone
to South Carolina.
    The Militia of Tryon County have had a very smart Engagement
with Johnson & his Indians & a Body of British Troops. It is said the
Militia consisted of 700. We lost about 100 men some of which are
the most active leading Whigs in that County. The Enemy were defeated & lost fifty or sixty Indians and some of their best Officers.
There was another Brush by a Party under Capt. Willet who drove
another Party of the Enemy and took a considerable Booty. Genl.
Schuyler writes that the van of Burgoyne's Army he is informed has
moved forward to Saratoga. I wish our affairs in that Quarter bore
a more pleasing Aspect. The New England States disgusted with
Schuyler & his officers have been very slow in giving him Assistance.
Gates perhaps will please them & get them to exert themselves.
    S.C.[2] says he has wrote you fully and therefore I need not be more
particular in my Intelligence. Pray what Success have we with our
Salt Works?
    Wishing you every Success and Happiness, I am, dear sir, yrs aftly.
                                                    W Paca

RC (MdAA).
¹ See Maryland Delegates to Washington, this date, note.
² That is, Samuel Chase.

John Adams to Abigail Adams

Philadelphia August 20th. 1777

My best Friend   Wednesday

This Day compleats three Years since I stepped into the Coach, at Mr. Cushings Door, in Boston, to go to Philadelphia in Quest of Adventures. And Adventures I have found.

I feel an Inclination sometimes, to write the History of the last Three Years, in Imitation of Thucidides. There is a striking Resemblance, in several Particulars, between the Peloponnesian and the American War. The real Motive to the former was a Jealousy of the growing Power of Athens, by Sea and Land. . . .¹ The genuine Motive to the latter, was a similar Jealously of the growing Power of America. The true Causes which incite to War, are seldom professed, or Acknowledged.

We are now afloat upon a full Sea: When We shall arrive at a safe Harbour, no Mariner has Skill and experience enough to foretell. But, by the Favour of Heaven, We shall make a prosperous Voyage, after all the Storms, and Shoals are passed.

5. o Clock afternoon

It is now fair sunshine again and very warm. Not a Word, yet, from Hows Fleet. The most general Suspicion, now, is that it is gone to Charlestown S.C. But it is a wild Supposition. It may be right however: for Howe is a wild General.

We have been hammering to day, upon a Mode of Tryal for the General Officers at Ti. Whether an Enquiry will preceed the Court Martial, and whether the Enquiry shall be made by a Committee of Congress or by a Council of General Officers, is not determined, but Enquiry and Tryal both I conjecture there will be.

If How is gone to Charlestown, you will have a little Quiet, and enjoy your Corn and Rye and Flax and Hay, and other good Things, untill another Summer.

But What shall We do for Sugar, and Wine and Rum? Why truly I believe We must leave them off. Loaf Sugar is only four Dollars a Pound here, and Brown only a Dollar, for the meanest sort, and Ten shillings for that a little better. Every Body here is leaving off loaf Sugar, and most are laying aside brown. As to Rum and Wine—give me Cyder and I would compound. N.E. Rum is but 40s. a Gallon. But, if

Wine was Ten Dollars a Bottle, I would have one Glass a Day, in Water, while the hot weather continues, unless I could get Cyder.

RC (MHi). Adams, *Family Correspondence* (Butterfield), 2:320–21.
¹ Suspension points in MS.

Benjamin Harrison to George Washington

Dear General   Philad. Augst. 20 1777
I remember well a Conversation's passing betwixt you and I on the subject of the Marquis de la Fyattes Commission, & that I told you it was merely Honorary, in this light I look'd on it, and so did every other member of Congress. He had made an agreement with Mr Deane, but this he gave up by Letter to Congress, not wishing as he said to embarrass their affairs. Mr Duer who presented this Letter assur'd he did not wish or desire Command, but gave us to understand his chief motive for going into our Service was to be near you, to see Service, and to give him an Eclat at home, where he expected he would soon return. These you may depend on it were the Reasons that induced Congress to Comply with his request, and that he could not have obtain'd the Commission on any other terms; The other Day he surprised every body by a letter of his, requesting Commissions for his officers, and Insinuating at the same time that he should expect a Command as soon as you should think him fit for one. Depend on it Congress never meant that he should have one, nor will not countenance him in his applications, I had it not in my power yesterday to get their opinions on the subject, but will do it soon.¹

Where can Howe be gone. We begin to be under great Apprehensions for South Carolina, and think he must have been heard off if he had taken any other course, can not a blow be given Burgoyne in his absence? If something can not be done in that quarter, N York will certainly be lost. Our eastern *Friends* have behaved most shamefully. Where the Devil is Gates, why dos he loiter so on the Road. The weather has been hot it is true, and so is the Service he is going to. I am my Dear Sir, your affect Hble Servt,   Benj Harrison

RC (DLC).
¹ In his August 19 letter to Harrison, Washington had requested clarification of the conditions under which Lafayette had been granted a commission as major general on July 31. See *JCC,* 8:592–93; and Washington, *Writings* (Fitzpatrick), 8:95–96. For Lafayette's August 13 letter, which had been referred to the Board of War, see Lafayette, *Papers* (Idzerda), 1:103.

Henry Laurens to Joseph Clay

20th August 1777

I had determined to have done my self the pleasure of giving you[1] a general State of our public affairs in this Central part of the United Colonies but have been so much & so often interrupted I have not time by the present opportunity. I must therefore beg you will be referred to the News papers which I shall put under cover with this.

Since my arrival here I have done every thing in my power to impress upon the mind of Congress the value & importance of Georgia & to recommend it to their particular protection which your Delegate will do me the justice to confirm. I apply in politics St. Paul's remark, if one member Suffers all the Members Suffer. The loss of Georgia or South Carolina or even their distress will be Sensibly felt by all the northern States. I think this important truth has not hitherto been properly considered.

I moved for a Committee to take the State of Georgia into consideration.[2] This produced certain determinations of which you will be advised fully by Colo. Walton to whom I also took the liberty of mentioning your name for Dep pay Master General & you will find you are accordingly appointed.[3] You must not refuse to Act. Tis an Office honourable & genteel, an Office requiring the knowledge, diligence & integrity of a Clay, therefore for your Country's Sake & for the honour of human nature I intreat you to act. The Office of paymaster has too generally been an Office of plunder. Your Accounts will shew that there are Men who can act with accuracy & Strict justice even for the public. This will induce an endeavour upon every occasion to Seek for such Men to serve the public & counteract the assertion of designing Men who when they mean to thrust a favorite or dependent into place Say that all Men when in Office are alike, & too often find it easy to refer to proofs in Support of so dangerous a doctrine. If Security Should be required I beg you will permit me to be one. Indeed I have already in order to Shew my Sentiments of your valuable Character made an offer to that purpose. Had you been near I would first have consulted you, in our present circumstances I trust you will not censure me for being too forward.

If I can render you any Service during my Stay in Philadelphia I beg you will give me Some opportunity; & believe me to be with great regard &ca.[4]

LB (ScHi).

[1] Joseph Clay (1741–1804), a Savannah, Ga., merchant, was chosen as a delegate to Congress in 1778 but did not attend. *DAB;* and *Bio. Dir. Cong.*

[2] For the August 1 resolves Congress adopted on the basis of the report of this committee, of which Laurens was a member, see *JCC,* 8:579, 590, 596–98.

[3] Congress made this appointment on August 6 and Clay informed Laurens

of his acceptance of it in an October 16 letter. See *JCC,* 8:616; and *Collections of the Georgia Historical Society* 8 (1913):46–51.

⁴ This day Laurens also wrote a brief letter to William Hunter of Norfolk, instructing him "when tis convenient & agreeable to you to remit the Money for return of the Sum received from me in Charles Town, please to direct at Mr. Aries in Market Street not the post office." Laurens Papers, ScHi.

John Adams to Abigail Adams

Philadelphia August 21. 1777.

My best Friend   Thursday

This Morning, We have heard again from the Fleet. At 9 o Clock at Night, on the 14 Inst. upwards of an hundred Sail were seen, standing in between the Capes of Cheasapeak Bay. They had been seen from the Eastern shore of Virginia, standing off, and on, for two days before. This Method of coasting along the shore, and standing off, and on, is very curious. First seen off Egg Harbour, then several Times off the Capes of Delaware, standing in and out, then off Sinepuxent, then off the Eastern shore of Virginia, then standing in to Cheasapeak Bay. How many Men, and Horses, will he loose in this Sea Ramble, in the Heat of Dog days. Whether he is going to Virginia to steal Tobacco, to N. Carolina to pilfer Pitch and Tar, or to South to plunder Rice and Indigo, who can tell? He will seduce a few Negroes from their Masters let him go to which he will. But is this conquering America?

From the Northward We learn that Arnold has marched with about 2000 Men to the Relief of Fort Schuyler.

Our People have given Sir John Johnson and his Regulars, Tories and Indians, a very fine Drubbing. The Indians scarcely ever had such a Mauling. The Devils are so frightened that they are all run away to howl and mourn.

The Papers, inclosed with this, will give you, more particular Information. Can nothing be done at Rhode Island at this critical Time. Opprobrium Novangliæ!

What is become of all the Massachusets continental Troops. Every Regiment and every Man of them is at the Northward, under Gates— and yet We are told they have not 4000 Men fit for Duty Officers included. And there are 3 Regiments there from N. Hampshire too.

10 o Clock at Night

Just come in from Congress. We have within this Hour, received Letters of G[enerals] Schuyler and Lincoln, giving an Account of the Battle of Bennington, wherein Gen. Starks has acquired great Glory, and so has his Militia. The Particulars are to be out in an Hand Bill, tomorrow Morning. I will inclose you one.[1]

RC (MHi). Adams, *Family Correspondence* (Butterfield), 2:321–22.
[1] This day Congress received the news of Gen. John Stark's August 16 victory
at Bennington, Vt., in letters from Gens. Philip Schuyler and Benjamin Lincoln.
These August 18 letters were published on August 22 by order of Congress in a
handbill printed by John Dunlap. See *JCC*, 8:663, 9:1086; and Evans, *Am.
Bibliography*, no. 15686. See also Committee of Intelligence to Washington,
September 2, 1777.

Board of War to George Washington

Sir, War Office Augt 21st. 1777
Col. Bland informed me that the Enemy had thrown into the Rariton
on their Departure from Brunswick two Cannon, one of 32, the other of
24. If these Cannon could be raised & sent in to this Place they would be
very useful in the Defence of the Chevaux de Frize as we have no spare
Guns of that Weight of Ball. I mentioned this Matter to the Board who
gave it in Direction to me to request your Excellency would order Search
to be made after the Cannon & if practicable direct them to be raised
out of the River & sent on to Philadelphia immediately. There are here
about 20 Eighteen Pounders belonging to the State & the Board are
collecting a Number of twelves which were intended for the Frigates,
Monsr. Du Coudray's Plan requiring a vast Number of Guns. But
whether twelve Pdrs. will answer much Purpose or whether it will be
prudent to trust any great Number of Cannon on the Jersey Side where
it seems a great Proportion of them are to go, are Matters which *future
Events* will determine; at present they are *at least* doubtful.[1] I have the
Honour to be, with the greatest Esteem & Respect, your very obed hble
Servt, Richard Peters Secy

[*P.S.*] There are here two Frigates without Guns. Query would it not be
better to make Batteries of these & put the Guns except a few at Billins-
port & Red Bank on Board them as they could be moved off in Case of
Accident, than to trust them where they must be lost if the Enemy prevail on the East Side of Delaware?

RC (DLC).
[1] For Washington's August 22 response to this letter, see Washington, *Writings*
(Fitzpatrick), 9:117–18.

John Hancock to George Washington

Sir, Philada. August 21st. 1777.
Upon the Resignation of Mr. Philips as Commissary of Hydes, the
Congress have been pleased to appoint Mr. George Ewing in his Place,

who is ordered to carry into Execution the Plan you have proposed; which I make no Doubt he will do with Application and Success.[1]

Your Favour of yesterday I had the Honour of receiving with the Inclosures from General Schuyler, and am extremely pleased to hear that our Affairs in that Quarter wear so favourable an Aspect.[2]

The enclosed Resolve to relieve the New York Militia, who at present garrison the Forts on Hudson's River, and to garrison them with a like Number of the New Jersey Militia, in Order that the former may be employed in defending their own State against the Attack of our Enemies, I must beg you will carry into Execution in the Manner therein pointed out.[3]

The inclosed Letter[4] I have just received by Express from Virginia, who informs that the Fleet was seen last Thursday standing in for their Capes. I inclose you also a Copy of Colo. Nelson's Letter to Colonel Harrison.[5] I have the Honour to be, with the greatest Respect, Sir, your most obed. and very hble Servant.

John Hancock Presidt

P.S. Col Harrison desires me to present his Complimts. to your Excellency, & begs you will order Robin Randolph to Camp. (Col H has his reasons.)

RC (DLC). In the hand of Jacob Rush, with signature and postscript by Hancock.

[1] See *JCC,* 8:607, 656. In his August 16 letter to President Hancock, Washington had suggested that exorbitant charges for leather could be avoided by "the Establishment of public Tanneries, in three or Four of the States, under the care of a Judicious Commissary or Director, to which all the Hides of the Cattle killed for the Army should be carried and tanned." Washington, *Writings* (Fitzpatrick), 9:72–73. Worthington C. Ford printed a report of the Board of War instructing Ewing to carry out this plan in the journals under the date August 19.

[2] Washington's August 20 letter to Hancock enclosed an extract of an August 15 letter from Gen. Philip Schuyler containing "an agreeable account of the face of Affairs at Fort Schuyler." PCC, item 152, 4:505; and Washington, *Writings* (Fitzpatrick), 9:101.

[3] See *JCC,* 8:659.

[4] See John Page to Washington, August 15, 1777, Washington Papers, DLC. Washington's August 21 reply to Page is in Washington, *Papers* (Fitzpatrick), 9:112–13.

[5] Thomas Nelson's August 15 letter to Benjamin Harrison is in the Washington Papers, DLC.

Henry Laurens to John Lewis Gervais

Dear Sir   21st August 1777

I have by this Conveyance per Capt Hornby troubled you with two or three packets already. My Heart is now Swelled with alarming apprehensions for my Country & my friends. I feel for all without distinction even for Some whose envy has made them often very unfriendly to me. I have long viewed Carolina as a fair bait for the Enemy—unguarded & even inviting. At length by false policy we have compelled them to take the most valuable jewel in the American Crown & to ruin our United Cause, for in the capture of Charles Town I see the destruction of the confederacy. God grant my feelings may upon the present occasion be without cause, I take it for granted the British Armament which lately disappeared from the Coast of Maryland is gone to So Carolina & Georgia in order to destroy our Trade, to make immense plunder of Negroes & perhaps Rice & Indigo & if we suffer them, to supply the West India Trade with Lumber & provision. In this view can I forbear grief?

You may remark from my direction to Loveday to make a clean House, that I had always lively apprehensions of our danger, & upon the first intimation of a fleet from New York I urged my Colleagues partly from common maxims of policy to Sound the Alarm to our Constituents by an express notification that 250 Sail of Ships with 7000 Men well appointed were in motion, but they judged it unnecessary—but I had Stronger motives for giving the information. I knew the value of my Country to ourselves & to the Enemy. I knew they only wanted to be rightly informed to induce them to attempt it. I knew that we had unfortunately sent persons to them who could give them the best information. I knew they had among them an enterprizing Genius whose ambition & avarice would prompt him to use every artifice, every means in his power to gain a Command upon an expedition which held out to him Glory & Rich pillage. If the Enemy are gone to you, my old friend Grant[1] will be the first or second in Command & will have the merit of having been the projector.

This Morning I will move Congress to believe the danger real & to take some measure to hem the assailants within a narrow Circle if unhappily they Should get footing.[2] I have Strongly pressed Colo. Horry & Colo. Pinckney to fly homeward, they will go next Monday.

I send inclosed Copy of a Letter from a Gentleman of Rank to his friend here, it gives a melancholly true picture of our late affairs in the Northern department. Shew it to the president. If it meets you in the Woods it will rather mortify than console but we ought to know the truth. I pray God protect you all, you & yours in particular.

22d & 23d. Wrote to Mr Gervais again by the same hand. Sent an Account of the fleet in Cheasepeak, our late delay & now hurry. Sent hand Bills Coupdemain—for General Howe.

LB (ScHi).

[1] Maj. Gen. James Grant (1720-1806), whom Laurens had known since

Grant's service as the governor of East Florida the preceding decade.

2 On this day Congress appointed a committee consisting of Laurens and four other delegates to consider the state of Georgia and South Carolina, and on the 28th it instructed them also to consider the state of North Carolina. This committee never submitted a report to Congress because it soon became apparent that Philadelphia, not the southern states, was General Howe's objective after all. *JCC*, 8:660, 688.

James Lovell to Oliver Wolcott

Sir   Philada. Augst. 21st. 1777

This gratefully acknowledges the receipt of yr. favour of the 31st Ulto. from Litchfield. The probable "slow pilgrimage" of every written testimony of my esteem towards you makes it useless to endeavour to convey any *novelty* respecting matters to the east & north of my present situation; and the known simularity of our ideas of the leaders old and new in the FATAL DEPARTMENT annuls every call for my comments or reflexions upon their conduct. If the final decision in regard to Arnold's claim should draw any strictures from you, I shall not be backward to answer them in turn. It may be fresh to you that Genl. Starks from N Hampshire refuses to act with continental troops but upon his own terms; I believe the state gave some option whether to join the regular army or not; all, beyond that, is his own freak.[1]

We think we have reason to conclude that Howe is gone to surprize the Ports in North and South Carolina & Georgia. That he means to garison the places proper; to block the harbours, & to return to this or N. Yk. In the mean time our main strength will lay midway, instead of reinforcing Gates & Putnam to destroy Bourgoin & the last mentioned Capital; which are easy conquests in the absence of Genl. Howe's body of forces.

As to indoor matters they are like unto like. Our agents will pay the interest of our borrowings at the Loan Offices for 5,000,000 Dollars or more. Some of us therefore think that, by informing the public they shall either receive 6 per Cent here, or bills of Exchange upon our Commissioners at 5, mercantile men would be induced to lend. Others are for making new tickets carrying upon their face 5 per Cent in France so as to make them negotiable, supposing they would be bought abroad at par on a small discount. But even if this was probable, which it is not in my opinion, the consequence would be giving foreigners a demand upon us at some certain future Period for millions. These we could not *oblidge* like our own people to wait till we could sink our tickets by taxes in a course of years. You will guess who are for turning things into rapid mercantile courses with a motto of the devil take the hindmost. In both schemes attention is paid to *present* exigencies; for, Taxes are indubitably our only wise Plan for a continuance; and every day we omit to tax we pass a precious opportunity. One of the schemes is built upon certainty; the other upon chance with the highest probability of ill consequences. The principal of the Tickets is to be paid here upon our plighted faith. If they do not obtain currency in Europe we shall be disgraced immediately; for, the face of the Paper shows our views & expectations. If they do pass freely, we shall have a sad after-reconing. If fresh encouragement to lenders, by bills of Exchange for their interest as it becomes due, does not give an immediate spring to our Loan business, we must emit directly, till a tax can supply. We should consider that we have only gone two years into our annual income; we can bear much more; and our circulation is most amazingly extended, so as not to leave the depreciation a charge against the *quantity* of Bills, by any means so strong as the prevalent opinion. Other causes have a more powerful influence. If Silas[2] and his York connexions could have a good opening to transfer their whole property to the other side of the water it is not impossible that they would *gladly* do it.

Sir   22d Augst

Since scratching an attendant half Sheet we have had several sorts of intelligence that may produce changes very considerable in our domestic plans. In the first place there has been a proper council of war and *determination* as things *then* stood. We have in the next place information that on the 15th the Enemy's fleet was at the Capes of Virginia. The Genl. & Council had thought Sth. Carolina or the eastern States the Object of Howe's pursuit.[3] I still believe that Virginia is visited thro meer necessity, if the present appearance of the ships is any thing more than an allarm. On the 5th of July the Troops went on board; they sail'd from Sandy Hook the 23d, appeared at the mouth of the Delaware the 31st, at Sinepuxent the 8th of Augst. and within the Capes of Virginia the 15th. It was said they had 40 days forrage on board, which must now be expended. Suppose Virginia is to be ravaged in part, some negroes and tobacco stolen, and a few stragling houses burnt; this is not forrage, or *that* conquest of America which is desired by Britain. It will furnish the Soldiery with plunder and revive their spirits a little. In the mean time,——————. But, I leave that matter to futurity.

Starks & his *militia* have made even Genl. Chase willing to overlook a foolish rashness about rank. The Bennington affair may spur up to general vigour in the northern Department. Schyler has been *petitioned* by the Genl. Officers to tarry & influence the militia, and he has *consented* to do it. If he is not a valliant man, he certainly knows how to *use* the world; he is far from a foolish man. He advises to send other indian Commissioners because Mr. Woolcot &c. are *so far off*. I will give you the extract. This also is not *foolish*.

4. Clock P.M.

Yesterday & this day we adjourned to dine. We were particularly induced to it, now, by an Express declaring the fleet high in the Bay of Chesepeak.[4] It appears we must at length fight it between Head of Elk and Philadelphia.[5]

RC (CtHi).
[1] See George Frost to Josiah Bartlett, August 19, 1777, note 2.
[2] Silas Deane.
[3] Congress received a report of the council of war in Washington's August 21 letter to President Hancock and immediately endorsed Washington's plan to march toward the Hudson River. See Hancock's first letter to Washington of August 22, 1777, note 1.
[4] See *JCC,* 8:665.
[5] For the continuation of this letter, see Lovell to Wolcott, August 25, 1777.

John Hancock to Richard Caswell

Sir,   Philada. August 22d. 1777.
The Congress having received Intelligence from Virginia that the Fleet of the Enemy were seen near the Capes of Chesapeak, on the 15th inst and not knowing what may be their Views upon the Southern Coast, have come to the enclosed Resolve, earnestly recommending to you to have all the naval and military Stores removed, with the utmost Expedition, to Places of greater Security.[1]

I have the Pleasure to congratulate you on the Success of Genl. Stark, who commanded a Party of two thousand mostly Militia, in the Northern Department. For the Particulars I beg Leave to refer you to the enclosed printed Account.[2]

I have the Honour to be, with the greatest Respect, Sir, your most hble Servt.   John Hancock Presidt

RC (OClWHi). In the hand of Jacob Rush and signed by Hancock.
[1] See *JCC,* 8:660.
[2] See John Adams to Abigail Adams, August 21, 1777, note.

John Hancock to James Nicholson

Sir,   Philada. Augt. 22d. 1777.
As the Enemy's Fleet are in Chesapeak Bay and may possibly turn their Views agt. Baltimore, or at least make an Attempt to seize the Shipping in that Harbour, I have it in Charge from Congress to inform you, that it is their Desire, in Case your Vessel cannot be saved from falling into the Hands of the Enemy otherwise than by destroying her that in this Case you should destroy her, and at the same Time save as much of her Tackle, Apparel, & Stores as you possibly can.[1]

Being thoroughly persuaded of your Zeal and Attachment in the Service of the United States, I make no Doubt of your exerting yourself on this and every other Occasion when called upon, in a Manner becoming your Character & the Trust reposed in you by your Country. I am, with Respect, Sir, your most obed. & very hble Servt.

J.H. Presid.

LB (DNA: PCC, item 12A). Addressed: "Captain Nicholson, Commander of the Continental Frigate Virginia at Baltimore."
[1] See *JCC*, 8:665–66.

John Hancock to George Washington

Sir,   Philada. August 22d. 1777. 7 O'Clock A.M.
Your several Favours—by Colonel Hamilton—by Lieutenant Ewing —and also of the 21st Inst. I have had the Honour of receiving in the Order of their respective Dates.

The Congress having had your Letter and the Proceedings of a Council of War under Consideration, highly approve the same, and have come to the enclosed Resolution on the Subject, to which I beg Leave to refer you.[1]

Since my last, we have received no farther Information respecting the Fleet. Every Intelligence on the Subject shall be instantly forwarded, that you may be fully acquainted with the Movements of the Enemy, and the better enabled to form a Judgment of their Views and Intentions.

I congratulate you on the Success of General Stark. Lest you should not have received so perfect an Account of the Matter, I do myself the Pleasure to inclose you a printed Copy of Genl. Lincoln's Letter to Genl. Schuyler and by him transmitted to Congress.

I have the Honor to be, with the greatest Respect, Sir, your most obed & very hble Servt.   John Hancock Presidt

RC (DLC). In the hand of Jacob Rush and signed by Hancock.
[1] In his August 21 letter, Washington asked for Congress' opinion of his plan to move his army back to New York since it then appeared that the British fleet with General Howe's expeditionary force was headed for Charleston, S.C. Congress considered this letter on the 21st and approved "the plan of marching the army towards Hudson's river, and then that General Washington act as circumstances may require." See *JCC*, 8:663; and Washington, *Writings* (Fitzpatrick), 9:107–10. As the very next entry shows, however, this plan immediately became outmoded when word reached Philadelphia the next day of the arrival of the British fleet in Chesapeake Bay.

John Hancock to George Washington

Congress Chamber 22d Augst. 1777
Sir,   1/2 past 1 oClock PM
This moment an Express is Arriv'd from Maryland with an Accott.
of near Two hundred Sail of Mr Howe's Fleet being at Anchor in
Chesapeak Bay, a Copy of the Letter brought by the Express I inclose you, & to which I Refer you.[1] In consequence of this Advice Congress have order'd the immediate Removal of all the Stores & Prisoners
from Lancaster & York in this State to places of greater Safety.[2]
Congress have this moment come to the Inclos'd Resolution[3] to which
I beg leave to Refer you, & indeed I need not Add, as the whole matter
is submitted to you. I will not Detain the express only to Say that I
am with every Sentiment of Esteem & Respect, Sir, your very hume
Servt,   John Hancock Presidt

RC (DLC).
[1] The letter in question was written by William Bordley to William Paca at
5 P.M. on August 21. Washington Papers, DLC.
[2] See *JCC,* 8:665.
[3] This resolve informed Washington that Philadelphia was the probable
British objective and urged him to reconsider his plan to march his army to
New York. *JCC,* 8:666.

New Hampshire Delegates to Meshech Weare

Sir   Philadelphia Agust 22d. 1777.
The Inclosed is a coppy of general Lincolns letter to general Schyler
and the Resolution of Congress on Receiving it, which was the 19th
Insant.[1] Some of the Southern gentlemen made themselves Very warme
on the occation, threw out many Illiberal Reflections on general Stark,
and some on the legisltive authority of the state of New Hampshire
which made your deligates sit very uneasy in thair chairs even to give
them time to go through, but in our turn we informed Congress that
we had no information from the State of Newhampshire to informe us
what the Resons waire that induced them to give such orders to general Stark, but that we had Recd. a letter from the Honel. Josiah
Bartlet a member of the council of that State and lately a member of
congress which had given us some of thaire Reisons and ware such
in ouer opinion as ware concluscive and would justify the conduct of
that state in the eyes of the whol world. That in the first Place the
militia of that State had lost all confidence in the general officers who
had the comand at Tyconderoga when it was evacuated and given up
to our enemies. That they would not turn out nor be commanded by

such officers. That the Preservation of the lives of the inhabetints on
ouer frunteers and the cause in which we weire all engaged mad Such
orders at that critical time absolutely necessary. That we ware not
abought to justify general Stark for making a demand of Rank in the
army at that Critical time but we well know that he hase a great deal
to Say for him salf on that head, and that he had been in allmost all
of the engagements to the northward and distinguished him Self while
others ware advanced [over?] his head. Yesterday a motion wase made
by Maryland and seconded that a Resolve of Congress might be Paste
to Censure his Conduct in Refuseing to submit to the Rules & Regulations of the armay on which a large debate insued in which we ware
Suported by all the Newengland Delegates and some of the Ver-
ginians. On motion being made it was agreed it Should lie on the table
and carried by a grate majority.[2] We informd Congress that a motion of
that Sort came with a Very bad grace from Maryland who only of the
thirteen United States had Seen fit to make laws Diracktly in oppersion
to Congress, by Refuseing that thaire militia Should be Subjacted to
the Rules and Ragulation of the army when Joynd. And we informd
Congress that we had not the lest Doubt but the first batle thay heard
of from the north would be faught by Stark and the troops he
Comanded, notwithstanding that Some gentleman in thaire warmthe
had Said Some things Disrespectfull of them and that I Should not be
affraid to Risk my honer nor my Life thay wood do as much towards
the defence of that Part of the Cuntrey and the Coman Cause as the
Same number of any of the troops in that department. I will leve you
Sr. to Judge of ouer feelings when the Very naxt day we had a Con-
formation of what we had asserted by an Express from general
Schuyler Giveing an account of the Victory obtained by general Stark
and the troops under his Command. We beleive this Curcumstance only
will make those Easy who have been trying to Rase a dust in Congress.
We have this day an account by express from Maryland of the arivel
of a hundred Saile of Hows fleet in Chesepeek bay and a hundd.
moore turneing into Said bay. It is the opinion of Congress thaire
design is to attack this City as it is but abought fifty miles a Cross
from whare thair Ships are at anchor to this Place. General Washington is incampt abought thirty miles to the northward of this Place with
abought half of his army the Rest Chefly on Hudsons River. The above
information no Doubt will turne his attenshon this way. As the enemy
are within two Days march of this Place orders are given to the In-
habetents to drive back thaire Stock that they may not fall in to the
enemys hands. General Gates Reacht Albany the 17th Instant in
order to take the Command in that department. The Congress are not
in the lest discoraged and have not the lest doubt but ouer effairs will
bare a more favourable aspect in the north and had rather How should

come to this Place than anywhare else as general Washington is so
handy. The militia in this and nabouring States aire orderd to be
drawn forth and Several Places of Randervoes appointed. We aire with
the grates Respect Sr. your most obdent. Humle. Servents.

Nathel. Folsom

Geo. Frost

P.S. 23d. General Washington is with his division I have heard this
moment is within teen miles of this City. General Santclaire is arrived
this day agreeable to a Reselution of Congress in order for tryel.

RC (Nh–Ar). Written by Nathaniel Folsom and signed by Folsom and Frost.
  [1] For further information on the controversy surrounding Gen. John Stark,
see George Frost to Josiah Bartlett, August 19, 1777, note 2.
  [2] See the lined-out entry in the journals for August 20, 1777. *JCC,* 8:657.

New York Delegates to the New York
Council of Safety

Honor. Gentlemen,   Philad. 22d August, 1777.
  Your despatches of the 15th instant we had the honour of receiving,
with so minute an account of the situation of our distressed country,
and your efforts for its preservation, as you have been pleased to
furnish.[1] We left nothing undone to procure the reinforcements which
were in our opinion indispensably necessary for your safety. Van
Cortlandt's and Livingston's battalions will be a seasonable relief, but
Col. Morgan's corps of riflemen will, we flatter ourselves, be of decisive advantages.
  The battles in Tryon county and at Bennington, so favourable to our
affairs at the most critical juncture, will undoubtedly raise the spirits
of our fellow citizens; and as New-Jersey is called upon for 1,000 men
to garrison forts in the Highlands, with an express design to give the
militia of our State an opportunity of repairing to the northern
frontier and reinforcing the army there,[2] It is to be hoped General
Burgoyne will meet with an effectual check, if not a total defeat.
  General Howe's fleet were seen the 14th instant plying off the Capes
of Virginia; what are his real intentions still remains an uncertainty.
South Carolina is the only object worth his pursuit; but against such
an enterprise the season seems to be an insurmountable obstacle. Should
this however be the case, the army must look to the northward, for
vain will it be to attempt to follow General Howe through the distant
and unhealthy climes of the southern States, from which he can vanish
at pleasure.

PHILADELPHIA, *August* 22, 1777.

By an Exprefs arrived laft Evening from General SCHUYLER to CONGRESS, we have the following important Intelligence.

Van Schaick's Ifland, in the mouth of the Mohawk River, Auguft 18th, 1777.

SIR,

I have the honor to congratulate Congrefs on a fignal Victory obtained by General STARK; *an account whereof is contained in the following Letter from General* LINCOLN, *which I have this moment had the happinefs to receive, together with General* BURGOYNE's *inftructions to Lieutenant-Colonel* BERN; *Copy whereof is inclofed.*

Bennington, Auguft 18th, 1777.

" DEAR GENERAL,

"THE late fignal fuccefs of a body of about 2000 troops, moftly Militia, under the command of Brigadier-General STARK, in this part of the country, on the 16th inft. over a party of about 1500 of the enemy, who came out with a manifeft defign to poffefs themfelves of this town, as will appear by the enclofed, is an event happy and important—Our troops behaved in a very brave and heroic manner; they pufhed the enemy from one work to another thrown up on advantageous ground and from different pofts, with fpirit and fortitude until they gained a compleat victory over them.

" The following is the beft lift I have been able to obtain of the prifoners, their killed and wounded, viz. One Lieut. Colonel, 1 Major, 5 Captains, 12 Lieutenants, 4 Enfigns, 2 Cornets, 1 Judge Advocate, 1 Baron, 2 Canadian Officers, and 3 Surgeons, 37 Britifh Soldiers, 398 Heffians, 38 Canadians, and 151 Tories taken—The number of wounded fallen into our hands, exclufive of the above, are about 80.—The number of their flain has not yet been afcertained, as they fought on the retreat for feveral miles in a wood, but fuppofed to be about 200. Their artillery which confifted of 4 brafs field pieces, with a confiderable quantity of baggage likewife fell into our hands. We have heard nothing of Burgoyne or his army for thefe two days paft. The prifoners are fent into the State of Maffachufetts-Bay except the Tories; fhall wait your directions refpecting them, as moft of them belong to the State of New-York.

I am, dear General, with regard and efteem, your very humble Servant,

B. LINCOLN.

N. B. We had about 20 or 30 killed in the action, and perhaps 50 wounded."

Copy of Orders from Lieut. General BURGOYNE, *to Lieut. Colonel* BERN. *Dated near Saratoga, Auguft* 14, 1777.

SIR,

The accounts you have given me are very fatisfactory, and I doubt not every proceeding under your direction will be the fame.

I beg the favour of you to report whether the route you have marched would be practicable for a large corps with cannon, without repair, or with what fort of repair.

The defirable circumftance at prefent for your corps is to poffefs Bennington, but fhould you find the enemy too ftrongly pofted, and maintaining fuch a countenance as would make a coup-de-main too hazardous, I wifh you to take fuch a poft as you can maintain till you hear further from me, and upon your report, and other circumftances, I will either fupport you in force, or withdraw you.

Will you pleafe to fend to my camp, as foon as you can, waggons and draft cattle, and likewife fuch other cattle as are not neceffary for your fubfiftance; let the waggons and carts bring off what flour and wheat they can, that you do not retain for the fame purpofe. I will write to you in full to-morrow, in regard to purchafing horfes out of the hands of the favages; in the mean time let them be affured that whatever you felect from them fit to mount the dragoons, fhall be paid for at a proper price.

I have the honor to be, with great efteem, Your's, &c.

Lieut. Col. BERN.   J. BURGOYNE, Lieut. General.

I am in hopes that Congrefs will very foon have the fatisfaction to learn that General Arnold has raifed the fiege of Fort Schuyler: If that takes place, I believe it will be poffible to engage two or three hundred Indians to join this army, and Congrefs may reft affured that my beft endeavors fhall not be wanting to accomplifh it.

I am informed that General Gates arrived at Albany yefterday.

Major Livingftoo, one of my Aids, will have the honor to deliver you this defpatch.

I am, Sir, with every fentiment of refpect, your moft obedient humble fervant,

PHILIP SCHUYLER.

The Honorable JOHN HANCOCK, *Efquire.*

Publifhed by Order of Congrefs,

JOHN HANCOCK, Prefident.

Printed by JOHN DUNLAP.

Bennington Broadside, August 18–22, 1777

We have the honour to be, with the utmost respect, honor. gentlemen, Your most obedient and very hum. servants,   Jas. Duane,

Wm. Duer.

P.S. Since writing what precedes, an express is arrived from Baltimore, giving us a certain account that the enemy's fleet have entered Chesapeek's Bay, and yesterday morning were near its head; their army by this time is probably landed. General Washington, with the American troops, lies about 20 miles from this city, and we presume will immediately move to the southward and attack the enemy, to whom he is probably superior in numbers, independent of the militia.

Reprinted from *Journals of N.Y. Prov. Cong.*, 1:1050–51.
[1] For the council of safety's letter to the New York delegates of August 15, which dealt with the invasion of northern New York, see ibid., pp. 1042–43.
[2] See *JCC*, 8:659.

John Adams to Abigail Adams

My best Friend   Philadelphia August 23 1777
It is now no longer a Secret, where Mr. Hows Fleet is. We have authentic Intelligence that it is arrived, at the Head of Cheasopeak Bay, above the River Petapsco upon which the Town of Baltimore stands.
I wish I could describe to you the Geography of this Country, so as to give you an Adequate Idea of the Situation of the two great Bays of Cheasopeak and Delaware, because it would enable you to form a Conjecture, concerning the Object, he aims at. The Distance across Land from the Heads of these Bays is but small, and forms an Istmus, below which is a large Peninsula comprehending the Counties of Accomack and Northampton in Virginia, the Counties of Somersett and Worcester in Maryland, and the Counties of Kent and Sussex on Delaware. His March by Land to Philadelphia, may be about sixty or seventy Miles. I think there can be no doubt that he aims at this Place, and he has taken this Voyage of six Weeks, long enough to have gone to London, merely to avoid an Army in his Rear. He found he could not march this Way from Somersett Court House, without leaving G. Washington in his Rear.
We have called out the Militia of Virginia, Maryland, Delaware, and Pensilvania, to oppose him, and G. Washington is handy enough, to meet him, and as G. Washington saved Philadelphia last Winter, by crossing the Delaware and marching to Morristown, and so getting in the Rear of Howe, so I conjecture he will still find Means to get in his Rear between him and Chesapeak Bay.

You may now sit under your own Vine, and have none to make you afraid. I sent off my Man and Horse at an unlucky Time, but, if We should be obliged to remove from hence, We shall not go far.

If Congress had deliberated and debated a Month they could not have concerted a Plan for Mr. Howe more to our Advantage than that which he has adopted. He gives Us an Opportunity of exerting the Strength of all the middle States against him, while N.Y. and N.E. are destroying Burgoine. Now is the Time, never was so good an Opportunity, for my Countrymen to turn out and crush that vapouring, blustering Bully to Attoms.

RC (MHi). Adams, *Family Correspondence* (Butterfield), 2:325.

John Adams to Abigail Adams

Philadelphia August 23d. [1777]
My best Friend   Saturday 4 O Clock
We have an Express, today from Governor Johnson, Captn. Nicholson and several other Gentlemen with an Account that the Fleet, to the Number of Two hundred and Sixty Three Sail, have gone up towards the Head of Chesapeak Bay. They lie over against the Shore between the River Sassafras and the River Elke.

We have also a Letter from General Washington acquainting Us that Tommorrow Morning at seven O Clock, he shall march his Army through the City of Philadelphia, along Front Street, and then turn up Chesnutt Street, in his Way to cross over the Bridge at Schuylkill River, so that General How will have a grand Continental Army, to oppose him, in very good Season, aided by a formidable Collection of Militia.

I like this Movement of the General, through the City, because, such a show of Artillery, Waggons, Light Horse and Infantry, which takes up a Line of 9 or 10 Miles upon their March and will not be less than 5 or 6 Hours passing through the Town, will make a good Impression upon the Minds of the timourous Whiggs for their Confirmation, upon the cunning Quakers for their Restraint and upon the rascally Tories for their Confusion.

I think there is a reasonable Ground for Confidence with the Favour of Heaven that How will not be able to reach this City. Yet I really doubt whether it would not be more for our Interest that he should come here and get Possession of the Town.
1. Because there are Impurities here which will never be so soon or so fully purged away, as by that Fire of Affliction which How inkindles wherever he goes.

2. Because it would employ nearly the whole of his Force to keep Possession of this Town, and the rest of the Continent would be more at Liberty.
3. We could counteract him here better than in many other Places.
4. He would leave N. England and N.Y. at Leisure to kill or catch Burgoine.

In all Events I think you may rejoice and sing, for the season is so far gone, that he cannot remove to you.

RC (MHi). Adams, *Family Correspondence* (Butterfield), 2:326–27.

Samuel Chase to Thomas Johnson

My Dear Sir   Philada. Augst. 23rd. 1777.

I received your Letter of the 17th by Thursdays Post. Yesterday Noon I received an Express from Mr. W. Bordley, informing that the fleet were off Rock Hall. The Intelligence was immediately communicated to his Excellency Gen. Washington, by whose Answer, received last Night, we are informed that he has ordered the Division under Gen. Nash, about 1500 & 300 artillery at Trenton, to march directly to Chester; that Sullivanes Division, now at Morris Town are also ordered down & the Army under his Command, at Nashameny, about 20 Miles from this, are to march this Morning.

You will receive, by Express, a Requisition to call out 1250 of the western, and 750 of the Eastern Shore Militia. They are desired to collect at Baltimore & Harford & George Town on Sassafras. Virginia is desired to march from her back Counties about 2000 to Frederick Town. The Intention is to cover our Country from the Incursions & Depredations of the Enemy, & to hang on the Rear of the Enemy. Gen. Washington never intends to join our or any Militia with his Regulars, but in Case of an absolute Necessity. Orders are sent to remove the prisoners and Stores from Lancaster, to prevent their Loss by a Coup de Main of Gen. Howe. This City is certainly the great object of Gen. Howe, & I believe he will not only be disappointed in that Design, but totally ruined, if the Militia turn out.

I greatly lament your Want of Arms. I hope you will be able in a little Time to render those lately arrived, fit for Use.

Genl. Smallwood & Colo. Gist are directed to repair to our State to arrange, march & command our Militia.[1] The places of Rendezvous were named, that provisions might be conveyed to some certain Place.

I sent you by Express going to Virginia the Intelligence of a victory gained over a Body of Genl. Burgoynes army.

I beg you to give Notice to my Family if any Circumstances should render their Removal necessary. My Compliments to the Gentlemen of the Council.

Your affectionate Friend,   S Chase

RC (DNDAR).
¹ See *JCC,* 8:667–68.

James Duane to Philip Schuyler

My dear General   Philad 23d Augt 1777
I am now to thank you for your kind and confidential favour of the Instt.¹

With the papers transmitted me by Mr Jay they have and shall be seen by those whose good opinion deserve your Solicitude.

Your Conduct in my Judgement wants no Apology. Instead of Censure it merits thanks. Your Friends in Congress echo this Sentiment freely. Your Enemies relentless and bent on your Destruction woud willingly involve you in the Odium of loosing Ticonderoga. The Change of Command was not however founded on this principle but merely on the Representation of the Eastern States that their militia suspicious of your military Character woud not turn out in Defence of New York while you presided in the Northern Department. So Confident were they in these Assertions and such from your Own representations was the gloomy Aspect of our Affairs there, that the Southern members were alarmed, and we thought it prudent not to attempt to Stem the Torrent. It was however agreed and declard, as I hinted before, that the Eastern prejudices against you were the only motive to your recall, and it was understood that you might take your time in coming down. Indeed to have ordered otherwise, at so critical a Time, wou'd have been inhuman considering your family, fortune and Influence in that Country. Your Resolution to stay & exert yourself while she remains in such imminent danger is worthy of a Virtuous, brave and patriotic Citizen. All your Friends wish that fortune may put it in your power to give some signal Proof of the only military Talent which you have not Evidenced in the Course of your Command for want of an Opportunity. They all pronounce that this woud put your Enemies to Silence and to Shame and elevate you to the highest Rank among the American Commanders.

The Application from the Eastern Generals for your Continuance in the Department, and the respectable Reinforcement from New Hampshire which so palpably contradict the Assertions which were the Basis of your Removal are no small Occasion of Triumph to such of us as predicted that you woud be supported, and will not readily be forgotten. Probably a few weeks will give a decisive and fortunate turn to our Affairs in the North. The Loss already sustaind by the Enemy must be severely felt, and Mr Burgoine's Temerity cannot fail of exposing him to inextricable Embarrasment. Shoud his Army be cut off it will be a capital stroke indeed. With God's blessing our Western frontier will be safe for this Season. We long impatiently to hear from our gallant Friend Arnold. We have much too to expect from the Northward. Give us the earliest Intelligence. Every mouth is full of the Praises of Herkimer, Stark, Gansevort & Willet. They have established their Reputations effectually.

I beg you'l present my Compts to all our Friends. Excuse my not writing sooner; I saw no messenger I coud trust which is the only Reason. Believe me to be with the greatest Respect Dr Genl., your most obedient hum servt.   Jas Duane

[*P.S.*] Col. Duer joins in respectful Complimts.

RC (NN).
[1] An extract of General Schuyler's August 19 letter to Duane is in Benson J. Lossing, *The Life and Times of Philip Schuyler,* 2 vols. (1873; reprint ed., New York: Da Capo Press, 1973), 2:309.
[2] Schuyler had sent John Jay "Extracts of all my orders relative to Tyonderoga, since my Return from Philadelphia, and a short account . . . of what Measures I took . . . for the Security of that Post," and Jay forwarded them to Duane. Jay, *Papers* (Morris), 1:434–35, 444.

John Hancock to Certain States

Gentlemen,   Philada. Augt. 23d. 1777.

In the present critical State of Affairs the Congress have come to the enclosed Resolves for the Defence of the several States therein mentioned which I have no Doubt you will immediately carry into Execution.[1] The absolute Necessity of Exertion & Vigour on this Occasion is too apparent to be pointed out. It is sufficient to observe that a spirited and active Behaviour in the Militia will have the most beneficial Effects, by convincing our Enemy of our Determination to oppose ⟨their Progress⟩ them with the utmost Firmness and Resolution. I am, Gentlemen, your most obed. & hble Set.   J.H. Presid.

LB (DNA: PCC, item 12A). Addressed to the assemblies of Delaware, Maryland, Pennsylvania, and Virginia.
[1] These resolves, which were passed on August 22, recommended a number of military measures to repel the British invasion force that had just appeared in Chesapeake Bay. *JCC,* 8:666–68.

John Hancock to George Washington

Sir,   Philada. August 23d. 1777. 6 O Clock A.M.

I am this Moment honored with your Favour of yesterday by the Return Express.[1]

Considering the Necessity of strengthening the Army under your Command, and of giving all possible Opposition to the Enemy, the Congress have come to the inclosed Resolves, Copies of which I shall forward in a few Minutes by Express to the sevl. States with the utmost Expedition. I beg Leave to refer your Attention to them, and am with every Sentiment that Esteem and Respect can inspire, Sir, your most obedt. & very hble Servt.   John Hancock Prest.

[*P.S.*] I have just Rec'd an Express from Baltimore,[2] the Intelligence the same as heretofore transmitted you, that I will not trouble you with the Copies.

RC (DLC). In the hand of Jacob Rush, with signature and postscript by Hancock.

[1] This letter is in PCC, item 152, 4:535, and Washington, *Writings* (Fitzpatrick), 9:118–19.

[2] See *JCC,* 8:668.

Cornelius Harnett to Richard Caswell

Sir   Philadelphia August 23d. 1777

I have the Honor to Inclose your Excellency a hand Bill published by order of Congress.[1] Genl. Stark has in some measure retrieved our Affairs in the Northern Department. He is a Militia Brigadier from N Hampshire & has acquired great Honor. The fleet of the Enemy are arrived in Chesapeke Bay, what may be their Intensions Congress is not informed, but are prepared, I hope, to disconcert their Plan whichever way it may be pointed.

As Congress seem at present Inclinable to fortify Sea Ports at the Continental Expence, I could wish Your Excellency would be pleased to forward to the Delegates of your State, the Plans of Cape Lookout Bay and C Fear River. I hope for the Assistance of Congress in this business, I have, ever since I arrived in this City, proposed to my Collegues to write Official Letters Jointly, this has not as yet been thought necessary, I only therefore can Lay before your Excy. my own Crude & Indigested thoughts on Subjects as they Occur to me.

Would it not be adviseable to Collect the Arms Drop'd by our Battalions in Virginia & Maryland, perhaps an Application to the Governors of those States would Effect this purpose, bad as those Arms are, they are better than none.

General Howe by his late Maneuvers seems to have acknowledged the Superiority of the American Forces. I should not be surprised if in future he should Continue to alarm us in different Quarters, he may by these means distress the States but I trust he can not Conquer them by this kind of war. I have heard of an intended Insurrection in your State & that Felix Keenan was at the head of it.[2] I shall be much obliged to your Excy. for the Particulars of that affair. I am with the Greatest respect, Your Excellencys Most Obedt. & very huml Servt.   Cornl. Harnett

RC (CSmH).
[1] See John Adams to Abigail Adams, August 21, 1777, note.
[2] In July 1777 North Carolina authorities had ordered the arrest of Felix Keenan, a loyalist, for complicity in an otherwise undescribed "plot" and "combination." *N.C. State Records,* 11:290, 523.

John Adams to Abigail Adams

My dearest Friend   Philadelphia August 24. 1777
We had last Evening a Thunder Gust, very sharp and violent, attended with plentifull Rain. The Lightning struck in several Places. It struck the Quaker Alms House in Walnut Street, between third and fourth Streets, not far from Captn. Duncans, where I lodge. They had been wise enough to place an Iron Rod upon the Top of the Steeple, for a Vane to turn on, and had provided no Conductor to the Ground. It also struck in fourth Street, near Mrs. Cheesmans. No Person was hurt.

This Morning was fair, but now it is overcast and rains very hard which will spoil our Show, and wett the Army.

12. O Clock. The Rain ceased and the Army marched through the Town, between Seven and Ten O Clock. The Waggons went another Road. Four Regiments of Light Horse—Blands, Bailers, Sheldons, and Moylands. Four Grand Divisions of the Army—and the Artillery with the Matrosses. They marched Twelve deep, and yet took up above two Hours in passing by.

General Washington and the other General Officers, with their Aids on Horse back. The Colonels and other Field Officers on Horse back.

We have now an Army, well appointed between Us and Mr. Howe, and this Army will be immediately joined, by ten Thousand Militia. So that I feel as secure here, as if I was at Braintree, but not so happy. My Happiness is no where to be found, but there.

After viewing this fine Spectacle and firm Defense I went to Mr. Duffields Meeting, to hear him pray, as he did most fervently, and I believe he was very sincerely joined by all present, for its success.

The Army, upon an accurate Inspection of it, I find to be extreamly well armed, pretty well cloathed, and tolerably disciplined. Gill and Town by the Mottoes to their Newspapers, will bring Discipline into Vogue, in Time.[1] There is such a Mixture of the Sublime, and the Beautifull, together with the Usefull, in military Discipline, that I wonder, every Officer We have is not charmed with it. Much remains yet to be done. Our soldiers have not yet, quite the Air of Soldiers. They dont step exactly in Time. They dont hold up their Heads, quite erect, nor turn out their Toes, so exactly as they ought. They dont all of them cock their Hats—and such as do, dont all wear them the same Way.

A Disciplinarian has affixed to him commonly the Ideas of Cruelty, severity, Tyranny &c. But if I were an Officer I am convinced I should be the most decisive Disciplinarian in the Army. I am convinced their is no other effectual Way of indulging Benevolence, Humanity, and the tender Social Passions, in an Army. There is no other Way of preserving the Health and Spirits of the Men. There is no other Way of making them active, and skillfull, in War—no other Method of guarding an Army against Destruction by surprizes, and no other Method of giving them Confidence in one another, or making them stand by one another, in the Hour of Battle.

Discipline in an Army, is like the Laws, in civil Society.

There can be no Liberty, in a Commonwealth, where the Laws are not revered, and most sacredly observed, nor can there be Happiness or Safety in an Army, for a single Hour, where the Discipline is not observed.

Obedience is the only Thing wanting now for our Salvation—Obedience to the Laws, in the States, and Obedience to Officers, in the Army.

12 O Clock. No Express, nor accidental News from Maryland to day, as yet.

RC (MHi). Adams, *Family Correspondence* (Butterfield), 2:327–28.

[1] The *Continental Journal* published in Boston by John Gill carried on its masthead the motto: "The Prussian monarch tells us that the Entire Prosperity of Every State rests upon the Discipline of its Army." Benjamin Towne, publisher of the *Pennsylvania Evening Post* in Philadelphia, was then printing on the *Post's* masthead: "The finest spectacle, and the firmest defence, is the uniform observation of discipline by a numerous army. Archidamus."

John Hancock to George Washington

Sir   Philada. 24 Augst. 1777, 8 oClock Eveng

By a Return Express, this moment Rec'd from the Northern Department the Inclos'd Letter for your Excellency.[1] I inclose you Copy of

Genl Gates's Letter to me,[2] in which he mentions Genl Schuyler's having wrote me particularly, but I have not a Line from him unless one should be Inclos'd in your packett; should that not be the case, & you should have any material Intelligence, I shall be much oblig'd by being favour'd with such Extracts. I have just Rec'd a Letter from Head of Elk[3] Copy of which I inclose also, & to which beg to Refer you.

We have a Report, which seems to be confirm'd several ways, that a Detachmt. of Continental Troops have been on Staten Island, burnt some houses, brought off some Cattle & about 160 Prisoners, among whom are Two Colonels, Dungan & Allen.[4]

Should I Receive any further Intelligence you may Depend on having the earliest Notice.

I am with respect, Sir, your most Obed set,

John Hancock Prest.

RC (DLC).
[1] Benjamin Lincoln's letter to Washington of August 19, 1777, is in the Washington Papers, DLC.
[2] See Horatio Gates to Hancock, August 20, 1777, ibid.
[3] Henry Hollingsworth's August 24 letter to President Hancock gave intelligence about British forces in Chesapeake Bay. Ibid.
[4] Gen. John Sullivan's August 22 raid on Staten Island, which was less successful than Hancock supposed, is described in Charles P. Whittemore, *A General of the Revolution: John Sullivan of New Hampshire* (New York: Columbia University Press, 1961), pp. 54–56. See also Samuel Chase's second letter to Thomas Johnson, August 25, 1777, note.

Henry Marchant to Nicholas Cooke

Honored Sir,   Philadelphia August 24th. 1777

I have by no Means been unmindful of the unhappy Situation of the State of Rhode Island. A very large Body of the Enemy long since took Possession of near a quarter Part of that State, and altho' the Enemy have called off from Time to Time great Part of Their Forces there, yet Their having gained a Possession, aided still by Their Ships; the Force of the State with the small Aid received from Our Sister States have not yet enabled Us to dislodge the Enemy. In the mean Time, the whole Trade and Commerce of the State, as well as the Continental Ships have been blocked up. Taking into Consideration that the Enemy have seen proper to make this Campaign so far to the Southward and Northward as I am in Hopes will give an Opportunity to raise a sufficient Force of Militia and State Battallions to induce Our State joined by Massts and Connecticut to make an Attempt upon Rhode-Island: And in Order to give a Spring to such a hoped for Design; and wishing at least to get Our Shipping and Continental

Navy out to Sea, I ventured to draw up the enclosed Resolutions and to prefer Them to Congress. They were by Congress referred to the Marine Committee, and obtaining a favourable Report from that Board, I finally got Them passed by Congress nearly as I had at first drawn them up.[1] If they should be thought by the Navy Board for the Eastern Department and the Councill of War of Our State, to have been idle, inexpedient or unadviseable, I shall but have lost my Pains, not doubting but they will be candidly considered. If on the other Hand, they should meet the Approbation of the State I have the Honor to represent, I shall feel myself amply rewarded. And should They prove effecatious in delivering Our Trade and Commerce and the Continental Navy from its present Embarassments my every Wish will be unspeakably gratified. I thought I could not well answer it to the distressed State of Rhode-Island &c to remain an Idle Spectator of the Calamities to which it has been reduced without receiving any Continental Aid, while so many Thousands have been expended in the particular Defense of Delaware Bay and River; not less than ten Fire Ships, besides several large Gallies having been ordered by Congress, exclusive of very great Continental Assistance in constructing and raising of Batteries &c &c. I would by no Means however wish to see the publick Monies expended in Our State, without a hopeful Prospect of its being really beneficial. And I would therefore strongly recommend that it be first well considered. I doubt not you will have the same Resolves inclosed to you by the President; but I have hitherto made it my Duty to transmit you all Resolves that respect Our State. I could wish the Hints I offered some Time past, of sending out two armed Briggs on a Cruize, and to France for Cloathing &c four Our Soldiery, may be thought worthy of Attention; especially if Our Harbour should be opened.

Just as Congress as well as Genl. Washington had concluded, Mr. How had most certainly sailed for South Carolina, and an Expedition was forming four Our Army, and some of Them had began to move again Eastward, An Express denounced Mr. How's Appearance with a Fleet of 260 Sail almost up to the Head of Cheaspeak Bay, Genl. Washington immediately ordered his Army to march this Way. The main Body of His Army this Morning passed thro' this City. From the State House We had a fair View of Them as They passed in Their several Divisions. The Army alone with the necessary Cannon and Artillery for each Division, exclusive of their Baggage Waggons, Guards &c which took another Rout, were upwards of two Hours in passing with a lively smart Step.

I congratulate your Honor upon the Victory obtained by Genl. Stark, Genl. Harkimer, and by Col. Witlet. These are happy Presages I hope of future Success.

It is just reported that How has begun a landing about seven Miles below the Head of Elk. We have also a Report of a Skirmish upon Staten Island, terminating to Our Advantage; but have not the Particulars. With great Respect I am, Honored Sir, your most Obedient, humble Servant, Hy. Marchant

RC (R–Ar).

[1] On August 21 Congress approved resolves calling upon Rhode Island to launch fireships against the British fleet stationed there and urging Gen. Joseph Spencer to support this effort "by such attacks or feints as he may judge proper with the troops and boats under his command." *JCC*, 8:661–62. The Rhode Island authorities never carried out the incendiary attack envisioned by these resolves, apparently because of an acute shortage of shipping in the state. William R. Staples, *Rhode Island in the Continental Congress, 1765–1790* (Providence: Providence Press Co., 1870), pp. 154–55.

John Adams to Abigail Adams

Phila. Aug. 25. 1777

Yours of Aug. 12 and 13, came by this Mornings Post.

A letter from Cheasopeak Bay, dated Yesterday Morning, informs that the Enemy had not then landed.[1]

This Morning General Nash, with his Brigade of North Carolina Forces, marched thro the Town with their Band of Musick, their Train of Artillery, and their Bagage Waggons, their Bread Waggons, travelling Forges &c.

General Washingtons Army encamped last Night at Derby. Sullivans Division is expected along in two days.

Our Intelligence of the Fleet has been as good as could be expected —they have been 6 Weeks at sea.

If our People do not now turn out and destroy Burgoines Gang root and branch, they may justly be reproached as lost to Honour and to Virtue. He is compleatly in our Power. Gates writes to congress, that Burgoine is lessened 1200 Men by the Bennington Action.

I inclosed Needles from Turner to Hardwick lately. But Turner is gone home and reached it eer now.

RC (MHi). Adams, *Family Correspondence* (Butterfield), 2:329.

[1] Col. Henry Hollingsworth's August 24 letter to President Hancock. See *JCC*, 8:670.

Samuel Chase to Thomas Johnson

Dear Sir Philada. Augst. 25 1777 Monday

We are informed from the Head of Elk, by Letter from Hollingsworth dated yesterday, that a person he sent to view the Enemies fleet,

gives account that 200 Sail lie from Turky Point to the Mouth of
Sassafras, & that Troops are on board, none were landed on Saturday
late in the Evening.

On yesterday Morning Gen. Washington passed thro' this City with
the Troops under his immediate Command, about 8,000. On this Morning Gen. Nashes Brigade bet[ween] 12, & 1500 marched thro' this City
about two Hours ago. Genl. Sullivane will be here in three Days.

Things remain in the same State in the North as they were when
We received the account of Starks Victory.

We hear We have made 160 prisoners on Staten Island, no account
is come to Congress.

I beg Leave to remind You of the State of the fort at Whetstone
and the Defects mentioned in Genl. Gates Memorandum.[1] I believe
Nothing has been done in Consequence of his advice, which You may
See in a Bundle of the late Council of Safety.

Your affectionate Friend, S. Chase

RC (Facsimile, *Stan V. Henkels Catalog*, no. 969, 1907, item 81).

[1] Apparently a memorandum on the vulnerability of the fort at Whetstone
Point, which must have been prepared the previous February when Gates was
in Baltimore on a brief visit and the British fleet was menacing Maryland
towns and posts on Chesapeake Bay. No such memorandum has been found,
but for a cryptic reference to General Gates' opinion on Baltimore's defenses
at that time, see Chase to the Maryland Council of Safety, February 6, 1777.

Samuel Chase to Thomas Johnson

My Dear Sir. Philada. Augst. 25, 1777. Monday Evening.

I am favoured with your Letter of last Fryday by this Days Post.
Your Expresses arrived here Saturday afternoon. Eer this an Express
to you must be arrived. I wrote You this Day, that we were informed
by a Letter from Hollingsworth of yesterday that 200 Sail were lying
between Turky Point & Sassafras River, & that on Saturday Evening
not one Person had landed. Troops are undoubtedly on board. Gen.
Washington marched at the Head of his army, between 8 & 9000,
thro' this City yesterday Morning. Genl. Nashes Brigade of N. Carolina forces between 12 & 1500 passed thro' this Morning. Genl. Sullivane will be here in three or four Days.

I must approve your Proclamation for Calling forth the Militia, and
am glad the Wish and Intentions of Congress and Gen. Washington
so exactly correspond with yours. I beleive Gen. Washington will be
posted on the Heights before Howe can land & march there. It will
greatly assist Us to be in Possession.

I am satisfied neither Annapolis or Baltimore can, at present, be
defended against any considerable Sea or Land force, and yet I would

by no Means have them abandoned, especially the latter. I am convinced Mr. Howe will be fully employed, and can spare no Land force against either, if he means to prosecute any attempt against this City. If I may be permitted to suggest my opinion, I would endeavor to obstruct the Passage between Queenbury and Horn Points, and would keep the Gallies & Xebeck in the Harbour, put the Forts in the best Condition, & keep 200 Militia in the City. I would give considerable attention to Baltimore. I would compleat the present works, erect new temporary works on some advantageous place between the Town & Pataspsco River, capable of being defended by 500 but capable of Holding 1000 Men, & I would station 500 Militia in Baltimore. In that Situation neither could be taken or destroyed without a Landforce that Howe cannot spare. It is probable if Mr. Howe should fail in or decline his Design on this City, or be beaten, he will make an Attempt to possess himself of one or both of those Places for his Winter Quarters. If you could only delay him a few Days, our Army would follow him. Expence must be incurred & some Danger risked. I am very unwilling to lose our only trading Towns. Be assured that a few fire-Rafts, procurred at a little Expence, will greatly terrify the Enemy. Gen. Washington will consider of sending you an Engineer.

I think you perfectly right to remove the public Stores & Money, but I hope You will consider well before You dismantle the fortifications.

This Moment, while writing, Colo. Hazen showed Me a Letter, giving an account of an attempt by Gen. Sullivane on the Enemy on Staten Island last Thursday. One party under Colo. Ogden of 500, surprised the Enemy, killed a few, made 100 prisoners & returned. Sullivane commanded Deborres Brigade, he killed 5 & made 30 prisoners. Gen. Smallwood had no Luck. He was discovered & the Enemy escaped. So far Success. About 9 o'Clock the two Brigades joined, & began to cross at the old blazing Starr. Before all our Men got over, the Enemy came up & attacked 150 of our Men. Our People behaved bravely, drove the Enemy several Times, but were overpowered. We had but a few killed. We lost 130 privates prisoners. Colo. Antill, Major Woodson, Major Stewart, Major Tillard, Capt. Carlisle, & Duffee a Surgeons Mate are taken. Capt. Hoven, Lieut. Campbell, Lt. Anderson & Ensign Lee were not mentioned in the flagg & are suffered to be killed. Several Field & Commd. officers fell into our Hands. The above is the substance of the Letter.[1]

If Howe should issue a proclamation I wish You would answer it by another. Their perfidy to, and Robbery & Murders of those who were so credulous as to trust them would be excellent Subjects. Our press should rouse our People. I am convinced in no Manner can our Friend Mr Carroll so effectually serve his Country as by publishing a weekly Paper.

Our affairs look very favourably in the North. Farewell, tis now almost 12 oClock. If any thing ocurs tomorrow before the post leaves this I will write again. I expect Mr Paca here tomorrow with his Lady.

Your affectionate Friend and Obedt. Servant,   Saml Chase

RC (DNDAR).
¹ For General Sullivan's lengthy report to Washington on this engagement, see Sullivan, *Letters* (Hammond), 1:437–42.

Samuel Chase to George Washington

Dear Sir.   Philadelphia. Augst. 25. 1777.

From an opinion that your Excellency would wish to be acquainted with the Country which will probably be the Seat of this Summers Campain, and that a Knowledge of such Persons there, in whom You may repose a Confidence, would be acceptable to You, I take the Liberty to solicit, for a Moment, your attention to this Subject.

You will receive, by Dr. Shippen, a pretty exact Map of the Country, and which will afford a general Idea of it. The Distances & natural advantages can only be known by you on observation. Mr. Henry Hollingsworth is active and well acquainted; Mr. Jos Gilpin, Patrick Ewing, ——— Hyland, Jos. Baxter, Charles Rumsey, Dockery Thompson and Wm. Clark, all of Cæcil County, may be relied on.

If any Intelligence should be wanted, or service rendered, in Kent County, John Voores & J. Henry at George Town, and Capt. ——— Kent and ——— Leathrbury, assembly Men, Joseph Nicholson Senr. and John Cadwallader Esqr. may be depended on.

In Harford County, on the South Side of the Susquehanagh, your orders will be readily & faithfully executed by Aquila Hall, Frank Hall and John Paca, Benjamin Rumsey & Jacob Giles.

Colo. Patterson, near Christeen Bridge bears a good Character.

One Charles Gordon, a Lawyer, and one ——— Pearce, near George Town, and ——— Millegan on Bohemia, and Danl. Heath, near Warwick, are very suspicious Characters. Would it be improper for the above Gentlemen of Cæcil to give You an alphabetical List of all doubtfull & suspected Persons?

If wanted, I am informed 50,000 Flints may be purchased in Baltimore. Mr. William Lux will execute any of your orders there. A Considerable Quantity of Continental Powder is near that Place.

I am Dear Sir, with Sincere Esteem, Your very affectionate, obedient Servant.   Saml. Chase

[*P.S.*] I had almost forgot to request You to send an Engineer, if one can be spared, to Baltimore and Annapolis, to advise in their Fortifications. Could Genl. Conway be spared to go there? I believe Baltimore might be defended.[1]

RC (DLC).
[1] For Washington's August 27 response to this letter, see Washington, *Writings* (Fitzpatrick), 9:137–38.

Connecticut Delegates to Jonathan Trumbull, Sr.

Sir   Philadelphia August the 25th. 1777
Since ours of last Monday when it was apprehended Genll. How was gone for South Carolina he has appeard with his whole fleet as it is supposed entering Cheesepeek Bay & by the last Accounts was up as far as where the river Elk enters the Bay. It is Conjectured he Intends landing at a place called Charlestown, from whence it is probable his first design may be upon Lancaster where we have large Stores & some hundreds of Prisoners. On Notice of the fleet coming up the Bay Immediate Orders were sent to Lancaster to remove the Stores & Prisoners from thence to some place of Safety but Philadelphia may yet be his principal Object as he will have but about fifty miles March to this place. If this is his design the only reason of his Changing Delaware for Cheesepeek must be the Concern he had of the Fire ships & rafts of which we had large Numbers in this river. Genll Washington with his Army had lain about 20 miles from this City towards the Jerseys untill Thursay last when Supposing Genll Howe to have gone far Southward beyond his reach had determined to push up the North River & Indeavour A total rout of the Enemy Northward if possible, at the same time to have attempted dislodging the Enemy from New York & have drove them in their detached parts from all their posts in the Northern & Eastern Department. Providence seemed to point out this season when How was at so great a distance, to Accomplish all this before his return but having that day received Intelligence of the Fleet pushing up Chesepeek altered his rout & is now on his March to Meet the Enemy wherever he may find them on this side Cheesepeek. He marched thro this City yesterday morning about 8 oClock with his whole Army which made a very respectable appearance. The Militia from this State, Delaware, Maryland & the nearest Countys in Virginia are ordered to join him. It is rather thought that Genll Washingtons forwardness to meet him in this quarter & especially if the Militia join him as is expected will again discourage Hows attempts this way but if not have the greatest hopes with the blessing of Heaven that here he may receive his final Overthrow. And we are yet in hopes Notwithstanding Genll Washingtons being Diverted from the Northward And Eastward Yet if New England (on the present divided State of How

& Burgoins Army) will properly exert themselves And rightly Improve the Advantages put into their hands they may by the blessing of Heaven Effect a most happy close to the present warr before this Year expires. We hope Burgoins Success (however blame worthy the Genll officers in that quarter may have been) will by the disposals of Providence prove his ruin & destruction. Congress have done what lay in their power to remove the Complaints of the People, recalled the Officers concernd, ordered the Strictest Scrutiny & are making every preparation for a full, fair & Impartial Tryal. They have sent such Officers to Command in their room in that Department as they thot most Acceptable to the people & in whom they might confide both for skill & fidelity, that we shall have no excuse for ourselves or the people whom we represent if they should now fail to offer themselves readily & Chearfully in the Cause of their bleeding Country. We hope, we trust, they will no longer drouse or Sleep untill the Tommohawk awake them in their own dwellings & habitations. The Notable Affair of Genll Stark with his party, seems to open a happy prospect of future success in that quarter if properly followd & pursued which God grant. This, with the Success of Coll Herkemer & Willet near Fort Stanwix & the distruction of so large a Number of the Savages at their first onset are most seasonable Interpositions of Providence in our behalf when every thing looked gloomy in that quarter. The great & weighty affair of our Confederacy, the Supplies of our Treasury giving Credit & Stability to our depreciating Currency are Objects which we trust will very soon be attended to, tho we have been unhappily diverted therefrom by other matters tho not so Important yet Necessary to be done.

We have the honour to be with the greatest Esteem & regard, your Honors most Obedt Hble Servts. Eliphalet Dyer

Richd. Law

Wm. Williams

[*P.S.*] By the best Computation we can make Genll Washington Army of Continental Troops amount to between Ten & Eleven thousand fit for Duty, expects to be joined by about 7 or 8 thousand Militia.

RC (Ct). Written by Dyer and signed by Dyer, Law, and Williams.

James Duane to George Clinton

Sir Philad 25t August 1777

We have the Honour of your favour of the 10th Instant and shall on all Occasions worthy of your attention, or of Importance to the publick, communicate to you our Sentiments with the utmost Freedom and Candour. Since you left Kingston the Council of Safety have been pleasd to resume their former Correspondence with us, which is the Reason you have been so long without an Answer; as we concluded our Letters to that honourable Body would be presented to you with the first Opportunity.

We have the Satisfaction of finding a perfect Correspondence between your Excellency's and our Sentiments on the Subject of the Northern Department; and can bear our Testimony That General Schuyler is sacrificd to unworthy Suspicion and unprovoked malice: and our State left to struggle almost alone under a powerful Invasion attended with every Circumstance of savage Barbarity and Devastation. The Change of our Affairs will have some Tendency (but much greater the Strange plan which general Howe is pursuing) to call forth our Massachusetts & Connecticut Neighbours into Action. Besides, as their favourite[1] commands they will be destitute of the Shadow of an Excuse if they do not Join the Army with the utmost Diligence and Alacrity. With the brave New Hampshire Militia, Morgan's, Livingston's & Van Cortlandt's Corps, joined to our own militia, I cannot but think, Heaven not being unpropitious, that General Burgoine will be obliged to consult his Safety by a precipitate Retreat. Perhaps, from his great Confidence, even that may become impracticable.

General Howe is now between Turkey point and Charles Town near the Head of Chesapeak bay. We have not learned that he has yet landed his army: but expect the news every Hour. General Washington marched part of his Army thro this City yesterday morning. Other Divisions will soon follow with a considerable body of militia. General Howe will therefore meet with a very warm Opposition. The Spirits of the People here are high. They have had time to regulate their militia and We have Reason to think they will turn out Very chearfully. We shall be able in all probability to give you some material Inteligence from this Quarter very soon. In the mean time we remain, with the greatest Respect, Sir, your Excellency's most obedient, humble Servants,

Jas Duane for self & Colleague

P.S. General Sullivan has made an attack on Staten Island which has terminated rather unfortunately for us; the rear guard being cut off. The Enemy's Loss is the greatest, ours 150 officers & privates. It appears to have been ill conducted.[2]

RC (CtY).
[1] Horatio Gates.
[2] See John Hancock to George Washington, August 24, 1777, note 4.

John Hancock to the Rhode Island Governor and Council of War

Gentlemen,   Philada. August 25th. 1777.

The enclosed Resolves which I have the Honour of transmitting, will inform you that Congress have referred the Propriety and Expediency of preparing Fire Ships to attack the Fleet of the Enemy at Rhode Island to the Governor and Council of War of that State, and the Navy Board of the Eastern Department, who are directed to consult together on the Subject. The Resolves themselves are so full and explicit, and point out so clearly the Mode of carrying the Plan into Execution, that I shall not add; any further than to recommend the greatest Secrecy in whatever you may think proper to undertake on the Occasion.[1] I beg Leave to refer your Attention to the Resolves, and have the Honour to be, Gentlemen, your most obed. & very hble Servt.

John Hancock Presidt

RC (R–Ar). In the hand of Jacob Rush and signed by Hancock. Addressed: "Honl Govr Cooke & Council of War." The same letter was also sent to Gen. Joseph Spencer and to the Eastern Navy Board. PCC, item 12A, fol. 256.

[1] On this point, see Henry Marchant to Nicholas Cooke, August 24, 1777, note.

John Hancock to the New Hampshire Assembly

Gentlemen,   Philada. Augt. 25th. 1777.

I have it in Charge from Congress to transmit you the enclosed Copy of a Letter from Genl. Lincoln, accompanied with the Resolve of Congress founded thereon.[1]

It is with the utmost Regret the Congress hear that Genl. Stark has Instructions to act independant of the Army of the United States, if he should be so inclined. As Nothing can be more destructive of military Subordination, or produce greater Confusion in the Service, than the Existence of any Corps or Body of Men free from the Controul of the Commander in Chief and the Rules of Discipline that bind the Rest of the Army, it is the earnest Desire of Congress that Genl. Stark may be subject to the same Regulations by which all other general Officers of the Militia have been hitherto governed when called out at the Expence of the United States. I am therefore to request you will give Genl. Stark Instructions to govern himself accordingly.

I beg Leave to refer your Attention to the enclosed Resolve, and to entreat your immediate Compliance with it, as the only effectual Means of preventing Discord, and restoring that Harmony so indispensibly necessary at this Juncture in the Army of the United States of America.

I have the Honour to be, Gentlemen, your most obed & very hble Sert.　　　　　　　　　　　　　　　　　　J.H. Presid.

LB (DNA: PCC, item 12A).
¹ This issue is discussed in George Frost to Josiah Bartlett, August 19, 1777, note 2.

Richard Henry Lee to Thomas Jefferson

Dear Sir　　　　　　　　　　　　　　　　　Phila. August 25. 1777

It will not perhaps be disagreeable to you in your retirement, sometimes to hear the events of war, and how in other respects we proceed in the arduous business we are engaged in. Since the loss of Ticonderoga (into the cause of which, and the conduct of the commanding Officers, Congress have ordered inquiry to be made) and Gen. Burgoynes speedy march to Fort Edward, our affairs in that quarter begin to wear a favorable appearance. In addition to Burgoynes force, another Body of Men came down the Mohock river, by way of Oswego, and laid seige to Fort Stanwix, or Schuyler, as it is now called. At this place a battle ensued with the Tryon County Militia, in which the enemy were driven from the ground with the loss of more than 200 Indians and several regulars. Colo. Willet making a Sally from the Fort did great injury to the enemy and took from them a great quantity of baggage with 2 or 3 field pieces. However, the Militia having lost many Men in this Action and their best officers having been killed or wounded, they retired and left the enemy to return and lay Seige to Fort Schuyler, which the Garrison was bravely defending, when Gen. Arnold was detatched with a body of men to relieve the place. We expect every day to hear of his success. To the northward of this, in the N. Hampshire grants, Gen. Stark with 2000 Militia attacked Colo. Baum and 1500 Regular Troops behind works, and with Cannon. The consequence you will find in the inclosed Hand bill.¹ This was an important victory, well timed, and will probably occasion Mr. Burgoyne to retire very quickly. If he does not, I can venture to *Augur* his destruction. He is at Saratoga and Fort Edward, with our main Army a few miles in his Front at the mouth of Mohock river. I expect Generals Lincoln and Arnold will presently be in his rear, after which, his chance of returning will be very small. Gen. Gates has joined the Northern Army and now commands in that quarter. Putnam with 5000 men commands on the heights of Hudsons river above N. York, in which place Gen. Clinton is left with about 3000 men. After Gen. Howe had long raised the curiosity of this part of the world, to know what could be his view in embarking his Army and coasting it for 5 weeks in a most oppressively hot season; at length, he appears at the very head of Chesapeake Bay where he remains with more than 200 sail of Vessels. His Troops not yet landed that we know of, but imagine they were put on shore yesterday. We are left yet to guess his Object. It may be supposed either for this City, or to conduct a line from Chesapeake to Newcastle and thereby inclose a large tract of Country between that Bay, Delaware, and the Sea. Let his plan be what it may, Gen. Washington, with a gallant Army is gone to enter a Caveat. The General with his Army passed thro this City yesterday, and they made a fine appearance. To aid the Army, and make the business secure, Congress has called for Militia from this State, Delaware, Maryland, and the Northern Counties of Virginia. Should Gen. Howe venture to enter the Country against this force, I think his ruin will be sure, notwithstanding we are told his Master depends on the "desperate efforts that Generals Howe and Cornwallis must make to redeem their Bankrupt honor." So, we learn from France, the King of England hath said. We have no reason to suppose, from our foreign intelligence that a war in Europe will immediately take place, but that every preparation for it is making remains without doubt; and in the mean time we shall surely receive most substantial Aid from our friends there. The fleet of France grows stronger daily, and with it, the spirit of the Court rises, as appears by the answer made to Lord Stormont when he told the french Minister that "the peace cannot continue long if N. America continues to draw supplies from France." *"Nous ne desirons pas la Guerre, et nous ne le craignons pas."* In truth, every art of falsehood and fraud has been practised to prevent a war there, but it seems clear that this will not *long* prevail. Dr. Lee is returned from Spain and is gone to the Prussian Court. That Monarch is fond of commerce and is desirous of being acquainted with the whole nature of ours. He is offended with the Court of London, and has no reason to fear its resentment. We have good reason to expect considerable advantage from his friendship. If our funds fail us not, and our Union continues, no cause was ever safer than ours. To prevent the former, most extensive and vigorous taxes should immediately take place. The sum in circulation is immense and no corrective can be applied but Taxation, nor was there ever a time when the vast plenty of money rendered that business more easy. The Loan Office, with that, will I believe answer, and upon the success of our funds will probably depend the Unity of our exertions. The Confederation goes on but slowly, occasioned by the immensity of business created by the war. But I find our right to our Charter bounds, as stated by our Act of Government will be strongly contested.[2] The Charter of 1609 it is said has been vacated, and that no transfer of that Charter right can be shewn from the Company to the people of Virginia. That therefore the ungranted lands were the property of the Crown, and being taken from it by common exertions, must become common Stock. Will you be so kind as favor me with your reasons and authorities in support of our right? I am with great regard & esteem, dear Sir Your most affectionate and obedient [Servt.],   Richard Henry Lee

RC (DLC). Jefferson, *Papers* (Boyd), 2:29–31.

¹ See John Adams to Abigail Adams, August 21, 1777, note.

² Another recent development concerned with land claims that would have interested Jefferson was related to the protracted controversy between Virginia and Pennsylvania over their disputed western boundary. In a July 5 letter, George Bryan, vice president of the Pennsylvania Council, had notified the Virginia delegates of the Pennsylvania Assembly's June 17 counterproposals to Virginia's proposals of December 17, 1776. RG27, PHarH. Jefferson had been chairman of the committee appointed on November 5, 1776, to draft proposals for a permanent boundary between the two states, and it was the resulting resolutions, approved by the Virginia Assembly on December 17, 1776, to which the Pennsylvania Assembly's resolutions were responding. Pennsylvania also stated "that if the foregoing proposal be not accepted" Pennsylvania would consent that Congress "(excluding the Delegates of Virginia and Pennsylvania,) having heard both parties by their Council, shall finally determine the boundary in dispute. . . ." Journals of the Pennsylvania Assembly, June 17, 1777, pp. 80–81. DLC(ESR). Late in the next session of the Virginia Assembly the Pennsylvania proposals were read but consideration was postponed and no further action was taken until December 19, 1778, when the Virginia Assembly proposed that a mixed commission representing both states meet to work out a permanent agreement. The commissioners who met in Baltimore in August 1779 reached an agreement that was ratified by Pennsylvania in November 1779 and by Virginia in June 1780. A summary of the Virginia Assembly's actions on this issue from June 1776 to December 1779 is in PCC, item 71, 1:323–32. See also Jefferson, *Papers* (Boyd), 1:594–97; 3:77, 200, 489. For further background on the Virginia-Pennsylvania dispute, see Virginia Delegates to the Speaker of the Pennsylvania Convention, July 15, and to a Committee of the Pennsylvania Convention, September 12, 1776.

James Lovell to William Whipple

Dear Sir,   25th August 1777

I have only time to say I rec'd your favor of the 12th. I shall soon acquaint you who are on the Committee for obtaining authentic facts relative to the evacuation of Ty.¹ St. Clair is in the City urging for a speedy decision. Schuyler has *yielded* to the *petition* of the General Officers, so far as to act in a militia Line. Gates intends to *seek* the enemy.

I wished to fill the Banks of North River with the names of places which Duer promised to insert, but he has not returned my original, therefore I will not longer detain the enclosed.² I will send you the ground which Howe shall occupy if he lands. At present he is at the mouth of the Elk. He will land at Turky Point, formed by Elk and North East rivers.

Adieu.

[*P.S.*] We hear of a pretty little invoice from Bilboa at Portsmouth—naval stores &c.

Tr (DLC).
¹ John Adams, Henry Laurens, and Richard Henry Lee were named to this committee on August 28. *JCC,* 8:688.
² Although Lovell's enclosed map has not been found, for a similar map, which he sent to Abigail Adams a few days later, see Adams, *Family Correspondence* (Butterfield), 2:262, illustration 9.

James Lovell to Oliver Wolcott

[August] 25th [1777].

I have not got the Extract¹ hinted at but it is not matereal.

The Enemy's fleet continues at the mouth of Elk, and is known now to have troops on board, which was doubted yesterday. We have army enough to swallow Howe and all his troops including his Horses as well as their Riders. The militia turn out with alacrity, better armed than those of any other State, I dare say. I desire to be known with Affection and Respect, Sir, Your humb Serv, James Lovell

[*P.S.*] I hear regularly from Coll. Whipple, who is well. A Quantity of Cordage, some anchors, Broad Cloth, Sail Cloth and Shirting has arrived at Portsmouth by the Friendship of Spain.

RC (CtHi). A continuation of Lovell to Wolcott, August 21–22, 1777.
¹ A reference to passages in an August 15 letter written by Philip Schuyler to Congress, from which, in his August 21–22 letter to Wolcott, Lovell promised to send an extract.

Marine Committee to John Stevens

Sir   August 25th 1777

Your Letter of the 18th June advising your arrival at Charles Town with 500 stand of Arms has come to hand, and we are pleased with your success. The Commercial Committee has now given Orders to the Agents to load your Vessel with a convenient Cargo which you must receive and proceed therewith to the Island of Martinico where you are to deliver the same as the said Agents shall direct.¹

When this is done you must again return to Charles Town where the Agents will employ your Schooner agreeable to orders now given them, therefore you must follow such directions as they give you in future advising us when you arrive. We doubt not you will be extreamly cautious to prevent your Vessel from falling into the hands of the enemy and that you will be diligent for dispatch in Port and at Sea. Wishing you success, We are Sir, Your hble servants

LB (DNA: PCC Miscellaneous Papers, Marine Committee Letter Book). Addressed: "Lieutenant John Stevens Commanding the Schooner Lewis."
[1] For information regarding a previous voyage by Stevens to Martinique, see Secret Committee to William Bingham, November 22, 1776. The Commercial Committee's orders to the South Carolina agents have not been found.

John Adams to Abigail Adams

Philadelphia August 26th. 1777
My best Friend   Tuesday
Howes Army, at least about 5000 of them besides his Light Horse, are landed, upon the Banks of the Elke River, and the Disposition he has made of his Forces, indicate a Design to rest and refresh both Men and Horses.

General Washington was at Wilmington last Night, and his Army is there to day. The Militia are turning out with great Alacrity both in Maryland and Pensilvania. They are distressed for Want of Arms. Many have none—others have only little fowling Pieces. However, We shall rake and scrape enough to do Howes Business, by the favour of Heaven.

Howe must have intended that Washington should have sent his Army up to fight Burgoine. But He is disappointed.

The Kindness of Heaven, towards Us, has in nothing appeared more conspicuous, than in this Motion of Howe. If the Infatuation is not so universal as to seize Americans, as well as him, it will prove the certain Destruction of Burgoines Army.

The New England Troops and N. York Troops are every Man of them at Peeks Kill and with Gates. The Massachusetts Regiments are all with Gates.

Gen. Washington has none but Southern Troops with him, and he has much the largest Army to encounter.

If My Countrymen do not now turn out and do something, I shall be disappointed indeed. One fifth Part of Burgoines Force has been totally destroyed by Starks and Herkermer. The Remainder must be shocked and terrified at the Stroke. Now is the Time to strike. New Englandmen! strike home.

RC (MHi). Adams, *Family Correspondence* (Butterfield), 2:329–30.

Thomas Burke to Richard Caswell

Dr Sir   Philadelphia Aug. 26th 1777
I have been in daily expectations of setting off for the Southward for

some time past, and therefore have omitted writing to you, and indeed we have not until very lately had any thing to write about. At length the campaign begins to be active, and I am, though exceedingly anxious to get home, induced to defer my journey until something material shall happen between the two grand armies who are now approaching each other.

After many unaccountable movements the fleet and army under the Hows has reached so far up Cheseapeak as to have their rear above Baltimore, and their van a good way into the Susquehana. No accounts are yet received of their landing. General Washington has already marched with a gallant army composed of Southern Troops to oppose them; and a few days will bring him sight of them. He will we hope be powerfully supported by the brave and martial militia of Maryland and Pennsylvania. In short, Sir, our hopes are very high that a capital blow will be given to the enemy in every quarter. Burgoin already feels the force and spirit of the New York and Eastern Militia. A choice body of 1500 men were encountered by about two thousand New Hampshire Militia, and routed with the loss of 12 hundred killed and taken with all their artillery. Another brave action was fought by a party of New York militia, who, tho' surprised by an ambuscade, fought with most obstinate perseverance from nine until three o'clock, when the enemy were forced to retire, having suffered great slaughter. What renders this action remarkable is, that, upon the first surprise 200 out of seven hundred were panic-struck and fled; the commanding officer was wounded, and many brave officers were killed very early in the engagement, yet the men, with a courage that would do honour to the best veterans in Europe, sustained the engagement under every disadvantage, and under a very bloody slaughter, until they gained an undisputed victory. The particulars of these actions you will find in the inclosed papers, and I touch upon them here only because I deem them happy presages of the accomplishment of what I have always hoped and wished for, that our militia would become good soldiers. Happy improvement! What foreign force, or domestic ambition should we then have any thing to fear from?

General Nash with his Brigade has passed through this City, and they appeared very well. I saw Captain Caswell, he is well, but had no time to talk with me.

I wish, Sir, I could tell you the Congress improve in wisdom and virtue, but as I hope soon to see you, I shall reserve what I have to say of them.

I have the honour to be, Sir, with the greatest respect and esteem, your very obdt hum. Sert.   Thos Burke

P.S. The Enemy are landed near the head of Elk.

Tr (Nc–Ar).

Samuel Chase to Thomas Johnson

Dear Sir,   Philada. Augst. 26. 1777.
I am informed by Mr. Paca, now at Chester Town,[1] Kent County,
that the Militia of the Eastern Shore are generally willing to turn out,
but they have few Arms, and there are no Magazines of Provisions. Mr.
Paca is extremly anxious that your Excellency would order Colo. Rich-
ardson to march his Battalion to the Head of Sassafras. If you consent,
Mr. Houston will carry your orders, & may be entrusted.[2]
I am with Sincerity, Your affectionate and Obedt. Servt,
                                                                S Chase

RC (PPRF).
[1] William Paca's letter to Chase has not been found, but his August 25 letter
to Governor Johnson is in *Md. Archives,* 16:344–45. Five days later Paca also
wrote Johnson another lengthy letter, but the document fails to indicate whether
Paca was still at Chester on August 30. Ibid., pp. 352–54.
[2] This day Chase also sent the following note to Delaware Gov. John McKinly
"Extract of a Letter from the Head of Elk. dated Monday, 11 oClock A.M. 'Mr.
Brown, Express from Elk ferry, informs he saw a large Number of Troops land
& form in the Field, above Mr. Thomas [Savins?] not less than 2,000, & were
still landing from all the Ships, so that the whole will be landed this Evening.
Henry Hollingsworth.' " Slack Collection, OMC.

Elbridge Gerry to James Warren

My dear sir   Phila August 26. 1777
As the post goes off soon I have only Time to acknowledge the rect of
your Favours of the 9th & 13th Inst the Contents of wch are communicated to Congress. The Commercial Comitee have not given Orders
relative to the other Cargoes in Consequence of their wanting Information from the eastern Navy Board of their Readiness to act in that Department; but Mr Morris informs me that he shall order the Cloathg to
be deliverd to the Cloathiers Agents by this Conveyance & that a Disposition of the other Articles will soon be made & conveyd to your Board.
Should this be neglected from the Approach of the Enemy to this City
or the Engagemt of the Commercial Comee. I think it will be best on
the rect hereof to deliver to the Agents afored the Cloathg, to the
D Q M G the Tent Cloth & for the use of the Continental Frigates
Such articles as they may need. Mr Morris desired me to inform You
that your expenses should be remembered & Services acknowledged by
the earliest oppertunity.
I think You have conducted prudently in sendg Charters for the
Goods while at Casco bay; & not able to determine whether You determine to order them by Land or Water from Portsmouth I have not sayed

any thing to the Commercial Committee on that Head, but shall mention it this morning & doubt not that they will be fully Satisfie.

P.S. I think it will be best to order the Goods from Portsmouth by Land as the Distance is not great & Roads good.

FC (MB).

¹ Warren's August 9 letter to Gerry has not been found, but his August 13 letter to Gerry asked for orders regarding a shipment of supplies that had just arrived in Portsmouth, N.H. C. Harvey Gardiner, ed., *A Study in Dissent: The Warren-Gerry Correspondence, 1776–1792* (Carbondale: Southern Illinois University Press, 1968), pp. 76–77.

Cornelius Harnett to William Wilkinson

Dr. Sir   Philadelphia Augt. 26. 1777
     I am really surprised that you will not give me one line. I fear some terrible Accident has happened in my family I have not had a line from Mrs. Harnett since I left Cape Fear. For Gods sake write me by every Post. This is the last you may expect to receive from me unless you Comply with your promise of writing to me Often. I am anxious to hear from My family as well as my friends. I refer you to the N. Papers inclosed, for News. I am, Dr Sir, Your sincere friend &c,
                                                                                Cornl. Harnett

[*P.S.*] The Post just Setting off.

RC (ICHi). Endorsed: "Recd. the 19th of Sepr. 1777."

Robert Morris to Jonathan Hudson

Sir   Philada. Augt. 26th. 1777
     Having recd. yours of the 19th Inst¹ & growing a good deal anxious for the fate of the Bacon, Pork &ca. you had at the Head of Elk, I determined to accept an offer made me by the Commissary & sold him the same. Pork for £12 per barrell & the Hams &c 18d per lb. This Price was not so high as I might have got had the Circumstances of these Goods been more favorable. I have since recd. a letter from Mr. Irwin mentioning his having sent these articles forward but fancy he will be Stopped therein by the Commissary who now must take charge thereof & these will ease you of all trouble & risque on this Score.
     I am, Sir, Your Obedt. hble Servt.   Robt Morris

P.S. As the Enemy are landed near Elk its plain they mean this way which will give you time to sell your other Goods.

RC (PHarH). In a clerical hand, with signature and postscript by Morris.
[1] Hudson's August 19 letter to Morris is in the Robert Morris Papers, DLC.

William Williams to Jonathan Trumbull, Sr.

Hond Sir   Phila Augt 26 1777

Since my last of abt the 19th Inst[1] I have by the good hand of Providence been regaining my Health, have been able to attend Congress ever Since, tho I recover Strength very slowly; am not able at this Time to write Mrs. Williams. You will please to let her & my other dear Friends know the better State of my Health.

In a joint Letter of last Even'g We informd you of the Intelligence We have of the Howes Fleet & Army. There is a report the army is landed at George Town & Frederic Town, up Sassafrass River in Maryland, but I believe very uncertain, as no Express has brot it. It is said They had a most remarkably safe & quick Passage up Cheasapeak Bay, that there is commonly more danger in that Navigation than a West India or European Voyage, & that a Single Ship is generally 8 days in getting as high as the whole Fleet arrivd in Three. I trust their Design must have been to attack this City, that They were detered from attempting it up this River by finding our Army so near, & so much Fire Craft, &c prepared to meet them, (They have minute Intelligence from those Enemies of God & Man the Tories). It seems probable their next Intention was to come up the River Elk at the head of the Bay. They are in, & within about 12 miles of New Castle & make their attempt that Way, & have lain out of sight so long on purpose that Genl Washington might return to his Station, which by the united opinion of his Genl. Officers he had determined & which was approved by Congress, & beginning to execute the moment we were advised of their being in the Bay, which occasioned his return. He passed thro the City on Sat. morn'g last, another Brigade passd yesterday morn'g. 4000 Militia of this State are ordered & on the proper ground, 1000 from Delaware, 2000 from Maryland & upwd of 2000 from the nearest parts of Virginia are called upon & hope will be seasonable.

Whether the Enemy on getting Intelligence of these Things will think it prudent to hazard so much I cant say, but believe it is more than They expected.

Indeed were it not for the abounding Sins & wholly unreformed State of the Country, I shod dare to hope that God in Mercy had blinded the minds & darkened the councils of Enemies & turned them into foolishness. I know not what may yet be, but it wod seem they had lost the Season, & must render their troops sickly on Ship board so long in extream Heat & neglected for Them a happy Season to join & cooperate with Burgoyne, or fall upon other parts of N England, & effectually prevent any succours to the Northward, & so leave in Burgoynes power to accomplish his Rage, which Howe might have ravaged & desolated our Country & reduced Us to amazing distress & effected more than the conquest of this city. But We know not what certainty what is before Us, & may be sanguine. But this is certain N England has vast Occasion to bless & praise the Lord, for his wonderous Mercy in our Deliverance from the dreadful Scourge. The distress had been beyond all discription had our Enemy invaded them in so critical a Moment. O that there was an heart in our Countrymen. May God in infinite Mercy pour out his Spirit upon Us, I hope & trust is the earnest Cry of all that Love his Name.

I am glad to See a Day of Fasting is appointed in Contt & Massa. May We no longer mock the Almighty with deceitfull Words from feigned Lips. The Time is elapsed & the Post on the point of Setting out.

With Compliments to the Gent. of your Councill & tender rememberance to my dear Friend I am & shall ever be with great respect & highest Esteem Your most dutiful & Obed Son & Servt.   W Williams

[*P.S.*] I hope you recd mine by Sa. Hunt.[2]

RC (Ct).
[1] Not found.
[2] Williams' letters to Trumbull of August 2.

James Duane to Robert Livingston

My dear and honourd Sir   Philadelphia 27h Augt. 1777

Mr Thorne deliverd me your favour of the 15t Instant. I participate in the Distress & Anxiety you must have felt at the prospect of Genl Burgoine's Approach attended by murdrous Savages and no less cruel European Troops. That gracious Being who has hitherto protected us will I trust disappoint the destructive Projects of our Enemies. To him let us look up for Protection; and our Efforts for our own self preservation will be blessed with Success. The signal Victory gained at Bennington; the severe blow given to the Indians by our Tryon militia, and the Courage and Perseverance of the Garrison at Fort Schuyler, join'd to General Burgoine's Temerity, and Genl Howes great Distance which must effectually prevent his giving[1] any Succour in Season; Above all the present Security which the Eastern States derive from the remote Situation of General Howe—which leaves them at full Liberty to employ their whole Strength to the Northward—All these Circumstances united will probably give a happy turn to our affairs, and oblige Mr Burgoine to retreat with more Rapidity than he advanced.

We have Reason to hope that General Arnold will raise the Siege of Fort Schuyler as he writes that the militia of Tryon support him with the utmost alacrity. This we may reasonably conclude will settle the minds & secure the Fidelity of the six nations and our western frontier. Indeed we have the strongest assurances that on this Event they will take an active part and retaliate on General Burgoine who under the guise of Religion and Humanity has Been the Author of Cruelties at which his Countrymen must blush, and which must stain the page of British History with indelible Infamy.

Col. Ogden has made a successful Sortie on Staten Island and took a hundred Prisoners, but this fortunate maneuvre was unhappily marr'd by General Sullivan who attempting a like Enterprize suffered his rear Guard to be cut off, so that tho' nothing coud equal the Cowardice of the Enemy, nor exceed the gallantry of the Continental Troops, the Account is nearly balancd.

General How has certainly landed his army near the Head of Chesepeake about 48 miles from this City. General Washington is on his way from this city to meet him. He writes Congress that the militia shew the greatest alacrity to support him. Those who are Judges assure me that General Howe coud not have Chosen a place in this part of the Continent to which more good men coud have been drawn on a sudden Emergency to oppose him. I need not tell you, who are so great a master of Geography, that his army is now near 230 miles from the Sea. What Advantages he proposes by taking this ground is hard to be conceivd. His Object is undoubtedly Philadelphia; nothing else is of sufficient moment. To obtain it he must leave his shipping at a great distance and give G Washington an oppertunity of taking his own Time, and his own Ground, to harrass and oppose him. A few weeks, perhaps days, will settle the point between the Competitors. The people here in general are firm and pleasd with the Hopes of success. I have not seen a single family moving out of the Town, nor a single Feature discomposed with Fear.

I am Dear & hond Sir, your Dutiful Son & most obed Servt,

Jas. Duane

[*P.S.*] Be pleased to present my affectionate Regard to every branch of your & my Families & tell my Polly that I wrote to her yesterday by Major Livingston.[2]

RC (N).
[1] Duane wrote "receiving" above "giving" but did not line out the latter.
[2] Duane's letter to his wife has not been found.

John Hancock to Delaware and Pennsylvania

Gentlemen,   Philada. Augt. 27th. 1777.

As the State of Pennsylvania is threatned with an immediate Invasion, the Principles of good Policy require that all those Persons should be secured who may be reasonably suspected of aiding or abetting the Cause of the Enemy, and thereby injuring the general Weal. I am therefore to request you will cause all those who are notoriously disaffected to be forthwith apprehended & secured till such Time as they may be released without any disadvantage to the Common Interest of America. I beg Leave to refer your Attention to the Resolve[1] and have the Honour to be, Gentlemen, your most obed & very hble Serv.

J.H. Presid.

LB (DNA: PCC, item 12A). Addressed: "His Excly. Thos. Wharton Esqr, Presid. & the Honble the Executive Council of the State of Pennsylvania. His Excy. John McKinley Esqr, Presid of the State of Delaware."
[1] See *JCC,* 8:678–79.

John Hancock to George Washington

Sir,   Philada. August 27th. 1777.

I have the Honour to transmit you the inclosed Resolves which Congress have passed at this critical Period, with a View to have the disaffected in the States of Pennsylvania and Delaware immediately apprehended and secured.[1] I shall forward Copies of them to those States with the utmost Expedition, that a Measure of such Consequence may be carried into Execution as soon as possible.

I have only Time to refer your Attention to the Resolves, and have the Honour to be, with the greatest Respect, Sir, your most obed. & very hble Servt.   John Hancock Presidt.

[*P.S.*] The Inclos'd Letter[2] I have just Rec'd, & judging it of Consequence I sent it by Express. We have a report that General Parsons has been on Long Island, & brought off some Prisoners & Cannon, but have no particulars. I wish it may prove true.

RC (DLC). In the hand of Jacob Rush, with signature and postscript by Hancock.
[1] See *JCC,* 8:678–79.
[2] Not identified.

Henry Laurens' Heads of Inquiry into the State of the Northern Army

In Congress 27 August 1777.[1]

Resolved &ca.

By corresponding with pub. Bodies or private persons by Letter or otherwise in this & the neighboring States

1st. To collect the fullest & clearest evidence of the state of the Army in the Northern department.

Agreed. to apply to the Board of War for all Letters from General Schuyler & Gen. St. Clair from 1st May last to 31st July & to the Board of War & Treasury for all the Returns*

2d The state of the Troops, military Stores & provision at Ticonderoga & Mount Independence.

Agreed—see Returns* for state of the Troops. For Military Stores, enquire of Commissary [M S?], for Provision, of the Commissary of P² what provisions were there the 1st May & sent afterwards up to the time of abandoning the post.

3d To call for & examine the minutes of the Council of War what orders were given from time to time by the Commander in Chief of that department.

4th Were the Barracks & Stores destroyed?

5th Enquire of the Quarter Master & Commissary Gen—the quantity of Provision laid up at Ticonderoga or near it. What measures were taken or taking for throwing in further supplies. See 2d.

6th The number, appointment & movements of the Enemy from the time of their Landing to the time of Evacuating the Fort.

7th. And also the number, quality & condition of the Garrison. See the 2.

8th. What measures were taken to gain Intelligence of the strength of the Enemy by the Commander in Cheif or the Commanding Officer of the Garrison.

Agreed to enquire of Officers who were in Garrison.

9th. To Enquire of the Clothier general—what Cloathing had been issued from time to time for use of the Northern department & from other public Officers into the expenditure of such issues.

Agreed—to enquire at the War Office for returns by Mr. Measom,³ of Mr. Maese⁴ & his deputies & of proper persons for the expenditure.

10th. The number, equipment & behaviour of the Militia, the terms for their service, at & before the time of the evacuation.

11th. The situation & condition of the Lines at Ticonderoga⁵ & the Fortifications upon Mount Independence.

Agreed—to inquire of Colonel Putnam, Engineers.

12th. What works thrown up by the Enemy at what distance & what posts they had taken.

Agreed—to enquire of Engineers & other proper Officers.

13th. What Orders by the Commanding Officer directing & regulating the Retreat, the manner in which the Retreat was conducted, what care taken of the Sick.

Agreed to enquire of Feild Officers & others.

14th. Were any Continental Troops & what number at Albany or in the Neighborhood, how long they had been there & why not ordered to Ticonderoga.

Agreed—Enquire of the Adjutant general, his deputy, also of General Officers.

15th. The number & size of the Cannon—Were any removed before evacuating the Posts? The qnty & species of Military Stores? were the Troops furnished with Bayonets? were there Pikes & Spears & what number proper for defending Lines?

Agreed—Enquire of Engineers, of Officers of Artillery, Commissary of Military Stores, Colonels & others.

Agreed to send Copies of the Resolve to the Governor of Connecticut, Councils of Massachusetts & New Hampshire & to Governor Clinton of N. York.[6]

MS (ViU). In the hand of Henry Laurens.

[1] This document represents the work of two committees of which Laurens was a member—the committee appointed on August 1 to determine the mode of investigating the evacuation of Ticonderoga and Mount Independence and the committee appointed on August 28 to carry out this investigation. The numbered sections of this document summarize the points of inquiry set forth in a report by the first committee that was written by Laurens and approved by Congress on August 27. Those prefaced by "Agreed" are decisions concerning how the second committee planned to answer the questions raised by the first committee. Although this document is clearly dated August 27, it was probably not written before August 28, the day the second committee was appointed. *JCC*, 8:681–86, 688. For a fuller discussion of the work of these two committees, see John Hancock to Arthur St. Clair and Philip Schuyler, August 5, 1777, note.

[2] That is, "enquire of the Commissary Military Stores, for Provision, of the Commissary of Purchases."

[3] George Measam, commissary of clothing for the northern department.

[4] Clothier General James Mease.

[5] MS damaged; last two words supplied from *JCC*, 8:685.

[6] See Committee of Congress to Meshech Weare, September 4, 1777.

Henry Laurens to Solomon Legare

Dear Sir,   27th August 1777

The Carolina News papers had announced my loss by the Sudden death of our late friend Doctor Air some days before your favor of the 24th July came to hand. The first Stroke affected me deeply, I felt myself marked again by a Shadow, but from the frequent alarms which have been repeated in my history by Similar disappointments

I have learned that all events are directed by Supreme Wisdom &
from that persuasion I would not hesitate, even in the gush of irresistible Tears, to acknowledge, "Whatever is is best."

I wish it was in my power to join other friends in Offices of consolation to the distressed Widow, the big tear which at this Instant over-
flows each Eye, Sympathises in her complaints, but at this distance I
can offer nothing but wishes that She may Submit with Christian
fortitude to the desire of providence & learn betimes to Say, "Thy Will
be done."

I had paid so little attention to my own affairs for a long time before
the public commanded me upon this unreasonable Service, that I cannot remember particular accounts. My Books & papers were carried
to my Mepkin Plantation where I had intended to have devoted three
or four days to the Service of arrangement, but I was soon convinced
my hopes were ill founded, therefore I huddled them into Trunks con-
fiding in providence for a future opportunity. In this State of the Case
I cannot recollect the Amount of Mr. Air's debt. There is a Bond for a
much larger Sum than he owes me. It was taken in that Style, when
we were in England in order to include such Sums as he might be
Supplied with on my Account after I should leave that Kingdom. I
impressed the advice of frugality upon his mind for his own Sake, &
when we arrived in Carolina I had the Satisfaction to find he had paid
proper attention to my Sentiments, for he had room enough under my
indulgence to have used Several, perhaps four or five hundred pounds
Sterling more. As I remember, his Balance to me was between fifteen
hundred & two thousand pounds Currency out of which he had a right
to a considerable deduction for his Accounts of Medicine &ca; the
real Balance therefore cannot be great. Be that as it may, I request
you to take upon you the trouble of the Administration of his Estate
& when please God we meet my Account shall be adjusted in a manner
perfectly to your Satisfaction. If he had left a poor & friendless Widow
my Love for him would have prompted me to offers which would now
be improper. But if it shall appear that he has not left enough to pay
off all his engagements I shall not count any deficiency towards me a
loss. You now know my mind, & I know you to be an honest & good
Man, therefore act in the premises as you Shall judge proper.

You will have heard before this reaches you of the many extraordinary Movements of the Grand Army of our Enemy, which at
length have terminated so far as to effect a landing at the head of Elk
River, about 45 or 50 Miles from this place within the State of Maryland. General Washington with upwards of 12000 Continentals & an
innumerable hive of Militia are waiting their approaches. It seems
the long Voyage from New York to Chesepeak Bay had greatly hurt
their Cavalry, these are turned into Corn feilds & pastures to recruit &

when they are a little recovered the grand March for this City *may be* attempted, in the meantime they are Sustaining losses every day. We have already possession of 84 Soldiers & Sailors by Capture & desertion without the loss of a Man on our Side. Some of these assure us that the Navy & transports are not above half Manned & these very sickly & also that both Soldiers & Sailors are a tiptoe for desertion, they add that many more than these 84 had deserted but had taken different routes into Maryland & Virginia.

'Tis reasonable from many circumstances to beleive Mr. Howe would not have attempted his present Seeming plan if he had not been amused by that fop Burgoyne with hopes of being joined by his "retired Arm" of which he [. . .] boasts in his proclamation. The Checks which that Braggadocia has already received will stop his Career. He will be fortunate even if he can tread back his Steps with half his Troops & cross the Lakes again. You will learn many particulars from the News papers which I shall put under Cover with this. One would naturally ask why did we Suffer Burgoyne to come so far, if 'tis in our power to drive him back, it certainly was in our power to have hindred his advances? This is very true, but it is equally & lamentably true that people on this side are all too eagerly scrambling for the fruit before they have effectually secured the property of the Orchard. Every Body bent upon making Money by every possible practice, & those who ought to be watchful & attentive to public Safety will not act but upon the Spur of occasion. The evacuation of Ticonderoga in the manner & at the time of the Act was shameful. I spent some hours last Night in examining papers relative to that Incident which prove to me that our Guardians had been all Nodding—the Commander in Chief of the Northern department absent from the post of Duty, present they say at his own Farms & Estates—the Commanding Officer at the post so totally inapprehensive of danger he had not made one disposition for removing the Military & other Stores, nor the Sick, untill the very hour of retreat—which in that extremity resembled the most precipitate flight & was consequently followed by a very heavy loss—all our Cannon & Stores & not a few Lives.

I wish I could even excuse Congress from a share of general blame. But to do them justice they must participate. They were lulled by misplaced confidence & that kind of timidity which makes Men too often neglect their most important duties through fear of offending popular Men. However although I would no more excuse any who were the means of losing that important post because good consequences may & are likely to spring from their neglect or misconduct than I do Judas because he was an Instrument in the work of Redemption, yet I begin to see in a new instance that whatever is is best. Our apparent Loss will be our gain. We shall probably ruin Burgoyne's

Army & contend with Mr. Howe's at much less risque than we could have done if the two had united in any part of the Jerseys or on the Pennsylvania Shore any where within the Capes of Delaware. Mr. Burgoyne's ill success will damp Mr. Howe & I hope in a few Weeks you will learn that these blustering Heroes have ended the Campaign by escaping with fragments of their pretended omnipotency.

The present hour is teeming with the fate of our Union. Thank God, notwithstanding some things in the Cabinet as in the field, look unto-ward, I feel confident of a happy event. You must expect in Carolina a brush from the tail of this Comet & should be upon guard. Dear Sir, I repeat my good wishes to yourself & Daughters & am with great regard &ca.[1]

LB (ScHi). Addressed: "Solomon Legare Charles Town."
[1] Laurens' letter books also contain copies of two routine letters he drafted on August 25 and 26. The former, directed to his brother James, consisted simply of instructions to draw on his account for £150 to the order of William Stepple; the latter, to South Carolina merchant and planter John McQueen, explains the expenses he had incurred in looking after "Your Man Martin" during Martin's recent brief stay in Philadelphia. Laurens Papers, ScHi.

Marine Committee to James Maxwell and Paul Loyall

Gentlemen   August 27th. 1777
The Honorable the Marine Committee has ordered me to com-municate their apprehensions for the safety of the Frigates now building by you for the Continental service,[1] should the enemy attempt to destroy them on their return or during their continuance in Chesapeake Bay. They request that you will give your opinion on this head, and should you think it Necessary to form any plan for the preservation of those Vessels wherein their interposition or assistance will be required please to inform them thereof.

I am Gentlemen, Your obedient Servant, By order of the Committee,
John Brown Secy

LB (DNA: PCC Miscellaneous Papers, Marine Committee Letter Book).
[1] Maxwell and Loyall had been appointed in January to superintend the con-struction of two Continental frigates at Gosport, Va. Morgan, *Naval Documents*, 7:1065–66.

Robert Morris to George Washington

Dear Sir   Philada. August 27th. 1777
I cannot withstand the solicitations of Monsr. Epiniers the nephew

of Monsr. Beaumarchais (whose Services to America I fancy you are not unacquainted with), but take the liberty to introduce this Young Gentn. to your Excellencys patronage & protection. He has just obtained from Congress a Captains Commission, and seems to possess an Active Mind with a large fund of Good Nature that will not fail to recommend him to those who have an opportunity of observing his Conduct.[1] I shou'd be very unwilling to trouble you on any occasion but the present is indispensible. I have the honor to remain, Your Excellencys Most obedt. & very hble servt.   Robt Morris

RC (DLC).
[1] For the August 21 resolve granting a captain's commission to Augustin F. Des Epiniers, see *JCC,* 8:663.

John Adams to Abigail Adams

Philadelphia August 29. 1777
My dearest Friend   Fryday
    The Newspapers enclosed, will give you, all the Intelligence, of any Consequence.
    General Washington with a very numerous Army, is between Wilmington and the Head of Elke. How will make but a pitifull Figure. The Militia of four States, are turning out, with much Alacrity, and chearfull Spirits. The Continental Army, under Washington, Sullivan and Nash, besides is in my Opinion more numerous, by several Thousands, than Howes whole Force. I am afraid that He will be frightened and run on board his ships and go away, plundering, to some other Place.
    I almost wish he had Philadelphia, for then he could not get away. I really think it would be the best Policy to retreat before him, and let him into this Snare, where his Army must be ruined. However this Policy will not be adopted.
    In a Letter from good Authority, Mr. Paca, we are informed that many dead Horses have been driven on the Eastern shore of Maryland. —Horses thrown overboard, from the Fleet, no doubt.
    Price current. £4 a Week for Board, besides finding your own Washing, shaving, Candles, Liquors, Pipes, Tobacco, Wood &c. Thirty shillings a Week for a servant. It ought to be 30s. for the Gentleman and £4 for the servant, because he generally eats twice as much and makes twice as much trouble.
    Shoes five Dollars a Pair. Salt, 27 dollars a Bushell. Butter 10s. a Pound. Punch twenty shillings a Bowl.
    All the old Women and young Children are gone down to the Jersey shore to make Salt. Salt Water is boiling all around the Coast, and I

hope it will increase. For it is nothing but heedlessness, and shift-lessness that prevents Us from making Salt enough for a Supply. But Necessity will bring Us to it.

As to sugar, Molasses, Rum &c. We must leave them off. Whisky is used here instead of Rum, and I dont see but it is just as good. Of this, the Wheat and Rye Countries can easily distill enough, for the Use of the Country.

If I could get Cyder, I would be content.

The Business of the Continent has been in so critical and dangerous a situation for the last 12 Months, that it was necessary the Massachusetts should have a full Representation, but the Expences of living are grown so enormous, that I believe it will be necessary to reduce the Number of Delegates to three after this Campaign is over.

RC (MHi). Adams, *Family Correspondence* (Butterfield), 2:332–33.

Samuel Adams to Samuel P. Savage

My dear sir   Philade. Augt 29 1777

I have stepped aside to write you this Letter. It will be deliverd to you by Daniel Clymer Esq, who is warmly attached to our great Cause. He is besides Nephew to General Roberdeau whose Character is well known to the Publick. Your friendly Notice of Mr Clymer & Introducing him into the Circle of your Acquaintance will much oblige me. He tells me he has some Effects in Boston which he wishes to transport out of the State of M.B. If you can assist him consistently with the Law you will add to the favor.[1] I am with Respect to our Friends very affectionately yours,   S Adams

RC (MHi).
[1] Daniel Clymer (1748–1810), was a lieutenant colonel in the Philadelphia Associators, 1775–76, and in 1778 was appointed deputy commissary general of prisoners. "Clymer Family Genealogy," *PMHB* 9 (July 1885): 353–55; and "Letters and Documents from the 'Clymer Papers'," *PMHB* 31 (January 1907): 43–47. This day James Lovell also wrote a letter of introduction for Clymer to the Massachusetts Board of War, of which Savage was chairman. Board of War, vol. 152, M–Ar.

Eliphalet Dyer to Samuel Gray

Dear Kinsman   Philadelphia August 29th 1777

I have wrote you two or 3 times since my Arrival here.[1] I have Informed you of your Appointment as a Deputy Commissy Genl of

Issues (supposed for the Eastern department).[2] I sent you a printed Copy of the New Regulations in the Commisy Department tho the sad Wages are since raised, yours to 100 doll per month, your Deputy I think 75. You have the sole Appointment of all who are to Act under you in the Various posts Eastward of Hudsons River. There will be one or two wanted at Providence & near there. Mr. Phillips who used to Act under Mr Trumbull suppose will not Act. Mr. Stelle of Providence (who Married Huldah Crawford) is now here. Came to see the Commissy Genll Trumbull but missed of him in his way. He tells me he has Acted Under Mr Phillips is used to the business. I know him to be a Gentn of Carracter & fidelity. I can heartily recommend him for your appointment as one of your Deputys if he Inclines which suppose he will as it will be About his Home. I should like to have Oliver that way if there wants another, that is if he Chooses it unless there is some post in Connecticut you can place him at. I hope John White will be provided for at some proper place for him. I wish you would write to me, I think you have been a little Negligent in not writing me. I begin to fear you have not received mine. The post comes from your quarter every week. I sent you one to the care of Majr Gray. I wish you would let me hear from Oliver. From your loving Kinsman,   Elipht Dyer

[*P.S.*] Mr Stelle can acquaint you with News this way, have not time to add.

RC (NhD).
   [1] Not found.
   [2] Dyer's brother-in-law Samuel Gray (d. 1787) served as Windham, Conn., town clerk and treasurer, 1755–86, and had been performing commissary functions in Connecticut for some time before he was elected deputy commissary general of issues for the eastern department on August 6. Ellen D. Larned, *History of Windham County, Connecticut,* 2 vols. (Worcester, Mass: C. Hamilton, 1874–80) 2:47, 186, 213, 227; *A Historical Collection, from Official Records, Files, &c., of the Part Sustained by Connecticut, during the War of the Revolution,* comp. Royal R. Hinman (Hartford: E. Gleason, 1842), pp. 410, 413, 432, 439; and *JCC,* 8:617.

James Lovell to Abigail Adams

Dear Madam   Philada: Augst. 29th. 1777
   It is probable that Genl. Howe will waste the fall of this year between Chesapeak Bay and Delaware River. I send you a copied sketch of part of the country to which the Gazettes will frequently refer;[1] as I know You give singular attention to the interesting concerns of America in the present struggle.

This knowledge is only part of the foundation of my affectionate esteem of you. Nor will I mention the whole.

I shall rather apologize for what there is already of Gallantry in my manner of conveying this little Present to your hand.

I could, it is true, have delivered it to your Husband. But, I could not with delicacy have told him, *to his face,* that your having given your heart to *such* a man is what, most of all, makes me yours, in the manner I have above sincerely professed myself to be.

James Lovell

RC (MHi). Adams, *Family Correspondence* (Butterfield), 2:333.
[1] For this manuscript map in Lovell's hand, see ibid., illustration 9, following p. 262.

Robert Morris to Matthew Irwin

Sir   Philada. August 29th. 1777
Mr. Lawrison informs me that you are like to disapoint him of the money he came after notwithstanding the long time he has waited & the heavy expence of his journey. I apprehend you have no doubt of Mr Watson being in advance & if so I think you shou'd certainly send him some money to relieve his present wants & I am confident if you apply at the Treasury Board & represent that an advance is necessary to support the Public Credit they will not let you want. Mr Watson is strongly recommended to me by Colo Hooe in whom I place the most unlimited Confidence & you may shew this note at the Treasury if you think fit.[1] I am sir, Your Obedt Servt.   Robt Morris

RC (PHi).
[1] Congress advanced $50,000 to Commissary of Purchases Matthew Irwin on September 1, "to discharge contracts he is engaged in for provisions," but it is not known whether that advance pertained to the recommendation Morris made to Irwin in this letter. See *JCC*, 8:702.

John Adams to Abigail Adams

Philadelphia August 30th: 1777

My Friend   Saturday
A Letter from General Washington, was received last Night by the President, which I read. It is dated the 29th Yesterday.[1]

The Enemy are in Possession of the Head of Elke, a little Town, at the Head of the River Elke, in which they found a Quantity of Corn and Oats, belonging to the States. Waggons were so universally taken up, in conveying away the valuable Effects of the Inhabitants, that none could be procured to transport this Grain. Part of their Army, is advanced to Grays Hill about two Miles from the Head of Elke, but whether to take Post there, or only to cover while they remove their Plunder, from the Head of Elke is uncertain.

Our Army is at Wilmington. We have many Officers out reconnoitring the Country and the Enemy. Our Scouting Parties have taken between Thirty and Forty Prisoners, and Twelve Deserters are come in from the Fleet and Eight from the Army.

They say the Men are generally healthy, but their Horses have suffered much by the Voyage.

These Prisoners and Deserters are unable to give any other Intelligence. The Enemy give out, that they are Eighteen Thousand strong. But these are like Burgoines "Make Believes" and "Insinuations." We know better; and that they have not Ten Thousands.

The Militia from four States are joining General Washington, in large Numbers.

The Plan of their military Operations, this Campaign, is well calculated for our Advantage. I hope We shall have heads and Hearts to improve it.

For my own Part, I feel a secret Wish, that they might get into this City, because I think it more for our Interest that they should be cooped up here than that they should run away again to N. York. But according to present Appearances they will not be able to get here. By going into Cheasapeak Bay, they have betrayed a Dread of the Fire Works in the River Delaware, which indeed are formidable. They must make the most of their Time, for, They cannot rationally depend upon so fine a Season, late in the fall, and Early in Winter, as they had the last Year. September, October, and November are all that remain.

We expect Hourly, Advices from Gates and Arnold. We have Rumours of an Expedition to Long Island under Parsons, and another to Staten Island, under Sullivan, but no regular Accounts. I suppose it certain that such Expeditions have been made, but know not the success.

RC (MHi). Adams, *Family Correspondence* (Butterfield), 2:333-34.
¹ See *JCC*, 8:697.

Samuel Chase to Thomas Johnson

Dear Sir.   Philada. Augst. 30th. 1777.

By Letters from Gen. Washington of yesterday we are informed that the Enemies advanced Body, supposed 2,000, are about two Miles on this Side the Head of Elk. We have taken 20 prisoners and 14 Deserters. We hear Colo. Hollingsworth is slightly wounded thro' the Cheek. We have lost some Stores at the Head of Elk, about 10, or 12,000 Bushells of Corn. Private property to a considerable amount was removed in Time. General Smallwood and Colonel Gist passed thro' this City yesterday, one to the western, and the other to the Eastern Shore. I am in Hopes they will be of Service. Colo. Gist is very desirous You could send him, one, if possible two field Pieces, and a proper Number of Artillerists and officers.

I am strongly impressed with an opinion that Mr. Howe will not detach any of his forces either to Annapolis or Baltimore, before he either is checked, or succeeds against Genl. Washington. I do not beleive he has above 12,000 effectives, & rather suspect his force does not exceed 10,000. It is not very improbable in either Event he will send a small force to possess himself of those Places. If he should find himself unable to penetrate to this City, he may think of wintering in our State.

Congress has recommended to Genl. Washington to send an Engineer and an Artillerist to our State, but I am informed by the General that he cannot spare any at present.[1]

We have no Intelligence from the North.

Major Powell is dead. Major Steward has gained great Credit.

My Compliments to the Gentlemen of the Council.

Your affectionate and Obedient Servant,   Saml Chase.

[*P.S.*] I had no Letter from you by the Post.

RC (NN).
[1] See *JCC*, 8:692. For Washington's response to Chase's August 25 request that he send an engineer to Baltimore, see Washington, *Writings* (Fitzpatrick), 9:138.

John Hancock to William Livingston

Sir,   Philada. Augt. 30th. 1777.

The Congress having received such Information of the Disaffection of the Quakers as to leave the Matter no longer doubtful, they have come to the enclosed Resolves recommending it to the different States forthwith to apprehend all Persons of that Society, and indeed all others, who have evidenced by their Conduct & Conversation a Disposition inimical to the Cause of America. It is also recommended to the different States to take Possession of the Records & Papers of the *Meeting of Sufferings* and that such Parts of them as are of a political Nature be transmitted to Congress.[1] I beg Leave to refer your Attention to the whole of the enclosed Resolves, and shall only add that the greatest Secrecy is highly necessary touching the Premisses. I have the Honour to be, with Respect, Sir, your most obed. & very hble Set.

J.H. Presid

LB (DNA: PCC, item 12A).

¹ On August 25 Gen. John Sullivan wrote a letter to President Hancock in which he enclosed "a Number of Important papers" which alleged "that the Quakers at their meetings Collected Intelligence & forwarded [it] to the Enemy." These "papers," which were found among some "Baggage" captured during Sullivan's recent raid on Staten Island, consisted of three items: an undated set of queries about the Continental Army, a July 28 intelligence report about its movements, and an August 19 "Information" from the "Spanktown Yearly Meeting" about General Howe's Chesapeake Bay landing and the location of Washington's and Sullivan's forces. The first two documents were of undetermined origin, but the third seemed to support Sullivan's contention that some Quakers were giving vital military intelligence to the British. Yet as contemporaries and later scholars have pointed out, there is good reason to believe that this document was a forgery. There is no evidence that a Quaker meeting was ever held in Spanktown, N.J., and Howe's August 25 landing in the Chesapeake could not have been known on August 19. Despite the fact that the Spanktown "Information" appears to be spurious, no one has been able to identify the person or persons responsible for the fabrication. See PCC, item 53, fols. 83–101, item 160, fol. 47; Sullivan, *Letters* (Hammond), 1:443–44; Thomas Gilpin, *Exiles in Virginia* . . . (Philadelphia: C. Sherman, 1848), pp. 36, 58; and Robert F. Oaks, "Philadelphians in Exile: The Problem of Loyalty during the American Revolution," *PMHB* 96 (July 1972): 302.

In Congress, on the other hand, Sullivan found a receptive audience for his charges against Quakers owing to the proximity of General Howe's army to Philadelphia and the disposition among many delegates to equate Quaker pacifism with disloyalty. Congress read Sullivan's August 25 letter and enclosures on the 28th and referred them to a committee of John Adams, William Duer, and Richard Henry Lee. Later that day the delegates approved a report hastily prepared by this committee, which charged that "a number of" Quakers were disaffected and likely to aid the British, called upon the Pennsylvania Executive Council to arrest eleven Quakers suspected of maintaining "a correspondence and connection highly prejudicial to the public safety," urged every state to apprehend "all persons . . . who have, in their general conduct and conversation, evidenced a disposition inimical to the cause of America," and recommended a seizure of the records of Quaker meetings. Interestingly enough, it did not cite Sullivan's enclosures, but shortly afterward Congress procured publication of them as well as several official Quaker statements urging Friends to remain true to their pacifistic principles. See *JCC*, 8:688–89, 694–95; and Gilpin, *Exiles in Virginia,* pp. 282–300.

Congress' resolves had immediate repercussions in Pennsylvania. On August 31 the executive council ordered the arrest of forty-one men thought to be "dangerous to the State," Quakers and non-Quakers alike, in consequence of which twenty-six, mostly Quakers, were confined without a hearing. Congress approved a proposal by the executive council on September 3 to remove them to Staunton, Va., though on the fifth it also advised the council that it would not object to the release of any of the prisoners who swore or affirmed loyalty to the state. Few prisoners took advantage of this concession, however, and most demanded a hearing before the council or Congress. Congress read a remonstrance from eight imprisoned Quakers on September 6 and asked the executive council to grant such hearings, but the council sternly replied that it had no time for niceties in the midst of the present military emergency. Therefore on September 8 Congress resolved that as "it would be improper for Congress to enter into any hearing of the remonstrants or the other prisoners . . . they being inhabitants of Pennsylvania . . . that . . . the said Council . . . order the immediate departure of such of the said prisoners as yet refuse to swear or affirm allegiance to the State of Pensylvania, to Staunton, in Virginia." As a result, twenty-two Philadelphians were exiled in Virginia until April 1778, without benefit of a judicial hearing and in consequence of suspected disloyalty, not because of any overt acts they had committed. See *JCC,* 8:707-8, 714, 718-19, 722-23; *Pa. Archives,* 1st ser. 5:574, 584, 586, 589, 593, 600-601, 603-5, 607-10; *Pa. Council Minutes,* 11:283-85, 287-97; and Oaks, "Philadelphians in Exile," pp. 303-25.

In regard to the transfer of the prisoners to Virginia, John Adams, in his capacity as chairman of the Board of War, wrote the following brief note on September 13 to the county lieutenant of Frederick County, Va.: "The Continental Board of War have directed me to communicate to you their consent, that the said prisoners be stopped at Winchester, and there accomodated according to instructions." Gilpin, *Exiles in Virginia,* pp. 161-62.

Finally, the prisoners who remained behind in Philadelphia caused fresh alarm among some delegates soon thereafter when Pennsylvania Chief Justice Thomas McKean issued writs of habeas corpus to twenty of them. These critics, who viewed former delegate McKean's action as particularly lamentable in view of the British advance on Philadelphia, prompted McKean to defend his conduct in the following September 19 letter to John Adams. "I am informed," McKean explained, "that some of the Members of Congress are dissatisfied with my allowing, as Chief-Justice of this State, writs of habeas corpus for twenty persons confined in the Free-masons Lodge in Philadelphia. Next to the approbation of a good conscience I esteem the good opinion of good men, and of my friends in particular. This occasions you, Sir, the trouble of reading the following brief account of that transaction, and the reasons for it, which, I flatter myself, will convince you of the propriety of my conduct, and, by your candid explanation, all others, who may not have had the same opportunities with you and me of studying & understanding the laws.

"The writs were applied for in form, agreeable to the directions of the statute of the 31 Car. 2 ch. 2; and the only authority for the confinement, that I saw, was the copy of a letter from the Vice Presidt. to Colo. Lewis Nicola. My situation was such, that I had not received a letter, nor seen a news-paper from Philadia. for a fortnight, nor could I learn any particulars respecting this affair from any one whom I met, excepting the two persons who brought the writs to me: they offered me a pamphlet written by the prisoners stating their case, which I refused to accept or read, saying, I shou'd determine upon the returns that should be made to the writs and nothing else.

"The habeas corpus Act forms a part of the Code of the Pennsylvania laws, and has been always justly esteemed the palladium of liberty. Before that statute the habeas corpus was considered to be a prerogative writ, and also a writ of *right* for the subjects; and if the King and his *whole* Council committed any subject, yet by the opinion of all the judges (in times when the rights of the people were not well ascertained nor sufficiently regarded) a habeas corpus ought to be *allowed and obeyed;* and the distinction taken was, that in such a case *upon the return* the prisoner was to be remanded, but if the commitment was by *part* of the Lords of the Council, he was to be bailed, if not for a legal cause he was to be discharged. I need not mention to you the many cases on this head on our books, had I any now to recur to. By the statute all discretionary power is taken away, and a penalty of £500 sterling imposed for a refusal of any judge in the vacation to allow the writ: so that if I had forgot the oath I had taken but a few days before, common prudence would have prevailed upon me not to have incurred the forfeiture of ten thousand pounds sterling, and also as a judge to have subjected myself to the just censure of the judicious and dispassionate; and the more especially when no injury could arise by returning the writs & bringing the parties before me, save a little delay, the expense being borne wholly by the prisoners, agreeable to the statute. If upon the return of the process I had shewn any partiality to the prisoners, or sought occasion to favor men inimical to a cause I have espoused with as much sincerity, and supported and will support with as much zeal, as any man in the Thirteen United States, then indeed I might have been deservedly blamed & stigmatized; but censure previous to this was, to say no more, premature and injudiciously bestowed. No Gentleman thought it amiss in the judge, who allowed the habeas corpa. for Ethan Allan & his fellow-prisoners upon the application of Mr. Wilks &c. Even the Ministry despotic as they were, did not complain of it, but evaded them by sending the prisoners out of reach. Fiat justitia, ruat calum, pleases me as a sentiment and faithful judges ought not to be subjected to unnecessary difficulties.

"I acquainted the Vice-President with every particular of what had happened by an Express sent for the purpose; enquired of him, if the ha. cor. act had been suspended, or was about being suspended, for a limited time; and requested, if an act had passed for that purpose, to favor me with an exemplified copy. I told him, that, in almost every war since the making the statute, the like had been done in England, and that it was now in fact done there. You know however the struggles in Parliament from time to time, whenever this has been moved by the Ministry. I could no more. On Tuesday, last a law was enacted for the purpose, a copy of which was made out under the proper seal, and delivered to my express the same day, which has relieved me from any farther difficulties. I am anxious notwithstanding that the virtuous should think *me* so, and must therefore beg leave to re-iterate my request, that you will be so kind on proper occasions to explain this matter. I know how apt many are to disapprove of proceedings that are disagreeable, without duly reflecting upon their propriety & necessity." Adams Family Papers, MHi.

McKean's defense doubtless was also prompted by the recent retaliation of the Pennsylvania Assembly, which on September 14 overturned McKean's writs and subsequently moved to suspend all such future writs emanating from the state supreme court. See Gail S. Rowe, *Thomas McKean, the Shaping of an American Republicanism* (Boulder: Colorado Associated University Press, 1978), p. 106.

Henry Laurens to John Wereat

Dear Sir,[1]   30th Augst 1777

I am much indebted for your friendly Letter of the 4th Ulto. which Mr. Donaldson delivered me three days ago. 'Tis true the present or the late measures in your State Seem untoward, but good Men must not therefore desert their posts, 'tis their duty through good Report & through evil Report to strive against the powerful Stream of popular error without uniting in party Spirit on either Side, & from a persuasion that the majority never mean to hurt themselves, labour by good examples & seasonable advice to lead them into a better way. We ought to look with the most watchful attention in order to discover if there be any, our most rooted Enemies blazing in the guise of enthusiastic patriotism. Such, when found out, are easily removed without blows. The prescription by one of the early Christians for marking out a vain Religionist, will apply extremely well in detecting a Sinister patriot, but we must not be too hasty in our conclusions. All Men are liable to Err, & often we see the best become dupes of their own policy. Our freind General McIntosh will remember my Sentiments upon his very favorite Constitution & acknowledge that the best Rules may not only lose their efficacy but even become pernicious perhaps destructive by misapplication. 'Tis more essential to know how to apply with advantage, than merely to know, I foresaw that a Stark-naked democracy which might have been in times of tranquility a happy form of Government in Pennsylvania, would be a rueful project for the conservation of a handful of Men of dissiminated affections & attachments within, engaged at the same time in a public & violent War which demanded the purest wisdom to contrive & the utmost vigour to execute means even for Self defence, & now with great grief & concern I learn of the bad effects. But for all this we must not dispair, we must not turn our backs & conclude that all is lost. Every honest Man, indeed every discreet Man who means to promote his own, as well as the welfare of the Community, when he discovers that neither Men nor measures have a tendency to that point will exercise all his powers to effect a happy Resolution. Perhaps after a little time even your present form of Government may be made happy. God forbid you should Sink under the present convulsions. Of all the Mad Schemes you have been pestered with that of uniting the opposite Shores of Savanna within one State appears to be most frantic & no doubt has been the provocative to that frenzy for indiscriminately mixing the best friends & most bitter Enemies of Georgia & attempting to rob the former of their unalienable property. Severe & unjust as the attack is upon me in that Incident I will not abate of my Zeal for the Interest & happiness of that branch of the thirteen United Independent States of America. I am of opinion that when the Ruling powers & people of Georgia in general have reflected on the evil consequences which must follow the execution of the "Act for opening a Land Office & for the better Settling & Strengthening the State" in its full extent they will hasten to make Such alterations & exemptions as justice & Sound policy shall dictate.[2] I can hardly indulge my Self in thinking it necessary to prompt them on this occasion, nevertheless that I may not be charged with remissness of Duty to my Country & to my Children I shall make a proper representation & every Suitable effort to deprecate greater evils.

I beleive Congress will interpose a recommendation if I ask for it. If

I do, my representation shall be in terms which will not dishonour Georgia nor its Government. I may seek & obtain redress to my Self & for others in Similar circumstances without attempting to obstruct any of those good effects which the Majority of the Legislature must have had in view when they framed the Law.

One circumstance which has Soured minds of your people is undoubtedly that in which the indiscreet Geo. McIntosh has had so great a Share.[3] As we are all friends I may venture to Speak voluntarily as well as freely to you. I cannot bring my Self to be Advocate for the transgressions, wittingly committed, even of a Brother. I have carefully read the printed Case of that unfortunate Gentleman & upon my honour from that very Paper he may be charged to have been wilfully highly Criminal. The testimonies which set forth his Zeal in promoting the general Association prove at the Same time the most flagrant violation of that Sacred band by his close, intimate & Interested connexions with Men who were not only Nonassociates but notorious Enemies to the Cause which America at the hazard of Life & fortune was Strugling to Support. If he was forward openly to keep Committees together in the part of the Country where he resided he has proved by the most favorable affidavits of Mr. Baillie & Mr. Demere that he was secretly counteracting & even Sapping their Resolutions. In a word I never will beleive a Man very chaste who delights in private meetings with harlots & debauchers & who affords means for promoting their Commerce although he Should produce a thousand witnesses of his constant repetition of the 7th Commandment at the regular Striking hours of a Town Clock. I shall attempt to open Georges Eyes that he may see his indiscretion that he may acknowledge it too, to his Countrymen & promise hereafter to take every opportunity to make atonement. The General[4] knows my Sentiments pretty clearly already on this Subject. If he had taken a wise part in the beginning, if he had not attempted to knock down Suspicions too well founded, much trouble might have been Saved. By misconduct this affair has become not only a party & family but a national quarrel & God only knows when & in what intent it will end. For his sake will we pretend to Love Mercy let us also deal justly. A transgression against our Associations against our Laws is a greater Crime than Housebreaking, & by a Man vested with public confidence is aggravated in proportion to its pernicious influence & effects. Let us in this day of tryal divest ourselves of partial affections, extend every warrantable kindness of humanity even to conquered Enemies but let us know no Man as a friend or a Brother who in the Strictest Sense of the term, falls Short of the Duty of friend & Brother. To Neutrals let our Love be neutral, our eyes & Ears attentive—to apostate Guardians, Chiefs & Trustees becoming severity should be exercised, they know that times of Civil War exclude the virtues of Charity & forgiveness &c &c. Sir I have written the impressions of my heart, a Heart which never deliberately consented to an uncharitable or Cruel Act, but which had ever fortitude enough to blame a criminal friend, without fearing consequences of resentment, & I have detained you so long on this painful topic because from that Source I am persuaded much of the Evil complained of in Georgia has Sprung. All may be rectified & made Smooth again by prudent & wise exertions on the part of those who have given offence to the public & furnished such Characters as you have depicted in the Sequal of your Letter with opportunities of figuring in the Language of public Spirit. For the Sake of a bleeding Country I hope the General will reflect on these circumstances in an hour of composure. If he does I am sure his good sense will prompt him to do what he must know will be right.

I will take the liberty of inclosing with this a few News papers. You will learn from them many particulars relative to the Belligerent powers in this Neighborhood. In general I may say & with much Satisfaction we are Stronger & the Enemy much weaker than the parties respectively were nine or even two Months ago. Our Army is better than ever it was, theirs is worse. Our finances are streched, theirs are broken to pieces. The present hour is big with the fate of America, the proximity of Armies within 50 Miles so. west & two hundred & fifty North East of this Center shew me that our grand dispute is drawn to an important Crisis. I feel confident it must be from an assurance which has never failed me that our Cause is good.

I remain with great truth, Dear Sir &ca.

LB (ScHi).

¹ John Wereat (1730–99), Savannah, Ga., merchant and conservative patriot leader, was a Continental prize agent in Georgia. George R. Lamplugh, " 'To Check and Discourage the Wicked and Designing': John Wereat and the Revolution in Georgia," *Georgia Historical Quarterly* 61 (Winter 1977): 295–307.

² Laurens owned extensive tracts of land in Georgia, and consequently he objected to this act because it contained a clause designed to deprive absentee landowners of their property in the state. On October 16, 1777, however, Joseph Clay, another of Laurens' Georgia correspondents, wrote and informed him that the Georgia legislature had recently repealed this offending clause. *Collections of the Georgia Historical Society* 8 (1913): 47–48.

³ The case of George McIntosh, who was accused of illegally trading with the British in East Florida, is discussed in John Hancock to Archibald Bulloch, January 8, 1777, note.

⁴ George McIntosh's brother, Gen. Lachlan McIntosh.

John Adams to William Gordon

Phil. Augt. 31, 1777.¹

The loss of Ty is in a train of serious enquiry. Altho' this disaster for the present is grievous, yet I think it has put Burgoyne into our power, and I hope he will not be suffered to slip out of it. Mr. Howe has planned his operations in such a manner, as to give us a vast advantage, both of him and Burgoyne. He is at the head of Elke about 55 miles from this city. Genl. Washington is at Wilmington, about 15 miles on this side of him, with a noble army of continental troops, and a large body of militia, which is constantly and rapidly increasing. Whether the General will be compelled to depart from his Fabian System or not time will discover. A general action, successful to us is destructive to them, and even if they should be successful and keep the field, they will loose so many men, as to be crippled after it. Whereas I think we should be able speedily to reinforce our army, notwithstanding the panic and consternation which would follow a defeat.

MS not found; reprinted from "Letters of the Reverend William Gordon, Historian of the American Revolution 1770–1799," *Proceedings of the Massachusetts Historical Society* 63 (June 1930): 364–65.
    1 William Gordon included this extract, which he identified as a letter from John Adams, in a letter to an unknown recipient. Ibid., pp. 360–65.

John Adams to Abigail Adams

My dear   Philadelphia September 1. 1777. Monday
    We have now run through the Summer, and altho the Weather is still warm, the fiercest of the Heats is over. And altho the extream Intemperance of the late Season has weakened and exhausted me, much, yet I think upon the whole I have got thro it, as well as upon any former Occasion.
    A Letter from General Washington, dated Saturday, informs that our light Parties have brought in four and twenty Prisoners, more.[1] So that the Prisoners and Deserters, since Mr. Howe landed is near an hundred.
    The Question now is, whether there will be a general Engagement? In the first Place I think, after all that has past it is not good Policy for Us to attack them unless We can get a favourable Advantage of them, in the Situation of the Ground, or an Opportunity to attack a Detachment of their Army, with superiour Numbers. It would be imprudent, perhaps for Us, with our whole Force to attack them with all theirs.
    But another Question arises, whether Mr. Howe will not be able to compell Us to a General Engagement? Perhaps he may: but I make a Question of it: Washington will maneuvre it with him, a good deal to avoid it. A General Engagement, in which Howe should be defeated, would be ruin to him. If We should be defeated, his Army would be crippled, and perhaps, We might suddenly reinforce our Army which he could not. However all that he could gain by a Victory would be the Possession of this Town which would be the worst Situation he could be

in, because it would employ his whole Force by Sea and Land to keep it, and the Command of the River.

Their principal Dependence is not upon their Arms, I believe so much, as upon the Failure of our Revenue. They think, they have taken such Measures, by circulating Counterfeit Bills, to depreciate the Currency, that it cannot hold its Credit longer than this Campaign. But they are mistaken.

We however must disappoint them, by renouncing all Luxuries, and by a severe Œconomy. General Washington setts a fine Example. He has banished Wine from his Table and entertains his Friends with Rum and Water. This is much to the Honour of his Wisdom, his Policy, and his Patriotism, and the Example must be followed, by banishing sugar, and all imported Articles, from all our Families. If Necessity should reduce Us to a Simplicity of Dress, and Diet, becoming Republicans, it would be an happy and a glorious Necessity.

Yours—Yours—Yours.

RC (MHi). Adams, *Family Correspondence* (Butterfield), 2:335–36.

¹ General Washington's August 30 letter to President Hancock was read in Congress this day. *JCC*, 8:699; and Washington, *Writings* (Fitzpatrick), 9:148.

Eliphalet Dyer to Samuel Gray

Dear brother   Philadelphia Septr. 1st 1777

Received your kind favour of the 19th this day and trust before now you have receivd my second Inclosing one to Mr Wales & some to my family. Am rejoiced to hear my son Thos is on the mending hand, Amelia recovered and the rest in health. May a kind Providence still protect them. You must every so Unwilling be Oblidged to hear of Genll How once more. He is at length appeard up Cheesepeek Bay landed his Army at the head of the river Elk about 50 miles from this City not so well of it to appearance even for this City as he was at Brunswick for Genll Washington is within about 14 miles this side of him with an army of about 20 thousand men Including Militia who flock in to him on this Occasion. Providence has seemed to give a favourable turn in our Affairs to the Northward which hope will be most gratefully Acknowledged. Every thing at present looks favourable this way but all our dependence must be on the same kind Providence for Success which God Grant. Be so good as to write me as often as you can & let me hear a little about affairs at home. Does the house goe on over the River or Stand still. These matters I know are of but little Concern compared with the whole but one at a distance wants to hear. Tell our folks to make as much Cyder as possible, we have scarce any thing to drink here but Water. Board here now about £5 per week bare & spare, horse dollar a night, loaf sugar more than 20/ per lb, rum 50 &c &c & rising but hope matters may soon take a turn for the better. My love to Sister, my wife & family, Mr White & Sister & am yours,   Elipht Dyer

RC (ICHi).

Eliphalet Dyer to Jonathan Trumbull, Sr.

Sir   Philadelphia Septr 1st 1777
    Since our last[1] when we Informed you Genll How had landed his Army at the head of Elk the Enemy have made but little progress and have extended their Army but about 4 miles. Genll Washington has made his head quarters at Willmington about 14 miles from the Enemy. Genll Green about 4 miles advanced towards them with about 4000 men. The Militia of this Country are daily reinforcing Genll Washington and Are employed in harrassing Genll Hows partys which oblidge them to keep pretty close & Compact. It is supposed our Army now Consists of near Twenty thousand men under Genll Washington & Increasing, our parties have taken about a hundred since their Landing Including some deserters, the Enemy have lost a Considerable Number of their horses since they landed Nothing appears discouraging in this Quarter, if the Enemy Should Advance it would give us an Advantage of throwing a large body of Men in their rear. Appearances are favourable but Success is of the Lord, to whom we would Commit our Cause & hope for a prosperous issue. Congress are Deeply engaged in financiering in Contriving ways & means. All agree in taxing largely but that will not afford us Immediate supplies, France & Spain Offer to Lend us, will it do to borrow at least so much as to pay the Interest by bills drawn on our Commissioners there? Will that Induce our Continental bill holders to place their money in the Loan Offices as fast as we want it? Ought we or does policy require now our Streights are great for speedy Supplies that in order to obtain them we may be oblidgd to borrow on France & Spain sufficient to pay the Interest by Bills drawn in favour of our Lenders on our Commissioners there which will serve their Interest not only in Specie but payable in Europe whereby the great risque & Charge of Transportation is saved & will bring us Considerably in Debt to those foreign Powers. I ask does Justice or policy require we should put all the past Lenders & who have obtained their Certificates at 6 per Cent payable here in the same bills they put in on the same footing which will much Increase our Debt abroad & will not help at all in bringing in present money into the Loan offices. I know the old Lenders will say yea, but what will prudence & Impartial Common sense say. I hope we may Act with Discretion on these & other Important Subjects but advice once in a while would be Very refreshing.

Have the honor to be with the greatest Esteem, Your Honors Obedt
Humle Servt,   Elipht Dyer

[*P.S.*] My partners not present when I sign & seal up this letter.

RC (Ct).
¹ See Connecticut Delegates to Trumbull, August 25, 1777.

Elbridge Gerry to Joseph Gardoqui & Sons

My dear Sirs   Philadelphia 1st Sepr 1777
My last to You was dated the 1st July,¹ since wch. am favoured with
yours of the 27th April & 30th May per the Lydia, Capt. Willm.
Andrews, who is arrived at Portsmouth in New-Hamshire. I have delivered to the commercial Committee of Congress the Invoice of Goods
which You shipped by this Oppertunity, & have furnished them with an
Extract of your Letter relative to Remittances. I beleive they will find
a Difficulty in making Returns whilst the Coast continues to be so infested with British Ships of War previous to the Winter Season, but
must refer You to the Committee for further Information on this Head.
If the amount of these Cargoes is placed to my Acct. You will please
to credit me therefor, with the Invoices by Capt St Clair & Williamson
as heretofore requested.²
In the Bale No 6 per Capt Hodges, was 1 Ps of russia Duck more than
was charged in the Invoice, which is passed to your Credit in 270
[Rrtn?].³
Agreable to your Request, an Extract of your last Letter relative to
the Indulgence of your Court to Adventurers in the Article of Tobacco
is inserted in the publick prints.
When I wrote You last, We left General Howe at Amboy a Seaport
Town in the State of New Jersey, to which he retreated for the Security
of his Army. After he had there taken Post, & recovered from the
Fatigue & Confusion which generally attend a Retreat, several attempts
were made to surprize Part of General Washingtons Army, & to manœuvre
him out of the Strong Post which he possessed in that State, but these
proving unsuccessful induced General Howe to remove his Troops to
Staten Island, which is about 18 miles in Length, & lays on the Jersey
Shore extending from Amboy towards New York, & forming Part of the
Harbour of that City. Here he continued a few days & again embarked
his Troops on a secret Expedition, intending as was supposed for the
Delaware, or for the North River which leads up to the back Part of the
State of New York, against which General Burgoyne was bringing his
Army. About the 23d of July he sailed from New York Harbour, with a
Fleet of 280 Sail including Ships of War, appearing after a few Days

off Egg Harbour about half Way to the Capes of Delaware, & about the first of August at the Capes. General Washington in the Interim, leaving 4 or 5000 Men at the North River, marched about 12 or 14000 towards Philadelphia, where an equal number of the Militia were ordered to be in Readiness to join them; but to the Surprize of most people the Fleet again disappeared, and was not seen from the Land for three Weeks, when Information was sent from Virginia, that It appeared off their Capes, & in a few Days that the Whole Fleet had reached the Head of Cheesepeak Bay, which is about fifty Miles from hence. There General Howe has debarked his Troops, & General Washington with the Army aforesd, reinforced by the Militia, who voluntarily collect in Numbers far exceeding the Requisitions of Congress, has taken Post within six Miles of him, & is constantly harrassing him. What the Event will be, Time must determine, but I think We have not much Reason to be apprehensive, unless providence should remarkably frown on our Cause.

Philadelphia is evidently the Object of General Howe's Wishes, but this is vastly inadequate to the risque of marching from his shipping, since the Loss of it on our Side would not be much felt, & a Defeat on his would decide the Cause against him, & compell the whole of the British Troops to evacuate the Continent.

With Respect to General Burgoyne on the Western Frontiers, about the Beginning of July he made his approach to Tyonderoga, & to the Surprize of the whole Continent, Our *General Officers* in that Department at a Council of War determined to evacuate the Fort without firing a Gun, or securing or destroying the Stores & Baggage, notwithstanding they had 3000 effective Men in the Garrison, Plenty of Stores, & in ten or fifteen Days Time would have been reinforced with 6 or 8000 Men, if so many were necessary to raise the Seige. *Their* Conduct is highly resented, & a Court martial is ordered to [be] held on all the Generals aforesd.

By this Misconduct of four or five of our officers, General Burgoyne was flushed with Success, & published a pompous proclamation which being somewhat diverting is herewith inclosed.[4] This performance has answered the purpose of Amusement to our Wits, & of making the Author compleatly rediculous. He however thot the Country would be affected by it & pushed towards Albany (to which the North River is navigable for Transports) but has met with severe Checks, having lost at Fort Schuyler by a Sortie from the Fort about 300 Men, at Bennington about 900, & is now obliged to raise the Seige of the former. I sincerely hope that General Burgoyne whose Army does not exceed 6, or 7000 Men, will be hardy enough to attempt a March to Albany, as the Militia of the New England States who are ordered to oppose him, must be able to accomplish it with little Trouble. We have now a Number of Troops on that quarter equal to G. Burgoynes Army, & such large Reinforcements are ordered to General Gates who is an experienced officer

& has the Command there, that I fear Mr Burgoyne will be on the Retreat, before he can be brot to Action.

In Consequence of the Movement of General Howe to Cheesepeak Bay, I shall be glad if You will order one of the Salt Vessels (which I desired You to load for my Account), to Boston or any Port between that & Portsmouth, & the other to North Carolina consigned to Messr. Hughes & Smith of Edenton.

I remain Gentlemen with much Esteem, Your very hum Sert. E G.

N.B. In the publication of the Extract I have somewhat deviated from the *Letter,* but have endeavourd to retain the Speech of the Original.

Tr (British Museum, Additional Manuscripts 24322).

[1] Not found.

[2] On Gerry's complex business relations with Joseph Gardoqui & Sons, in both his private and public capacities, see George A. Billias, *Elbridge Gerry, Founding Father and Republican Statesman* (New York: McGraw-Hill Book Co., 1976), pp. 125–29.

[3] For complications arising from this shipment of "Russian Duck," see Gerry to James Warren, June 30, 1777.

[4] For Gen. John Burgoyne's June 20 proclamation, see Henry Laurens to John Lewis Gervais, August 17, 1777, note 5.

John Hancock to George Washington

Sir,   Philada. Septr. 1st. 1777.

Your several Favours to the 30th ulto. (inclusive) I have had the Honour of receiving in the Order of their Dates.

From the enclosed Resolves you will perceive, the Congress have appointed a Committee to collect and arrange the Evidence relative to the Evacuation of Ticonderoga, which will be afterwards transmitted to you, that a Court Martial may be thereupon instituted for the Trial of the general Officers who were in the Northern Department when the Evacuation took Place.[1]

The great Demand for Arms to equip the Militia who are called into Service, has induced the Congress to pass the enclosed Resolve, directing that a Number of Workmen (conversant in the Business of repairing Firelocks) should be immediately detached from the Militia to be employed in repairing the Arms in this City there being between two and three Thousand that in a short Time may be rendered fit for Use.[2]

I have the Pleasure to congratulate you on our farther Success in the Northern Department in raising the Seige of Fort Schuyler. The Enemy, on the Approach of Genl. Arnold, fled with the utmost Precipitation, leaving behind them their Tents, Ammunition, Provision, &c. As I forward herewith several Letters for you from that Quarter which

I make no Doubt contain an Account of the Matter, I beg Leave to refer you to them for further Particulars.[3]

I have the Honour to be, with the greatest Respect, Sir, your most obed & very hble Serv.   John Hancock Presidt

RC (DLC). In the hand of Jacob Rush and signed by Hancock.
[1] See *JCC,* 8:684–86; and Hancock to Arthur St. Clair and Philip Schuyler, August 5 ,1777.
[2] See *JCC,* 8:698.
[3] Gen. Horatio Gates' letters to Washington of August 25 and 28, 1777, as well as Gen. Benedict Arnold's August 24 letter to Gates, are in Washington Papers, DLC. See also Washington, *Writings* (Fitzpatrick), 9:154–55.

Henry Laurens to Lachlan McIntosh

Dear sir.   1st Septem 1777.

Since my last of the 11th Ulto. by Capt. Hornby our affairs in the Feild have acquired a more pleasing aspect. General Howe who we apprehended had been gone Eastward in order to form a junction with the foppish Burgoyne, has been floating round to Chesepeak Bay in a fleet of thirty Men of War & 280 Transport Vessels. The tediousness of his Voyage, hurt his Cavalry very much & 'tis not to be doubted that his Troops must also have suffered by sickness. About a Week ago he effected a Landing on the Banks of Elk River some 50 to 60 Miles distance from this spot upon which his Eye is fixed. The Horse were turned into Corn fields where many of them finished their Campaign by improper food. The Troops were stretching their Legs. Some of these also, perhaps upwards of ninety, have finished *their* Campaign, by Capture or voluntary desertion—among the latter about 15 seamen who unanimously report that the fleet is very sickly, not above half Manned, the Men exceedingly discontented & only waiting favorable opportunities to get off. General Washington at the head of a large well appointed Army 10 to 12 Thousand regulars, a fine train of Artillery & an uncertain but very numerous collection of Militia lie stretched along from Head Quarters at Wilmington to an encampment near the Enemy's Van watching & waiting for their motions. Our light Horse are employed in galling their flanks & seizing straglers in which they have been very successful. It appears to me this circuitous fetch by Mr. Howe must have been made in consequence of Burgoyne's rapid Entrance through the Country on this side Tyconderoga & in confidence of the "Stretch of his Arms" which he so much boasts of.[1] You will read in the News Papers our successes against that Brute who pays ten Dollars for the Scalp of an Infant. The Check which he has received will undoubtedly leave Mr. Howe to play all the future game in this Quarter without his Partner. This places us in a situation much less to be regretted than that which we should have been driven into, had the fop penetrated New York & approached this City through New Jersey. I am told he cannot attempt, even if he should escape across the Lakes, to bring his division round by Sea till the ensuing Year. Sir William Howe has published another kind invitation to Rebels to go in to him & accept Pardon.[2] This he styles a Declaration & the language is more Courtly than any of his former Addresses of that kind. Nevertheless I believe he will receive more blows than proselytes. Our People seem to be very much in earnest to fight & a good watch is kept on the few disaffected in the environs of the Enemy's Camp.

We are now at the Eve of a grand Crisis. Much blood will be spilled & possibly the fate of American Independence suspended or confirmed in the course of this Month. I feel confident of success persuaded that our Cause is good & that it cannot fail. Indeed the many false steps which have been taken by the mighty omnipotent British Generals, are enough to make every man on this side confident. However the event of War is uncertain. I am therefore not free from a suitable concern for our freinds.

Yesterday the Executive Council of this State caused divers persons chiefly of the people called Quakers to be seized & their Papers inspected. Among the suspected are Israel & John Pemberton & others of the most respectable people of that profession. The ground for this exertion of power is an information of correspondencies carried on between the Quakers & the Enemy. That information is supported by Papers which had been lately found at Staten Island & indeed by the very unfreindly declarations openly made by the Quakers in general. What or whether any discoveries have been made has not transpired.[3]

Governor Penn & Mr Chief Justice Chew who had been on Parol are both removed from this State into a remote part of Jersey.[4] The Powers here act as we too often do to the southward, upon the spur of the occasion. All these & many better things ought to have been done if necessary, with more deliberation & consequently with more decency.

Congress is now engaged in ways & means for filling an almost exhausted Treasury without repeating an Emission of Paper Dollars. The favorite scheme is that of borrowing from France, which I esteem the most destructive step we can take, so far as for all internal demands & will be to all intents & purposes a further emission of Paper Money, infinitely more detrimental in its consequences than the evil which is dreaded from a further Issue of Dollars. It may deprive us too of the use of so much Money as we shall want in France for the most important occasions to which Paper Dollars are inadequate. I have endeavoured to point out ways & means by which our Treasury might be filled without either of the modes abovementioned. Make the Conditions of your Loan more favorable I might say more equitable to Lenders, & practice that frugality & œconomy in Public & private affairs which was our boast in 1774 & from which particularly in Public Œconomy we have departed as widely as prodigality lies from discretion & virtue. This may employ a future hour between you & me. You will be astonished when you know all that may with too much truth be said upon the subject in one hour. At present be assured that affairs in the grand Circle are very unsatisfactory to every thinking disinterested Man. I judge so, because I not only feel my self dissatisfied but because I perceive a great majority are so, & hear them at different times acknowledge it. The cause *may be,* we begin to feel the weight of our grand contest & have not yet quite resolution enough to change our mode of living suitable to our circumstances. Luxury abounds here as it does in the more southern States & Luxury if we persevere in it will return us to dependence either upon Great Britain or transfer us to some less tolerable Master.

I now turn my attention to your favor of the 15 July which I received by the hands of Mr. Donaldson. The principal subject relative to your Brother Colo. George McIntosh is very affecting.[5] I have perused the printed Case according to your request with care & attention & I am sorry to tell you, he appears, from the most favorable representation in that State, to have acted, if not designedly a criminal part, yet a part extremely indiscreet & meritting Censure. This you may depend upon, it is the opinion of every person to whom I distributed that Paper, as far as I have learned, & you may almost infallibly rest assured it is the opinion of some who have not ventured to speak quite so plainly to you or him. I say this, alluding to one very particular Instance. The affidavits of Mr. Bailley & Mr. Demere which set forth strong appearances of Mr McIntosh's attachment to the American Cause, at the same time prove his close connexion with the declared inveterate Enemies of that *Cause* & this is confirmed by himself. Had this connexion been confined to common Civilities & innocent intercourse those disputes which our friend maintained in support of the Cause which he had espoused, might have been produced as evidence in his favour, but when it extended to *Partnership in exportation* & the management of the Voyage left to a Man who was notoriously a violater of the American Associations & a known fugitive from a Neighbouring State, suspicion lies hard against him, & rather gains strength from the Circumstance of Mr McIntosh's clearing the Vessel for Surinam. To judge charitably your Brother gave way to temptation & to say the least, acted very indiscreetly. He seems to have been in the class of those who wished the American Cause very well, but not *so well,* as to make any sacrifice of his Interest in order to promote its welfare, & I remember to have heard you declare your sentiments to this effect about a Month before the unlucky transaction which has occasion'd him & his friends so much trouble. I think he has severely smarted for his folly, for I am persuaded there was no Criminal design. I shall as soon as he recovers from the Small Pox speak in the most friendly terms to him upon this business & every thing that my own honour & my allegiance will warrant I will do for restoring him to his family & I think it will be in his own power to restore himself to the favour & protection of his Country.

I must take every method in my power to shield my property in Georgia against the attacks of violence. I think however your Assembly upon reflection will before the 12 December either repeal or make such an explanation of the Act of Assembly which I suppose you allude to as will distinguish friends from Enemies.[6]

My good wishes attend Mrs. McIntosh & your whole family. I hope soon to take you by the hand & to assure you by every respectful & friendly Office how truly I am, Dear sir, Your most obedt servt.

Henry Laurens

RC (ScHi). LB (ScHi).

[1] See Laurens to John Lewis Gervais, August 17, 1777, note 5.

[2] General Howe issued this proclamation on August 27, and Congress officially received a copy of it from Washington on September 2. See *JCC,* 8:703; Washington, *Writings* (Fitzpatrick), 9:152n.25; and Roger P. Bristol, *Supplement to Charles Evans' American Bibliography* (Charlottesville: University Press of Virginia, 1970), item B4477.

[3] See John Hancock to William Livingston, August 30, 1777, note.

[4] See Laurens to John Rutledge, August 12, 1777, note 10.

[5] See John Hancock to Archibald Bulloch, January 8, 1777, note.

[6] See Laurens to John Wereat, August 30, 1777, note 2.

John Adams to Abigail Adams

My dear Friend   Philadelphia Tuesday September 2. 1777

I had Yesterday the Pleasure of yours of   [1] from Boston, and am happy to find that you have been able to do so well, amidst all your Difficulties. There is but one Course for Us to take and that is to renounce the Use of all foreign Commodities. For my own Part I never lived in my whole Life, so meanly and poorly as I do now, and yet my Constituents will growl at my Extravagance. Happy should I be indeed if I could share with you, in the Produce of your little Farm. Milk and Apples and Pork and Beef, and the Fruits of the Garden would be Luxury to me.

We had nothing Yesterday from the General. Howes Army are in a very unwholesome Situation. Their Water is very bad and brackish, there are frequent Morning and Evening Fogs, which produce Intermittent Fevers in Abundance. Washington has a great Body of Militia assembled and assembling, in Addition to a grand Continental Army. Whether he will strike or not, I cant say. He is very prudent, you know, and will not unnecessarily hazard his Army. By my own inward

Feelings, I judge, I should put more to risque if I were in his shoes. But perhaps he is right.

Gansevoort has proved, that it is possible to hold a Post. Harkermer has shewn that it is possible to fight Indians, and Stark has proved that it is practicable, even to attack Lines and Posts, with Militia. I wish the Continental Army would prove, that any Thing can be done. But this is sedition at least. I am weary however, I own, with so much Insipidity.

St. Ledger and his Party have run away. So will Burgoine. I wish Stark had the Supream Command in the Northern Department. I am sick of Fabian Systems in all Quarters. The Officers drink a long and moderate War. My Toast is a short and violent War. They would call me mad and rash &c. but I know better. I am as cool as any of them and cooler too, for my Mind is not inflamed with Fear nor Anger, whereas I believe theirs are with both. If this Letter should be intercepted and published, it would do as much good, as another did two Years ago.

Adieu.

RC (MHi). Adams, *Family Correspondence* (Butterfield), 2:336–37.
[1] Blank in MS, but Adams is answering Abigail's letter of August 22, 1777. Ibid., pp. 323–24.

Samuel Adams to Henry Bromfield

My dear Sir[1]   Philada Sept. 2, 1777.

I am requested by a Member of Congress from South Carolina for whom I have a particular Regard, to introduce his Friend Mr Henry Crouch to some of my Boston Friends. He is a Merchant of Charlestown and will set off on a Visit your Way tomorrow. I take the Liberty of addressing a Letter to you by him. Your friendly Notice of him will greatly oblige me.

I heartily congratulate you on the happy Change of our Affairs at the Northward. The Feelings of a Man of Burgoyne's Vanity must be sorely touched by this Disappointment.

Howe's Army remains near where they first landed and is supposed to be ten thousand fit for Duty. Washington's Army exceeds that Number, is in health & high Spirits, and the Militia have joynd in great Numbers, well equip'd and ambitious to emulate the Valor of their Eastern Brethren. Our light Troops are continually harrassing the Enemy. The Day before yesterday they attack'd their out Posts & drove them in, killing & wounding a small Number. By the last Account we had taken about seventy Prisoners without any Loss on our side. Our Affairs are at this Moment very serious and critical. We are contending

for the Rights of our Country and Mankind—May the Confidence of
America be placed in the God of Armies! Please to pay my due
Respects to my old Friend Mr Phillips & his Family and be assured that
I am very cordially, Yours,

MS not found; reprinted from Adams, *Writings* (Cushing), 3:410–11.
[1] Henry Bromfield (1727–1820) was a prominent Boston merchant.

Thomas Burke to Richard Caswell

Dr Sir   Philadelphia Septr 2d 1777
The inclosed paper will give you all the public intelligence since my
last. The complexion of affairs is not yet become so determined that I
can set off for home; but I am in daily expectations of some events
which may determine my resolutions to that purpose.
Our finances have long engaged our attention in Congress, but we
have not yet come to any conclusive Resolutions thereon. The subject is
of the greatest importance, and truly too great for our talents. One
thing every one seems clear in, that Taxation in a very liberal degree
must take place. This, Sir, is so necessary that it must at all events be
attempted every where. The quantity of money in circulation, and its
consequent depreciation, and the accumulating debt of the public makes
it inevitably necessary. I fear the system under consideration will not
be so far mature before my departure that I can carry it with me, or
know how to apply my endeavours at home to the perfection of it. I
shall however make myself as much master as possible of the prevailing
opinions thereon.
You will find by the intelligence that our affairs every where bear a
promising aspect. I have the most sanguine hopes that this campaign
will give a severe blow to the British arms; and I even look forward to
an end of the war, much sooner than has hitherto appeared probable.
I have, Sir, troubled you too long in this Letter, and shall only add
that, I have the honor to be with the greatest respect & regard your
very obedt, hum. Sr,   Thos Burke

Tr (Nc–Ar).

Samuel Chase to Thomas Johnson

Dear Sir,   Philada. Septr. 2nd. 1777.
I am favoured with your Letter of the 30 of August, this Morning.
Our Intelligence from the North are very agreeable. The Enemy re-
main inactive in the same Situation as I mentioned in my last. An ad-

William Howe

vanced Body of about 2,000 are a little on this Side the Head of Elk—their main Body lies a little to the South of Elk River. Genl. Washington has detached 1000 light Troops to watch Mr. Howes Motions and to annoy them as much as possible. Our Army is encamped on the Heights about Wilmington. Lines & small Redoubts are making in our Front. Sullivane's Division, about 1400 effectives, will join the main Army this Day. The Militia of this and the Delaware State turn out very generally, but Complaint for arms is universal. I hope Genl. Smallwood will be agreeable to the western Shore, and Colonel Gist to the Eastern Shore Militia. If Congress should be blamed, I must take a considerable Share of the Censure. I thought Mr. Smallwood had some personal Influence, & I know no officer in our State equal to him. I beleive Colo. Richardsons Battalion will be ordered to join the Eastern Shore Militia. I submit to you the Propriety of ordering about 100 Militia to Jacob Giles or thereabouts to prevent the Enemy from sending small Parties to plunder.

I have just seen Genl. Howes Procla. of the 27th of Augst., inclosed by Gen. W. to Mr. Hancock, & will if possible procure & send You a Copy.[1] He offers Pardon to all Inhabitants of Delaware, Pennsylvania, and *the Eastern Shore Counties* of Maryland, who will surrender themselves to any Detachment of his army, & that he will hereafter make known the Day after which his gracious favor shall cease. He denounces Vengeance against all found in Arms, and promises Protection to all who remain quiet & peaceable. He excepts from his Pardon all who have acted in the legislative & judicial authority of the new Government. He acquaints the Inhabitants that his army is under the strictest Discipline; & yet an affidavit is sent to Congress of a most violent attempt by some of his Troops to ravish a Girl of Credit & Family. I wish to see it published in our Paper and in Hand-Bills & dispersed in every Part of our State, with observations & Remarks. No faith, no Confidence can be placed in any promises of the Nation of Britain or any of her Generals. Genl. Howe & Burgoyne promised protection, & plundered both Friends & foes. The Jersies & N. York are melancholy p[laces]. There has been a little Skirmish yes[ter]day—one officer & two or three privates killed of the Enemy, & one of ours wounded. I have got the proclamation & leave off to copy it.

Compliments to the Council & all Friends. Your affectionate & obedt Servt,   S. Chase

[*P.S.*] It is said Mr. Alexander remained on his planta. & that Harry Peaca is gone to the Enemy.

RC (MdFreHi).
[1] See Henry Laurens to Lachlan McIntosh, September 1, 1777, note 2.

Committee of Intelligence to George Washington

Sir,   Philadelphia 2d Septr. 1777

We have the honor to send your Excellency herewith a number of hand bills published by order of Congress, in that form, for the more easy dispersion thro the army, that the troops may be made acquainted with and emulate the conduct of their brave northern and eastern brethren.[1]

Wishing you health and success, we are with much esteem and regard your Excellencies most obedient humble servants,

| Richard Henry Lee | Jona D Sergeant | ⎱ Committee of |
| Thos. Heyward Junr. | Wm. Duer | ⎰ Intelligence |

RC (DLC). Written by Lee and signed by Lee, Duer, Heyward, and Sergeant.

[1] Under the supervision of the Committee of Intelligence, letters reporting the victory of Gen. John Stark at Bennington, Vt., had been published on August 22 as a broadside. See John Adams to Abigail Adams, August 21, 1777, note.

Henry Laurens to Joseph Clay

Dear Sir,   2d September 1777.

I had the pleasure of writing to you by Capt Hornby of the Georgia Troops under the 20th Ulto.

A few days ago by the transmission of a friend I was informed of an Act of Assembly lately passed in your State for vacating the Lands of all absentees after the 12 December next, notified by your Governor's proclamation.[1] It is not to be doubted but that all my Lands at Altamaha & Turtle River will come within the Letter of that Law although I cannot believe it possible to have been meant by an Individual of the Legislature. It should be considered that I continued the improvement & Cultivation of those remote frontier Settlements not only after all my Southern & Western Neighbors had removed but even long after the Cathiad Settlement & other interior inhabitants had left me—that Broughton Island & New Hope had been for Several Months exposed to the plunder & ravage of the Enemy—that five of my Negroes had been actually Stolen & carried away to St. Augustine—that the Man who had perpetrated that act of villainy had returned with a party in order to carry off as many more as he could take, that my escape from the heavy loss which would have happened if my Negroes had been at home was owing to mere accident—that I was left defenceless & that to have remained in that Situation would been an Act of temerity which would have encouraged the Floridians to persevere in their predatory War & eventually have been injurious to the States.

Perhaps it may be worthy of consideration too that I am now upon Duty in the Service of the thirteen United States, unable to quit my Post without permission.

In these Circumstances I request your friendly interposition to shield me against a damage which would on one hand be intolerable & on the other would Subject the State of Georgia to the charge of injustice & ingratitude. Perhaps the rigour of that Law in the particular Instance of my property might be eluded by Sending an overseer & a few Negroes to dig a Spade full of Earth & build a hut alternately on each Tract—but this is not what I aim at nor what I wish for; I have never in any part of my life practiced Jockeyship nor do I owe to dishonest artifice one farthing of my Estate. I mean to claim the protection of the State in which my property lies, where, while I held it, my constant practice was to make it as far as possible Subservient to the good of the State, & which I did not abandon until it was impracticable for the State to afford me a defence against the threatned attacks of a contiguous Enemy.

I intreat you to take proper Counsel & to make proper Addresses by Remonstrance, Memorial or petition to the Governor & his Council & to the House of Assembly & obtain a reasonable Suspension of the impending Escheat or an explanatory Act of Assembly establishing such exceptions as shall to the House seem consistent with Justice & good policy, I may say consistent with the happiness & well being of the State. From your friendly Offers of Service & from your attachment to the Interest of your Country as well as from your known love of justice, I flatter my Self in a dependence upon your exertions in the premises & therefore I will not take upon another moment of your time upon this head, but to say that for the honour of Georgia I trust there will be a discrimination between its warmest friends & most inveterate Enemies.

Our Arms in the Northern department have lately been Successful. Mr. Burgoyne has failed in every attempt except in too many acts of infamous Butchery upon Women & Children by his Indian Allies, since he made the halt at Fort Edward by a moderate computation he has lost Two Thousand Men killed & taken prisoner. The loss of Indians proved too heavy for them to bear—in order to prompt them to action they were made Drunk & Mad—the Survivors therefore when they soberred returned mourning & murmuring to their respective Countries. This Circumstance added to the great loss before Fort Schuyler & the total defeat of Colonel Baum has obliged the fop who boasted of extending his Arms far to contract his remaining forces within the compass of a strong-post, where he has hedged himself between a River & a Woody Mountain, on the defensive he will soon from necessity be obliged to remove in three or four Weeks. The

Season & the want of provision & necessaries will compel him. Our Troops will in the mean time make his Situation extremely incommodius, & will hang on his Skirts in a retreat. The evacuation of Tyconderoga will probably prove a profitable event. No thanks by the bye are due to those who should have defended it.

The Check which the puffing Burgoyne has received will probably operate as a Check upon Mr. Howe who no doubt had been taught to expect that his Coadjutor would before this day have been Marching through Jerseys towards Philadelphia & have facilitated his own from Elk River. The Road is now Thorny—many a bruised head & wounded heel will there be if he Should make the attempt. I hold it impossible that he Should finesse & embark without a tryal, but there are wiser Men of a different opinion. His force is computed at 10,000. General Washington's regulars exceed that number & the Militia are innumerable. They are very many daily increasing & very willing to come to action. We are drawing to a Crisis, probably while I am writing the Fate of 13 United States is in decision. Delay will be pernicious to both, but most to the Enemy, however they have many resources & advantages. Our trust is in the Righteousness of our Cause which is intitled to the favour of providence. I will enclose with this 2 or 3 latest News papers. Believe me to be &ca.

LB (ScHi).
¹ This issue is discussed in Laurens to John Wereat, August 30, 1777.

New Hampshire Delegates to Meshech Weare

Dear Sir,   Philadelphia Sepr. 2d. 1777

Genl. & Admirel Howe with their fleet arrived in Elk River on the 22d Ulto. and was wel Informed by two Intelligent salors (one belonging to Boston, 1 deserter from the Admirels Ship) that their fleet Consist of 280 Sail five of which is 64 guns 1 of 50. 1 of 40. Three frigets and a Number of tenders such as Brigs, Sloops & Schooners, that the Salors are Very Sickley with the scurvey, Spotted and yealo feavours, and that they lost many of their horses on the passage, that many of them has died Since they landed them, by turning them into Cornfeilds. The 25th they begun to land their Troops, it is uncertain what numbers they have, is Suposed to be about 10,000, that many of them has deserted and those deserters Says that all the Hessians will desert if they have an Oppetunity. The place were they now are is in the midst of their Countrimen and it is Said good Wiggs. The Congress has chosen a Committee to Collect what Evidence they can for the triel of Officers at Ticondaraga, as you'l see more at large by the news papers, and how fer the State of New Hampshire is concerned in that

Collection.[1] Here has been lately a discovery as is Soposed a plot by the Quakers in this place against the States by furnishing our Enemies with Inteligence &c. (I fear we shall fail of that proof that is Expected) which has in som degree laid the sencure on all those People in the United States and the Congress has passed some Resolves to be sent to the United States in order to apprehend som of those People.[2] I trust our Court will act with their known prudence and Caution in that affair. The Treasure board has not made any Report on our Request for money but are daly promising to do it. Am Still in doubt wether we Shall Succeed, as the Congress is in want of all our money for the public Use.[3] It is greatly wished by Congress that the Monied Men would Supploy the loan office faster, and that all the States would go largely into taxation.[4] Genl. Washingtons head quarters at present is in Wilminton, State of Deleware abot 12 miles from Howes main Armey and 26 Miles from this place. Has about 14,000 Continentel Troops, and the Militia is turning out in great bodyes or Numbers from all quarters this way, and in high Spirits. We trust (through the Goodness of God) we Shall be able to Repel the force of the Enemy. There is no Commission Appointed as yet in the Eastern department to Settle the Accopt. of those States, except what is Relating to the Armey but sopose there will be some Appointed soon, as we have Requested of Congress to Appoint such to Examin the State of New Hampshire Accot.[5] It would be no Small advantage to your Deligates If we Could be honord. with the Acts or Resolves of our Honoble. Court so fer as Relaites with our Dutey we oe the State and Court in Congres. We ware left to guse the Reasons the State had in giving Genl. Starkes his orders as it is Said he had and trust we have given the Congress Sufficent Reason to Justify the State therein and to prevent any Sencure on the State in Supposing they had any desine from Acting in a Seperate or distinct line but in Conjuntion and Steady union with the whole United States and for the general welfare of the same. We sent by Mr. Bass three books of the journels of Congress which was all he could carrey of the 20 Voted to Each State. Shall Send the Remainder 17 first oppetunity.

We are with great Esteam, sir, your most Obt. & Most Humble Servts.   Nathel. Folsom

Geo. Frost

RC (NhAr). Addressed: "The Honble Meshech Weare Esqr. Presedent New Hampshire." Written by Frost and signed by Frost and Folsom.

[1] See JCC, 8:686–88; and Henry Laurens' Heads of Inquiry into the State of the Northern Army, August 27, 1777.

[2] See John Hancock to William Livingston, August 30, 1777, note.

[3] On September 15 Congress authorized an advance of $100,000 to the state of New Hampshire. JCC, 8:746.

[4] The money problems that continued to plague Congress were also reflected

in the activities of the Board of Treasury, which at this time was attempting to overcome the obstacles that had been delaying implementation of the lottery since its authorization in November 1776. Thus at the board's direction, Auditor General John Gibson sent 800 lottery tickets with the following appeal to Maryland governor Thomas Johnson on September 3. "The Congress have deeply at Heart the success of this Lottery, and have great reason to apprehend that it has not met with attention and Encouragement equal to its vast importance. It is not only to be considered as a fund to defray the enormous expences which the United States in the prosecution of this most just and necessary War are and must continue to be exposed; But if the scheme should be so much neglected by the Friends of our cause as to prove abortive, it will have a most unfavourable aspect upon our public affairs: in other view, it will deeply wound our Public reputation, discourage our Creditors at home and our friends abroad, and be urged by our Enemies as a proof of our weakness and of the abatement of that public Virtue and generous ardour which have hitherto distinguish'd us in the course of this conflict; and sustain'd us under Divine Providence against the Efforts of our powerful and implacable Enemies." *Md. Archives,* 16:360; and *JCC,* 8:619.

⁵ The appointment of auditors for the northern and eastern departments was considered on January 3 and 5, 1778, but the appointments were postponed. *JCC,* 10:17, 22.

James Duane to Robert R. Livingston

My dear Sir   [September 3? 1777] ¹
I recd your favour of the   written at a time our dear natale Solum was in the greatest distress, and our Friends had every thing disagreeable to expect. Thro' the Bravery & good Conduct of Herkimer, Gaansvourt, & Willet, our Western Hemisphere is changed, the Clouds are dispersd, and we can view it without discomposure. To the North-ward too the prospect brightens. The compleat Victory gaind by Stark with his militia over the large Detachment of Burgoine's Army sent to savage our North Eastern Frontier, cannot, under Heaven, fail of be-ing productive of a variety of good Consequences. It has undoubtedly disappointed and depressed our Enemies; not less than it has en-couraged and elated our Friends; And very probably deliverd our State from Ravage and Destruction which a vigorous Exertion of the Enemy, unsustaind as you then were, might easily have affected. Let us, my dear Sir, adore most thankfully that gracious Being whose Interposition on this trying Occasion seems to have been So manifest in our favour. At the same time the brave Men who so happily conducted those several Enterprizes ought to be forgotten.² On the Contrary they ought to experience the Gratitude of their Country by sensible Effects. Herkimer first reversd the gloomy Scene and with a Courage and perseverance that do him infinite Honour. But it is his misfortune to want the powers of Description, and we have a most lame and im-perfect account of this great Event—*great* I call it, since, from the

severe Loss the Savages sustaind, it will not only give peace to our State with respect to the Indians but probably overawe all the Indians to the Southward. In this Light it appeard to General Washington who with a Benevolence peculiar to himself lamented that a more distinct Relation was not obtaind of this action, that the merit of the Commander & the militia might be properly understood by the world, & the former rewarded by his Country. I recommend this matter to your attention and any Letter you communicate for the purpose shall have its' full weight. It is difficult to fix a Reward for Herkimer. He does not want a Continental Command nor money. The Thanks of Congress and a sword will be readily granted. Can you think of any thing more suitable? ³ Gansevoort & Willet are in the highest Degree of Fame. We have had such a train of disgrace at all our Forts, & lost them so unexpectedly—Let me except Sullivan's Island—that the brave Defence of Fort Schuyler has made the deepest Impression. The Reward due to these Gent. is not yet determined, but it is generally talked to raise Gansevoort to the Rank of Brigr. General, & Willet to that of Colonel.⁴ Stark will also be provided for tho' he is something under the Clouds for refusing to serve under General Lincoln to whom he refusd the Command of the Troops, assigning as a Reason that Congress had done him Injustice in not promoting him.⁵ General Schuyler prevailed on him to submit to Lincoln: but before that General's Arrival at Bennington he took Care to attack and defeat the Enemy. You'l allow this to be a handsome Apology for intemperate Expressions.

Doubtless you are anxious to know the Situation of the two grand armies. General Howe's main body lies South East of the Head of Elk about two miles. An Advancd party of about 2000 lie about the Head of Elk. General Washington's main Army lies on the Heights of Wilmington; an advanced party of 1000 picked Regular Troops and a number of militia hang on the Enemy's advancd party. The grounds about Wilmington are tolerably advantageous but the Country between that & Philad does not admit of any strong Post. Take for the rest an Extract of Hamilton's Letter to me of last Saturday. "We must rely wholly upon our Numbers; the goodness of our Troops and our own good managemt of them. I see clearly we must either beat the Enemy in a general Action, or they will carry their point with respect to Philadelphia. It will not be very difficult. I am in hopes, to give them a handsome drubbing if we only have time to bring our whole army together assisted by 5 or 6000 militia well embodied, and I think we shall not want time for the purpose," I only add that there have been some slight Skirmishes & our Army have taken about 70 Prisoners without loosing more than 2 or 3 men. About a dozen Deserters have come in. By every Account a powerful militia from Pensa., Delaware, Maryland & Virginia are collecting to Join General Washington; so that numbers will not be wanting. People appear here to be in perfect security—not a family has movd. The Conjecture is that General Howe will not risk a Battle. His situation, whatever may have been his Hopes, is certainly much worse than when he was at Somerset Court house, & ours infinitely better on every Account. He has issued another Proclamation to try the Affections, or, as Ld North expressed it, to sound the Country.[6] It has no Effect. Nothing but a superiority in Arms will now serve his purpose. John Dickinson is once more in the feild & with George Reade accompanies Caesar Rodney the General of the Delaware Militia. The want of Horses & Desire of securing a Retreat by Lines or Forts are supposed to detain General Howe which gives General Washington immense advantages; as he has not yet all his regular Troops assembled.

Present my affectionate Regards to Mrs Livingston and all our Friends at both Mannors & believe me with the utmost Respect, Dear Sir, Your affectionate & most obed huml Servant,

Jas Duane

P.S. Col. Wilson, Mr Morris, Mr Duer, the President &c &c present their Respects to you.

RC (NHi).

[1] Duane probably wrote this letter on September 3, the day Congress ordered the Board of War to consider suitable rewards for the American officers discussed in the second paragraph. It is virtually certain that Duane did not write it after the third, the day the *Pennsylvania Journal* carried the news of the death of one of these officers, Nicholas Herkimer, whose death Duane was obviously unaware of as he wrote.

[2] Duane meant of course to write "ought not."

[3] On October 4, 1777, Congress resolved to ask the governor and council of New York to erect at Continental expense a monument to Nicholas Herkimer, a brigadier general in the state's militia who had been mortally wounded at the battle of Oriskany. *JCC*, 9:770.

[4] In recognition of the officers' role in the defense of Fort Schuyler, Congress resolved on October 4, 1777, to make Col. Peter Gansevoort "colonel commandant" of that post and to give "an elegant sword" to Lt. Col. Marinus Willet. *JCC*, 9:771–72.

[5] On October 4, 1777, Congress resolved to thank Gen. John Stark for his part in the battle of Bennington and to make him a Continental brigadier general. *JCC*, 9:770–71. See also George Frost to Josiah Bartlett, August 19, 1777, note 2.

[6] See Henry Laurens to Lachlan McIntosh, September 1, 1777, note 2.

John Hancock to Israel Putnam

Sir,   Philada. Sepr. 3d. 1777.

Your Favour of the 27th ulto.[1] I have been duely honored with, and immediately laid it before Congress.

From the enclosed Resolves you will percieve that Provision has been made for Major Generals while they act in a seperate Department— and as Congress consider you as acting in that Line for the present, the same Pay is to be extended to you from the Time you took the Command at Peeks-Kill, until it shall cease.[2]

The Congress have been induced from your Recommendation of Rose & Ackerly to consent that you should pardon them both. The Manner in which you propose to employ them appears to be extremely proper.[3]

Every Resolve of Congress relative to the Department under your Command shall be forwarded with all necessary Dispatch. I beg Leave to refer your Attention to those transmitted herewith.

I have the Honour to be, with great Respect, Sir, your most obed. & very hble Serv.   J.H. Presid.

LB (DNA: PCC, item 12A). Addressed: "The Honble Major Genl. Putnam. Peeks-kill."
    [1] This letter is in PCC, item 159, fols. 75–76.
    [2] See JCC, 8:704. Putnam, who had been placed in command at Peekskill by Washington in May 1777, needed the extra pay allowed the commander of a separate department in order to meet his expenses. PCC, item 159, fols. 75–76; and Washington, Writings (Fitzpatrick), 8:50–51.
    [3] See JCC, 8:704. In his August 27 letter to President Hancock, Putnam explained his request for clemency for Amos Rose and Lemuel Ackerly—both of whom had been sentenced to death by a court-martial, the former for having fired his musket at a superior officer and the latter for having been a British spy—and stated that he wished to have them "Secured & employed on board the Ships in the north river where they are wanted." The records of their courts-martial are in PCC, item 159, fols. 79–84.

John Hancock to George Washington

Sir,   Philada. September 3d. 1777.

I have Nothing in Charge from Congress at this Time, but to transmit the enclosed Resolves, to which I must refer your Attention.

General Sullivan's Expedition on Staten Island having ended in the Loss and Defeat of a considerable Number of the Troops under his Command;[1] the Congress have directed a Court of Inquiry to be instituted relative to the Expedition.[2]

You will please to order Colonel Richardson's Battalion on such Duty as you may judge most proper.[3]

Your two Favours of the 1st inst.[4] I have been duely honoured with.

I forward herewith a Number of blank Commissions for the Use of the Army in two Bundles and have the Honour to be, with the utmost Respect, Sir, your most obed & very hble Servt.

                                                    John Hancock Presidt

RC (DLC). In the hand of Jacob Rush and signed by Hancock.
  [1] At this point the following words were crossed out in the MS: "and it appearing from some Circumstances that his Conduct is not altogether free from Censure."
  [2] See *JCC*, 8:700. On October 12 a military court of inquiry decided that Gen. John Sullivan's August 22 raid on Staten Island had been well planned and that its failure was due to circumstances beyond his control. See Washington, *Writings* (Fitzpatrick), 9:379–80; and Charles P. Whittemore, *A General of the Revolution: John Sullivan of New Hampshire* (New York: Columbia University Press, 1961), pp. 54–56, 75. For another instance of congressional dissatisfaction with Sullivan's generalship, see Hancock to Washington, September 14, 1777, note 2.
  [3] See *JCC*, 8:706.
  [4] These letters are in PCC, item 152, 5:13–18, and Washington, *Writings* (Fitzpatrick), 9:151–52.

Henry Marchant to Nicholas Cooke

Honord Sir,   Philadelphia Sepr. 3d. 1777.
  In my last I referred to certain Resolves of Congress as enclosed, but thro' great Hurry, fearing the Post might leave my Letter, the Resolves slipt aside, and were not enclosed. This would have given me more Uneasiness, had I not immediately upon Enquiry, found that They were forwarded to the Govr. and Compy. by the President. However I now enclose Them.[1]
  I sincerely congratulate you Sir, Upon the Success of Our Arms to the Northward. A fatal Blow is struck to Burgoin's Enterprize, How has left him to his Fate, And I hope will receive his Own at the Head of Chesepeak. The Tory Thermomiter will sink below 0. And could there be a generous Ardor and Love of Our Country universally diffused, could we but extinguish the present too prevalent grasping engrossing Spirit, We might expect soon by the Blessing of God to establish the Peace and Happiness of the States. That this may be effected is the ardent wish of Honord Sir, your most obedient and very humble Servt.
                                                        Hy. Marchant

RC (R–Ar).
  [1] See Marchant to Cooke, August 24, 1777.

Committee of Congress to Meshech Weare

Sir   Philadelphia September 4. 1777
  In Obedience to an order of Congress, We have the Honour of transmitting the enclosed Copy of their Resolution of the Twenty Seventh

of August, whereby we are appointed and authorized to correspond
with public Bodies, or private Persons in order to collect the clearest
and fullest Evidence of the State of the Army in the Northern department, and also of the State of the Troops, military Stores and Provisions at those Posts, before and at the Time when the Evacuation was
determined on.[1]

As this Event is of much Importance to the united states and has
So greatly, and So justly excited the public Attention, it is necessary
that the most effectual Measures Should be Speedily taken, in order
to obtain an impartial State of the Facts. To which End, We have the
Honour to request of you, sir, to lay this Letter with the enclosed
Copy, before your Assembly, if Sitting, if not, before the Council, for
their Aid in procuring Evidence from Records and Witnesses, relative
to the Several Objects of Inquiry, enumerated in the Resolution.

The Testimonies of Witnesses, Should be in Writing Subscribed by
themselves, and authenticated in Such manner, as you shall think
proper: their Places of abode also should be pointed out.

Justice to the Public, as well as to the officers whose Conduct is to
be inquired into, requires, that all the Dispatch, which is consistent with
the Nature of the Business, Should be made.

When your Inquiries shall be finished, We have to request that you
would transmit the Result of them to the Chairman of this Committee
by Express, or at least by a quick and safe Conveyance. We have the
Honour to be, Sir, your most obedient and most humble, Servants,[2]

Henry Laurens

Richard Henry Lee

RC (NjMoHP). Addressed: "The Honourable the President of Council of the
State of New Hampshire." Written by John Adams and signed by Laurens and
Lee. The committee sent identical letters to Connecticut governor Jonathan
Trumbull, Sr., on this day and to New York governor George Clinton on Sep-
tember 8, copies of which are in the Jonathan Trumbull, Sr., Papers, Ct, and
Sparks MSS, MH–H, respectively.

[1] See *JCC*, 8:684-86, 688; John Hancock to Arthur St. Clair and Philip
Schuyler, August 5, note; and Henry Laurens' Heads of Inquiry, August 27,
1777.

[2] On September 5 the committee sent the August 27 resolve to Joseph
Trumbull with this brief note: "We request you to transmit to us by the
earliest good opportunity the fullest intelligence in your late department of
Commissary General & you will further oblige us by adding any further information properly authenticated relative to the enquiries which we are ordered
to make." Joseph Trumbull Papers, Ct. Extracts from the committee's September 5 letter to Richard Varick, deputy muster master for the northern
department, and his October 10 response are in *Autograph Letters and Documents Relating to the History of America from the Private Collection of Mr. &
Mrs. Philip D. Sang* (Iowa City: State University of Iowa, 1956), pp. 18–19.

Francis Lightfoot Lee to Landon Carter

My dear Col.   Philadelphia Sept. 4. 1777

Mr. Jackson will deliver you a Letter which I wrote some time agoe,[1] by Mr. Crump, who was stoped at Elk by Mr. Howe. I hope it will arrive time enough for your sugar making business. I cou'd have procured the Sickles at 10/ & 12/ a peice, but the impossibility of conveying any thing from hence to Virginia at present, will oblige me to hold my hand, till I hear further from you.

Genl. Howe is now within 40 miles of us with his whole force, yet we are in good spirits having our Genl. & a spirited Army to oppose him. By the papers sent to Col. Tayloe, which I know you will have the benefit of, you will see that we have little to apprehend from the valorous & most puissant Burgoyne, we fear he will make his retreat good.

If Howe should be obliged to betake himself to his ships, we hope the Virginia Militia will prevent his pillaging the Country on his return. Our best respects to Sabine Hall.

I am Dear Col. Your afft. friend & hble Sert.

Francis Lightfoot Lee

RC (NN).
[1] See Lee to Carter, August 13, 1777.

Robert Morris to William Whipple

Dear Sir,   Philada. Septr. 4th. 1777

I have seen letters from Cap McNeil to the Marine Committee wherein he blames Manly for some part of his Conduct, it was a great pity they did not push into some port with their Prize where the whole might have been manned & gone out fresh again, they wou'd have formed a Clever little squadron, however as that can not be, we must attend to what is in our power & if Thompson, Hinman, Jones & McNeill are not gone they will now receive orders to cross the Ocean, this point I carried yesterday in Committee & the orders will be sent immediately.[1]

I am much engaged in winding up the Accounts of the Secret Committee & it will be a Herculean labour, & in order to do it compleatly I moved for a New Committee which was appointed & is Stiled the Commercial Committee who are to carry on the business in future.[2] They have chosen me Chair Man but I am very averse to engaging deeply in this New business untill the old is closed, & indeed I now wish to be released from public business totally. I have had a long spell, my own affairs suffering amazingly the whole time & having no Ambition to gratify I wish to resign my honors & powers to somebody that may be better pleas'd with them. Whether I shall be permitted to retire or not I dont yet know, but the meeting of our assembly is at hand & I hope they will leave me out of the new appointments. The Commercial Committee agreed at their last meeting that it was better to lay by awhile as the Enemies Cruizers are too numerous on our Coasts for any thing to escape in the Summer Months, but I suppose they will commence some operations soon as hard Winds begin to blow. I shall want a vessell or two to load in Carolina or Georgia & wish you had told me the prices or terms of Charter. If you meet with any very good bargain of a vessell I wou'd either be concerned with you or wou'd wish a purchase on any Account for which you may draw on me with assurance that your bills shall be punctually paid, & you may dispatch her for Charles Town South Carolina Consigned to Mr. John Dorsius writing him to Load her with Rice for Havre de Grace Consd to Mr. Andw. Limozin, or if she cannot get into Charles Town she may go to Savannah in Georgia & apply to John Wereat Esqr. You may direct your letter to both those Gentn & they will comply with your orders as they have Funds of mine in hand. You may direct the Captain to go North about Scotland & keep well in with the Dutch & French Coast coming down to Havre. He must return to America with Salt.

Genl. Howe is preparing to disturb us but we hope to disapoint him. The Militia turn out with Spirit, they want arms but still we shall be able to Cope with him. Genl. Washington is taking possession of the Strong grounds whilst the Militia & a Body of Light Troops harass the Enemy. I am Dr sir, Your Obedt hble servt.   R. Morris

RC (MdHi). Addressed: "To Willm. Whipple Esqr., Portsmouth, New Hampshire." Endorsed: "This letter from the great American financier, was given to me by Mrs. Elwyn, granddaughter of General Whipple, to whom it is addressed. R. Gilmor, 1829."
    ¹ See Marine Committee to John Paul Jones, September 6, 1777.
    ² See Secret Committee Minutes of Proceedings, June 13, 1777, note 3; and Robert Morris' Statement, January 7, 1779.

Board of War to George Washington

Sir,   War Office Septr 5th. 1777
I have the Honour of enclosing you Copy of a Letter which was addressed to a Member of Congress, & laid before the Board for their Consideration. It is sent to your Excellency for the Purpose of pointing out the Grievances complained of & which the Board is very willing to use their Endeavors to redress if they could be furnished with your Excellency's Assistance in forming the Plan.¹ It is said the Salt, Meat

& Bacon is consumed in some Part by the General Officers but chiefly by the Commissaries & Followers of the Army. If so the latter Instance is a great Abuse & ought by all Means to be checked. But how to keep so constant a Watch upon these People as to prevent their Mal Practices is a Question of some difficulty. A large Quantity of Vinegar has been purchased for the Use of the Army & yet it is said by many Officers that their Regiments have not had a Drop. The Board directed me to mention this Matter also that Enquiry might be made into it & Measures taken if possible to oblige the Commissaries more faithfully to discharge their Duty.

I have the Honour to be, with the greatest Respect, your very obed Servt, Richard Peters Secy

RC (DLC).

[1] In his September 10 reply to the board—which is in Washington, *Writings* (Fitzpatrick), 9:204–5—Washington stated that the specific complaint against commissaries practising partiality in distributing provisions could not be redressed because the complaining Virginia officer had not been identified, but that the problem would be reported to the commissary of issues. In the same letter, Washington also commented on a question regarding ration regulations that had been raised by commissary Robert White in an August 28 letter that Peters had forwarded on September 6. White's letter to the board, a copy of the Virginia officer's August 30 letter to an unidentified member of Congress, and Peters' September 6 letter to Washington are all in the Washington Papers, DLC.

John Hancock to William Livingston

Sir, Philada. Sepr 5th. 1777.

In the present Exigency of public affairs, the Congress have come to the enclosed Resolve, which I have the Honour to transmit—and which I am to request you will comply with as soon as possible.[1]

The Militia of the State of New Jersey by their late Conduct agt. our cruel Enemies have distinguished themselves in a Manner that does them the greatest Honour; and I am persuaded they will continue to merit on all Occasions when called upon the Reputation they have so justly acquired. Those which the Congress now request you will order out, it is their Desire you will order to rendezvous at Bristol.

It will be highly agreeable to Congress to give the Command to Genl. Dickinson, should the Appointment fall in with your Judgment; and I have Reason to believe he will chearfully accept of it, if you shd. think proper to put them under his Direction.

I have the Honour to be, with the greatest Respect, Sir, your most obed. and very hble Servt.

LB (DNA: PCC, item 12A).

[1] On September 4 Congress resolved to ask Governor Livingston to send

3,000 New Jersey militiamen to reinforce "the army under General Washington, the said militia to rendezvous at Bristol, with as much despatch as possible." *JCC,* 8:712.

Henry Laurens to John Lewis Gervais

Dear Sir,   5th September. 1777.
I sit down this Morning with a design to trouble you with a very long Letter, God knows whether I shall be permitted to accomplish. The Main body of the Enemy were within thirty Miles of us yesterday morning & about four or five from our Army. We expect every moment to hear of an important clashing, but what I think most probable, admitting General Howe to be so Strong as he is reported to be 18000 men or even 15 thousand, is, that he will keep General Washington at Bay with one part & March the other by a different route to this City. These & a thousand as Idle conjectures employ the conversation of Men at this distance. The time is big with fates, Somewhat very important will be brought forth before we are three days older. Congress has not yet determined to adjourn from this City but I am taking time by the forelock. James is gone to get the Horses Shod, will have our little All packed up to day & be ready for a March in case of need. Before the meeting of the House I will endeavour to say the needfull in reply to your very kind Letters of the 26th & 29th July.[1]

All that you had done or had intended to do respecting my Brother's affairs, appears to be extremely proper. The House in which Mr. McKay lives ought to be repaired. Mr. Motte should be at one half the expence & pay that half in Cash, but I doubt whether he will do so. He does not use my Brother well, he refuses to pay the Interest on his Bond under a pretence that my Brother receives the whole Rent of that House, although he knows the latter has not been for a considerable time past equal to the former & I have reason to beleive it never has been quite equal after deducting Repairs & Taxes. I wrote to my Brother on this head Some time ago; 'tis probable we shall hear from him. In the mean time Mr. Motte Should advance money for his part of the expence to be incurred by Repairs.

Betty is very troublesome & it appears by a memorandum of her Masters she has been always so. To hire her in a family will certainly be best. If she does not behave well in that Station & Ishmael still absent I think it will be best to send her in the Country. I believe while Ishmael was at home he maintained her & paid the principal part of her Wages. She is very Idle.

In a Letter which I wrote to you Somewhere on the Road to this place or perhaps since my arrival, I requested you not to part with the Gold, but to keep it as on my Accott. which I now repeat & I will improve it for my Brother agreeable to his desire by assigning him a proper Sum to be received in London. I shall be obliged by your opinion what the Exchange ought to be.

The circumstance of March at Wright's Savanna shocks & effects me exceedingly, nor is it less amazing because he was ever a man of placid & obliging disposition & always as far as I knew a good & faithful servant until he unhappily became connected with Mary. He has since that Union been guilty of Robbery. It was for such a Crime he was really shipped by Morgan. I am really grieved for the poor fellow. It appears to me best to send Mary to Georgia & order her to be Sold there, she has very great abilities & when she is cut off from her old acquaintance she may find it her Interest to exert them. If you will take the trouble to correspond with Mr Clay on this matter & he gives hopes of obtaining £200 Georgia Money for her, order her to be sent to him. As to March I think the mode of punishment which you propose is due to the public, otherwise from the reluctance I feel, I believe he would escape. When his wound is healed he must be kept at such work as he is capable of performing & from the necessity of the Case great rigour Should be exercised upon him until he gives proof of humility which will soon be, after he is Seperated from that wicked Devil.

Casper seems to be held in contempt by the Negroes & I am afraid of Some fatal accident. I shall write to him by this conveyance & submit my opinion to yours.

My Dear Sir, it makes me very unhappy to give you so much trouble as I am in my present circumstances obliged to do. It is extremely unreasonable in my Country Men to compel me to this useless Service, if they had only considered how much of my time had been devoted to theirs & how very little to my own affairs I think common gratitude would have induced them to give me a moments respite. Did they know how their delegates are now mis spending time I am sure they would recall them or give them very Special orders. Congress is not the respectable body which I expected to have found. To be particular on this point would be improper, but I mention so much from that feeling which is irresistible. I see my own private affairs going to Wreck, I am helping forward the heavy loss by most amazing expences here. I am adding to the load of trouble which my friends must have from attending to their own concerns & am rendering my Country no intrinsic Services. This latter consideration grieves me most. I think I have been instrumental in averting two pernicious schemes & except these my time 5 or 11 hours every day has been Squandred. The most necessary work we have to do at present is that of Confederating—& that of making a State of past Expences, to be fully informed of the application of those Millions already Issued to govern our future proceedings by wiser measures & to fill our exhausted Treasury by means least likely to involve us in difficulties. My attempts to accomplish these great purposes have hitherto proved fruitless & I have too much reason to fear, from a discovery of the cause, will ever prove so—unless very particular Instructions from some of the States should be charged upon their Delegates to demand of Congress an adjustment of Accounts. I wish we were half an hour together. I would say many things to you, as an Assembly Man, in favour of our little honest State. What I have Said you may think of in that Character but as being said to your Self only.

I have wandered into this digression of hints from a reflection which Suddenly took place in my mind, of the vast trouble which an attention to my business has already occasioned to you while I my Self am detained in a State of worse than Idleness. I shall write to the president requesting His Excellency to obtain leave for me to return to Charles Town if my health Should fail me as I fear it will when the Cold weather comes on. In such case even attempts to Serve must fail & therefore I request your aid if a question should be made in your House. Mr. Middleton will leave us in October. You should really send us two or three Men of business & Spirit, if I am to stay here, Maugre all the disadvantages that your absence from Carolina will work to my Estate I wish you may be one—but come who will the Assembly Should in common justice allow them to live at least half as well as they had been accustomed to at home & pay their bare expences. Pray what is the present allowance? I have lived in a very humble style compared with the humble style of Ansonburgh yet including travelling expences (not Carriage & Horses) have already nearly exhausted 2300 Dollars. Mr. Middleton tells me he lives upon public money & offered me a supply but I will have none, I never touched any in my life. Admitting General Howe is so complaisant as to allow us to remain here the Winter expences will be Still more enormous. Judge from this one item, James tells me I must pay four Dollars for a pair of Strong coarse Shoes for George, & this, paid a Taylor for making a Single coat. I found the Cloth 24 Dollars—every article in proportion but to return to your Letters from which I have strangely wandered, my mind is rended with Ideas which March out with all the regularity of Militia Soldiers. It is scarcely possible to make an exact arrangement when one expects every moment an alarm. James is now packing up in order to be in readiness for a move. I must go to the House of Idleness, Shall probably not see this table again till 4 or 5 oClock P.M. after having been witness to the transaction of business which would require no more than half an hour judiciously applied. I know where the defect lies & may tell you by & by. At 5 oClock I returned from Six hours Session without doing one hours business. Took half an hour to dine & am now proceeding in this Address because at 7 I must attend a Committee upon a Wild Goose chase.[2] You see I am thoroughly out of humour, my Colleagues are not less so. I told you Mr. M[iddleton] is to leave us in October, Mr. H[eyward] says he will follow him in November. These are serious matters & demand the attention of Assemblies. For your own Sake do not leave the burthen of your whole State upon my insufficient abilities—but as I said a little while ago to return to your Letter.

As Bailey had not finished the business of my Georgia Estates the 9th July I should have been extremely glad to have heard from himself or Mr. Clay what progress he had made. The Georgia proclamation relative to our Chief Justice was a Secret to me before your intimation[3] & there was one published the 12 June relative to the forfeiture of the Lands in that State owned by Absentees which must have been a Secret to you the 29th July otherwise you would have Spoke to a matter of Such magnitude in my dwindling Estate.[4] I have written on the Subject very fully to Mr. Clay[5] as you will see by my Letter to him which will accompany this & left undone flying Seal for your perusal & information. I commend the Subject to your attention requesting you wod do every thing in your power to ward off the impending unmerited attempt to rob me of near half my Estate.

If your House of Assembly is setting & you think it necessary you will apply for their interposition, in their recess I am sure the President will not refuse his utmost assistance & if nothing less will do than my personal appearance I beg you will obtain permission for me & transmit it with dispatch. I shall scarcely have a day to Spare, even if I should receive a return to this the 1st November.

Mr. W.B.[6] was formerly of a different opinion from that which you now intimate relative to the source of the Water at Wrights Savanna, but other Mens sentiments upon different views have also varied whence I conclude the fact requires a more full investigation than was entered into by those unkind neighbors who gave powers which would have been inconsistent with Law & justice even after the strictest scrutiny. James Brisbane holds those Lands near my plantation without any Titles from the Owners Messrs Wright nor has he ever paid one farthing of purchase Money.

My agreement with Gruber was £35. His additional claim of £10 is for assisting to conduct the Chariot from George Town, this part at least Mr. Heath was to pay but I think I made it a condition that he was to pay the whole if I purchased the Carriage. My memory will not furnish me with particulars but my Letters to Mr. Heath or your Self will testify. Soon however Gruber ought to be paid the £45, & by me rather than keep him longer out of his Money.

I owe Mr. Nephew something but dont know how much. Himself only is to blame that I remain in his debt. I had Money with me in March 1775 for cancelling his Account, he appointed a day to meet me at Boston Island, I waited for him one or I beleive two days extraordinary for no other purpose, but he did not come. There were some questions to be asked which would not have been pleasing to him—at my return to Charles Town I was ordered into the Chair of the General Committee, soon after into those of Genl Congress & Council of Safety. You know the burthen which the people laid on me how diligently I applied my whole time to public & how totally I neglected my private concerns, my Books & papers were in so disorderly a State when I left Mepkin I was ashamed to show them even to you. I have therefore no regular Idea of the State of Mr. Nepher's Account but there is among my papers the ground work for building a just & fair reckoning between us. I should be sorry to keep from him one farthing that is due & as I hope he will not demand more I shall have no objection to Mr. Clay's paying him on my Account Seventy Pounds Georgia Currency taking from him a proper Stipulation promising to account with me. I Say Georgia Currency because I beleive our agreement was so, if he Shews the contrary, then I would pay him £400 Carolina Money, I mean to do him complete Justice but I remember there are one or more large charges againt him & he will acknowledge the delay which has happened was owing to the disappointment above mentioned. I now recollect he was to have called on me on a Tuesday. I had intended to have left the Island on Wednesday or Thursday according to the arrival of an expected boat from Sunbury, but I did not leave it 'till Saturday.

Payment of Mr. McCulloghs order to Byers, of Parkinson's Note & Balance I believe are very right & so may be the £5 to Mamma Narvo. I dont exactly remember the Old Womans last version but judge your payment will fully cancel it to the midle of September, from whence her Stipend may recommence at 40/ per month. In the meantime I beg you will give her as from me £4 & shall I request you also to give to Mr. Joseph Roper Fifty Pounds & Twenty five pounds to Sam's Wife or if he has behaved well I would wish to add some indulgencies to bare necessaries for himself.

The prize which you mention to have been made by Seymour was an excellent favor of fortune, the more valuable by the Capture of so inveterate an Enemy as Lofthouse. As a rooted Enemy to our State & by no means from any resentment for his imprudence to me I hope you will not part with him before you obtain an adequate Exchange. Pray what is become of Bishop. If he is at large in Augustine 'tis high time he Should fulfill his promise of remitting by Gold or Bill the money I advanced for him of which he has the Account.

If Mr. Arthur comes here he will probably have cause to regret a fruitless journey. Your Letter to Fosdick is very good, but since Jimmy Debatt's marriage into the Noble family he is turned a Sad Rascal, if I had been at home I would have sold him & so I would Doctr. Cuffee & Montezuma, & I earnestly request you to do so by all or any of those Villains, ungrateful villains if they give farther cause for complaint. The two last mentioned, if they are not carefully watched & kept low will Slip further off than Wright's Savanna whenever an opportunity presents. If they know as much of my intentions towards them as I do, my Negroes would esteem a change of Masters to be the heaviest punishment that could be inflicted upon them.

I hope Mr. Clay will very Soon inform me the State of my affairs under his protection, therefore I do not trouble him on that Subject, nevertheless his long delay induces me to request you will acquaint me with all you can learn from Bailey or to procure from him a Letter.

I propose to leave all the Letters under your Cover open for your perusal. You will be so good as seal & cause them to be delivered as Soon as possible. One to Mr. Legare will shew you some thing of my poor James Air's Account. From those to Mr. Wereat & General McIntosh you will learn my Sentiments on the Georgia Land Act in addition to what I have Said to Mr Clay as well as on Colo G. M's Case.[7] The general has been very pathetic in a late Letter on this Subject, but concerning my Land he touches so Slightly I should not have understood his meaning without the aid of the other Gentleman who has taken a very friendly part. The little which my old friend has said seems to have been postulated more to impress upon my mind a harsh opinion of the prevailing party in Georgia than for my Service. In each of these Letters you will gather some fragments of intelligence, more you will collect from the News papers which will accompany them & upon Monday Morning when I intend to dispatch this Messenger you Shall be informed of every material branch of intelligence which shall in the mean time come to my knowledge relative to our Armies on Delaware, the middle & Northern departments.

I feel a Strong disinclination to plague you with minute directions on any parts of my Estate. I am confident you will give in general & in Special proper orders together with such attention as your health & leisure will admit of & I will prefer great losses to the cruelty of pressing an overload upon you, but what a load do you think I have been contriving & were you here, if it should from Love of the Cause we are engaged in even cost me two thousand Guineas, you should bear it, I am sure you would be requested to undertake it. It is necessary to recal Mr. Deane from the Court of Versailles, his conduct has not given Satisfaction. I do not know a man in America nor have we yet employed one according to my opinion so equal to the Task in all respects as my friend Gervais. If you were here many an hundred pounds should I suffer by your absence from Charles Town, but I wish you were here.

We have had a little Skirmish between advanced posts. Baron Holzendorff this minute from Camp tells me one of our Generals misbehaved. The Enemy had Cannon, we had none, our Troops retreated. General Washington writes our loss is not very considerable; that of the Enemy he thinks was, from certain circumstances which he mentions & he is ever candid. The Baron whispers—"Your Soldiers my Dear Colonel are very good Mans, so good as any brave Mans in the World, but your Officers my Dear Colonel your Officers"—& then bursts his soft Laugh. I understand him & believe he is pretty just in his meaning. If we are put to the Block it will not originate in the Ranks. Here I left off at 1/2 past 10 Clock (the 6th) & went to Congress; am this moment returned 1/2 past 3. Five hours debating one Silly point whether certain persons chiefly Quakers who have given the Strongest proofs which in these times can be expected of their avowed attachment to the cause of our Enemies, who have peremptorily refused to take an Oath or affirmation of Allegiance to the State or to give a parol to the Executive power, should have a hearing in their own defence. The hearing which they aim at is not intended, but a hearing *they may have,* if they will accept the mode prescribed. Congress have recommended to the Executive Council to hear what they have to allege *"for removing Suspicion that they are Enemies to the Independence of the United States."*[8]

I am much mistaken if by this shifting ground the Cry of persecution will not be raised to a tone higher, & that Congress & Council will eventually make ridiculous figures.

You will see either by this or the next opportunity a chain of publications on this affair. What other hearing can reasonably be required or granted when a Country is actually invaded, the Enemy within a few Miles of the Capital City, denouncing vengeance on the Rulers & principal Inhabitants of the State?—see Genl Howes late Declaration—but an honest explicit answer to a reasonable, fair & necessary question. Will you behave inoffensively in all respects & neither directly nor indirectly by Act or deed desire or work damage or injury to this State? or, do you profess to owe allegiance to this State or to the King of Great Britain? Determine this affair as it may, the weakness of Congress will be marked, they Should have directed the measure in the first Instance or not have Submitted to be driven into it. This is an important question, if it shall be decided as there is too much reason to fear it will, Toryism will stalk triumphant & the first Assembly in America will be held in light esteem. If the Law of necessity will not justify us in the Act of confining notorious Enemies of the State when that State is actually invaded, what shall we Say to the late Suspension of the Habeas Corpus in England not Invaded? To the denunciation of Military Execution by Genl Howe & General Jones in New York, or to the Rules prescribed in Burgoyne's Orders to Baum in general, & particularly for distinguishing the *good* & imprisoning such as Governor Skeen Should *think* bad? If the Quakers pretend to claim protection of the Laws of the Land, it should be remembered they refuse to obey those Laws & deny allegiance to the State? In a word while the British powers Seize & confine the persons of our Subjects or friends upon *Suspicion* & we suffer their professed friends to be at large & to go through all the Ceremonies & chicanery of Courts of Law in their defense, we proceed upon very unequal terms. We go without Arms, to War with determined & well appointed Armies. I am anxious for a determination of this great question.

It appears to me there was no ground for raising it. Are you not surprized at hearing that Congress has forgot her own Resolutions or will not exert powers which she has vested in all the States? You know Men have been Seized & confined because their going at large was judged by the Executive power to be dangerous to the State. A dangerous Rule I confess this would be in days of tranquility, but you well know it is absolutely necessary for the Safety of each State in our present Circumstances. But will you not be more Surprized when you reflect that the Gaols here are *now* full of prisoners Committed upon *Suspicion,* or for refusing to give their parol or to swear or affirm allegiance, nay that many have been put to death upon *well-grounded suspicion only,* of being Spies & yet that Congress should do & undo, determine & hesitate, Resolve & reconsider & Suppress the Resolve— when a few powerful Men called Quakers come to be the objects? No, you would not be surprized if you knew as much of certain affairs as I do. No Man has more Love for the Society of Quakers than I have, they are good friends, good neighbours, good Citizens in times of peace & tranquility & in time of War exceedingly useful in their own ways to the Side to which they are attached, but they are the most dangerous Enemies in the World. They now profess themselves to be "real & true friends to America," but read their testimonials particularly No.   *9 & No.   & answer, are they friends to the Independence of the 13 United States? Are they friends to the Laws & Constitution whose protection they claim in the State of Philadelphia? Can there be more dangerous Inmates than Men who are in close correspondence with & giving intelligence, to the open Enemies of those with whom they dwell & to whom they outwardly profess Love & friendship? Can there be an instance produced of more refined insulting hyprocrisy than an artful declaration of Specious truth calculated to deceive? "We profess Love & Friendship to you in our open Addresses, but in our Secret Testimonials we declare the strongest attachment to your inveterate Enemies, we *there* call you unjust—tyrants usurpers of power & authority & we demonstrate that the true meaning of our Love & friendship for you is, opposition to you, & an ardent desire that you may be Subdued by your Enemies who we know will imprison some of you, put others to death & confiscate your Estates & this you are also to understand to be the genuine interpretation of our professed, real friendship to America." The Devil himself would be too honest, none but a thorough bred Jesuit would have the hardiness to call such duplicity "that Wisdom from above which is first *pure* then peaceable, gentle & easy to be entreated, full of Mercy & good fruits, without *partiality* & without *hyprocrisy*" (Pemberton's Address 20 December 1776).[10] The calling God who is the fountain of truth, or the quoting his Holy Scriptures, which are the Oracles of Truth, to witness a Lie, or any Species of deceit is blasphemy. And to such men as we have in view it may very fairly be retorted "they wrest the holy Scriptures to their own damnation."

I am sure you will not mistake me, that I mean to condemn the whole Society of Quakers. You are too well acquainted with my Maxim that I know no man by his Country or his Religious profession. No I am persuaded that every honest sensible Man in that Society will upon due reflection censure their Brethren & many will detest the principles of those double-minded leaders & their adherents. Sentiments Similar to these I have already heard from one speaking the language of others. To Speak in their Style, "my mind being deeply impressed with a fervent & anxious concern for the honor of Congress & for the welfare & preservation of the 13 United Colonies in the true Spirit of Liberty & Independence I am constrained to impart to you this detail of an extraordinary occurence & to signify my apprehensions of ruin to our Cause, or much detriment to say the least, if these Crafty Men succeed in their present attempts. To put an end to the Subject at present & to hope for the best, the Council will determine with becoming spirit on Monday & Send these Seditious dangerous Men to a place where they will be deprived of the means of doing harm. But you will ask what ground I have for such hope when I know that we have in another instance even in this very day Jockeyed ourselves? Governor Penn & Chief Justice Chew as Kings Officers were ordered to be sent out of the State in case of Invasion & it was understood they were to go to Virginia where few Tories are & where they would have little influence & little opportunity of corresponding with the Enemy—the trust was reposed in the Board of War. The Board has ordered these Gentlemen, I should Say connived at their going, to Union Iron Works in Jersey, the property of William Allen Esquire a confirmed Enemy of our Independence two of whose apostate Sons are gone over to

General Howe & one or both of them in his Army, from whence they may safely correspond with & transmit plans to our Enemies all around.[11] Is not this enough to make an honest man who has staked his Life & all on our side exclaim with faithful Mercutio, "a pox on both your Houses" & wish he never had had any thing to do with such Citizens? Better never to have offended Mr P & Ch by the stigma of Imprisonment & banishment than to provoke them by the Act, & lose to the people the intended effect & benefits. I speak plainly to you, General Washington's Life, his virtues are the only present proofs of our Cause. Should he drop Suddenly, I will not determine that so good a Cause would be lost but I cannot err in avering that we should undergo most violent convulsions. When I first arrived here I was told by way of caution that in Congress there were parties—I soon perceived there were. In the Short span of seven weeks I have discovered parties within parties, divisions & subdivisions to as great a possible extent as the number 35 (for we have never more together) will admit of. As it is wholly contrary to my genius & practice to hold with any of them *as party,* so I incur the censure of not being *long* with any. These will continue & the evil effects of them increase every day until we confederate & adjust Accounts & until we Resolve to banish & punish Luxury & to practice œconomy public & private suitable to the Circumstances of people whose means for Exports are almost all & will soon be totally, cut off, until we sift the chaff from the Corn, the Enemies from the friends of the United States, until we determine to depend more upon our Selves under the protection of God Almighty, than upon a Crafty designing Court, who never has done, & who never will do, any thing for our Interest but what has been or shall be subservient to their own & who by every Act has demonstrated a disposition to make Tools of us for promoting their own ends.

When we are driven by hard Strokes to virtuous frugality, to a firm dependence upon our own Strength, then we shall help our Selves, we shall be really & truly independent, then we shall receive offers of Service which we may accept or reject as dear bought wisdom shall dictate, but from our present proceedings & from all appearances we are yet to be reduced to the State of a Rudderless ship in a boistrous Ocean. What can be more affecting than to reflect, that our Congress were last Year so wanton, so young & incautious as to make propositions, very injudicious propositions, for a Treaty with France which that Court has betrayed to our Enemy but has not deigned to favour with an answer. Yes, there is something more affecting—the avidity of some Men (too many I fear from Selfish veiws) for borrowing unlimmitted Sums of money from that Court which will be to Sell your Soil & your selves into a worse State of dependence than that from which we are endeavouring to escape. Judge from certain authentic extracts.[12]

"Our Treaty of Commerce is not yet proceeded upon. Their plan is not to have any transactions with us which shall acknowledge American Independency but to make us more easy they tell us we enjoy all the advantages which we propose by such a Treaty." Strange.

"Capt Cunningham is imprisoned at Dunkirk & the prizes which he took will be restored, this will serve to lull the British Ministry & then Cunningham & his Vessel will be released *through favour,* but we must put up with the loss of his prizes. This is a matter of Triumph to our Enemies which we Suffer them to enjoy for the present while we have the most Substantial proofs of the friendship of this Court & of Spain which will Soon be manifested to the World." Substantial proofs indeed!

"Feeling our Selves assisted in other respects we are induced to let them take their own time." Aye! & their own time they will take!

"Mr   received the same *professions* of good Will at Madrid but was refused the Character of Ambassador or to be received or acknowledged openly." Manifested to the World!

"We applied for the naval aid you require & received a *possitive refusal.*" "Also for the two Millions Sterling on Loan & was told it was *impossible to lend* so large a Sum."—"but are promised certain quarterly payments to make good the payment for Interest on 10 Millions of Dollars if you should borrow so many." (I beleive it is extended even to the Interest of 20 Millions at 4 to 6 per Cent.) This may be in the whole about two hundred & seventy thousand pounds per Annum if we should borrow so much as 20 Millions Dollars per Annum. This of 20 Millions is grounded only upon *"we hope"* how long any part of it is to last we have no assurance. The change of a minister would put an immediate Brake [. . .][13] other demands which will absorb the greatest part if not the whole of the first intended grants for paying the Interest of the hoped for 20 million Dollars & farther that tis expected we shall enable the Court to collect by Duties in Tobacco which we have engaged to *Send* to the Farmers General, great part of the proposed Loan." Immense *friendship!* Enable me, & I will lend you a Sum of Money. Will you believe it, upon this Slender Basis a bold attempt has been made to draw plumply & immediately for ten Million of Dollars, next for five Million; the former equals £2,250,000 Sterling, the latter £1,125,000. Did I say Slight basis? Are we not told in the Strongest language it is impossible to lend us any such Sum? Is this going hand over head? Is it governing 13 United States by random Strokes of policy? or did it spring from sinister motives? I cannot suspect the latter. Yet Such projects were the megrims of Men who hold themselves of the first rank & first importance in our political system. I told you I had been Instrumental in averting two pernicious schemes. This is one of the Instances. The other was a proposed mad expedition,[14] but I have not succeeded to my wish. Far from it. By a Majority of one voice we have Resolved to draw on France at all hazards, Tobacco or no Tobacco or whether the fund may be exhausted by other demands or not, to draw I say for the Amount of Interest of all past & future loans.[15]

I cannot persuade Gentlemen to believe that Bills of Exchange on France bearing 6 per cent interest is a farther emission of paper Money, but so much more dangerous than an emission of Square Dollars by the Interest which will accumulate to be repaid abroad & thereby in effect mortgaging to a foreign Crafty power so much of our Soil. I cannot prevail upon them to beleive that if their Loan Certificates were made payble in one Year instead of three or five years & the Interest quarterly or half yearly, Money holders could be induced to lend more freely. I cannot prevail by my reasoning, to prove that either, from the *tenour* of their present loan Certificates or *from the insufficiency* of the Sums Emitted to answer the amazing circulation of paper Currency & also for a return into the public Funds *arises* the Slackness & deficiency of Loans. I beleive it arises chiefly from the former because there can be no man so Stupid, as to think *Congress money* in *many Bills* more permanent & secure by lying in their Desks useless & Subject to many ordinary risques than it would be if it was comprised & expressed in *one Certificate* of *Congress Money* & bearing 6 per Cent Interest.[16] Neither can I prevail on Interested Men to acknowledge that 20 Millions of Expence per Annum all paid in ready Money whether the Expence be for Soldiers, Waggons & Rations or for Broad Cloth & Silk requires more money for circulating Currency than the expence of 8 or 10 millions per Annum—of which 7/8th at least was entered into Books not paid for in twelve or 18 months & even then not 1/3d paid for in Paper Money but in produce of the Ground— nor can I persuade such Men to own although they must know, that however hard they may Struggle & rant in order to accomplish impossibilities the Value of their paper Currency whether in Bills of Exchange hawked about in France or in Paper Dollars contemned in Philadelphia—But Market will continue to decrease until we can open our Ports & obtain a free exchange for the products of our Land. We may indeed find some temporary relief by Sale of Forfeitures within. What is worse than all I cannot prevail upon them to listen to the alarm—that going in debt to France how be it this may afford us present means & put our debt out of sight for a little while will be mortgaging our Soil, will induce that Court to persevere in her plan "*to do no act which may seem to acknowledge our Independency*,"[17] will encourage the British Ministry to protract the War, will infallibly Create Jealousies & engender broils & divisions among the States & will in a very few years burst our Childish bubble of Independence. That from these awful considerations Wisdom dictated to us to draw upon

France for no more Money than is absolutely necessary to purchase &
pay for articles essential to our defensive War. That we should contract
our expences public & private, recommend Taxation in each Colony,
borrow at home upon the best terms, clear the States of Enemies, Sell
vacant & forfeited Tracts & other Estates, encourage manufactures, strive
more ardently to improve our marine force & do a Thousand other
things which we know to be necessary which we ought immediately to
engage in & which we would do, if Luxury & Avarice were discounten-
anced & banished. If we have not virtue enough to save our selves, easy
access to the Treasury of France will only hasten our ruin. These Sir
are very serious considerations. I have suffered much distress of mind
on the occasion, I have been told that my arguments were very pretty
for theoretic writers but I appeal to experience, it is from experience
I draw my reasoning. I do not contend for a further Emission of paper
Money, I wish to avoid it. I am sure we may avoid it if we please. I
contend against the most dangerous of all Emissions drawing Bills on a
foreign Court, but if we must emit for domestic purchases & Services,
of two Evils I would choose the least. Many other arguments I have at
different Stages introduced, too many to trouble you with, I hope my
endeavors will be acceptable to my Constituents, I am void of understanding if my reasoning will not bear the test of experience & sound
judgment. The subject is as familiar to me & as clear as that Indigo in
such circumstances as we have been reduced to for the three years past
is a preferable Commodity for exportation to Rice & Lumber (uncommon Cases excepted). Had we been so wanton as to have drawn for
10 or 5 M[illion] Dollars, the purposes of those whom we have no
reason to befriend might have been Served; Tories would have thrown
back your paper money if they had any faith in your Bills of Exchange
& taken leave of you, a few Merchants would have attempted to introduce a flood of French articles which we may & ought to do without.
In fine we should have incurred a solid ponderous debt without the
benefit of one Solid article in return.[18]

LB (ScHi).

[1] An extract of Gervais' July 29 letter to Laurens is in *South Carolina Historical Magazine* 66 (January 1965): 17–19.

[2] Perhaps a reference to the committee investigating the evacuation of Ticonderoga. See John Hancock to Arthur St. Clair and Philip Schuyler, August 5,
1777, note.

[3] In the July 29 letter to Laurens cited above, Gervais explained that the
government of Georgia had recently offered a reward of £100 for the appre-
hension of Chief Justice William Henry Drayton of South Carolina because of
Drayton's efforts to bring about the annexation of Georgia to South Carolina.
There are a number of contemporary sources relating to this episode in Robert
W. Gibbes, ed., *Documentary History of the American Revolution*, 2 vols. (New
York: D. Appleton & Co., 1855–57), 2:75–87.

[4] See Laurens to John Wereat, August 30, 1777, note 2.

⁵ See Laurens to Joseph Clay, September 2, 1777.

⁶ William Brisbane.

⁷ For a discussion of George McIntosh's "Case," see John Hancock to Archibald Bulloch, January 8, 1777, note.

⁸ In regard to the issue of Pennsylvanians suspected of disloyalty, see John Hancock to William Livingston, August 30, 1777, note.

⁹ Laurens inserted this asterisk to key a partially torn sentence he wrote at the bottom of this page in his letter book: "I see they are not Numbered in [. . . .]" Approximately five words appear to be missing.

¹⁰ See *To Our Friends and Brethren in Religious Profession, in These and the Adjacent Provinces . . . . Signed in and on Behalf of the Meeting for Suffering, Held in Philadelphia, for Pennsylvania and New Jersey, the 20th Day of the Twelfth Month, 1776* (Philadelphia, 1776). Evans, *Am. Bibliography,* no. 14770.

¹¹ For a discussion of the case of these two former proprietary officials, see Laurens to John Rutledge, August 12, 1777, note 10.

¹² The following quotes are generally accurate paraphrases of passages from letters of the American commissioners in Paris dated March 12, April 9, and May 25, 1777. Wharton, *Diplomatic Correspondence,* 2:284–86, 322–24.

¹³ LB damaged; approximately four words missing.

¹⁴ See Charles Thomson's Notes of Debates, July 24 and 25, 1777.

¹⁵ Laurens must be referring to a vote taken in the committee of the whole, because Congress did not formally enter its approval of this policy in the journals until September 9. *JCC,* 8:724–25.

¹⁶ Laurens inserted a double asterisk at this point, apparently to remind himself that he resumed discussion of this subject in his September 8 continuation of this letter to Gervais.

¹⁷ See the letter of the commissioners at Paris dated May 25, 1777, in Wharton, *Diplomatic Correspondence,* 2:324.

¹⁸ For the continuation of this letter, see Laurens to Gervais, September 8, 1777.

Board of War to William Atlee

Dr Sir   War Office Septr. 6th. 1777

The Board have perused your Letter & approve of your Proceedings as to the Prisoners.¹ There is no other County but Lancaster & Northampton where an application is necessary for Guards. However I will desire the Executive Council to write to all their Lieutenants to furnish Guards for Prisoners when required by the Commissaries in the different Counties.² The Barracks to be built at Lebanon would I apprehend be very expensive when Nails & other Materials are so dear. Please to send an Estimate of the Expence that the Board may judge of the Expediency & Propriety of building them. The Prisoners at York must remain as they are. They are sufficiently distant from the Enemy especially as York Town will hardly be an Object worth their risquing a great Deal for. If we should be successful in our Operations the Prisoners will be remanded to Lancaster. In the meantime the Inhabitants of the Towns must put up with some Inconveniencies which would not have been thrown upon them had not Necessity & Prudence compelled us to it.

I am your very obed Servt,   Richard Peters Secy

RC (DLC). Addressed: "William Atlee Esq, D Commissary Genl of Prisoners, Lancaster."

[1] On August 22, after learning that the British fleet was in the upper Chesapeake Bay, Congress had directed the Board of War to move prisoners "from Lancaster and Yorktown, to places of greater safety." *JCC,* 8:665.

[2] A letter on this subject, from the board to President Thomas Wharton dated September 5, is in *Pa. Archives,* 1st ser. 5:585.

Samuel Chase to Thomas Johnson

Dear Sir,   Philada. Septr. 6th. 1777. Saturday 12 oClock

I dropt you a line by Mr. Howard this morning.[1] Inclosed I send you the memorial of the Quakers and the form of the parole which the Quakers refused.[2]

I have not heard from Mr. Paca, and beleive no post can come up. I beg you would write to Mr. Carroll to come up, as I must come down to take care of my family & effects. Will the Assembly sit?

Your affectionate and obedient servant,   S. Chase

Tr (MdHi).

[1] A Tr of this letter—as well as a Tr of Washington's September 5 letter to President Hancock that Chase may have enclosed with another letter to Johnson that has not been found—was inserted by the copyist in the midst of the present document between the first and second paragraphs. For Washington's letter, see Washington, *Writings* (Fitzpatrick), 9:186–87. Chase's "line by Mr. Howard" reads as follows. "We have no letters from the Genll. since the one published giving an account of a little skirmish of which I sent you a copy by Adams. The information that Mr. Howe was in full march for our Army was premature. Mr. Howard waits; if anything occurs before the post leaves this I will inform you. No News from the North." Chase Papers, MdHi.

[2] See *JCC,* 8:718–19; and John Hancock to William Livingston, August 30, 1777, note.

Committee of Congress to George Washington

Sir   Philadelphia 6th Sepr 1777

The Representation made to your Excellency by a Board of General officers, touching the Inconveniences arising from the Mode in which regimental officers have drawn their Rations, having been committed to Us by Congress, We propose to report the inclosed Resolve, upon which We previously wish to have your Sentiments.

We are not to consider the proposal for drawing more provisions than are allowed by the Establishment, which appears to be attended with many Difficulties, & have therefore confined our Views to the Removal of the Inconveniences complained of,[1] being with much Esteem sir your very huml. Servts.   Richard Henry Lee

Nathel. Folsom

E. Gerry

RC (DLC). Written by Gerry and signed by Gerry, Folsom, and Lee.

[1] On August 11 Washington's August 9 letter to President Hancock and the enclosed report of a board of general officers concerning rations had been referred to a committee composed of James Wilson, Jonathan B. Smith, and William Smith, but there is no indication in the journals that this committee ever reported. On September 4 Folsom, Gerry, and Lee were appointed "to consider under what regulations and restrictions regimental officers shall, for the future, receive their rations," and almost simultaneously a Board of War report recommending that Washington "be empowered, if he thinks proper" to order regimental officers to receive their rations in messes was tabled. The second committee's report recommending that regimental officers "be empowered to divide themselves, as often as they shall think proper, into messes" was submitted to Congress on September 11. See JCC, 8:629, 710–11, 732–33; and Washington, Writings (Fitzpatrick), 9:38–39.

John Hancock to George Washington

Sir,   Philada. Septr. 6th. 1777.

You will perceive from the enclosed Resolves, that Congress, desirous of reinforcing the Army at this critical Period, have recommended to the States of Pennsylvania and New Jersey to order out immediately a considerable Part of their Militia; and I have no Doubt of their Compliance.[1]

I have wrote to Govr. Livingston on the Subject,[2] and informed him that should he think proper to appoint Genl. Dickinson to the Command of the three Thousand requested from that State, it will be extremely agreeable to Congress. That Gentleman has, I understand, signified his Readiness to act whenever called upon; and as he possesses the Confidence of the Militia, and has Talents equal to the Task, I am persuaded the Appointment will give general Satisfaction.

Your Favour of the 3d Inst, and likewise of yesterday by the Hands of Genl. St. Clair I have been duely honoured with.[3] The latter I shall lay before Congress this Morning.

I have the Honour to be, with the greatest Respect, Sir, your most obed. & very hble Servt.   John Hancock Presidt

RC (DLC). In the hand of Jacob Rush and signed by Hancock.

[1] See JCC, 8:711–12. Hancock also enclosed resolves of September 4 on the

resignations of Capt. Jacob Bower and Adjt. Charles Seitz and of September 6 on clothing for the army. *JCC,* 8:710, 715–18.

2 See Hancock to William Livingston, September 5, 1777.

3 These letters are in PCC, item 152, 5:25–27, and Washington, *Writings* (Fitzpatrick), 9:172–73, 186–87.

Marine Committee to John Paul Jones

Sir   In Marine Committee Philadelphia Septemr. 6th 1777

As soon as these Instructions get to Hand, you are to make immediate Application to the proper Persons to get your Vessel Victualled and fitted for Sea with all Expedition. When this is done you are to proceed on a Voyage to some Convenient Port in France, on your arrival there, apply to the Agent if any, in or near said Port, for such supplies as you may stand in need of.[1] You are at the same Time, to give immediate notice by Letter to the Honorable Benjamin Franklin, Silas Deane & Arthur Lee Esqr or any of them at Paris, of your arrival, requesting their Instructions as to your future Destination; which Instructions you are to obey as far as it shall be in your Power.[2]

If, however, in the Course of your Voyage a favourable opportunity should offer, of doing Service to the States by taking or destroying any of the Enemys Ships, you are not to omit taking advantage of it, but may go out of your Course to effect so good a Purpose. In this we trust to your Zeal & Discretion.

You are to take particular Notice that whilst on the Coast of France, or in a French Port, you are, as much as you conveniently can to keep your Guns covered & concealed, and to make as little war like appearance as possible.

Wishing you A Successful and happy Voyage, We are sir, Your Friends. In behalf of the Marine Committee

John Hancock Presidt

P.S. On your arrival in France send one of your Officers with the Letter you are to write to the Commissioners at Paris, to prevent its falling into improper hands.   John Hancock Pt.

RC (DNA: PCC, item 168). In a clerical hand and signed by Hancock. Addressed: "John Paul Jones Esquire, commander of the Continental Ship Ranger, Portsmouth, New Hampshire." This day identical letters were sent to Elisha Hinman and to Thomas Thompson, copies of which are in C.O. 101, PRO; and PCC Miscellaneous Papers, Marine Committee Letter Book, DNA.

1 Due to difficulties in outfitting the *Ranger,* Jones did not put to sea until November 1. Thompson, commanding the frigate *Raleigh,* accompanied by Hinman in the *Alfred,* had already sailed for France and arrived there in early October. See Gardner W. Allen, *A Naval History of the American Revolution,* 2 vols. (Boston: Houghton, Mifflin Co., 1913), 1:223–30, 249, 278; and William J. Morgan, *Captains to the Northward: The New England Captains in the*

Continental Navy (Barre, Mass.: Barre Publishing Co., 1959), pp. 97–102. For earlier instructions to Thompson, see Marine Committee to Thompson, April 29, 1777.

2 For the November 25, 1777, instructions of the commissioners at Paris to Thompson and Hinman, and their January 16, 1778, instructions to Jones, see Wharton, *Diplomatic Correspondence,* 2:428, 471–72.

Eliphalet Dyer to Joseph Trumbull

Dear Sir   Philadelphia Septr 7th 1777
    I recievd your kind favour of the 1st Inst from Lebanon. Am rejoiced to hear my family are so well, son Thos. you say a little better. Mr Wales writes me much better near fit to join the Army. I hope his account may prove true being the most favourable but shall expect after you get to Windham to have in your Next a little more particular home Accounts than have had. I now Consider you as one of my family. What I have left at home, House, pastures, barn and any thing else is as free to you as the rest of my Children & would have you look upon it as much your home as you please till you think best to set up house keeping which shall leave with you & my daughter. Tho am concerned for furniture you know it grows worse & worse, believe we must not stand on Niceties at these times, hope all will come right by & by. I think Congress now are in a pretty good Temper to do business if this plaguy fellow of an How does not disturb us, we are now very Sulky and determine not to move for him if we can help it. How long our Courage may last I know not. It will not be strange if at this time it should exceed our Conduct. We feel very Magnanimous, but a few days may decide—before Hows appearance this way, our removal from this Venial City became a serious topick, & believe would have been the case had not G How appeard but you know we Scorn to fly. Confederation & finances are now the great Objects but ten thousand Necessaries are dayly Crouding in but there is no design nor Art in keeping it off. All are agreed in the Object, differ only in the proportion of Representation & taxation. You may say that is enough. True it is but I think we shall not break upon these; it will now soon be agitated. Supplying our Army securing & appreciating our Currency is now first attended to. France & Spain offer us money to pay the Intrest of all our Loan. Will not sure Bills on our Commisrs in France for the Intrest at 6 per cent in Specie make money Catchers fond of our Bills & eager to put them into the Loan Office on recieving their Intrest in Europe by bills of Excge drawn on our Commisrs. It would in fact be equal to 15 per Cent. For the present if you have any to put in you had best wait a few days for a decision for I yet know not whether that advantage will be given only as Incouragement to those who will now throw in their money into the Office as it may soon be wanted or shall

extend to those whose money we have allready got, I mean to past Loans.[1] For my part if this takes place I should think it my Intrest to sell the most of my landed Estates, ie, if it will sell high in proportion to other things and place Avails in the Loan Offices as am persuaded in a few years when these loans are paid of[f] the same money will buy more than double the land in Value & Quantity especially in the heart of our Country. Should be glad to hear Whether Lands rise & Whether there is still a demand. Mr. Webster offers me about 17 hund pounds for Scotland farm. Believe should Venture to take 2000. Hope you will soon write me a little particular of family & Affairs & when I had best come home &c &c. I have wrote to Benjn. once or twice telling him I could get some very necessary articles here in his way if he wanted them such as could send by a post. There is now Morris & Brown both here who would be glad to carry some artickles for him but he never will write me one word. I wrote Mrs Dyer a few days agoe by Majr Still. My most sincere affection to Wife & Children, regards to all Friends & am sincerely Yours,   Elipht Dyer

[*P.S.*] Am discouraged writing to my Children. Have wrote 2 or 3 times to Coll. Thos but recieved no answer, only one from Amelia one for Jabez. What to do for Jabez I know not; do steer him as well as you can. I wish he could learn French. There is a Young Gent'n from France going or gone to reside at Wethersfield this fall & Winter. Would be glad of Jabez Company & they might learn each Other (ie the one English, the other French. I wish he would attend to it I should Value it 10 times as much as all his Lattin &c.   E D

Coll Williams & Mr Low well & send their Compliments to you. Brown is gone to head quarters. Will bring you the News if any, the Armys Near togeather, must rub Noses soon if one or the other [do not] run away.

RC (CtHi).
[1] This arrangement for payment of interest on future loans in bills of exchange drawn on the commissioners at Paris was approved by Congress on September 9, and it was extended to previously issued loan office certificates on the 10th. See *JCC*, 8:724–26, 730–31; and Henry Laurens to John Rutledge, September 10, 1777.

James Lovell to Joseph Trumbull

Dear Sir   Philada. Sepr. 7th. [1777]
   I find by yours dated the 1st of this Month that you will probably be a little more stationary than you have been for many weeks back. Therefore I shall scratch something or other upon paper for you, at least weekly; as is my practice to others of the few in whom I intirely confide.

I can excuse you, upon your *first* meeting with your lovely Amelia, for that descriptive Sketch which you have given me of your Happiness. But I charge you in future to avoid even Hints about dear domestic Joys. Consider that my Duty has fixed me in unsocial Philadelphia; and do not heedlessly make me the Victim of Envy which is its own severe Tormentor.

As to Journals—be persuaded that no Expence or Industry has been wanting on the Part of Congress to get them up to the present Time. The Flight of Printers & the Want of paper has impeded the Work till now, when we have a good prospect. We are up to Octr. 25th. and shall very shortly have the Year —76 in a Volume.[1]

When the main Army is at our Elbow, and while we are situated in the Capital of such a State as Pensylvania we shall never want ten thousand Interruptions to the Settlement of the Articles of Confederation & the Establishment of our Currency.

As to losing the Confidence of the people, I shall be sorry for their own Sakes; But, by Way of Scare Crow to an honest Heart, I value it as little as any other natural Phenomenon of Nature. There is a majority in every State of the Union, and in every great Assembly, which can be depended upon, at this Day; But there are also heavy Clogs in each. The Cause of the people is safe. But their Patience must have full Exercise. Virtuous themselves they cannot be ruined by their present Assailants.

Had there been due Vigour in this Government, Congress would not have been obliged to have pointed out Individuals of this State for Arrest. But the Safety of the Union called for it. And you may depend upon it every step we have taken can be handsomly defended. Freely did old Israel and the Tribe in general turn out armed when scandalous Oppression had stirred up the Paxton Boys. Read the hypocritical Cant of these Days. Hear the Appeal to the Freemen of Pensylvania, and Quotations from the Bill of Rights of this *Independent* State, from Wretches who will not affirm themselves faithful *Subjects* of it; and who since the Declaration of Independency complain, in the Registries of their meetings of Sufferings, that they are forced to aid in a War *against Government*.

I will suppose Coll. Dyer has written on the Subject of giving a Spring to the Loan Offices, therefore I shall omit that Topic at this Time.

Before this reaches you, a Number of New England Shippers will be about you, who have left their Vessels at the Head of Elk. There has been a most horrid Delay in the Management of the Persons to whom they were consigned. I have written to Coll. Aylett[2] to desire he would confide the Settlement of his private Accounts as well as public to you so far as concerns the 6 Captains particularly Taylor my old Fellow prisoner & Perkins my half LandLord. You can empower Tracy or

Deacon Smith to go through with it. The poor Fellows are heartsick of public Employ. They have about ruined themselves by their Late Tryal. Four in Five would have got to Boston long ago if they had been in private Service.

My Wife gives me a useful Account of the Scarcity of Bread, in Boston. How is it? artificial? Has it not been fruitful in the Eastern States? There is a vile Jewlike Struggle in every part; I wish Howe was nearer to his old pen in 42 Deg. 30' Latitude. Not indeed that I find he mends the People of this City by coming into their Neighbourhood. But he would have different materials to operate upon in my Country from what Quakers are constructed of.

You tell me you have nothing new. It cannot be long so with us. The Enemy's Fleet has fallen down Elk, our Genl. thinks it is to water at the mouth of Susquehannah. Time must discover. Though both Armies are exposed to the Fever & Ague, yet there is a great Difference to be expected in the Consequences. A Stranger with his Teeth chattering will think himself dowright sick. Our Countrymen will sweat off their Fever & go instantly upon Duty, as they have practised in regard to Field Labour. I close, Your affectionate Friend,   J Lovell

RC (CtHi).
[1] For Lovell's appointment to the committee for printing the journals and bibliographic information on the published journals for the year 1776, which the committee was still working on at this time, see *JCC,* 6:1128, 7:101.
[2] Not found.

John Adams to Abigail Adams

My dear   Philadelphia Monday Septr. 8. 1777

There has been a very general Apprehension, during the last Week that a general Action would happen, as on Yesterday. But We hear of none.

Our Army is incamped between Newport and White-Clay Creek on advantageous Ground. The General has harrangued his Army and published in General orders, in order to prepare their Minds for something great, and has held up the Example of Starks, Harkemer, Gansevoort and their Troops, to animate his Officers and Men with Emulation. Whether he expects to be attacked, or whether he designs to offend, I cant say.

A General Action which should terminate in a Defeat of How would be compleat and final Ruin to him, if it should terminate only in a drawn Battle, it would be the same Thing. If He should gain a Victory, and maintain Possession of the Field, he would loose so many Men killed and wounded, that he would scarcely have enough left to march to Philadelphia, surrounded as he would be with Militia, and the broken remains of the Continental Army.

But if there should be no general Battle, and the two Armies should lounge away the Remainder of the Campain, in silent Inactivity gazing at each other, Howes Reputation would be ruined in his own Country and in all Europe, and the Dread of him would cease in all America. The American mind, which I think has more Firmness now than it ever had before since this War begun, would acquire a Confidence and Strength, that all the Efforts of Great Britain afterwards would not be able to relax.

You will see by the Papers inclosed, that We have been obliged to attempt to humble the Pride of some Jesuits who call themselves Quakers, but who love Money and Land better than Liberty or Religion. The Hypocrites are endeavouring to raise the Cry of Persecution, and to give this Matter a religious Turn, but they cant succeed. The World knows them and their Communications. Actuated by a land jobbing Spirit, like that of William Penn, they have been soliciting Grants of immense Regions of Land on the Ohio. American Independence has disappointed them, which makes them hate it. Yet the Dastards dare not avow their Hatred to it, it seems.[1]

The Moments are critical here. We know not, but the next will bring Us an Account of a general Engagement begun—and when once begun We know not how it will end, for the Battle is not always to the strong. The Events of War are uncertain. All that We can do is to pray, as I do most devoutly, that We may be victorious—at least that We may not be vanquished. But if it should be the Will of Heaven that our Army should be defeated, our Artillery lost, our best Generals kill'd, and Philadelphia fall into Mr. Howes Hands, still America is not conquered. America would yet be possessed of great Resources, and capable of great Exertions. As Mankind would see. It may for what I know be the Design of Providence that this should be the Case. Because it would only lay the Foundations of American Independence deeper, and cement them stronger. It would cure Americans of their vicious and luxurious and effeminate Appetites, Passions and Habits, a more dangerous Army to American Liberty than Mr. Howes.

However, without the Loss of Philadelphia, We must be brought to an entire Renunciation of foreign Commodities, at least of West India produce. People are coming to this Resolution, very fast here. Loaf sugar at four dollars a Pound, Wine at Three Dollars a Bottle, &c. will soon introduce Œconomy in the Use of these Articles.

This Spirit of Œconomy would be more terrible to Great Britain, than any Thing else—and it would make Us more respectable in the Eyes of all Europe.

Instead of acrimonious Altercations between Town and Country and between Farmer and Merchant, I wish, that my dear Countrymen would agree in this Virtuous Resolution, of depending on themselves alone. Let them make salt, and live without sugar—and Rum.

I am grieved to hear of the Angry Contentions among you. That improvident Act, for limiting Prices, has done great Injury, and in my sincere Opinion if not repealed, will ruin the state, and introduce a civil War. I know not how unpopular, this sentiment may be: but it is sincerely mine. There are Rascally Upstarts in Trade I doubt not, who have made great Fortunes in a small Period, who are Monopolizing and oppressing. But how this can be avoided entirely I know not, but by disusing their Goods and letting them perish in their Hands.

RC (MHi). Adams, *Family Correspondence (Butterfield)*, 2:337–39.

[1] Adams was one of the committee appointed on August 28 by Congress to examine the Quaker documents that had been sent to Congress by Gen. John Sullivan. *JCC*, 8:688–89. The committee ultimately recommended the arrest of several prominent Philadelphia Quakers suspected of disloyalty. For further information on the events surrounding this incident, see John Hancock to William Livingston, August 30, 1777, note.

Charles Carroll of Carrollton to Thomas Johnson

Dear Sir,   Swan Creek 8th Sept 1777.

I beg the favor of you to forward the inclosed by the first Safe opportunity: my father will be anxious to hear from me.[1]

G. Smallwood writes to you by this opportunity & transmits a return of the militia here, their arms, ammunition, & accoutrements & I suppose will inform you he proposes to order the militia to rendevouze at Johnson's Ferry. The militia at this place will march tomorrow for that ferry. I shall proceed to head Quarters. No doubt you have better information from Mr. Jones of the enemys position & motions than I can collect at this out of the way place. Howe I hear is at Aithim's Tavern 5 miles from head of Elk. Col. Rumsey, who is now here, was Saturday at head of Elk & made some prisoners. Cornwallis is at Crouch's mills, Kniphausen at Fisher's mills, the last distant from Newark 3 miles. Poor Alexander is gone along with the enemy with all his Family. He can never remain in this country unless in the disagreeable situation of seeing it conquered by the enemy. If he has any virtue, this thought alone must pain him. Dr. H. Stevenson, it is said, cried like a child when he left his plantation in this neighbourhood. Unfortunate misguided men! G.W. made a speech (I am told by one Rogers who keeps Susquahanna Ferry) to his army which was recd with great applause. Officers & men desired to be led to battle. Washington is said to be at the head of 30 thousand men. I believe this number exaggerated by at least a third. I believe Gen. Smallwood does not intend to cross Susquahanna till he receives the feild pieces, at least not to proceed near the enemy. Gen. Washington I am sure will not hazard a general battle. We this day had a full view from stony point of the Enemy's fleet lying from the mouth of Elk to Sasafras, but chiefly about the mouth of Sasafras. If Mr. Smith should be desirous to return home, as it appears he is by a letter of his I this day saw written to Col. B. Rumsey, I shall proceed to Congress, & not return to join Smallwood's brigade of militia.[2] Indeed I already find this kind of sauntring life extremely disagreeable & fatiguing & hard lodging & irregular hours of eating begins to disagree with my puny constitution & habit of body; but perhaps I shall soon be more inured to & better able to support the fatigue of a campaign. I heartily wish you well & am yr. affectionate friend,

Ch. Carroll of Carrollton

RC (MeHi).

[1] Carroll's September 8 letter to his father is in the Carroll Papers, MdHi.

[2] Carroll was still with Gen. William Smallwood (at "Nottingham") on September 14, at which time he appended the following brief note to Johnson at the bottom of Smallwood's letter of that date to the governor. "I shall proceed with General Smallwood till he joins the main army and shall then on this go to Congress or return home. I am well and desire you will inform my father thereof by the first opportunity." Brown Books, MdAA.

George Frost to Josiah Bartlett

Dear Sir,   Philadelphia Sept. 8th. 1777

I Recd. your favr. wrote in Kingstown Augst   Wherein you say you were just returned from Springfield and the result of the Commissioners from the several states laid before Congress which we have Recd. but have not as yet acted on it.[1] The Avarice, Venality and disipation prevaling among all Ranks here in this quater and Increasing more & more in the Eastern states I fear it will be impractable to addop the Measures Recomended by your Committee, altho I think with you that it is Very Alerming and fear it will be Attended with Very ill consequences. As to the support of the Credit of our Money I can conceive of but two ways. First our Commisrs. in France & Spain has procured for us a loan to pay the Interest of all the Money we shall borrow by our loan office certificates at the rate of five livers France for every Dollar Interest which we sopose will give great encourragement to the Monied Men to lend the United States. The Other is that all the States go Immediately into large Taxation by which Means we shall be able to pay our Armey &c but if those two Measures should fail and we are obliged to Emit more Money (which I hope that wont be the case), it will sink it Very low indeed. As to the Northern affairs they have been Very Alerming but at present through the Goodness of God I trust they are at present Very favourable. You'l see more perticuler by the News papers and that Congress has adopted measures for Inquirry in that Affair. We Could have wished Borgoyne had pushed his armey lower down then he has that we might have marched an Armey in his Rear as well to Attack him in the front, we hope however that our brave Starke will be able to perform the former wile Genl. Gates attacks their front. Genl. Howes armey is some weare nigh Caskeen bridge, and Genl. Washingtons head quarters at Wilmington whose Advance parties has had several scermishes (as they are Called) according to fortain of war some times they gitt the better and sometime we have the better of them, we dayle Expect to here of a General Battle. I have not seen the Map you mention but am Informed by Good Judges its a pore one. I'l make further Inqy. and see it. If I think it will answer your Expectation will send it you by first good oppetunity. (We have been greatly perplex'd with a number of French officers. Some came over under Extradany Contracts by Mr. Deane and others to seek Rank & service in our Armey no les then five or six Majr. Generals, Briga. Genls, Cols. &c &c. To have plas'd them all we must have superseeded nigh half of our Officers, trust we shall send 'm for the greater part Back to France. I should be glad to be informed wether our Troops has Recd. their Clowes as we are Informed Clothing at the Northen Armey is scarce. You'l see by the papers Inclosd. what Situation we are in With regard to some principel quakers &c. I fear we shall meet with a great Deale of trouble with them. Am, sr, With great Esteam, your most Obt., Humble Sevt.   Geo. Frost

RC (MiU–C).
[1] See Henry Marchant to Nicholas Cooke, August 18, 1777, note 2.

Henry Laurens to John Lewis Gervais

[September 8, 1777]
It is now Monday Morning the 8th. We have nothing yet from the Camp except that both Armies seemed to be preparing for Serious Action. General Washington had approached the Enemy within three or four miles of Contact, had issued a very sensible animating public order a Copy of which I have seen & will endeavor to send you,[1] by this it would seem as if he meant to attack. General Howe on the other hand has sent on board the fleet all his Sick & wounded & ordered as [of] the 6th Inst four days provision to be Issued. This comes by a deserter who came in to General Washington yesterday morning, if this be true Mr. Howe expects to dine here on Wednesday, I hope we shall disappoint Sir William here as we did Sir Peter at Charles Town. The wounded arrived from the Skirmish the other day in which some of the

lower County Militia behaved Infamously, threw down their Guns & fled without stopping till they got home, but others made great amends & the Enemy altho they had Cannon & we had none suffered exceedingly. Colo. Martin of North Carolina & his Regimt have gained glory in that affair. I say as I have nothing new from the Camp I will trouble you a little further on the Subject which I droped the 6th.[2]

It was said, "many people hold Congress money to purchase Lands & other bargains or would even lend it at a low Interest to private persons in preference to putting it into the Loan Offices." Answer, admit these to be facts—what is proved, but that there is a circulation for money either by purchases or by Loans, & that there are some people who have as good an opinion of Congress money as to Exchange Land for it & some who have opportunities of improving it in different ways otherwise they would not borrow, & the loans to them being at a low interest prove these to be men of substance.

Again, "Many people will not take Congress Money who will by some means or other find Money to purchase Bills & fill your Loan office." Granted, but who are these people? Surely our *freinds* do not refuse to take Congress money, & shall we Involve the States in a debt which may involve their ruin in order to accomodate our *Enemies?* But is it certain that Tories who will not Credit us here at home where there *is* a Stamina, will take our paper money Payable in a Country where we have *no* foundation?

"But it has been the practice of all Nations to borrow"; true when necessity obliged them, & so far & no further, I consent *now* to borrow. But so extremely cautious wise nations have been of borrowing from other powers, so jealous even of a Balance of Trade against them has Great Britain been, that they broke off connexion with France & Submitted to drink muddy port instead of sparkling Champaign & brilliant Claret.

"But Great Britain owes now about 40 Million to the States of Holland for money borrowed." This lies on you to prove, but I believe I may safely deny it. The Dutch subjects I will grant have money in the British Loans, I dont know to what amount perhaps six or eight Millions, so have the subjects of other States as *Individuals.* But if nations have been accustomed to borrow of other Nations have they not given security? Did not Holland put some of her Port Towns into the hands of the Queen of England! Did not Prussia Mortgage Selissia for the Credit established in London? Which of the United States will you put into the hands of France as guarantee for the Sums intended to be borrowed. But why will you borrow when by a reassumption of that Virtue which we boasted of & dropped in the same year, you may go on & Succeed without borrowing?

"But France asks us no Guarantee, she offers to lend without any Security & when we are in her debt it will be her Interest to Support us." True she has as yet Courted us to take trifling Sums & magnified "*The K——s generosity*" in demanding no Security. She has also told us it is impossible to let us have the trifling Sum of two Millions Sterling. How long shall we remain free from a demand for guarantee? Can anyone answer? If it will be consistent with the Interest of France to Support us when we are in her debt, it will be equally consistent with her Interest & her practice too to send a few Men of War, Troops & Officers into one or more of our ports to protect us from insults from our old Enemies & at the same time to collect the Revenues due for the Loans. We have a recent proof of the Value France has put upon our Lands in our present Circumstances a "*Livre or 10½ d. Sterling per Acre*". What folly, what madness will it be to involve our selves in debt to that power. We should at least refrain until we have Resolved upon the Port for the reception of the French Men of War.

I compare our present attempt to the folly of a Young Man borrowing money from a designing Sharper upon the Credit of an expected Heirship. We are unwary & love ease & pleasure, we will borrow because it will save trouble. France pleads poverty in order to enhance the favor—will lend as much as she can (if you will enable her) & asks no Security. This magnifies the Royal & National Generosity. To whom are these manifique Offers proposed? To free & Independent States? No. To puppets whom she keeps behind the Curtain, to Squeak her purposes, for tis her plan "to do no Act which shall seem to acknowledge our Independency." She will not openly receive our Agents. Her Minister tells them "it will be well taken if they communicate with no other persons about the Court but himself, that he will at all *convenient Seasons* be ready to confer with them." They treat our Agents "with *all Civility* but are cautious of giving *Umbrage* to England."

"They (the French Ministry) take every Step to gratify England publickly—attend to their Remonstrances, forbid Ships with Military Stores for America to depart, recal leave of absence to their Officers going out to America & *in presence of the British Minister* give Strict Orders that American Prizes should not be sold in France, At the same time all these things are nevertheless done & they assure us (American Agents) of their good Will." [3] Can there be Stronger proofs adduced of French dissimulation & American Puppetism?

Would wise Men, would the Guardians of thirteen Orphan States incautiously trust their Wards in the power of such a Court? If you profusely borrow from her you will, you must be in her power. I tremble at the prospect. I would almost rather return to Subjection to England, but I would surely rather recall our Agents than Submit any longer to such Insults. France will not for her own Interest let you go back to England. Be Virtuous, She will also for her own Interest Seek you, she will continue to supply you with every thing needful & to keep her ports

open to your Ships. In a little time such virtuous Resolution will render
you Independent both of France & England. I must have tired you good
Sir & yet I have not minuted here one half that I thought myself
obliged to say & repeat upon this important business in the Course of
5 or 6 days debate & adjournment. Many good men see into the danger
of contracting a debt with France but they do not see clearly. They
say "what shall we do, the Treasury is Empty." This shews our Error
in having neglected so long a business which is one of the main pillars
of our Independence. It shews our folly too in the wanton terms proposed for Treaty last year—there the Court of Versailles has again
made puppets of us & treated us with the Contempt we deserved. God
Grant Mr. Washington, that brave & virtuous, that disinterested, Patriotic Hero, success in a Conflict which is probably now in agitation
& we shall have further time to retrospect our proceedings & to mend
what shall appear to have been amiss. If he fails a New Scene will
open. Nothing but virtue then can Save us. We never shall call in her
aid until we feel Severe distress. Tis time to attend Congress, maybe
when I return I may tell you more of the Quaker affair & trouble you
with another Sheet, but before I go let me suggest a danger which we
seem to be drawn into. A whole week is passed & nothing is said or
done further for replenishing our Treasury, if the proper means are
neglected until that is nearly or *more nearly* exhausted, we may be
frighted into a measure big with ruin, that of drawing for five or ten
Million Dollars for doing which we have neither permission nor encouragement. If this shall happen remember I have foretold it to you
& other my Constituents who are concerned in the event.

I am happy in having Mr. Middleton exactly coincide in Sentiments
with me altho he has not spoke to the point. Mr. H[eyward] differs
but I would not have it taken notice of for whatever his opinions may
be, he is a Man of Candour & Integrity & I wish not to name any
Body.

9th September. I did not return from business yesterday till the Sun
had Set, eat a Scanty dinner & was obliged to go out again upon
business. When I came home I felt a much stronger propensity for the
Bed than the writing Table. It was mortifying to sit from 11 oClock
to 1/2 past 6 without respite, spend four hours of that time wrangling
a point which I think had employed us five days before—receive &
pocket a well timed & spiritted reprimand from the Council & end
the business relative to the Quakers & other self disaffected, where it
might have been ended & in the manner in which it ought to have
been ended in five minutes from the very outset, by recommending to
confine at an appointed place Stanton in Virginia, all the mischeivous
& active ones who shall refuse to take the Oath or affirmation of
Allegiance to the State. I will not say the business is quite ended, for

as the Council feel or rather express themselves as if they were chaffed by our conduct, it may be they will have nothing further to do in it.[4]

These are weighty Considerations. Every weak, every impolitic step in Congress tends to lower it in the Esteem of the World, to sink its power & influence & to strengthen the hand & hopes of our Enemies abroad & at home. Many such steps are taken which the World do not know of. Those which are the subject of public canvassing make a rapid progress to our detriment. Observe among other reasons given in the House of Commons by Ld Geo Germaine for continuing the War in America he gives particularly this one—"that he had further formed his opinion from the circumstance of the Congress having given up the Government confessing themselves unequal to it & creating Mr. Washington dictator of America."[5] London May 16th. In the same speech he remarks on our Liberality giving the British West India Islands to the French, a foolish project which our Auctioneer friend must have betrayed & asked who will bid more? If people in America are once impressed with an opinion that Congress is inadequate to the business of Government, this Assembly will be presently blown up & our circumstances will become deplorable. I must observe that no part of the blunders or misconducts which I have been Witness to are chargeable upon the Men of business & plain good understanding. One bold patriot with few hairs on his Chin & endless fun & joke in his Brain, who boasts much of his knowledge in Law & Logic, who delights to discountenance a modest man & to baffle reason by ridicule, Strove as ardently to involve us in a serious quarrel with the Executive Council in this moment of danger as he did to plunge us into an enormous debt to France. Thank God we have hitherto repulsed him in both attacks. You will be again surprized when I tell you that during the important debates on the Subjects of borrowing money & removing Enemies from our bosoms we have Seldom seen more than twenty members upon the floor, & more than once, business has been interrupted by want of Members (9 States) to make a Congress. I may add to "weighty" that these are *melancholy* considerations. The Evil demands attention from the Several States—there must be a thorough Renovation. I can do you no good here. I am wasting time to no good purpose.

I am persuaded you will make the best use you can of these intimations, you may depend upon it I have neither by word or energy misrepresented any fact, I have Spoken pretty freely to His Excellency the President. Mr. Middleton I beleive has delivered his Sentiments & will deliver them very fully when he returns, but I Speak more to your Self in the Character of one of my Representative Constituents. I wish what I have said may be useful. I hold it dangerous that the public Should know our "Infirmity" as it was yesterday properly termed in debate by my Colleague last mentioned.

I beleive I shall scarcely have time to write by this opportunity to

Mr Manigault. You will be so good as to present me to him & to Mrs. Manigault in the most cordial terms. I beleive the good old Gentleman will not differ in opinion with me on the Subject of depending on or going wantonly in debt to the French. He will pity as I sincerely do the State of all people of quiet peaceable dispositions among the Quakers who no doubt are greatly distressed for the present Circumstances of their turbulent friends, for although many of them censure the Pembertons & others for having indiscreetly as they say interfered with affairs of State, yet they have deep feelings & many are apprehensive the Stroke may be aimed at their whole Society, this is not by any means intended.

I have not heard from Mr. John Laurens since the 31st August. He keeps close to duty with the General whom he greatly admires.

The Enemy at New York & Staten Island threaten to return the late compliment by General Sullivan on a visit to the Jerseys which is at present undefended except by their own Militia, these lie scattered & Estates & persons may be much injured before a respectable body can be collected & whereever the Enemy prevail they lay all waste & commit horrible Cruelties on the Inhabitants especially on the Women.

We have Submitted to General Washington for the propriety of ordering three Thousand Men from Peeks Kill for the protection of Jersey or for forming a Corps de reserve for enabling him in case of need to give second battle to General Howe's Troops.[6] It is said from Camp that General Howe has with the Sick & wounded embarked his Baggage & Tents, his Army retired a little way & Camped in Bowers on & near Iron Hill. If this be true the fleet will soon reappear in Delaware. I must now go again to Congress, when I return or early to morrow Morning will close this very long Epistle. We are more than three days older yet nothing extraordinary is brought forth so vain are all our conjectures.

Just returned from Congress 4 oClock. I cannot sit to dinner before I disburthen my mind by giving you a further Idea of our Confused proceedings.

I have been Witness to a Report made by a Committee of the whole, which had been entered upon the Journal, Superceeded by a new Resolution even without reference to the Report. A Resolution carried almost nem con—entered, & half an hour after reconsidered & expunged.[7] When I add that such irregularity is the work of almost every day, you will not wonder that I wish to be any where but in Congress.

The great question upon borrowing Money & paying in Bills upon France for the Annual Interest at 6 per Cent was this morning confirmed which *if our* Bills are *accepted* is meant to involve us further at least Two hundred & Seventy thousand pounds Sterling per Annum in a debt to France. 21 Yeas against 5 Nay. The Nays Colo Harrison,

Mr. John Adams, Mr. Duane, Mr. Middleton, Mr. Laurens. A very thin house for deciding the fate of America—time will Shew who are in the right.[8] £ 27000 Sterling per Annum. I Should have added besides the disadvantage of Remittances & besides vast other debt, but we have now temporary access to Money we shall continue to squander until we receive some very severe Check. This may possibly be within 48 hours for we this moment learn by express that Genl Howe has Stolen a march upon our great General. He must be stopped this night or tomorrow morning he will be on our Skirts. We are all now talking of adjourning to the Country. The question is, where?

I take up another sheet chiefly with a design to ask your pardon for this long detaining you & to conclude. If any thing momentous or any thing worth your notice comes to pass before I seal it shall be added in a Postscript. This had been intended by an Express Messenger, my Colleagues judge it proper to detain him a few days. It will therefore go by the hands of Doctor Houston of Savanna.

Adieu. My Compliments to Mrs. Gervais & best wishes to the Little folks & all of you. I am with great regard & affection &ca[9]

LB (ScHi). A continuation of Laurens to Gervais, September 5, 1777.

[1] See Washington, *Writings* (Fitzpatrick), 9:188–89.

[2] See Laurens to Gervais, September 5, 1777, note 16.

[3] The quotations in the last two paragraphs are taken from the letters of the American commissioners in Paris dated March 12 and May 25, 1777. Wharton, *Diplomatic Correspondence,* 2:284–85, 324.

[4] On this issue, see John Hancock to William Livingston, August 30, 1777, note.

[5] Germain was referring to the extensive grant of powers Congress made to Washington on December 27, 1776. *JCC,* 6:1045–46.

[6] There is no mention of this issue in the journals but the question may have been "submitted" to Washington via Col. David Forman, who this day delivered a verbal communication to Congress from the general. On September 8, however, Congress did order Gen. Israel Putnam, the American commander at Peekskill, to hold 1,500 men in readiness for Washington. See *JCC,* 8:720, 726.

[7] The actions referred to here by Laurens have not been otherwise identified.

[8] See *JCC,* 8:724–25.

[9] At this point in his LB, Laurens added the following note to himself: "In a P.S. informed him that the Letters for Georgia as they go by Mr. Houston will be carried on by him but enclosed him Copy of a Letter to Mr Clay. The letter to Mr Legare being too large for this Packet goes separate but he will see it— send double-sets of News Papers & desired him to give some to J. Wells."

Richard Henry Lee to Patrick Henry

Dear Sir, Philadelphia 8th Septr. 1777

Nothing new hath happened that we know of since my last. But it seems extremely probable that a general engagement will take place in a day or two between the American Army and Gen. Howe. The Quaker m[otto] ought to be "Nos turba sumus" for if you attack one, the whole Society is roused. You will see by the inclosed *Testimonies* a uniform, fixed enmity to American measures, which with the universal ill fame of some capital persons, has occasioned the arrest of old Pemberton and several others, to prevent their mischievous interposition in favor of the enemy at this critical moment when the enemies army is on its way here, with professed design to give this City up to the pillage of the soldiery. They have taken infinite pains, according to custom, to move heaven and earth in their favor, and have transmitted copies of their indecent remonstrances over the Country. Congress have, to prevent ill impressions, ordered their several inimical Testimonies to be published in one Handbill. Altho nothing can be more certain than that Allegiance & protection are reciprocal duties, yet these Men have the assurance to call for the protection of those laws and that government, which they expressly disclaim and refuse to give any evidence of their Allegiance to. There is no doubt but that they will endeavor by means of the "Friends" in Virginia to make disturbance and raise discontent there, but this may serve to put you on your guard. We understand that Gen. Howe has put all his heavy baggage and even his Tents on board ship and that all his fleet except a few Ships of war have fallen down to the mouth of Sassafrass, and many of them gone down the Bay. The Army has three or 4 days victuals cooked and by all their Manœuvres it seems clear that they mean to urge their way to this place. Gen. Washington is within 6 miles of their main Body and determined not to remove without a battle. By your letter of the 30th last it would seem that you have not received many letters from me that I have written, not one post since my arrival here on the 12 of August having gone without a letter to you with all the material news, besides one by Express. It is realy discouraging to write so much as I do having so little time, and yet my friends not receive my letters. This day Congress have proposed that the Quaker Tories should be sent forthwith to Stanton in Augusta, I hope you will have them well secured there for they are mischievous people. Should Howe be disappointed here, as it seems very likely that he will, it is more than probable that he will endeavor to do us all the injury in his power as he returns, and therefore it will be wise to be as well prepared for him as possible. I am dear Sir most affectionately yours   Richard Henry Lee

P.S. The worthy Baron Kalb desires me to aid your good offices in procuring his baggage to be forwarded by sending you the inclosed which shews the rout travelled and where his Trunks were left—at Wrights Ordinary.   R.H. Lee

RC (PHi).
[1] Lee may have enclosed the special September 5 "Appendix" of the *Penn-

sylvania Evening Post, which contained a December 20, 1776, address urging Quakers to refuse to assist in the American war effort and a September 4, 1777, remonstrance of Israel Pemberton, John Hunt, and Samuel Pleasants, claiming the rights of freemen against arbitrary confinement. Pemberton and other prominent Philadelphia Quakers had been arrested by Pennsylvania authorities at the recommendation of a congressional committee of which Lee was a member. On September 6 Congress had approved this committee's recommendation that Quaker records seized from the confined Quakers should be published, and nine of the "testimonies" and "epistles" presented at various Quaker meetings held in 1775–77 were printed in the September 9 issue of *Dunlap's Pennsylvania Packet.* For information on the origin of this episode and the developments that led to the arrest and removal to Virginia of several Quakers, see John Hancock to William Livingston, August 30, 1777, note.

² Henry's August 30 letter to Lee is in William Wirt Henry, *Patrick Henry, Life, Correspondence and Speeches,* 3 vols. (New York: Charles Scribner's Sons, 1891), 3:89–90.

³ For Henry's September 12 response to Lee acknowledging this request, see ibid., pp. 94–95.

James Lovell to Vicomte de Mauroy

Philada Sept 8th 1777

In answer to the letter with which you favoured me of the 5th from Darby, I would assure you that I have been continually attentive to the very disagreable situation in which, as a man of military spirit, you must have thought yourself, ever since the near approach of the enemy.¹ But, Sir, as something is begun, at length relative to your departure for France, I am of opinion that you should not now be desirous of exposing yourself as a volunteer in the field of battle for us.

I hope to inclose to you to morrow a final determination of your business.

With much respect for your very worthy character and with a Due sense of your zeal towards these states, I have the honour to be Sir, Your most humble Servant,   James Lovell

Tr (DLC). Tr (Archives nationales, Papiers Broglie).

¹ Charles Louis, vicomte de Mauroy (1734–1813), was a lieutenant colonel in the French army who had come to America with Lafayette, for whose arrival see Lovell to William Whipple, July 29, 1777, note 2.

Mauroy's September 5 letter to Lovell has not been found, but Mauroy wrote another letter to President Hancock of the same date pressing his demands for a commission in the American army commensurate with the rank promised by Silas Deane. Copies of Mauroy's letter to Hancock and his October 23, 1777, letter to his patron, the comte de Broglie, are in the Burnett Papers, DLC, and Papiers Broglie, no. 61, K 1364.59, dossier no. 2, Archives nationales. An August 9, 1777, letter from Mauroy to Hancock with a copy of his contract with Silas Deane is in PCC, item 78, 15:239–48.

On September 8 Congress voted not to honor Deane's contract with the French officers, including Mauroy, and instead offered to pay their expenses to return to France. *JCC,* 8:721–22, 733, 743. Mauroy's reflections on his American experience are in Lafayette, *Letters* (Idzerda), 1:53–55. See also Lovell to Samuel Adams, December 8, 1777, for Mauroy's bitter response to Congress' action.

Samuel Chase to Thomas Johnson

Dear Sir,   Philada. Septr. 9th. 1777. Tuesday

I have no letter from you by yesterdays Post. Mr. Lux informs me that you have regular and quick Intelligence from Head Quarters. We are in daily expectation of a Battle. Howe's whole army are on this side of Iron Hill, in three Divisions. Howes head-quarters are at Aitkens tavern, Cornwallis at Coaches Mill, and Kniphausen near Christiana Bridge.

Mr. Rittenhouse has a claim against our state for 103 1/2 Dollars for the plates for printing our money. Shall I pay it?

If the fleet is gone down our Bay, I think Annapolis and Baltimore will be safe this Year.

My compliments to the Gentlemen of the Council. Your Affectionate and obedient Servt.   Saml Chase

P.S. An officer just from Camp informs the Enemy are advancing.[1]

Tr (MdHi).

[1] The next day Chase sent Johnson another letter—under the dateline "Philada. Sept. 10. 1777. Wesday. P.M. 1 o'Clock"—which consisted of nothing but Washington's September 9 letter to President Hancock and a concluding sentence: "I have but a Moment & send You all the Intelligence in my Power." Etting Signers Collection, PHi. For Washington's letter, see Washington, *Writings* (Fitzpatrick), 9:197–98.

John Hancock to Israel Putnam

Sir,   Philada. Sepr. 9th. 1777.

The Congress having received Information from Govr. Livingston that there is great Reason to apprehend the Enemy on Staten Island are collecting with a View to make an Interuption in the State of New Jersey—and having requested of that State three Thousand Militia to reinforce the Army under Genl. Washington, they have, in this Situation of Affairs, come to the enclosed Resolve directing you immediately to hold a Detachment of 1500 Men in Readiness under the Command of a Brigadier to cross the North River when ordered by Genl. Washington to whom I have also transmitted a Copy of the enclosed to act therein as he may think proper.[1] I am to desire your Compliance with it, & have the Honour to be, with great Respect, Sir, your most obed. & very hble Sev.   J.H. Presid.

LB (DNA: PCC, item 12A). Addressed: "The Honble Major Genl. Putnam, Peeks Kill."

[1] See *JCC,* 8:720. The passage of this resolve was prompted by a September 7 letter to President Hancock from Gov. William Livingston of New Jersey, which is in PCC, item 68, fol. 277.

John Hancock to George Washington

Sir,   Philada. Septr. 9th. 1777.

I have the Honour to transmit at this Time Copies of two several Letters from Governor Livingston and Genl. du Coudray to Congress. As Govr. Livingston seems apprehensive of an Irruption from the Enemy on Staten Island, and says they are collecting there for this Purpose, the Congress have directed Genl. Putnam to hold in Readiness fifteen Hundred Men under the Command of a Brigadier; to cross the North River when you may think proper to order it. A Copy of the Resolve, I shall immediately forward to Genl. Putnam.

The enclosed Letter from Monsr. du Coudray contains a Proposal of forming a Camp between Wilmington & Philadelphia—the Propriety of which, the Congress have referred entirely to you.[1]

Colonel Harrison's Favour of the 7th Inst. was duely received.[2]

I beg Leave to Request your Attention to the Inclosures, and have the Honour to be, with the greatest Respect, Sir, your most obed. & very hble Servt.   John Hancock Presidt.

RC (DLC). In the hand of Jacob Rush and signed by Hancock.

[1] Philippe Du Coudray's September 7 letter to President Hancock is in Washington Papers, DLC. Washington wrote to Hancock on September 10 and stated that there was not enough time to carry out the French officer's plan. Washington, *Writings* (Fitzpatrick), 9:203.

[2] This letter from Col. Robert H. Harrison, one of Washington's aides, is in PCC, item 152, 5:31, and Washington, *Writings* (Fitzpatrick), 9:195–96.

Thomas Burke to Richard Caswell

                              Head Quarters near Shad's Ford on Brandywine Creek
Dr Sir   Sept. 10th 1777

Our army is disposed to receive the Enemy who are about three miles distance & advancing, every person is in high spirits, and expect a very important engagement. Our army is supposed superior, & the enemy is very shy. I have delayed my journey home for some time in expectation of this (now expected) event, and hope before many hours to have the satisfaction of seeing our enemies put to rout. I can write you no more at present, but that I have the honor to be, Your very obdt huml Sert,
                                              Thos Burke

Tr (Nc–Ar).

Elbridge Gerry to Unknown

My dear sir   Philadelphia Sepr 10 1777
    I have only Time to inform You, that my next will probably hand
You an Account of an important Event, which is hourly expected to
take place between the Armies of Generals Washington & Howe. The
particulars of their present Situation, with a Newspaper containing the
proceedings of Congress on the Tory quakers & a manly Address of
General Washington to his Soldiers, I have sent to our Friend Doctor
Cooper who will undoubtedly communicate the same if requested. I am
sir in great Haste yours sincerely,   E Gerry

[*P.S.*] The Enemy are about 27 Miles from this City; The Army & inhabitants in high Spirits. The Measure relative to paying the Interest
of Loan office Certificates that shall hereafter be issued in Bills of Exchange is adopted by Congress. Whether those already issued will be
on the same Footing, I cannot yet determine.[1]

RC (ViU).
    [1] See Eliphalet Dyer to Joseph Trumbull, September 7, 1777, note.

John Hancock to George Washington

Sir,   Philada. Septr. 10th. 1777
    The great Desire of Congress to be informed of the Movements and
Positions of the two Armies as early as possible, at this critical and
important Period, has induced them to pass the enclosed Resolve, to
which I shall only refer your Attention.[1]
    Your Favour of yesterday I was honoured with last Night.[2]
    With warmest Wishes, that Victory and Success may attend you, and
that the Campaign may terminate in such a Manner as to encrease
your Fame and Glory, I have the Honour to be, with the greatest
Respect, Sir, your most obed Servt.[3]   John Hancock Presidt

RC (DLC). In the hand of Jacob Rush and signed by Hancock.
    [1] This September 9 resolve requested Washington "to appoint a proper person
at head-quarters to write to the president twice a day, or oftener if necessary,
advising the position and movements of the armies," and directed the Board of
War to appoint "proper persons for conveying the said letters." *JCC*, 8:726–27.
In keeping with the latter directive, the board's secretary Richard Peters had
sent Washington the following note on the ninth. "The Board have it not in
their Power to provide suitable Persons for the Purpose or they would not
lessen the Number of Combatants in the Army, but are obliged to request
your Excellency to appoint a sufficient Number of Expresses out of either
Blands or Sheldon's Regts of Horse & to carry into Execution the Resolve of
Congress with all convenient Speed." Washington Papers, DLC.

[2] This letter is in PCC, item 152, 5:33, and Washington, *Writings* (Fitzpatrick), 9:197–98.

[3] This day Hancock also wrote a brief letter to Gov. Jonathan Trumbull, Sr., of Connecticut, acknowledging receipt of his September 1 letter and informing him that it had been "laid before Congress, and is now under the consideration of a Committee—as soon as a determination is had, the result shall be communicated to you." Jonathan Trumbull, Sr., Papers, Ct.

Henry Laurens to John Rutledge

Dear Sir,   10th September 1777.

I had the honour of writing to Your Excellency the 12 & 15 August by Colo. Sumpter.

A very important question varied in different branches of borrowing Money from the Court of France has been Since agitated in Congress, I have been uniformly against the measure & think it my duty by the earliest opportunity to inform Your Excellency the grounds of my dissent.

The first question was for drawing Bills on our Commissioners for Ten Millions Dollars—which passed in the Negative.

A proposition was then made & a question put for drawing for five Millions of Dollars—passed also in the negative.

Yesterday by the most extraordinary motion & irregular proceeding that I have ever been Witness to in any other Assembly a Question was carried for drawing Bills of Exchange on our Commissioners at the rate of 5 Livres of France for a Spanish Dollar for payment of Interest at 6 per Cent per Annum of all Money already brought into the Loan office & that shall be brought in before the 1st March next.[1]

It is expected that upon this encouragement Money holders will bring Supplies to the Loan Office & that we may without another Emission of paper raise before the 1st March 20 million Dollars, the Annual Interest of which will be about £270000 Sterling besides the risques of loss & delay by Remittances.

'Tis true the Commissioners have given Congress assurance of Money received & promised Sufficient to pay the Interest of five Million Dollars annually & added "we hope" also to find Sufficient by subsidies to pay the Interest of 20 Million if we should be obliged to borrow that Sum. At the Same time they inform us, that upon application to the Court of France to borrow two Million Sterling they were told it was "impossible" to Spare Such a Sum. That they had been Strongly pressed & that the Minister was "anxious" to contract for the delivery of 20,000 Hogsheads of Tobacco as a ground for raising Money by Taxes. That they had actually engaged to deliver 4000 Hogsheads & had received a very considerable advance on the Stipulation & "earnestly intreat" Congress to enable them to comply with their part of the agreement, which while our ports are Stopped will be impossible.[2]

It appears to me that the foundation for drawing Bills is not Substantial, the practice dangerous & the measure except for articles absolutely requisite for carrying on our defensive War not necessary.

The Commissioners Speak possitively of Money advanced & expected by periodical payments only for payment of the Interest of five Millions, which Sum & a much larger I apprehend will be consumed by a variety of other demands on them, which 'tis impossible from our mode of transacting business & our total ignorance of the public debt contracted & increasing, to form an Estimate of. This forbids in the Strongest terms the Act of borrowing Money abroad. They say in a Subsequent dispatch that we may rely on punctual payment of Congress-Bills drawn for the discharge of the Interest of Sums borrowed, but refer I apprehend only to the Five Million Per Annum & here they recommend that the Interest should be reduced to 5 or 4 per Cent,[3] but Congress upon a question confirmed 6 per Cent against 5 & have put former loans upon a level with such as may be hereafter made.[4]

The Court of France on failure on our part of the Contract for Tobacco, our continued demands on them for Money, for Ship building, Cloths, Arms & many other articles will have ground for Complaint & may make a pretext of failure on our side for withholding further payments to the Commissioners.

The drawing Bills of Exchange is to all intents & purposes emissions of Paper Money upon the very worst terms aggravated by 6 per Cent per Annum to be discharged under all disadvantages in a foreign Country, it is putting our debt out of Sight for a little time but it will infallibly return upon us with accumulated force.

Although France has peremptorily told us it is impossible to lend us two Million Sterling we are hastening to make a demand for that & for aught we know a much larger Sum.

The seeming temporary relief which we shall receive by draughts upon France will draw off our attention from enquiring deeply into the State of our funds & debts & lull us in our present alarming course of extravagance.

We should pay proper regard to the conduct of the Court of Versailles, in refusing to receive our Commissioners openly in their Ambassadorial Character, in "avoiding every act which should seem to acknowledge our Independence," in "refusing positively" the Naval Aid which we had applied for, in neglecting to consider or give any answer to our plan for a Treaty & in betraying part of our proposals & possibly the whole of them to the British Ambassador, in a taunting Sarcastical remark to one of our Commissioners that we had not bid high enough, in Imprisoning one of our Captains, Seizing his Vessel, ordering a restitution of his prizes & in a word in carefully avoiding to give "umbrage" to the English.

To borrow Money from a foreign power is to Mortgage our Soil.

That the boasted generousity of the K of F. in feeding us lightly & demanding no Security, is, when compared with the conduct above-mentioned liable to suspicion of being insidious. It will be the Interest of the French Minister to ensnare us by degrees into a considerable debt & the knowledge of the Negotiation will be a Strong incentive to the British for protracting the War.

That by altering the tenor of our Loan Certificates making the payment of Capital at one instead of three Years & of Interest quarterly or half yearly, Money holders would be induced to bring Supplies into the Office—that the expectation which the public have been held in of an emission of Bills of Exchange for 5 or 10 million of Dollars had been no small impediment.

When the loan Office Certificates are put on a beneficial plan, if Money shall not be brought in Sums equal to the public exigency, it will be a proof that past emissions are not excessive. The demand for Money at this time is not confined to the Capital Towns & Cities & within a Small Circle of Trading Merchants, but spread over a surface of 1600 Miles in length & three hundred broad nor is it now the practice to give Credit for one & more years for 7/8th of the whole traffic. Every Man is a Moneyholder & every article is paid for in Cash. It is hence obvious that an immense Sum is necessary for a compleat circulation. No Man would be so void of understanding as to keep Continental Bills Idle & at a risque of loss in his Desk when he might upon the Same Security improve them at 6 per Cent per Annum.

The Sudden rise of price for domestic necessaries of Life is not wholly owing to great Emissions of paper, but in fact principally to the total Stoppage of Imports & the consequent Scarceness & dearness of such articles as our real wants cannot, & too many which our Luxury will not forego.

Borrowing of a foreign power will not increase the value of our paper Money, it may & probably will be the source of extending the depreciation to several years beyond the term when we might if we were in debt at home *only* have redeem'd it.

Such & many other arguments I used upon this occasion particularly recommending Taxation & the most vigorous exertions for opening our Ports & promoting exportation. I had the mortification to fail in my endeavors. The question being put & the yeas & Nays demanded there appeared 21 yeas & 5, Colo. Harrison, Mr. Jno. Adams, Mr. Duane, Mr. Middleton, Mr. Laurens, Nays. If I have erred in my attempts it is fortunate for my Country that I have done no harm, but the measure appears to me big with danger & as I am apprehensive a further attempt may be made to draw for some Capital Sum on the Commissioners I request to be instructed by Your Excellency whether to consent or protest.

I beg your Excellency's pardon for having delivered my Self on this important Subject so unconnectedly, but I am reduced to a very short Space for writing, my Colleagues have intended to have sent our dispatches as tomorrow by an express Messenger. We have now determined to stay him till we learn the event of an approaching general battle between our Army & the British now very near each other & within thirty Miles of this City. I intend this by the hand of Doctor Houston who waits for it. I shall inclose half a dozen News papers & refer to them for past intelligence & add only that I am with great regard & esteem &ca.

P.S. Casting my Eye upon the Resolve I perceive the time for bringing Money into the Loan office on the terms above mentioned Stands unlimited. The Report of a Committee of the whole House had Limitted 1st March which was passed over without a question so very irregularly do we transact business every day. This Resolution being made known in our State will give an opportunity to our people to prepare for partaking the proposed benefit if they choose to lend.[5]

LB (ScHi).
[1] See *JCC,* 8:724–26, 730–31; and Laurens to John Lewis Gervais, September 5 and 8, 1777.
[2] See the letters of the American commissioners in Paris dated January 17, March 12, April 9, and May 25, 1777, in Wharton, *Diplomatic Correspondence,* 2:249, 283–87, 324.
[3] See ibid., pp. 285, 324.
[4] See *JCC,* 8:724–26, 730–31.
[5] Contrary to Laurens' statement, the resolve approved by Congress on September 10 retained the March 1, 1778, limit. Congress did approve a motion without this limit on September 9, but this motion was superseded by the resolve passed on the 10th. *JCC,* 8:724–26, 730–31. On October 6 Congress resolved that its resolution "for paying the interest of money lent the Continent with bills of exchange on the commissioners at Paris, be without delay transmitted to the executive powers of the several states, with a request, that they will order the same to be published in their respective gazettes for six months, successively." *JCC,* 9:777–78.

Henry Marchant to Nicholas and John Brown

Gentlemen,   Philadelphia Sepr. 10th 1777
    Yours of the 22d of August came to Hand by Mr. Olney. I immediately attended to your Wishes. Mr. Morris President of the Secret Come. informed me that there were some Vouchers &c which you had not sent, altho' requested long since, and was not very willing to send any Money till those Papers came, and the whole Account could be properly adjusted. However upon my pressing the Matter, and the Consideration of the Time you had been kept out of the Money, it was agreed that You should have an order upon the Loan Office for the

State of Rhode-Island for the Sum you drew for save a Charge I think
of about £90 which he had some Objection to and which he says he
will write you upon. I would wish you to send that Committee all the
Papers they require, with the remaining Charges, so that the whole
may be settled.[1]

I shall at all Times make it my Pleasure & Happiness to oblige you,
and am your very humble Servt.[2]   Hy. Marchant

RC (RPJCB).

[1] See also Secret Committee to Nicholas and John Brown, this date.

[2] The preceding day Marchant wrote the following letter to his daughter
Sarah. "It is no small Pleasure to find a growing and improving Correspondent
in my Daughter Sally. Go on my Dear thus improving, and add daily one Virtue
to another. And may God grant that his Grace may really affect your Heart
with suitable Impressions of His Goodness. Remember that God made You, that
God keeps you alive, and preserves you from all Harm, and gives You all the
Powers and the Capacity whereby you are able to read of Him, and of Jesus
Christ your Saviour and Redeemer, and to do every other needful Business of
Life. And while you look around you and see the great Priveleges and Advantages you have above what other Children have, of learning to read and write,
of being taught the meaning of the Great Truths of the Bible, you must
remember not to be proud on that Account, but to bless God, and be thankful
and endeavour in your turn to assist others with the knowledge you may gain.
And be kind and good to all poor People, and poor Children that have not
your Opportunity, especially in a kind and tender Manner assist your Sister and
Brother. And at all Times remember the great Obligations you are under to
your Parents for their Care of you, especially think from Day to Day how
kind a Mama You have, how when you are sick she Nurses and provides for you.

"I am much obliged to you for the Information You give me of the farming
Business. Let us all be thankful to God for giving us such a Plenty of the
Fruits of the Earth." Marchant Papers, RHi.

Marine Committee to Stephen Hopkins

Sir   September 10th 1777

This Committee have examined the accounts of the Gentlemen you
employed to build the Continental Frigates at Providence[1] and have no
objection thereto save the charge of an Anchor which Mr. Olney
agreed to take out of the Account, and also a charge of Interest which
never has been and cannot be allowed, the balance therefore being
£1506,18,8 1/4 Lawful Money it is expected you immediately discharge out of the sum of 20,950 dollars which it appears by the
Treasury Books you have drawn for the Purpose of building these
Frigates over and above the sums you have advanced, and that the
remainder of the Money which you will still be accountable for being
15926 8/9ths Dollars you pay to Mr Tillinghast as Continental Agent
for the State of Rhode Island in whose favour we have drawn an order

therefor.[2] The particular Account of the Monies you have from Time
to Time drawn is now enclosed. We are Sir, yr hble servants

LB (DNA: PCC Miscellaneous Papers, Marine Committee Letter Book).
[1] The frigates *Providence* and *Warren* were completed in the spring of 1776,
but the British blockade of the lower Narragansett Bay kept them virtually
idle throughout 1777. William J. Morgan, *Captains to the Northward: The New
England Captains in the Continental Navy* (Barre, Mass.: Barre Publishing Co.,
1959), pp. 66, 77–78.
[2] This day the Marine Committee also wrote the following brief note to
Daniel Tillinghast, Continental agent for Rhode Island: "We enclose you herein
a draft on Stephen Hopkins Esquire for 15,926 8/9 Dollars in your favour which
you will find by the enclosed Copy we wrote him this date is the balance of
Moneys which he drew for the use of the two frigates building at Providence
more than was expended in building those Frigates. We expect this draft will
be immediately paid and you will place the same to the Credit of this Committee." PCC Miscellaneous Papers, Marine Committee Letter Book, DNA.
Actually Hopkins did not owe such a large sum. For the Marine Committee's
acknowledgement of their error, see their letter to Daniel Tillinghast, November
17, 1777.

Secret Committee to Nicholas and John Brown

Sirs,   In Secret Committee. Philadelphia Septemr. 10th 1777
    As the accounts you have furnished to this Committee are not yet
fully examined, we now enclose you An order on the Loan Officer of
your State for 2500 Dollars in part of the Ballance due to you thereon,
and as you will have other Accounts to render before a final Settlement can be made, this sum must suffice for the present, until such
Time as the Necessary Papers can be had to close the transaction.[1]
    We observe some charges in these accounts which we think ex-
ceptionable, and shall furnish you with our remarks thereon in due
Time, but we now think it necessary to mention that Captain Bunkers
account is unprecedented and can by no means be allowed.
    We find you have Ommitted sending us Receipts for the Goods you
have delivered, which are essentially necesary and should have accompanied the accts now before us, in order that the Persons who got
them might be charged therewith, wherefore we must demand those
receipts from you, together with an exact list of the goods that now
remains in your possession. We are Gentlemen, Your obedt servants,
                                    Robt Morris ChairMan

RC (RPJCB). In a clerical hand and signed by Morris.
[1] The Secret Committee was in the process of closing its accounts and trans-
ferring balances to the Committee of Commerce. See *JCC*, 8:533–34; and Secret
Committee Minutes of Proceedings, June 13, 1777, note 3.

CHAD'S FORD, September 11, 1777. 5 O'Clock. P. M.

SIR,

WHEN I had the honor of addressing you this morning, I mentioned that the enemy were advancing and had began a cannonade. I would now beg leave to inform you, that they have kept up a brisk fire from their artillery ever since. Their advanced party was attacked by our light troops under General Maxwell, who crossed the Brandywine for that purpose, and had posted his men on some high grounds on each side the road. The fire from our people was not of long duration, as the enemy pressed on in force, but was very severe. What loss the enemy sustained cannot be ascertained with precision, but from our situation and briskness of the attack, it is the general opinion, particularly of those who were engaged, that they had at least three hundred men killed and wounded. Our damage is not exactly known, but from the best accounts we have been able to obtain, it does not exceed fifty in the whole. After this affair the enemy halted upon the heights, where they have remained ever since, except a detachment of them which filed off about eleven o'clock from their left, and which has since passed Brandywine at Jones's Ford, between five and six miles above Chad's; the amount of it is not known, accounts respecting it being various—some making it two or three thousand strong, and others more. Generals Sullivan, Stirling, and Stevens, with their divisions, are gone in pursuit and to attack it, if they can with any prospect of success. There has been a scattering loose fire between our parties on each side the brook, since the action in the morning, which just now became warm, when General Maxwell pushed over with his corps, and drove them from their ground, with the loss of thirty men left dead on the spot, among them a Captain of the 49th, and a number of intrenching tools, with which they were throwing up a battery.

At half after Four o'clock the enemy attacked General Sullivan at the Ford and above this, and the action has been very violent ever since. It still continues. A very severe cannonade has began here too, and I suppose we shall have a very hot evening. I hope it will be a happy one.

I have the honor to be, in great haste,
Sir, your most obedient servant,
ROBERT H. HARRISON.

The Honorable JOHN HANCOCK, *Esquire.*

Published by Order of Congress.

CHARLES THOMSON, Secretary.

CHESTER, September 11, 1777. Twelve o'Clock at Night.

SIR,

I AM sorry to inform you that in this day's engagement we have been obliged to leave the enemy masters of the field. Unfortunately the intelligence received of the enemy's advancing up the Brandywine, and crossing at a Ford about six miles above us, was uncertain and contradictory, notwithstanding all my pains to get the best. This prevented my making a disposition adequate to the force with which the enemy attacked us on our right; in consequence of which the troops first engaged were obliged to retire before they could be reinforced.—In the midst of the attack on the right, that body of the enemy which remained on the other side of Chad's Ford, crossed it, and attacked the division there under the command of General Wayne and the light troops under General Maxwell; who after a severe conflict also retired. The Militia under the command of General Armstrong, being posted at a Ford about two miles below Chad's, had no opportunity of engaging. But though we fought under many disadvantages, and were from the causes above mentioned, obliged to retire; yet our loss of men is not, I am persuaded, very considerable; I believe much less than the enemy's. We have also lost seven or eight pieces of cannon, according to the best information I can at present obtain.—The baggage having been previously moved off is all secure; saving the men's blankets, which being at their backs, many of them doubtless were lost.

I have directed all the troops to assemble behind Chester, where they are now arranging for this night.—Notwithstanding the misfortune of the day, I am happy to find the troops in good spirits; and I hope another time we shall compensate for the losses now sustained.

The Marquis La Fayette was wounded in the leg, and General Woodford in the hand. Divers other officers were wounded, and some slain, but the numbers of either cannot now be ascertained.

I have the honor to be, Sir, your obedient humble servant,
G. WASHINGTON.

P. S. It has not been in my power to send you earlier intelligence; the present being the first leisure moment I have had since the action.

Published by Order of Congress,

CHARLES THOMSON, Secretary.

Brandywine Defeat Broadside, September 11, 1777

Samuel Chase to Thomas Johnson

Dear Sir,   Sept. 12th. 1777. Fryday Morning. 11 oClock

I am this Morning favoured with your Letter of the 6th. I immediately applied to Congress & now enclose You an order on Mr. Harwood for 30,000 Dollars & I have a Draft on the Treasury here for 20,000 more, which I will receive and send to you by the first safe Conveyance.[1]

The enclosed Letters from Genl. Washington will give You all the authentic Account of a Battle fought yesterday. A thousand various Accounts are circulating.

We just hear the Enemy moved this Morning, by Day light, leaving their Dead unburied, & with Design as supposed, to gain the Swedes ford on Schullkill, about 16 Miles from this City.

The above is confirmed.

We have heard Nothing of Genl. Smallwood or Gist since they left this City.

Our Resolve to pay the Interest in Bills will bring Us Money, if any thing will do it.

I write this by an Express which goes to Genl. Smallwood to know where he is, & what force he has with him, & to Colo. Gibson at Alexandria to march his Regimt. to Head Quarters.

I shall write You constantly. Farewell. Your Friend,

Saml. Chase

5 oClock. A.M. Mr. Wm. Smith, who was in the action within a little Time after it began informs no officer of our Troops is missing. Maryd. forces gained no Honor. They were Commanded by Gen. Debore [who was?] ignorant of his Duty. The Conduct of our Troops is imputed to their being led agt. the Enemy without being formed. Sullivane Commanded the three Divisions, Sterlings, Stephens & his own, in which our Troops were.

Our army is now within a few Miles of this City. I will give You every Occurrence worthy of notice.

RC (MdFreHi).

[1] See *JCC*, 8:737.

Eliphalet Dyer to Joseph Trumbull

Dear Sir   Philadelphia, Septr 12th 1777

The last Accounts I gave you of the two great Contending Armies this way was that Genll How had left the head of Elk & had Marched for this City sending his Ships down Cheesepeak Bay supposed with a design to have them come round to this, that he had Cast the die & put all at Hazard upon his Success & that the two Armies were near togeather not far from Willmington parted by the River Brandywine where was a pass way over a Bridge near Willmington, & a ford way about 12 miles farther up in the Country. After This Genll Washington passd with his Army over the bridge to meet the Enemy, formed a line of Battle waiting for Hows Attack which for that day was hourly expected but it seems Howe declined, & in the Night after (Wednesday) stole a March up the river towards Chads ford on which Genll Washington repassed the Bridge & pushed up on this side the river towards the same ford where he Arrived just at time enough to oppose How in his passing that Ford where a sharp Cannonading insued on each side. During this, How sent a part of his Army about 6 miles above where was another ford way. For fear of this Genll Washington ordered Genll Sullivan towards that Ford & to watch the motions of the enemy, but Sullivan having false Intelligence from a Country man, that the Enemy were not passing that way which he sent back to Genll Washington which prevented him sending the reinforcement Intended, & thereby the Enemy passed that ford without any body to oppose them & was in their full March to flank our Army. Genll Sullivan by the sudden appearence of the Enemy had not time to form in the best manner, & before he was reinforced His division was thrown into Confusion, the reinforcements coming in rather in small parties tho they faught with utmost bravery yet were overpowered with Numbers were oblidged to give way. To Support them Genll Washington was oblidged to Weaken his force opposing the Enemy at Chads ford by which means the Enemy at length forced their passage through that & our Army were oblidged to retreat from the ground being thrown into Considerable Confusion. The greater part of this day was taken up in very severe Attacks & very heavy & sharp firing. Our loss is Computed from 400 to a thousand. It is said & affirmed by most, that the Enemy have lost more than double the Number. Our Army were oblidged to retreat to Chester & were coming in from their dispersions this day. At the same time the less fatigued part of our Army are on the way to the Schuylkill & now at Evening some divisions have passed it against this City & are moving up towards German Town. The Enemy by the best accounts have lain still this day to bury their Dead, to take care of their wounded &c but are expected very soon to Move & supposed to pass Schuylkill about 15 miles above this City at a smooth shallow ford way there called Sweeds ford. Genll Washington is bringing over his Army this side by a bridge against this City & moving up to oppose him & Another Battle is very soon expected which most likely will decide the fate of this City or of Genll Hows Army. We wish Providence might order a delay for 2 or 3 days for some reinforcements coming in from the Jerseys & a body of Troops from Maryland & from that quarter who are now on their way, & will soon be close on Genll Hows rear. We fear but do not despair. We were too self Confident before the late disaster. That has given a little seriousness & hope may direct us Heaven ward for Help & that before I finish this letter a kind Providence will Interpose for us and that I may close it with giving you a more favourable Account of our Affairs.

Saturday Evening. I had no design of finishing my Narrative in two or three days expecting something further material would happen before that time but Morris calling upon me this Evening going out very early in the Morning must Close it with only mentioning that we expected Genll How would have pushed on rapidly for this City, but we find his Victory has cost him so dear that he has been Willing to lye still to this time, has sent in a flag to Genll Washington requesting protection for a Hospital for [His?] Wounded which we learn amounts to 18 hundred.[1] What answer Genll Washington has given him am not yet Informed. Our Army are much fatigued but not at all discouraged but on the Contrary are said to be very alert & in high spirits. We hope for rest two or 3 days when we expect 3 or 4000 Jersey Militia. Tho this City were thrown into great Consternation on finding the retreat of our Army before the Enemy but their Spirits now revive and they are turning out Militia & Volunteers to join Genll Washington, & now instead of Genll Hows making for the City we begin to Imagine he will return to Willmington & wait for a reinforcement from New York & Rhode Island which we hear he sent for sometime agoe as also for his shipping up this river, but all is Uncertain at present. Genll Washington has again repassed the Schuylkill with that part of his Army which came over & has by this time his main Body at Darbey about 8 miles from hence & believe designs soon to take his turn & attack How. The Event must leave to That Being who Governs All. Congress tho much Alarmd yet determined not to move till the last Extremity tho they had began to be in earnest about moving from this City before Genll Hows approch. We are Still in great hopes How will never be able to get to his Shipping again. My sincere affection to family & am Your,   Elipht Dyer

RC (CtHi).

[1] Dyer's information was not accurate. Howe had offered to permit American surgeons to attend the wounded among the 400 American officers and soldiers captured at Brandywine. Washington's September 13 acceptance of Howe's offer is in Washington, *Writings* (Fitzpatrick), 9:217. While it is estimated that the Americans lost 200 killed and 500 wounded in addition to those captured, the British only lost 90 killed and 448 wounded in this engagement. See Howard H. Peckham, ed., *The Toll of Independence* (Chicago: University of Chicago Press, 1974), p. 40.

John Hancock to George Gibson

Sir,[1]   Philada. Septr. 12th. 1777

I am directed by Congress to forward the inclosed Copy of a Resolve requiring you to hasten up the Battalion under your Command to join Genl. Washington, unless you should have received Orders from the State of Virginia to the Contrary; in which Case it is their desire you immediately dispatch an Express to Williamsburgh to inform the Govr. & Council that it is the earnest Wish of Congress you should be sent forward to execute the orders you shall receive from the Governor for the Purpose afsd.[2] I have the Honour to be, Sir, your most obed. & very hble Sert.   J.H. Presid

LB (DNA: PCC, item 12A).
  [1] Col. George Gibson (d. 1791) was in command of the First Virginia Regiment at Alexandria. F. B. Heitman, *Historical Register of Officers of the Continental Army during the War of the Revolution* (Washington, D.C., 1892), p. 189.
  [2] See *JCC*, 8:736–37. Hancock also wrote letters this day to Gen. William Smallwood and Col. Mordecai Gist, asking them to send the Maryland troops under their command to reinforce Washington. PCC, item 12A, fols. 271–72; and *JCC*, 8:736. Congress requested all these reinforcements because of the American defeat at Brandywine on the 11th.

John Hancock to William Livingston

Sir,   Philada. Septr. 12th. 1777.

It is the earnest Desire of Congress, and I have it in Charge to inform you of it, that you will immediately order out four Thousand of the Jersey Militia to reinforce the Army under Genl. Washington with all possible Expedition. If you should not be able to call out that Number, it is the Request of Congress, that you will call out as many as possible in this critical State of our Affairs.[1]

I have the Honour to be, with great Respect, Sir,[2] your most obed. serv't,   John Hancock, Presid't

RC (Nj). In the hand of Jacob Rush; signature clipped. *Selections from the Correspondence of the Executive of New Jersey, from 1776 to 1786* (Newark, N.J.: Published by Order of the Legislature, 1848), pp. 99–100. RC damaged; missing words supplied from Tr.
  [1] This day Hancock also wrote to Gen. Philemon Dickinson and urged him "to bring forward the Jersey Militia with all possible Expedition to reinforce the Army under Genl. Washington at this critical Juncture." PCC, item 12A, fol. 271; and *JCC*, 8:736.
  [2] Remainder supplied from Tr.

John Hancock to Israel Putnam

Sir   Philada. Sepr. 12th 1777.
I am directed by Congress to send you the enclosed resolve with the utmost dispatch and to intreat your immediate compliance with it. The situation of Affairs calls for your utmost exertion on this occasion, and I have no doubt of your sending forward the troops with all possible expedition.[1]
I have the honour to be, your most obedt. hble Servt.
John Hancock Presidt

RC (Privately owned original, 1974). In a clerical hand and signed by Hancock.
[1] The enclosed resolve requested General Putnam to send 1,500 Continental soldiers to Washington. *JCC,* 8:736.

John Hancock to George Washington

Sir,   Philada. Septr. 12th. 1777. 4 O'Clock A.M.
I am this Moment favoured with yours by the Express.[1] I am sorry for the unfortunate Issue of the Day, but from the Troops keeping up their Spirits, I flatter myself it will still be in our Power to retrieve the Loss of yesterday.
I have thought proper, in Consequence of the Intelligence received this Morning, to call the Congress together at six O'Clock. I have the Honour to be, with the utmost Respect, Sir, your most obed. Servt.
John Hancock Presidt

RC (DLC). In the hand of Jacob Rush and signed by Hancock.
[1] Hancock received letters of September 11 from Washington and his aide, Col. Robert H. Harrison, describing the American defeat at Brandywine. PCC, item 152, 5:49–54; and Washington, *Writings* (Fitzpatrick), 9:206–8. Congress read these letters on the 12th and ordered them to be published, in consequence of which they soon appeared in the form of a John Dunlap broadside. *JCC,* 8:735–36; and Evans, *Am. Bibliography,* no. 15636.

Samuel Chase to Thomas Johnson

Dear Sir,   Philada. Septr. 13. 1777, Saturday 11 oClock A.M.
I wrote to You by Express yesterday afternoon, inclosing an order on Mr. Harwood for 30,000 Dollars. I have received 20,000 Dolls. which Mr Smith or Myself will send in a Day or two. I have seen several of our Generals & many of our officers, & it is universally agreed that We have not above 600 killed and wounded, & that the Enemy have killed and wounded above double that Number. Our

Troops are in high Spirits. We have Intelligence that Genl. Howe has
sent for to N York & Rhode Island for an immediate Reinforcement
of 4000. We have ordered 1500 from Peaks Kiln. The Jersey assembly
have voted & preparing & will send in three Days 4000 of their
Militia. They give a Bounty of £4 a Man. In a Captains Pockett was
found a Copy of Mr. Howes orderly Book & Gen. Washington says
he collects from thence, that Howe's force is between 8 & 10,000 Men.
Mr Howe has no Tents, none but officers. We had before the Battle
14,000 Regulars including officers & 5,000 Militia, We are encreasing.
    Yesterday Noon Mr. Howe was not removed from the Place of Battle.
    Congress have given Brevet Commissions to the officers who came
with Mr DuCoudray. Two of them Monsieur Auguste Le Brun, an able
Engineer, and Monsieur ——— Pierre a skilful artillerist will be sent to
You to give You their advice & assistance in Defending our Towns and
teaching our Artillery.[1] They are both Gentlemen & experienced officers. I doubt not You will give them a Polite Reception. Would it be
amiss to get some Person Master of their Language to be generally with
them & attentive to their wants & to prevent their being imposed on?
They complain of Disrespect & Imposition here. Would it not be
proper for some of our young Gentlemen to endeavor to learn their
art? Would it not be proper to have an accurate Survey & Plot of the
Harbours & Grounds near Balt. & Annapolis? Adieu. Your Friend,
                                                          S. Chase

[*P.S.*] Where is Smallwood & Gist? Where Nat Gist with his Indians?

RC (NjP).
    [1] There is no mention in the journals of commissions for Captain Pierre and
Captain Augustin Le Brun, but for Chase's previous efforts to secure an engineer and artillery officer for assistance in preparing the defenses of Baltimore,
see Chase to Johnson, August 30, 1777, note. The two were among the several
officers who received money from Congress in November for their expenses to
return to France. See *JCC,* 9:875–77.

John Hancock to George Washington

Sir,   Philada. Sepr. 13th. 1777
    In consequence of some information Congress have received respect-
ing the Conduct of brigadier general Borre, they have come to the
inclosed resolve, which I do myself the honour to transmit you, & am
to request you'l be pleased to pay immediate attention to it.[1]
    I have the honour to be, with the greatest respect, Sir, your most
obedt. & very hble Servt.[2]   John Hancock Prest.

RC (DLC). In a clerical hand and signed by Hancock.
    [1] On this day Congress ordered Washington to investigate the conduct of Brig.

Gen. Philippe Preudhomme de Borré, whose brigade had collapsed under the weight of the British flank attack at the battle of Brandywine. De Borré offered his resignation to Hancock this day and Congress accepted it on the 14th. Shortly afterward, however, de Borré complained to Congress that he had been unfairly condemned before he could be heard in his own defense and asked to be promoted to the rank of major general. Congress turned down his request on October 4 and informed him that it had no further need for his services. *JCC,* 8:740, 760; and PCC, item 78, 2:265, 279.

² This day Hancock also wrote a brief note to Washington, transmitting a resolution calling upon him to complete "the defences of Delaware river." Washington Papers, DLC; and *JCC,* 8:739.

Cornelius Harnett to William Wilkinson

Dear Sir   Philadelphia Sepr. 13th 1777
   I received your favour of the 26th August, that of the 15th is not yet come to hand. The arrival of Cap Merredith with his Prize gives me pleasure. I am in hopes this will be a saving Voyage perhaps a Profitable one. This is the 5th letter I have wrote you since my Arrival and you have not acknowledged the receipt of one of them. I every time Inclosed you the Last papers. You have them again now, by which you will find we have had a Battle at Shad's ford upon the Brandywine, and Our brave troops Obliged to leave the field entirely owing to a mistake in the intelligence received. Our Army however are in high Spirits & very desirous of having another Brush with the Enemy who by the last Accounts still remain on the field. By the best Accounts as yet received of the Loss sustained by us is about 400 killed & wounded, and a gentleman who was lately near the field of Battle was informed by the inhabitants of that part of the Country who had viewed the Dead that there were at least three to one killd of the Enemy. It is supposed Genl. Howe will, as soon As he recovers from the late fatigue, proceed to the Sweeds ford upon Schoolkiln about 16 Miles from this City, where they will meet with (as I hope) their Deserts. I have Often requested that you would send me every Intelligence you can meet with relative to the Southern Colonies, surely you may now & then meet with a So. Carolina paper.
   I must beg you will let Mrs. Harnett know when the Post sets off that I may have the pleasure of one Letter from her which I beg you will Inclose to me. Let me know if you have received any intelligence of our Other Brig. It is amazing to what a price every Necessary & Convenience of life is arisen to. Such a Still as we last purchased would now sell for £2000 this Currency—Common rum 32/6 per Gall, Jamca. Spirits 60/ & every other Article in proportion, a Common riding horse £150.
   Altho' the Enemy's Army are so very near this City, Congress have

not determined to remove neither will they, unless they are forced. In hast, I am, D Sir, Your most Obed Servt.   Cornl. Harnett

RC (NcU).

Richard Henry Lee to Patrick Henry

My dear Sir,   Phila. Septr. 13. 1777
    On the 11th instant at Chads ford on the Brandywine about 10 miles above Wilmington we had a most bloody battle with Gen. Howes whole Army which ended after 4 hours engagement in the enemies keeping the field and our Army retiring. But Gen. Howe may say with Pyrrhus, such another victory will ruin me. Every account of Officers and Country people who have been in the field since the Action say the enemies loss in killed & wounded must be between 2 & 3000. Nothing proves this more strongly than their remaining yet upon the field of battle, when every interest called upon them to push. Our loss in killed & wounded scarcely comes up to 500. The Militia were never engaged, nor was a strong division of our Army much in battle. The Virginia Troops have gained immortal honor. No capital Officers are lost and none wounded except the Marquis Fayette in the Leg & Gen. Woodford in the hand, but neither badly. Our Army is now the greatest part between Darby & Schuilkill—Two Brigades on this side—All in high spirits and wishing for another trial with the enemy. We are collecting reenforcements with all diligence and hope yet to give a good account of Gen. Howe. Gen. Smallwood with 1500 Maryland Militia is coming fast upon the enemies rear.
    Farewell dear Sir,   Richard Henry Lee

RC (MdHi, Middendorf deposit).

Robert Morris to John Ross

Dear Sir   Philada. Septr. 13th. 1777
    Genl. Howe is now aiming to possess this City and as my worthy partner Mr. Willing is determined to remain here at all events, it is probable he may be in Want of money. I have therefore desired him to draw on Messrs. Geo. Clifford & Teysett of Amstm. the amount of Five hundred pounds Sterlg & have wrote them to pay such drafts, but shou'd you have taken the Funds out of their hands I beg you will confirm this Credit and provide them with the means of paying his bills which will only be drawn as his occasions may require.[1] I depend

on your Complyance & am Dr Sir, Your affectionate Friend & Obedt
hble servt.   Robt Morris

RC (DLC).
¹ This day Morris also sent the following similar letter to his brother Thomas.
"I hope [you] will never see this letter as I write it for the purpose of leaving
it with our Worthy partner Thos. Willing Esqr. who is determined not to remove
from this City even if Genl. Howe shou'd succeed in his present attempt on it.
This being the case, and the events of War so very uncertain it is possible
Mr. Willing may be in want of Money as I have removed most of our effects.
I therefore desire you may pay his drafts on you to the amount of Five hundred
pounds Sterling shou'd he have occasion to draw; he will do it sparingly & only
as he wants Money from time to time." Bloch Collection, PPAmP.

William Williams to Jonathan Trumbull, Sr.

Hond Sir   Philadela. Sepr. 13th. 1777, Saturd. Eveng.
In my last I hinted my & the common apprehention that Howe did
not intend to fight till his Ships had got into the Delawar, but the
Event has shewd it otherwise. Thursday last was a day of most severe
Conflict, & it has pleased the holy God to suffer it end for that Time
to our great disadvantage. Between 8 & 9 oClock in the morning the
Enemy attempted to force a passage over the Brandywine river at
Chads Ford near which our main Body was placed, they began a
heavy Canonade which was returnd & brot on a prodigious Fire,
wherein we had great advantage &ca in an Engagemt which lasted
till about 11. The Gen. had advice They were moving their main body
about 6 or 8 miles higher up to another Ford near to which was Gen
Sullivan &c., who had sent the Genl. that advice, on which Gen
Stephens, Green, & one more division were ordered to the assistance
of Sullivan, but the Genl received again Intelligence from him that the
first advice was a mistake,¹ on which their march was countermanded,
but unhappily, as the first advice was true, & about 5 oClo. they forced
the Passage before Sullivan was able to form, tho he attacked them with
great Bravery as did many others posted there about. A very heavy &
tremendous Fire took place for considerable time; old officers & all I
have seen say beyond what they conceived possible from Musquetry.
Our men fought with great Bravery, but were obliged to yield to superior numbers, & broke & fled, about 15 min. before Green's Division
came up, who was however of great advantage in covering the Retreat
& in the defence of so many, sent to the upper Ford. The Enemy also
forced a passage at Chads & our Army retreated as fast as cod well be
& brot off all the amunition & Baggage Waggons &c &c which were
very numerous, but lost 9 pieces of Cannon (they are replaced from
the City tis said). The Enemy were left masters of the Field, the Con-

William Williams

fusion of the Day was great. Genl Washington retreated to Chester, abt
12 Miles below us, & endeavord to collect his Army there, as they
went & scatterd in such Confusion, I trust he will never find them all
again by many, who are alive. The Genl is now got to German Town,
6 mi. from this northward, where his headquarters are, & I take it the
main of his army. The Loss on our side is very much unknown even
to the Genl, some are confident not more than 400 of killd, wounded
& missing, & others are Confident it is at least 1000, & every one
inclines to think the Enemys is much larger, some say at least 3 to one,
but doubtful to me. We always think in this way. As our Army was
much dispersed having many Posts & Passes to defend, not near all
were ever engaged & few or none of the militia. Tis said by every one
that they behaved with great bravery, but were under many disadvantages of ground &c, & also that They are yet in good Spirits & not
dismayed. The Genl also has strong Faith, yet effectually to resist
them, both which I believe are true.

The Storys are very many & various & volumes wod not contain
them.

It is said & believed the Enemy have not moved from the field, but
reports have been that they are moved up to the Sweeds Ford over
the Schuykill about 15 miles & will come by the way of Germ Town
& also that part are gone to Wilmington &c. I rather think the first is
true, & that They are much galled, & wait for 4000 Recruits from
Rhode Island, N York, & parts adjacent, which we learn from Peekskill They had sent for before the Battle, & are probably hard bye.
Congress had also sent for 1500 from that place before the Action.
4000 Jersey Militia are on the move & expect them in 2 or 3 days.
The whole Militia of this State are called upon & 5000, to march, but
I cant say they turn out with Spirit, tho some worthy men of the City
affirm They Do. Tis said 1500 Maryland Militia are in their rear
coming on, have heard nothing from Virgin. but hope They are moved.
The People of the City seem to be a little stirred & but very little. They
are amazingly stupid & seem to think no harm will come to them, tho
there is little doubt but the murderers are promised the plunder of the
Town. Indeed tis hard for me to say whether the greater part will be
well pleased with Howe's success. A flag is come to the Genl this day,
it is said, with proposals to succur our wounded prisoners in their
hands & with promise that the rest shall be treated as those of War &c.
Some are disposed to make light of what has happened, & others to
aggravate it to the highest degree. Most certainly it is a serious &
important affair, to have such an Army so full of confidence & Spirit,
so worsted, as to find it proper to retreat above 30 miles, & make their
last stand, where such another Encounter will certainly be fatal as to
this City.

It is an awful Frown of divine Providence, but we are not at all humbled under it, a sad sign that more dreadful Evils await Us. We are indeed at a most critical & tremendous Crisis, a powerful Army, flushed with victory & animated by the strongest motives, Riches & Glory before them, no hope of Escape from Shame & Death but by Conquest, pursuing & at the Gates of this great City. Yet if we have a few Days & the People turn out & behave as They ought on such an Occasion, we might have yet great hope & to be sure, I am far from Despairing, that God will yet save Us. Yet We have reason to tremble. Our amazing Sins totally unrepented of to all appearance, is the burden of my perpetual Fear, & apprehentions, but such Language is most exceedingly ungrateful & unattended to here. What can we then expect but God's Mercy is infinite & greater than our Sins. Yet does he usually save a People that wont be saved & fight against him. Yet I must & cant but hope, but perhaps it is a false & illgrounded Hope. I must however entertain, till I know it is so.

The next News you receive from hence will be of vast importance, God grant in his infinite mercy, it may be happy. Shod They succeed, tho the blow must be terrible & the Wound deep, but I hope not incurable, the Effect it may have on our Credit & currency will not be the least dangerous. What will become of us in such a Case, God only knows. Congress are not disposed even to consider where we shod remove to, if we are not able to stay here, & I dont expect They will till the last minute. We are in the hands of an infinitely wise & great Being, who orders all Things well. O that every Soul was joining with you in ardent Supplications for the Reformation of this People & for the deliverance & Salvation of this Land. Have wrote a very imperfect Sketch of the thousand things said &c., in great haste, not knowing of Morrises going till abt 9 oClo. With tender remembrance to my dear wife & other dear friends, I am most Affectionately your dutiful Son & Servt   W. Williams

[*P.S.*] It is believed 6 or 8 Ships of War &c are got into the Bay.

RC (Ct).
    [1] At this point Williams keyed the following marginal note: "Great blame is laid to G. Sullivan, for not geting better Intelligence & not forming his Men &c tho he fo't with great personal Bravery & I expect He will be suspended as his Brigadr. De &c. Borre is already, one of Mr D's officers from France."

John Adams to Abigail Adams

My dearest Friend   Philadelphia Septr. 14. 1777
    You will learn from the Newspapers before this reaches you, the situation of Things here. Mr. Howes Army is at Chester, about fifteen Miles from this Town. Gen. Washingtons is over the Schuylkill, await-

ing the Flank of Mr. Howes Army. How much longer Congress will stay here is uncertain. I hope We shall not move untill the last Necessity, that is untill it shall be rendered certain, that Mr. How will get the City. If We should move it will be to Reading, Lancaster, York, Easton or Bethlehem, some Town in this state. It is the Determination not to leave this state.[1] Dont be anxious about me—nor about our great and sacred Cause—it is the Cause of Truth and will prevail. If How gets the City, it will cost him all his Force to keep it, and so he can get nothing else. My Love to all Friends. Yours,

John Adams

RC (MHi). Adams, *Family Correspondence* (Butterfield), 2:342.

[1] Congress convened in an unusual Sunday session this day and resolved to meet at Lancaster if it were obliged to leave Philadelphia, and after adjourning for the day on the 18th intelligence arrived "which intimated the necessity of Congress removing immediately from Philadelphia; Whereupon, the members left the city, and, agreeable to the resolve of the 14, repaired to Lancaster." *JCC*, 8:742, 754.

John Hancock to Nicholas Cooke

Sir,   Philada. Septr. 14th. 1777

Should the Information Congress have received of the British Troops having left Rhode-Island be true, it is the Request of Congress that you will immediately order a Battalion of your State to march to Peeks Kill, armed and equipped in the best Manner you are able; And in Order that they may march with the greater Expedition, you will disencumber them of all Baggage, such as Tents &c which may be sent after them.[1] I beg Leave to request your Attention to the Resolve and have the Honour to be, Sir, Your most obed. & very hble Servt.

John Hancock Presidt

RC (R–Ar). In the hand of Jacob Rush and signed by Hancock.

[1] This intelligence about the British evacuation was false. The journals do not mention its source. *JCC,* 8:742.

John Hancock to Philemon Dickinson

Sir[1]   Philada. Septr. 14. 1777. Sunday In Congress

I was this morning honour'd with your two Letters of yesterday's Date, which I laid before Congress.[2] I inclose you a Letter from the General, & one from him to Genl Putnam, one to General McDougall & one to Major Murray,[3] which when you have perused you will please to Seal & forward with all dispatch by Major Putnam, but should the Major have left you, please to Send them as early as possible by a safe Express.

I have the honour to be, Sir, Your very huml set,   J H Pt.

LB (DNA: PCC, item 12A). Addressed: "Honl Majr Genl Dickinson, Trenton."
  [1] Philemon Dickinson (1739–1809), the younger brother of John Dickinson, was the commander of the New Jersey militia. *DAB.*
  [2] General Dickinson's September 13 letters to President Hancock, the second of which reported British advances into New Jersey, are in PCC, item 78, 7:119, 123. Worthington C. Ford erroneously states that the second letter was dated September 14. *JCC,* 8:740n.3.
  [3] Washington's letters of this date to all four officers are in Washington, *Writings* (Fitzpatrick), 9:218–19, 221, 223–24.

John Hancock to George Washington

Sir,   Philadelphia 14 Septr. 1777 Sunday Morng
  I have just Rec'd by Express a Letter from General Dickinson at Trenton, the Subject is of such importance that I Judged proper to Transmit you a Copy by Express, which is Inclos'd & to which I beg leave to Refer you.[1]
  Your favr. by the Return Express I Rec'd & shall lay before Congress this morng.[2]
  I have the honour to be, Sir, Your most Obedt Servt.
                                                John Hancock Presidt

RC (DLC).
  [1] Hancock enclosed a September 13 letter from Gen. Philemon Dickinson reporting British advances at Elizabethtown and Second River, N.J. PCC, item 78, 7:123.
  [2] Washington's September 13 letter to Hancock is in PCC, item 152, 5:55–56, and Washington, *Writings* (Fitzpatrick), 9:215–16.

John Hancock to George Washington

Sir,   In Congress Philada 14 September 1777
  I have just Rec'd your Letter of this Day's Date, & have forwarded on the Dispatches you inclos'd.[1]
  The Resolution inclos'd has this moment pass'd Congress respecting Major General Sullivan, to which I must beg leave to Refer you.[2]
  I Transmit you a Letter I just Rec'd for you, and also Coppies of several Letters Rec'd this day from General Gates.[3]
  I am with much respect, Sir, Your most Obedt Set.
                                                John Hancock Prest

RC (DLC).
  [1] This letter is in PCC, item 152, 5:59, and Washington, *Writings* (Fitz-

patrick), 9:225. For the enclosures in question, see Hancock to Philemon Dickinson, this date, note 3.

² By this resolution Congress ordered Gen. John Sullivan's recall from the Continental Army pending the inquiry into his handling of the August 22 raid on Staten Island that Congress had ordered on September 1. Congress passed this resolve because of its disapproval of Sullivan's conduct during the battle of Brandywine where, as at the battle of Long Island in 1776, he had fallen victim to a flanking movement by General Howe that was the turning point of the engagement. Congressional dissatisfaction with Sullivan was further fueled not only by the general frustration among the delegates at the army's inability to check the British advance, but also by the specific criticisms of North Carolina delegate Thomas Burke, who had been present at Brandywine and was chagrined by Sullivan's generalship. Despite mounting criticism of Sullivan in Congress, however, Washington successfully argued that in view of the "critical and delicate" military situation, it would be unwise to remove the New Hampshire general from his command until the court of inquiry completed its work. After this court decided on October 12 that the Staten Island raid had failed because of circumstances beyond Sullivan's control, Washington promptly forwarded its decision to Congress. There the general's supporters took this opportunity to procure passage of a resolution on October 20 expressing Congress' pleasure with the decision and ordering its publication "in justification of the injured character of that officer." As a result, Sullivan, who had been threatening to resign his command, was mollified and agreed to remain in the army.

See *JCC*, 8:700, 727, 740, 742, 749–50, 9:808, 822–23; Washington, *Writings* (Fitzpatrick), 9:227–29, 241–42, 253, 347, 367–68, 379–80; and Thomas Burke to Richard Caswell, September 17, and to John Sullivan, October 12, 1777. Sullivan's own correspondence about his conduct at Staten Island and Brandywine is in Sullivan, *Letters* (Hammond), 1:453–566. Henry Laurens to John Laurens, October 10; and Eliphalet Dyer to John Sullivan, October 11 and 23, 1777, indicate that some of Sullivan's critics were supporters of Gen. Philip Schuyler who were eager to retaliate against a New England general.

Sullivan's critics probably overstepped themselves in their hostility, and as a result may have contributed to his ultimate exoneration. In this regard it is interesting to note the following extract of a letter from an unidentified "member of Congress" that Sullivan received "A few Days after the Battle of Brandywine" and quoted in a letter he wrote in January 1781 to Gen. Alexander McDougall. "I find Some of the Southern members are Determined to ruin your reputation, one of them has Accused you of the most Shameful Conduct at the Battle of Brandywyne in which action he pretends to have had a Considerable hand & asserts that he assisted to rally your broken Troops which you had not Sufficient Skill to do yourself & that to your ill Arrangement, bad Disposition of your Troops & misconduct the Loss of the Battle Ought to be attributed: Congress have in Consequence Suspended you from the Service." Sullivan, *Letters* (Hammond), 3:271–72.

³ See *JCC*, 8:741, for a list of the enclosed letters by and to Gates.

Joseph Jones to George Washington

Dr. Sr.   14th Sept. 1777.

Being in want of a light Phæton I directed my Servt. to inquire abt. the City for one. He tells me he has found a single light carriage wch.

belongs to you and has been lying here for some time. I have not seen it but from his account of it expect it will answer my purpose and if you choose to sell will purchase and give any price you may think it reasonably worth. If it is your inclination to keep it and get it out of the way of the Enemy I will take it to Lancaster if we are obliged to move there, which you will please to determine by a line.[1] I am, Yr. aff. hum. Sevt. Jos. Jones

RC (DLC).

[1] Washington's September 17 reply, in which he requested his fellow Virginian to use his carriage until he needed it, is in Washington, *Writings* (Fitzpatrick), 9:232–33.

Another indication of the preparations being made to leave Philadelphia is contained in a letter Jones and his Virginia colleagues Benjamin Harrison, Francis Lightfoot Lee, and Richard Henry Lee wrote this day to Robert Morris. "As it will be very inconvenient for us to receive from you the balance of the Cash in your hands belonging to us as Delegates in Congress from Virginia, and which you desired to pay as you are about removing your Cash & effects from this City, We must therefore request you will send our Cash in your Chest with your own, taking the same measures for the security of ours that you do for your own and we hereby agree & declare that the same shall be entirely at our Risque & not yours." *Stan V. Henkels Catalog*, no. 1183 (January 16, 1917), item 39.

John Adams' Diary

Septr. 15. 1777. Monday.

Fryday the 12, I removed from Captn. Duncans in Walnutt Street to the Revd. Mr. Sprouts in Third Street, a few doors from his Meeting House.[1] Mr. Merchant from Rhode Island boards here, with me. Mr. Sprout is sick of a Fever. Mrs. Sprout, and the four young Ladies her Daughters, are in great Distress on Account of his Sickness, and the Approach of Mr. Howes Army. But they bear their Affliction with christian Patience and philosophic Fortitude. The young Ladies are Miss Hannah, Olive, Sally and Nancy. The only Son is an Officer in the Army. He was the first Clerk in the American War office.

We live in critical Moments! Mr. Howes Army is at Middleton and Concord. Mr. Washingtons, upon the Western Banks of Schuylkill, a few Miles from him. I saw this Morning an excellent Chart of the Schuylkill, Chester River, the Brandywine, and this whole Country, among the Pensilvania Files. This City is the Stake, for which the Game is playd. I think, there is a Chance for saving it, although the Probability is against Us. Mr. Howe I conjecture is waiting for his Ships to come into the Delaware. Will W. attack him? I hope so—and God grant him Success.

MS (MHi). Adams, *Diary* (Butterfield), 2:262.

[1] For John Adams' accounts for his expenses from January 9 to September 14,

1777, see ibid., pp. 252–56. Although Adams remained in Congress until November 11, 1777, his accounts end abruptly in mid-September, because, as he later explained to James Warren, "I was obliged to leave a small Trunk of my Baggage together with my Account Book and all my receipts behind me, in the Care of a Reverend Gentleman in the City." Ibid., p. 256n.1. On January 27, 1778, the Massachusetts General Court authorized the payment of £342.18.8 to Adams for his expenses from January 9 to November 27, 1777. *The Acts and Resolves, Public and Private of the Province of the Massachusetts Bay . . . 1777– 78* (Boston: Wright & Potter Printing Co., 1918), 20:261, chap. 685.

Samuel Chase to George Washington

Dear Sir,   Philada. Septr. 15. 1777

Mr. Buchanan, Commissary General of Purchases, informs Me this Morning, that he was at Christiana Bridge on Saturday Afternoon, that Colo. Gist was then there, with 400 Maryland Eastern Shore Militia, that he informed Mr. Buchanan he expected to be joined by 400 more in a few Days, that he had with him three Iron field pieces with 36 Artillerists, That he was informed by several, & by Colo. Gist that Brigadier Smallwood was at Nottingham on Saturday last with about 1000 Militia from the western Shore of Maryland, without any field Pieces. Colo. Gist informed Mr. Buchanan that by his Intelligence about 1000 British Troops entered Wilmington on Fryday Night & took full Possession of the Town and president McKinly before it was discovered they were in the Town.[1]

General Rodney and Mr. John Dickenson was at Christeen with Colo. Gist.

Mr Buchanan informs that Genl. Rodney had with him 150 of the Delaware State before he arrived at Christeen, but that so many of them deserted, that Genl. Rodney discharged the Remaining few.

Colo. Gist further informed Mr. Buchanan that Genl. Rodney had wrote to you on Fryday last, giving an account of his and Colo. Gist situation, & sent the Letter by the usual Road & therefore fears it has fallen into the Enemies Hand. If Mr. Howe is acquainted with the Circumstances of Colo. Gist, he may be in Danger. I am, Sir, with Regard & Respect, Your Affectionate and Obedt. Servant,

Saml Chase

[*P.S.*] Colo. Richardson is sick in Sussex County.

RC (DLC).

[1] For the capture of Delaware President John McKinly on September 13, and the difficulties encountered in obtaining his exchange for William Franklin, which was not effected until almost precisely one year later, see Gail S. Rowe, "The Travail of John McKinly, First President of Delaware," *Delaware History* 17 (Spring–Summer 1976): 21–36.

James Duane to George Clinton

Sir   Philad. 15th Septr. 1777

You have undoubtedly before this heard of the late Battle between the grand armies under General Washington & General Howe. General Washington's Account is enclosd.[1] I was in hopes to have had it in my power to collect a more particular Account of this sharp & bloody conflict founded upon satisfactory Evidence. But as the Enemy were last masters of the field of Battle my Expectations have hitherto been disappointed.

Several Countrymen have viewd the Field, before the dead were buried, who, according to their Report, amounted to 1500 at least, more than two thirds of them British & Hessian. There can be no doubt but the Loss was very great as the Enemy have not Attempted to improve their Advantage. Their main Army now lies between Namun's Creek and Wilmington about 24 miles from this City. General Washington has repassed the Schuylkil & gone towards them. A large Body of Militia, the Light Infantry Corps, & Light Horse are hanging about them. If I may be indulged a conjecture I presume that General Howe will strongly fortify the Camp he now occupies & wait the arrival of the Fleet which is expected up the Delaware: if not of the Reinforcement which it is said he has orderd from New York and Rhode Island.

I am sorry to inform your Excellency that my only Colleague here, Mr. Duer, is sick & has been incapable of attending Congress for about 10 days during which time the state has had no Vote. Mr. Duer is better this morning & probably will go to Bristol for a few days To reestablish his Health. I beg your Excellency to pardon this hasty scrawl. I have several Letters to write and detain a private Express.

I am with the greatest Regard, Sir, your Excellency's most Obedient, humble Servant,   Jas Duane

RC (NN).
[1] This enclosure was a John Dunlap broadside containing September 11 letters on the battle of Brandywine by Washington and Col. Robert H. Harrison. Evans, *Am. Bibliography,* no. 15636.

Richard Henry Lee to Mann Page

Phila. Sept. 15, 1777. Reports on the battle of Brandywine. "Gen. Washington marched his army here after the battle and having refreshed his men with a little rest &c he yesterday recrossed the Schuylkil and was this morning about 16 miles from hence and about 12 from the enemy. Our army is in very high spirits and eagerly wish to attack the enemy[1] . . . we every day expect another battle . . . We have sent for a reenforcement of 2000 men from Peeks Kill[2] . . . we shall be ready quickly to give Mr. Howe a third battle, if the second shoud not content him. We have strengthened our Army . . . by the addition of two able foreign Officers, Baron Kalb & Count Polesky. The former a Brigadr. General of great experience . . . the latter, a Nobleman of Poland who has commanded 18000 men in his own Country . . . he is arrived here to fight the battles of liberty over again. He is at the head of our Cavalry.[3] Gates writes us that he is strong & has got up to Stillwater very near to Burgoyne, and that a few days, perhaps hours, will shew whether the British General chooses to fight or fly[4] . . . I hope by next Post to congratulate you on a glorious victory over Howes whole force, & perhaps Burgoynes fate may come about the same time . . . Gen. Washington was this morning within 6 miles of Howe, and . . . we should have had a battle e'er this if the heavy rain now falling had not prevented it . . . We just now hear that the enemy having collected their force from Rhode Island, N. York &c &c were pushing thru the Jersies with 4000 men under Gen. Clinton. The Jersey Militia are collecting under Gen. Dickinson to oppose them, and 2000 men are ordered from Peeks Kill to cross the North River and come on their rear . . ."

MS not found; abstracted from extract in *Charles Hamilton Autographs Catalog,* no. 6 (1955), item 73.

[1] Ellipses here and below in Tr.

[2] On September 12 Congress had ordered 1,500 Continental troops from Peekskill, N.Y., to reinforce Washington's army. *JCC,* 8:736.

[3] This day Johann de Kalb was appointed major general and Casimir Pulaski, brigadier general in the Continental Army. *JCC,* 8:745–46.

[4] Horatio Gates' September 10 letter was read in Congress on the 14th and is in PCC, item 154, 1:256.

New Hampshire Delegates to Meshech Weare

Worthey Sir,   Philadelphia Sepr. 15th. 1777
    No Doubt but that you'l here of the battle of the 11th Instant (before this Reaches you) which begun at Chads ford on Brandiwine River. Vearious and Uncertain are the Accounts of the loss on both sides. Several Members of Congress was present at the battle who Reports as their oppinion that our loss did not Exceed 400 and by Information this day by a man who lived nigh the field of battel who says he was called on with some others by Genl. Howe to bury the dead that they buried of the Enemy on that part where our Right wing was Ingaged 1274 and that in said place we lost but 200. What numbers was Slain on our left wing were the battle first begun is not as yet Asertained. They have lost a great many officers, and a very great many wounded, one hundred waggen loaded with sd. wounded went off the field togeather, on the

whole they ware so sore that they have continued in their Camp ever since the battle haveing full Imployment to take care of their wounded and to bury their Dead. Altho we lost the field with Six peices of Cannon another such Victory would ruin Howes Armey. General Washington has Collected his Armey and (in high Spirits) taken an advantages post about five Miles from the Enemy and as soon as the reinfostment from Pekskill of 2500 Joynes him to Attack the Enemy. We have Obtained an order from Congress for one hundred thousand Dollars one half on the loan Office in Boston, the other half on the loan Office in our State. Mr. Frost being in a pore State of Helth Desires leave to Return home and proposes to Set off from this place next week and bring the Orders on Sd. Office's with him.[1] We are with great Respect, Sr., Your Most Obt. and Most Humble Servts.   Nathel. Folsom

Geo. Frost

RC (Nh–Ar). Written by Frost and signed by Frost and Folsom.
[1] Frost was granted leave of absence by Congress on September 17. *JCC,* 8:753.

John Adams' Diary

1777. Sept. 16. Tuesday.

No Newspaper this Morning. Mr. Dunlap has moved or packed up his Types. A Note from G. Dickinson that the Enemy in N. Jersey are 4000 strong. How is about 15 miles from Us, the other Way. The City seems to be asleep, or dead, and the whole State scarce alive. Maryland and Delaware the same.

The Prospect is chilling, on every Side. Gloomy, dark, melancholly, and dispiriting. When and where will the light spring up?

Shall We have good News from Europe? Shall We hear of a Blow struck by Gates? Is there a Possibility that Washington should beat How? Is there a Prospect that McDougal and Dickinson should destroy the Detachment in the Jersies?

From whence is our Deliverance to come? Or is it not to come? Is Philadelphia to be lost? If lost, is the Cause lost? No—the Cause is not lost—but it may be hurt.

I seldom regard Reports, but it is said that How has marked his Course, from Elke, with Depredation. His Troops have plunderd Henroosts, dairy Rooms, the furniture of Houses and all the Cattle of the Country. The Inhabitants, most of whom are Quakers, are angry and disappointed, because they were promised the Security of their Property.

It is reported too that Mr. How lost great Numbers in the Battle of the Brandywine.[1]

MS (MHi). Adams, *Diary* (Butterfield), 2:263.
¹ As chairman of the Board of War, Adams this day wrote the following brief letter "To the Officer who has the Charge of the Hessian Prisoners" at Lancaster, Pa. "I am directed by the Board of War to desire you to deliver to Coll. Bird forty of the Hessian Prisoners in your Custody, to work with him as Artificers and Labourers, if they consent." Force Collection, DLC.

Samuel Chase to Thomas Johnson

Dear Sir,   Philada. Septr. 16. 1777. Tuesday Morning.
By the Post which left this City on Saturday I acknowledged the Receipt of your Letter of the 6th, & I am now to thank you for your favor of the 11th. I sent you by Mr. Wm. Hammand 20,000 Dollars. I hope he got safe to you. We hear Colo. Gist was at Christeen Bridge on Saturday with 400 of our Eastern Shore Militia, & that Genl. Smallwood was the same Day at Nottingham with 1000 of the western Shore Militia. I wish You had or could inform Me of the Number of our Militia under each of these Gentlemen.

It will be impossible to obtain a Declaration from Congress that our Militia should be subject to their own Articles of War. I pressed it with every Argument in my Power when the Requisition was made for our Militia. I before mentioned to you that our Militia will not be joined to the Regular Troops. Mr. John Adams, Chairman of the Board of War & who constantly attends, knows of no such Letter to Mr Peale, & is inclined to think no such order ever issued.

On Fryday Night the Enemy, to the Amount of 1000 or 1500, entered into Wilmington, without the least Discovery by the Town or Governor McKinlay who they made Prisoner.

On Sunday Morning Genl. Washington marched with his army from the Heights of Schuykill, near German Town, and on yesterday at 3 o'Clock A.M. he was at Bucks Tavern (near Radnor Meeting) on the Lancaster Road, about 16 Miles from this City, & was moving up that Road to get in between the Enemy & the Swedes ford. The main Body of the Enemy, from the best Intelligence G.W. has been able to get, lies near *Dilworth Town* near *Birmingham,* not far from the field of action, where they have been busily employed in burying their Dead, which from accounts amounted to a considerable Number.

We are informed the Enemy from Staten Island have made an Excursion into the Jersies & landed 1000 at Elizabeth Town point, & 1000 more at Second River. They have possessed themselves Elizabeth Town & Newark; this Movement is designed to keep their Militia at Home.

By Letters from Genl Gates of the 10th ulto. from Still Water he is moving towards the Enemy. I before mentioned that Burgoyne was at fort Edward. Baton Kiln is in his front & Hudsons River on his left. I am informed by a Letter from Mr. Wells from Albany, that Gates has above 7000, and Lincoln 5,000.

Mr Smith sends to Dr Boyd an [account?] received from Gen. Dickenson of Howe's force which he got from N York.

Mr. McHenry waits. Adieu.

Your Friend,   S Chase

P.S. Would it not be proper to publish the *Substance* of what Intelligence I send you? Send to Paca—no Conveyance to him from thence—his Son is well, & all his Relatives here.

Genl. Deborre was recalled & resigned. Genl. Sullivane was recalled but G.W. is unwilling to part with him.

RC (MdFreHi).

James Duane to George Clinton

Sir   Philad. 16th Septr. 1777

I had the Honour to write to your Excellency Yesterday. Every moment is now become interesting and the Prospect of a general Engagement on which much depends cannot be contemplated without the utmost Anxiety. The British Army since the late bloody Engagement moves with the utmost Caution. They are now at Dilworth Town not far from the late field of Battle. Our main army about 12 miles distant from them stretches between the Enemy and the Sweeds ford on the Schuyl-kill. The Light Infantry under General Maxwell & 2000 Pensylvania militia are gone on some Enterprize I imagine in the rear of the Enemy. Col. Gest with about 700 Maryland militia lies at Christiana about Twelve miles above the Town of Wilmington, Genl Smallwood with about 1100 at Oxford 9 miles South of the field of Battle. There are other parties at different places. I suppose General Washington will soon bring on an Action to deprive General Howe of the Advantage of cooperating with his shipping for which he is very probably waiting; tho' the bloody battle of the Brandywine undoubtedly demanded for the Survivors some Repose. A few days will decide the Fortune of the two Generals, & probably the Fate of this City; so far as respects its being either consigned to Plunder, or delivered from that dreadfull Calamity: for that General Howe shoud be able to hold it with an Army of not 10,000 men when they left New York woud be too extraordinary to admit of serious Apprehension unless we can first be perswaded that the Patriotism and the promises of the Southern states were meer Puffs and Delusions. I look, Sir, to the North with the utmost solicitude. Pleasing as are the Prospects I await the important Event with the utmost Impatience. Good news from thence woud animate every Breast. Oh may it arrive, and arrive speedily! that my poor bleeding Countrymen, after all their severe Labours and sufferings, may enjoy Security and Repose.

I have the pleasure to inform you that my worthy Colleague[1] has shaken off his billious Fever, and will I hope be soon able to attend Business.

I have the Honour to be, with the utmost Respect, Sir, your Excellency's most obedt huml Servant, Jas Duane

RC (NHi).
[1] William Duer.

John Hancock to the Pennsylvania Council

Gentlemen, Philada. Septr. 16th. 1777.

From the enclosed Resolve you will percieve, that Congress concurring in opinion with General Washington, that the Provisions now in this City should be removed to some Place of Safety, except only such as may be necessary for the Use of the Inhabitants, and the Army under his Command, have directed me to request in their Name, you will take the most speedy and effectual Measures to have the same removed agreeably to his Desire.[1]

The unhappy Situation of many of the Troops for Want of Blankets, has induced the Congress earnestly to entreat you will exert yourselves to collect in this City all the Blankets you possibly can for their Use. I enclose to you an Extract of the General's Letter to Congress on this Subject,[2] and have the Honour to be, Gentlemen, your most obed. & very hble Servt. John Hancock Presidt

RC (PHC). In the hand of Jacob Rush and signed by Hancock.
[1] See *JCC*, 8:747–48. The council's September 17 response to this letter is in *Pa. Archives*, 1st ser. 5:630–31.
[2] See *JCC*, 8:748; and Washington, *Writings* (Fitzpatrick), 9:229–30. This day Hancock also wrote a brief note to Commissary General of Issues Charles Stewart, instructing him to comply with a resolution directing him to transfer the supplies under his care to "Trenton . . . Bethlehem, or some other place of safety." Charles Stewart Papers, MH–H; and *JCC*, 8:748.

John Hancock to George Washington

Sir, Philada. Septr. 16th. 1777.

I have only Time to enclose you the Resolves of Congress passed yesterday and to request your attention to them.[1]

As I am not acquainted with the Name of Count Polaski, I must beg you will give orders for his Commission to be made out; and delivered to him. As he is at Head Quarters, it may be done with Exactness by consulting him as to his Name and Titles.[2]

Your Favour of yesterday I was duely honoured with & shall lay it before Congress this Morning.[3]

I have the Honour to be, with the utmost Respect, Sir, your most hble Serv.   John Hancock Presidt

RC (DLC). In the hand of Jacob Rush and signed by Hancock.

[1] These resolves concerned actions taken by Congress with respect to certain foreign officers. *JCC,* 8:744–46.

[2] Count Casimir Pulaski came to America equipped with letters of introduction from Silas Deane, Benjamin Franklin, and Madame de Lafayette. With the support of the marquis de Lafayette, who recommended him to James Lovell as "one of the first member of the confederation of Polland, the most distinguished officer, and the most dangerous enemy of the tyrants of his country," Pulaski asked Congress on August 24 to give him the command of a volunteer cavalry company, subject only to the authority of Washington and Lafayette. Congress rejected this request on the 25th as "highly impolitic," but on September 15, after having received letters from Washington in Pulaski's behalf, it did agree to give the count an appointment as "commander of the horse . . . with the rank of brigadier." *JCC,* 8:631, 673, 687, 698, 711, 745; PCC, item 41, 7:21, 25; Washington, *Writings* (Fitzpatrick), 9:112, 143–44, 244; and Lafayette, *Papers* (Idzerda), 1:97–98, 106–7.

[3] This letter is in PCC, item 152, 5:61–63, and Washington, *Writings* (Fitzpatrick), 9:227–30.

John Hancock to George Washington

Sir,   Philada. September 16. 1777.

I have this moment Rec'd a Note from Genl. Dickinson desiring the Inclos'd Letter from him might be Sent to you by Express; he Judges the Enemy's Force in Jersey to be 4000 strong.[1]

I will not Detain the Express longer than just to Inclose you the Resolution of Congress submitting to you the Execution of the Resolve respect. General Sullivan.[2]

Your favr. of this Day I have just Rec'd;[3] I am with the utmost Respect, Sir, Your most Obed servt.   John Hancock Presidt

RC (DLC).

[1] Gen. Philemon Dickinson's September 15 letter to President Hancock is in PCC, item 78, 7:131. The enclosed letter of the 14th from Dickinson to Brig. Gen. John Cadwalader is in Washington Papers, DLC.

[2] On this day Congress acceded to Washington's request to defer the recall of Gen. John Sullivan until a more favorable moment. *JCC,* 8:749–50; Washington, *Writings* (Fitzpatrick), 9:227–29; and Hancock to Washington, September 14, 1777, note 2.

[3] This letter is in PCC, item 152, 5:65; and Washington, *Writings* (Fitzpatrick), 9:230.

Henry Laurens to George Galphin

Dear Sir,[1]   16th Septmber 1777.

Although from Circumstances of our affairs 'tis impossible for me to reply so fully as I would otherwise have done to your favour received by the hands of the Reverend Mr. Holmes yet a total Silence would be inexcusable.

I congratulate with you on your success in treating with the Creek Indians.[2] I hold the States of So. Carolina and Georgia as well as all the United States much indebted to your unwearied labours for the present good disposition of those Savages & as their continuance in this temper depends much upon your exertions so we are all bound to pray for your life & health.

I had intended to have presented the Indian Talk to Congress & to have made a proper representation of your merits, but from the day of Mr. Holmes' arrival to the present moment we have been engaged in attentions to the attempts of baptized Savages at our very door to murder, Burn & imprison in different Classes every one in this quarter who have virtue enough to refuse their proffered pardons for doing their duty in the Cause in which you are also engaged.

Mr. Holmes will relate to you the Substance of our present accounts of the Battle of Brandywine fought on Thursday the 11th Inst. in which our brave American Troops shewed they were not to be intimidated by Cannon or fixed Bayonets, both which they opposed with undaunted Courage from 9 in the Morning to Sunset & although from an unlucky mistake they lost the Feild & 7 or 8 Peices of Cannon, yet they made their antagonists pay for the purchase very dearly. This is proved by their inability to pursue the advantage. They have remained ever Since on the Same ground, their principal employment burying their dead & dressing & housing the wounded, which from the modest accounts exceede the losses on our Side at least Quadruple.

General Washington is on the Skirt of the same feild again & determined not to wait to be attacked. I expect if the Enemy is not averse & the present very bad weather does not hinder, there will be another very bloody conflict tomorrow. The event may incline one party or the other as the Scale may rise or fall to talk of terms for Suspension of Arms. If we are successful here, Great Britain will see the futility of her measures as clearly as we see the wickedness of them. If we are beat, the Enemy will be in possession of so much Sea Coast & the infamous Tories, the worst Enemies of America, will become so insolent, it may & probably will be necessary to make a total change in our mode of action. In the Northern department our affairs look well. Mr. Burgoyne has been Severely checked & he is now so hemmed in as to render it necessary for him to fight or fly. One of these we expect to hear of in a very few days. In either case he will be under very great

disadvantages. Ten days more will bring forth the most momentous
events.

Congress in the present Situation of affairs think it necessary to
prepare for adjourning to Lancaster about 66 Miles West. Perhaps
before Sun rise to morrow I shall be on my journey. Some of us are
already gone. I will continue here as long as most of the Company, but
as I have ever loved free air & exercise & hate to be confined to a
Small room, I will not stay the very last Man. When we are restored
to tranquility wheather here or elsewhere you shall hear again from
&ca.

LB (ScHi).

¹ George Galphin, a South Carolina Indian trader, was serving as a Con-
tinental Indian commissioner for the southern department. James H. O'Donnell,
III, *Southern Indians in the American Revolution* (Knoxville: University of
Tennessee Press, 1973), pp. 20–24.

² On April 4, 1777, Congress had approved Galphin's plan to meet with the
Creek Indians in order to discuss a peace treaty and instructed him to send
some Creek leaders to Philadelphia at Continental expense. Galphin met with
the Creeks in Georgia in June, and although the Indians signed no treaty and
sent no representatives to Philadelphia, they did indicate their intent to maintain peaceful relations with the United States. Ibid., pp. 59–61; and *JCC*,
7:223–24.

Henry Laurens to John Rutledge

Dear Sir   16th September [1777]

Since my arrival at this place I have had the honour of twice addressing Your Excellency, the 12th Ulto. by Capt. Hornback & the
10th Inst. by Doctor Houston.¹

The present is intended by the Revd. Mr. Holmes who calls late in
the evening to acquaint me of his intention to begin his journey to
Carolina early to Morrow Morning, tis probably the last trouble I shall
give your Excellency from this Station, it may be the last I shall ever
give.

As my Colleagues have been Some days absent, gone with their
families to a place of Supposed Safety & as I may find it necessary to
leave Town this very night I think it my duty to devote a few minutes
to transmit a brief State of our affairs at the present Instant.

Colonel Horry who went away yesterday & who will probably be
with you before this, will inform Your Excellency in general & in many
particulars the rise & progress of last Thursday's battle. I will therefore only add on that head, that by accounts which Congress has received this day we are confirmed in beleif that the loss of the Enemy
was very great, not less than one Thousand killed & probably as many
or more wounded, had it been otherwise tis not to be doubted that

General Howe would have improved the advantage which one unlucky mistake on our Side had afforded him & have been in possession of Philadelphia upon Friday. I Speak from appearances & accounts which deserve Credit.

General Washington as Speedily as circumstances would admit of recollected his forces, recrossed the Schuylkil Sunday the 14th. This morning he informed Congress of his being within a few Miles of the Enemy, that as his Troops had been hard Marched he had halted & given them an opportunity of refreshing themselves, that the British Commander had discovered a "violent inclination" to get again on his right & intimated the Signs of an approaching Second battle. He strongly recommends the immediate removal of all public Stores from hence & the most Speedy efforts to Supply his Troops with Blankets & Clothing.

The recommendation to remove Stores is construed by many Members of Congress to imply their own removal, which they Suppose & Some have Said he wishes for, although he may not think plainer terms becoming from this circumstances. If we do not learn Some event very favourable to us, the Representatives of the 13 United States will be Scattered to morrow & proceed in hopes of reuniting at Lancaster or York Town.

General Washington commenced his last March determined against waiting to be attacked. The nearness of the two Armies therefore puts it beyond a doubt that a Second general battle, provided the Enemy is not averse, will happen to morrow if the Weather Shall not forbid. At this moment it rains tremendously & the air does not promise to favour Gunpowder in a few hours. For my own part I feel under all discouraging appearances confident of Success. I have learned from Officers who were in the heat & the hottest of that heat of the 11th Inst. that our Men are firm, that they showed no fear of Superior power of Cannon nor of fixed Bayonets. They are gone out now determined to recover the honour lost on that day by the Shameful misconduct of Some of the Officers. These I flatter my Self will behave better & be doubly anxious to bury in oblivion the remembrance of their Crimes. 'Tis much to be lamented as a part of those Crimes we cannot obtain returns of our late loss nor of the present State of the Army. The latter from the best guess accounts I compute to be nine to ten Thousand Continental & five to Six Thousand good Militia if any Militia besides those under General Starks can be called good. From an orderly Book found in the pocket of a Slain Captain of the 49th British, General Washington had computed General Howe's whole force embarked at New York to have been under 9000, & from an authentic Account which we have obtained from New York of the whole forces under his Command, a Copy of which I shall here inclose, Your Excellency will beleive it could not have been greater.

Yesterday Congress was informed of the landing of 2000 Troops from Staten Island & New York at Elizabeth Town & this day General Dickinson has advised that the number landed there was 4000, in consequence of which he was that minute going to Assemble all the Militia who had been otherwise intended as auxiliaries to General Washington. We have also advise of nine Ships of War being as high up the River as Reedy Island, of a very dangerous plot concerted in this State & part a Neighbouring Colony extending from Fort Pitt to the Enemy's Army & that some of the chief conspirators were apprehended & Committed to Gaol.[2]

If Townes Evening post comes abroad this Evening Your Excellency will find also inclosed an extraordinary history of Correspondence between the invincible Burgoyne & General Gates from whence it appears that our affairs are in a pleasing State in the Northern department.[3]

All the Stores, Sick & wounded which had been removed hence to Trenton are now ordered to be carried to Bethlehem. The New Frigates & some other Navigation are as high at Burlington if the Enemy should penetrate so high these will form funeral pyres.

Other Frigates, Fire Ships & Wrafts, Gallies, Gondolois & Gun Boats are below. What defence or destruction these will make is very uncertain but as Billings port is abandoned & Fort Island not in a full posture of defence, I am apprehensive the Enemy's fleet will meet with no great resistance from them. The land battle will decide their fate.

General Caudre unfortunately drowned this morning in Schuylkill. Baron duKalb yesterday appointed a Major General his Commission if he accepts to be dated one day anterior to that of Marquis delafayette who lies wounded in his Leg at Bristol where If I am obliged to run I mean to call for him.[4]

We are drawn to an important Crisis. If we are blessed with Success, my native Country will probably enjoy another Winter unmolested; on the contrary, she must expect a Severe attack before Christmas. It will be her wisdom to prepare immediately without hesitation or waiting for events to increase her honour & military fame.

I must now go through the weather to learn if any thing momentous has happened Since I came home & if necessary at my return a postscript shall be added, mean time I beg leave to Salute your Excellency with repeated assurances of being with respect Esteem &c.

LB (ScHi).

[1] Laurens had also written to President Rutledge of South Carolina on August 17 and 19.

[2] Laurens may be referring to the episode described in John Hancock to William Livingston, August 30, 1777, note, but see also *JCC*, 8:745–46.

[3] These letters are listed in *JCC*, 8:741.

[4] See *JCC*, 8:745–46. At de Kalb's request, Congress later erased from the journals its resolve antedating his commission to Lafayette's and decided on

October 4 that both men should hold commissons as major general from the same date. *JCC*, 9:769; Lafayette, *Papers* (Idzerda), 1:145–46.

Samuel Adams to Elizabeth Adams

My dear Betsy   Philada. Sept 17. 1777

Your kind Letter of the 29th of August is now before me. You therein take a very proper Notice of the signal Success of our Affairs at the Northward. I hope my Countrymen are duly sensible of the obligation they are under to Him from whose Hand, as you justly observe, our Victory came. We had a Letter from General Gates yesterday, from which we every hour expect another great Event from that Quarter. The two Armies this Way had an obstinate Engagement last Thursday. The Enemy have gaind a Patch of Ground but from all Accounts they have purchasd it as dearly as Bunkers Hill. Two or three more such Victories would totally ruin their Army. Matters seem to be drawing to a Crisis. The Enemy have had enough to do to dress their wounded and bury their dead. Howe still remains near the Field of Battle. Genl. Washington retreated with his Army over the River Schuylkill through this City as far as[1] [Germantown]. There he recollected his Forces and [recrossed] the River again & posted himself [. . .] the Enemy. Our Soldiers [. . .] eager for Action and we are every day expecting another Battle. May Heaven favor our righteous Cause and grant us compleat Victory. Both the Armies are about 26 Miles from this City.

I am pleasd to hear that Col Crafts invited Mr Thacher to preach a Sermon to his Regiment. He discovered the true Spirit of a New England Officer. I dare say it was an animating Discourse. Religion has been & I hope will continue to be the ornament of N England. While they place their Confidence in God they will not fail to be an happy People.

I am exceedingly rejoycd to hear that Miss Hatch is in hopes of recovering her Health.

Remember me, my dear, to my Family and Friends. I am in good Health & Spirits and remain with the warmest Affection, your

S A

RC (NN).

[1] MS torn; approximately ten words from four lines missing.

Samuel Adams to James Warren

My dear Sir   Philade Sept. 17 1777

I receivd your favor of the 1st Instant. I have not Time at present to give you a particular Account of our Military Movements in this Quarter. I suppose you will have it from our Friend Mr J A. There was an obstinate Engagement last Thursday. The Enemy were left Masters of the Field, but by all Accounts the Advantage was on our side. Howe & his Army remain near the Field of Battle. They have had much to do in dressing their wounded & burying their dead. General Washington retreated over the Schuilkil to Germantown a few Miles above this City, where he recruited his Soldiers. He has since recrossed the River and is posted on the Lancaster Road about 12 Miles distant from the Enemy. His Troops are in high Spirits & eager for Action. We soon expect another Battle. May Heaven favor our righteous Cause & grant us compleat Victory! Both the Armies are about 26 Miles from this Place. A Wish for the *New England* Militia would be fruitless. I hope we shall do the Business without them.

I have a favor to ask of you in behalf of my very worthy Friend R. H. Lee. He supposes that Mr Gardoque of Bilboa has sent him some Jesuits Bark. I wish you would inquire of the Captains from Bilboa & forward it to him, if any is arrivd, by the first safe opportunity. I have requested the same thing of Capt John Bradford, not knowing but the Multiplicity of publick Affairs might render it impossible for you to attend to it, although I am sure you will oblige so good a Patriot as Mr Lee if it may be in your Power.

We are told that the Enemy have landed in the Jerseys, 4000 strong. You can tell whether they have left Rhode Island. I have Reason to hope that an equal Number of spirited Jersey Militia are musterd under the Command of General Dickinson, Brother of the late Patriot. These were designd for a Reinforcement to the Army here. If the Report be true, these Militia joynd with 1500 Troops from Peeks Kill (undoubtedly now in Jersey) under the Command of Brigd General McDougal, will be sufficient to give a good Account of them.

I think our Affairs were never in a better Scituation. Our troops are victorious in the North. The Enemies Troops are divided & scatterd over a Country several Hundred Miles. Our Country is populous & fertile. If we do not beat them this Fall will not the faithful Historian record it as our own Fault. But let us depend, not upon the Arm of Flesh, but on the God of Armies. We shall be free if we deserve it. We must succeed in a Cause so manifestly just, if we are virtuous. Adieu my Friend.   S A

RC (MHi).

Thomas Burke to Richard Caswell

Dr Sir   Philadelphia Sept 17th 1777
I wrote you a few Lines from Head Quarters on Brandywine near

Chads Ford on the Tenth Instant, and in them gave you the hopes I then Entertained of seeing in a few hours our Arms triumphant over our Enemies. I am sorry I can not now tell you those hopes were realised. I am constrained to give you a detail of Circumstances which have grieved me to the Soul, and I know will give you and my Country great concern.

On the morning of the eleventh about Eight oclock the Enemy appeared on hights to the southward of the Creek and a little to the westward of Chads ford. They drew up in order, and erected Barbet Batteries from whence they kept up a Cannonade on our Lines which were formed on the North side of the Creek in a Meadow flanked by Hills to the right and left, on which we had several pieces of Artillary posted to advantage and from whence a well directed fire was kept up very hot until eleven, by which time the Enemy's Batteries were Silenced and their Troops driven from the Grounds on which they had first formed in the morning. During the Cannonade the Light Troops on both sides skirmished very warmly and always with advantage to us. Lower down the Creek Extended General Washington's left Wing composed of four thousand Pennsylvania Militia who had no Opportunity of engaging. Up the Creek extended the right commanded by Major General Sullivan. About two oClock the General received advice that a Body of the Enemy amounting to five thousand had moved up the Creek in order to pass at a ford about four or five miles distance. He immediately made the necessary dispositions for encountering them so as to prevent their getting on his right Flank. Soon after this General Sullivan was Informed by a Country man, a Major of Militia, that he had come along the road which immediately led from that Ford and had seen no Enemy, whereupon he dispatched Information to General Washington that he was Convinced from the Countryman's Intelligence that no Enemy was upon that rout, and the General in Consequence thereof halted the Troops destined to resist them. The Error was not discovered until it was to late to bring the Troops up in good order. The Consequence was that the Brigades which first formed were attacked before they Expected it, and those who were forming were thrown into disorder, and soon routed. The right and left Flanks of those who were first formed were then exposed, and the Enemy gained such advantage thereby that they overpowered our Troops and defeated them with the loss of their Field pieces, five in Number. The Evil did not end here. Green's division and Nash's Brigade which formed the chief strength of the centre were ordered to the right to reinforce the Troops on that Wing. By this General Wayne was left to sustain an fierce engagement for an hour and an half against Numbers greatly superior, and under a heavy Cannonade which the Enemy now renewed from Batteries lower down. He and his Troops behaved with exemplary Gallantry and after destroying great Numbers of the Enemy retreated without losing their

Artillary or leaving their wounded behind them. Coll. Proctor with some Artilary was posted on the right of Wayne and was attacked by a strong Column of the Enemy who forced their way within Pistol shot before our men gave way and at length they brought off their Guns except two whose Horses a Waggoner had run away with.

None of the reinforcement had time to get up so as to engage except Weedons Brigade who checked the Enemy and very Gallantly covered the retreat of the whole Army. The Enemy did not dare to pursue but retired from the field of Battle that night.

During this action I had an Opportunity of observing that our Troops and Inferior Officers are exceedingly good, but that our Major Generals (one only excepted) are totally inadequate. They were so disconcerted by the unexpected attack of the Enemy that they knew not what to do but to permit, (some say to order) a precipitate retreat. Sullivan to compleat his Blunder made a circuit of two Miles when one quarter in the direct road would have brought him to his Ground, and he arrived so late that it was preoccupied, but as he was Commander in that Wing he insisted on Changing the disposition, and while he was attempting it, his Troops which were brought up in great confusion, were pressed by the Enemy, and not being able to form into any order fled without resistance. These Miscarriages snatched from my Hopes the Glory of a Compleat Victory which was certainly in our Power if Sullivan had not by his Folly and misconduct ruined the Fortune of the Day.

Judge Sir how disagreeable must be my reflections on this Occasion, when my Sanguin and well founded hopes were at once cut off not by the Superiority of the Enemy but by so glaring an Insufficiency in our Officers. Could the Commander in Chief's Ideas be executed I should deem our Success certain. But I have the Melancholy Conviction that his principle Officers are Incompetent, and I fear it is an Evil that cannot be remedied.

Sullivan was for three days posted on the right Wing, and furnished with Horse and light Troops for reconnoitring. Yet so uninformed was he of the Ground that he knew not even the roads by which the Enemy might march to attack his flank, and altho he was warned by the General that the Enemy would in all likelihood make that movement, and was ordered to keep out reconnoitring parties in order to know certainly their force and motions, yet he relied on the Information of a Country man who passed along One road while the Enemy were marching on the other. This unfortunate General has ever been the Marplot of our army, and his Miscarriages are I am persuaded owing to a total want of Military Genius, and to One of that sort of understandings which is unable to take a full comprehensive view of an object, but employs it's Activity in Subtle Senseless refinement. Thus persuaded, I thought it my Duty to Endeavour to have him removed from his Command, and I succeeded so far as to have a resolution passed for recalling him. But General Washington remonstrated against it at so critical a time and the Execution is now left to his discretion.[1]

In a word Sir, so long as our army is Conducted by such Officers I shall not be very Sanguin in my Expectations of Success. However I shall hope for the best, and as our army is composed of good Troops, and in general of good Officers from the Major Generals downwards, and under the auspicious Command of General Washington, I shall keep up my expectations until I know the Issue of our other Battle. Our loss was not very considerable tho I know not the particulars. The Enemy have suffered so much that ever Since they have not attempted to advance. General Washington has put his Troops again in order, and has disposed his army so as to hang on their flank if they attempt to cross the Scuylkill. I wish we could Once bring ourselves to attack them instead of waiting for them to attack us. We should certainly have the advantages which they now have over us.

Our affairs in the northern department bear a very promising aspect. General Gates has a formidable army under his Command, and was by the last Accounts on the point of attacking General Burgoin.

There are certain accounts of a plot of a very Extensive Nature formed in this State for blowing up Our Magazines and destroying our Stores. The particulars are not yet come to light but the Execution is prevented.[2]

Captain Caswell is well. I shook hands with him on the Field of Battle.

I have the honor to be, with the greatest respect and Esteem, Your very obdt hum Set. Tho Burke

RC (MeHi).
[1] See Hancock's second letter to Washington, September 14, 1777, note 2.
[2] See *JCC*, 8:745–46.

James Duane to Philip Schuyler

Dear General Philad. 17t Sept. 1777

I have the Honour of your favour of the 3d Instant: on the various subjects of which I have no Time to comment; nor is it necessary, since you may be assurd that I return every Sentiment with regard to you which I was impressed with when we separated. Accounts daily come in of the severe Losses of the Enemy in the late bloody Battle of the Brandywine. Their Killed and wounded are estimated between 2 & 3000, a large proportion of Officers and one General being of the number. You see from this Account that there is no certainty, all depending on the Conjectures of the Country people. To keep up the

Spirits of the British Troops reports are propogated among them that General Washington was totally defeated, his army dispersed, & that they woud not be able to give the least Opposition to General Howe's designs. However they doubtless changd their opinion yesterday: for at 1/2 past 2 oClock P.M. they met General Washington at the Head of his army about 24 miles up the Lancaster Road prepard to give them another battle—which was only prevented by a violent Shower of Rain. General Washington's Army is in good order and Superior to General Howe's exclusive of the Militia—which last is not inconsiderable. Every moment we expect an Express from the Army with the important Issue of the Battle; If this Express does not set off before we receive further Intelligence I will furnish you with the News.

The Troops from Staten Island & the City of New York to the amount it is said of 4000 have enterd East Jersey & will probably gain Morris Town before a competent Force can be collected to oppose them, tho' it is not doubted they will be driven back when the Country can be raised.

I long most ardently to hear of the Issue of the Campaign to the Northward where Genl Burgoin seems to be much inferior to the American Army. Adieu. I present my Complt. to Mrs. Schuyler, the young Ladies & all our other Friend & believe me to be, with the greatest Respect, Dear Sir, your most Obedt. & very hume servt,

Jas. Duane

RC (NN).

Elbridge Gerry to James Warren

My dear Sir   Philadelphia Sepr 17. 1777

Since my last I am favoured with yours of August 31st with the Agreable Intelligence of Capts. Lee's & Harris's Arrivals.[1] The Contents of your Letter & of the Invoices inclosed by Messrs. Gardoqui's were communicated to Congress, in Consequence of which You will receive Orders by this Conveyance from the Committee of Commerce, for the Delivery of the Goods; unless the general Hurry, which the Approach of the Enemy to this City occasions, should prevent it; in which Case You'll please to deliver the Duck & Tent Cloth to the D Q M General, the Cloathing to the Agent of the Cloathier General, the Salt to the order of the Commissary or D Commissary General of Issues for the eastern District, the naval Stores to the navy Board of the District, & the Medicines to the Dep. Director General or his order. An Order passed Congress on the Loan office of your State, in Favour of the Commte. mentioned, for 5000 Dollars, wch is to be sent to You by this Conveyance for the purpose of defraying the Expences mentioned in your Letter.[2] The Circumstances of Capt Harris's Conduct have also been mentioned to Congress, & no objection was made to the proposal of his continuing in the Command of his Vessel, which will probably be ordered to Carolina for a Load of rice. Duplicate Receipts being taken for all the Articles delivered, one of each may be forwarded to the Committee.

Inclosed are printed Copies of two Letters from General Washington & his Secretary of the 11th Instant wch. may serve to give You some Idea of the Battle of the Brandywine, wch happened on that Day.[3] This Creek empties into the Delaware about 26 Miles below the City, & runs a considerable Way into the Country. At the Mouth on the other Side is Wilmington, & it is there crossed by a fine Bridge. About twelve Miles from the Bridge into the Country is Chads Ford, & 5 or 6 Miles from thence higher up is Jones's Ford, at & near which was fought the Battle. General Washington was a few Days before posted on the Heights of Chrystine Creek, about 8 or 10 Miles on the other Side the Brandywine, but General Howe declined giving him Battle on that Ground & passed him on the Right, which left the Delaware in his Rear, the Brandywine on his Right Wing & White Clay creek on his left, with the Enemy to the Westward & in Front. This occasioned the Removal of our Army to the N E Side of the Brandywine, on the Banks of which opposite Chads Ford they posted themselves. The Enemy approached this Ford on the Morning of the 11th, abt 3/4 after 8, & began a Cannonade, which We distinctly heard at this place & wch was returned by our Army untill 11, when it ceased for the most part. Here General Maxwell twice crossed with about 1000 of the continental Troops, which were picked from the several Brigades & formed into a Corps of light Infantry. The first Time he advanced about a Mile or two, & as the Enemy came on retreated to a pass or Defile, where he formed a Kind of an Ambuscade & poured on them a very heavy Fire. This did considerable Execution, as is agreed on all Sides, & their Loss is by the General's Computation which by far is the most modest, above three hundred killed & wounded. The second attack of Maxwells, by the Secretary's Letter left 30 of the Enemy dead on the Spot, & of Course the wounded were double the Number. Mean while General Sullivan, who was posted on the Right to guard Jones Ford, was informed by some Scouts that the Enemy were marching up the Country, but discredited it from the Information of a Farmer not having seen them, could not confirm the first Account. Lord Stirling & Stevens with their Divisions, who in the Afternoon were posted near to Sullivan, on hearing the Account that the Enemy had crossed the Creek marched towards them, & soon meeting them formed for Battle. Sullivan also marched, but by the best Information to be had, was attacked before he could form. Whether it was owing to Chance or Misconduct, I must leave You to judge. A very warm engagement ensued, in which was as heavy a Fire from the Musketry as *perhaps* has been known this War in America, but the Disorder into which Sullivan's Division was soon thrown, was communicated to the others, & obliged the three Divisions after a severe Conflict of between one & two Hours to retire in Haste. General Washington however arrived in Time to cover the Retreat with Green's Division, which with General Conway's Brigade in Sterlings Division behaved incomparably well. The Enemy at Chads Ford at this Time pressed on, & obliged Maxwell & Wayne, who were unsupported by the Militia wch were posted three Miles below them towards the Bridge, to give up the Ground. What the Loss on either Side is, I cannot ascertain, but that the Enemy have received a severe Check is evident from their Silence since the Battle. I have not any Doubt that they are at least 1500 weaker (killed & wounded) by this Action, which We have Reason to think much exceeded our Loss. Indeed the people from the Country make their Loss much greater, but to avoid Disapointments, it becomes necessary to form moderate Expectations. General Washington two Days after the Battle, marched his Army to Philadelphia, from whence he went to German Town about five Miles from hence up the Schulkyll River, there he crossed & is now about fifteen Miles from this City on the Northwest, & the Enemy about the same Distance on the Southwest. 1500 of the Maryland Militia are to joyn him in a Day or two, & 2500 of the Continental Troops are ordered from Peeks Kill, also 3 or 4000 of the Jersey Militia are ordered to be embodied, which must soon make him powerfull. The Enemy have lately landed two Divisions of 1000 Men each, in New Jersey, & will probably find Employment for most of the Jersey Militia. The Governor & Council of that State do not however appear to have much Apprehension of their Power to penetrate the Country, having ordered their western Militia to reinforce General Washington. A Reinforcement of two thousand Men is also expected from Virginia, but these I presume will not be in Time for an Engagement wch is daily Expected & in our present Situation will put General Howe between G Washington & this City. The Enemy's Ships of War are as high up as Wilmington, & probably mean to co'opperate with their General. Thus You will see, that the Campaign opens briskly, altho late, in this quarter. The publick stores & papers are removed to places of Safety, it being tho't improper to keep them in a place for wch the Armies are at present contending; & our Troops are in high Spirits.

9 oClock in the Morning. I am just now informed that last Evening the Armies were so near to each other as to have a warm Skirmish, which would have ended in a General Engagement had not the Rain wch fell very plentifully prevented it. If General Howe should be tripped, he will find it difficult to recover, whilst our situation may admit of Recovery under repeated Misfortunes.

Our Affairs at the Northward, by late Advices looked very favourable, & e'er this reaches You I think something important may happen in that Quarter.

With respect to foreign News, We have none, save a Continuance of the friendly Disposition of the Courts of France & Spain, so far as it respects their assisting us by Supplies; I think their Conduct in not immediately recognizing our Independence, to wch the former early professed to be a Friend, shews that they so far regard their own Interest as to run as little Risque as possible. Indeed if the Credit of our Currency is established, wch We are in a fairer Way of accomplishing than We have yet been in, I think We can oppose Great Britain without their declaring War; but this will not justify their Conduct in the Matter, when they well know that the power of G Britain was sufficient to overcome their united Exertions during the last War. We have however the strongest assurances from some of our Commissioners that War will be declared before the next Campaign, if the present is attended with tolerable Success.

The Confederation will I hope be finished before the Winter comes on, but this also depends in some Measure on the Success of our Arms. I can only add that with much Esteem I remain sir yours sincerely,

E Gerry

P.S. As I have not Time to write to my Freinds at M[arble]head, I shall be much obliged to You if a Copy of the Letter relative to the Action of the 11th can be taken by your Clerk & sent to Mr Gerry.

RC (ICarbS: Elsie O. and Philip D. Sang deposit, 1971).
[1] James Warren's August 31 letter to Gerry is in C. Harvey Gardiner, ed., *A Study in Dissent: The Warren-Gerry Correspondence, 1776–1792* (Carbondale: Southern Illinois University Press, 1968), pp. 78–80. For further information on the disposition of the Spanish cargoes of these ships, see Gerry to Joseph Gardoqui & Sons, September 1; Warren to Gerry, September 15 and October 5, 1777, ibid., pp. 81–85; and *JCC,* 8:748.
[2] *JCC,* 8:749.
[3] See John Hancock to Washington, September 12, 1777, note.

John Hancock to Dorothy Hancock

My Dear   Philada. 17 September 1777
Nothing could have happened more fortunate, than your leaving this City at the time you did, for in a very few days we were much Alarm'd, & proceeded to Pack up all our publick Papers, to be ready in case we were under the necessity of Removing, & indeed most of the publick papers are remov'd, mine still Remain here, tho' I Expect Congress wil this Day Adjourn to Lancaster, unless we should hear of General Washington's gaining a Victory. The Enemy are within 26 or 30 miles of us,

& an Action Expected as soon as the weather clears up. It is said 4000 of the Enemy from New York have landed in the Jerseys, with what design is not known. I hope we shall Rout Genl Howe's Army, & that will put a fine face on our affairs.

I was much pleas'd to hear that you got safe over the North River, I wish this may find you all well. I have but a moment to spare. Mr Bant will inform you all the news. Remember me to all Friends. I will write you as often as I can. Take care of yourself. Poor Monsr Du Coudra was yesterday Drown'd in the Schulkill, he Rode on his horse into the Ferry Boat, & the Horse jump'd out with him.

Let me hear from you as often as you can. The Inclos'd Letter is for Mr Rees the Waggoner.[1] Send back the Waggons as quick as you can. Take care of the Box of plate & all the things.

I am greatly hurried. I am, your affecte Husband,

John Hancock

[*P.S.*] Give Mr Rees the waggoner the Inclos'd pass.

RC (DLC).
[1] Not found.

John Hancock to George Washington

Sir,   Philada. Septr. 17th. 1777.
I have the Honour to transmit the enclosed Resolves, conveying the most extensive Powers to you, in Order that the Army under your Command may be more effectually supplied with Provisions and other Necessaries; & that the same may be prevented from falling into the Hands of the Enemy. The Congress have likewise empowred you to suspend all Officers for Misbehaviour, and to fill up all Vacancies in the Army, under the Rank of Brigadier General, until their Pleasure shall be known.[1]

In Consequence of your Letter advising that the Provisions in this City should be removed to some Place of Safety, & requesting a Supply of Blankets, the Congress came to the enclosed Resolves, which were immediately communicated to the Executive Council of this State. In obedience to the Order of Congress, I enclose you a Copy of their Answer on the Subject,[2] and have the Honour to be, with the greatest Respect, Sir, your most obed. & very hble Servt.

John Hancock Presidt.

P.S. In Consequence of the Resolution of Congress transmitted some Time ago, two Thousand of the Virginia Militia have rendevouzed at Fredericksburg, where they wait only for your Orders, to march as you shall think proper to direct.[3]

This Morning, Genl. De Coudray, in attempting to cross the Schuyl-kill, was unfortunately drowned; and was this Afternoon interred at the public Expence.[4]

RC (DLC). In the hand of Jacob Rush and signed by Hancock.

[1] See *JCC,* 8:751–52.

[2] See *JCC,* 8:747–48; and *Pa. Archives,* 1st ser. 5:630–31.

[3] See Hancock to George Gibson, September 12, 1777.

[4] This day Hancock also wrote a brief note to Washington enclosing letters of the 16th and 17th by Gov. William Livingston and Gen. Philemon Dickinson on New Jersey affairs. Washington Papers, DLC. See also Washington, *Writings* (Fitzpatrick), 9:236.

James Lovell to William Whipple

My Dear Sir,   Philadelphia Sept 17. 1777.

Your favor of double date the 25th and 30th is before me. That same "military check" will justly rank for its consequences with the most capital blows given to the enemy this war, while in circumstances of bravery it not only exceeds them but the actions of any modern campaign. It has been proposed as a stimulus in General Orders to the Continental Army in this quarter.

As to the affair at Brandywine last Thursday I doubt whether you will even accurately know whether fortune alone is to be blamed, or whether Sullivan and the Chief should not share with her in the slanderous murmurs. Knowledge of the enemy's intentions on the right wing of our army was certainly wanting. General Washington and some good military men especially the highest officers do not charge the want to Sullivan. But as he was under the order of Congress for a Court of Enquiry as to Staten Island the Maryland officers in his division, the delegates of that State, the great Burck, the friend of St Clair and the connexions of Schuyler accomplished to cast such reflections upon his want of capacity to direct a wing of our army in this critical day, that a majority, after first demolishing old De Borre affected the Resolve to recall Sullivan till his conduct should be enquired into as per former order. You are to take with you that an attempt to send St Clair to join the Army had been baffled. Agreeable to the prophecy of the Minority the Commander in Chief has written in the most pressing manner for a suspension of the Order of recall which being carried Ch——e moved that a direction might go to put the Maryland troops under some other M. G[enera]l which would have been in effect throwing out S——n, for the soldiers of other divisions would be unwilling to serve under a man discarded by the Marylanders if the Generals would consent to exchange. R——d joined and had the Delaware inserted with Maryland.[1] But these States were the only yeas which agreeable to modern petty practice were booked with the Nays by the request of M——d. The foreign officers showed themselves to great advantage in the battle. Brevets are given to Du Coudray and all his officers; he having modestly, for once, asked a Captain's for himself and Lieutenant's for his attendants. In crossing the Scuylkill his horse leaped out of the boat with him, who was foolishly in the saddle and so was drowned yesterday. Count Pulaski who headed the Polanders, is now Commander of our Cavalry, having first signalized himself greatly in the battle of Brandywine. Baron de Kalb who speaks English well and has been in Pennsylvania formerly and who in manners and looks resembles our Chief is made a Major General, but I am not certain he will return having left this City on Monday for South Carolina though I imagine he is yet at Bristol.

The intention of the enemy is to gain upon our right wing, but I think we are so posted as to render it impossible. The Lancaster road must be so perfect a clay pit, that no cannon can move in it for some days after the present very heavy rain. Phil. Dickinson, General of the Jersey militia writes that 4000 of the enemy have visited them. McDougal must join him very shortly as our Order went last Thursday. I doubt not they two will give Courland Skinner and the Tory levies a full beating; for there cannot be above 1200 British, if there is no mistake as to 4000—we heard of only 2000 at first.

Howe's whole command in America is said to be the 16th and 17th regiment of Light Dragoons, 1 Brigade of Guards, 5 Companies of Artillery, 9 regts of Foot, 2 Battalions of Marines, British—Hessians, 2 Companies of Chasseurs, 18 regts Foot, 1 of Artillery.

Ships	50 to 28 guns	34
	20 to 10 "	22
	Bombs	2
	Armed Vessels	10

With this trifling force and some Torries he is plaguing several States. Oh Shame! But he will not long continue to do it. I think our affairs are very favourable, among other things a fine Continental cargo from Bilboa at Boston.

Yours affectionately,   J.L.

[*P.S.*] Esq Frost sets out for home tomorrow.

Tr (DLC).
¹ George Read was the Delaware delegate who joined with Samuel Chase in this unsuccessful attempt to obtain Sullivan's removal from the command of Maryland and Delaware Continental units. See *JCC,* 8:749–50.

Henry Marchant to the Rhode Island
Governor and Assembly

Gentlemen,   Philadelphia Sepr. 17th. 1777

You have doubtless seen the Resolution of Congress, for paying the Interest of the Money they borrow by Bills of Exchange to be paid in France, or in Contl. Bills, at the Election of the Lender.[1] This must give a Spring to the Loan offices and thereby considerably appretiate the Currency. Let this be followed with large Taxes, which the Country were never so able to bear, And we may fully establish Our Credit. In short rightly considered, every Man must see that how great soever the Tax he pays, if proportioned with others, he does not lessen his Estate, because what he still has left is of more Value, than the whole was before, and this will continue to be the Case, till the Quantity of Money is reduced to so much as may be necessary for a Medium of Trade.

Congress have the utmost Assurance that those Bills of Exchange will be punctually paid.

The 11th of this Month is famous for the Battle of Brandewine—a River leading out of Deleware thro' part of the State of Deleware and into Maryland. The Battle was at Chadsford and Birmingham. It began a little before Nine in the Morning with a heavy Cannonade, which was very distinctly heard in Our State House yard about 30 miles from the Place of Action. It lasted till dusk; and tho' we were obliged to leave the Enemy Masters of the Field, yet we may esteem it a Victory, as our whole Loss did not exceed in killed, wounded and missing more than 700. By the best Information from some steady Countrymen who lived near the Spot and were obligd by the Enemy to help bury their Dead, they had 1200 killed, and at least 1500 Wounded. They had not dressed all their wounded in three Days after the Battle, and have remained near the Spot ever since. Genl. Washington marched in a Day or two after, his whole Army this Side Schuylkill, save some reconoitering Parties, and having well refreshed his Men marched again and was yesterday by his Letter,[2] upon the left Flank of the Enemy, and not more than five or seven miles from them. Our Army are in high Spirits and wish for a second Battle which is hourly expected.

We had Information Yesterday that four Thousand of the Enemy had landed in the Jersey, a large Body of Millitia had collected, and Genl McDougall from Peekskill with 500 men, ordered sometime before to march this way, was in the Jerseys, that we are in good Hopes a proper Account will be given of the Enemy. Our Accounts from the Northward are very favourable. By the Blessing of Heaven (and I most sincerely wish we more deserved it) we have Reason to expect a happy Issue to this Campaign. We had Intelligence that all the British Troops had left Rhode Island, but I doubt it. Congress have requested, if the Fact be true that One of your State Battallions may be forwarded to Peekskill, that we may be able to draw the Continental Force from thence as Circumstances may Require.[3] A Requisition of the like kind is gone to Connecticut,[4] And will I presume to Massts.

I hope some Expedient will be found for getting Our Vessells out of Providence River, And that One or two State owned Vessells will be employed to go to France for Arms, Blankets and other Cloathing ballasted with Salt. They may very probably clear the whole Adventure by Prizes. I have offerd this Hint before; I hope my Zeal for the Good of my Country will plead an Excuse for those or any other Observations I have made and am with great Truth, Your most obedient and humble Servant,   Hy. Marchant

RC (R–Ar). Addressed: "The Honorable The Govr. & Company, State of Rhode Island."
    [1] See JCC, 8:730–31.
    [2] See Washington, Writings (Fitzpatrick), 9:230.
    [3] See John Hancock to Nicholas Cooke, September 14, 1777.
    [4] This action is not recorded in the journals.

Robert Morris to Abraham Whipple

Sir   Philada. Septr. 17th. 1777
    The Attempt Genl. Howe is now making to get possession of this City has caused me to remove my Family, Books, Papers &ca. to a place of Safety. Consequently I can not attend closely to my Correspondents till something decisive is done & this is all I have to offer in extenuation for my not answering by this post your favr. recd. by yesterday's, Time not permitting me to add any thing more than just to assure you that indeed I am, Sir, Your Obedt. hble Servt. For Robt. Morris,[1]   John Swanwick

RC (Capt. J. G. M. Stone, Annapolis, Md., 1973). In the hand of John Swanwick.
    [1] Swanwick also wrote a similar letter this day for Morris to John Langdon. See PMHB 23 (October 1899): 401.

North Carolina Delegates to Richard Caswell

Sir   Philada. Septr. 17th. 1777
    On the 11th Instant there was a very severe Ingagement between the Armies of General Washington and Howe, on the Brandywine twelve Miles above Wilmington. The enemy made the attack at 8 oclock; it

lasted with little intermission untill dark. The officers say the fire from the Cannon and small arms was the hottest they ever heard of, they kept the ground but paid dearly for it having from the best accounts we have had, lost upwards of 2000 men, one General & several Field officers killed & wounded supposed to be their best men. Our loss is said to be 700 killed & wounded tho' the greatest part of the latter were brought off. Only one field officer was killed a Major Bush. The enemy got seven pieces of Cannon from us.

General Washington retreated over the Schuylkill but the next day marched towards the enemy, taking an upper road. He soon got near the place where the late action was, the enemy having been the whole time busily imployed in burying their dead & taking care of their wounded. The armies have been manuvring for two days, we expect there will soon be another action. It is with pleasure we can inform you that our officers & soldiers are in good spirits anxious for an opportunity of obtaining revenge.

You will observe from General Washington's letter to Congress[1] that our loosing the ground was owing to some mistake as to Intelligence relating to the movement of the enemy.

Our affairs to the Northward are in a promising situation. General Burgoyne has met with such a check as will make him more attentive to effect a retreat to Ticonderoga, than any thing else, as Genl. Gates has nearly the double of his force & a large body are getting into his rear.

General Howe is making his last effort. If he meets with a defeat, he is undone, as he is a considerable distance from his ships, his situation is truly critical. We hope soon to be able to give your Excellency the agreeable news of the success of the American arms. The North Carolina Troops were not ingaged in the late action. Inclosed are some papers for your amusement and are with due respect, Sir, Your most obt. Servts. Thos Burke

J. Penn

Cornl. Harnett

RC (PHC). Written by Penn and signed by Penn, Burke, and Harnett.
[1] See John Hancock to Washington, September 12, 1777, note.

William Williams to Jonathan Trumbull, Sr.

Hond. Sir   Philadel the 17 Sepr. 1777 Wed. Morn

I have nothing material to add, since my last by Morris, no important movements of the Armys have taken place since the late action of BrandyWine. Genl Washington is encamped, I cant describe where as

Places have no names here. I take it about 15 Miles westerly, or south-
westerly from this, at the crossing of sundry Roads, & the way is open
for Howe to Us. I take Washingn intends to attack them on the rear,
on his attempt to get here. Howes main army the last we heard lay
near the place of Action, being doubtless much galled & probably to
wait reinforcements, which they have sent for before the action, from
R Island, N Y &c & their Ships, We have no certainty about any
being in the River, tis said they are & that they have per York or
S. Island invaded Jersey agn with 4000 men & they destitute of
Amunition, & were supplied from hence yesterday. Probably they hope
to penetrate thro to Us or however it will effectually answer their great
End of stoping their Militia from Washns assistance, otherwise their
Genl Dickinson says he shod have brot 4 or 5000. Tis Confidently said,
but we have not sufficient Evidence, that the Enemy buried 1070 at the
upper ford, beside what were killed at Chads. Report this morning is
that a Skirmish happened yesterday between advance or picquet Gards
of the two Armies, but that the rain parted them. The last was an exceeding rainy night. Somthing very important will soon take Place.
May every Heart & every Soul be lift up to God for Mercy & Deliverance. Tis most ardently to be wished but alass, alass, how little to
be expected, by appearances here, I pray God it may be otherwise in
Connecticut!

Congress remain here, but begin to talk & have indeed voted to
move to Lancaster if They are obliged to remove. It is about 60 miles
west of this. Tis sorely against my Will to move that Way, & as the
Time is very nearly expired that I intended to Stay I have some
thoughts of returning home but less Ill Nature shod call it Timidity,
beleive I shall not.

The two last Posts brot me no Letters, which was very greivous. If
my Freinds have all forgot me, I must bear it.

Intended to have wrote largely about Mr Erkelens, with whom I
have had much Conversation, I am fully convinced he is a firm, solid,
principled friend to America, & his Stay & manufactures in our Colony
wod be a most valuable Acquisition. He is determind if he cant go on
there to move to this, the Center & cherisher of all Manufactures, to
their immense advantage. (the Wethersfd Peace Maker carries on a
great stroke here). The Crops are very large here & thro the Country
there is no possible Danger of the armys suffering for want of Bread &
I shod think the Spirit for them wod be of very great Importance. They
want it exceedingly in this Army. I hope we shall be too wise to loose so
valuable a Business, but He wishes most heartily & he mut be rid of the
Tory Shaler if it shod be discouraged, for a Time, to make Shaler sell
out to him, possibly it wod promote it.

But also what is all this, if God is pleased to give us up to Slavery &
Destruction, but I hope in his Mercy, let us not faint nor be discouraged,

but wait patiently for the Lord, & he will not fail them that trust in him. They begin to be alarmed here so as to run out with Effects &c but not so much to fight as I cod wish. With tender Rembrance to yr dear Daughter &c &c I am most respectfully yours &c,

W. Williams

[*P.S.*] This minute I hear in Congress that the Enemy certainly carried 100 waggon load of Wounded to Wilmington. One Genl officer killd &c. They say our army is intirely cut to pieces.

Brandy Wine emties into Delawar, between Wilmington & New Castle, not below, as I believe I have wrote, some time since.

RC (NN).

John Adams' Diary

1777. Septr. 18. Thursday.

The violent N.E. Storm which began the Day before Yesterday continues. We are yet in Philadelphia, that Mass of Cowardice and Toryism. Yesterday was buryed Monsr. Du Coudray, a French Officer of Artillery, who was lately made an Inspector General of Artillery and military Manufactures with the Rank of Major General. He was drowned in the Schuylkill, in a strange manner. He rode into the Ferry Boat, and road out at the other End, into the River, and was drowned. His Horse took fright. He was reputed the most learned and promising Officer in France. He was carried into the Romish Chappell, and buried in the Yard of that Church.

This Dispensation will save Us much Altercation.

MS (MHi). Adams, *Diary* (Butterfield), 2:263.

John Hancock to John Armstrong

Sir,   Philada. Septr. 18th. 1777. 10 O'Clock P.M.

I have the Honour to enclose you a Resolution of Congress for the Removal of the printing Presses in this City (except one) which you will please to carry into Execution in the Manner you may think most proper.[1] I beg Leave to refer your Attention to it.

Should you receive any Intelligence of the Movements of the Enemy, I must request you will immediately forward it to Congress, that they may have all possible Information of their Views and Intentions.

I have the Honour to be, with great Respect, Sir, Your most obed. & very hble Servt.   J. H. Presid.

LB (DNA: PCC, item 12A). Addressed: "Honble Major Genl. Armstrong."
  [1] See *JCC*, 8:754.

John Hancock to George Washington

Sir,   Philada. Septr. 18th. 1777 10 O'Clock P.M.
    Last Night I was duely honoured with your Favour of yesterday,[1]
and this Day communicated the same to Congress.
    A few Minutes ago I received a Letter by Express from Genl. Dickin-
son (a Copy of which I enclose) covering one to you, which I also
forward.[2]
    A certain Joseph Burns of Chester County, who had been sent out
by Genl Wayne to reconoitre the Situation of the Enemy, has this
Moment called on me. He says he found them within seven or eight
Miles of the Swede's Ford; and being unable to get back again, was
under a Necessity of making the best of his Way to this City. He further
says, that some of the Pennsylvania light Horse on their Return to
Town, had made Prisoners of two British Soldiers within eighteen Miles
of this City on the Lancaster Road. I thought it best to lay this Intelligence before you, and to transmit it immediately by Express, and have
the Honour to be, with the greatest Respect, Sir, your most obed. &
very humble Serv.   John Hancock Presidt.

[*P.S.*] The Inclos'd Letter from Col Wood Congress Refer to you.[3]

RC (DLC). In the hand of Jacob Rush, with signature and postscript by Hancock.
    [1] This letter is in PCC, item 152, 5:67–68, and Washington, *Writings* (Fitz-
patrick), 9:230–31.
    [2] Gen. Philemon Dickinson's September 17 letter to Washington and Sep-
tember 18 letter to President Hancock are in Washington Papers, DLC.
    [3] This letter is not in PCC or Washington Papers, DLC, nor is it mentioned
in Washington's correspondence for 1777.

Henry Laurens to John Lewis Gervais

Dear Sir,   18th September 1777.
    I had the pleasure of writing to you two or three days ago[1] by favor
of Colonel Horry. This will inclose a couple of News Papers. If any
thing contained in them valuable to Mr. Wells be so good as to communicate & tell him I have never missed one opportunity of Sending
News papers to him directly or through you.
    I have written fully in general terms to the president who will let
you know what I have Said if worth hearing. Perhaps Letters by express ten days hence will make my intelligence Stale.

All our affairs are undoubtedly in a better appearance than they were three days ago, but fright has driven Some great Men to do precipitantly what I Strongly urged as necessary to do early & deliberately as soon as we learned of Mr. Howe's landing at Elk. But I suffer the fate of all wise Men, my counsel is not always attended to. No wise man however can suffer with more patience & indifference. Some who smiled at the proposition are gone in a hurry, embarrassed, others are now on the wing, we keep enough to make a Congress & that's all. I shall remain as long as any. I sent my baggage forward some days ago & can easily transport my self, but I am really in a comfortable State of confidence that General Washington will be victorious in the next engagement which will probably happen this Evening or to morrow, be that as it may I am ready to go or to remain & may do either with a good face. My advice was not to go, but to prepare for going, that we might not be endangered to have our last moments which ought to be Spent in the most Serious & solemn deliberations & orders, perplexed by a thousand different opinions & reflections how to dispose of our bodies & wordly Estate. We Spent lately upwards of 4 hours in that sort of confusion & considered & reconsidered 4 times, & what was then determined I believe by a reconsideration is now undoing. I came out of the House to forward barely two lines to you & I find I have scribled above twenty—the effect of being at leisure in mind (though hurried by the party who is to be bearer). My baggage is ahead, my Horse is ready, before the Enemy can cross Schuylkill, which I hope he will never do in any character but prisoner, I may be 15 or 20 Miles on Bristol Road & Strike off into the interior Country. Wherever I am I shall endeavor to let you hear from me & will always be wishing the happiness of you & yours. This moment I got here, a friend comes in to dine with me 'till 1/2 past three & in a burst of Laugh tells me we are to meet at 6 oClock this evening & to morrow to enter upon the weighty business of the Confederation. Fright sometimes works Lunacy. This does not imply that Congress is frighted or Lunatic but there may be some Men between this & Schuylkill who may be much one & a little of the other. Dinner & the messenger for this waits.

LB (ScHi).

[1] Laurens noted in his letter book that on September 15 he wrote Gervais "A brief Accot. of the Battle of Brandywine & enclosed Papers of intelligence," but no copy of the letter has been found.

Index

In this index descriptive subentries are arranged chronologically and in ascending order of the initial page reference. They may be preceded, however, by the subentry "identified" and by document subentries arranged alphabetically—diary entries, letters, notes, resolutions, and speeches. An ornament (☆) separates the subentry "identified" and document subentries from descriptive subentries. Inclusive page references are supplied for descriptive subentries; for a document, only the page on which it begins is given. Eighteenth-century printed works are indexed both by author and by short title. Other printed works are indexed when they have been cited to document a substantive point discussed in the notes, but not when cited merely as the location of a document mentioned. Delegates who attended Congress during the period covered by this volume appear in **boldface type.**

Accounts: marine committee, 11, 57, 128, 206, 646–47; secret committee, 19, 43, 65, 91, 142–43, 161, 170, 180, 187, 194, 603, 645, 647; teamster, 32, 93; delegate, 34, 304, 664–65; Gen. Schuyler's, 41, 51; John Langdon's, 65, 166; printers, 117; *Montgomery,* 172–73; prisoner, 195, 503; board of war, 221; state, 503, 596
Ackerly, Lemuel, pardoned, 600
Adams, Abigail Smith (Mrs. John): letters to, 12, 25, 28, 43, 57, 81, 83, 88, 98, 103, 113, 119, 137, 161, 167, 175, 194, 195, 207, 240, 262, 278, 292, 293, 317, 329, 334, 339, 347, 350, 354, 356, 375, 386, 394, 400, 403, 411, 432, 439, 449, 450, 473, 478, 491, 504, 505, 517, 520, 531, 533, 538, 542, 554, 567, 569, 570, 579, 588, 626, 660; husbandry extolled, 83–84
Adams, Abigail (1765–1813), 263
Adams, Elizabeth Wells (Mrs. Samuel): letters to, 200, 404, 440, 506, 677; mentioned, 241
Adams, Jenifer, 465
Adams, John: diary, 664, 668, 693; letters from, 12, 13, 21, 25, 28, 29, 30, 43, 48, 57, 59, 81, 83, 88, 98, 99, 103, 113, 119, 120, 137, 161, 162, 166, 167, 175, 176, 181, 194, 195, 207, 208, 220, 240, 249, 262, 278, 293, 305, 307, 317, 329, 334, 339, 347, 375, 384, 386, 394, 400, 403, 405, 411, 432, 439, 460, 473, 478, 491, 501, 504, 505, 517, 520, 532, 533, 538, 542, 554, 567, 570, 574, 578, 579, 588, 601, 626, 660, 669; ☆ elected to Congress, xvi; attends Congress, xvi; recommends Nathan Brownson, 13; on foreign affairs, 21, 221; on inflation, 21; on British barbarity, 25; on Danbury raid, 28; on filling Continental quota, 28–29; on fiscal policy, 29, 121, 176, 501, 506, 628, 636, 644; proposes eastern navy board, 30; on trade, 43, 627; on heroism, 48–49; on military discipline, 48, 163, 176, 439, 505; describes Henry Strachey, 49; on Gen. Arnold, 49;

Lee, Francis Lightfoot (*continued*)
conjectures British strategy, 177, 202, 478; protests Richard Henry Lee's displacement, 180–81; mentioned, 363
Lee, John, apprehended as loyalist plotter, 84–85
Lee, Ludwell, letter to, 63
Lee, Richard Henry: letters from, 6, 20, 32, 52, 53, 55, 63, 75, 76, 79, 86, 94, 97, 104, 105, 121, 125, 158, 498, 499, 512, 550, 593, 601, 620, 636, 656, 664, 666; letters to, 202, 249, 263, 343, 359, 363; notes, 111; ☆ elected to Congress, xx, 34, 125, 262, 316, 327; attends Congress, xx, 362; secret committee, 3, 19–20, 43, 52–57, 65, 79, 91, 123, 142–43, 193–94; marine committee, 6, 86–87; requests additional delegate, 32–33; educates sons, 63–64; on recruitment, 75; on fiscal policy, 76, 551; commercial transactions, 76; on British propaganda to inhibit Continental recruitment, 94–95; on foreign officers, 104–5; recommends Mr. Demmere (of Georgia), 105; committee on commissary regulations, 111; accused of depreciating paper currency, 121–26; on sectional discord in Congress, 123–24; leaves Congress, 125, 127; superseded as delegate, 125, 139–40, 180–81; on promotion of useful knowledge, 126; opposes Gen. Schuyler's reappointment to northern command, 139–40; committee for foreign affairs, 282–83; quoted, 282–83, 361; urges frequent reporting to commissioners at Paris, 282; committee on Ticonderoga inquiry, 417, 553, 601–2; on Anglo-French relations, 498–500; conjectures British strategy, 513, 551; lauds Lafayette, 514; committee on Quaker disaffection, 573; committee of intelligence, 592; committee on Continental rations, 620–21; on Quaker sedition, 637; mentioned, 281, 328, 358, 478, 678
Lee, Thomas, letter to, 63
Lee, Thomas Ludwell, 126
Lee, William: appointed commissioner to Austria and Prussia, 59, 282–83, 316, 362, 364; mentioned, 54, 63, 159, 300, 436
Legare, Solomon: letter to, 563; mentioned, 611, 636
Le Maire, James, employed by secret committee, 185–87
Leonard, Abiel, 48, 131
Leonard ,David, 360
Leonard, Lucy, 179
Le Pelletier & Du Doyer, 56
Lewellen, Mr. (son of John Lewellin), 134
Lewis, Mr. (Maryland), 164
Lewis, Francis: letters from, 172, 173; ☆ elected to Congress, xvii; attends Congress, xvii; and James Nicholson dispute with Maryland, 118; secret committee, 142–43; and *Montgomery* prize shares, 160; visits Baltimore, 172; procures salt, 173; secret committee contract, 270; mentioned, 194, 255, 325
Lewis (schooner), 554
Liberty (ship), 142
Limozin, Andrew, 237, 238, 604
Lincoln, Benjamin, 211, 411, 510, 511, 520, 521, 528, 549, 550, 598
Linen, price, 470
Livery, cost, 26, 424, 449, 455, 470, 581
Livingston, Henry Brockholst, 44, 560
Livingston, James, 132, 530, 548
Livingston, John, 130
Livingston, Philip: letters from, 6, 20, 50, 52, 53, 55, 65, 86, 111, 159, 203, 205, 232, 253, 254, 256, 284, 325, 329, 393; ☆ elected to Congress, xviii; attends Congress, xviii; marine committee, 6, 86–87, 203–6, 253–56; secret committee, 20, 43, 52–57, 65, 142–43, 161, 170, 179–80, 193–94; defends Gen. Schuyler, 41; on Hudson River defense, 160, 326; on New York politics, 225–26; on Gates-Schuyler conflict, 232; secret committee contract, 270; committee of

Advisory Committee

Library of Congress American Revolution Bicentennial Program

John R. Alden
James B. Duke Professor of History Emeritus, Duke University

Julian P. Boyd*
Editor of The Papers of Thomas Jefferson, *Princeton University*

Lyman H. Butterfield
Editor in Chief Emeritus of The Adams Papers, *Massachusetts Historical Society*

Jack P. Greene
Andrew W. Mellon Professor in the Humanities, The Johns Hopkins University

Merrill Jensen*
Editor of The Documentary History of the Ratification of the Constitution, *University of Wisconsin*

Cecelia M. Kenyon
Charles N. Clark Professor of Government, Smith College

Aubrey C. Land
University Research Professor, University of Georgia

Edmund S. Morgan
Sterling Professor of History, Yale University

Richard B. Morris
Gouverneur Morris Professor of History Emeritus, Columbia University

George C. Rogers, Jr.
Yates Snowden Professor of American History, University of South Carolina

*Deceased.

749